Marketing TODAY
Second Edition

David J. Rachman
Baruch College
City University of New York

With Cases by
W. Wayne Talarzyk
Ohio State University

The Dryden Press
Chicago New York San Francisco
Philadelphia Montreal Toronto
London Sydney Tokyo

Part Illustration Sources

Part One: Courtesy of Canandaigua Wine Co., Inc.
Part Two: Courtesy of *ADWEEK* Magazine.
Part Three: Courtesy of Buck & Pulleyn Advertising.
Part Four: Courtesy of Isuzu Trucks of America, Inc./Evans/Weinberg Advertising.
Part Five: Courtesy of United States Borax Chemical Corporation.
Part Six: Courtesy of The Potato Board, Denver, CO.

Acquisitions Editor: Rob Zwettler
Developmental Editor: Rebecca Ryan
Project Editor: Karen Vertovec
Production Manager: Barb Bahnsen
Permissions Editor: Doris Milligan
Director of Editing, Design, and Production: Jane Perkins

Text and Cover Designer: Alan Wendt
Copy Editor: Nancy Moudry
Indexer: Lois Oster
Compositor: The Clarinda Company
Text Type: 10/12 ITC Baskerville

Library of Congress Cataloging-in-Publication Data
Rachman, David J.
Marketing today.

Includes bibliographies and indexes.
1. Marketing. I. Title.
HF5415.R2354 1988 658.8 87-22239
ISBN 0-03-013573-7

Printed in the United States of America
789-032-98765432

Address orders:
111 Fifth Avenue
New York, NY 10003

Address editorial correspondence:
One Salt Creek Lane
Hinsdale, IL 60521

The Dryden Press
Holt, Rinehart and Winston
Saunders College Publishing

Cover Photo: Joe Burull—*Porsche* Magazine.

The Dryden Press Series in Marketing

Balsley and Birsner
Selling: Marketing Personified

Barry
Marketing: An Integrated Approach

Blackwell, Engel, and Talarzyk
Contemporary Cases in Consumer Behavior,
Revised Edition

Blackwell, Johnston, and Talarzyk
Cases in Marketing Management and Strategy

Block and Roering
Essentials of Consumer Behavior,
Second Edition

Boone and Kurtz
Contemporary Marketing,
Fifth Edition

Churchill
Basic Marketing Research

Churchill
Marketing Research: Methodological Foundations,
Fourth Edition

Czinkota and Ronkainen
International Marketing

Dunn and Barban
Advertising: Its Role in Modern Marketing,
Sixth Edition

Engel, Blackwell, and Miniard
Consumer Behavior,
Fifth Edition

Futrell
Sales Management,
Second Edition

Hutt and Speh
Industrial Marketing Management: A Strategic View of Business Markets,
Second Edition

Kurtz and Boone
Marketing,
Third Edition

Park and Zaltman
Marketing Management

Patti and Frazer
Advertising: A Decision-Making Approach

Rachman
Marketing Today,
Second Edition

Rogers and Grassi
Retailing: New Perspectives

Rosenbloom
Marketing Channels: A Management View,
Third Edition

Schellinck and Maddox
Marketing Research: A Computer-Assisted Approach

Schnaars
MICROSIM
A marketing simulation available for IBM PC® and Apple®

Sellars
Role Playing the Principles of Selling

Shimp and DeLozier
Promotion Management and Marketing Communications

Talarzyk
Cases and Exercises in Marketing

Terpstra
International Marketing,
Fourth Edition

Weitz and Wensley
Readings in Strategic Marketing: Analysis, Planning, and Implementation

Zikmund
Exploring Marketing Research,
Second Edition

Preface

The purpose of the second edition of *Marketing Today* is the same as that of the first edition: to teach basic marketing principles by demonstrating the link between theory and practice. This revision, however, goes a step further by reflecting the interests of today's students. Unlike most principles texts, *Marketing Today,* Second Edition, captures the excitement and vitality of the modern marketing environment. Students will enjoy learning from this textbook because it speaks to them.

Organization of the Book

The second edition of *Marketing Today* is organized into six parts. Each part presents basic marketing concepts and describes how these concepts relate to marketing decisions and activities. Part One, "Overview of Marketing," covers the scope of marketing, management and planning, and the marketing environment. Part Two, "Markets and Segmentation," focuses on marketing research and information systems and consumer and industrial buying behavior. The next three parts discuss the marketing mix variables: Part Three, "Product and Pricing Strategy"; Part Four, "Placement Strategy"; and Part Five, "Promotion Strategy." The chapters in Part Six, "Special Marketing," cover international marketing and marketing activities in not-for-profit organizations. Three appendixes especially helpful to students are "Marketing Arithmetic," "Career Resource Guide," and "Marketing for Small Businesses."

Special Features of This Edition

Each chapter contains the following pedagogical aids designed to provide information that promotes learning.

- ☐ **Learning Objectives.** Each chapter begins with "Sounding Out the Chapter," a list of 10 to 12 learning objectives that highlight chapter concepts, guide individual study, and facilitate review of chapter material.

- ☐ **Opening Vignettes.** An actual marketing situation introduces students to the main theme of each chapter.

- ☐ **Contemporary Examples.** A criticism of many textbooks is that examples of concepts are not fully integrated into the text but instead appear "tacked on." In *Marketing Today,* current examples enhance students' understanding of key marketing practices and activities. The examples focus on topics and events that students are familiar with, thus encouraging them to learn how marketing relates to their everyday lives.

- ☐ **Marketing Today Boxes.** These special features take a look at marketing principles in action. They give students the chance to relate concepts to actual marketing decisions and strategies.

- ☐ **Services Marketing Boxes.** Called "At Your Service," these boxes reflect the growing importance of services in our economy by providing a real-world application of the marketing of services as they relate to specific chapter topics.

- ☐ **Marginal Glossary Terms.** Key terms are defined in the margin of the page on which they are first mentioned. Ready access to key terms and their definitions permits students to concentrate on each chapter without flipping back and forth to an end-of-book glossary. In addition, a complete text glossary of all definitions is included at the end of the book. Each glossary term and the page on which it is defined are highlighted in the subject index in boldface type.

- ☐ **Chapter Summaries.** The "Chapter Replay" summarizes key points that correspond to the learning objectives that begin each chapter.

- ☐ **End-of-Chapter Questions.** Two types of questions test knowledge of chapter content. Recall questions test concept recognition, while discussion questions present scenarios for applying these concepts.

- ☐ **End-of-Chapter Cases.** Two cases at the end of each chapter allow students to evaluate and apply marketing practices discussed in the chapter. Focal questions accompany the cases, which include completely updated selections and some old favorites. Written by Professor W. Wayne Talarzyk of Ohio State University, the cases primarily deal with real-world situations in marketing.

Other Features

- ☐ **End-of-Part Cases.** New to this edition, these longer cases help instructors who use the case approach to integrate chapter concepts within each part of the book.
- ☐ **Marketing Arithmetic Appendix.** This section will help students review basic mathematical techniques necessary for studying marketing principles.
- ☐ **Career Resource Guide Appendix.** Particularly useful to today's career-minded student, this new end-of-text supplement serves as a resource guide for students to familiarize them with realistic entry-level job possibilities in the field of marketing. The guide was put together by Dee Smith of Lansing Community College.
- ☐ **Marketing for Small Businesses Appendix.** In today's economy, nearly 70 percent of the organizations are small businesses. This appendix, written by Peggy Lambing of the University of Missouri—St. Louis, discusses special marketing issues relevant to small businesses and presents an extended case study of a successful small company.

Ancillary Materials

A complete, carefully developed support package accompanies the second edition of *Marketing Today.* It includes a *Study Guide, Computerized Marketing Simulation Game, Instructor's Manual, Test Bank, Computerized Test Bank, Full-Color Transparency Acetates,* and *Enterprise Videos.*

Instructor's Manual

The *Instructor's Manual,* written by Blaine Greenfield of Bucks Community College and Karen Schenkenfelder, parallels the text and includes the following items in each chapter: a chapter synopsis that includes learning objectives; a chapter outline that indicates where the corresponding transparency acetates and masters can be used; lecture notes that include current event highlights; key terms and definitions; answers to end-of-chapter discussion questions; classroom projects and activities; and answers to the case questions.

Test Bank

Written by Michael Fowler of Brookdale Community College, the *Test Bank* has been completely rewritten for this edition. It includes more than 2,200 test items and is organized by quiz-type and exam-type questions. True/false, multiple choice, mini-case, and essay questions are provided in each chapter along with the correct answer, text page reference, major subject area, and level of each question.

Computerized Test Bank

The questions on the diskettes are identical to those that appear in the printed version of the *Test Bank.* This system gives instructors the flexibility of entering the program and adding or deleting questions. The test bank is available for the IBM or Apple personal computer.

Color Transparency Acetates

Full-Color Transparency Acetates are available to accompany *Marketing Today.* They include charts, graphs, tables, and illustrations that do not appear in the text.

Study Guide

Written by Constantine Petrides of the Borough of Manhattan Community College, each *Study Guide* chapter corresponds to the text chapters. Each chapter contains a summary, learning goals, key concepts, programmed review, marketing riddle, exercise, and self-quiz.

Computerized Marketing Simulation Game

Developed by Steven Schnaars of Baruch College, the game allows students to work independently or in a group to apply their understanding of marketing principles to current marketing situations.

Enterprise Videos

A group of 11 videos from the *Enterprise* series are available upon adoption of *Marketing Today.* Ideal for classroom use, the videos are accompanied by a separate booklet of teaching notes that explains how to use them in teaching key marketing topics. The notes are written specifically to accompany *Marketing Today.*

Acknowledgments

This book is truly the result of a team effort. Many individuals devoted enormous amounts of time and energy to ensure that the second edition of *Marketing Today* is the best it can be. My colleagues and students worked together to produce *Marketing Today,* along with the editorial and production professionals of The Dryden Press—Becky Ryan, Rob Zwettler, Susan Riley, Karen Schenkenfelder, Karen Vertovec, Alan Wendt, Jane Perkins, Mary Jarvis, Barb Bahnsen, and Nancy Moudry. In addition, a special thank you is in order to Michael Czinkota, of Georgetown University, who reviewed and provided information for the revision of Chapter 17 on International Marketing and Dale and Wayne King, of Lenoir Rhyne College, who provided invaluable research assistance.

I extend my sincere thanks to the following people who guided me through the development and writing of this new edition:

- **Jim Berson**
  Borough of Manhattan Community College
- **Thomas R. Blackshear**
  Lincoln Memorial University
- **Jim Boespflug**
  Arapahoe Community College
- **Howard Budner**
  Borough of Manhattan Community College
- **John Cantrell**
  Cleveland State Community College
- **Robert Carter**
  Columbus College
- **Gary Donnelly**
  Casper College
- **Bob Dwyer**
  University of Cincinnati
- **Mike Fowler**
  Brookdale Community College
- **William George**
  Villanova University
- **Richard Giudicessi**
  Des Moines Area Community College
- **Richard Goodwin**
  Broward Community College
- **Blaine Greenfield**
  Bucks County Community College
- **Jack Heinsius**
  Modesto Junior College
- **Ed Kirk**
  Vincennes University
- **Darwin Krumrey**
  Kirkwood Community College
- **Ron Lennon**
  Towson State University
- **Jay McKee**
  Champlain College
- **Roger McKinney**
  Auburn University—Montgomery

- ☐ **Randall Mertz**
  Mesa Community College
- ☐ **Paul Metzger**
  Houston Community College
- ☐ **Milledge Mosby**
  Prince George's Community College
- ☐ **H. Reed Muller**
  Salisbury State College
- ☐ **Debra Murphy**
  North Virginia Community College
- ☐ **Carol Pingitore**
  Brookdale Community College
- ☐ **Ben Recarey**
  University of Miami
- ☐ **Tom Schiller**
  University of Puget Sound
- ☐ **Dee Smith**
  Lansing Community College
- ☐ **Kathy Smith**
  Towson State University
- ☐ **Robert Sorensen**
  Rider College
- ☐ **Bill Vincent**
  Santa Barbara City College

To all of these marketing educators, and others who have provided ideas and suggestions over the years, I extend a grateful thank you.

I would like to dedicate this book to my wife, Barbara.

David J. Rachman
Baruch College
City University of New York
November 1987

Contents in Brief

Contents

ADWEEK readers make waves.

Chapter 5 Information for Marketing Decisions 124

Chapter 6 Consumer Buying Behavior 158

Chapter 7 Organizational Buying Behavior 194

Part Four

Placement Strategy 321

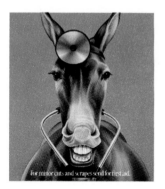

Part Six
Special Marketing 517

Overview of Marketing

1 The Importance and Scope of Marketing

Sounding Out the Chapter

In this chapter, you will learn:

1. **The definition of marketing, including some examples of marketing activities.**
2. **The distinctions among products, goods, and services.**
3. **How marketing adds value to a product.**
4. **Three orientations to doing business.**
5. **The nature of a seller's market and a buyer's market.**
6. **Key ideas underlying the marketing concept.**
7. **The four elements of the marketing mix.**
8. **Issues critics have raised about the marketing concept.**
9. **How marketing reconciles today's concern for social responsibility with company profit motivations and individual wants.**

Source: Courtesy of the Jolt Company, Inc.

Need a Jolt?

Jolt cola is audacious. In an age of sugar-free, caffeine-free, fruit-juice-added soft drinks, Jolt cola's slogan is "All the sugar and twice the caffeine." Jolt contains 5.9 milligrams of caffeine per fluid ounce, just under the 6-milligram maximum allowed by the Food and Drug Administration and one-fifth the caffeine of coffee. The cola is sweetened only with sugar, rather than the corn sweeteners or artificial sweeteners other soft drinks contain.

C. J. Rapp, president and founder of Jolt Co., explains that Jolt cola was created for those who buy soft drinks purely for taste and fun. "Soft drinks were created for sheer enjoyment and pleasure," observed Rapp, "but the industry has become awfully serious."

Others take a dimmer view of the product. The *Nutrition Action Health Letter,* published by the Center for Science in the Public Interest, criticizes the product as unhealthy because of its high caffeine content. The group nominated Rapp for a "personal niche in the nutrition hall of shame."

Jolt Co. defends itself by comparing Jolt's caffeine content to that of coffee and by pointing out that its advertising is straightforward. Many consumers seem to share Rapp's enthusiasm for the product. Within three weeks of its introduction, Jolt had achieved a market share in its home city that put it number 3 behind Pepsi and Coke. Several months later, the company was expanding distribution a year ahead of schedule. And Gay Mullins, the Seattle man who led the Old Cola Drinkers of America to boycott new Coke and force a return to the old formula, has switched to Jolt.

Many of the issues involving Jolt cola are common in marketing. For example, what kinds of products will appeal to consumers? How does an organization let consumers know about those products? Does an organization have a responsibility not to produce anything that may cause harm? This chapter explores these and many other questions as it defines marketing and describes the many activities involved in marketing.

Sources: "C. J. Rapp Has Formulated a Jolting Drink That's Creating Plenty of Fizz in the Cola Biz," *People,* September 15, 1986, p. 67; "Jolt Jump Starts America!" undated press release from the Jolt Company, Inc.; Richard W. Stevenson, "Jolt Cola's Contrary Strategy," *The New York Times,* August 20, 1986; and Nancy Webster, "Jolt Gets Lightning-Fast Start," *Advertising Age,* July 28, 1986.

A well-known management theorist, Peter Drucker, once noted, "Any business enterprise has two—and only two—basic functions: marketing and innovation."[1] Many of America's largest and most successful organizations—Procter & Gamble, IBM, and Wal-Mart among them—have built their businesses around this philosophy. Marketing sets the tone of doing business in these organizations, just as it does in many smaller companies.

Innovation depends on marketing. Many developers of personal computers and related products have learned this the hard way. They have found that sometimes an exciting new product flops because it is too expensive, fails to meet a perceived need, or is not delivered at the promised date.

Some Basic Concepts

As a child, did you ever ask for a toy you saw on TV? Did you ever try selling lemonade or Girl Scout cookies? When you selected a college, did you get information from promotional brochures? Did you ever try a new pizza place or oil-change service because you had a discount coupon? If so, you have been involved in marketing. Advertising, selling, brochures, and coupons are all part of this broad field.

What Is Marketing?

Marketing
Activities performed by individuals, businesses, and not-for-profit organizations that satisfy needs and wants through the process of exchange.

Exchange
Process by which two or more parties freely give something of value to one another to satisfy needs and wants.

Those who sell lemonade or college educations or oil changes need to find buyers. **Marketing** comprises the activities performed by individuals, businesses, and not-for-profit organizations to satisfy needs and wants. This satisfaction occurs through **exchange**—the process by which two or more parties freely give something of value to one another. For example, a student might exchange money for a textbook. Exchange is basic to all marketing. The academic discipline of marketing studies exchanges to find out how they can be made better or more efficient.

Marketing is an important but often misunderstood activity. Some of the confusion arises from the use of the word *marketing* to mean selling. For example, many companies call their salespeople marketing representatives. One commentator observed that the word may be "the most widely abused term in the business lexicon today."[2] In fact, much more than selling is involved in satisfying needs and wants through exchange. Some of these other activities are suggested by the American Marketing Association's definition of marketing:

Marketing is the process of planning and executing the conception, pricing, promotion, and distribution of ideas, goods, and services to create exchanges that satisfy individual and organizational objectives.[3]

Besides selling, marketing includes product development, market research, distribution, pricing, and many other activities. This course will show you how all the elements of marketing work together.

Over the past 50 years, the proportion of the work force involved in marketing has grown largely because of expanding marketing tasks. The U.S. Department of Labor considers workers to be in marketing if they participate in a marketing exchange either directly by selling or indirectly. Indirect participation includes product delivery, communication of product availability, or research into demand for products. Under this broad definition, an advertising copywriter, a supermarket clerk, a long-distance truck driver, and Bill Cosby could all be engaged in a joint marketing venture—selling Jell-O pudding.

What Can Be Marketed?

Almost anything that people need and want can be marketed. And in a society as sophisticated as ours, people need and want much more than simple food and shelter. Consequently, the variety of things that can be marketed ranges from the most concrete, such as furniture, to the very abstract, such as investment advice.

The marketing term for anything offered to meet a want or need is *product.* Products can be goods, ideas, or services.

Goods and Services When you go into McDonald's and trade a couple of dollars for a hamburger and a Coke, you are engaged in a marketing exchange. You receive tangible items—a sandwich and a drink. In marketing terms, tangible items received in an exchange are **goods.**

Goods
Tangible objects exchanged in marketing.

But what about when you deposit a token in the fare box of a bus and ride nine blocks? Or when a stylist trims your hair into a new cut? Money is exchanged, but what goods do you have to show for the transaction? In these cases, instead of a tangible object, you receive a **service,** or intangible benefit.

Service
Intangible benefit exchanged in marketing.

The United States is now a service economy. About 50 percent of the average family's budget is spent on services.[4] Besides transportation, the most important services that individuals and families purchase are:

1. Shelter: use of housing in exchange for rent or mortgage payments.
2. Medical care: health insurance, dental and physical checkups, and hospital care.
3. Household operation services: heating, electricity, water, and telephone service.
4. Personal care services: hair and beauty care, use of exercise facilities, and so forth.
5. Recreation and travel: theater-going, eating out, vacationing.
6. Education: tuition and related expenses.

In addition to the money individuals spend on services, businesses expend billions more for such services as transportation, advertising, legal advice, and machine repair. If individual and business purchases are taken together, more money is now spent on services than on goods.

One of the most profitable growth areas in the economy has been the expanding foreign market for U.S. services. Foreign countries are eager to import American skills in engineering, management consulting, and computer software design, among others. In 1985, the international market for American manufactured goods was relatively poor, resulting in a trade deficit of $148 billion. But when the value of export services is figured into the nation's balance of payments, the overall balance for 1985 registered a less troublesome deficit of $79 billion.[5]

Impressions Marketing is not confined to goods and services in the narrow sense of those words. Marketing is also used to create impressions about the following:

- ☐ People in the public view, from Ronald Reagan to Joan Collins to Mr. T.
- ☐ Places, using slogans such as "I Love New York" and "I think I'd rather be in Colorado."
- ☐ Ideas—for example, the Sierra Club markets the idea that conservation is important.
- ☐ Organizations that want to be viewed favorably by potential customers, donors, or employees. For example, the army and navy attempt to create the impression that enlisting is a way to learn a valuable skill and improve one's career prospects.

Most marketing experts agree that a substantial part of any marketing exchange involves intangible elements, even when the item exchanged is as unmistakably solid as a car. The typical automobile purchaser, for example, buys not only an assemblage of rubber, steel, and glass, but also convenience, a feeling of independence, and perhaps a sense of prestige. GM's advertising slogan "the spirit of Cadillac" is based on selling these intangible benefits. (See Marketing Today 1.1.)

When you buy almost any product, you are buying certain symbolic or psychological benefits along with the product itself. For example, when you purchase Reebok shoes, you are also purchasing the psychological benefits of owning goods that are highly regarded by your peer group. A marketing exchange can therefore be much more than simply an exchange of goods or services for money.

Intangibles Some marketers have taken the question of what constitutes a marketing exchange one step further. They suggest that the objects of exchange might be entirely intangible and symbolic. One theorist maintains, for example, that a marketing exchange takes place when a person decides to watch a television program.[6] Figure 1.1 on page 8 shows how this might work.

Marketing Today 1.1
Cadillac's Hopes for Spirited Design

Source: Cadillac Motor Car Division

Why would car buyers who in 1986 refused to spend $25,000 on a car that seats six want to pay $50,000 for one that seats two? General Motors is hoping that the Cadillac Allante's benefits will make the higher price worthwhile.

The Allante offers the features that consumers expect in a high-priced car, such as ten-way adjustable power seats, a leather-wrapped tilt and telescoping steering wheel, and a fancy sound system. But what makes the car unusual for Cadillac is its design. To give this Cadillac added prestige, GM hired an Italian designer, Pininfarina, to create a new model. The Allante they have created is a sleek convertible designed to appeal to young, wealthy car buyers who might otherwise favor imports.

GM expects the Allante to boost sales of its entire line of Cadillacs. The company's advertising emphasizes the Cadillac division over individual Cadillac lines. The theme of the advertising campaign is "the spirit of Cadillac," with the Allante being called "the new spirit of Cadillac," the Seville "the elegant spirit of Cadillac," and so on. GM hopes that the prestige generated by the Allante's new design will make Cadillac's "spirit" seem like a desirable benefit to buyers of the entire Cadillac line.

Sources: Ralph Gray, "Cadillac Line, Led by New Allante, Refocuses on Spirit," *Adweek,* September 15, 1986, p. 4; Stephen Koepp, "A Passion for Italian Bodies," *Time,* September 15, 1986, p. 46; Jim Mateja, "Cadillac Gambling on Allante," *Chicago Tribune,* September 14, 1986, sec. 17, p. 1; Raymond Serafin and Patricia Strand, "Financing Fallout: '87 Ads Facing Heavy Challenge," *Advertising Age,* September 15, 1986, pp. 3, 30.

If you watch a television program with commercials, you exchange your attention and potential purchasing power for entertainment and information. This initial marketing exchange makes possible several other exchanges that happen to involve money. For example, suppose you see an ad for Diet Pepsi. Besides exchanging your attention for information about the soft drink, you may decide to give a supermarket $1.25 or so for a two-liter bottle of the product. The supermarket, in turn, exchanges a certain percentage of that price with a distributor, who exchanges a portion of that with the Pepsi-Cola Company. Pepsi-Cola, in turn, exchanges a portion of its share of the purchase price with an ad agency for producing and placing a television commercial, and the ad agency exchanges a certain amount of that sum with the TV station for running the ad.[7] All of the transfers are marketing exchanges, from your initial viewing to your final purchase, because something of value (whether money, goods, information, or attention) is offered for something else in order to satisfy a need.

Figure 1.1
From Pepsi to the Consumer—A Marketing Exchange

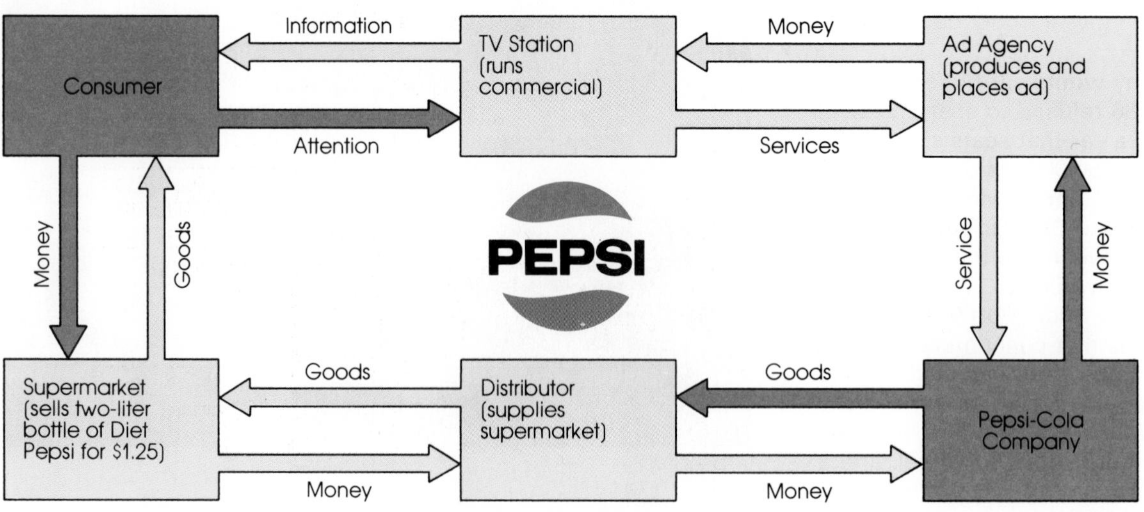

Marketing's Primary Activities

Estimates indicate that 40 to 60 cents of every dollar the consumer spends help to pay for marketing costs.[8] Figure 1.2 shows the breakdown of cost for an 11-ounce box of Ritz crackers, purchased for perhaps $2.00. Of this, $1.12, or 56 percent of the price, goes for marketing activities—advertising, packaging, shipping and warehousing, and paying both the Nabisco sales force and the grocer. Meanwhile, the cost of actually manufacturing the crackers accounts for only $.88, or 44 percent of the price.

In an age of heightened consumer awareness and scarce resources, critics have charged that such marketing costs are excessive. They maintain that manufacturing, not marketing, has produced the goods and services Americans enjoy. They also claim that the American genius for technology, not marketing, has brought us the wide variety of products that characterize our economy.

But the manufacturing process is only one of the many activities that bring a box of crackers to your pantry. The product must be developed to meet actual wants and needs, and it must be delivered to where the consumer can buy it. The consumer must know that the product is available. In sum, without the services the marketing sector provides, the product would simply pile up at the factory, languishing for lack of customers.

Figure 1.2
Costs of Producing and Marketing Ritz Crackers

Source: Information from William J. Taylor and Roy T. Shaw, Jr., *Marketing: An Integrated Analytical Approach,* 3d ed. (Cincinnati, Ohio: South-Western Publishing Company, 1975), 5.

Values Provided by Marketing

Economists distinguish four kinds of "utilities," or values, that can be added to a product. **Form utility** is given to a product by converting raw materials into a finished good. A shoe factory that transforms leather and rubber into a wearable item creates form utility. Creating form utility is the role of the manufacturing sector.

Form Utility
Value added to a product by converting raw materials into a finished good.

Time Utility
Value added to a product by making it available when buyers need it.

Marketing adds other kinds of utility. It creates **time utility** by making goods or services available when consumers want them. It creates

Place Utility
Value added to a product by making it available where buyers want it.

Ownership Utility
Value added to a product by giving consumers a way to obtain ownership of it.

place utility by making goods and services available where they are accessible to consumers. Marketing also creates **ownership utility** by giving the consumer a way to obtain the rights of owning and using a product, say, by mailing in payment with an order form or by using a charge account at a store. These utilities are necessary for a product to have value.

Consider the Ritz crackers again. Nabisco, the manufacturer, performs a service by converting flour, eggs, and other ingredients into an edible product, thereby creating form utility. When the firm packages and transports the crackers to a grocery store, it provides place utility. The retail grocer, also a marketer, helps satisfy the need for crackers by storing the product until the customer's regular shopping day, thus creating time utility. The grocer creates ownership utility by providing a place (the checkout counter) where money or a check is given in exchange for the product.

Marketing may increase demand for products to the point at which mass production (and savings in costs) may become possible. Before 1958, for example, toys were not widely advertised and were sold mainly through department stores. After that time, they were heavily promoted on television, and discount stores began to sell them as well. This additional marketing activity led to an increase in demand, a drop in manufacturing costs, and a consequent lowering of prices. Customers benefited directly by lower prices resulting from increased marketing activity.[9]

Functions of the Marketing Sector

Various experts disagree on the precise number of activities in which marketers engage, but they usually include some of the following:

1. Searching out buyers and sellers.
2. Matching goods, services, and other offerings to the needs of customers.
3. Finding an acceptable price in the marketplace.
4. Informing buyers and sellers of product availability and convincing them to purchase.
5. Transporting and storing goods.
6. Settling details for the final exchange (arranging credit, delivery, and so forth).
7. Assuming risks (absorbing losses for unwanted products or paying the cost of keeping products until wanted).[10]

Marketing people help create and bring about exchanges by performing certain functions. Some organizations may stress one function or another. Manufacturers take responsibility for transporting goods to convenient locations. Advertisers alert the public to the product's availability. Retailers are responsible for the details of the final exchange. Some functions—such as providing information, setting a price, and assuming risk—may be shared by many marketers. The point to keep in mind is that someone must perform these functions in order for an exchange to occur.

The History of Marketing

Marketing is probably as old as civilization itself. It's not hard to imagine a Stone Age person convincing a neighbor to trade food for a spare tool. By getting together and trading their respective surplus, both would benefit.

As occupations became more specialized, exchange became more regular. Towns grew, with central marketplaces where people could meet and exchange what they produced. Soon money became an acceptable substitute for goods.

The Middle Ages brought trade between nations and the development of brands and trademarks. A craftsman belonging to a guild (a trade organization for merchants and artisans) would put the association's distinctive mark on his product. Consumers would know from the mark that they were buying from a reputable craftsman. Thus the concept of buying "name brands" dates back to long before the promotion of designer jeans.

In the late 1700s, the Industrial Revolution brought the beginning of modern marketing. Factories began turning out items in quantity, prices dropped, and it became more desirable to buy than to make many products. The development of railroads made it easier to move goods to consumers, and larger cities made it easier to sell the products.

As modern marketing has developed, the philosophy of doing business has changed. Businesses were first based on a production concept, then on a sales concept; today they are based on a marketing concept. The following paragraphs explain the development of these philosophies.[11]

The Production Concept

In the early 1800s, American colonists depended on trade with England for products ranging from tea to textiles. During and after the Revolutionary War, the country had to become more self-sufficient, and a new era of production began. The Civil War further spurred the growth of industry. When the war was over, factories turned from making armaments to producing consumer goods. The result of the seemingly boundless supply of customers and natural resources was the first Industrial Age business philosophy—the production concept.

The **production orientation** emphasized the importance of producing goods. Three assumptions basic to this concept are:

1. Anything that can be produced can be sold.
2. The most important task of management is to keep the cost of production down.
3. A company should produce only certain basic products.

Production Orientation
Business philosophy emphasizing that (1) anything that can be produced can be sold; (2) the most important managerial task is to keep the cost of production down; and (3) a company should produce only certain basic products.

GRANDMA'S
BISCUITS.
FLEISCHMANN & CO'S
None Genuine without our Facsimile Signature
Fleischmann & Co
COMPRESSED YEAST.
Behold each merry, happy girl!
'Tis Grandma's Biscuits Charm them.
Their expectation's in a whirl,
A panfull can not harm them.
They know the secret of the feast,
They're raised with Fleischmann's Compressed Yeast.

Getting
his own
Breakfast
Shredded
Wheat
Ready-Cooked –
Ready-to-Eat

BARNUM'S
ANIMALS
Delicious Crackers
Fun and good eating
for the children
P. S. Uneeda
Biscuit
NATIONAL BISCUIT COMPANY

DRINK
Coca-Cola
DELICIOUS
AND
REFRESHING
CALL FOR IT BY FULL NAME
NICKNAMES ENCOURAGE SUBSTITUTION

This way of thinking arose naturally from the state of American business. Manufacturing, using specialized labor and complex machinery, was new. Industrialists had to focus on working out the bugs in the production process. Efficiency experts, not marketers, were the policysetters.

Probably the best representative of the production orientation was Henry Ford. By concentrating on production and simplifying it through assembly-line procedures, Ford was able to offer consumers a car for less than $300. Of course, he turned out only one type of car, the Model T, and he offered it to the public "in any color they wanted it, as long as it was black."

Businesses took a similar approach to other products. Consumers could purchase only a limited range of products, such as basic black telephones and white kitchen iceboxes. From 1865 to 1920, businesspeople could ignore the problem of selling their goods because demand greatly exceeded supply. Figure 1.3 shows selected advertisements for products during this period.

The Sales Concept

After World War I, the business environment changed. Competition grew, and there were more goods to sell than demand warranted. Companies began thinking about how to stimulate sales of their products, thus they developed a **sales orientation.**

Sales Orientation
Business philosophy emphasizing that (1) finding buyers for products is management's chief concern; and (2) convincing buyers to purchase a firm's output is management's chief task.

Sales-oriented businesses emphasize that:

1. Finding buyers for products is the chief concern.
2. Management's main task is to convince buyers—through varying degrees of persuasion—to purchase a firm's output.

The sales orientation prevailed from 1920 to about 1950. Particularly during the Great Depression of the 1930s, businesses found it necessary to "push" products coming off the assembly line. Sales departments were started to oversee sales personnel. Advertising also grew in importance.

The Pillsbury Company, for example, became sales oriented in the 1930s. The firm spent millions of dollars advertising its limited line of baked goods. Pillsbury also trained a sales force to find out what grocers needed in order to sell the company's products successfully.[12] Characteristic of the sales orientation was the advertising campaign for Listerine used in the 1920s, described in Marketing Today 1.2.

Figure 1.3
Selected Ads for Products, 1865–1920

Marketing Today 1.2

New Uses for an Established Product: Listerine

According to the sales concept, consumers must be persuaded to buy a product. When consumers haven't been interested in one use for a product, some advertisers have invented new uses.

A case in point is the advertisements for Listerine during the 1920s. For years, Listerine had been marketed as a general antiseptic. To sell more of it, advertising copywriters Milton Feasley and Gordon Seagrove, along with company president Gerard B. Lambert, set about to induce the public to discover a new need for Listerine.

They succeeded with an ad picturing a beautiful girl and containing a story titled "He Never Knew Why." The story was of a rising young businessman spurned by the beautiful girl after a single encounter. The young man had many advantages but a major handicap: "halitosis."

The copywriters had found the term *halitosis* in an old medical dictionary and chose it because of its scientific sound, which dignified the subject. The ad developed into a series patterned after personal interest stories and advice columns in the tabloids of the day. Soon, using mouthwash became an accepted part of one's daily routine.

But Gerard Lambert was not content to stop with this new need. He began to proclaim Listerine's virtues as a cure for dandruff. This claim was followed by ads promoting the use of Listerine as an after-shave, a cure for colds and sore throats, an astringent, and a deodorant.

Often a bridesmaid but never a bride
EDNA'S case was really a pathetic one. Like every woman, her primary ambition was to marry. Most of the girls of her set were married—or about to be. Yet not one possessed more grace or charm or loveliness than she.
And as her birthdays crept gradually toward that tragic thirty-mark, marriage seemed farther from her life than ever.
She was often a bridesmaid but never a bride.
* * *
That's the insidious thing about halitosis (unpleasant breath). You, yourself, rarely know when you have it. And even your closest friends won't tell you.
Sometimes, of course, halitosis comes from some deep-seated organic disorder that requires professional advice. But usually—and fortunately—halitosis is only a local condition that yields to the regular use of Listerine as a mouth wash and gargle. It is an interesting thing that this well-known antiseptic that has been in use for years for surgical dressings, possesses these unusual properties as a breath deodorant.
It halts food fermentation in the mouth and leaves the breath sweet, fresh and clean. Not by substituting some other odor but by really removing the old one. The Listerine odor itself quickly disappears. So the systematic use of Listerine puts you on the safe and polite side.
Your druggist will supply you with Listerine. He sells lots of it. It has dozens of different uses as a safe antiseptic and has been trusted as such for a half a century. Read the interesting little booklet that comes with every bottle.
—Lambert Pharmacal Company, Saint Louis, U. S. A.
For HALITOSIS use LISTERINE

Source: Roland Marchand, "The Golden Age of Advertising: Two Legendary Campaigns," *American Heritage* 36 (April/May 1985); 74–77.

The Marketing Concept

The stage was set for a new way of doing business when, at the end of World War II, the economy shifted from a **seller's market** to a **buyer's market.** A seller's market is one in which there is a shortage of goods and services. A buyer's market is one in which there is an abundance of goods and services.[13] Companies occasionally adjust production to create a seller's market for their goods so they can keep prices high and make their product seem especially desirable, but a buyer's market is more common in the U.S. economy. Usually there is a greater supply of laundry detergents, hamburgers, pocket calculators, and four-door sedans than existing demand alone would warrant.

Seller's Market
Market in which there is a shortage of goods and services.

Buyer's Market
Market in which there is an abundance of goods and services.

In the buyer's market of the 1950s, Pillsbury and many other companies realized that the sales-oriented approach was no longer effective. Customers had become both more affluent (better able to afford a wider range of products) and more sophisticated in taste (less willing to accept whatever was for sale). Competition for buyers' attention in the marketplace was keener. Once again, business needed a new philosophy to reflect important changes, and a new approach to business was formulated—the **marketing concept.** (See Figure 1.4.)

Marketing Concept
Business philosophy emphasizing that (1) companies should produce only what customers want; (2) management must integrate all company activities to develop programs to satisfy those wants; and (3) long-range profit goals should guide management.

The marketing concept proposes three basic ideas:

1. Companies should produce only what customers want.
2. Management must integrate all company activities to develop programs to satisfy those wants.
3. Long-range profit goals rather than "quick" sales should guide management decisions.

Managers who adopt the marketing concept no longer support the idea that customers must be "sold" whatever the company produces. Instead, they seek to uncover desires through research and to design products as a result of that research. Marketing departments take on the overall responsibility for this work. Other departments work with marketing to satisfy customers and keep them loyal.

Pillsbury management expressed this concept when they stated, "We are in the business of satisfying needs and wants of consumers."[14] This is a far cry from using advertising to persuade consumers to find a need for a product, as Listerine did in the 1920s.

Key Elements of the Marketing Concept

Successful implementation of the marketing concept requires that a company pay close attention to three basic principles: (1) discover what customers want (a customer orientation); (2) mobilize the entire organization to meet those wants; and (3) pursue long-term profit.

Figure 1.4
Changing Business Philosophies at Pillsbury

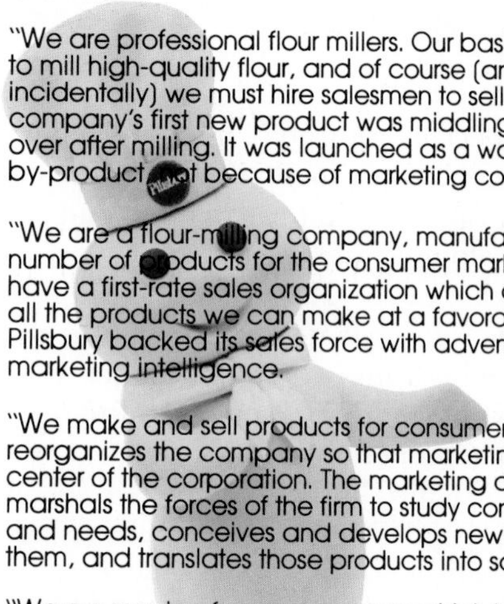

Era	Philosophy
Production Orientation (1869–1930)	"We are professional flour millers. Our basic function is to mill high-quality flour, and of course (and almost incidentally) we must hire salesmen to sell it." The company's first new product was middlings, the bran left over after milling. It was launched as a way to get rid of a by-product, not because of marketing considerations.
Sales Orientation (1930s–1950s)	"We are a flour-milling company, manufacturing a number of products for the consumer market. We must have a first-rate sales organization which can dispose of all the products we can make at a favorable price." Pillsbury backed its sales force with advertising and marketing intelligence.
Marketing Orientation (1950s–1960s)	"We make and sell products for consumers." Pillsbury reorganizes the company so that marketing is at the center of the corporation. The marketing department marshals the forces of the firm to study consumer wants and needs, conceives and develops new products to fill them, and translates those products into sales.
Marketing Control (1960s–present)	"We are moving from a company which has the marketing concept to a marketing company." Marketing sets the company's short-term policies and influences long-term planning. Marketing guides technical research, production, inventory control, advertising, and sales.

Source: Courtesy of The Pillsbury Company.

Customer Orientation

Companies that adopt the marketing concept organize their businesses around consumers' wants and needs. This may sound like an obvious idea. After all, what company would intentionally disregard what consumers want? American automobile manufacturers did just that in the late 1970s when they failed to take changing consumer preferences for smaller, energy-efficient, high-quality cars into account in their planning. After years of losing millions of dollars in sales to the Japanese, Detroit finally began to design cars more in keeping with what the marketplace was demanding.

While a marketing orientation benefits a company, it also makes marketing exchanges more complex. Customers must be sought out not only for their purchasing power, but also for their opinions about products. Often companies develop marketing research departments or hire firms that specialize in marketing research to keep them up to date about changing consumer preferences and activities of their competitors. Marketing research is a method of collecting information about a particular marketing problem or opportunity. (Chapter 5 discusses how marketing research works.)

Market researchers do more than simply analyze how consumers feel about particular products. They must also determine if consumers have needs that no product on the market currently satisfies. Often consumers themselves do not know exactly what they want. Few men, for example, actually demanded a twin-blade razor from Gillette. What they wanted, according to research, was a better shave. Gillette's marketers and engineers worked together to devise an improved product to meet that need. As one board member at Procter & Gamble noted, "We expect (our research people) to search for needs and desires that the consumer perhaps has not yet perceived, but that the consumer will regard as important, once recognized."[15]

Integrated Organizational Approach

When a company adopts the marketing concept, it often finds it must reorganize staff to reflect changes in the way it conducts business. For the marketing concept to work, many other aspects of a company must be coordinated with the plans and goals of the marketing department. Often the executive in charge of marketing oversees activities in departments as diverse as research and development, production, sales, distribution, and even personnel.

Commitment to the marketing concept requires top management to completely reorganize how the company works. As one marketing director put it:

The true marketing concept guides a firm's progress by monitoring the needs and wants of the marketplace, enabling management to identify market segments . . . that will most profitably utilize available resources.[16]

Managers ideally take a flexible approach that emphasizes cooperation within the organization to meet the common goal of satisfying consumers.

An interesting illustration of how marketing may influence personnel selection is provided by the following incident:

One leading package delivery system limits the weight of packages it will handle to those below the standard 50-pound breakpoint because it wants its delivery personnel to present an attractive appearance; management feels that the "big bruisers" it would have to hire to handle heavy packages would give the company the wrong customer image.

An integrated effort requires more than just the coordination of a firm's departmental activities, however. The marketing department must also develop *a unified plan,* known as the **marketing mix,** which specifies what will be offered to customers and how. The marketing mix specifies the policies a firm intends to adopt with respect to the **four "Ps"** (Figure 1.5):

Marketing Mix
Plan that specifies what will be offered to customers (the product) and how (its price, promotion, and placement).

Four "Ps"
Elements of the marketing mix, which are product, price, promotion, and placement.

Figure 1.5
Elements of the Marketing Mix

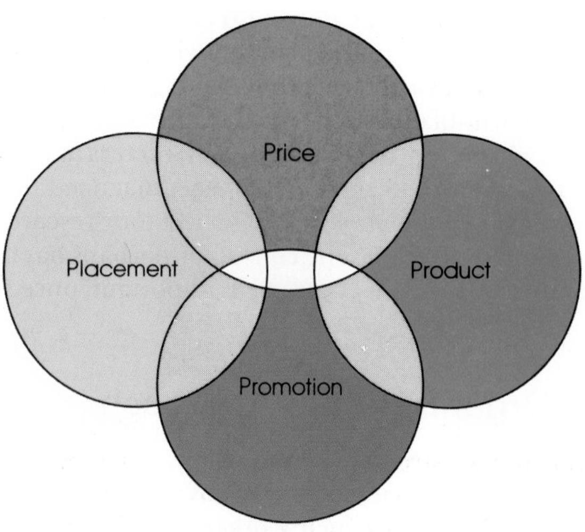

Product
Good, service, or idea offered for exchange and providing benefits for customers.

Pricing
Placing a value on a product.

Promotion
Communication to inform, persuade, and remind customers of a product's benefits.

Placement
Means of delivering a product; also called distribution.

1. **Product:** the offering (a good, service, or idea) that embodies benefits consumers seek. Determining a product's packaging and name are among the decisions product designers must make. Apple computers, for example, combined a nonthreatening name with user-friendly technology.
2. **Pricing:** the value placed upon the product by the firm. A product's price is often affected by competitors' prices for similar products. Price often is also influenced by psychological issues. Apple's early success was at least partially a result of its products' prices, which were low enough to be affordable to a nonbusiness market.
3. **Promotion:** the firm's communications with customers to inform, persuade, and remind them of the product's benefits. For example, when Apple introduced the Macintosh computer, its advertising and sales promotional efforts went into high gear. The computer was launched with a $50 million media blitz that included lavish 20-page, four-color inserts in national magazines, a three-page ad in *The Wall Street Journal,* and TV spots during the Super Bowl and the Winter Olympics.
4. **Placement:** also called distribution, is the means of delivering the product. This aspect insures that a product is in the right place at the right time. Taking a path unlike that of IBM, which is building Product Centers to sell its computers, Apple's executives met with dealers to stress that Apple is committed to selling through them. The company also built a $20 million, highly automated factory to make sure that demand would not outpace supply.

These areas of decision making are known as the four "Ps."[17] Each area is relatively complex. For example, advertising, personal selling efforts, publicity, and sales promotion are all part of the area of promotion. To master the whole field of promotion, or even a part of it, such as advertising, may take a lifetime. Nevertheless, marketing generalists are expected to know their way around not just promotion but the other three areas as well. Failure to plan any one of the four "Ps" can lead to a costly error. The various aspects of the marketing mix are explored further in Chapter 2 and at length in Chapters 8 through 16.

Long-Term Profit Goal

Besides requiring customer orientation and an integrated effort, the marketing concept also stresses the importance of long-term **profit.** No business can survive without making a profit. Businesspeople have always recognized this, but they have sometimes misinterpreted what it means. In a sales-oriented firm, the goal is often to make a quick profit, an objective that can cripple the firm eventually. A pushy car salesperson may pressure a customer into buying, but the customer, remembering the experience, may never return.

Profit
What remains for a business after expenses are deducted from revenues or income.

The marketing concept says that businesses should think in terms of the long run. They may have to sacrifice profits in the present for a better return in the future. New products often lose money when they are first introduced until they attract enough buyers. Lacking a long-run outlook, many managers would never have marketed such products as pocket calculators and instant cameras, which were not overnight successes.

A long-term perspective also fits better with the idea of customer satisfaction. No company can afford to jeopardize the loyalty of its customers. According to one study, brands that have lost brand loyalty are the ones that lose some of their share of the total market.[18]

While brand loyalty has apparently remained steady from the late 1970s to the mid-1980s, consumers' loyalty toward specific products rises and falls. Shampoo, for example, is known for the brand *dis*loyalty of its buyers. A Los Angeles research firm found that 24 percent of adults have a new favorite shampoo every year. Intense competition makes it hard to achieve customer loyalty for a particular brand of shampoo, as hundreds of brands are available. The challenge of competition extends to many products; companies that compete for the consumer's dollar in supermarkets must share shelf space with about 12,000 products.

Because the most brand-loyal consumers are thought to be those who have purchased the product at least once, marketers try to keep their current customers. This may mean spending some money and forgoing some profits. Many companies find it worthwhile to spend dollars to achieve loyalty if in the long term they may recoup their initial investment many times over. A customer orientation and a future orientation are in many ways two sides of the same coin.

Issues Raised by the Marketing Concept

The marketing orientation is widespread in American business. A survey of chief executive officers in 30 major U.S. corporations disclosed that those executives believe marketing is the most important management function in their business and will become more important in the future.[19] Despite its pervasiveness, however, the marketing concept has its detractors. Criticism has centered on three basic areas: consumerism, profit orientation, and long-term competitiveness.

Consumerism

Consumerism
Movement to increase the influence, power, and rights of consumers in their dealings with institutions of all types.

Consumerism has been defined as a movement to increase the influence, power, and rights of consumers in their dealings with institutions of all types.[20] Advocates of consumerism are skeptical about the sincerity of marketing's claim to be consumer oriented. They suggest that being consumer oriented means more than providing a product consumers ask for; it also includes accepting responsibility for the impact of that product on users and the general public.

Marketing analysts recognize the problem. Peter Drucker, who pioneered the marketing concept, has referred to consumerism as "the shame of marketing."[21] He believes that the consumer movement developed because many firms only gave lip service to the marketing concept, while remaining basically sales oriented.

The marketing concept, as we have seen, seeks to identify consumer wants and to satisfy them. You may prefer the lower price of leaded gasoline. But in meeting the demand for low-cost transportation, critics say, automobile and oil companies must also weigh the consequences to the public of breathing in lead from exhaust fumes.

In another vein, C. J. Rapp determined that some consumers prefer a soft drink that contains caffeine and sugar. But some people criticize him for making available a product containing the maximum caffeine allowed when this ingredient is considered harmful. Others contend that Rapp's approach is at least frank. Some of these people question whether it is really more in the public interest to make a soda containing 10 percent apple juice or added vitamin C and represent it as being nutritious.[22] Soft-drink manufacturers need to weigh both views in developing their products.

Unless marketers respond to consumer criticism, they may be subject to government regulation. Many businesspeople fear government regulation as a threat to the free enterprise system. But failure to examine ways to cope with the conflicting demands imposed by the marketing concept may force more government action.

Advocates of consumerism demand that companies respond to consumer needs in the broadest sense. This argument says that companies must bear in mind their social responsibility to make products that are safe and that do not harm the environment. How to achieve the company's goals while meeting the demands of consumers and fulfilling social responsibilities will continue to be one of marketing's greatest challenges.

Profit Orientation

Some observers contend that a contradiction is inherent in the marketing concept. It is the conflict between providing customer satisfaction and the basic goal of any business: to make a profit. For-profit or otherwise, organizations do not exist to satisfy the goals of others. In the words of one analyst:

The initiators of a commercial venture do so to satisfy their own needs. The initiators of a public program, such as an infant immunization program or a myriad of other public policy efforts, do so for the benefit of the citizens of that political body. It is the goals of the membership which define the organization's purpose.[23]

Can an organization have a marketing orientation if it sees a consumer demand and then does not try to meet it? It can, because the marketing orientation includes evaluating the position of the organization as well as that of consumers. The organization must decide whether meeting certain needs is in line with the organization's goals—profitability in the case of a commercial organization. In some situations, an organization with a marketing orientation may choose not to design a product to meet a certain demand.[24]

A church, for example, may be sensitive to its members and their needs, but it generally would not base its teachings on what members want to hear. Or a manufacturer of disposable pens may decide that, even though people's hands are of different sizes, it is uneconomical to make pens in many different sizes to accommodate them.

Of course, businesses cannot ignore what customers want. Eventually, consumers will patronize the organizations that are sensitive to their demands. If businesses want profits for the long term, they must maintain customer goodwill.

Long-Term Competitiveness

Another concern with the marketing concept has centered around its implications for American business in an increasingly competitive world market. Critics have accused the marketing concept of diverting attention from the product to advertising, selling, and promotion.[25]

An example of this diversion of attention is the automobile market of the late 1970s and early 1980s. While American automakers were emphasizing selling, Japanese automakers were developing models that consumers demanded. By 1980, imported cars had captured 30 percent of the market.

The problem, according to analysts, is that by allowing marketing departments to direct research and development, companies tend to develop only low-risk modifications of existing products. However, real technological breakthroughs usually result from the ideas of scientists and engineers. Consumers, in contrast, may not have much insight into what they will demand years from now or what the significance is of some technological innovation. For example, few consumers of 20 years ago would have expressed a need for microchips, but most consumers now buy them as integral parts of numerous products, including watches, radios, and microwave ovens. Market research has even transformed the traditional college bookstore into a supermarket of goods ranging from frozen food to videotapes. (See At Your Service 1.1.)

In fact, part of the marketing concept involves anticipating future wants and needs and drawing upon the insights of scientists and engineers. Marketing is not limited to meeting needs that are current and expressed. In the words of one observer, the marketing manager is an "orchestra leader" who brings into harmony all strategic thinking and planning across departmental lines.[26] When the marketing concept is used appropriately, it addresses both long-term and short-term concerns.

It is interesting to note that marketing goals of Japanese and American executives apparently continue to differ. In a recent study, executives of major U.S. and Japanese companies reported the most important elements in their long-range strategic marketing operations.[27] The top sales concern for the Japanese executives was establishment of innovative sales channels. For the American executives, the top priority was training of first-line salespeople. Note that neither group cited a product development goal as first. Only time will tell whether these objectives will lead to long-term competitiveness for Japan or the United States.

Marketing and Society

One of the most difficult problems marketers will face in the coming years is striking a balance between the needs and wants of individuals and those of society at large. Many states, for example, have passed "bottle bills" requiring consumers to return empty bottles and cans from beer and soft drinks. The purpose of this legislation is to help prevent litter and to recycle valuable resources such as aluminum. Most people would agree that these are commendable goals. But as an individual, you may find returning bottles to the supermarket an annoying obligation. How can marketing reconcile such diverse positions?

Once more, marketing has proved the old adage, "Necessity is the mother of invention." Several beverage manufacturers are now packaging their drinks in small cardboard containers that can be thrown away when the consumer is finished with them.

At Your Service 1.1
The New College Bookstore

Source: © Phyllis Woloshin

Students of 20 years ago would be amazed if they were to wander into a college bookstore today. Now, college bookstores are selling a lot more than books. Some stores stock computers, videotapes, and lunch meats. A few even sell frozen food to students who have microwave ovens in their dorm rooms or apartments.

Prompting this expansion is the increased spending power of college students. One survey shows that after paying for tuition, books, and room and board, students have median incomes of $123 a month. Over half of all college students have credit cards. Observes Leo Shapiro, head of a well-known Chicago-based marketing research firm, "College students are very good shoppers. They spend all they have and a little more."

Source: Ronald Alsop, "Firms Send Brands to College to Cultivate New Consumers," *The Wall Street Journal,* July 31, 1986, p. 27.

In a similar fashion, appliance manufacturers have responded to high energy costs by developing refrigerators and air conditioners that are energy efficient, and cereal manufacturers have begun to address concerns about excess sugar by promoting products with a diminished sugar content. Often these products prove to be profitable because they successfully integrate society's and individuals' needs.

This approach is the essence of a new marketing concept called **societal marketing,** which balances concerns for profits, satisfying individual wants, and meeting overall societal needs.[28] In some cases, these diverse goals have been happily reconciled, but in many industries resolving these issues is far more complex.

Societal Marketing
Concept that balances concern for profits with concern for satisfying individual wants and societal needs.

Social responsibility within a company involves three areas of concern: (1) philanthropic giving; (2) total compliance with international, federal, state, and local laws; and (3) moral and ethical standards under which the company will operate, stated in terms of what the company will and will not tolerate.[29] Specific issues companies address are as diverse as pollution control, pricing, and product safety.

A variety of factors—including a marketplace fragmented into many special interest groups, increased international competition, and rapid technological change—have combined to make marketing the top corporate priority. The future has never been brighter for people with marketing experience who understand how to develop a product strategy that can succeed in a highly competitive environment. A career in marketing offers not only many exciting personal challenges and opportunities, but often the chance to have a significant impact on a company's future.

Chapter Replay

1. **What is marketing, and what are some examples of activities included in marketing?**
Marketing consists of the activities that satisfy needs and wants through the process of exchange. It includes finding buyers and developing, pricing, promoting, and distributing products.
2. **What are products, goods, and services?**
A product is anything offered to meet a want or need. Goods are tangible items received in an exchange; services are intangible items.
3. **How does marketing add value to a product?**
Marketing adds value by creating time utility, place utility, and ownership utility.
4. **What three orientations to doing business have organizations used?**
After the Civil War, businesses developed a production orientation. After World War I, the emphasis shifted to a sales orientation. During the 1950s, many businesses led the move to a marketing orientation.
5. **What is a seller's market? A buyer's market?**
A seller's market is one in which there is a shortage of goods and services. In a buyer's market, there is an abundance of goods and services.
6. **What are the key ideas underlying the marketing concept?**
The three basic ideas are that (1) companies should produce only what customers want; (2) management must integrate all company activities to develop programs to satisfy those wants; and (3) long-range profit goals rather than quick sales should guide management decisions.
7. **What are the four elements of the marketing mix?**
The marketing mix consists of the four "Ps": product, pricing, promotion, and placement.
8. **What issues have critics raised about the marketing concept?**
Critics have contended that marketing is insensitive to the real needs of consumers, that the goal of providing customer satisfaction conflicts with the profit motive, and that the marketing concept causes long-term competitiveness to suffer.
9. **How does marketing reconcile today's concern for social responsibility with company profit motivations and individual wants?**
Societal marketing balances the objectives of increasing company profitability and satisfying individual wants with a concern for societal needs. Companies practice societal marketing when they give to philanthropic organizations, comply with all laws, and set moral and ethical standards.

Key Terms

buyer's market
consumerism
exchange
form utility

four "Ps"
goods
marketing
marketing concept
marketing mix
ownership utility
place utility
placement
pricing
product
production orientation
profit
promotion
sales orientation
seller's market
service
societal marketing
time utility

Discussion Questions

1. What is marketing? Are the people who prepare a mail-order catalog engaged in marketing? The people who decide the prices of the products in the catalog? The people who research what consumers would like to find in the catalog?
2. Give an example of a good and a service. Could either of these be considered products? Explain.
3. Mary and Martha went shopping for a coat for Mary. As they looked at the prices, however, Mary got increasingly aggravated. "You know, Martha," she complained, "I read that the actual cost of making a coat is only about one-third of what I'm paying for it. It's not right for the store to charge so much." Based on what you have read about the values provided by marketing, explain why a coat is worth more than the cost to manufacture it.
4. What functions are performed by the marketing sector? Do all organizations perform all the functions?
5. What assumptions are basic to the production concept? Does this concept work better when demand exceeds supply or when supply exceeds demand?
6. At Green Nursery, the main concern is finding customers for the company's products (chiefly decorative shrubs). Green Nursery's owner, Mr. Green, recently said to the sales personnel, "Our main task is to convince the people of our community that they need more decorative shrubs around their homes." Does Green Nursery have a production orientation, a sales orientation, or a marketing orientation?
7. What are the three basic ideas underlying the marketing concept? Did this concept emerge in a buyer's market or a seller's market?
8. Ellen Nelles just bought a concert hall. What product will she be selling? In developing a unified plan to sell her product, what elements of the marketing mix must she consider?
9. What is consumerism? Why should marketers be concerned about it?
10. Is a marketing orientation compatible with innovation? With social responsibility? Explain.

Case 1.1 The Coca-Cola Company

The Coca-Cola Company is a symbol of refreshment, enjoyment, and relaxation around the world. Coca-Cola, which celebrated its 100th birthday in 1986, is the world's best-selling soft drink, being consumed over 355 million times per day. The entertainment business sector is a major producer and distributor of films and television programs such as "Ghostbusters" and "Who's The Boss." The company's foods business sector has developed many new products around the popular Minute Maid trademark and also has introduced new categories in this growing segment.

Soft-Drink Marketing

Soft-drink products accounted for 76 percent of the company's net operating income in 1985. The company's soft-drink products include Coke, Coca-Cola classic, diet Coke, Fanta, Sprite, Minute Maid Orange and Lemon-Lime Sodas, Tab, Fresca, Mr. Pibb, Mello Yello, and Ramblin' Root Beer. The company now has over a 40 percent share of the U.S. soft-drink market.

The Coca-Cola Company manufactures soft-drink syrups and concentrates that it markets to bottling and canning operations and to approved fountain wholesalers. The bottling operations combine the syrup with carbonated water or combine the concentrate with sweetener and carbonated water, and package the final soft-drink product for sale to retailers. Packaged soft drinks are distributed to consumers in cans, returnable and nonreturnable glass bottles, and plastic packaging. Fountain wholesalers sell soft-drink syrups to fountain retailers, who in turn sell soft drinks to consumers.

During 1985, the company sold 67 percent of its soft-drink syrups and concentrate in the United States to approximately 475 bottlers. The remaining 33 percent was sold to nearly 3,500 authorized fountain wholesalers. Outside the United States, soft-drink concentrate is sold to approximately 950 independently owned bottling and canning plants.

The following represent recent major highlights of The Coca-Cola Company:

- ☐ In 1985, the company developed a new taste for Coca-Cola, which continues to earn superior preference ratings. As a national launch of the new formula got underway in April of that year, many consumers came forward with unexpected loyalty to the original taste of Coca-Cola. Responding promptly, the company introduced Coca-Cola classic in July—a new name for the original formula.

Source: Adapted from The Coca-Cola Company's annual reports and information provided by the company.

- In the major growth area of diet colas, diet Coke achieved a volume growth of 33 percent in 1985. Together with caffeine-free diet Coke and Tab products, the company's diet colas command more than 50 percent of overall diet cola sales.
- Cherry Coke was introduced nationally in 1985 and quickly established itself as a top-10 soft drink in the United States. Cherry Coke enjoyed the highest consumer trial level of any new product ever in the history of the company. A diet version of the popular drink is currently in test market.
- In 1986 the company acquired Merv Griffin Enterprises, a producer of programming for network television and first-run syndication. Among the company's current programs are "Wheel of Fortune" and "Jeopardy!"—the top two syndicated shows in the nation. The entertainment business sector also includes Columbia Pictures, Tri-Star Pictures, and Coca-Cola Television.
- The company formed Coca-Cola Enterprises in 1986 as part of an ongoing program to strengthen its bottling network. Coca-Cola Enterprises is the largest bottler of Coca-Cola in the world, distributing approximately 38 percent of the total bottle/can volume for the company in the United States. The Coca-Cola Company holds a 49 percent interest in this publicly held bottling entity.

Strategy for the 1980s

The following quotes have been extracted from the "Strategy for the 1980s," presented to the board of directors of The Coca-Cola Company by its chairman, Roberto C. Goizueta, on March 4, 1981:

In order to give my vision of our Company for 1990, I must first postulate what I visualize our mission to be during the 1980s. I see our challenge *as continuing the growth in profits of our highly successful existing main businesses, and those we may choose to enter, at a rate substantially in excess of inflation, in order to give our shareholders an above average total return on their investment. The unique position of excellence that the trademark Coca-Cola has attained in the world will be protected and enhanced as a primary objective. I perceive us by the 1990s to continue to be or become the* leading force in the soft drink industry *in each of the countries in which it is economically feasible for us to be so. We shall continue to emphasize product quality worldwide, as well as market share improvement in growth markets. In choosing new areas of business, each market we enter must have sufficient inherent real growth potential to make entry desirable. It is not our desire to battle continually for share in a stagnant market in these new areas of business.*

When we arrive at the 1990s, my vision is to be able to say with confidence that all of us in our own way displayed:

- *The ability to see the* long-term consequences *of current actions;*
- *The willingness to sacrifice, if necessary, short-term gains for* longer-term benefits;

- ☐ *The sensitivity to* anticipate and adapt to change—*change in consumer life styles, change in consumer tastes and change in consumer needs;*
- ☐ *The commitment to manage our enterprise in such a way that we will always* be considered a welcomed and important part of the business community *in each and every country in which we do business; and*
- ☐ *The capacity to* control what is controllable *and the wisdom not to bother what is not.*

Focal Topics

1. In light of the material in this chapter, how would you respond to the question, "Who needs The Coca-Cola Company?"
2. To what do you attribute the success of The Coca-Cola Company over its almost 100-year history?
3. In what ways do you think The Coca-Cola Company might become even more marketing oriented?

Case 1.2 Levi Strauss & Co.

Levi Strauss arrived in California in 1850 with a large supply of canvas that he hoped to sell to miners for use as tents and wagon covers. He quickly found that the miners' real needs involved pants that would hold up in the mines. Levi Strauss promptly took his roll of canvas to the nearest tailor and "those pants of Levi's" were born. Those extra-tough work pants, first of canvas and then of heavy denim, complete with copper rivets, became the "folk costume" of the American West. Eventually, however, the miners of pioneer days and the cowboys began to fade from the scene and the company considered liquidation.

To reposition the company, management started to redefine its markets and decided to concentrate on young males between 15 and 24 years old, and expanded from distribution only in the West to national and eventually international markets. Later, management continued to improve the product, expanded the variety of its line, and targeted new market segments such as young females, boys, and adult suppliers of sportswear.

Current Situation

Today, Levi Strauss is the world's largest brand-name apparel manufacturer. It designs, manufactures, and markets a diversified line of apparel for men, women, and children, including jeans, slacks, shirts, jackets,

Source: Adapted primarily from Levi Strauss & Co.'s 1982 10 K Report and D. C. Cleary, *Great American Brands* (New York: Fairchild Publications, 1981), pages 211–216.

skirts, hats, and accessories. The company's products are marketed principally under the Levi's® trademark in the United States and Canada and in numerous other countries throughout North and South America, Europe, Asia, and Australia.

Levi Strauss USA is organized into four operating divisions outlined below. Each division is essentially an integrated operation with its own staff, manufacturing plants, distribution centers, and sales force, although overlap exists among products marketed as well as retailers and consumers served by the division.

Jeanswear Division. This division is the largest in the company in terms of sales and profits and is the leading manufacturer of jeans in the U.S. In addition to basic and fashion jeans and slacks for young men, this division markets a broad line of western wear, knit and woven shirts, and casual jackets.

Menswear Division. This division primarily markets men's jeans, casual and dress slacks, sports coats, and vests. Additional products include participant and spectator sportswear, outerwear, and accessories as well as such items under the Oxford® clothes label for both men and women.

Womenswear Division. This division markets lines of casual sportswear, including jeans, slacks, knit and woven tops, blazers, and skirts. Sizes range from junior and miss to special sizes such as large, petite, tall, and maternity.

Youthwear Division. This division is one of the world's largest brand-name manufacturers of children's apparel. Its products include basic and fashion jeans, slacks, skirts, knit and woven tops, jackets, blouses, vests, and active wear.

A new subsidiary company, Battery Street Enterprises, has been created to market the diversified brands of Koret of North America, Oxford, and Resistol. Battery Street Enterprises will also house any new brands that Levi Strauss & Co. acquires.

Additional Information

The following points provide some additional information about Levi Strauss and its marketing activities:

- ☐ For the first time, beginning in 1982, the company's jeans were distributed in Sears and J.C. Penney stores, a move that expanded Levi's major retail outlets by 2,600 units, or approximately 7 percent.
- ☐ The company advertises on radio and television and in national publications. It also participates in local cooperative advertising programs under which it shares with retailers the costs of advertising its products. Levi's contracted with the U.S. Olympic Committee and the Los Angeles Olympic Organizing Committee to be the official outfitter and a major apparel sponsor of the 1984 Olympic games.
- ☐ For the first time in its history, Levi's has collaborated with a name designer, Perry Ellis. The new company, Perry Ellis America, will be headquartered in New York and will function as an independent

business unit within Levi Strauss USA. The Perry Ellis American collection for Levi's includes sweaters, shirts, and jackets as well as jeans. The new line will be more affordable than what Ellis had traditionally offered, but more expensive than the regular Levi's line.

- Another new line of clothing, Frank Shorter Sportswear, has been acquired and will report to the senior vice president of marketing for Levi Strauss USA. The line includes shirts, shorts, running suits, GoreTex® wind suits, and other runner's apparel.

Focal Topics

1. In light of the material in this chapter, how would you respond to the question, "Who needs Levi Strauss & Co.?"
2. To what do you attribute the success of Levi Strauss & Co. over its more than 150-year history?
3. In what ways do you think Levi Strauss & Co. might become even more marketing oriented?

2 Marketing Management and Planning

☐ Sounding Out the Chapter

In this chapter, you will learn:

1. The marketing manager's basic tasks.
2. What is involved in strategic marketing planning.
3. The elements of a marketing strategy.
4. Some special challenges of marketing management.
5. How to define a mission and objectives.
6. What goes into a marketing plan.
7. How marketers decide what segments of the total market will be the focus of their efforts.
8. The role of marketing mix in the marketing plan.

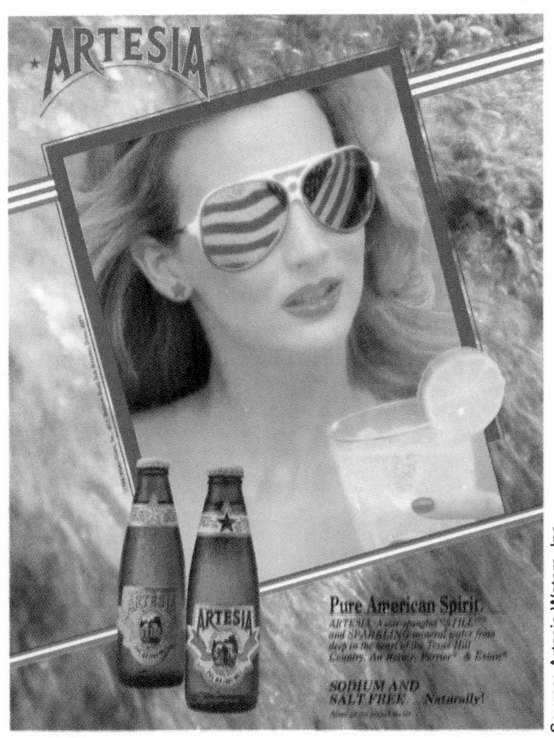

Source: Artesia Waters, Inc.

Artesia Finds a Niche in the Beverage Business

What's the fastest-growing beverage on supermarket shelves? Water. In the United States, consumption of bottled water is growing dramatically. Beverly Hills now boasts a trendy bar, called the Water Bar, that serves no alcohol, only 53 varieties of bottled water from 20 countries.

In 1979, Rick Scoville, of San Antonio, Texas, was inspired when he read about the dramatic rise of Perrier in the mineral-water business. Considering the growing demand for bottled water and the good taste of the water in San Antonio, Scoville decided to set up shop. He located an old bottling plant, dug a well, and began pumping.

Scoville decided to compete with Perrier by emphasizing the Texas origins of his water, which he named Artesia. In contrast to Perrier's 6½-, 11-, and 23-ounce bottles, Artesia comes in Texas-size bottles of 7, 23, and 32 ounces. The label on the bottles features a waterfall topped with a Texas Lone Star.

Artesia's first advertising campaign was a modest one, consisting of ads on billboards and radio. Scoville convinced bar owners to try Artesia by bringing in samples of Perrier, Artesia, and plain club soda for blind taste tests. In supermarkets, grocery managers would line up ten rows of Perrier to two of Artesia, so Scoville would walk down the aisles and quietly rearrange the bottles.

The first year, Scoville lost money, so he revised his marketing strategy. He focused more on distribution, offering premiums to retailers that gave Artesia prominence. Instead of paid advertising, he turned to public relations by pitching himself to the Texas media as a patriotic underdog. Revenues soared. Artesia became the best-selling sparkling water in Texas. In 1985, Artesia was number 95 on *Inc.* magazine's list of the 500 fastest-growing privately held companies in America.

In 1987, to keep up with a rapidly growing and changing business, the company expanded into flavored waters. Eight different flavors are available in a single eight-pack—along with a reply card so that customers can tell the company which their favorites are.

Like Rick Scoville, marketers must continually adapt their strategies to a changing environment. This chapter shows how to do that, using the tools of strategic marketing planning, the marketing mix, and target markets. Stated more broadly, this chapter describes the job of the marketing manager.

Sources: "Artesia Sparkling Water Seeking to Drown Out the Perrier Line," *Food People*, January 1987, p. 21; "Clean Fun in Beverly Hills," *Time*, December 1, 1986, p. 33; and Curtis Hartman, "The Great Texas Water War," *Inc.*, March 1986, pp. 68–70+.

What Do Marketing Managers Do?

Marketing Manager
Chief marketing executive who coordinates the work of the members of a marketing department.

A **marketing manager,** or chief marketing executive, is the person who coordinates the work of a marketing department. Depending on the size and organization of the company, the marketing manager may be responsible for marketing planning, new product planning, distributor and dealer relations, sales promotion, advertising, marketing research, and many other areas.

The job of marketing manager has been compared with that of a symphony conductor.[1] Both seek to bring harmony out of a potentially discordant situation by balancing the activities of the members they direct.

While the scope of marketing managers' jobs is defined by the company for which they work, every marketing manager engages in certain basic tasks. The most important are (1) *planning,* (2) *implementing,* and (3) *evaluating.* (See Figure 2.1.)

Planning

Strategic Marketing Planning
Process of establishing an organization's goals, assessing opportunities, and developing marketing objectives; results in marketing strategies.

The marketing manager is responsible for strategic marketing planning. **Strategic marketing planning** is the process of establishing an organization's overall goals, assessing opportunities, and developing marketing objectives.[2]

The marketing manager should establish marketing goals in accordance with the rest of the company's objectives. For example, when Steven Rothschild, marketing director for General Mills, wanted General Mills to buy the company making Yoplait yogurt, he had to work with General Mills executives to make sure that the acquisition was in line with the company's goals.[3]

Establishing goals also requires evaluating the marketing environment. The marketing environment includes the company's own resources, such as equipment and personnel; the competitive environment; relevant laws and regulations; and broad social issues, such as consumer safety and the environment. For example, in deciding whether to market Yoplait yogurt, Rothschild considered the existence of only one major competitor, Dannon, and whether General Mills had the resources to acquire Yoplait.

The next step in strategic marketing planning is to assess opportunities. When Rothschild weighed the opportunities in entering the yogurt business, he considered the rapid growth in yogurt consumption (3,400 percent from 1954 to 1976) and the large proportion of the population that had not yet tried yogurt. Perhaps those who had not tried yogurt could be convinced to do so.

Marketing Objectives
Stated goals of the marketing department that specify quantitatively how marketing will contribute to meeting overall organizational objectives.

The final step in strategic marketing planning is to develop marketing objectives. **Marketing objectives** specify what the marketing department intends to accomplish through marketing activities. These accomplishments should contribute to achieving the objectives of the organization as a whole. The manager should state the objectives clearly and set time limits for them. For example, Rothschild might have set the objective to

Figure 2.1
Stages in the Management of Marketing

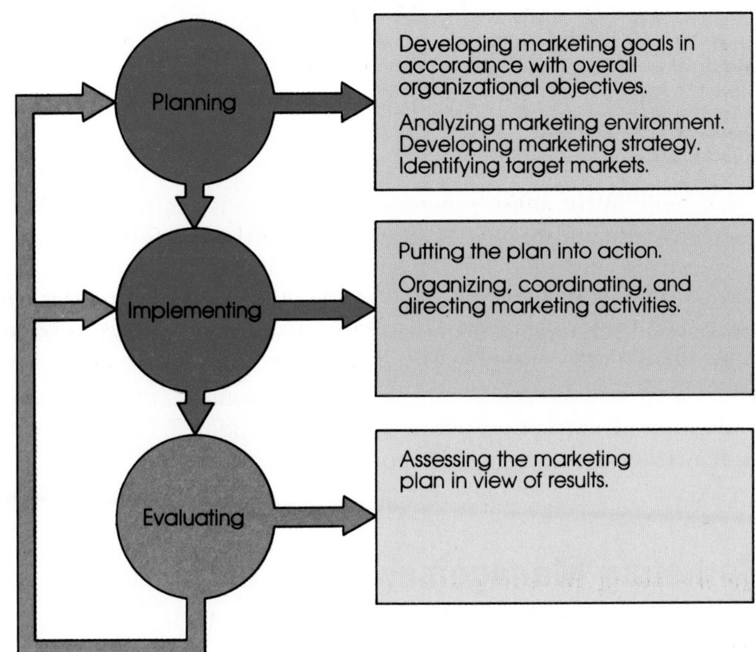

be the best-selling yogurt in California by 1981 or to have 40 percent of the national yogurt market by 1985.

Strategic marketing planning results in marketing strategies. A **marketing strategy** is a plan for achieving the marketing objectives. It describes the marketing mix that the company will use to reach a selected part of the market. For example, Rothschild decided to convince people who had not yet tried yogurt to try Yoplait. He targeted his efforts at "early adopters," people who like to try new products. To reach these people, he scheduled television ads for prime time and late-night shows rather than daytime shows. He also emphasized Yoplait's French origins, because French food has a positive reputation. Later, this chapter discusses marketing strategies in greater depth.

Marketing Strategy
Concrete plan for achieving marketing objectives by using a specified marketing mix to reach a specified target market.

Implementing

The second task of the marketing manager is implementing the marketing plan. To implement a plan is to put it into action. A plan for a new product may require many activities, from developing new manufacturing facilities to lobbying the government on issues that may affect the product.

One would expect Apple Computer's marketing plans, for example, to rely heavily on the development of technologically sophisticated products. Apple's plans have not stopped with machinery, however. Its strategy to capture the youth market included lobbying the California legislature for a change in tax laws that would give the company a tax write-off for donating computers to every elementary and secondary school in the state.

Evaluating

The third stage in the management of marketing is evaluating. This is the means by which a manager can ensure that the department is meeting its objectives, and that the department revises its plans if something goes wrong. One typical method of evaluation is the sales analysis, which measures actual sales against forecasts of sales. Other evaluation procedures are discussed in Chapter 16.

Broad responsibilities accompany the development, implementation, and evaluation of marketing plans. Marketing Today 2.1 describes the extent of marketing managers' responsibilities at Chrysler.

Is Marketing Management Different?

On one level, managers from various departments perform the same function: They are involved in a company's strategic planning and implementation of planning. They set objectives, develop plans, execute those plans, and evaluate their success.

Marketing managers are unique in that they direct their department's activities toward the goals of maintaining demand for the firm's products. This goal sets the marketing manager apart from the production manager, whose responsibility is to oversee the manufacture of the product, or from the financial manager, who is concerned with the supply of funds that support production and marketing activities.

Despite the differences in their responsibilities, a company's managers work toward the organization's primary goals. In most marketing-oriented companies, marketing is equal, but not superior, to other departments. Nevertheless, the interests of key managers in other departments may seem to conflict with those of the marketing manager.

A marketer, for example, may want to produce many different products tailored to various customer needs. However, this plan could create problems for a production head, who would prefer to stick with the efficiency of mass producing similar goods. The plan might also antagonize inventory managers, who may want to keep warehousing costs down by stocking as few products as possible.

A marketing manager must know the problems and capabilities of the other departments in the company. Before mounting a major advertising campaign, for example, a marketing manager for an automobile manufacturer should know if the assembly line can produce enough cars to satisfy projected demand. Similarly, although a marketing manager need not necessarily know the ins and outs of corporate finance, he or she should know if current interest rates make it unwise to borrow large

Marketing Today 2.1
What Marketing Managers Do at Chrysler

At Chrysler, brand marketing managers are being teamed up with product managers. That way, the people who plan and develop Chrysler products can work closely with those responsible for the rest of the marketing process.

The four brand marketing managers are responsible for marketing, advertising, merchandising, sales promotion, and strategic planning. They report to the company's vice president of marketing. One manager is responsible for the Chrysler brand, another for Plymouth, a third for Dodge cars, and a fourth for trucks. The vehicles are marketed around key themes for each line: Chrysler for luxury and comfort, Plymouth for value and integrity, Dodge cars for performance, and Dodge trucks for quality and toughness.

Formerly, Chrysler used a sequential system of planning, designing, engineering, purchasing, tooling, manufacturing, and then marketing. According to Joseph Campana, the marketing vice president, the influence of marketing in that system "depended on the individuals involved as opposed to the organizational structure."

Chrysler hopes the new structure will foster the sharing of information and speed the development of sharper brand identities.

Sources: William J. Hampton, "The Next Act at Chrysler," *Business Week,* November 3, 1986, pp. 66–69, 72, and Raymond Serafin, "Marketing in Chrysler Product Mix," *Advertising Age,* October 6, 1986, p. 22.

1987 Chrysler Conquest TSI

1987 Plymouth Voyager LWB

1987 Dodge Daytona Pacifica

1987 Dodge Dakota 4X4

Source: Chrysler Corporation

sums for new-product development. In sum, although company plans should be market-oriented, the marketing department's plans are not the plans of the whole company. But if the marketing manager is sensitive to the company's goals, the marketing department's plans can help establish the tone and direction for the whole company.

Because of the marketing department's special focus, the marketing manager faces unique challenges. Some of these challenges are:

1. *The highly changeable nature of the market.* This year's style may not be next year's fashion; competitors' new technology may make one com-

pany's product look outdated before it even gets a foothold in the market. Marketing managers must be alert to changing consumer preferences and new-product developments.

2. *Geographical complexities of the market.* The market for grits may be great in Georgia, but nonexistent in North Dakota. Now that many companies are marketing their products worldwide, marketing managers must be sensitive to local customs, language, and ways of doing business in a wide variety of locations.
3. *People variables.* A marketing department is much more dependent on people than most production or financial departments. The quality of the sales force, the creativity of the advertising personnel, and the skills of the market researchers are subject to wide variations.
4. *The need to rely on people outside the firm.* Particularly in the distribution area, marketing executives need to deal with large organizations over which they have little authority. Supermarkets must be persuaded to allot shelf space, and department stores must be convinced that an item fits in with their merchandising.
5. *Wide number of alternatives.* No other department in a company faces quite so many choices as marketing does. What product should we sell to what market? At what price? Should we sell through department stores or discount outlets? The wide range of choices, any combination of which may lead to success or failure, is one of the things that makes marketing such a challenging field.
6. *Marketing's influence on the success of the firm.* Costs for new-product development, advertising campaigns, and market research can run into the hundreds of thousands, or even millions, of dollars. A successful promotion can provide rewards far in excess of these costs. An unsuccessful one could be disastrous for a company. This high degree of uncertainty coupled with the potential for large profits—or losses—make the executive marketing decisions critical to the success of the firm.[4]

Marketing Planning

Successful marketing planning takes into account everything from a company's broadest, most abstract goals to the final details of distribution to the consumer.

Establishing a mission and objectives is the first step in any plan—and for a very good reason. Unless an organization knows what it is and where it is going, it will waste its resources.

Defining Mission and Objectives

As Chapter 1 noted, marketing seeks to serve consumer needs. Therefore, marketing managers have an important role in establishing a firm's mission, or overall goals.

Companies usually define their mission in short, general statements. IBM's corporate mission, for example, is "To meet the problem-solving needs of business." That statement may sound too vague to give any real direction. In fact, it is a good one for two reasons. First, it is not too specific. IBM might have said that its mission is "to sell computers." However, that would have confined the company to marketing only a limited line of computer hardware instead of the broad line of problem-solving equipment and computer services it now sells.[5] Second, it defines a group of customers to be served—namely, business.

Too often firms forget to do this. One analyst claims that the chief reason Chrysler lagged behind General Motors and Ford was that its mission did not define a customer group. Chrysler had thought of its purpose as the manufacture of a well-engineered car. In contrast, Ford's stated mission was "to produce a workingman's car." Lacking a customer-oriented purpose like Ford's, Chrysler repeatedly changed directions without gaining on its competitors.[6] Despite the company's profitability beginning in the mid-1980s, Chairman Lee A. Iacocca has conceded that Chrysler will not catch up to the size of GM and Ford: "We can be a first-rate company as long as we respect our size and don't try to have any delusions of grandeur."[7]

A well-defined sense of mission is important, but it is not enough. The mission must be translated into specific objectives.

Organizational Objectives
Overall goals a firm pursues, such as increasing sales or maintaining a quality image.

Organizational objectives specify goals for the organization to pursue as a whole. Many people think that businesses have only one objective—to maximize profits. Profit is important for business survival, but it is by no means the only objective that organizations pursue. General Foods once produced a line of gourmet foods to foster a quality image for the company's products even though the line lost money. Other common business objectives are to increase the company's share of the market, to achieve industry leadership, or to diversify the corporation's activities.

Goals
Organizational objectives that have been made specific with regard to size and time.

Organizational objectives are most helpful when they are linked with specific **goals.** Managers use the term *goals* to describe objectives that have been made specific in size and time. A possible organizational objective for IBM would be to increase long-term profitability. Using that objective, the corporate planners at IBM might set a goal of increasing profit by 5 percent each year for the next five years. Giving an organizational objective a numerical value and a time frame makes it more useful as a guide to action and a measure of performance.

Quantifying organizational objectives is only one way to make them more exact. Another is to indicate what each department in the organization can do to achieve those goals. Since marketing sets the tone in many firms today, marketing objectives are especially important. To be effective, marketing objectives should be quantified as well. "To expand the market by 5 percent in three years" or "to develop two new products for the office in seven years" could be marketing goals that IBM might pursue.

Once a marketing department has set specific goals, it can then go about mapping a strategy for attaining them.

Creating a Marketing Plan[8]

An important distinction must be made between marketing planning and a marketing plan. Marketing planning is an ongoing, continuous process. Every day a marketing manager may be engaged in some form of planning, such as mapping out the dimensions of a marketing research project, designing an advertising strategy, setting up a network of dealers, or devising ways to motivate the sales force. In contrast, a marketing plan sums up the insights gained in the course of that process and focuses them on a particular course of action for a specific period of time.

Most businesses now require written marketing plans. Plans may be long-term, covering a period of several years, or short-term, detailing proposed activity for a year or less. Short-term plans should always be in harmony with long-term plans, and both should be in keeping with a firm's long-term objectives.

Although firms' requirements for the structure of a marketing plan may differ, certain topics are generally included. The following elements are in most marketing plans:

I. Market Analysis
- A. Demand (see Chapters 5–7)
- B. Competition (see Chapter 3)
- C. Environmental Climate (see Chapter 3)
- D. Resources of the Firm (see this chapter, page 44)
- E. Distribution Factors (see Chapter 12)
- F. Political and Legal Constraints (see Chapter 3)

II. Problems and Opportunities

III. Marketing Strategy
- A. Marketing Objectives (see Chapter 2 or this chapter, pages 38 and 46)
- B. Target Markets (see Chapter 4)
- C. Marketing Mix
  1. Product (see Chapter 9)
  2. Price (see Chapter 10)
  3. Promotion (see Chapters 14–16)
  4. Placement (see Chapters 11–13)

Market Analysis In early 1980, the housing market was thriving. Buyers were scrambling to make deals, and prices were escalating rapidly. Then mortgage interest rates began to climb almost as quickly as housing prices. By late summer, rates were so high that few people could afford to buy. Demand for housing evaporated and remained depressed until early 1984 when rates dropped and the cycle began again.

The housing market may constitute an extreme example, but it demonstrates one of the primary difficulties marketers face: planning in the midst of constantly changing conditions. It is not enough for a marketer to plan on the basis of what is. The more critical question is, "What will be?" Marketers must examine several areas to determine what the future might bring and how it is likely to affect the marketing strategy they plan to pursue.

Demand The question basic to all marketing is, "Who are we going to serve?" The answer determines the organization's **markets.** For businesses, markets consist of people who are willing to buy a firm's output and have the purchasing power to do so. For nonprofit firms, markets are made up of individuals who have an interest in a product offering (whether a tangible good or an intangible service or idea) and a willingness to exchange something (attention, support, change of habit, and so on) in return.

Market
For business, those who are willing to buy a firm's output and have the purchasing power to do so. For nonprofit firms, those who have an interest in a product and are willing to exchange something in return (whether monetary or nonmonetary).

Consider some examples of markets. The market for rubber bands contains different kinds of rubber-band buyers—businesses of all types, students, crafts instructors who want to use them for projects, and children who want to use them as aerial weapons. But if you were a rubber-band manufacturer, would this market diversity matter? Most likely not; you would probably get the best return from making rubber bands in a few different sizes and using inexpensive, functional packaging.

But what about the market for shirts? For starters, people need shirts in different sizes. And men and women often prefer different styles or colors. Different occasions—weddings and golf outings, for example—call for different styles as well. Furthermore, 16-year-olds and 46-year-olds often have different preferences. A shirt manufacturer will not be in business long if it sells one style and size for everyone, so the company has to consider the differences in shirt buyers.

Few organizations know the exact wants and needs of every potential customer. Instead, marketers learn about the market by dividing it into submarkets, called market segments. A **market segment** is a group of individuals, groups, or organizations in a market that share similar characteristics that cause them to have similar wants or needs. A shirt manufacturer might consider one market segment to consist of men aged 35–50 who earn \$25,000–\$50,000 in white-collar jobs. In determining market segments, the shirt manufacturer also might take into account people's attitudes, say, toward clothing or toward trying new things.

Market Segment
Group of individuals, groups, or organizations in a market that share similar characteristics that cause them to have similar wants or needs.

In business, two broad market segments are the consumer and industrial markets. The **consumer market** consists of individuals who buy either for their own or their family's personal consumption. The **industrial market,** on the other hand, is made up of purchasers who buy for business, government, or institutional use, mainly for the purpose of resale or re-exchange.

Consumer Market
Individuals who buy either for their own or for their family's personal consumption.

Industrial Market
Purchasers who buy for business, government, or institutional use, mainly for the purpose of resale or re-exchange.

Within each of these broad categories are many subgroups that make up possible market segments. Customers can be grouped according to age, income level, interests, and a variety of other factors. The process of segmenting markets is investigated at length in Chapter 4.

Marketing managers cannot set realistic objectives without knowledge of the market they want to serve. Markets are an uncontrollable factor because customers have more influence in shaping marketing plans than managers have in shaping customer needs. Determining the extent to which consumers will want a firm's product or service is a key variable that marketers must address early in the planning process.

Demand is the one element on which much of the marketing plan hinges. It is often the least known, especially in the case of a new product, and the least predictable. But on it rests the weight of not only the marketing department's plans, but also those of production, finance, personnel, and other departments in the firm.

To assess the nature of demand for a product or service, marketers might ask such questions as: Who makes the purchase decision? Who influences the decision maker? How much brand awareness or loyalty does this product possess? Where is this product purchased? When?

After assessing the nature of the demand for a product, marketers must examine the extent of the demand. Marketers might ask the following questions: What is the size of the market now, and what does the future hold? What is our current share of the market, and is that share growing or declining?

The answers to these questions give marketers a basis on which to predict the company's profit opportunities and to determine how much of the firm's resources should be allotted to marketing and production.

Competition Demand is not the only key variable in a marketing plan. The number and types of competitors must also be analyzed.

Marketers view competition rather broadly. When marketers of RCA televisions evaluate their competitors, they think not only of Zenith, Panasonic, and Sony, but also consider alternate forms of entertainment, including movies, museums, books, sports, and a variety of others. All represent competing ways for consumers to spend their entertainment money. Thus the RCA marketers' job is to lure customers away from other entertainment media as well as from other TV set manufacturers.

Competition both within and between industries is keener today than ever before, partly because of the increasing strength of foreign marketers at home and abroad. Three of the top ten television makers, for example, are Japanese (Sony, Quasar, and Panasonic). Foreign competitors also are important in the markets for autos, steel, cameras, shoes, clothing, and chemicals.

Competition cannot be avoided, and the actions of competitors cannot be controlled. The effect of competition can be blunted, however, if marketers can convince customers that their product offers a clear advantage. Offering a product at a lower price than that of competitors is one source of advantage, but there are others.

Managers often try to establish customer preference by other means. Making a distinctive product is one way. In the highly competitive market for pocket calculators, Hewlett-Packard has survived by offering models with more functions than those of competitors, thus appealing to the professional end of the market. A distinctive means of distribution can also appeal to customers. Avon's door-to-door selling proved effective in competing with well-established cosmetics firms that sell mainly in department stores. Any element of the marketing mix, or some unique combination of elements, can help distinguish a company's products.

Environmental Climate Suppose you know that your neighborhood contains many pizza lovers but no pizzerias. Is this information sufficient for setting a goal of opening a pizzeria? No. The next step of your market analysis is to evaluate the environment. You might ask questions like these: What are the zoning restrictions that affect opening a restaurant

Figure 2.2
Environmental Levels

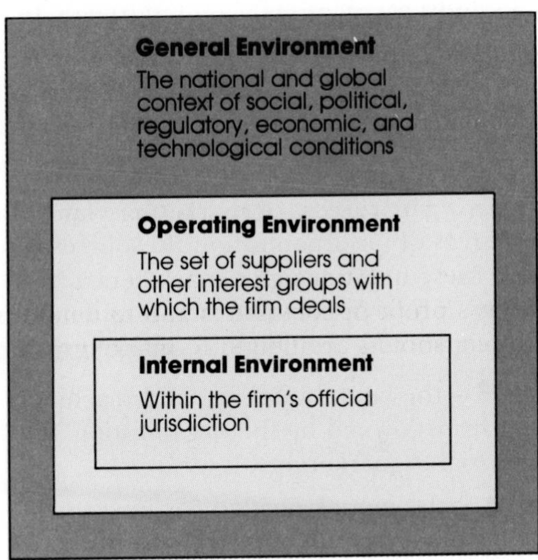

Source: Adapted from Philip S. Thomas, "Environmental Analysis for Corporate Planning," *Business Horizons,* October 1974, p. 28.

in this neighborhood? Are reliable suppliers accessible and reasonably priced? What laws apply to food service and liquor sales?

Marketing departments investigate questions such as these because a marketing department may succeed or fail for reasons unrelated to its effort. For example, workers at a supplying firm may go on strike. The government may decide to build a highway through your chosen pizzeria site. Or the economy may take a sudden downturn, so that consumers spend less.

Evaluating issues such as these is called **environmental analysis.** It involves examining the environment and identifying the circumstances and conditions that can cause the greatest problems or offer the greatest opportunities. An example of a potential problem is rumors that the truck drivers who deliver key supplies may go on strike. A possible opportunity for major banks is the banking deregulation of the 1980s.

Marketers often find it useful to divide the environment into the three "environmental levels" illustrated in Figure 2.2. The division is based on the immediacy and controllability of the circumstances and conditions within each level.

The most immediate and controllable environmental level is the **internal,** or **micro, environment.** This level contains factors that are outside the control of marketing managers but within the organization as a whole. For example, a marketing manager who sees an opportunity to increase revenues by expanding the sales force may run into problems if the organization's plans for that year include employee cutbacks or a hiring freeze. The next level is the **operating environment.** This level con-

Environmental Analysis
Examination of the environment and identification of the circumstances and conditions that can cause the greatest problems or offer the greatest opportunities.

Internal (Micro) Environment
Factors in an organization (such as financial resources and employees) capable of being influenced but not totally controlled by marketing managers.

Operating Environment
Individuals and organizations outside a firm (such as dealers and competitors) that help shape marketing plans and can, in turn, be shaped by them to some extent.

sists of individuals and organizations outside the organization that help shape marketing plans and can, to a limited extent, be shaped by them. Suppliers, distributors, and competitors are part of a firm's operating environment. The level least subject to marketing control is the **general, or macro, environment.** This level includes the national and global conditions that affect the success or failure of marketing plans. These conditions may be social, political, regulatory, economic, or technological.

General (Macro) Environment
Economic, technological, legal, and social forces that are largely outside the control of marketers and that affect the success or failure of marketing plans.

Resources of the Firm The success of marketing plans often depends largely on the resources of an organization. Resources can be both tangible and intangible.

Tangible Resources. The most obvious organizational resources contributing to marketing success are tangible. These include:

1. *The physical plant*—the land, buildings, and machinery (in the case of manufacturing firms) owned by the organization. The location of the plant can be crucial to marketing.
2. *Financial reserves*—the money needed for investment. More than one marketing department has discovered that it underestimated the amount of capital needed to market a new product—and failed as a result. Capital is especially important for "capital intensive" industries—those requiring a large initial investment. Even large companies like RCA and Westinghouse had to pull out of manufacturing computers because of the heavy expenses incurred.
3. *Raw materials*—the supply of basic products needed to produce a product. To ensure a steady supply of these, many large firms have bought a controlling interest in their source of supply. For example, the New York Times Company purchased a substantial share of a Canadian pulp supplier, the Spruce Falls Power & Paper Company. Small manufacturers who cannot afford this approach may suffer marketing disadvantages. They may attempt another approach—negotiating long-term contracts with their suppliers.

A firm can make use of any of these tangible resources to establish what marketers call a **differential advantage.** This is the special edge over competition a company may have or develop. A differential advantage may have a number of sources, including an organization's tangible and intangible resources.

Differential Advantage
Special edge over competition an organization may have or develop by working with the elements of the marketing mix.

Intangible Resources. Intangible resources include a firm's public image with customers, stockholders, suppliers, and others. Other intangibles are its reputation, the quality of its products, the fairness of its prices, and its willingness to service products or to replace or repair products that are defective.

Some companies have made major marketing mistakes by ignoring their intangible assets, such as company reputation. The German car manufacturer, Volkswagenwerk AG, prospered in the American market for years by producing homely but sturdy Volkswagen Beetles. Owners loved them because they were cheap to buy, cheap to operate, and remarkably reliable. Volkswagen owners also liked the idea that their car was a product of superior German engineering. But in an attempt to expand the market for its product, Volkswagen changed its character—with dire results.

The company built a plant in Pennsylvania and began manufacturing VW Rabbits. Quality control at the plant was poor, and VW's reputation for reliability suffered. The design was changed to "Americanize" the car, and the price climbed. Some prospective buyers came to view the Rabbit as a small, unreliable, overpriced American car. Between 1970 and 1983, VW's market share fell from 7.2 percent to 2.6 percent.[9]

Perhaps just as important as a company's reputation are the people the organization employs. Sometimes organizations develop a reputation for attracting and training talent in special areas. General Mills, Procter & Gamble, and General Foods are known for their outstanding product management programs.[10]

Distribution Factors No marketing plan can succeed without the cooperation of the people who deliver the product from the producer to the consumer. Dealers, or intermediaries, are another element in a firm's operating environment. The grocery store, the wholesale outlet, and the travel agency are all examples of dealers. Occasionally dealers are wholly owned by manufacturers, but frequently wholesalers and retailers are independents. They must be dealt with as outside forces that can benefit or harm a business.

Marketers often have less control over dealers than they would like. Dealers' cooperation in meeting marketing objectives cannot be guaranteed. Furthermore, the wrong choice of a dealer can spell disaster for a firm because it can affect costs and revenues. But with careful planning, a company can establish and maintain good relations with dealers. Chapter 12 discusses ways of winning dealers' cooperation.

Political and Legal Constraints Before 1978, airlines had little competition. As labor costs increased, they were passed on to consumers. Fares may have been high, but the airline profit picture was rosy. Then Congress passed the Airline Deregulation Act. The skies became an aerial free-for-all. Price wars broke out, profits plunged, and large carriers who found they could not cut costs enough to compete ultimately filed for bankruptcy.[11]

Similar scenarios followed the deregulation of the trucking industry in 1980 and intercity bus service in 1982 and have been forecast for the financial industry. Such events illustrate the enormous influence the political and legal environment has on marketers.

When developing a marketing plan, marketers today must take into account antitrust, antipollution, truth-in-lending, truth-in-advertising, and many other laws and regulations. Not only must marketers keep current laws in mind, but they also need to be aware of pending legislation that could drastically alter the way they do future business. Chapter 3 discusses ramifications of political and legal constraints in greater depth.

Problems and Opportunities Once the market analysis is complete, the marketer is ready to list the problems and opportunities that have been uncovered in the course of developing the preliminary phase of the plan. Each of the different factors can then be assigned a weight equal to its importance.

Parker Brothers, the 100-year-old producer of such board games as *Monopoly* and *Clue,* admits, for example, that it nearly missed the boat when playing games on the television set started to become popular. Realizing that it had to rethink its product and marketing strategy—and fast—the company moved to restructure its marketing staff into two groups: electronic and traditional. It then hired 20 software engineers to develop video games centered around popular movie figures and what had been arcade games such as Q-Bert.

In addition, the company increased its marketing budget enormously. In 1983, Parker Brothers allotted $30 million to promote video games alone; in 1981, the company's total marketing budget had been only $15 million. But while Parker Brothers was willing to make the leap into new technologies, it was not about to neglect its traditional strengths. The company also decided to begin promoting its most popular board games to adults, with a campaign stressing how such games bring people together as a group.[12]

Parker Brothers analyzed its problems and found a way to turn them into opportunities. See Marketing Today 2.2 for an example of how a manufacturer in the cable industry coped with the problems of intense competition and a declining market.

The process of developing a marketing plan is often an occasion for marketers to step back for a moment from handling day-to-day concerns and to assess the broader issues affecting the company.

Marketing Strategy Having analyzed the market and explored the various problems and opportunities that it presents, a marketer is ready to develop a marketing strategy to achieve specific objectives. Such a strategy uses the elements of the marketing mix—product, price, promotion, and placement—to reach targeted market segments. Because the elements of the marketing mix are the means for achieving the marketing objectives, much of the remainder of this book is devoted to discussing each element in depth.

Marketing Objectives This stage of the marketing plan involves translating broad objectives into specific, quantifiable goals for the marketing department. Generally, marketing objectives include (1) sales volume (in dollars or units), (2) market share (expressed as a percentage of the total market), and (3) profits (expressed as a return on investment). Each goal should specify size and time, so the marketing manager can measure results as the plan is put into action.

Target Markets The marketing department can meet its objectives most efficiently by focusing on the part of the total market most likely to want or need the company's products. Marketers do this by referring to their previous analysis of demand. Remember that part of this analysis involves dividing the total market into market segments. The marketer evaluates which of these segments are most likely to demand the com-

Marketing Today 2.2
A Marketing Success in an Adverse Evironment

In 1984, the outlook was bleak for TOCOM Inc., once a cable technology leader. Competition was intense, the cable market was declining, and the company had faced the expense of making corrections on one of its products. TOCOM was in deep financial trouble.

But the company turned around. It merged with General Instrument Corp. and adopted a marketing orientation. The merger supplied needed financing, and the marketing orientation enabled TOCOM to reclaim its market share.

TOCOM first determined its problems and opportunities. The company researched the market and learned that cable operators wanted a product that was feature-oriented, was compatible with consumer electronics, would retain subscribers, and offered a way to generate extra revenue. TOCOM also learned that although cable operators wanted support in marketing their products to subscribers, they currently received little from manufacturers.

TOCOM used the information it had gathered to devise a strategy for promoting its corporate image. The strategy had three stages:

1. Present a cohesive company image in new product literature, stationery, signs, and advertising.
2. Develop advertising featuring customers testifying to product reliability and good service.
3. Use advertising stressing TOCOM's extensive service and support.

TOCOM also incorporated many features into its new product and intensified quality control.

To stimulate sales, TOCOM initiated a four-part program:

1. Mailings telling cable operators about the product and company.
2. Follow-up telephone calls to generate sales leads.
3. Independent research to verify consumer preference for TOCOM's products.
4. Marketing support, including TV spots, brochures, and bill stuffers, to help cable operators promote their services and TOCOM products.

Source: *Marketing News,* November 7, 1986.

SUCCESS SPEAKS:
"We need more than a reliable product. We need good customer support...we get both from TOCOM."

GENERAL INSTRUMENT

Source: Courtesy of TOCOM Division, General Instrument Corporation.

pany's products or which segments demand something that the company can offer. When the company decides to concentrate on reaching these market segments, they become **target markets.**

Target Market
Market segment an organization designs its marketing mix to reach because that segment is considered likely to demand the product being marketed.

Quaker Oats Co. followed this process in devising a strategy for selling its rice cakes.[13] (See Figure 2.3.) Rice cakes are slabs of puffed grain, each containing 35 calories, that were previously available only in health food stores. Quaker hoped that they would become popular among consumers as a substitute for bread and crackers.

Research indicated that 30 to 40 percent of American homes are "fitness oriented." Quaker decided to make this market segment its target market for rice cakes. It based this decision on the low calorie count of rice cakes; a rice cake contains only half the calories of a typical slice of white bread.

Figure 2.3
Quaker Targets Rice Cakes to the Fitness-Oriented Consumer

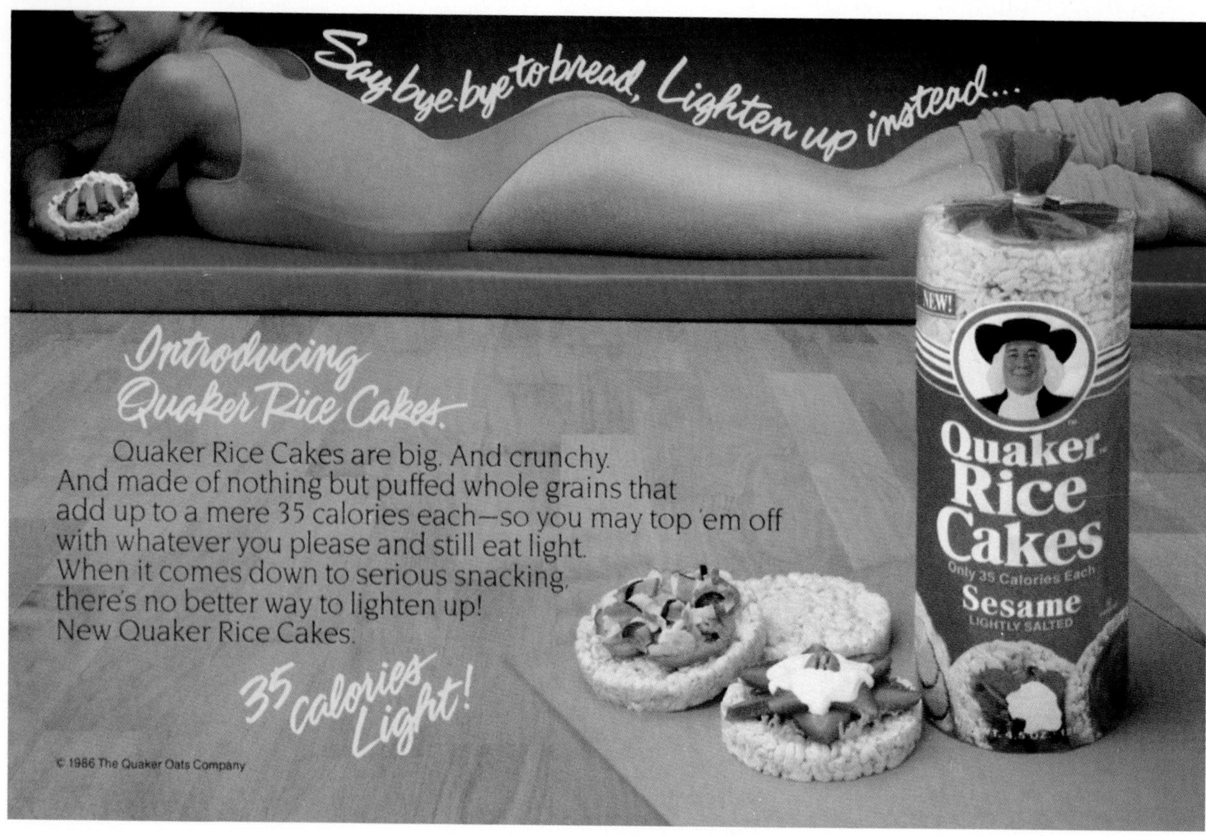

The chapters in Part Two offer a more in-depth look at target marketing and the analysis of markets.

Marketing Mix Chapter 1 discussed the four elements of the marketing mix: product, price, promotion, and placement (or distribution). A marketing plan comprehensively treats each of these elements:

☐ *Product.* Should we develop new products, change old products, or drop products from the line? How should our product(s) be positioned? How should they be branded—national brands, private, generic?

In the case of Quaker's rice cakes, the company decided to position an existing product as an alternative to sandwiches and as a base for a snack or light meal. Quaker used its established name as the brand for this unfamiliar product.

☐ *Price.* Should our price be above, below, or at the rate currently charged for similar products? Should we allow prices to vary based on discount structures or geography? What profit margin do we seek?

Rather than reduce the price of rice cakes to woo customers, Quaker improved their value by solving a problem common to the product. Rice cakes absorb moisture rapidly, so when they become stale, they become unappealing. Quaker redesigned the package with thicker plastic to ensure a six-month shelf life.

☐ *Promotion.* What should be our mix of advertising, sales promotion, personal selling, and dealer incentives? How should our budget be apportioned? What media should we use? What message do we seek to convey?

Quaker developed a message focusing on fitness and contemporary lifestyles. A series of TV commercials show scenes at beaches and health clubs. The message is "35 calories will fill you up, not out." These commercials are part of a national television and print advertising campaign, the most aggressive advertising effort thus far for a rice cake product.

☐ *Placement, or Distribution.* Should our products be available in many locations or few? What type of wholesaler and retailer should we use? Should these distribution channels be long or short?

In the past, buyers of rice cakes could find them only in health food stores. To reach a broader market, Quaker began distributing them to supermarkets.

A marketing manager's job is to mesh product, price, promotion, and placement into a workable plan so that the final result is more than the sum of its parts—all the while keeping budget considerations in mind. At the beginning of this chapter, the job of marketing manager was compared with that of a symphony conductor. Perhaps it is now easier to see why the analogy is apt. In both cases the concerns are many and the chances of disharmony great, but the rewards may be equally great for a job skillfully done.

Chapter Replay

1. **What are the marketing manager's basic tasks?**
   The marketing manager is responsible for strategic marketing planning, implementing the marketing plan, and evaluating the results of marketing efforts.
2. **What is involved in strategic marketing planning?**
   Strategic marketing planning includes establishing an organization's overall goals, assessing opportunities, and developing marketing objectives. This process results in marketing strategies.
3. **What are the elements of a marketing strategy?**
   A marketing strategy consists of the marketing mix selected to reach specified target markets in order to achieve marketing objectives.

4. **What are some special challenges of marketing management?** These challenges include the highly changeable nature of the market, geographical complexities of the market, heavy dependence on people's skills, the need to rely on people outside the firm, the great number of alternatives, and the marketing department's major influence on the firm's success.
5. **How does a company define a mission and objectives?** First, the company defines its mission in short, general statements, which are ideally customer-oriented. The mission is then translated into specific objectives linked with measurable goals.
6. **What goes into a marketing plan?** A marketing plan begins with an analysis of the market, including demand, competition, environmental climate, resources of the firm, distribution factors, and political and legal constraints. Based on this information, the plan evaluates problems and opportunities. It then sets forth a marketing strategy, using target markets and marketing mix to achieve marketing objectives.
7. **How do marketers decide what segments of the total market will be the focus of their efforts?** Marketers divide the total market into market segments. They evaluate which segments will most likely demand what the company offers. Based on this evaluation, they select segments to be target markets.
8. **What is the role of marketing mix in the marketing plan?** A marketing plan comprehensively treats these elements—product, price, promotion, and placement—in determining how each will help the company achieve its objectives in reaching target markets.

Key Terms

consumer market
differential advantage
environmental analysis
general (macro) environment
goals
industrial market
internal (micro) environment
market
market segment
marketing manager
marketing objectives
marketing strategy
operating environment
organizational objectives
strategic marketing planning
target market

Discussion Questions

1. What is the difference between strategic marketing planning and a marketing strategy?
2. What is wrong with the following marketing objectives?
   a. Have 65 percent of the automobile owners in Midtown try our car wash.
   b. Increase profits by 5 percent by the end of next year.

3. Why must marketing managers be aware of other departments' problems and capabilities?
4. Before a marketer can set objectives or devise a strategy for meeting them, he or she must analyze the market. What topics are typically included in a market analysis?
5. Researchers in the marketing department of A-1 Gloves, Inc., have divided the market for gloves into groups according to high, middle, or low income; region of the country; and high or low frequency of participation in winter sports. What is the marketing term for such categories?

   The marketing manager has learned of a new fabric that is expensive but has superior insulating properties. Gloves made of this fabric could keep hands warm at 50 degrees below zero. How might A-1 Gloves use the categories of consumers to select target markets?
6. Which of the following market segments describe the consumer market? The industrial market?
   a. Customers of a hair salon
   b. People who have enrolled in a stop-smoking workshop
   c. A gas station that buys gas from a major oil company
   d. Customers of the gas station
   e. An apartment building manager who buys a snow blower to clear the walks around the building
   f. A father who buys a balloon and then gives it to his child
7. How can organizations blunt the effects of competition? Who are the competitors of charitable organizations, such as Project HOPE or the Salvation Army? Do the same strategies for competing apply to these organizations?
8. What is a differential advantage? Give an example of a tangible resource and of an intangible resource that give a company a differential advantage.
9. John Doe and Ray Mead established a music school. John gives piano lessons, and Ray teaches guitar and voice. They have a steady stream of pupils, but after several years and much analysis of their local market, they have decided to expand. Together, John and Ray settle on a marketing objective: to double their business in three years. To achieve their marketing objectives, what should John and Ray include in their marketing strategy?

Case 2.1
California Beef Council (A)

Because beef producers throughout the state recognized their shared need for a single research, education, and promotion channel for beef, the California Beef Council (CBC) was established. In 1957, legislation

Source: Adapted from the California Beef Council's 1987 Marketing Plan and earlier ones.

was passed making the CBC one of the nation's three oldest beef councils.

Council Background

For the first 17 years, voluntary industry contributions supported the council. Then in 1974, legislation was passed providing a compulsory checkoff system. An assessment is deducted from the price that producers and handlers receive when an animal is sold. In 1982, new legislation increasing CBC funding went into effect. The assessment was raised from $.25 to $1 per head for live cattle produced in California, and an equivalent mil assessment was placed on beef shipped into the state.

The 1987 budget year is more different than ever before as the new national checkoff is now in effect. Half of every dollar collected is forwarded directly to the national program, as well as the entire dollar collected for animals that are transported to California for immediate sale or slaughter. The new national assessment changes CBC operating practices. Revenues for 1987 are projected to be lower than in 1986 as is the cash carry over, which is considerably lower than in previous years. A $2.5 million in-state assessment is projected to carry out the 1987 Market Plan goals in promotion, research, education, and public information. Half of the 1987 collections will be sent to the national program. The total 1987 budget projection is approximately $3 million.

The CBC staff is experienced in consumer marketing, advertising, research, promotion, communications, nutrition, and home economics. All CBC programs are approved by the director of the California Department of Food and Agriculture.

Much of the council's effort goes into coordinating activities with similar national programs. The CBC maintains a small staff and frequently calls upon consultants from promotional agencies and universities to increase its service to the industry.

Organizational Objectives

As a marketing organization, the CBC views the marketplace from the consumer's, rather than the producer's, perspective. Specifically, the CBC desires to:

- ☐ Understand consumer attitudes toward purchase and consumption of beef and its competitors.
- ☐ Determine how consumers currently perceive beef as a food and the beef industry.
- ☐ Identify opportunities to enhance those attributes of beef and the beef industry that the consumer views as important.

The CBC's basic mission is to increase consumer demand for beef in California and to generate positive attitudes about the beef industry, its products, and practices. The overall 1987 Market Plan strategy is to maximize the impact of the national Beef Industry Council programs in

California and, simultaneously, to develop and carry out programs that fit the regional needs of the California market.

The basic rationale behind this mission is that there are only three ways to achieve increased demand: (1) by gaining new customers, (2) by increasing volume per use among current customers, or (3) by increasing the frequency of usage among current users. Beef currently enjoys a 94 percent household penetration. Those who do not eat beef refrain because of health restrictions or personal convictions that offer little potential for conversion. Attempting to increase portion size, on judgment, runs contrary to current light eating trends. Therefore, increasing the number of beef meals per week offers the greatest potential for increased volume.

The secondary objective of the CBC is to generate a positive attitude among California residents concerning the cattle industry and the products they produce. To achieve that objective, the CBC will use every feasible means to communicate the value of cattle production as a vital resource in the manufacture of numerous consumer and industrial products in addition to food.

The rationale supporting this secondary objective is that the cattle industry has been the subject of negative publicity concerning feeding practices and, more generally, the allocation of limited natural resources to cattle production. It is imperative that the industry respond to these issues to give the general public a balanced perspective. On judgment, the CBC believes that the consumer's resistance to current retail prices is to some degree a result of a reduction in perceived value generated by negative publicity.

Focal Topics

1. Do you agree that the CBC should view the marketplace from the perspective of the consumer rather than the producer? Why, or why not?
2. Evaluate the rationales used to support the primary and secondary objectives of the CBC.
3. What other objectives might be appropriate for the CBC?

Case 2.2
Franklin International (A)

Franklin International

Franklin International can trace its roots to 1935 when the company started with a single product—animal glues for furniture. Today, the company still produces that initial product, Liquid Hide Glue, but it has grown from that single item to one of the most diversified manufacturers in the country of adhesives and sealants for home and industry. Franklin was the first to develop a synthetic aliphatic resin glue as a substitute for animal glues. The company continues its role today as an innovator of new products through its research and development laboratory, which also provides technical assistance to industry users of Franklin's products.

With manufacturing and corporate offices in Columbus, Ohio, the company operates warehouses located strategically throughout the United States to service its customers. From its base of industrial wood adhesives, the company has integrated backward into the manufacturing of the polymers that serve as the raw material for the wood glues. The company has also expanded forward into the manufacture of adhesive, sealants, and caulking for the consumer market.

Company Organization

The company is divided into four primary businesses. The Industrial Division, the original business, sells adhesives to furniture manufacturers. The Polymer Division, originally created to produce raw materials for the Industrial Division, now sells two-thirds of its production to other adhesive users, such as label manufacturers. The remaining third is sold to the Industrial and Consumer Divisions. The Plastics Division was created to ensure the Consumer Division a steady supply of bottles to package its products; 90 percent of its sales are now to outside customers.

The Consumer Products Division was created as a new natural extension of the Industrial Division to market wood glues to nonindustrial users. The current product line includes Titebond (the first aliphatic resin glue) and Franklin Construction Adhesive (the first construction adhesive sold to the consumer markets). These two products, in varying sizes, account for nearly 40 percent of the Consumer Division's sales. Other products include wood flooring adhesives, latex caulks, and paneling adhesives.

Marketing activities of the Polymer and Plastics Divisions are directed to a relatively small number of potential customers. The Industrial and Consumer Divisions, on the other hand, have a large number of present and potential customers.

Industrial Division The Industrial Division sells directly through company salespeople to furniture manufacturers and cabinetmakers. The salespeople also provide a technical support function to the manufacturer. The superior technical ability of the salespeople is believed to be a key differentiating factor in comparing Franklin to the competition.

The Industrial Division had always positioned itself as the quality, premium-priced producer in the marketplace. Management determined long ago that it did not want to participate in markets that are only based on price and that if satisfactory margins were not available from a product, they would not carry that product. With increased competition in the 1960s and 1970s, however, even products that had traditionally been only moderately price sensitive were being promoted and sold on the basis of lower prices by Franklin's competition as a means of gaining a foothold in the market. This was probably the key reason for the shrinking of the Industrial Division's market share in the 1970s. To counteract, or at least abate this erosion, the company decided to initiate a formal advertising program in 1978 that continues today.

With the decision to create some type of advertising program, several additional decisions were reached to maintain consistency of image. First, all advertisements were to reflect the quality image the company enjoyed in the furniture industry. Second, the advertisements were to highlight the technical capabilities and experience of the company as well as the different products. Third, to illustrate company commitment to quality and service, all advertisements would be full page and in full color.

Consumer Products Division The Consumer Products Division manufactures some private brands for major retailers and markets its own brands through a variety of channels such as:

- *Building material distributors*—who sell primarily to lumber yards, cabinet shops, and large contractors.
- *Hardware distributors*—who sell primarily to independent hardware retailers.
- *Building materials chains*—who act as purchasing agents for all the stores in a chain, usually home centers.
- *Hardware co-ops*—who act as purchasing agents for member hardware dealers; typical co-ops include True Value, Ace, and Trustworthy.

In the past, promotions normally took the form of a discount on specific sizes of a product and were usually introduced at a hardware or home center show. Special discounts of $1–$5 per case to the buyer were sometimes used as an additional incentive to purchase the sale merchandise. A co-op advertising fund was utilized as an aid to the hardware dealer in promoting Franklin products. Dealers were eligible for reimbursement of 50 percent of their advertising costs on Franklin products up to a maximum of 3 percent of their total purchases upon submission of the advertising copy and proof of purchase of Franklin products from their distributor or co-op. The division plans to make some major changes in its promotional strategies.

Focal Topics

1. What would you describe as the "real business" of Franklin International? From a marketing perspective, why does the firm exist?
2. How might the marketing concept be applied to a firm like Franklin?
3. Assume that the president feels that Franklin is too product or production oriented. How would you suggest that the firm become more marketing oriented?

3 Environments for Marketing Strategies

☐ Sounding Out the Chapter

In this chapter, you will learn:

1. **General categories of competitive markets.**
2. **How marketers can respond to the competition in each of these markets.**
3. **How the government protects fair competition.**
4. **How the government protects consumers.**
5. **Ways in which industries regulate themselves.**
6. **Issues marketers must address in responding to the social environment.**
7. **Responsibilities of producers and consumers.**
8. **How marketers can respond to changes in the economic environment.**
9. **How marketers can respond to changes in the technological environment.**

Source: Neil Leifer/Time Magazine.

Tobacco Advertising under Fire

The environment for cigarette advertisers is hardly a friendly one. In nations around the world, consumer and medical groups are pressuring governments to prohibit tobacco advertising. Opponents of tobacco advertising argue that if a product is harmful, it should not be promoted. The tobacco industry and advertisers respond that a product that is legal to sell should also be legal to promote.

Despite this argument, the worldwide trend seems to favor restrictions. According to James Neelankavil, a consultant for the International Advertising Association, "In the last five years, there seems to be more clamoring. For every ten times people jump up and down, three or four restrictions pass, and that's much more than before." In 1986 alone, tobacco advertising was under attack in Singapore, the Netherlands, Argentina, Australia, South Korea, Hong Kong, Brazil, New Zealand, Canada, and the United Kingdom.

In countries that already ban tobacco advertising, governments are restricting other moves by marketers to promote cigarettes. In Italy, for example, legislation was proposed to ban promotions such as displaying cigarette brand names on clothing.

Some governments are considering other avenues to reduce smoking, such as antismoking advertisements and higher cigarette taxes. In Germany, the government increased the tobacco tax 39 percent. Cuba has instituted a nationwide antismoking campaign. The country's president, Fidel Castro, has taken a leadership role by giving up cigars and urging others to do the same.

While the results of these efforts are unclear, there is no evidence that the pressure on tobacco advertisers will ease anytime soon. The pressure is more severe than other advertisers typically face, but every marketer is affected in some way by consumer expectations and government regulations.

Chapter 2 introduced you to the variety of issues that marketers must consider when planning a marketing strategy. Many of those forces are outside a marketer's control, but can, nonetheless, exert a powerful influence over the success or failure of a marketing plan. Taken together, those forces constitute the company's marketing environment. This chapter considers more closely the various forces that bear upon the way a company markets its products.

Sources: "Fidel on Cigars: 'No More,' " *Time,* September 8, 1986, p. 47; and "Pressure Is on for Tobacco Ad Ban Worldwide," *Advertising Age,* August 18, 1986, pp. 46, 48.

The Competitive Environment

The previous chapter discussed competition as an element of the operating environment that marketers have to take into account in market planning. But not all competition is alike. A marketing manager for Pacific Gas & Electric, which is the only supplier of those utilities in its service area, has quite a different job from that of the marketing manager for Warner Records—in more ways than are immediately apparent. The Warner manager, for example, must worry about the competition from Capitol Records, RCA, MCA, Arista, and A&M, not to mention the competition for young adults' spending money posed by movies, video games, and rock concerts. The manager of PG&E also may have many things to worry about, such as population shifts or consumer attitudes, but competition from other utilities is not among those concerns.

Types of Competitive Markets

The nature of the competitive market greatly influences a firm's marketing decisions, especially pricing decisions. Therefore, the marketing manager needs to understand the nature of the market in which his or her organization operates.

Competitive markets fall into four general categories: pure competition, oligopoly, monopolistic competition, and monopoly.[1] When deciding which category applies to a given situation, marketers should keep in mind that categories overlap, and a firm may actually operate in a combination of competitive markets.

Pure Competition
Situation in which there are many sellers, no seller dominates a market, and the products sold are interchangeable.

Pure Competition The competitive market is characterized by **pure competition** when the following conditions exist:

- ☐ Products are uniform—for example, potatoes, coal, chemicals, or laundry services.
- ☐ There are many buyers and sellers.

In this environment, sellers can do little to influence price. If a seller charges more than the going price, buyers will take their business elsewhere. The seller has no reason to charge less than the going price. Marketers facing pure competition seek primarily to ensure a wide distribution of their product at a competitive price.

Agriculture is typical of pure competition. Few consumers can distinguish between fresh green beans offered by various growers in Florida, so each grower must set prices in line with supply. If a drought destroys the bean crop in California, the Florida grower may be able to raise prices. But if New Jersey farmers have a bumper crop, farmers in Florida may barely be able to charge enough to recover their costs.

Oligopoly
Situation in which a few firms dominate the market, set similar prices, and make entry by other firms difficult.

Oligopoly An **oligopoly** exists when a few companies dominate an industry. Two examples of oligopolies are the U.S. steel industry, which is dominated by ten large companies, and the aluminum industry, in which five companies produce 78 percent of the country's supply.

When competition is oligopolistic, the dominant companies have great control over the product's price. The prices of competitive products tend to be similar, because price competition would reduce firms' profits.[2] Instead, marketers use other elements of the marketing mix to distinguish their products from those of competitors.

Monopolistic Competition The word *monopolistic* means having exclusive possession. In **monopolistic competition,** each firm tries to gain exclusive possession of a share of the market. Buyers perceive products as being diverse, so firms can gain differential advantages. Product diversity is one source of the competition in this type of market. Another source is the relatively large number of sellers, enabling dissatisfied buyers to find alternatives.

Under monopolistic competition, the role of marketing is to establish a brand difference in customers' minds. If these efforts succeed, the company may be able to influence the price at which it sells its products. Ray Ban sunglasses, for example, sell for premium prices because the company has carved out a distinctive style-conscious image in the marketplace.

Monopolistic Competition
Situation in which there are many sellers in a market who rarely engage in price competition but compete by trying to establish brand preferences among consumers.

Monopoly A **monopoly** exists when one company is the exclusive provider of a product or service. A pure monopoly is rare but can exist in one of the following ways:

- *As a government monopoly, such as the U.S. Postal Service.* The government sets prices to meet various policy objectives, such as encouraging or discouraging use.
- *As a private regulated monopoly, such as a utility company.* Under this arrangement, rates are subject to the approval of government regulatory bodies called public service commissions.
- *Temporarily as a private monopoly by holding a patent on a product.* In the United States, a patentholder may be the exclusive manufacturer for 17 years and may charge whatever price the market will bear. Companies may charge less than full price for a variety of reasons, including fear of government regulation or desire to penetrate the market quickly.[3]

Monopoly
Situation in which one company is the exclusive provider of a product or service.

Marketing to Meet the Competition

The type of competitive environment in which a company operates will dramatically affect its marketing strategy. Often, companies wage their competitive battles in the area of price. (Pricing to meet the competition is discussed in Chapter 10.) Some companies may choose to offer enhanced services to distinguish themselves from the competition. Others may offer a unique method of distribution.

In the case of pure competition, a company typically invests little in marketing, because consumers view one company's products as being basically the same as another's. For example, laundromats in a given com-

Betty Crocker

NEW

Suddenly SALAD™

GREAT TASTING SALAD IN NO TIME

BOIL

Just boil our special Fresh-Flo™ Pouch.

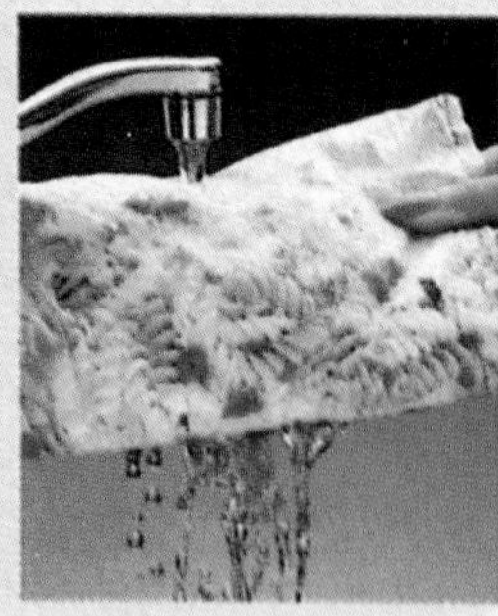

RINSE TO CHILL

Rinse under cold water to chill. No refrigeration needed!

TOSS

Add our special seasonings and toss with your own fresh oil or mayonnaise.

Live high—with Classic Pasta Salad, Creamy Macaroni Salad, Italian Pasta Salad, and Creamy Potato Salad from Betty Crocker. Look for Suddenly Salad on your grocer's shelf.

munity provide about the same service at the same price, and they don't take out ads in magazines, rent billboard space, or give away coupons.

In an oligopoly, although companies may engage in price wars, they avoid price competition. For example, in the automobile industry, major advertising campaigns tell consumers about the benefits of various models. In the fall of 1986, however, the major U.S. automakers engaged in a kind of price war when they followed each other in offering new-car loans at very low interest rates, even 0 percent. But by 1987, the companies had returned to touting the benefits of their cars.

Under monopolistic competition, companies look for a differential advantage. In the restaurant business, for example, each restaurant has many choices in devising a marketing mix to capture a slice of the total market. These choices include varying the atmosphere, menu, service, location, and prices. McDonald's has a large share of the fast-food market, but even though its prices are lower than those at elegant French restaurants, McDonald's will not sell to much of the market segment that consists of people who want a fancy dinner.

It might seem that a monopoly company would have no need of marketing, but such companies usually do market their products. For example, a patentholder might try to build a large base of loyal customers before its patent runs out. Or a utility might try to build goodwill to reduce consumer opposition to future requests for rate increases.

Sometimes the marketing environment changes, and organizations can help to bring about such change. For example, while produce has traditionally been sold in a purely competitive market, some large sellers of prepared vegetables have begun putting their name on fresh vegetables. Pillsbury has tried distributing cleaned and trimmed asparagus, broccoli, cauliflower, and two vegetable mixtures under its Green Giant name. Kraft Inc. has introduced a line of cut and packaged vegetables it calls VegiSnax. One industry observer forecasts that branded produce will eventually account for half of all produce sales.[4] Figure 3.1 shows an advertisement for another product developed to appeal to the branding of salad items.

The Legal and Political Environments

One of the strongest forces that marketing decision makers must face is the **legal environment.** It consists of laws and interpretations of laws that compel business to operate under competitive conditions and to observe various consumer rights.

Legal Environment
Laws that compel businesses to operate under competitive conditions and to observe specified consumer rights.

Legislation Regulating Business

Political and economic thinking in the United States assumes that the economy benefits from competition among many firms. Presumably, then, the public benefits from laws that protect competition. These laws are called **procompetitive legislation.**

Procompetitive Legislation
Laws that sustain and protect competition.

Figure 3.1
Betty Crocker Suddenly Salad

Table 3.1
Federal Legislation Protecting Competition

Sherman Antitrust Act (1890)

Prohibits contracts or conspiracies that would restrain trade and forbids monopolies or attempts to form monopolies.

Clayton Act (1914)

Prohibits practices such as price discrimination and tying contracts (requiring a customer to buy one product to get another) that would lessen competition or create a monopoly.

Federal Trade Commission Act (1914)

Created the FTC and gave it the power to prosecute unfair practices and to investigate industries.

Robinson-Patman Act (1936)

Outlaws certain price discrimination practices among wholesalers and retailers (such as giving discounts to buyers not based on cost savings to manufacturers) that would lessen competition.

Miller-Tydings Act (1937) and McGuire-Keogh Act (1952)

Amended Sherman Act to allow manufacturers to prevent price cutting by fixing the retail price of their goods (called fair trade laws).

Wheeler-Lea Act (1938)

Empowered the FTC to prosecute unfair practices that injure the public as well as competition—specifically the power to prosecute cases of false advertising.

Celler-Kefauver Antimerger Act (1950)

Forbids one corporation from acquiring the stock or assets of another if the result would be to lessen competition in that industry.

Consumer Goods Pricing Act (1975)

Prohibits the use of price maintenance agreements among manufacturers and resellers in interstate commerce.

Magnuson-Moss Warranty/FTC Improvement Act (1975)

Established standards for written consumer product warranties.

The first procompetitive laws were passed near the end of the last century. Following the Civil War, industries had expanded, and some of them became monopolies that raised prices and squeezed smaller companies out of the market. The wealthy men who controlled these monopolies were called robber barons. The first laws were a response to the monopolies and robber barons.

Some of the major laws protecting fair competition are listed in Table 3.1. The first was the Sherman Antitrust Act, passed in 1890. It prohibits contracts or conspiracies that would restrain trade and forbids attempts to create a monopoly. Subsequent laws have prohibited price fixing, bid rigging, and boycotts and mergers within the same industry.

Regulatory Forces

Marketing decisions are greatly influenced by the many laws affecting competition. The enforcement of the laws, in turn, is affected by the prevailing political climate and by public opinion. The priorities of governmental and nongovernmental regulatory forces are subject to change. Marketers must be constantly alert to subtle shifts in public and political attitudes toward business in general and their products in particular.

Governmental Regulatory Forces The first governmental body formed specifically to investigate cases of unfair competition was the Federal Trade Commission (FTC). It was established in 1914 as an independent five-member agency and given the power to proceed against all violators of the Sherman and Clayton acts. In 1938, the commission's powers were expanded by the Wheeler-Lea Act to allow it to prosecute cases of false advertising.

The Wheeler-Lea Act gave the FTC a consumer orientation. Since the passage of that act, Congress has enacted other laws that have made the commission one of the chief protectors of consumer rights. Its exact role has varied somewhat, as the federal government has responded in different ways to pressures from marketers and consumers. (See Marketing Today 3.1.)

Besides the Federal Trade Commission, the Justice Department is the principal agency for handling antitrust matters. Either of these bodies may start an antitrust suit in court, or an injured competitor may start the action.

Antitrust laws provide for punishment of violators, restitution to injured competitors, and relief from further violations. Punishment may take the form of jail sentences and fines for executives, as well as fines for the offending firms. Restitution is usually made through civil suits. Injured competitors may recover triple the amount of financial loss suffered because of the violation. To prevent further injury, the government may seek:

1. An injunction, or court order, to refrain from a practice.
2. A consent decree, or voluntary agreement by the company to abide by the rules of business behavior in the decree.
3. A dissolution or divestiture decree, or order to break up.

In addition to the FTC, Congress has established several other federal regulatory agencies to oversee specific industries:

- ☐ The Food and Drug Administration, which controls the product development, manufacturing, branding, labeling, and advertising of food and drugs.
- ☐ The Interstate Commerce Commission.
- ☐ The Consumer Products Safety Commission, which sets safety standards for products and imposes penalties for failure to meet the standards.
- ☐ The Civil Aeronautics Board, which regulates the airline industry.

Marketing Today 3.1
Politics and the Federal Trade Commission

Source: Copyright Field Museum of Natural

Not only does the Federal Trade Commission influence marketers, but marketers influence the power of the FTC. As a result, the agency's role has shifted throughout the years.

For many years the Federal Trade Commission was derided as "The Little Old Lady on Pennsylvania Avenue"—a fussy, nitpicking, but essentially ineffectual force for business regulation. Then came the consumer movement of the 1970s, and the FTC emerged as a powerful protector of consumer rights. Led by Carter appointee Michael Pertschuk, the agency aggressively went to work on issues as diverse as children's advertising, cigarette pack warnings, and the funeral industry.

By the end of the decade, the business community had begun to view the FTC as the *Tyrannosaurus rex* of regulation. The agency was criticized for regulatory overkill. Critics blamed it for undermining productivity and tying the hands of American business when Japan was providing stiff competition. Congress responded by limiting the agency's power. Beginning in 1980, Congress has each year prohibited the FTC from making industrywide rules against unfair advertising practices.

The Reagan administration has emphasized deregulation. In 1986, however, Congress voted not to permanently strip the FTC of its power to set rules for industrywide ad practices. Congress took this action despite two years of intense lobbying by advertisers, who feared a repeat of such actions as the FTC attempt to regulate children's TV programming in the late 1970s.

Sources: Steven W. Colford, "FTC Survives Ad Challenge," *Advertising Age,* May 10, 1986, p. 10; "A Farewell to Deregulation," *Fortune,* September 19, 1983, p. 49; and "The FTC's Miller Puts His Faith in the Free Market," *Business Week,* June 27, 1983, pp. 66–70.

- ☐ The Federal Communications Commission, which regulates radio and television broadcasting.
- ☐ The Environmental Protection Agency, which sets and enforces standards for pollution control.
- ☐ The Office of Consumer Affairs.

The regulations of these agencies may apply to the way a product is designed and manufactured, the design of and information on the product's packaging, the information in the advertising for the product, the price at which the product is sold, and other concerns of the marketer.

Political Influences Affecting Regulation Technically these agencies are independent, but they are greatly influenced by the political party in office. Often, when a new administration takes office, members of the various agencies resign. Since the president is responsible for appointing new members, he has a strong influence on the subsequent behavior of the commissions.

Other political and economic factors also influence the power these agencies command. When Jimmy Carter was president, for example, spiraling inflation was one of the country's chief economic concerns. After listening to critics who claimed that regulations added significantly to consumer costs, he initiated the use of **cost-benefit analysis** as a way of weighing economic costs against economic benefits. Such an analysis would seek to compare the cost of a factory's new air-quality equipment with the cost society might have to bear if it were not installed and workers subsequently became ill because of job-related pollutants.

Cost-Benefit Analysis System for weighing economic costs against economic benefits.

Under Carter's successor, Ronald Reagan, deregulation was a priority. In the different political climate of the Reagan administration, many laws were revised or revoked. As a result, marketers faced a different set of choices for developing and selling products. To be aware of all marketing opportunities while avoiding the consequences of violating the law, marketers must keep a careful watch over governmental actions, both in and out of the courts.

Industry Self-Regulation Many industries have formed self-regulatory bodies to oversee the activities of their members. The motives for forming such groups range from an attempt to ward off possible government regulations to the hope of establishing a favorable image for the industry in the public mind. The few named here are of special interest to marketers.

The *National Advertising Review Board (NARB)* was founded in 1971 to monitor national advertising for truth and accuracy. Complaints from the National Advertising Division of the Council of Better Business Bureaus, from consumers, and from competing advertisers are referred to a five-member panel for review. While the NARB can recommend that an ad it finds deceptive be modified or discontinued, the organization itself can take no disciplinary action. Following is an actual case that came before the NARB panel:

Complaint: *Advertising of Kal Kan Food Inc.'s Kal Kan dog food had the capacity to mislead many consumers into believing that certain ingredients used in a competitive brand may be harmful to the health of their dogs.*

Decision: *The panel ruled that the Kal Kan advertising falsely disparaged a competitor's product and made explicit and implied claims that do not have general acceptance in the field of veterinary medicine. The advertiser agreed to discontinue the challenged copy.*

Advertiser Statement: *The advertiser claimed in its own defense that its goal was simply to point out that Kal Kan used natural foods in its product while the competition used synthetic chemicals and supplements, so that consumers could make informed choices about the product they prefer for their pets.*[5]

The *Direct Marketing Association (DMA)* is made up of companies engaged in direct mail, telephone, and direct-response broadcast marketing. Its guidelines for ethical business practices for its members stress honesty in advertising (both in product claims and terms of payment), cautious use of the word "free," clear disclosure of rules governing sweepstakes, prompt shipment of prepaid merchandise, and strict attention to the proper handling of personal data. Because its members are in touch with consumers so directly, the association has been especially sensitive to consumer issues. It established a Mail Preference Service (MPS) that allows consumers to have their names removed from DMA members' lists. (See Figure 3.2.) It will provide the same service with regard to telephone marketing. Its Mail Order Action Line handles consumer mail-order complaints. While the DMA has no regulatory enforcement procedures, its Committee on Ethical Business Practices monitors the mails and investigates consumer complaints.

The *Council of Better Business Bureaus* (CBBB) is an international association of national and local businesses whose goal is to ensure consumer confidence in the marketplace. The council has offices in over 130 cities, where it tries to mediate between consumers and businesses. The bureaus operate largely through the voluntary cooperation of their members and have little real enforcement ability. Consumers may, however, contact their local bureau to determine if a particular business is known to be reputable.

Social Environment
Climate of public opinion that affects marketers' practices.

The Social Environment

You switch on your new stereo, only to discover that one of the speakers doesn't work. Your pants shrink two sizes the first time you wash them. You call three banks to find out where your savings will get the best return but can't make sense of what the bank's representatives tell you. How do you feel in situations like these? Many consumers have come to believe that they have a right to expect more from the suppliers of goods and services.

The Rise of Consumerism

Chapter 1 discussed the rise of consumerism, the social movement that increased the powers and rights of buyers. One of the major causes of consumerism was increased education and income in the 1960s; consumers bought more, were disappointed more often, and were better able to express their frustrations. Another cause was greater complexity of products, making an informed choice difficult. At the same time, consumers found it especially important to make informed choices as the inflation of the 1960s and 1970s eroded their buying power. Finally, writers and activists, such as Rachel Carson and Ralph Nader, drew national attention to environmental and consumer issues.

Many politicians were quick to sense a potential vote-getting issue. In 1962, President John Kennedy articulated a "consumer bill of rights." It noted the obligation of the government to protect the consumer's right to safety, information, freedom of choice, and the ability to be heard. The rights corresponded closely to specific complaints consumers were voicing about marketing practices.

Today, consumerism is less popular as a political issue, but it still carries weight. In the final weeks of the 1986 session, the Senate consid-

Figure 3.2
Coupon for the Mail Preference Service

YES! Our company wants to be a part of the direct marketing industry's commitment to the Mail Preference Service for consumers who do not wish to receive advertising in the mail.

IMPORTANT: Our company agrees that use of the DMA Mail Preference Service is strictly for the purpose of removing consumer names from mailing lists. We recognize that DMA authorizes use of MPS for no other purpose, and we agree to use MPS for its intended purpose.

Enter my subscription as follows:

Authorized Signature

Date

MONTH ☐ Jan. ☐ July ☐ Apr. ☐ Oct.

Company Name

Street

City State Zip

To the attention of

Telephone

dma TM

TAPES ☐ 1600 BPI ☐ 6250 BPI	DMA Member Cost	Non-Member Cost
4 PER YEAR	☐ $175	☐ $275
3 PER YEAR	☐ $150	☐ $225
2 PER YEAR	☐ $100	☐ $150
1 PER YEAR	☐ $ 50	☐ $ 75

Yes! Our company wants to be a part of the direct marketing industry's commitment to the Telephone Preference Service for consumers who do not wish to receive national telephone sales calls.

Important: Our company agrees that use of the DMA Telephone Preference Service is strictly for the purpose of removing consumer names from calling lists. We recognize that DMA authorizes use of TPS for no other purpose, and we agree to use TPS for its intended purpose.

Enter my subscription as follows:

Authorized Signature

Date

Company Name

Street

City State Zip

To the attention of

Telephone

dma TM

TAPES ☐ 1600 BPI ☐ 6250 BPI	DMA MEMBER COST	NON-MEMBER COST
4 PER YEAR	☐ $175	☐ $275
3 PER YEAR	☐ $150	☐ $225
2 PER YEAR	☐ $100	☐ $150
1 PER YEAR	☐ $ 50	☐ $ 75

Source: Direct Mail Marketing Association.

ered a bill that would limit court awards to victims of unsafe products. The bill never made it to a vote, however, as it was thought to favor business too heavily.[6]

Marketing Abuses—and Responses

Consumers voice most of their dissatisfaction in four areas. They are most concerned about (1) deficiencies in product quality, (2) lack of information, (3) unfair pricing practices, and (4) environmental pollution.[7]

Product Quality Consumers are concerned about the quality of the goods they buy and the quality of the services that accompany those goods. They complain that many products are unsafe, impure, or defective. They complain that it is nearly impossible to get honest and competent repairs.

Besides repairs, many types of services have been the target of consumer complaints. Marketers have had to face the challenge of trying to balance price and service to find a satisfactory mix. For example, the price cutting that has followed deregulation in the airline industry has led airlines to increase their overbooking of seats. As a result, passengers are more likely to be bumped from flights.

In stores, customers complain about the difficulty in finding helpful salespeople. Sears grouped its salesclerks around cash registers to speed up the check-out process, reducing the number of employees who were in store aisles to answer questions. The decline in service led Sears to reevaluate its decision, and it has since put more people on the sales floor. Other common complaints about service involve banks that discourage small accounts, gas stations that no longer sell service along with gas, and doctors who no longer have time to talk to patients.[8]

With regard to deficiencies in the quality of goods, Ralph Nader's report on defective cars was one of the first major exposés. But automobiles have not been the only culprits. At about the same time as Nader's report, one governmental agency reported that 20 million Americans each year required medical treatment for accidents resulting from faulty products. The news media have told many stories of product hazards: cancer-causing food additives, highly flammable children's clothing, radiation seepage from color televisions and computer screens, and many others.

In response to such complaints, the Consumer Product Safety Commission (CPSC) was established in 1972. It has two primary powers: (1) to order the recall, repair, or replacement of any product thought to be a risk to the consumer and (2) to set safety standards for industry groups to meet.

Recall
Power of certain federal agencies to require manufacturers to notify customers that a product may be hazardous and may be exchanged or repaired.

The power to **recall** is the commission's ultimate weapon. Manufacturers must notify the CPSC within 24 hours of discovering a product safety hazard; they must then notify consumers to bring products in for repair, replacement, or refund. Manufacturers who do not comply face stiff fines. The commission has recalled over 20 million unsafe prod-

Figure 3.3
FTC Health Warnings on Cigarette Packs and Print Advertisements

SURGEON GENERAL'S WARNING: Quitting Smoking Now Greatly Reduces Serious Risks to Your Health.

SURGEON GENERAL'S WARNING: Cigarette Smoke Contains Carbon Monoxide.

SURGEON GENERAL'S WARNING: Smoking Causes Lung Cancer, Heart Disease, Emphysema, And May Complicate Pregnancy.

SURGEON GENERAL'S WARNING: Smoking By Pregnant Women May Result in Fetal Injury, Premature Birth, And Low Birth Weight.

ucts—from TV sets to tires and toys. Recalls are expensive. Therefore, most companies are now spending more money on product testing before marketing.

Market Information Especially in light of the complexity of modern products, consumers need information to make intelligent buying decisions. They expect the information companies supply in their advertising and on their packaging will be truthful.

These expectations are backed up by the enforcement power of the Federal Trade Commission. The FTC requires marketers to provide documentation to support advertising claims and to run corrective ads when false claims are made.

Beyond the prevention of abuses, the FTC has taken steps to disclose information that may aid consumers in making purchases. The commission has led the fight to require health warnings and tar and nicotine levels on cigarette packs. (See Figure 3.3.) It enforces a rule that gasoline stations post octane ratings on pumps, and it requires clothing manufacturers to include instructions for cleaning garments on the labels attached to them.[9] (See Table 3.2 for a list of important legislation that protects consumers against misbranding or false advertising.)

The Fair Packaging and Labeling Act gives the Food and Drug Administration the power to require certain information on labels (such as the U.S. Recommended Daily Allowance of vitamins and nutrients),

Table 3.2
Protection against Misbranding and False or Harmful Advertising

Wheeler-Lea Act (1938)

Enlarged Federal Trade Commission's powers to cover deceptive acts or practices in commerce, and false advertising of foods, drugs, and cosmetics.

Wool Products Labeling Act (1939)

Required fabric labeling, actual percentage of fabric components, and manufacturer's name.

Fur Products Labeling Act (1951)

Required that furs name animals and country of origin.

Textile Fiber Products Identification Act (1958)

Prohibited misbranding and false advertising of fiber products not covered in the Wool or Fur Labeling acts.

Federal Hazardous Substances Labeling Act (1960)

Required warning labels to appear on items containing dangerous household chemicals.

Fair Packaging and Labeling Act (1966)

Required honest and informative package labeling and attempted to limit the increase in package sizes. Federal Trade Commission, in 1972, required the following to be clearly labeled: origin of the product, quantity of contents and representation of servings, uses and/or applications of the product.

Public Health Cigarette Smoking Act (1970)

Banned cigarette advertising on radio and television; strengthened the required warning on packaging.

Source: David J. Rachman and Michael H. Mescon, *Business Today,* 4th ed. (New York: Random House, 1987), p. 20.

and the Radiation Control for Health and Safety Act allows the FDA to ban color TVs and microwave ovens with excessive radiation.

Besides regulators, competitors give marketers a reason to be careful that their advertising is factual. In the makeup business, Maybelline has disputed Noxell's claim that its Cover Girl Clean Lash mascara is waterproof. Charging false advertising, Maybelline won a court order halting shipments and ads for the mascara. An appeals court then issued a temporary stay of the order, but Maybelline took the case back to court.[10] Court battles are expensive, so advertisers do well to avoid leaving themselves open to such challenges.

Pricing It might seem that price is one element of the marketing mix that has to be clear to buyers. However, when financing enters the picture, consumers can become confused. Different ways of stating the interest rate for credit cards or credit plans can make it nearly impossible for someone who is not a financial expert to determine the actual

Figure 3.4
Credit Card Statement Showing the Annual Percentage Rate

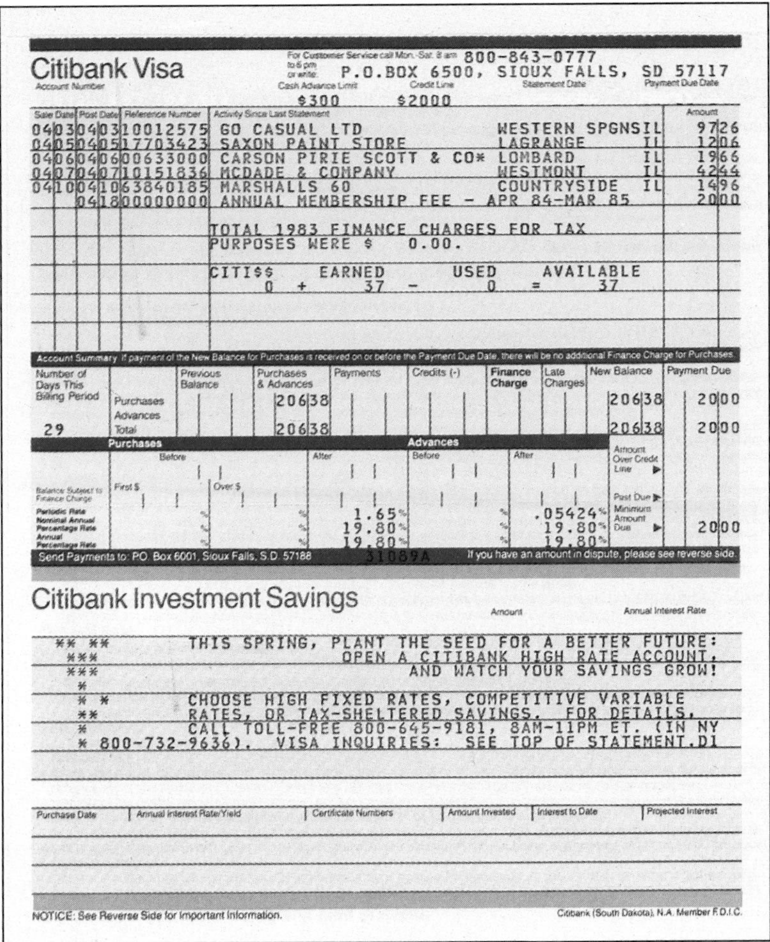

Citibank Visa

For Customer Service call Mon.-Sat. 8 am to 6 pm 800-843-0777
or write: P.O.BOX 6500, SIOUX FALLS, SD 57117

Account Number	Cash Advance Limit	Credit Line	Statement Date	Payment Due Date
	$300	$2000		

Sale Date	Post Date	Reference Number	Activity Since Last Statement		Amount
0403	0403	10012575	GO CASUAL LTD	WESTERN SPGNS IL	97 26
0405	0405	17703423	SAXON PAINT STORE	LAGRANGE IL	12 06
0406	0406	00633000	CARSON PIRIE SCOTT & CO*	LOMBARD IL	19 66
0407	0407	10151836	MCDADE & COMPANY	WESTMONT IL	42 44
0410	0410	63840185	MARSHALLS 60	COUNTRYSIDE IL	14 96
	0418	00000000	ANNUAL MEMBERSHIP FEE - APR 84-MAR 85		20 00
			TOTAL 1983 FINANCE CHARGES FOR TAX PURPOSES WERE $ 0.00.		
			CITI$$ 0 + EARNED 37 - USED 0 = AVAILABLE 37		

Account Summary If payment of the New Balance for Purchases is received on or before the Payment Due Date, there will be no additional Finance Charge for Purchases.

Number of Days This Billing Period		Previous Balance	Purchases & Advances	Payments	Credits (-)	Finance Charge	Late Charges	New Balance	Payment Due
	Purchases		206 38					206 38	20 00
	Advances								
29	Total		206 38					206 38	20 00

	Purchases Before		Purchases After	Advances Before	Advances After	
						Amount Over Credit Line ▶
Balance Subject to Finance Charge	First $	Over $				Past Due ▶
Periodic Rate	%	%	1.65%	%	.05424%	
Nominal Annual Percentage Rate	%	%	19.80%	%	19.80%	Minimum Amount Due ▶ 20 00
Annual Percentage Rate	%	%	19.80%	%	19.80%	

Send Payments to: P.O. Box 6001, Sioux Falls, S.D. 57188 31089A If you have an amount in dispute, please see reverse side.

Citibank Investment Savings

Amount Annual Interest Rate

** ** THIS SPRING, PLANT THE SEED FOR A BETTER FUTURE:
*** OPEN A CITIBANK HIGH RATE ACCOUNT,
*** AND WATCH YOUR SAVINGS GROW!
*
* * CHOOSE HIGH FIXED RATES, COMPETITIVE VARIABLE
** RATES, OR TAX-SHELTERED SAVINGS. FOR DETAILS,
* CALL TOLL-FREE 800-645-9181, 8AM-11PM ET. (IN NY
* 800-732-9636). VISA INQUIRIES: SEE TOP OF STATEMENT.D1

Purchase Date	Annual Interest Rate/Yield	Certificate Numbers	Amount Invested	Interest to Date	Projected Interest

NOTICE: See Reverse Side for Important Information. Citibank (South Dakota), N.A. Member F.D.I.C.

cost of a product. A television purchased for a seemingly reasonable monthly interest rate could turn out to be outrageously expensive when the interest rate is stated on a yearly basis. Consumers' problems are compounded when businesses deny credit unfairly or debt collectors harass those who have fallen behind in their payments.

Beginning in the late 1960s and continuing on into the 1970s, Congress enacted several important pieces of legislation to protect consumers against credit abuses. Two laws are of special note:

1. *The Equal Credit Opportunity Act,* which prohibits discrimination in lending based on sex, marital status, race, national origin, religion, age, or receipt of payments from public assistance programs.
2. *The truth-in-lending law,* which requires lenders to disclose the annual percentage rate of interest they charge. In the sample statement shown in Figure 3.4, this rate appears near the center of the form.

When marketers are planning advertising messages, they must make sure that any information about financing complies with the truth-in-lending law.

Environmental Pollution Marketers have been accused of contributing to pollution in a number of ways. They have prepared advertising to bolster the image of companies that damage the environment by dumping industrial by-products into the air and water. They have introduced products with injurious environmental effects, such as fluorocarbon sprays that damage the upper atmosphere's ability to filter out certain harmful rays. Sometimes a product that is not harmful has damaging side effects. Plastic wrappings and nonreturnable bottles, for example, both contribute to the solid waste problem.

The power to enforce federal antipollution laws is vested in the Environmental Protection Agency (EPA). The EPA's broad authority includes establishing environmental standards, suing polluters who violate such standards, and imposing fines (equal to the amount firms save by disobeying the law) on those who delay pollution control orders. If the EPA is lax in enforcing codes, citizens may sue a polluter directly or sue the agency itself.[11] For example, the Natural Resources Defense Council challenged the EPA decision not to set strict limits for emissions of vinyl chloride, a chemical used in making plastics and linked to cancer.[12]

Because of pollution control laws, a company may find that it is more expensive to pollute than to comply with the law. In the case of one major problem, toxic waste disposal, a 1986 law requires companies responsible for creating toxic waste to clean it up or pay the EPA for doing so. If a polluter refuses and the agency does the work, the company is liable for triple damages. Furthermore, the law makes any party contributing to a hazardous waste site liable for the cost of the entire cleanup project.[13]

Companies cannot afford to ignore the problem. Marketers can contribute to the solution when they weigh environmental issues in product and packaging design.

Special Interest Consumer Groups

In addition to the governmental agencies charged with the responsibility of protecting consumers, various special interest groups have arisen to inform the public of consumer issues and to exert pressure on business and government.

Consumers Union provides its subscribers and the public with product information on everything from antiperspirants to yogurt; and Action for Children's Television works to eliminate commercial abuses in programming targeted to children. Many other organizations lobby or disseminate information about particular areas of concern.

Figure 3.5
Boise Cascade Advertises Its Commitment to the Environment

HOW BLUE ARE THE SKIES OVER OUR PAPER MILLS? COME SEE FOR YOURSELF.
Pack the family in Old Reliable, aim it at one of our paper, lumber or plywood mills, and take a guided tour.
You'll not only be able to check out the sky overhead (and the water alongside), you'll also get a first hand look at how some of our society's more essential products get made.
We suspect you'll find the processes fascinating, maybe even magical, and we know you'll have a good time.
That's one of two reasons why we offer these tours. The other: We want you to see how seriously we take our responsibilities.
For tour locations, write Sharon Ramsey, Boise Cascade, One Jefferson Square, Boise, ID 83728.
Boise Cascade Corporation
Paper/Office Products/Packaging/Building Products/Forests

Source: Courtesy of Boise Cascade Corporation.

Beyond Laws: Social Responsibility

Marketing departments need to be aware of the company's reputation for responding to consumer and environmental issues. Heightened consumer awareness gives rise to a need for marketing that keeps consumers informed about the company's positive actions. Boise Cascade Corporation uses advertising to send such a message. (See Figure 3.5.)

Another reason businesses must keep the concerns of consumer groups in mind is that they have a **social responsibility** for their actions. Managers must consider the effects of their decisions on the external world so as to accomplish social benefits as well as traditional economic ones.[14]

Social Responsibility
Moral obligation of businesses to consider the effects of their decisions on society and to accomplish social benefits.

Social responsibility begins where the law ends. For example, the law requires fines for certain pollution-causing activities, such as dumping chemicals into waterways, but is silent about others, such as overpackaging, which contributes to solid waste. A firm guilty of wasteful packaging is acting within the law, though some would question whether it is acting in a socially responsible way.

Like many business decisions, choosing to be socially responsible involves a trade-off. Social responsibility costs money, but it also creates goodwill, which can lead to more business.

Responses of Individual Firms One organization that has committed resources to social responsibility is General Electric. Corporate officers are assigned responsibility for designing safety features into the products they want to market. To ensure that customers know about these features and the safe use of the firm's products, the company publishes safety tips for the home appliance user. The major complaint against appliance manufacturers is that repair service is difficult to secure. GE has removed many of the restrictions and clarified the legal language in its warranty statements.[15]

Other companies have instituted consumer hot lines with toll-free 800 numbers so that consumers with complaints or requests for information can be more readily in touch with the product's manufacturer.

Procter & Gamble claims to be an 800 pioneer, having experimented with the use of a toll-free number in 1974 for Duncan Hines Brownie Mix. Today, nearly every P&G product has its own number. By 1983, P&G was logging over 450,000 phone calls a year. (The question most asked: "What makes Ivory soap float?" The answer: "All the air it contains.")[16]

While ingredient labeling is now required on all packaged foods, some companies have voluntarily chosen to furnish consumers with even more information than the law stipulates. The label on Sugar-Free Kool-Aid, for example, explains why each ingredient is included; it also gives information on the artificial sweetener it contains.

Other businesses are sponsoring consumer panels to alert them to the issues that concern their customers. Stop 'n Shop supermarkets, a chain in the Northeast, instituted its Consumer Board Program in 1968. Because of Board members' concerns regarding sodium content in packaged foods, Stop 'n Shop introduced a line of no-salt-added products two years ahead of national brands. The line has since expanded from six to fifteen items, and is successful both in meeting consumer needs and in improving Stop 'n Shop's business.

These few examples show that socially responsible actions often pay for themselves. They also may generate a positive image in the public's mind. Good corporate citizenship is also good business.

Consumer Responsibility
Buyers' obligation to know their rights and to make informed judgments.

Consumer Responsibility Government can pass laws and businesses can supply product information, but eventually it is a **consumer's responsibility** to know his or her rights and to make an informed judgment based on the information provided. Mandating seat belts will not stop highway deaths if consumers do not use them. Instituting a "cooling-off rule," which allows a consumer to change his or her mind after buying something from a door-to-door salesperson, has no effect if consumers do not know about it.

Consumer leaders such as Ralph Nader have suggested that instead of demanding more legislation to secure rights, consumers must now do more for themselves. The laws at present offer consumers substantial protection. According to consumer activists, citizens could take better advantage of those laws if they used the courts more frequently, were better educated about their rights, and participated more directly in regulating businesses. How well do you know your consumer rights? Take the quiz in Table 3.3 to see how well you are informed.

The Economic Environment

Chapter 2 pointed out that the economy is an important factor in the marketing environment. In fact, an analysis of the general, or macro, environment is as important as an examination of the operating environment. One top corporate official noted, "The chief executive has to watch out for the killing variable in the external world that can change everything for his company."[17]

The killing variable can be any number of things. Many firms are keeping a close eye on the fluctuation of the dollar's value abroad. A decline in the dollar raises the price of imports, including the price of oil and raw materials. A rise in the dollar's value, while a bonanza for American tourists, also serves to dampen the world market for American goods. Or, when interest rates are low compared to inflation, students may be more likely to borrow money to pay their tuition. As a result, they might have more money available to spend on hamburgers or movies.

Such changes in economic conditions can dramatically influence business plans. Because the influence of the economy on marketing is so important, it will be considered more closely here to see how changes may affect market planning.

Economic Cycles

The economy of the United States goes through a recurring cycle of boom and bust. The full cycle consists of four phases: **prosperity, recession, depression,** and **recovery.**

1. *Prosperity*—a period of generally high income, employment, and business growth.
2. *Recession*—a phase of decreasing income, employment, and growth rate.
3. *Depression*—a radical drop in business activity and consequent high unemployment and business failure.
4. *Recovery*—an upswing characterized by a gradual rise in business and consumer economic well-being.

Economic cycles rarely occur in a neat pattern. Even skilled analysts have trouble predicting how long any one cycle will last or what cycles

Prosperity
Period in business cycle of generally high income, employment, and business growth.

Recession
Phase of the business cycle characterized by decreasing income, employment, and growth rate.

Depression
Phase of the business cycle characterized by a radical drop in business activity and consequent high unemployment and business failure.

Recovery
Upswing in the business cycle characterized by a gradual rise in business and consumer economic well-being.

Table 3.3
How Well Do You Know Your Consumer Rights?

Answer true or false to each of these statements.

1. **False or Deceptive Advertising**

   A children's commercial for toy race cars that exaggerates the speed of the cars is *legal.*

2. **False or Deceptive Retail Advertising**

   It is *not legal* to advertise a low-priced item and then only stock enough for the first few customers who enter the store.

3. **Credit Regulations**

   It is *legal* to deny a female college student a credit card on the basis of her sex.

4. **Credit Reporting**

   If you have been denied credit, you have the *legal* right to know the nature and substance of the information (except medical) collected about you by a credit reporting agency.

5. **Door-to-Door Selling**

   A door-to-door salesman in *not legally* required to furnish the purchaser with a fully completed contract until 24 hours after the sale has taken place.

6. **Automobile Sales**

   When selling a car it is *not legal* to turn the odometer (mileage meter) back on the car to show that the vehicle has fewer miles on it than it actually has been driven.

7. **Credit Cards**

   You are *legally* responsible for a credit card mailed to you that you did not request.

8. **Labeling**

   A manufacturer that produces merchandise subject to cleaning, such as clothing, is *legally* required to have a label in plain sight which tells the consumer how the product is to be laundered or dry cleaned.

9. **Truth in Lending**

   Retail stores are *legally* required to state the true interest rate and other costs of credit transactions.

10. **Deceptive Retail Practices**

    It is *legal* for a store to tell you that you have won a free gift of an oil painting if you have to pay $15.00 for the frame to receive the gift.

Source: William H. Cunningham and Isabella C. M. Cunningham, "Consumer Protection: More Information or More Regulation?" *Journal of Marketing,* April 1976, p. 65.

Correct Responses to Table 3.3

1. False; 2. True; 3. False; 4. True; 5. False; 6. True; 7. False; 8. True;
9. True; 10. False

will follow the current one. In the 1950s and 1960s, for example, the American economy went through an extended period of prosperity. Income rose nearly 70 percent, the unemployment rate was low, and the gross national product nearly doubled. Many economists expected that when the bubble burst in the early 1970s (with the oil crisis), the economy would slump into a recession and then a deep depression. In fact, throughout the decade, the economy fluctuated between recession and recovery without experiencing either prosperity or depression.

Although marketers cannot know exactly how long a phase will last or how to predict the onset of a new phase, they must plan to meet changes. Some economic indicators (such as the Wholesale Price Index and the rate of new construction) provide clues to the future. Marketing plans can be adjusted accordingly.

Economic downswings introduce a note of caution into marketing. In the recessionary 1970s, not only did the rate of new-product development slow, but the variety of products was cut back. For example, General Electric dropped the marketing of blenders, fans, heaters, humidifiers, and vacuum cleaners, and Philco eliminated 40 percent of its refrigerator models.[18]

The recession brought changes in other marketing areas as well. Some companies trimmed their sales forces and hired in their place less costly independent wholesalers. In other cases, advertising budgets were increased to stimulate demand, or the advertising messages themselves were changed to emphasize more economical products. (An old product, Bisquick, a multipurpose flour, made a major comeback.) Finally, some companies offered special low prices to encourage buying; for example, automakers and small appliance manufacturers offered rebates (or money back) for immediate purchase.

In periods of prosperity and recovery, marketing managers generally pursue growth-related objectives. They may introduce new products, increase advertising expenditures, hire additional salespeople, or add to the number of outlets through which products are sold. It was no accident that many of the goods and services we enjoy today—contact lenses, cassette recorders, one-hour dry cleaning, permanent press clothing—were commercialized in the prosperous 1960s. The era also saw a noticeable increase in the number of workers in marketing as well as in the number of retail outlets. At Your Service 3.1 describes how the mortgage industry coped with a boom in that market.

During the first half of the 1980s, the economy expanded much more slowly than in the 1960s. Companies had to pay special attention to the competition, because their own growth more often had to come from competitors' share of the market. At one time it looked as if International Business Machines Corp. couldn't lose in the rapidly growing market for personal computers, but in 1986 the company's earnings declined as it lost market share. One competitor making inroads was Compaq Computer Corp., which grew to Fortune 500 size in less than five years by making IBM-compatible computers with slight improvements and a lower price tag. Compaq introduced a personal computer that runs at twice the speed of IBM's PC AT and is as powerful as a minicomputer (a type of computer that costs about $10,000 more).

At Your Service 3.1
Banks Challenged by Mortgage Boom

When a journalist called a New York City bank to find out the ceiling, or maximum rate, on the bank's variable-rate mortgages in mid-1986, the person handling his call replied, "What's a ceiling?" At about the same time, the telephone sales staff at a San Francisco bank were so rushed that they often neglected to tell mortgage applicants what documents they needed to supply.

These incidents occurred because the mortgage industry was experiencing a dramatic boom. Interest rates had fallen to a six-year low, and Americans had gone on a binge of home buying and refinancing. Lenders were swamped.

Finding the employees needed to handle the flood of mortgage applications presented the major challenge. "The banks that saw the crunch coming prepared by transferring personnel, basically dredging up people in-house," reported Paul Havemann, vice president of HSH Associates, a New Jersey mortgage monitoring and counseling service. The banks started by transferring personnel from their consumer loan departments and trying to quickly teach them the complicated forms and many types of loans available.

Even when employees were transferred, the banks still needed more staff. They turned to temporary help agencies, settling for people who had no experience with mortgage applications. As a result, backlogs of applications continued to increase. Companies looked for other ways to handle the business, including greater reliance on computers. The banks learned that, for marketers, a boom can be as much of a challenge as a recession.

Source: Arthur Bragg, "Telemarketing Mayhem in Mortgage Land," *Sales and Marketing Management*, July 1986, pp. 46–48.

Slower growth in the microcomputer market means that the success of Compaq's new model can hurt IBM's performance.[19]

Consumer Spending

The state of the country's economic health greatly influences what marketing strategy a company might pursue. But it is not enough for a marketer simply to know when the country shows signs of slipping into a recession, or when the populace has finally moved over the arbitrary line marking the difference between recovery and full-fledged prosperity. More important than the economic cycle itself is how consumers are spending whatever funds they have during a given period.

Consumer spending has been called the nation's number one leading business indicator. Industries as diverse as metalworking, housing, and insurance keep a close watch on it because it accounts for nearly two-thirds of the spending power in the $4 trillion U.S. economy. Often the level of consumer spending is a barometer to industry of just what direction the economy is heading. For example, in October 1982, the country was in the grip of a serious recession. Nonetheless, consumers in that month outspent the rise in their personal incomes three times over. Analysts, noting the upturn in the consumer's willingness to spend, correctly began predicting that the recession was bottoming out.[20]

Disposable Income
Any money that remains after taxes are paid.

In addition to watching the amount of consumer spending, marketers must pay close attention to how those dollars are being used. Economists—and marketers—distinguish between two kinds of income. **Disposable income** is that amount of money remaining in a person's wallet after taxes are paid. A person's **discretionary income** is what remains after a person has paid for food, shelter, clothing, and other basic necessities. This money is what consumers use to buy furniture, automobiles, appliances, and vacations.

Discretionary Income Any money remaining from disposable income that a family or individual is free to spend for luxuries or save.

Although per-capita disposable income rose by more than two-thirds during the 1960s and 1970s,[21] most of the buying power of that increase was eroded by inflation. Household income has not regained the ground lost to rapid inflation. Median household income, in inflation-adjusted dollars, was $23,556 in 1979 but only $22,415 in 1984, despite the growth in the number of two-income families.[22] A decline in consumer income does not make the marketer's job impossible, but it requires marketers to consider emphasizing value in product design and advertising, as well as reducing prices.

Changing Patterns in Family Income

Marketers need to know not only how much money consumers have, but also how the income is distributed among families and who is spending it. Marketers use this information in targeting market segments and in planning how to use the marketing mix.

During the first half of the 1980s, the nation gained 6 million households. The pattern of growth suggested that the United States is not returning to the traditional nuclear family. The fastest-growing type of household was families headed by men or women without spouses. As of the end of 1985, the percentage of households made up of couples with children was declining even faster than in the 1970s.[23] Marketers of consumer products cannot assume that they are selling to mom, dad, and two children.

While the income of these households fell somewhat between 1979 and 1984, the pattern varies among types of households. The householders who were doing better in 1984 than in 1979 were the elderly, while the most dramatic fall in income was for householders under 25. The income of black and Hispanic households fell faster than that of white households; one reason given is that the proportion of households headed by women alone is greater for black and Hispanic households than for white ones. Also, the decline in income was less for two-earner families than for one-earner families.

Not only is a rising proportion of households headed by a single parent, the proportion of two-earner households is also growing. In many of these households, the wage earner is a mother with children under 18. In 1986, the percentage of mothers in the labor force reached 62.8 percent.[24] Marketers targeting these women consider the demands on their time, and they schedule less television advertising during the daytime soap operas.

The share of families earning at least $50,000 grew rapidly between 1983 and 1984. Nevertheless, these families do not represent the majority of households. One in five households in 1984 earned less than $10,000, two in five earned less than $20,000, and three in five earned less than $30,000. Households with incomes over $50,000 represented about one-eighth of the total. Businesses targeting an upscale market

Mozart By Toshiba.

The beauty of Mozart's impeccable operas, symphoni or chamber music reproduced faithfully is the beauty of Toshiba digital technology.

Toshiba's new CD player were created with uniquely developed digital technology. Only digitalized signals are picked up, eliminating unnece sary noise. Transmitting only the purest sound. Giving you music more accurate and more alive than the best live performance.

Digital technology enhances every product we create. From medical equipment to home electronics, offi automation to heavy electric equipment.

Over 100 years of technological innovation has made Toshiba the ninth largest electric and electronics manufacturer in the world.

At Toshiba, we're choosin a better tomorrow, creating the products that improve the quality of our lives.

Including musical reproduction that is as flawles as a Mozart quartet.

In Touch with Tomorrow

TOSHIBA

must therefore focus their efforts to reach this smaller segment of the population.

In marketers' minds, the key question is how households will choose to spend their income. Will they choose to live in the city or the suburbs? Will they spend their money on fast food or fast cars? What kind of furniture will they buy, and how will they outfit baby? The implications of buyer behavior are explored in future chapters. To a marketer, such economic changes are vitally important.

The Technological Environment

As recently as the 1970s, a college student in a technical field might spend about $100 to buy a pocket calculator that could add, subtract, multiply, and divide. For the same price today, that student can purchase a small calculator that can automatically perform almost 100 functions and even be programmed for specialized tasks. Most college students today also spend some time using a personal computer or the school's mainframe computer. And almost everyone has an inexpensive pocket calculator for balancing the checkbook or computing percentages.

Today we take for granted not only calculators, but many products that were unimaginable only decades or years ago—stereos and compact disc equipment, videocassette recorders, watches that wake us up as well as tell time, and 24-hour access to cash through automated teller machines. These products are the result of technological developments—changes that even influence things from the past. (See Figure 3.6.)

Technology applies science to the solution of practical problems. It has enormous implications for our everyday lives, and its growth and direction are often unpredictable. This makes the technological environment vitally important for marketers, and also extremely difficult to plan for. Companies have shot to the top of their industries or gone under because of changes in the state of technology. Bruce Culver saw a demand for people with technical expertise and started Lab Support, a business that provides high-tech temporary help: scientists, engineers, programmers, technical writers, and technicians. The business has grown three- to fivefold annually; by 1987 about 75,000 temporary employees were reporting to work at oil refineries, drug companies, analytic chemistry labs, and other companies.[25]

Technology
Application of principles of science to the solution of practical problems.

There is no sounder way to gain a differential advantage over competitors than to come up with a technologically superior product. Photocopying is now synonymous with the name Xerox and instant pictures with Polaroid because those companies were the first to exploit an advance in technology. Product advances give a company only a tempo-

Figure 3.6
Today's Technology Influences Sounds from the Past

Source: Reprinted with the permission of Mr. Yusuo Harada—Senior Manager, International Division, Advertising Department of TOSHIBA CORPORATION, Tokyo, Japan.

rary advantage, however. Kodak has challenged Polaroid in the instant picture market, and Canon and Toshiba have gained a share of the market for photocopiers.

The most important technological advance of recent times has been the development of semiconductors—tiny silicon chips now found in everything from wristwatches to microwave ovens and space shuttles. Advances in this field turn largely on the development of ways of packing ever-greater amounts of information on the little chips and in devising ways to process that information more quickly.

At one time, the United States was clearly in the forefront of computer technology, but Japan has made inroads. In 1986, the U.S. Commerce Department became concerned enough about Japanese companies' low prices and increasing sales that it negotiated a trade agreement with Japan's Ministry of International Trade and Industry. As a result of the agreement, prices of microchips rose rapidly.[26] One observer predicts that for the foreseeable future, U.S. companies will dominate the market for specialized microprocessors but will lose share to the Japanese in high-volume parts, where the Japanese benefit from greater production effectiveness.[27]

Computers are leading a revolution in the technological environment. By the year 2000 the electronics industry, which is already a $300-billion-a-year business, is expected to more than triple in sales to become the world's biggest business except for agriculture.[28] In addition, technology is bringing dramatic changes in the life sciences, the development of advanced materials, and the use of particles of light (called photons) to speed data processing.

While no one can be certain exactly where these developments will lead, their influence is certain to extend beyond high-tech companies. Many students of today will be joining the work force as employees of the companies that bring about or are affected by technological developments. Those who enter the field of marketing will have a special role in bringing together new products and the users who can benefit from them.

Chapter Replay

1. **What are the general categories of competitive markets?**
   Competitive markets fall into four general categories: pure competition, oligopoly, monopolistic competition, and monopoly.
2. **How can marketers respond to the competition in each of these markets?**
   Marketers facing pure competition seek to ensure a wide distribution of their product at a fair price. In an oligopoly, marketers try to avoid price wars and use other elements of the marketing mix to distinguish their products. In monopolistic competition, marketers try to establish a differential advantage. In a monopoly, marketers establish strategies based on company or government objectives.

3. **How does the government protect fair competition?**
The government protects fair competition through federal laws beginning with the Sherman Antitrust Act, as well as through investigation and prosecution by the Federal Trade Commission and the Justice Department.

4. **How does the government protect consumers?**
The Consumer Product Safety Commission has the power to set safety standards and take action against companies that fail to meet those standards. Congress has also established several other agencies to oversee specific industries.

5. **What are some ways in which industries regulate themselves?**
The National Advertising Review Board monitors national advertising for truth and accuracy. The Direct Mail Marketing Association sets guidelines for direct-response advertising. The Council of Better Business Bureaus strives to ensure consumer confidence in the marketplace.

6. **What issues must marketers address in responding to the social environment?**
Marketers must address consumer dissatisfaction about deficiencies in product quality, lack of information for making informed judgments, unfair pricing practices, and environmental pollution.

7. **What responsibilities do producers and consumers have?**
Businesses have a social responsibility to consider the effects of their decisions on the external world. Consumers are responsible for knowing their rights and making informed judgments based on the information provided.

8. **How can marketers respond to changes in the economic environment?**
Marketers can respond to economic downswings with cautious strategies and cutbacks, with advertising designed to stimulate demand, or with emphasis on low price. During more prosperous times, marketers can emphasize growth-related objectives. Changing patterns in disposable income also may affect marketing strategies.

9. **How can marketers respond to changes in the technological environment?**
Marketers can follow technological developments closely in order to prepare for actions by competitors and to learn of opportunities for using new developments to gain a differential advantage.

Key Terms

consumer responsibility
cost-benefit analysis
depression
discretionary income
disposable income
legal environment
monopolistic competition
monopoly
oligopoly
procompetitive legislation

prosperity
pure competition
recall
recession
recovery
social environment
social responsibility
technology

Discussion Questions

1. Every day at supermarkets and convenience stores, many shoppers select breakfast cereals from among the wide variety offered. What term describes the competitive market for breakfast cereals? How do companies compete in this market? Name a few products besides cold cereal that provide competition for cereal makers.
2. In which types of competitive markets might a new competitor be able to influence the price of a product? Explain your answer.
3. What practices are prohibited by procompetitive laws in the United States? How does the FTC help to protect competition?
4. In each of the following situations, how can industry self-regulatory bodies help you?
   a. You are planning to buy a television at a local discount store, and you want to know whether the business is reputable.
   b. You hear on the radio about a new brand of yogurt that contains twice the calcium of the major brands. You drive to the store, only to discover that this new brand contains twice the calcium merely because the carton is twice the size.
   c. You dislike getting advertising mail and want to have your name removed from as many mailing lists as possible.
5. The rise of consumerism has led the public to express dissatisfaction when companies fall short in four major areas. How can businesses respond to these consumer issues?
6. What is the role of the Consumer Product Safety Commission?
7. How do marketers adjust their strategies to times of economic prosperity? To times of economic recession?
8. How does disposable income differ from discretionary income? Why is this difference important to marketers?
9. Al Goodman runs an amusement park about 30 miles from a major metropolitan area on the East Coast. In the last couple of years, Al has noticed that business has fallen off somewhat. He wants to plan a marketing strategy to persuade more people to visit the park. What are some patterns of consumer spending and family income that Al should take into account in devising his strategy?
10. "Why are you reading about high technology in a marketing class?" Burt asked Lisa. "That's for engineers and computer programmers." Why do marketers need to keep abreast of technological developments?

Case 3.1
Christina Lane Cosmetics, Inc.

For almost a decade, Christina Lane had been one of North America's most sought after fashion models. She appeared on the covers of many leading magazines and did a number of television commercials for major consumer companies. Around Christmas, one year, two investors and a marketing executive for a large cosmetic firm approached Christina about forming a corporation to develop and distribute a full line of women's cosmetics bearing her name.

While it seemed logical that her name recognition and position as a model would provide instant market exposure for such a cosmetic line, the decision was not an easy one for Christina to make. The prospects of being part of a company carrying her name seemed exciting and potentially rewarding, but it did mean that her modeling career would be severely limited as she went into competition with some of her former clients. After much personal evaluation and counsel from trusted friends and business associates, Christina decided to go ahead with the idea. Christina Lane Cosmetics, Inc. became a reality.

Marketing Strategy

In many ways the company was an overnight success. National sales distribution was achieved by developing a field sales force that personally called on all of the major department and women's specialty stores that carried full lines of high-quality cosmetics. The company decided early in the development of its marketing strategy that the product line would not be distributed through drug or discount stores or smaller department stores.

A multimedia advertising and promotional campaign involving national television, most women's fashion and general interest magazines, and an extensive retailer cooperative program supported the Christina Lane line of cosmetics. Christina herself was highly visible in most of the company's advertising and frequently made guest appearances at trade shows and major fashion programs at leading retail stores. During the company's first five years, sales grew at an average annual rate of 125 percent and profits increased an average of 80 percent each year.

Potential Legal Problems

After five years of almost unparalleled success, management of Christina Lane Cosmetics learned of charges that several of their marketing activities were in possible violation of the Robinson-Patman Act and other federal legislation. Specifically, the areas included:

Appreciation is expressed to Professor John R. Grabner, Ohio State University, for his assistance on this case.

- ☐ A major department store on the West Coast complained that the company had sold identical cosmetics to a store in the Chicago area for ten percent less than it had paid. Another retailer complained that it had to pay Christina Lane $32.50 per case for certain cosmetics, while another store in the same city had paid only $27.50. Management acknowledged that both situations had occurred but that in the second instance the store paying $27.50 per case had ordered 50 cases while the other store had only ordered 25 cases. In another pricing issue, two stores in the same city had been charged different prices for the same product in equal quantities, but management of Christina Lane said that they were simply responding to a lower price that a competitor had quoted to one of the stores.
- ☐ One of Christina Lane's competitors complained that the company was misleading the public with its advertising. The competitor cited one of Christina Lane's advertisements: "Use of this moisturizer for 14 days will make you look ten years younger." The competitor also took issue with an advertisement that compared the two companies' products and stated: "Eight out of ten women who sampled both products preferred Christina Lane's."
- ☐ Since its founding, Christina Lane Cosmetics has provided its retailers with advertising support. The advertising program states that, if a retailer purchases more than $50,000 of the company's products during a calendar year, it can receive a 5-percent rebate as an advertising allowance to help promote the Christina Lane line of cosmetics. If annual purchases exceed $100,000, a retailer can receive a 7-percent rebate for advertising. One retailer complained that since its annual purchases amounted to only about $40,000, it received no advertising support from the company and was, therefore, put at a disadvantage compared to its larger competitors.

Focal Topics

1. In the three pricing situations, was the company in violation of the Robinson–Patman Act? Why or why not?
2. How would you respond to the claim that some of Christina Lane's advertising is misleading the public.
3. Does the complaining retailer have a legal basis regarding Christina Lane's advertising allowances?

Case 3.2 California Beef Council (B)

The California beef industry operates in a complex and dynamic environment. Effective marketing of the industry's products requires knowledge of the current status of this environment, anticipation of likely

Source: Adapted from the California Beef Council's 1987 Marketing Plan.

changes, assessment of the potential impact of these changes on the industry and its markets, and development of a plan for marketing products that considers such impacts. The purpose of this section is to identify both the current and anticipated 1987 status of key factors in the California beef industry environment. These factors are categorized into six specific areas: the California economy, the consumer market, the retail and foodservice industries, the U.S. beef industry, the California beef industry, and the competition.

California's Economy

During 1986, California's economy has continued to expand, but at a slower rate than in 1985. In keeping with its recent pattern, the California economy has again outperformed the U.S. economy. California's economy should continue to grow in 1987. The gross state product is expected to increase to $577 billion, a real increase of 4.2 percent.

California's Consumer Market

California's large and diverse population is more urban, more affluent, more mobile, better educated, and more experimental when compared to the nation as a whole. In general, the consumers in this population have seen their economic situation continue to improve during the last year. They have reacted by increasing purchases of luxury and novelty items, particularly those that better enable them to pursue their active lifestyles. In terms of food, this has meant a focus on convenient products and increased usage of take-out food. At the same time, consumers continue to be concerned with obtaining the best value for the prices they pay for all goods and services.

Some key insights to the consumer market include:

- ☐ California's population is expected to grow by 2 percent. The Hispanic population, in which consumers tend to be heavy users of beef, will continue its rapid increase of 7 to 8 percent annually.
- ☐ California's Asian population is expected to increase to 3 million by 1990 and then double by 2030 to 16 percent of the state's population.
- ☐ Per-capita personal income is expected to increase 5 percent.
- ☐ The fastest-growing segment of the population is the 35 to 44 year olds—the Baby Boomers—who are entering their prime wage-earning years and are having children, creating a Baby Boomlet.
- ☐ The number of one- and two-person households, two-income households, and women working outside the home will continue to increase.
- ☐ Microwave cookery will become increasingly important as an in-home food preparation technique, particularly in two-career households.
- ☐ Emphasis on "eating light" will continue to grow, and, as a result, consumer focus will remain on calories, fat, and smaller portion sizes.

Retail Grocery and Foodservice Industries

The retail grocery and foodservice industries are a significant portion of the beef industry, as they are the "agents by which beef is made available to the consumer market." Both industries continued to grow in 1986 and have shown increased interest in merchandising beef in ways that meet consumer needs and wants. There will be increased emphasis by these industries on new merchandising ideas for beef.

The U.S. Beef Industry

Ongoing beef herd liquidation and the Dairy Herd Termination Program have resulted in beef supplies much higher than expected in 1986. This large supply, in conjunction with increased poultry supplies, have offset the potentially positive impact of low feed costs and higher poultry prices. As a result, cattle prices have remained lower than anticipated and have put further pressure on a financially stressed beef industry. The year 1987 should bring some improvement in the beef industry as beef supplies tighten, beef prices show some improvement, feed costs remain low, and cattle prices increase.

The California Beef Industry

The California beef industry has faced even greater difficulties than in 1985. Low cattle prices, greater impact of the dairy herd buy-out program, cheaper feed in other parts of the United States, high transportation costs, and the lack of sufficient slaughter facilities in California have all played a role in further eroding the cattle market and the profitability of beef operations.

The Competition

In terms of price, 1987 is expected to bring a decline in beef's position relative to both pork and poultry, as poultry and pork supplies increase relative to beef supplies. How this will affect the beef industry will depend largely on the willingness of consumers to absorb beef price increases. The willingness of consumers to do so will, in turn, depend on the rate at which beef prices increase, the magnitude of the price differential between beef and competitive products, and how well the industry communicates the benefits of beef relative to competitive products.

Focal Topics

1. What do you feel are the major reasons for the declining per-capita consumption of beef?
2. Discuss the key problems and opportunities for the marketing of beef.
3. What other types of environmental issues would you consider in developing a marketing plan for beef?

Case for Part One

Wendy's International, Inc.

"Does America need another hamburger chain?" was the question asked by R. David Thomas as he opened the doors to his first Wendy's Old Fashioned Hamburgers restaurant at 257 East Broad Street in downtown Columbus, Ohio, on November 15, 1969. At that time, many food industry experts and some skeptical observers had commented that the fast-food growth curve had already peaked during the late 1960s, ending the rapid expansion of the industry.

On March 21, 1978, after operating only 8 years and 4 months, Wendy's opened its 1,000th restaurant at 1000 Memorial Boulevard in Springfield, Tennessee. Never before had such an accomplishment been achieved in such a short period of time. During 1986, the company opened 300 new units, bringing the total number of Wendy's restaurants to nearly 3,700.

Product Offering

Wendy's places primary emphasis on consistent quality in all areas of food preparation and presentation. The firm uses 100-percent pure beef, which is delivered in bulk and pattied fresh every morning in each of its restaurants. The patties are cooked slowly to retain their natural juices and flavors. Whether the customer orders the quarter-pound single, the half-pound double, or the three-quarter-pound triple, the hamburger is served directly from the grill. By mixing and matching the nine available condiments, a Wendy's customer can specify one of 1,024 different ways to have his or her hamburger served. Hamburgers account for about 40 percent of all sales; of these, approximately 65 percent are singles, 33 percent are doubles, and 2 percent are triples.

Chili, another menu item popular with customers, also serves a unique secondary purpose. To keep the hamburgers fresh for customers, no cooked patties are kept on the grill for more than 4 minutes. To eliminate this potential meat waste factor, hamburgers not served within the 4-minute time period are steamed in a kettle and used for the next day's chili. French fries, Frosties, coffee, tea, milk, and soft drinks round out the basic menu. The Frosty, a Wendy's exclusive, is a thick, creamy

This case has been edited from an earlier one that appeared in *Cases and Exercises in Marketing*, by W. Wayne Talarzyk. Copyright © 1987 by CBS College Publishing. Reprinted by permission of Holt, Rinehart & Winston, Inc.; and updated with information from "Wendy's Battles Fast-Food Competition," by Richard Koenig, *The Wall Street Journal*, November 12, 1986, p. 6; "Marketing Strategy Looms Large in Wendy's Future," by Ann Holifield, *Business First of Greater Columbus*, November 10, 1986, p. 7; and Wendy's International, Inc. 1986 Annual Report. Logo courtesy of Wendy's International, Inc.

blend of chocolate and vanilla (much like a very thick milkshake), served with a spoon.

Addition of Salad Bars In 1979, seeking ways to improve customer traffic, Wendy's turned to a strategy that had worked fairly well for other foodservice organizations—an expanded menu. The company's desire to diffuse its dependence on beef products, and yet not interfere with its extremely efficient in-store operating setup, led to salad bars as the first menu addition.

Salads represented a logical extension of the menu by being compatible with Wendy's operational system while enhancing the company's adult image. The salad bar also widened Wendy's appeal to families and increased its lunch and dinner business. Salads also helped attract the health- and weight-conscious and smaller-appetite consumers, both of which are growing market segments.

Breakfast Menu In May 1979, Wendy's began testing a breakfast menu that included omelette and scrambled egg platters, bacon, sausage, biscuits, hashbrown potatoes, and french toast. Breakfast is prepared primarily on the grill, with relatively minor additions to kitchen equipment, and is compatible with Wendy's system. It is designed to utilize the restaurants from 7 a.m. to 10:30 a.m., before the lunch part begins. Breakfast represents an attractive opportunity to increase sales and utilization of the restaurants. Customers view Wendy's offering as a superior product. By late 1983, the breakfast menu—narrowed down to omelettes, breakfast sandwiches, and french toast—was offered in about 200 restaurants. Breakfast was implemented systemwide in June 1985.

In March 1986, Wendy's decided to give individual restaurants the option of continuing a breakfast offering. By early 1987, the original breakfast menu was available in only about 15 percent of company-owned restaurants and in about 30 percent of franchised restaurants. Plans are now underway to develop a new breakfast menu.

Advertising Activities

Since 1982, the major hamburger fast-service chains have been fighting what the media has dubbed the "Burger Wars." Wendy's, the world's third-largest hamburger chain, is outspent in advertising eight to one by its major competitors—McDonald's and Burger King. Accordingly, the company has been compelled to communicate by using creative treatments and media extension techniques that break through the clutter and dramatize product benefits in a unique and often humorous and exaggerated manner.

When the Burger Wars began anew at the start of 1984, Wendy's again found itself in this position. McDonald's promoted a $.39 hamburger. Burger King launched its "flame-broiling versus frying" campaign. At the same time, research findings showed the consumers perceived McDonald's and Burger King's hamburgers to be larger than

Wendy's, although in reality Wendy's single hamburger contains more beef.

Seizing its hamburger-size advantage, Wendy's created the "Where's the Beef?" campaign, airing its first spots on January 9, 1984. Its goal was to create consumer awareness of its larger-size hamburger and leverage a comparatively small ad budget to extend the reach and frequency of the ad message beyond purchased media impressions. In other words, Wendy's planned to use public relations to do more with less—to bring the advertising theme into the American vernacular, to create awareness of Wendy's larger hamburger, and to underscore the inherent value of all Wendy's menu items.

Recent Results

Wendy's sales were up slightly in 1986 following an 18 percent increase in 1985. While both years benefited from the additional company-operated restaurants that were open, 1986 reflected an 8 percent decrease in average sales per restaurant and the elimination in the fourth quarter of sales from restaurants in the realignment program.

The realignment program involved selling, leasing, or closing 164 unprofitable or marginally profitable company-owned restaurants. This resulted in a charge of $51.8 million, which led to the company recording a $4.9 million (5 cents per share) net loss for 1986. This compared to net income of $76.2 million (82 cents per share) in 1985 and $68.7 million (75 cents per share) in 1984.

In the 1986 annual report management offered the following observations for the future: "Looking into 1987, the first half of the year is expected to be difficult. However, we anticipate gradual improvement in the second half, based on a continuation of the current sales trends. Higher sales should alleviate the present pressure on margins over time. The company has weathered difficult periods before and we have emerged stronger each time. We believe that we can do it again by laying a firm foundation for the future—not by quick fixes. We enter 1987 with a renewed determination toward long-term success."

Marketing Strategy

Company officials have told stock analysts that the challenge is to improve Wendy's price/value image with consumers. Slower inflation rates in recent years may have harmed the value image of the total fast-food industry.

Robert Barney, Wendy's chairman and chief executive officer, says he is confident "the worst is behind us." The firm's plan is to concentrate on a back-to-basics recovery plan. Two essentials of the strategy are better service and hamburgers. One of the largest Wendy's franchisees states, "I think our future hinges on our ability to do the best big hamburger in America."

Some of the major elements of Wendy's marketing plan are:

- ☐ Concentrate on improving the company's price/value image by creating smaller products that can be sold for lower prices. Cutting prices on existing products may also be a possibility.
- ☐ Slow new-store development and focus on the company's existing operations.
- ☐ Develop brand-name hamburgers, such as the new "Big Classic," that will be directly identified with Wendy's. Company officials believe that brand names will improve Wendy's product and company identification with consumers.
- ☐ Develop an "arsenal" of new products that can be rolled out at any time to spur customer interest.
- ☐ Focus advertising on the company's hamburger line-up.
- ☐ Concentrate on streamlining restaurant design to reduce construction costs and improve efficiency during operations.
- ☐ Streamline drive-through operations to improve delivery time.

Focal Topics

1. Discuss the environmental factors that have contributed to meals being eaten at fast-food restaurants as opposed to home.
2. What do you see as the "real business" of Wendy's?
3. Why do you think Wendy's breakfast offering was withdrawn from many of its restaurants?
4. Based on your analysis of the case and your knowledge of the existing business environment, what are the basic problems facing Wendy's and the industry in the future?
5. Based on your response to question 4, what recommendations would you make to Wendy's at this time, and why?

ADWEEK readers make waves.
ADWEEK readers make waves.

Part Two

Markets and Segmentation

Market Segmentation and Sales Forecasting

□ Sounding Out the Chapter

In this chapter, you will learn:

1. **The differences between mass marketing and target marketing.**
2. **Ways to segment the consumer market.**
3. **Ways to segment the industrial market.**
4. **The difference between concentrated marketing and differentiated marketing.**
5. **Issues marketers consider in deciding how many market segments to target.**
6. **What criteria make a market segment a good candidate for targeting.**
7. **What types of forecasts marketers use.**
8. **How marketers estimate demand.**

Source: © Sam Emerson/ONYX

Radio Stations Zero In On Baby Boomers

How do radio stations decide whether to play Madonna or Springsteen, the Beatles or the B-52s? They start by deciding who they want to have listening.

In many cases, the desired listeners are the Baby Boomers— that large chunk of the population who are in their mid-20s to mid-50s. The reason for the popularity of this group as a target market is that it is the largest age group and has the most money to spend. Therefore, advertisers are most interested in buying time on radio stations that reach Baby Boomers.

This aging group of listeners is considered by many in the radio business to be a relatively passive audience of people who want to hear familiar tunes. According to music consultant John Parikhal, Baby Boomers have less interest in new music because they have already accumulated 15 years' worth of music they like. The result, in the opinion of many, is a boring trend toward "classic rock" programming. Says Parikhal, "People are bored with what they're hearing, but there is an inability to accept too much that's new."

Other radio stations have found success by targeting less popular market segments. In Los Angeles, for example, KPWR switched from an adult-contemporary format to playing current dance hits. In just one rating period, the station went from ranking 22nd to 2nd, with a core audience of teens and young adults.

Like most companies, radio stations find that they cannot appeal to everyone. Each radio station must evaluate which group of listeners it can reach most effectively. As you learned in Chapter 2, such groups are called market segments. This chapter describes ways to segment a market. It also discusses how marketers decide which segment or segments to target, including how marketers estimate whether a segment will be profitable enough to warrant targeting.

Source: Gail Belsky, "Boring In on Baby Boomers—And We Mean *Boring*," *Adweek*, July 21, 1986, pp. R.R.2, R.R.4–5.

Two Ways to Think of Markets

The market for a product consists of all the people who buy and sell it. As you learned in Chapter 2, some marketers find it most efficient to think of all the buyers of their product as being one great mass. Other marketers find it more effective to divide the market into segments and to target specific market segments. Because most marketers use this approach, it will be the focus of most of this chapter.

Mass Marketing

Mass Marketing
Practice of directing the marketing mix at all potential buyers rather than a particular subgroup.

In **mass marketing,** all of the customers in a particular market are thought of as having the same, or homogeneous, needs. Those needs are easily satisfied by a single product and a single marketing program or mix.

In the 1920s, the Ford Motor Company pursued a mass marketing approach by offering only one car, the Model T, in one color, at one price, with no options. In fact, mass marketing was the basic approach to target marketing before the adoption of the marketing concept. A few companies today still adhere to mass marketing. Ace Playing Cards, for example, offers essentially the same product—laminated cards—to all customers in the playing card market at the same price and through the same outlets (variety stores).

Firms that opt for a mass marketing approach do so for one basic reason—to save money. These firms keep production, inventory, and transportation costs low by producing only one standardized product; administrative costs are lower because only one marketing program must be planned and executed.

Mass marketing works as long as consumers demand no variety. But few products can satisfy everyone's tastes. As consumers have become more affluent, they have come to expect a wider product choice. In the automobile market, some people buy a car for its styling and class distinction, others give priority to gas mileage, and still others buy for price. No one car can satisfy all of these requirements.

Some staple food items such as sugar and salt still lend themselves to a mass market approach, but even these products are gradually being diversified for different markets. Sugar, for example, is available as regular granulated sugar; as unrefined, blonde turbinado sugar for natural food lovers; as super-sweet fructose for dieters; as very fine crystals for bartenders; as confectioners sugar for bakers; and as light, dark, granulated brown, and liquid brown sugar. It also comes in one- and five-pound sizes, as dots and tablets, and in packets. And we have not even started to mention the various sugar substitutes that now abound.

Farm products, such as fruits and vegetables, are also among the few items that may still be mass marketed. (See Figure 4.1.) Because consumers may not be able to distinguish produce from different growers, marketers may use various promotional strategies to differentiate products from those of competitors. Oranges stamped "Sunkist," bananas with "Chiquita" stickers, and "Perdue" chickens are all distinctively labeled to distinguish them from everybody else's oranges, bananas, and chickens.

Figure 4.1
Mass Marketing California Strawberries

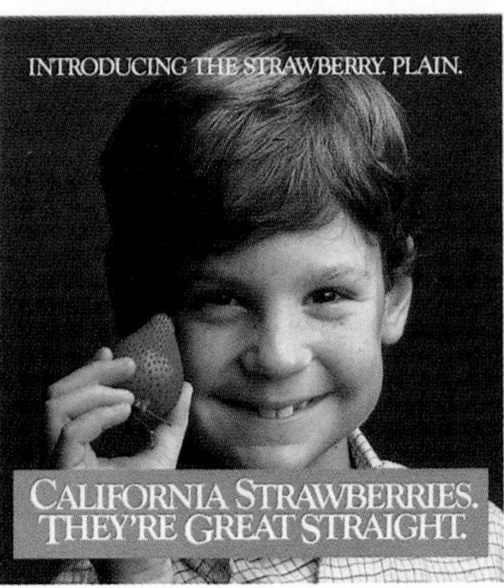

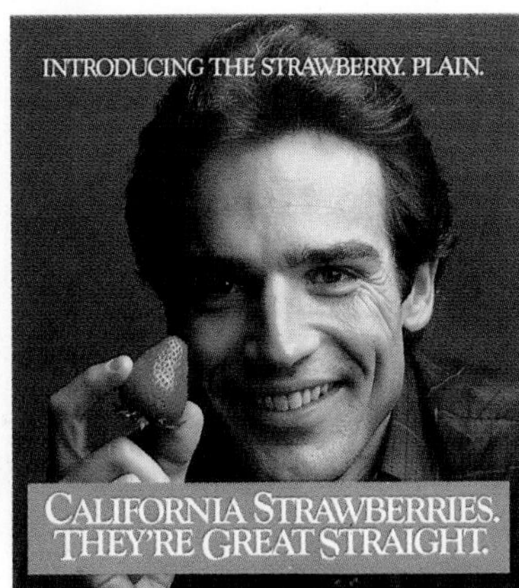

Source: Courtesy of California Strawberry Advisory Board

Target Marketing and Segmentation

The increased acceptance of the marketing concept has resulted in the rapid adoption of **target marketing** as the most productive strategy for most companies to pursue. In contrast to mass marketing, target marketing to a market segment divides the market into groups of customers with different, or heterogeneous, needs. Each group requires a different product, a unique price, a suitable outlet, and a distinctive advertising appeal.

Target Marketing
Practice of dividing the market into segments and devising a marketing mix to appeal to one or more targeted market segments.

Target marketing is practiced by firms in both the consumer and industrial markets. For example, the slogan for General Motors at one time was "a car for every price, purpose, and personality."

The main advantage of target marketing is that it usually results in more sales than mass marketing. Customers with no choice may simply drop out of the market. Given alternatives, more people may buy.

The chief drawback of target marketing is that it raises costs. General Motors, for example, must have special tools and limited runs for each automobile model it produces. Each different advertising campaign it plans costs extra. Thus the success of an organization that uses this approach depends on how well it identifies market segments and selects appropriate segments to target.

Different market segments are identified, depending on whether the marketer is considering the consumer market or the industrial market. As explained in Chapter 2, the consumer market consists of people who buy a product for personal use; when you buy milk at the grocery store, you are part of the consumer market. The industrial market is made up of businesses that buy products for resale or to operate their establishments. The purchasing agent at Kraft Foods who buys hundreds of tank cars full of milk to make Philadelphia cream cheese is part of the industrial market.

Segmentation Bases for the Consumer Market

A marketer can segment a consumer market in four primary ways: (1) by demographic factors; (2) by rate of product usage; (3) by perceived product benefits; and (4) by psychographic, or life-style, characteristics.

Some segmentation data, such as demographic information, are more easily obtained than others, such as psychographic information, which may require special research. No one basis for segmentation is best for all situations. In many cases, marketers resort to a combination of bases to obtain an adequate picture of their market target.

Demographic Segmentation

Demographic Segmentation
Division of a market into classes on the basis of geographic proximity or some shared socioeconomic trait.

Demographic segmentation groups customers on the basis of geographic proximity or some shared socioeconomic trait (e.g., age or social class). The theory behind demographic segmentation is that customers who live in the same locale or belong to the same age, income, or other grouping have common needs and will buy similar products.

Geographic Factors Before the Industrial Age, local tradespeople produced goods to meet local needs. This was a kind of natural, or unplanned, geographic segmentation of the market. Today most consumer products sell to a national market, but a growing number of firms tailor their products to regional or local needs or concentrate their marketing effort in one region or a few regions.

Campbell Soup Company, for example, makes two versions of its Nacho Cheese Soup, one spicier than the other. The spicier version contains substantially more jalapeno peppers and is sold only in the West and Southwest. Similarly, Domino's Pizza offers different toppings for its pizza in different regions of the country.

A company can adapt other elements of the marketing mix besides its product. General Foods Corporation varied its promotions for Maxwell House coffee, holding a series of regional events such as rodeos in Dallas and a show at Radio City Music Hall in New York.[1]

Companies can identify broad differences among people who live in different geographic regions by conducting research or by using consumer profiles developed by advertising agencies and consultants. The companies can reach the regional market segments in many ways, such as through local radio and television stations, in regional editions of magazines, and through mailings to people in the targeted regions.

Socioeconomic Factors General Motors was one of the first nationally known firms to use socioeconomic factors to distinguish segments for branded products. Alfred Sloan, GM's chief executive from 1923 to 1945, hit on the idea that cars could be sold as visible symbols of the climb up the social ladder. He produced different makes of cars to sell to different income groups at six price levels ranging from $450 to $3,500. The models were positioned so that practically all of the buying public—from the most price conscious to the most affluent—was covered.[2]

Figure 4.2
Jordache Advertises to a Specific Age Segment

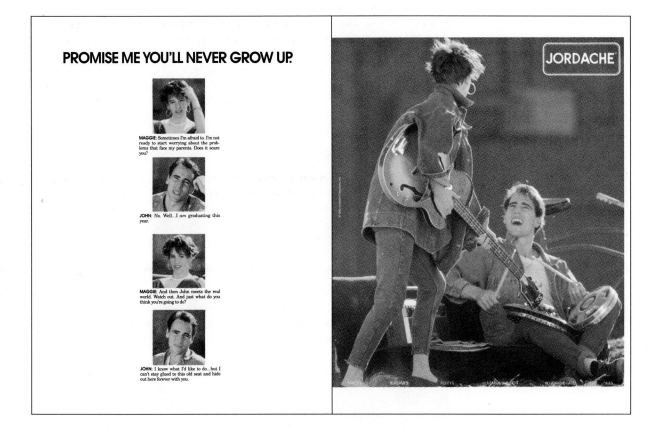

Sloan's idea caught on. Soon other socioeconomic factors were used to describe market segments. Age, for example, has proved to be a successful way of dividing the market. Jordache jeans are advertised to consumers in their late teens and early twenties. (See Figure 4.2.)

Because many variables may be at work in a buying decision, marketers rarely use only one socioeconomic factor to segment the market. Sloan's exclusive use of income to distinguish segments of car buyers would not work today.

Automobile manufacturers now are likely to use multiple socioeconomic factors to identify buyers of specific brands and models. Saab, which calls itself "the most intelligent car ever built," has targeted a sophisticated, responsible, well-established man, probably the head of a family, who is interested in a car that combines sports-car virtues, such as performance and handling, with practicality. (See Figure 4.3.) In a few paragraphs of copy, the ad speaks to such diverse variables as age, sex, income, educational level, family size, family life cycle, home ownership, and social class, and those only begin to suggest the various psychographic appeals at work.

Figure 4.3
Targeting the Family Man Who Wishes for a Sports Car

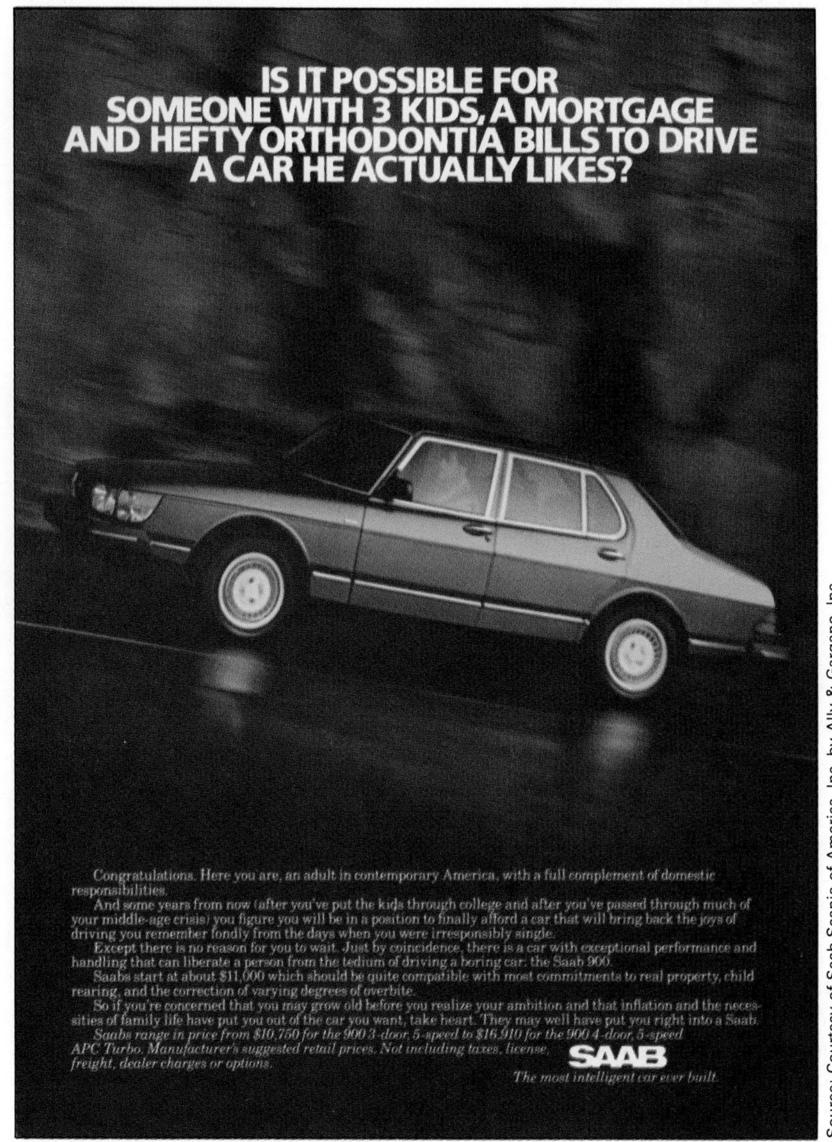

Source: Courtesy of Saab-Scania of America, Inc. by Ally & Gargano, Inc.

Socioeconomic factors, especially when used together, can help pinpoint a target market. These factors are widely used because they produce segments whose sizes can be measured easily (by the use of census data). In addition, because the various advertising media (among them magazines, television, and radio) use the same socioeconomic factors to describe their audiences, marketers can easily find an appropriate medium for reaching their target effectively.

Figure 4.4
Variations in Demand for Three Beverages

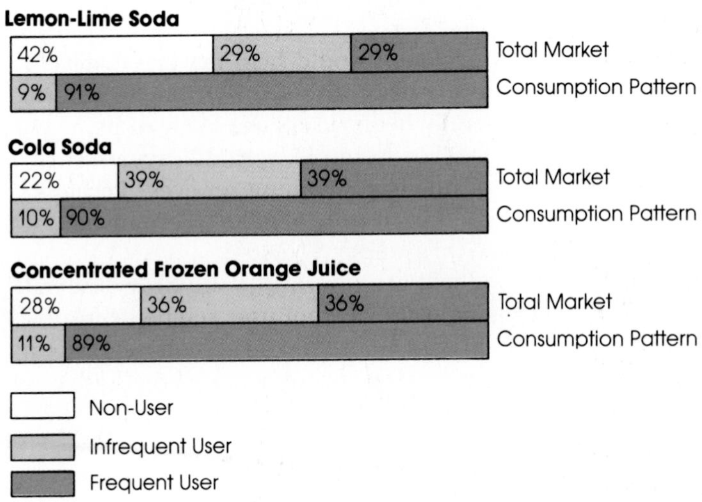

But marketers cannot always relate product or brand choice to differences in age, income, sex, or family size. People with an identical demographic profile may still exhibit different tastes. Other criteria may also be needed to zero in on the most likely buyers.[3] For that reason, marketers also segment the market based on the use of products, the benefits consumers seek, and consumers' life-styles and personalities.

Usage-Rate Segmentation

In addition to demographic differences, consumers also exhibit differences in the rate at which they buy and use products. Research results have shown that in many product categories, a few consumers account for most of the sales. Figure 4.4 shows this graphically for several product categories. In the category of lemon-lime soft drinks, for example, 58 percent of the households sampled use the product. But half of these users (29 percent) did most of the buying. They purchased 91 percent of all lemon-lime soft drinks sold—ten times as much as the light users.

Usage-Rate Segmentation Division of a market into classes on the basis of the rate at which members buy and use products.

Usage-rate segmentation takes into account variations in demand among different groups and divides the market into heavy, light, and nonusers. Usually marketers combine usage-rate segmentation with demographic segmentation; they look for demographic differences between heavy, light, and nonusers of a product.

Naturally, marketers are usually most interested in the small number who buy in the greatest quantity. Marketers for *True Story* magazine ran an ad to encourage companies to advertise in their pages, claiming that "more heavy users of more products are heavy users of *True Story*." They supported their claim by reporting that *True Story* readers used

134,459 tons of laundry detergent and bleach in 1981—more than the average household of any other women's service magazine. But in addition to usage-rate statistics, marketers would also want to know demographic information about *True Story* readers, such as their age, income, and educational level.

This demographic information would help marketers develop advertising that would appeal to the heavy users, and it might help marketers decide whether these generally heavy users are likely to be heavy users of a specific good or service. For example, would heavy users of *True Story* also be heavy users of financial planning services? Perhaps yes, if they are typically over 25 and earn over $30,000. Perhaps not, if they are typically under 18 and earn under $15,000.

If most marketers in a field are catering to the heavy users, it may pay to concentrate on the light-user or nonuser segments instead. Businesspeople, for example, may compose the largest share of the market for hotel rooms in midtown Manhattan. But many hotels advertise special weekend rates to the tourist market to fill those rooms when businesspeople go home.

Although many firms have benefited by employing usage-rate segmentation, the method does have limitations. Segmenting the market into heavy and light users and nonusers does not explain why consumers fall into one category rather than another. The labels may actually disguise the real subdivisions of the market and hide key information. The term "heavy coffee drinker," for example, actually describes two distinct types—compulsive coffee drinkers and those who drink for taste. The former usually buy cheap house brands, but the latter may prefer premium products.[4] (Marketing Today 4.1 describes in greater depth the market segment of specialty coffee drinkers.) Often such differences within a segment become apparent only when the marketer considers other segmentation bases, such as those described below.

Benefit Segmentation

Benefit Segmentation Division of a market into classes on the basis of benefits that members of each class seek.

One way to discover possible hidden segments within the broad categories of light and heavy users and nonusers is to apply **benefit segmentation,** which attempts to identify the benefits people seek in a product as a basis for grouping them together. For example, in a study conducted in 1983, researchers were able to divide MBA candidates (the market for business schools) according to whether they were seeking quality, specialty programs, a degree, convenience, career flexibility, or a low-cost program involving minimal effort.[5]

The market for many products is divided up quite naturally by the benefits people seek. Consumers usually want a combination of benefits, but they tend to stress one or two when deciding to buy. For example, you might want free checking but would rather pay a small service charge if you can open an account that offers you the convenience of withdrawing cash on campus. Similarly, buyers of Timex watches seek a good product with a low price; buyers of Lean Cuisine frozen dinners seek a convenience food with reduced calories; and high-volume readers

Marketing Today 4.1
Hot Market Segment for Coffee Makers

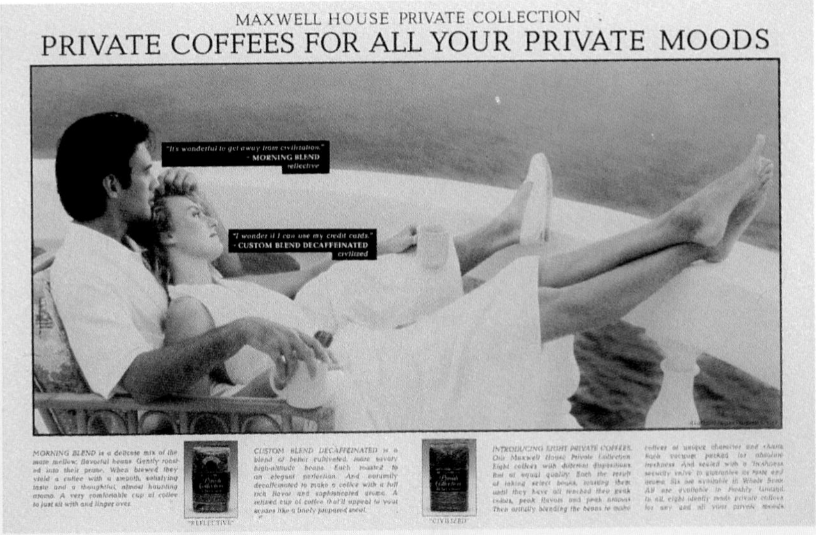

MAXWELL HOUSE PRIVATE COLLECTION
PRIVATE COFFEES FOR ALL YOUR PRIVATE MOODS

Source: Courtesy of General Foods Corporation. MAXWELL HOUSE is a registered trademark of General Foods Corporation.

Coffee drinking has declined over the past two decades, as young adults stick to soft drinks. However, the gourmet coffee segment has actually grown 15 percent. The consumers behind that growth are 25 to 49 years old and affluent. These consumers, who have been willing to spend as much as $9 to $10 a pound for good coffee, have sparked a new industry of gourmet coffee roasters and retailers.

Having discovered this promising market segment, major coffee sellers have wasted no time moving in. In 1986, General Foods and the Great Atlantic & Pacific Tea Company both introduced lines of gourmet coffee, each featuring similar exotic varieties. General Foods' line, called Maxwell House Private Collection, includes whole bean and ground roast coffee packaged in clear plastic bags. A&P's line, called Eight O'Clock Royale Gourmet Bean Coffee, is sold in gold-colored bags. For both lines, the packaging includes a new innovation for longer shelf life: a one-way valve that allows the coffee to release gases without letting oxygen in.

Source: Patricia Winters, "GF, A&P Grind It Out in Specialty Coffees," *Advertising Age*, July 21, 1986, pp. 3, 77.

of romance or adventure novels may be seeking an inexpensive "escape" from their day-to-day lives.

Sometimes market researchers cannot immediately determine exactly what benefits different groups look for in a product. Could you, for example, explain the differences between how you decide which shampoo to use and how your parents make the choice? Often the researcher must apply sophisticated statistical tools to distinguish between the benefits people see in marketed products and the benefits they would ideally like to see. The techniques are complex but may reveal new product possibilities.

The classic study of benefit segmentation was performed by Russel I. Haley in the toothpaste market. He discovered that the market could be divided into four benefit segments, each with its own characteristics. One group in the study, composed primarily of large families, sought decay prevention. Another group, mostly teenagers and young adults, cared most about cosmetic features such as brightness and breath fresheners. Men looked for the brand with the lowest price, and children wanted a brand with the best taste or the most novel appearance. Each group could be linked with a brand demonstrating the benefits considered most

Table 4.1
Life-Style Dimensions

Activities	Interests	Opinions	Demographics
Work	Family	Themselves	Age
Hobbies	Home	Social issues	Education
Social events	Job	Politics	Income
Vacation	Community	Business	Occupation
Entertainment	Recreation	Economics	Family size
Club membership	Fashion	Education	Dwelling
Community	Food	Products	Geography
Shopping	Media	Future	City size
Sports	Achievements	Culture	Stage in life-cycle

Source: Joseph T. Plummer, "The Concept and Application of Life-Style Segmentation," *Journal of Marketing* (January 1974), p. 34.

important.[6] Although the research was completed in the 1960s, toothpaste companies still use the results of the study.

Psychographic Segmentation

The basic question left unanswered by demographic and usage-rate segmentation is *why* consumers purchase what they do. Benefit segmentation does not answer why people emphasize certain benefits. Psychographic segmentation tries to answer these questions by focusing on a potential consumer's life-style and personality traits.

Life-Style
Person's pattern of living expressed in activities, interests, and opinions.

The concept of **life-style** refers to a person's pattern of living in the world as expressed in his or her activities, interests, and opinions.[7] By examining a person's life-style, you can learn things that information about social class or other demographic data would fail to reveal. Two women of the same age and with the same family size and income might live next door to each other in an affluent suburb. One might be a top executive with a Fortune 500 firm, while her neighbor might be a traditional homemaker.

Psychographic Segmentation
Division of the market into classes on the basis of the life-styles of members.

To determine the best approach to reaching either of these women, marketers might turn to psychographics. Using the methods and insights of motivation and personality research, **psychographic segmentation** seeks to divide the market according to people's life-styles, or distinct approaches to living.

Marketers identify different life-styles by measuring three factors: activities, interests, and opinions. (See Table 4.1.) To probe these areas, marketers administer lengthy questionnaires consisting of general statements (such as "I enjoy going to concerts") and product-specific statements (such as "Instant coffee is more economical than ground coffee"). Consumers must rate the extent of their agreement or disagreement with the statements on a seven-point scale. Usually, they are also asked to give information on their product usage and demographic characteristics. Marketers then group those with similar responses into psychographic categories and develop a profile of each group's demographics and product usage rates. Each group represents a different market segment.[8] The description of the teenage market in Marketing Today 4.2 includes psychographic as well as demographic information.

Using this method, the marketers at Colgate identified a new segment of the market for soap. After administering a psychographic questionnaire to a group, researchers were able to isolate three life-style categories among respondents. The first category, "rejuvenators," were other-directed, insecure, and in need of social reassurance. They sought the deodorant protection of a soap like Dial. The second group, "compensators," were pleasure seekers who liked to feel pampered by a beauty bar like Dove. But research uncovered another group distinctly different from these two. It was composed of self-assured, practical, rugged people—primarily men—who used a soap simply to get *clean.* Colgate, at the time, had no soap specifically targeted to this group, which they labeled "independents."

On the basis of this information, Colgate marketers tailored a marketing mix for the "independent" segment. The name given to the new soap, Irish Spring, was chosen to express the benefit that independents most desired—cleanliness. The distinctive black package was designed to catch the eye of the independent thinker. Commercials featured Sean, a rugged-looking guy, to stress the mood of outdoor "manliness." This strategy netted Colgate third place in the market for soap.[9]

The psychographic method is not infallible, however. It is costly, and information can be misinterpreted. Psychographics that richly describe a market segment do not always succeed in predicting how consumers will behave in the marketplace. Because research into the theory underlying psychographic segmentation has been limited, marketers lack a reliable procedure. Nevertheless, psychographic research provides marketers with descriptive detail that helps them in developing marketing strategies. Psychographic segmentation has therefore achieved widespread use.[10]

Segmentation Bases for the Industrial Market

Most of us are relatively familiar with the strategies companies use to reach consumer markets. But many marketing students may eventually find themselves employed by industrial firms whose target markets are not individuals but other industries.

Industrial buying behavior is different in many ways from consumer buying. Although certain segmentation strategies are similar to those practiced in consumer markets, others are unique to industrial marketing. The most common ways of segmenting an industrial market are by customer location, type of industry, company size, and end use of product.

Marketing Today 4.2
Targeting Teenagers

According to Charles Mittelstadt, manager at the Center for Advertising Services, today's teenagers are a lot different from teenagers of past years. "You can't go back," says Mittelstadt, "because the cultural differences between today and yesterday are so great."

One difference is the spending power of today's teenagers. One estimate for 1986 predicted that teenagers would spend $30 billion of their own money that year. In addition, many also shop for their family because both their parents work. As a result, they may be spending as much as $40 billion of family money, mainly on groceries. One study estimates that teenagers make up to 20 percent of all supermarket purchases among families with teenagers.

Changing family patterns also affect teenagers' values. Because of high divorce levels, most teens rate family continuity as being extremely important. They tend to admire grandparents more than parents. Thus, ads including grandparents in family settings may appeal to teenagers. Mittelstadt summarizes teenagers' values this way: "They are very disciplined about acquiring money, very goal oriented. But there's a major change in the work ethic. It's no longer work hard and save for a brighter future. Now it is work hard and get what you want today."

Source: Jeffrey A. Trachtenberg, "Big Spenders: Teenage Division," *Forbes*, November 3, 1986, pp. 201, 204.

Zittles:
Et Zitera:
Zits, zits and more zits.
Sneakattacne:
A zit that surprises you right before a date.
"Zittles" are brand new words for the same old bummers—acne pimples. What can you do about them? Launch a major Zitskrieg with the unbeatable medicine in Oxy 10®, Oxy 10® Cover, Oxy 5® and Oxy 10® Wash. They all contain a potent measure of benzoyl peroxide, the very stuff that brought acne medicine out of the Dark Ages.
In fact, to kill acne bacteria and help prevent new pimples from forming, there's nothing stronger you can buy without a prescription.
Next question: How clean can you get your skin? You know all those little embedded blackheads that like to call your nose home? Oxy Clean® softens them up—helps send them floating down the drain.
Oxy Clean Medicated Pads, Cleanser, Soap and Scrub lift away dirt and oil so well you can actually prevent new pimples from starting in the first place.
So, remember: the next time that Sneakattacne attacks your face, get Oxy and launch a Counterattacne.

OXY Because zits are no laughing matter.

Source: © Illustration, Scott Pollack. © 1987 Norcliff Thayer, Inc.

Table 4.2
The Standard Industrial Classification System

Industries Classified	First Two-Digit SIC Numbers Involved for Major Industry Groups
Agriculture, forestry, and fishing	01, 02, 07, 08, 09
Mining	10–14
Construction	15–17
Manufacturing	20–39
Transportation, communications, electric, gas, and sanitary services	40–49
Wholesale trade	50–51
Retail trade	52–59
Finance, insurance, and real estate	60–67
Services	70, 72–73, 75–76, 78–86, 88–89
Public administration	91–97

Source: Office of Management and Budget, *1972 Standard Industrial Classification Manual* (Washington, D.C.: U.S. Government Printing Office, 1972), pp. 5–7.

Customer Location

As in consumer markets, industrial demand for products varies by geographic location. Companies seeking to market to high-tech firms would concentrate their efforts on California's Silicon Valley, Boston's Route 128, and North Carolina's Research Triangle. Similarly, firms targeting the automobile industry would make Detroit the focus of their efforts. But even when industries are highly concentrated, opportunities exist for smaller suppliers who may be able to provide superior service to local clients.

Industry Type

One of the most valuable tools for an industrial marketer is a U.S. government coding system called the **Standard Industrial Classification (SIC) Code.** SIC is a numbering system for categorizing businesses by economic activity. (See Table 4.2.) Each industry within these groups has a distinct code number. The industry group "manufacturing" codes (20 through 39), for example, includes manufacturers of food products (SIC 20). These major groups are then divided into three-digit industry groups. Food processors (SIC 20) is further broken down into bakery products (SIC 205), which is then further divided into the subgroup cookies and crackers (SIC 2052). SIC is divided into 10,000 different products, each assigned a seven-digit code.[11]

Standard Industrial Classification (SIC) Code
Numbering system followed by the U.S. government for categorizing businesses by economic activity.

Marketing managers can learn a great deal about potential customers by knowing their SIC codes. A number of government and private sources, including the *U.S. Industrial Outlook,* Dun & Bradstreet's *Market*

Identifiers, and the *U.S. Census of Manufacturers,* publish information about industries identified by SIC codes. By using these sources, marketers can acquire information such as where customers are located, how much of the market they control, and who the companies' key executives are. This information can then be used to identify target markets and to develop a marketing strategy.[12]

Customer Size

A marketer may want to segment the market further on the basis of the size of possible customers. Large buyers may have special requirements for purchasing procedures, delivery schedules, or price. While it may be worthwhile for some firms to service large and sometimes demanding customers, other companies might do well to concentrate on the smaller end of the market.

Richards Consultants, Ltd., for example, learned that small can be profitable when they first launched their executive search firm. The two founders originally thought large high-tech firms such as Digital Equipment Corporation (DEC) and Honeywell would be the best places to offer their services. But when they set out to investigate how they might develop a competitive edge over these companies' existing search firms, they realized there was a better way to approach the problem. Instead of fighting an uphill battle for the already well-serviced industry giants, why not target the many small, rapidly growing companies that were hungry for management talent? The two owners have since built a thriving firm serving the DECs and Honeywells of the next generation.[13]

In the industrial market, firms may also be segmented as to usage rate. Paper manufacturers, for example, may want to target book, newspaper, and magazine publishers who are heavy users of paper rather than companies who may occasionally use paper to print an in-house newsletter or brochure.

End Use of Product

Because an industrial product may be used many different ways, a marketer may want to segment the market by the way the product will ultimately be used. A paper manufacturer may decide to target companies that manufacture paper party goods, toilet tissue, greeting cards, or product packaging rather than publishers. Again, SIC data would be a valuable source of information about potential customers.

Selecting Markets to Target

After a marketer has divided a market into segments, the next step is to decide which segments to target. This decision involves weighing whether to pursue one segment or many, as well as selecting the market segments the company can target most effectively. American Express,

At Your Service 4.1
American Express Hopes New Services Will Appeal to Multiple Markets

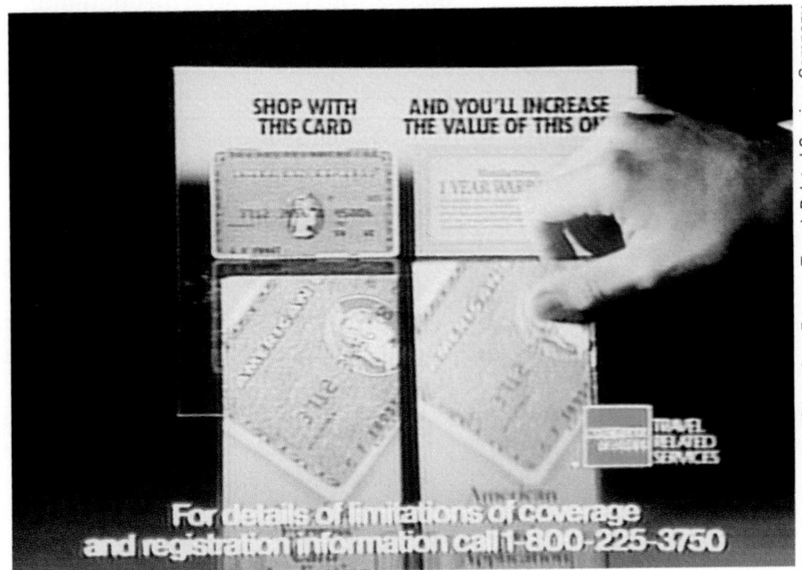

SHOP WITH THIS CARD
AND YOU'LL INCREASE THE VALUE OF THIS O
TRAVEL RELATED SERVICES
For details of limitations of coverage and registration information call 1-800-225-3750

Source: Courtesy of American Express Travel Related Services Company, Inc.

When American Express wanted to target new markets, it revised its marketing mix. The company had selected several target markets; specifically, its objective was to increase the card's use among women, students, affluent elders, and empty nesters (parents whose children have grown up and left home).

The company adopted an advertising campaign promoting its new services, including 24-hour customer service, a 24-hour legal and medical referral hotline, and an innovative service called Buyers Assurance. Buyers Assurance extends the repair period on manufacturers' warranties for merchandise charged on an American Express card. According to the company, this service is a first for the industry.

The company's advertising focuses on describing these services. American Express has, since introducing its card in 1958, made a practice of adding services to differentiate its card from competing credit services. Explains one senior vice president for personal card marketing, "It's great to have services, but what we've found from time to time is we had to communicate those services in an intrusive way."

Source: Sarah Stiansen, "American Express Drops 'Do You Know Me'; Shifts to Services," *Adweek,* August 18, 1986, p. 3.

for example, plans to expand its business by increasing its appeal to several target markets. (See At Your Service 4.1.)

One Segment or Many?

Marketers can target a single market segment, or they can diversify their efforts to try to appeal to several segments. For example, Cable News Network caters to television viewers who want news and information, whereas NBC tries to schedule a variety of programs that will attract a broad audience.

Concentrated Marketing When an organization focuses all its efforts on one segment with a single marketing mix, it is engaging in **concentrated marketing.** Playschool, for example, concentrates its marketing on toys for preschoolers. In Los Angeles, the Wilshire House was built for

Concentrated Marketing Practice of dividing the market into market segments and selecting only one segment to serve with a marketing mix.

people who could afford condominiums ranging in price from $1,500,000 to $11,000,000—a specialized market indeed.

The advantage of concentrated marketing is that it allows a firm to thoroughly know and understand its market and thus to meet its specialized needs in a way that would not be possible with a more diversified strategy. Concentrated marketing may also be the best tactic for a firm with limited resources, since it may be able to serve its customers better than its larger competitors can.

Concentrated marketing does have drawbacks, however. By focusing efforts on one particular segment, a firm may be vulnerable if marketing conditions change and it has nothing to fall back on. When the bottom fell out of the housing market in the early 1980s, developers of the Wilshire House, for example, resorted to offering a free Rolls Royce to anyone who would buy an $11,000,000 condo.[14]

Another disadvantage of concentrated marketing is that a company's strength in one market may be a deterrent should it seek to expand its base. Disney Studios, for example, had trouble breaking into the market for young adult films because the company was so heavily identified with movies for children.

Differentiated Marketing
Practice of marketing to many market segments, each with a different marketing mix.

Differentiated Marketing When an organization markets to many segments, each with a different marketing mix, it is practicing **differentiated marketing.** The soft-drink industry provides good examples of this approach. Royal Crown, for instance, sells different colas to different market segments: RC for those who want the basic product, Diet Rite for weight watchers, and RC 100 for those who want to avoid caffeine.

A policy of differentiated marketing allows a firm to pull out of a segment that proves unprofitable and to rely on other segments. For example, when R. J. Reynolds' low-tar cigarette Real failed to capture a following, the company simply pulled out of that segment and supported its offerings to other segments (Winston, Salem, Vantage, More, and Now).[15]

The production and marketing costs of servicing many different segments, as Reynolds does, are very high. Marketers must weigh the risk of specialization against the cost of diversification. Three other questions relevant to deciding how many segments to pursue are:

1. *What is the financial condition of the firm?* Small firms with limited resources may need to restrict their marketing effort to one segment in order to survive.

2. *What is the competition doing?* If competitors are covering the major segments with a broad line of products, they may be ignoring smaller segments that can be pursued.

3. *Is the market new to the firm?* It may be better to concentrate on one segment when entering a new market and expand to other segments after a foothold is established.

Which Segments?

In deciding which segments to target, marketers evaluate which segments the organization can reach most effectively. A segment is a good candidate for target marketing if it meets three general criteria:

1. *A market segment is identifiable.* Marketers should be able to spot a common need or characteristic of some people that is different from that of other people in the market. It may be determined, for example, that when certain people are depressed, they become heavy consumers of snack foods. But how could a marketer reach people with just those tendencies? It is much easier to use a variable like income as a way of distinguishing groups of people in a given market because a great deal of information on the composition of the American population by income groups is available.

2. *A market segment is accessible.* Even if a marketer can identify a subset of consumers, segmentation may not be worthwhile if that market cannot be reached economically. A real estate office may recognize that the market for a five-bedroom, $175,000 house would most likely be a family earning more than $60,000 per year, with three or more children. But not all families with those characteristics in a given area are in the market for a house, and the potential buyer may even be someone who does not match those standards. The office may advertise in local papers knowing that most readers will not be interested in the offering. Compare that scattershot approach to the ability of marketers of expensive cookware to reach potential customers through such magazines as *Gourmet* and *Bon Appétit.*

3. *A market segment is large enough to be profitable.* There must be enough people in a potential segment to justify the high costs of marketing and production. While there may be a market in the United States for romance novels written in Portuguese, it is likely to be too small for a marketer to justify the cost, especially since such novels usually are marketed in inexpensive paperback editions. Conversely, while the market for very specialized scientific books is also small, some publishers find this segment a worthwhile market. Scientific and technical books can command a premium price, and potential customers—usually professionals and libraries—are easily reached using highly targeted mailing lists. The determination of profit potential is so crucial to marketers that various techniques for measuring demand have been devised. They are explored at the end of this chapter.

Forecasting in Marketing

Forecasting
Predicting demand in the marketplace over a given period of time.

The strategy of target marketing is worthwhile only if the segments targeted have enough sales potential to warrant a special marketing program. To estimate the size of that potential, marketers engage in **forecasting,** which is the art of predicting demand in the marketplace over a given period of time. Forecasts may be short-range (one year or less), medium-range (one to five years), or long-range (more than five years).

Forecasting is complicated because demand can be expressed in a variety of ways. Sometimes demand refers to actual sales—the amount of money a company can expect to make in a given market segment. At other times demand refers to **market potential**—the total of all sales that might be generated in a market segment. If a company is the sole seller of a product in a certain segment, then the two meanings converge. But because competition exists in most segments, a single company's sales rarely equal all that buyers are willing and able to purchase.

Market Potential
Total of all sales that might be generated in a market segment.

Properly speaking, the term **sales forecast** refers only to the prediction of actual sales a company can expect to make in a certain market or segment. But in order to arrive at this, marketers must first determine market potential, which sets an upper limit on what can be sold. Two other types of forecasts—economic and industry forecasts—enable them to gauge market potential.

Sales Forecast
Prediction of actual sales a company can expect to make in a certain market or segment.

Forecast Types: A Comparison

Economic, industry, and sales forecasts are distinct yet related. A general understanding of the economy underlies an accurate prediction of industry sales, which in turn serves as the foundation for predicting company sales.

Economic Forecasts An **economic forecast** detects how changes in the national and international business climate will affect specific industries. As noted in Chapter 3, marketing activity varies with the phases of the business cycle (depression, recession, recovery, and prosperity). Marketers recognize that the general health of the economy may seriously affect sales in an industry. Hence, they pay close attention to variations in economic cycles before stepping into a new market segment or undertaking new programs in an established segment.

Economic Forecast
Prediction of how the economy will fare as a whole in light of changes in the national and international business climate.

The gross national product (GNP) and the unemployment rate are two of the most widely used economic indicators. Researchers have found that sales in many industries are closely correlated to these measures. For example, when there is a rise in the GNP, auto sales usually increase.

Other, more specific, indicators may successfully predict sales trends for various industries. The level of housing starts, for example, is an excellent indicator for companies that supply the construction industry. Businesses as diverse as lumber companies, appliance manufacturers, and real estate offices watch this indicator to help estimate what their sales might be in coming months. In the area of consumer products, an increase in average hours worked may signal a rise in sales, since overtime produces more income for discretionary buying.

The indicators needed to make an economic forecast are compiled by the U.S. government. Two of the most useful government publications containing information are the *Survey of Current Business* and the

Federal Reserve Bulletin, both published monthly. Many firms enter data from such sources in their computer banks for forecasting. Other firms depend on outside organizations (universities, banks, and brokerage houses) for economic forecasts. While the use of computers has made economic forecasting more accurate, unexpected world events can undermine even the most sophisticated predictions. For example, the 1974 Arab oil embargo and the drought of the summer of 1986 had widespread economic reverberations that could not have been anticipated in economic forecasts.

Industry Forecasts Economic forecasts set an upper limit on potential demand in a given segment. They tell how much income may be *available* for purchase of a particular product. However, they do not indicate how much income people are *willing* to spend on that product (rather than save or spend elsewhere). For such information, marketers require an **industry forecast,** the prediction of likely sales for a class of products.

Industry Forecast
Prediction of likely sales for a class of products.

In addition to the economic climate, industry sales are affected by two factors: (1) the amount of industrywide marketing activity and (2) the prevailing social and legal climate.

Marketing activity by fellow industry members can increase or decrease demand for a product. The growth in sales of personal computers, for example, has created a boom market for manufacturers of software, disks, and terminal tables, as well as for publishers of computer books.

A marketing manager who must predict the sales of products must anticipate how the marketing activities of other companies may influence total demand. Also, as you learned in Chapter 3, marketers must take into account the current social and legal environment for their industry. For example, beginning in the summer of 1987, California has permitted banks from certain western states to do business in California. Preparing for the expected onslaught of out-of-state competitors, Wells Fargo Bank hired experienced salespeople to promote its commercial loans.[16]

Marketing departments can obtain information about social and legal issues for their industry from trade association publications, which report estimates of future patterns of industry growth and decline. Marketers in the energy business, for example, might be interested in supply and demand forecasts for natural gas reported in *World Oil* and *Oil and Gas Journal;* marketers in the computer industry might check the forecasts reported in *Electronic Business.*

Company Sales Forecasts An economic forecast tries to set an upper limit on income available for purchases, and an industry forecast predicts how much of a specific product people may be willing to buy. A sales forecast is needed to determine how much of the market a company may expect to capture. This figure is known as a company's **market share,** the percentage of the total industry sales that a particular firm can claim.

Market Share
Percentage of total industry sales that a particular firm can claim.

A company's share of market demand is directly related to its marketing effort. Market share increases or decreases with changes in the marketing mix. A change in product formulation or design, price, distribution methods, or the amount of advertising may affect market share. The relation between market share and marketing effort is a key point to remember. Some marketers mistakenly believe they must have a sales forecast before they can plan for marketing, forgetting that marketing strategy itself often affects how much is sold.

The forecast of company sales is arrived at by applying the company's historical share of the market—adjusted by marketing plans for the upcoming year—to industry forecast figures. For example, Lipton was for many years the only national marketer of bagged and instant tea. Sales of tea had been flat for years, but Lipton had not worried. It historically had sold half of the 90 million pounds of bagged tea bought each year. Sales forecasting was simple. But all that changed when Procter & Gamble and Nestlé both decided to move into the market. Lipton responded by launching new products, substantially increasing advertising budgets, and strengthening its sales force. With new competitors, new products, and a dramatically revamped marketing mix, sales forecasting at Lipton is no longer a simple task.[17]

The hardest part of sales forecasting is determining expected market share. The task is especially difficult when the forecast is for a new product with no track record. Even when past information is available, it is difficult to translate into hard figures how a change in strategy will affect demand. Various techniques for estimating demand are available to marketers.

Techniques of Demand Estimation

The methods for estimating demand can be simple or elaborate. Some involve merely a survey of opinion, others a manipulation of statistics, and still others a use of market tests. Marketers choose from among them on the basis of market stability (whether the demand is changing), the number of potential customers, the availability of historical data, and the amount of money available for forecasting.[18] Sometimes a combination of methods is used to increase forecast accuracy. Table 4.3 summarizes the major techniques discussed below.

Survey Techniques All of the survey techniques for estimating demand rely on soliciting the opinions of some of the people involved in the marketing process.

Executive-Panel Survey
Means for sales forecasting using opinions of company officials.

Executive-Panel Survey An **executive-panel survey** is often used when funds are limited or when a new product is being introduced. Before introducing its line of heat- and cold-resistant glass cookware, Corning commissioned an economic feasibility study to determine if there was a market for such a product. Results of the study indicated there was not a market. But a panel of executives at Corning claimed that, based on their previous experience in marketing other types of cooking products, this line would succeed. The company chose to ignore the report and rely on its own managers' judgment. Corning has since gone on to be-

Table 4.3
Demand Estimation Techniques: A Comparison

Type	Use	Advantages	Disadvantages
Survey			
1. Executive panel	For new products in particular	Inexpensive; draws on marketing experience	Subjective and unreliable
2. Sales force	For few customers	Improves accuracy because of closeness to customers; provides psychological motivator	Often results in conservative, uninformed estimates
3. Customer sampling	For many customers	Relies on first-hand information	May not predict actual purchase; is costly
Statistical Methods			
1. Time-series projection	For products with stable demand; for firms with many products	Is more objective than survey methods	Requires years of data; cannot predict pattern changes
2. Correlation analysis	For products with stable demand over a long period	Can be quite reliable when many correlations are found	Associations are difficult to find, and sometimes unreliable
Market Tests	For new products	Provides information about actual, not just intended, purchases	Is expensive; can fail to be predictive if sample is poorly chosen

come one of the leading manufacturers of this type of cookware.[19] Executive opinion is not always that reliable, however. The past experience of executives is often not a good guide to the future. Many times different executives come up with radically different figures, and an average of them all may be far off the target.

Sales-Force Survey A **sales-force survey,** in which a company asks its salespeople to estimate sales in their territories in the upcoming year, may be more reliable. The sales force is closer to the market and may know customers better than executives do. In addition, if salespeople participate in estimating their own sales quotas, they may have more of an incentive to meet them.

Sales-Force Survey
Means for sales forecasting using estimates of company salespeople.

However, marketers should exercise caution when estimating demand based on sales-force surveys. Salespeople often are not aware of planned changes in the company's marketing mix or of possible changes in the economic climate that may affect sales. When a salesperson's estimates are also to be used as a measure of performance, the potential demand may be underestimated so sales quotas can be easily exceeded. On the other hand, if money for sales promotions and advertising is keyed to a territory's potential sales, a salesperson may be tempted to overestimate demand. A sales-force estimate is useful, but only in concert with other estimates of demand.

Customer Sampling
Survey conducted to sample customers' intentions to buy.

Customer Sampling Direct **customer sampling,** a survey of consumers' intentions to buy, may also provide useful information about the strength of market demand. The National Lead Company surveys its largest buyers each year to determine likely demand for its paint, paper, and rubber products; General Electric maintains a panel of consumers to keep the firm informed of their intentions to buy appliances.

Samples of customer intentions can be expensive to obtain, however. And an "intention to buy" often does not result in an actual purchase. Like all survey methods, a sampling of customers is subjective and can give inaccurate results. But in the case of new products, a survey of opinion may be the only feasible method.[20]

Statistical Methods Although forecasting is not an exact science, some techniques are more objective than others. Statistical methods, which make use of past data, attempt to take some of the guesswork out of demand estimation.

Time-Series Projection
Statistical method for forecasting sales based on past patterns projected into the future.

Time-Series Projection **Time-series projection** uncovers patterns of movement in past sales and projects these patterns into the future.[21] At least five years of past sales data are usually required for an accurate prediction.

Researchers look for four patterns of movement. Sometimes a product's sales move upward along a trend line, as lite beer has done over the past few years. More often, sales patterns are cyclical, changing every few years with the general business climate. As previously noted, car sales are closely tied to economic conditions. The sales of some products exhibit a seasonal pattern of movement, soaring at one or more times of the year and trailing off at others. Sales of toys at Christmas and suntan lotion in July are typical examples. Finally, some products' sales move up and down randomly, exhibiting no apparent pattern.

When a past pattern is discernible, marketers can determine the rate of change mathematically and project a continuation of that rate. The assumption is that the future will be like the past. Of course, that is not always so. Time-series projections cannot detect radical turning points, so they are generally more reliable when applied to the immediate, rather than the distant, future.

Correlation Analysis
Statistical method of forecasting used to find factors that change in advance of changes in product demand.

Correlation Analysis Another statistical technique, **correlation analysis,** is more sophisticated. It is used to find factors that change in advance of changes in product demand. One industrial packaging manufacturer found that changes in the Index of Industrial Production tended to precede a change in company sales by three months.

When many correlations are found, predictions of future demand tend to be even more accurate. However, finding correlations can be difficult and, at times, impossible.

Test Marketing
Trial marketing in a limited area chosen as representative of an entire market.

Market Tests Historical data for making time-series projections or a correlation analysis are not available for new products. Customers can be sampled, but, as noted previously, what customers say they will purchase and what they will actually purchase can be quite different. An alternative method is **test marketing,** during which a product is sold in a limited area chosen as representative of the entire market.

Test marketing is expensive. Moreover, if test cities are not properly chosen, the results can be deceptive. But small-scale tests are sometimes the only way to gauge demand. The advantages and drawbacks of this method are discussed in Chapter 5.

Combining Approaches Since each of the methods for estimating demand has some disadvantages, many companies use two or more of the techniques as a check on accuracy. For example, the estimates of an executive panel are often weighed against estimates from the sales force. The executives supply the knowledge of long-term economic trends and marketing plans that salespeople often lack, and the sales force provides knowledge of local markets, customer reactions, and competitors' activities in the field.

Accuracy is important because companies use sales forecasts for many purposes other than marketing. Based on the sales forecast, production is scheduled, raw materials and equipment are purchased, inventory is planned, and the effectiveness of the sales force is monitored. Many managers strive for accuracy to within 10 percent of the actual sales.

Chapter Replay

1. **What are the differences between mass marketing and target marketing?**
   In mass marketing, all the customers in a market are thought of as homogeneous. Target marketing divides the market into market segments and develops a marketing mix to attract a particular market segment.
2. **What are some ways to segment the consumer market?**
   A marketer can segment a consumer market based on demographic factors (including regional and socioeconomic factors), rate of product usage, perceived product benefits, and psychographic characteristics.
3. **What are some ways to segment the industrial market?**
   A marketer can segment an industrial market based on location, industry type, company size, and end use of the product.
4. **What is the difference between concentrated marketing and differentiated marketing?**
   Concentrated marketing focuses on one segment with a single marketing mix. Differentiated marketing uses different marketing mixes to reach many market segments.
5. **What issues do marketers consider in deciding how many market segments to target?**
   Marketers consider the cost of diversification, the risk of specialization, the financial condition of the firm, the actions of competitors, and the firm's experience with the market.

6. **What criteria make a market segment a good candidate for targeting?**
A market segment is a good candidate for targeting if it is identifiable, accessible, and large enough to be profitable.
7. **What types of forecasts do marketers use?**
Marketers use economic, industry, and company sales forecasts.
8. **How do marketers estimate demand?**
Marketers use survey techniques, such as the executive-panel survey, the sales-force survey, and customer sampling. They also use statistical methods—including time-series projection and correlation analysis—as well as market tests.

Key Terms

benefit segmentation
concentrated marketing
correlation analysis
customer sampling
demographic segmentation
differentiated marketing
economic forecast
executive-panel survey
forecasting
industry forecast
life-style
market potential
market share
mass marketing
psychographic segmentation
sales-force survey
sales forecast
Standard Industrial Classification (SIC) Code
target marketing
test marketing
time-series projection
usage-rate segmentation

Discussion Questions

1. What assumptions does mass marketing make about customers and products? Three-ring binders are a fairly uniform product used for one basic purpose: to hold paper. Can marketers of three-ring binders use target marketing? If so, what market segments can they target and how?
2. In segmenting the consumer market, what demographic characteristics might a maker of air conditioners consider?
3. Middletown officials commissioned a study of who is using its public library, hoping to use that information to get more people to visit the library. According to the study, 15 percent of Middletown citizens—mostly students—use the library several times a week, 40 percent visit the library at least once a year, and the remaining 45 percent rarely if ever use the library. To convince more people to use the library, which of these groups might the library target? Suggest some ways in which the library might adapt the elements of the marketing mix—product, price, promotion, and placement—to reach the target market(s).

4. What is psychographic segmentation? How do marketers measure life-style?
5. Don Deluxe runs a word-processing business, Deluxe Word Processing. In deciding which companies to sell his services to, what segmentation strategies might Don use?
6. What are the advantages and disadvantages of concentrated marketing and differentiated marketing?
7. What criteria make a market segment a good candidate for target marketing? How do marketers evaluate whether a segment is likely to be profitable?
8. Marsha McCloud, who works in the marketing department of Best Consumer Products, is responsible for estimating the market potential for refrigerator sales. What kinds of information will help Marsha make this estimate?
9. How can Marsha use the information in question 8 to forecast company sales?
10. Acme Software Developers is planning to introduce a revolutionary new program for students that automatically does homework while entertaining the user with video games. What techniques could the company use to estimate demand for this product? Describe the advantages and disadvantages of each technique you suggest.

Case 4.1 Woods Gordon

Woods Gordon, a wholly owned Canadian partnership, is a leading management consulting firm that provides clients with professional expertise in a wide variety of disciplines. The firm offers comprehensive management, audit, tax, valuation, insolvency, and financial services from 22 offices throughout Canada. Based on a detailed analysis of national economic and market trends, *Tomorrow's Customer in Canada* is a report prepared by Woods Gordon each year as a service to its clients and friends. The following information has been extracted from the section on the people of Canada.

Population Trends

Population growth has been slowing for the last decade. Increases are expected to average only 0.8 percent per year between 1986 and 1991 and 0.5 percent per year between 1991 and 1996, resulting in a population increase from the present 25.6 million to 27.3 million in 1996. As a result, the markets for many products are not expanding at the same rates they did in the 1960s and 1970s.

Source: Adapted from *Tomorrow's Customers in Canada,* 1986, published by Woods Gordon, a member of Arthur Young International.

Canadians Get Older

As a nation, Canadians are getting older. Over the next decade we will see a 7 percent decline in the number of Canadians under 35. There will be 370,000 fewer children under 9, 50,000 fewer teens, and nearly 600,000 fewer young adults 20 to 34.

The contraction in the number of school-age children will continue to create pressure for downsizing the educational system. Offsetting this will be a 25 percent increase in the number of people 35 and over.

As the Baby Boomers begin to enter middle age, there will be nearly 1.6 million more adults 35 to 49, an increase of 32.4 percent from 1986. The "gray revolution" will be increasingly apparent. By 1996, almost 7.6 million Canadians, slightly less than 28 percent of the population, will be over 50 years old (compared to 22 percent in 1976), and nearly 3.6 million of these, or 13.1 percent, will be over 65 (compared to 8.7 percent in 1976).

The 50 to 64 Age Group In 1996, about 4 million Canadians will be in the 50 to 64 age group, nearly 450,000 more than today. Disposable income for this group will be particularly high as their children leave home and mortgages are paid off. However, with couples now starting their families later in life, the average age of parents when their children leave home is expected to increase. As members of this group become grandparents, they may be expected to be both willing and able to spend on their grandchildren for toys, clothing, baby items such as cribs and strollers, and scholarship trust funds. Members of this age group are hardly "old" in outlook or physical well-being and retain many of the spending patterns of their younger days.

The Over 65 Age Group In 1996, nearly 3.6 million Canadians will be 65 or older—850,000 more than today and 1.5 million more than 10 years ago. For these older Canadians, physical well-being and nutrition will be key concerns. The elderly living in their own homes will require assistance with many of the maintenance tasks they once did themselves.

Number of Households Growing

While the population growth is expected to be modest, households will continue to grow nearly three times as fast. Between 1986 and 1991, the number of households is expected to increase 2.7 percent per year on average—an addition of nearly 1.2 million new households over the next 5 years (from 9.5 million in 1986 to just over 10.6 million in 1991). By 1996, there will be nearly 11.4 million households.

The rising number of divorces is contributing to new household formation. While the annual number of marriages declined between 1972 and 1984, averaging just over 190,000, the number of divorces doubled to 70,000. Despite the rising divorce rate, Canadians continue to marry, reflecting the triumph of hope over experience.

Changing Role of Women

The changing social and economic climate has had a dramatic impact on the family structure of Canadians. One example is the decline in the number of families in which the wife is at home with the children. Of *all* Canadian households in 1971, one in three was the traditional unit with the wife at home with the children. By 1981, the ratio dropped to one in five. The 1986 Census is expected to show a further substantial decline. For marketers, the declining number of households with the typical housewife means reevaluating positioning and advertising of products and services that once were the domain of the housewife.

Between 1973 and 1985, the number of women in the labor force increased by more than 60 percent, from 3.3 million to 5.4 million, at a compound annual growth rate of 4.1 percent.

While the participation of men in the labor force has declined marginally from 98.2 percent in 1973 to 76.7 percent in 1983, the participation rate of women has increased from 42 percent in 1973 to 54 percent in 1985. Compared to many other industrialized nations, the participation rate of Canadian women in the labor force is high.

Focal Topics

1. Why is it important for a firm like Woods Gordon to prepare a report on changing consumer trends?
2. What other types of information about consumers would be helpful?
3. How would you use the information in the case if you manufactured and marketed baby products? Consumer foods? Household furniture? Children's toys?

Case 4.2
Viewdata Corporation of America, Inc.

"The Waiting Is Over; Touch the Future with Viewtron. Welcome to the Future! Tomorrow has arrived. A historical moment in the United States is upon us, and all of us who live in South Florida are a part of this historic event." With those words, Viewdata Corporation of America, Inc., introduced Viewtron®, a videotex service, to the marketplace. The company described videotex as a new communications medium that combines space-age technology with a consumer's television and telephone line to bring information and services into the home.

Edited Viewtron News Release

Miami—A futuristic communications and information medium is about to move from the scientific lab into the American living room. Viewtron,

Source: Adapted from news releases and company information about the videotex service. Viewtron is a registered service mark of Viewdata Corporation of America, and Sceptre is a trademark of AT&T Company.

Viewtron Facts

What Is It?

The first full-scale consumer videotex system in the United States, combining the features of television, telephone lines, and computers, and offering instant, two-way communications. It provides an information and transaction service, Viewtron®, which is accessed by an electronic terminal called Sceptre™.

Who Created It?

The Sceptre™ terminal was developed by Bell Laboratories and is being manufactured and marketed by AT&T Consumer Products.

Viewtron was created by Viewdata Corporation of America, Inc., a wholly owned subsidiary of Knight-Ridder Newspapers, Inc.

Viewdata Corporation is the system operator, collecting, packaging, storing, providing, and maintaining the service.

What Does It Do?

Viewtron provides consumers, in words and graphics, at-home banking, in-home shopping, news, reference material, entertainment, education, messaging, and more. The Sceptre™ terminal is used to obtain the Viewtron service.

How Does It Work?

The Viewtron subscriber uses the Sceptre™ terminal to send a message over his telephone line to tell the Viewtron computer what information or service he wants. The information is instantly displayed on the home television screen.

Where Does It Operate?

The first U.S. fully commercial videotex system is being inaugurated in Dade, Broward, and Palm Beach counties in South Florida. Once it is established there, Viewdata Corporation plans to extend Viewtron to other major market areas throughout the country.

When Does It Operate?

The Viewtron service is available to subscribers at all times except on Mondays from 12:30 a.m. to 5:30 a.m., from 2:30 to 5:30 a.m. on all other days, and at other unscheduled times when maintenance is necessary.

What Can It Tell Me?

Masses of information stored in the Viewtron computers cover categories of news, sports, money, education, games, shopping, messaging, home and family, entertainment, food and dining, health, travel, books and reference material, and classified advertisements.

How Was It Developed?

Knight-Ridder Newspapers/Viewdata Corporation of America spent seven years in research and development. This included a 14-month field test of the Viewtron system in 204 homes in Coral Gables, Florida, in 1980–1981.

How Much Does It Cost?

The cost of the Sceptre™ terminal is $900. A special introductory price of $600 will be offered to South Florida consumers for a limited quantity of terminals. The monthly subscription is $12 for nearly all Viewtron services. There is a charge of about $1 per hour for use of the telephone line to communicate with the Viewtron computers, which will be billed directly by Southern Bell.

When Does It Begin?

October 30, 1983

Where Can I Get One?

In South Florida, plans are to market the Sceptre™ terminal through department stores, AT&T Phone Centers, and video and computer retail outlets.

---

the nation's first full-scale commercial videotex service, will begin operation in South Florida this fall. Subscribers will shop, bank, get the latest news, educate and amuse themselves, and send and receive messages—instantly and at all hours—without stirring from their easy chairs at home.

Viewtron subscribers will simply connect a new videotex terminal called Sceptre™ to their telephones and TV sets, enabling them to send requests for information or services over their phone lines to the Viewtron computers. Information and messages are then instantly displayed on the home TV screens.

The Viewtron service provides a steady stream of news from the Associated Press, *New York Times, Miami Herald,* Dow Jones, and other news sources. Its computers also are stocked with a vast supply of information on business, finance, travel, people, history, current affairs, health, consumer advice, the community, shopping, and hundreds of other items.

Viewtron subscribers also are linked directly to the computers of seven major national corporations—American Express, J.C. Penney Company, E.F. Hutton, Commodity News Services, Grolier's *Academic American Encyclopedia, Official Airline Guide,* and VideoFinancial Services (a banking network).

Viewtron communication is interactive (two-way). By pressing the keys on the Sceptre™ keypad, subscribers can post public notices, order goods or services from merchants, banks, and other financial institutions, and communicate privately with each other.

System Termination

By March 1986, Viewtron had reached a local subscriber base of about 3,000, with another 17,000 personal computer owners receiving the text-only version of the service. In announcing the decision to withdraw the Viewtron, Knight-Ridder's president James K. Batten stated, "We went into the Viewtron project with the primary purpose of determining what videotex might mean to the future of newspapers, which represent 90 percent of Knight-Ridder's revenues. It is now clear that videotex is not likely to be a threat to either newspaper advertising or readership in the foreseeable future."

Focal Topics

1. What do you think were the major reasons why Viewtron was not successful?
2. How will an understanding of consumer behavior help other companies market similar systems?
3. In the future, how might videotex systems change the ways in which firms perform their marketing activities?

5

Information for Marketing Decisions

☐ Sounding Out the Chapter

In this chapter, you will learn:

1. How marketers get information for routine operations and for making nonroutine decisions.
2. The kinds of information that go into a marketing information system.
3. The steps in the marketing research process.
4. Ways to conduct an exploratory investigation.
5. Advantages and disadvantages of the basic methods of conducting research.
6. Why researchers often use samples rather than trying to survey everyone.
7. What types of samples are available to researchers.
8. The role of analysis, intuition, and communication in interpreting data.
9. Why marketing research is important to organizations.

Pleasing Pets' Palates: An Experiment in Good Taste

At the Ralston Purina Research Farm in the rolling countryside of Missouri, almost 1,100 dogs and more than 800 cats give Ralston Purina answers about the food preferences and nutritional needs of pets. Every morning, 54 uniformed Ralston employees go to work watching, clocking, and monitoring mealtime activities. They watch out for such potential problems as "left eaters," dogs that can skew test results because they tend to eat from the bowl on the left.

Every morning, workers serve 2,000 pounds of dog and cat food, filling 4,000 shiny aluminum bowls. Many animals are fed two dishes of food that weigh the same and may look the same but that differ in flavor, texture, or nutrients. The foods to be tested are manufactured in a special pilot plant; they arrive at the research facility in plain brown wrappers coded in a way that only the scientists at corporate headquarters can understand.

What do the animals like to eat? Dogs prefer garlic and onion tastes, as well as cheese. In dry foods, they like smooth to rough chunks. Cats are fond of food that tastes of fish and dislike foods that are exceedingly hard.

Of course, pets are not the ones who do the shopping—owners are. So ultimately the research is intended to help Ralston Purina develop products that pet owners will buy. In contrast to the 1960s, when owners wanted pet foods with new flavors, today's pet owners are interested in fitness. As a result, Ralston Purina introduced Fit and Trim, a blend of dry food that has almost three times as much fiber and 300 calories per pound less than the standard Dog Chow blend.

Not all companies conduct research as elaborate as what Ralston Purina does. However, to meet marketing goals and keep abreast of changes in the environment, marketers do need to obtain information. This chapter describes ways of collecting information for ongoing operations and special marketing decisions.

Source: Bonita Brodt, "Finicky? Who's Finicky?: Fidos and Felines Relish Duty at Ralston Purina's Test Kitchens," *Chicago Tribune,* September 12, 1986, sec. 2, pp. 1, 3.

Marketing can be risky. This is particularly true for new products, which fail about 80 percent of the time. No doubt marketing managers are acutely aware of this at Procter & Gamble, which for years has been struggling to make its Wondra skin lotion a market leader. Observers in 1985 predicted it would take the company another ten years to accomplish this goal.[1]

Imagine that you are an executive at a major consumer products company. The time has come to make a decision about a new product that could cost your company millions of dollars. The deadline for the decision is fast approaching. Your job—and your company's future profits—are on the line. Naturally, you want as much information as possible on which to base your decision. But you have no time to wade through oceans of data that may be only marginally useful. Clearly, having the right information at the right time is crucial.

Every day marketers in major companies face decisions like this. Since it can cost as much as $80 million or more to launch a new product nationally,[2] marketers cannot afford to gamble with inadequate information. As the stakes have become higher, methods have been developed to accommodate decision makers' needs for critical information. The information generally can be broken down into two categories: (1) data important for staying on top of day-to-day operations and (2) facts on which to base important nonroutine decisions.

Consider, for example, the information needs of General Motors marketers. To plan for production and distribution, they must have continuous updates on which GM cars are selling, how many are in stock, and how many are on order by retail dealers. But to plan for the design of automobiles to be marketed in three years, they need a different kind of data. They must keep abreast of possible changes in consumer preferences by reviewing information such as trends in family size and the price of gasoline. They also must stay informed about what legislation Congress might pass that could affect design—for example, requirements for seat belts or air bags and regulations concerning minimum fuel efficiency.

Major Sources of Information

To meet needs for information, marketers turn to marketing information systems and marketing research. These two sources of information are closely related, but they serve different purposes.

Marketing Information Systems

Marketing Information System (MIS)
Orderly procedure for regular collection of raw data internally and externally and conversion of those data into information for use in making marketing decisions.

A **marketing information system,** or MIS, is an orderly system for collecting data from inside and outside the firm. The MIS converts the data into information that managers can use in making marketing decisions. A useful marketing information system meets three criteria:

1. *Data are collected regularly*. As conditions in the environment change, the changes are reflected in updated information. In a retail clothing

store, for example, managers want to know which items are moving quickly and which are moving slowly, so that the store can order more of the popular items and put the unpopular ones on sale to move them out.[3] To learn this information, the store can set up an MIS, using sales slips or data entered into a computerized cash register.

2. *The data collected from both inside and outside the organization.* Inside information could include figures on sales, costs, and inventory. Outside information could include figures on competitors' sales and costs, overall economic conditions, and changing consumer attitudes.
3. *The data are converted into useful information.* For example, a store manager might want to compare present sales of a line of gloves with past sales, with sales of a competing line, or with the store's goals for sales. This information could confirm that the store's activities are succeeding or could alert the manager that he or she needs to take corrective action. If the manager had to look at individual sales figures with nothing to compare them to, these data would provide little useful information.

Increasingly, managers who use an effective MIS view the available information as a *resource* for decision making.[4]

Marketing Research

Marketing Research Method for collecting, on a one-time basis, data pertinent to a particular marketing problem or opportunity.

In contrast to an MIS, **marketing research** involves collecting data in order to solve a particular marketing problem or take advantage of a particular opportunity. Marketing research differs from an MIS in three ways:

1. The researchers collect data once, not continuously.
2. The data collected are pertinent to a single problem or situation, such as developing a new product or preparing an advertising campaign.
3. Much of the data must come from outside the firm—from customers, competitors, or the government.

Marketing research and marketing information systems can involve collecting data in similar ways, but the data serve different purposes. Consider, for example, the electronic scanners commonly used in grocery stores today. The checkout clerk passes your cans and boxes over a glass scanner, which reads the black and white bars printed on the packages. Those bars tell the supermarket's computer what you are buying and how much it costs.

The store uses this information for inventory control—to decide when to order more of an item and which items to discontinue because they are purchased infrequently. When used this way, scanners are part of a marketing information system. The makers of the products you buy also use this information. These companies obtain scanner-collected data on a product to determine how well a new product is doing or whether a new promotion has boosted sales.[5] When the company uses the data to

Marketing Today 5.1
What Goes into a Data Bank?

Source: © 1987 Phyllis Woloshin.

Most organizations would agree that their customers are their most important assets. It makes sense, then, that the company would want to maintain a bank of information about customers, to make sure that the company is succeeding in its efforts to build up that asset.

One company that obtains such information is Benetton, the Italian textiles group. Benetton obtains a daily report of consumer purchasing patterns from its 2,000 European shops. This information enables the company to adapt production to meet changes in market demand. In addition, the company conducts an annual audit; by comparing data for the current year with data from the previous year, Benetton officials can establish whether its customer base is growing or declining.

In establishing a data base of customer information, a company can ask questions such as: How many customers do we have? How many of these customers are new since last year? Which are the top 20 customers? What is the average purchase per customer? What do customers consider important when buying the company's goods or services? How likely are customers to display similar purchasing patterns next year?

Source: Alan Melkman, "Why the Customer Is King," *Management Today* (May 1985), pp. 43, 46.

widely scattered throughout different departments in the company and frequently existed in a form marketing managers found difficult to use. Most companies now rely on the computer to process such information and to present it in a way useful for various departments, each with different needs.

In an internal accounting system, the chief source of data is the sales invoice, the record of a customer's order. The data on that form are invaluable. When data from all customers' sales invoices are totalled, they give a picture of how well a company is doing in sales. The total can then be put through **sales analysis,** which breaks down sales according to:

Sales Analysis
Breakdown of a company's sales data by product or customer demand, territorial volume, and salesperson performance.

1. *Product*—to indicate which products or lines are in greatest demand.
2. *Territory*—to show where products are selling best or most poorly.
3. *Salesperson*—to point out those who are meeting goals assigned them and those who are not.
4. *Customer*—to shed light on which customers are the largest buyers.

Sales analyses are important for spotting significant sales patterns. For example, Skil, second to Black and Decker in the sale of power tools, undertook a thorough sales analysis and discovered that too much of its sales representatives' time was devoted to serving small customers. By trimming accounts by 40 percent and concentrating its sales effort, Skil increased sales by 21 percent and cut market costs by 13 percent.[7]

In some companies, 80 percent of sales come from 20 percent of the firm's customers or from the purchase of a small part of the product line. A close watch on these key customers or products by the computer is crucial. At Time, Inc., the internal accounting system produces weekly circulation charts in color to help management decide where to focus special marketing and promotion efforts.

Managers can apply the information in an internal accounting system in a number of ways:

- ☐ They can pinpoint reasons for a sales decline.
- ☐ They can evaluate the progress of a promotional campaign and, if necessary, reallocate funds to an area that is behind target.
- ☐ They can analyze sales by market segments.[8]

Managers and information specialists are continually refining new ways to use internal data.

Marketing Intelligence System

As demonstrated in previous chapters, to make wise decisions, marketers need information from outside their companies. Consequently, many firms supplement their internally generated information with data from external sources such as government agencies and private organizations. Data on total industry sales gathered from such sources can be helpful in evaluating a firm's standing in an industry.

The sales force can often provide information about competitors' activities. And business periodicals, trade journals, and trade shows can supply valuable intelligence about economic conditions and how developments in the social and legal environments might affect marketers. Companies may also purchase information from outside intelligence suppliers such as the A. C. Nielsen Company, which amasses data on retail prices and brand shares and evaluates television ratings, and Market Research Corporation of America, which accumulates data from 7,500 households on brand shares, sizes, prices, and other matters.[9]

As firms become increasingly aware of the need for up-to-date information, more and more are establishing company libraries. The key to the growth and management of all this information has been the data base, a computerized file containing information on specialized topics.

While great strides have been made in developing the technology for a sophisticated MIS, some problems remain in implementing such a system. Unless top management is committed to the development of a truly functional system, the design of the system may not adequately address the problems that its users ask it to solve. In some cases, the technical

TURN UP THE VOLUME WITH AGREE

Agree
shampoo

Turn up the volume. Turn heads.

Turn on to big soft beautiful hair.

AGREE SHAMPOO AND CONDITIONER

staff develops a system that provides impressive feedback, but not in a form that managers find useful for decision making. Thus it is important for managers to clearly state their specific information needs and in what form that information should be presented.

If such issues are addressed in an early stage of system design, the resulting benefits can be enormous. For marketing managers, a system's potential to help design effective strategies, to oversee their performance, and to act quickly as the results emerge should prove an invaluable asset.

The Scope of Marketing Research

Marketing information systems are useful for controlling day-to-day activities and planning for the efficient use of people and money. But sometimes they uncover problems without giving any clear indication of solutions. In those cases, in-depth marketing research studies are needed to reveal the real causes of the trouble.

Tandem Computers Inc. enjoyed initial success by marketing a fault-tolerant computer—one in which parts could fail but the computer could keep on working. The reliable design attracted users who absolutely had to keep their computers running: banks, hotels, manufacturing plants, travel agencies, and the like. After several years, however, other companies were making fault-tolerant computers, and Tandem lost its technological edge. The company protected its position with extensive marketing research. Tandem learned that its customers were initially attracted to its product by the novelty of fault tolerance but actually bought Tandem computers because they had an efficient modular design. Tandem shifted its marketing message to emphasize this benefit, and has maintained its strong position in the market.[10]

Besides seeking the underlying causes of specific problems, marketing research can also be used to explore opportunities in the marketplace. Thus, when S. C. Johnson & Son Company decided to get into the hair-care market for women, it first conducted extensive marketing research to determine market sizes and trends. After having narrowed the growing markets to shampoos and creme rinses, it surveyed a national sample of women by mail to explore hair-care practices. The survey indicated that "oiliness" was the number one hair-care concern. To combat the problem, the company responded by developing a 99 percent oil-free shampoo and creme rinse. Advertising for its Agree brand claimed that the products would "help stop the greasies." Agree shampoo and creme rinse went on to become the most successful new products in the company's history.[11] (See Figure 5.2.)

Marketing research is most useful when marketing researchers work as partners with management. In this role, researchers help managers

Figure 5.2
Agree Shampoo Is a Successful Entry into the Hair-care Market for Women
Source: Photograph by Bert Stern for S. C. Johnson & Son, Inc.

Table 5.1
Research Activities of 798 Companies

Activity	Percent of Companies
Measurement of market potentials	93%
Sales analysis	89
Competitive product studies	85
Short-range sales forecasting	85
New-product acceptance and potential	84
Establishment of sales quotas, territories	75
Distribution channel studies	69
Studies of advertising effectiveness	67
Packaging research	60
Export and international studies	51
Social values and policies studies	40

Source: Data from Dik Warren Twedt, ed., 1978 Survey of Marketing Research (Chicago, Ill.: American Marketing Association, 1978), p. 41. Table reprinted with permission from *Marketing,* 2nd ed., by David L. Kurtz and Louis E. Boone, p. 134. Copyright 1984 by The Dryden Press.

identify researchable issues and then conduct research or analysis to address these issues. Marketing researchers are best able to adopt the role of partner when three conditions are present:

1. Researchers do objective, professional work of the highest standard of integrity.
2. Management is receptive to the value of research.
3. Researchers and management share a sense of clearly identified research needs and issues. This requires researchers to be sensitive to the concerns of managers.[12]

When researchers work as partners with management, they try to solve problems, not merely gather data.

The usefulness of marketing research has been recognized for over a century. The first formal piece of research is credited to an advertising agency, N.W. Ayer and Sons. In 1879, the agency surveyed state officials about expected grain production. It used the results of the survey to plan the advertising schedule for a manufacturer of farm equipment.

Since then, the scope of marketing research has expanded considerably. More than two-thirds of all firms having sales over $5 million have marketing research departments of their own. In addition, the federal government conducts extensive research pertinent to marketing, and many nonprofit organizations are beginning to establish market research departments.

Not only has the number of firms engaged in marketing research grown, but the variety of research projects has also expanded. Table 5.1 lists the most common areas of research undertaken by businesses. Most

Figure 5.3
Stages of the Research Process

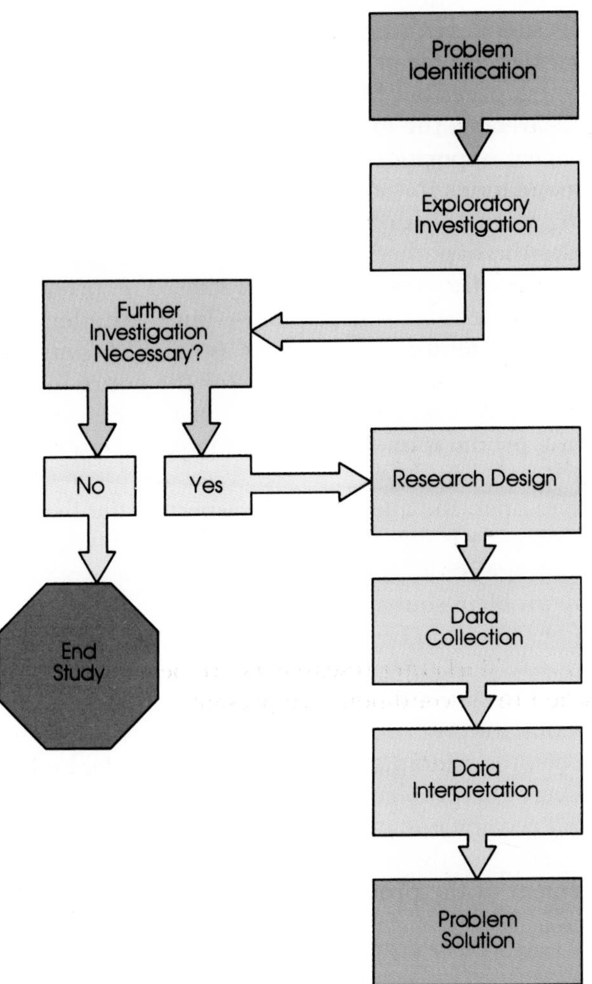

firms use marketing research to measure market potentials, determine market characteristics, and analyze sales and market shares.

According to one author, the purpose of all such research is "to find holes"—holes that may be fatal to an organization unless plugged or holes that provide an opening for a new venture.[13] The method for finding gaps in marketing knowledge is similar in all research situations.

Marketing Research Methods

Most definitions of marketing research note that it involves the methodic gathering of data. A method is an orderly way of proceeding. The order generally followed in marketing research studies is shown in Figure 5.3.

Problem Identification

Most experienced market researchers say that after the problem is identified, half the work is done. The reason is not difficult to understand. Most students soon learn when doing a term paper or special report that one of the trickiest problems is finding an area narrow enough to be handled in a few pages but broad enough to be of interest. In the case of market researchers, the most difficult task is defining underlying causes or areas of opportunities without so narrowing the definition that final recommendations for action are trivial.

Beginning researchers often mistake symptoms for the problem itself. Consider the hypothetical case of the New England soft-drink manufacturer who discovers a decline in sales. The problem for researchers is not the decline itself—a symptom—but the underlying causes.

The firm's MIS may give some clues as to which causes can be eliminated from consideration. Thus, if sales for the entire industry are up, the problem does not lie in the economy. Or if salespeople report no new competing products on the market, the problem probably does not originate there.

That leaves open for question some aspect of the firm's marketing mix. Again, some areas may be less promising for investigation than others. If the beverage is a well-established brand, the product formulation is an unlikely problem source. Similarly, if all sodas on the market cost about the same, price too can be eliminated as the cause of declining sales.

By proceeding systematically, marketers can narrow down the source of the problem. However, during the first phase of problem identification, the problem is seldom clearly defined. The soft-drink researchers may know where the problem does *not* lie, but that is far from having a set of working recommendations on how to raise sales. After their preliminary narrowing of the problem, the researchers must search for a testable statement of the problem.

Exploratory Investigation

Hypothesis
Educated guess about the relationship between things or what will happen in the future.

The purpose of exploratory investigation is to develop a **hypothesis,** or an educated guess about the relationship between things or what will happen in the future. This investigation, often called situation analysis, may involve either (1) talking to informed people in informal interviews or (2) investigating literature that may pertain to the possible problem areas.

Informal Interviews Researchers talk to informed people to get their views on the source of a problem or on possible areas for research. For example, researchers for the soft-drink manufacturer might talk to at least some of the following people:

1. *Customers.* A discussion with some users and perhaps nonusers of the company's brand may give researchers an idea of how customers view the product or how advertising messages are received.

2. *Intermediaries.* This group might include franchised bottlers for the firm's product, some retailers who sell the product, and perhaps owners of restaurants who serve the beverage.
3. *The firm's own staff.* Interviews with the sales force, for example, may uncover possible customer dissatisfaction or rumors circulating in the industry.

Focus Group Interview One technique researchers have found useful for talking with customers is the **focus group interview.** In this approach, a group of people with something in common—such as owning a home or going to the movies at least once a month—assemble with a moderator or interviewer to discuss a topic. Usually the group exchanges views about a new product, an advertising approach, or some other marketing concern of the company sponsoring the interview. The moderator directs the interview based on a guide that indicates which subjects the group is to cover. This guide is not a questionnaire, however; the moderator uses it flexibly.[14] Often, observers watch from behind a one-way mirror.

Focus Group Interview
Method of determining customer attitudes by interviewing a relatively homogeneous group assembled to discuss a topic.

Focus groups provide information relevant to a variety of situations. Newspapers, for example, use the groups as a guide in planning news features, improving graphic design, and deciding on how to approach certain stories. Universities use them in planning how to tailor their recruiting efforts and fund drives. A computer manufacturer used a focus group to find out why owners of businesses with sales of $2 to $5 million weren't buying its products. Participants in the group quickly made it clear that they weren't as technologically sophisticated as the company's marketers had assumed. They weren't buying the computer systems because they didn't understand them and were afraid of them.[15]

Focus groups can consist of in-house personnel as well as potential customers, an approach that may be particularly suitable for those who sell to the industrial market. The researcher gathers all company personnel who have contact with users of the company's product; these people might include product managers, accounting personnel, repair workers, and secretaries. The discussion in such a group would cover customers' expressed or hidden problems. For example, in one in-house focus group, it became evident that company maintenance people needed more training.[16]

While focus groups provide helpful information, this approach has limitations. The people chosen for focus group interviews are seldom scientifically selected; therefore, the results can be biased and should not be taken as conclusive. Researchers observing the interview are susceptible to preconceived notions and to hearing only what they want to. Because the groups are small and not randomly selected, what group members say is not necessarily representative of the total market. Nevertheless, when interpreted properly, the results of focus group interviews can give important clues for further research. Examples of some clues uncovered in actual focus groups are described in Marketing Today 5.2.

Secondary Data
Information that exists before a particular study is conducted and that was collected for another purpose.

Literature Reviews Researchers can save time and expense when they can find relevant **secondary data,** information that already exists some-

Marketing Today 5.2

The Marketer As Detective: Using Clues from Interviews

Corona, the leading beer brewed in Puerto Rico, asked researcher John Lister to solve a problem: Corona had been a local favorite but was losing ground to competitors. Part of Lister's initial investigation was to discuss the product with a focus group.

From the focus group interview, some clues emerged: Years before, the brewery's steel cans had had a leakage problem that had caused the beer to spoil. Although Corona had corrected the problem, consumers still associated the brand with flaws and flatness. Also, as Puerto Rico's population grew more cosmopolitan in outlook and more U.S. products entered the market, Corona had come to be perceived as second-rate. The singing farmer who illustrated each can had become a symbol of the beer's poor status. In blind taste tests, the beer performed well, however.

Based on this information, the research team redesigned the can, giving it an international appearance and switching to aluminum cans. With the new can, the beer's performance improved.

Three years later, Corona's market share was declining again, and again blind tests showed that taste was not the problem. More interviews showed that beer drinkers perceived U.S. beers as being more full-bodied. Adding a deep red to the can's design gave it a stronger look. Tests showed that drinkers thought the beer in the redesigned cans was much improved.

Source: John Lister, "That Delicate Concept of Nuance," *Advertising Age,* September 29, 1986, p. 40.

where, having been collected for another purpose.[17] Because such information is relatively inexpensive to gather, and because there is no point in repeating work already done, researchers often investigate secondary data before turning to other sources of information.

The firm's own internal data might be classified as secondary data if they were collected for purposes other than the study. Such internal data might include sales call reports, product performance reviews, company profit and loss statements, or analyses of marketing expenditures. In addition to internal data, the secondary data of most interest to researchers at this stage of the investigation are found in the published material of other organizations.

Some of the more useful publications for marketers are listed in Table 5.2. The organizations chiefly responsible for such publications are:

1. *The federal government,* whose various agencies (particularly the Bureau of the Census) provide marketers with statistics including the

Table 5.2
Secondary Data: Some Useful Publications

Government Publications

Statistical Abstract of the United States: A summary of business, economic, social, and demographic statistics published yearly by the U.S. government.

Historical Statistics of the United States: A collection of government statistics from colonial times to the present, updated periodically.

County and City Data Book: Breakdown of government statistics (on population, manufacturing, sales, etc.) by city and county, published every 3 years.

U.S. Industrial Outlook: Projections of industrial activity by industry, including production, sales, shipments, and employment.

Survey of Current Business: A monthly updating of important economic statistics (income, employment, construction, etc.).

Monthly Catalogue of U.S. Government Publications: A monthly updating of books and pamphlets (some free) issued by government departments and agencies.

Private Publications

Business Periodicals: Those dealing principally with marketing include *Advertising Age, Sales and Marketing Management, Product Marketing, Industrial Marketing, Stores,* and *Distribution Worldwide.*

Professional Journals: See especially *Journal of Marketing, Journal of Marketing Research, Journal of Advertising, Journal of Advertising Research, Journal of Retailing.*

Indexes to Periodicals: See especially *Business Periodical Index* and *Wall Street Journal Index.*

Standard and Poor's Industry Surveys: Updated statistics and analyses of industries.

Private Marketing Guides

Consumer Market and Magazine Report: An annual report of U.S. consumer ownership and purchase of goods and services as well as readership of magazines.

A Guide to Consumer Markets: An annual report on U.S. population, employment, income, and expenditures.

Market Guide: An annual report of statistics (on population, industries, retail sales, and outlets, etc.) for 1,500 major American and Canadian cities.

Marketing Information Guide: A monthly bibliography of studies of interest to marketers.

Sales Management Survey of Buying Power: Market data (on population, income, retail sales, etc.) for counties, cities, and other statistical areas, published annually.

Rand McNally Commercial Atlas and Marketing Guide: Population breakdowns and maps for 100,000 American cities and towns, published annually.

---

size and composition of markets, the sales volume of industries, and the types and locations of wholesalers and retailers.

2. *State and local governments,* which provide information such as traffic on roads, retail sales tax revenues, and consumption of various taxed products.
3. *Trade associations,* such as the Automobile Manufacturers' Association and the National Association of Retail Druggists, which sponsor special studies for members.
4. *Magazine and newspaper publishers*, who report on business trends, report the results of periodic surveys, and provide news of impor-

tant legal developments and technological trends that may affect a marketer's business.

5. *Computer-assisted literature searching,* which is the computerized version of thumbing through a card catalog. In the lobbies of an increasing number of libraries are computer terminals that contain information on whether a library has a book and whether or not it has been checked out. In addition, computers that can hook up to a telephone with a modem can be used to obtain information from bibliographic data bases. The user enters the desired topic, and the computer lists the publications available on that topic.
6. *Commercial market researchers,* such as the Market Research Corporation of America and A. C. Nielsen Company, which sell marketing information gathered from consumer and trade surveys on the rate of product usage or turnover in stores, the amount of advertising by brand, market share by product, and other vital indicators.
7. *Consumer attitude and public opinion research,* such as that provided by the *Yankelovich Monitor,* an annual census of changing social values and how they can affect consumer marketing.[18]

The soft-drink manufacturer's researchers might benefit by consulting some of these sources. If the firm is a member of a trade association, data on the kinds of distributors used by other firms may reveal inefficiencies in the researching firm's distribution policies. Or information from A. C. Nielsen may suggest a link between increased advertising outlays by other companies and the firm's declining sales. One industry that has acted on secondary data is the health care industry. At Your Service 5.1 describes how hospitals have responded to such information.

All information from secondary sources must be interpreted carefully. The reasons for caution are related to the nature of secondary information. Because it is collected for purposes other than the specific study, it can be faulty. The information may be unreliable because it is biased. Because trade associations often act as boosters for their members, they may put data in a highly favorable light. Another problem with secondary data is that they may not be completely relevant to the problem at hand.

An interesting example of the latter problem arose when Skippy introduced a new brand of peanuts to compete with Planters. Based on reports purchased from a commercial firm, Skippy brought the brand to market at what was supposed to be the height of the snack sales season—around the holidays in November and December. When heavy sales for the product failed to materialize, the brand was pulled from the market. A postmortem examination showed that the original information was misinterpreted. Retailers stocked up heavily in November and December, but sales of the product remained the same throughout the year. The secondary data had shown only heavy movement from factory to warehouses during the period, not heavy sales.[19]

Hypothesis Formation The preliminary investigation should have produced enough information for researchers to develop a hypothesis about

At Your Service 5.1
Hospitals Act on Research Results

Source: Courtesy of Rose Women's Center.

Much research has been done on the demand for hospital services. One pattern this research has uncovered is that women are an important submarket. They make most of the health-care decisions for a family and account for over half of patient visits and almost two-thirds of surgeries. However, women are frequently dissatisfied with the limited and often impersonal care they receive.

As a result, many hospitals have scrambled to appeal to women. In Denver, Rose Women's Center offers consumer education programs on topics of interest to women. For example, the financial concerns of young working parents prompted the hospital to team up with a local bank in offering a session on financial planning.

In Fargo, North Dakota, Lutheran Hospitals and Homes Society offers an extended product line of women's services based on the principle that although obstetrics is a one- to two-month concern for providers, a child is a lifelong concern for parents. Therefore, the facility offers education about family planning, nutrition, parenting skills, housekeeping, day care, and well-baby care.

Source: "In Health Care, Women Rule the Roost," *Sales and Marketing Management* (December 1986), p. 116.

---

the problem. The hypothesis must be carefully worded to avoid possible errors in future research.

Let us assume in the case of the soft-drink manufacturer that the preliminary investigation strongly indicates that the reason for declining sales is ineffective advertising. The researchers believe that sales are down because competitors are spending heavily on new advertising. Their hypothesis might read: "Sales will increase by at least 40 percent if the advertising message is changed to emphasize a new plastic bottle." This is only a hypothesis. It may or may not be true. Only further research will reveal whether the problem lies there or elsewhere.

Further Investigation? The organization's research objectives, plus the amount and quality of information gained from exploratory research, help the marketing manager decide whether to continue researching. Sometimes the company needs more precise and reliable information than it can obtain from exploratory research. In many cases, however, research may be concluded after the inspection of secondary sources. If several studies report similar findings, the problem may be solved without further research and with a considerable cost saving. Or, if secondary sources hint that the problem can be solved only after more comprehensive and costly study, researchers may decide that further study is not worth the expense.

The high cost of marketing research often leads researchers to end the investigation at this stage. For example, it would not make sense for the soft-drink manufacturer to spend $1 million to learn how to increase sales by $500,000. But if the company were planning to spend $50 million to launch a new product, an additional $1 million spent to avoid a marketing catastrophe might sound like a bargain. In that case, the marketing department would be more likely to continue on to the next stage of research design.

Research Design

Primary Data
Original information gathered for a specific research project.

At the third stage of marketing research, marketers prepare to collect **primary data**—original information produced specifically for the present study. While primary data are almost always more costly and time consuming to gather than secondary data, any doubt about the reliability of published sources or accuracy of the hypothesis must be resolved by primary research.

Research Design
Method for carrying out a marketing study.

Research design refers to the method of carrying out the study, using one of three methods—observation, experimentation, or survey. The correct method for doing research depends on the project. As one author has noted, "A research method for a given problem is not like the solution to a problem in algebra. It is more like a recipe for beef stroganoff; there is no one best recipe."[20]

Observation
Research method that involves either the personal or mechanical viewing of subjects or physical phenomena.

Observation Data collection by **observation** involves either the personal or mechanical viewing of subjects or physical phenomena. There are many varieties of observational studies. One common observation technique is the traffic count—of pedestrians or cars—used, for example, to determine the site of a new gasoline station or the popularity of a display. Another staple observation method used by American marketing researchers is the Nielsen audiometer; attached to a TV set, it estimates audience size for sponsors by recording how many sets are turned on and to what channel. The number of supermarket scanners grew from barely 200 in 1978 to more than 10,000 today.[21]

An advantage of mechanical observation is that it records exactly *what* peole do, not what they *say* they do. For example, a group of electric utilities hired a researcher to find out why their fuel-use projections, based on poll-takers' reports of customer interviews, were falling short of reality. The researchers set up television cameras trained on the thermostat in 150 homes. Homeowners had claimed to keep them set at 68°, but other people in the house—teenagers, older relatives, visitors, and cleaning ladies—fiddled with them throughout the day.[22]

The problem with observational research is that it reveals only *what* is happening, not *why*. To overcome this limitation, observation may be used in conjunction with one of the other methods.

Experimentation
Research method that establishes cause and effect relationships.

Experimentation In recent years, **experimentation,** which establishes cause and effect relationships, has attracted more interest. Market researchers have conducted experiments both in laboratory settings and under real field conditions. In this technique, two matched groups of subjects are exposed to situations that are identical except for one or two elements called variables. The subjects' responses to the differences in those variables can then be measured.

The soft-drink manufacturer might commission a field experiment to test the hypothesis regarding advertising the new plastic bottle. Researchers could run a television commercial stressing the new packaging in one city and simultaneously run the regular commercial in another city. (This technique is referred to as a "split run.") Researchers might then contact viewers for their reactions to the commercials and then compare the results. The small-scale test marketing of new products in different cities uses a similar approach.

A somewhat different approach is the laboratory experiment, in which researchers try to duplicate market conditions in an artificial setting. One example of such testing is the laboratory that tests the food preferences of cats and dogs, described in the opening vignette for this chapter.

Experimentation is an increasingly important marketing tool. The method does have some shortcomings, however. Experiments can be very expensive and time consuming. (Test marketing often goes on for about a year at a cost sometimes of over a million dollars.) Experiments are also difficult to control. Competitors have been known to sabotage field experiments by running heavy advertising of their own in test cities or lowering prices drastically. For example, when Campbell Soup Company tried to test market a dry soup mix, salespeople from Lipton, the market leader, stormed into stores and pasted high-value coupons on Lipton soups.[23] Another shortcoming of experimentation is that in laboratory settings consumers may behave differently because they know they are being observed. But despite these drawbacks, marketers will continue to use experimentation because they want to discover cause-and-effect relationships.

Surveys The most widely used and useful method for marketers is **survey research,** which involves interviewing people. Surveys may range from the most informal—perhaps a few questions from an interviewer in the supermarket—to elaborately designed, computer-read questionnaires.

Survey Research
Study using direct or indirect interviews.

The survey may directly ask consumers their reasons for buying or not buying, or it may use questions to uncover motives indirectly. Mason Haire used indirect questioning in a classic piece of marketing research almost 40 years ago. Instant coffee had just been introduced, and Haire wanted to investigate why consumers resisted buying it. When he had asked homemakers directly, they had replied that they disliked the flavor; however, in blindfold tests, they could not tell the difference.

So Haire prepared two shopping lists that were identical, except that one included Nescafé instant coffee, and the other Maxwell House drip-grind coffee. Haire asked the homemakers to describe the kind of women who would compile such lists. They replied that the instant coffee buyer was lazy, a spendthrift, an inefficient manager, and a poor wife. Haire concluded that consumers were avoiding instant coffee because they feared that serving it would project a negative image of themselves.[24]

The popularity of survey research stems from its flexibility.[25] Surveys can be used to obtain a variety of kinds of information in a variety of situations. However, respondents may be unwilling to respond or unable to supply accurate information.

Additional advantages and limitations apply to each of the three basic survey methods. These methods are personal interviews, mail surveys, and telephone interviews.

Personal Interviews The most favored method for conducting a survey has been the personal interview. It may be conducted either in the home or at the offices of a research company. In the latter case, a group of individuals, constituting a panel, may be interviewed. Marketers prefer the personal interview for several reasons. It can be long, so that a good deal of data can be secured. Doubts about the meaning of questions can be clarified, and visual aids can be used to increase understanding. In addition, the interviewer can report on the social and economic status of those interviewed—an aid for interpreting results.

But the fear of loss of privacy (and, in urban areas, of admitting a stranger into a home) now limits the effectiveness of personal interviews. The high cost of hiring personal interviewers and then training them so they do not bias results by inappropriate remarks is another disadvantage.

Mail Surveys Researchers may avoid some of the problems of personal interviews by conducting a mail survey. Mail surveys are less costly than personal interviews and can reach working people who might otherwise be missed. People seem to prefer mail surveys because they can answer at leisure and often remain anonymous.

But mail surveys also have limitations. The response rate may be only 25 percent or even less.[26] Questionnaires tend to be answered only by the better educated, so that the survey may be unrepresentative. (The section on sampling later in this chapter illustrates the importance of representativeness.) Also, since 20 percent of Americans move yearly, an accurate mailing list may be impossible to obtain. Finally, respondents in mail surveys often misunderstand questions or skip them altogether.

Researchers can improve mail surveys to reduce or overcome some of these limitations. For example, researchers can test surveys on a few people to see whether they understand the questions. Testing is an inexpensive, trouble-shooting technique that applies to other kinds of surveys as well. In addition, researchers can try to improve response rates by making it easier to respond, say, by including a stamped return envelope and even a pencil. Including a small gift, such as a dollar bill, also can improve response rates; often people feel uncomfortable about accepting even a small gift without doing something in return.

Telephone Interviews For many research purposes, a good compromise between the face-to-face interview and the impersonal mail survey is the telephone interview. The telephone allows some probing by the inter-

Table 5.3
Advantages and Disadvantages of Three Survey Methods

Personal Interview	Mail Survey	Telephone Interview
Advantages		
Obtains detailed information.	Covers widespread area cheaply.	Reaches wide area inexpensively.
Allows interviewer to probe.	Eliminates interviewer bias.	Speeds data collection.
Obtains socioeconomic data on respondent.	May reach otherwise inaccessible people.	Allows respondent some anonymity.
Permits use of visual aids.	Allows respondent to answer anonymously and at leisure.	
Disadvantages		
Can be expensive.	Can lack representativeness.	Difficult to reach those with unlisted numbers.
May introduce interviewer bias.	May produce low rate of return.	Must use short questions.
May raise fears for privacy.	Does not allow probing or follow-up questions.	

viewer and still permits some privacy for the respondent. Because organizations can shop for lower-than-normal long-distance rates, the expense of personal interviewing may be cut. Finally, telephone interviewing allows immediate response. The soft-drink researchers could get same-day reaction to a particular commercial by using this method.

Telephone interviews do raise a few problems, however, that researchers should keep in mind. People tend to be more impatient over the phone than in personal contacts. Therefore, questions must be brief. Also, many people now have unlisted phones, though through a technique called "random digit dialing" researchers can get around this limitation.

The advantages and disadvantages of each form of survey are summarized in Table 5.3. The survey method selected depends ultimately on the nature of what must be probed. In-depth questions about motivation for purchasing a product are best handled through personal interviews. A simple knowledge of fact ("Did you see our ad?") may be secured over the phone. Whatever the form of survey, however, almost all methods employ a questionnaire.[27]

Questionnaire Design All surveys, including personal interviews, require a data collection instrument, or form, so that all participants answer the same questions. People unfamiliar with research tend to think that almost anyone can write questions for a questionnaire. Researchers know that constructing a questionnaire requires genuine skill. Many kinds of mistakes can be made in questionnaire writing, but most are either errors of bias or of communication.

Errors of bias are common but not always obvious. Experienced researchers know that one source of bias is placement of an answer at the head of a list. Thus, the seemingly innocent question:

Figure 5.4
Test Your Skills as a Questionnaire Writer

Imagine that a private university (we'll call it Gradgrind U.) developed this questionnaire to get information from the parents of its incoming freshmen. Can you detect any problems with these questions?

1. What was your total family income last year?

People often balk at giving such personal information. If this question were necessary, it should appear later in the questionnaire when a spirit of cooperation has been established, and in a less threatening form, i.e., "Check one: $15,000–19,999; $20,000–24,999, etc."

2. How many colleges and universities did your son/daughter investigate before choosing Gradgrind U.?

Who can remember this? Besides, what does "investigate" mean? Look at the brochure, or visit the campus?

3. Don't you think the government should give financial assistance to bright students who want to attend private colleges?

Biased question. What parents, faced with a hefty tuition bill, would answer "no"—especially since all parents fondly assume their kids are very bright?

4. Is your son/daughter eager to attend Gradgrind U.? yes ( ); no ( )

Who's to say what "eager" means? And can it be answered "yes" or "no"? The kid may be eager to get away from home, less eager to leave his or her girlfriend or boyfriend, and not eager at all to take English Comp I. Besides, what useful information does this question provide?

Based on Don A. Dillman's chapter on "Writing Questions," in *Mail and Telephone Surveys* (New York: Wiley, 1978), pp. 79–118.

Which soap do you prefer?

☐ Ivory

☐ Dove

☐ Dial

☐ Irish Spring

will collect some votes for Ivory that it would not ordinarily receive if it were not listed first. The ongoing struggle among politicians to secure the first line on the ballot in a voting booth provides evidence of such a bias. To overcome it, market researchers sometimes rotate the order in multiple-choice questions or leave the question open-ended so that the respondent can supply an answer.

Perhaps the greatest source of error lies in faulty communication, or a misunderstanding of what the question means. In a survey for a new detergent, one question asked respondents where they might use the product in their homes. One specific reference was to "germ-ridden" areas. "I want a germ-ridden kitchen," one woman responded. "What do you mean by that?" asked the surprised interviewer. The woman answered, "Well, I want to be ridden of all my germs."[28]

Can you spot the problems with each of the questions in the "questionable" questionnaire in Figure 5.4?

Data Collection

Regardless of the research design chosen, researchers must decide from whom they want information and how they want to go about collecting it. One way to proceed is to collect data from every member of a population under study. Such a complete canvass is called a **census.** An alternative way is to collect information from only a part of the population. The theory is that the part of the population that is selected, called a **sample,** may yield information about the larger group.

Census
Complete canvass of every member of a population under study.

Sample
Limited canvass of a representative part of a population under study.

Most people are familiar with sampling as it is used to predict the outcome of elections. Major television networks have developed this technique to a high degree, and they have been criticized for "calling" elections even before polling places on the West Coast have closed.

Market researchers prefer to sample, rather than take a census, for several reasons. First, complete counts are usually time consuming and prohibitively costly. Second, it is sometimes physically impossible to check all members of a population. For example, researchers simply could not count everyone who had his or her television set on last night between nine and ten o'clock. Finally—and surprisingly—samples are often more accurate than complete censuses. In the case of a survey, the more people questioned, the greater the probability of the surveyor introducing errors.

Types of Samples Just as there is no one best research design, there is no ideal sampling method. Researchers recognize two broad types of samples—probability and nonprobability.

Probability Sample
Sample in which each member of a given population is selected on some objective basis not controlled by the researcher.

In a **probability sample,** each member of a given population is selected on some objective basis not controlled by the researcher. This is called random selection. In a **random sample,** each member of a population under study has an equal chance of being selected from a list. A firm wanting to sample automobile owners in Arizona might obtain a registration list from the state motor vehicle department and select every tenth name on the list.

Random Sample
Probability sample in which each member of a population under study has an equal chance of being selected.

If a population has subgroups that differ markedly, random sampling may produce inaccurate results. For example, corporations vary tremendously in size. If a sample of corporate attitudes toward social responsibility is taken, results may differ if all corporations are considered together, rather than if they were polled in groups according to size. In **stratified sampling,** important subgroups are identified and then randomly sampled.

Stratified Sampling
Probability sampling in which subgroups are identified and then randomly sampled.

Both random and stratified sampling work best when there is a precise list of the population being studied. Sometimes, however, no such list exists. There is no list of soft-drink consumers, for instance. In such cases, people may be divided by geographic area and then parts of the area (such as city blocks) may be sampled. This is known as **cluster sampling.** Note that such area sampling upholds the principle of probability sampling: All residents within the blocks selected have an equal chance of being chosen.[29]

Cluster Sampling
Probability sampling in which the population under study is divided into subgroups and then parts of the group are chosen at random to be sampled.

Nonprobability samples are less objective than probability samples since they involve personal judgment in the selection of sampled items.

Nonprobability Sample
Sample that involves personal judgment in the selection of sampled items.

Convenience Sample
Nonprobability sample in which subjects are chosen on the basis of convenience to the researcher.

Judgment Sample
Nonprobability sample composed of subjects who are specially qualified in the area of interest of a study.

Quota Sample
Nonprobability sample composed of subjects chosen on the basis of characteristics thought pertinent to a study.

The researcher, rather than chance, decides who will be chosen to participate in the study. In a **convenience sample,** such as a man-on-the-street interview, members are selected because they are close at hand. In a **judgment sample,** the kind often used in award nominations, experts who are thought to be specially qualified in the area of interest are chosen. Participants in **quota samples** are singled out by researchers on the basis of characteristics thought pertinent to the study. For example, the soft-drink manufacturer may instruct researchers to sample an equal number of men and women, half between the ages of 15 and 24 and half between 25 and 34.

In some circumstances, nonprobability samples are the preferred way of collecting data—for example, when special expertise, such as knowledge of an award category, is important. Frequently, however, researchers resort to nonprobability samples because they must collect data quickly or work with limited funds. In those cases, the results of such samples must be interpreted cautiously because those selected may be unrepresentative. Merely stopping someone on the street, for instance, is no guarantee that the opinion volunteered is representative of the population. The nature of the street itself may seriously bias the answers given. To cite an obvious example, we would expect different responses from people sampled on Fifth Avenue in New York City from those on the Bowery. There may be less pronounced, but still significant, differences among various neighborhoods in any city. In short, the unknowns in nonprobability sampling frequently make the results uncertain.

Errors in Collecting Data Probability samples are more objective than nonprobability samples because they avoid subjective judgments that may lessen the representativeness of the sample. That does not mean that probability samples are free of error. Sampling is done by people, after all, and people do make mistakes. The human factor is an important source of error in both probability and nonprobability samples.

In random sampling, for example, an interviewer assigned to canvass randomly selected homes may substitute a home because residents of the chosen home were out. The effect is to substitute subjective judgment for objective criteria of selection. Canvassers may also introduce errors by misreading a question or recording an answer incorrectly. Or they may bias results by asking questions in a certain tone of voice or by altering the wording.

The training of people who collect samples therefore becomes very important. Many companies use the services of outside polling firms such as the Louis Harris organization, which have highly trained professionals who can handle any research design from a simple count to an in-depth interview. Error can never be completely eliminated, but in this way it can be minimized.

Data Interpretation

Good market researchers, like efficient marketing information systems, must convert raw data into usable information. This is the critical step in the research process. At this stage, a researcher must draw upon many talents, including analytical skills, intuitive understanding, and an ability to communicate.

Role of Analysis Data can be analyzed in a number of ways. Analysis may simply involve reviewing the data. Even if the amount collected is not large, it may be sufficient to produce conclusions and recommendations.

In most cases, however, researchers confront a mass of data. For example, researchers for the soft-drink manufacturer we have been following might have statistics on audience awareness of commercial messages in test cities. This information must be sifted to determine if there is a relationship between a particular kind of message and rising sales.

Various statistical techniques can be applied to yield information. The tools of analysis are too numerous to mention here, but skilled researchers must be aware of all of them.[30] They are the means of distinguishing the forest from the trees.

Role of Intuition Statistical techniques by themselves cannot ensure reliable research results. Intuition—the ability to see what is relevant in the data—plays an important part. For example, the failure of researchers at two food companies to see the relevance of information they had collected cost their companies millions of dollars. The companies had seen an opportunity in the dry-soup market, which had barely been tapped at the time. They conducted extensive marketing research, and researchers recommended a go-ahead on the basis of their findings. But they chose to ignore an important piece of information they had learned: that consumers used existing brands of dry soup mainly as a flavoring for gravies and snacks. The companies produced dry-soup flavors that were unsuitable for nonsoup uses. Consequently, sales were small and the companies pulled out of the market.[31]

Intuition is not infallible. But without it, statistical analyses may produce totally useless information.

Role of Communication After the researchers have interpreted the data, they must write a report. Frequently, the decision makers who read the report are unskilled in research and statistical methods. The job of the researcher is to translate highly technical material into understandable English.

A good research report must be readable, objective (based on evidence revealed by the data), and pointed (answering questions important to managers).

It is usually best to start the report with the conclusions and recommendations—parts that most interest executives. Details of the research process can be included in an appendix or in a separate technical report.

Problem Solution

All the efforts of the marketing research process lead to the final step: solving the problem. Often, the person who decides how to solve the problem and the person who conducts the research are different people. However, the researcher typically recommends possible solutions.

Marketing Research Prospects

Good marketing researchers need the abilities to think mathematically and to write clear English. Researchers who combine those skills are prized by both business and nonbusiness organizations.

The marketing concept emphasizes attention to customer needs. Marketing research is the key to carrying out that purpose. Researchers are usually staff members who feed marketing managers information about customer reaction to the four "Ps." On the basis of this information, managers plan for the markets they serve. As long as firms continue to practice the marketing concept, there will be a need for marketing research. For that reason, the field offers excellent career opportunities.

The risks of conducting a business today are greater than ever before. Fluctuating economic conditions, increased competition, more government regulation, and less consumer confidence are all factors that contribute to this uncertainty. Advance information on changing conditions is a must for survival. Since marketing researchers can supply this information, their position in the organizational world of the future seems secure.

Chapter Replay

1. **How do marketers get information for routine operations and for making nonroutine decisions?**
   Marketers get information for routine operations from an ongoing marketing information system. They get information for making nonroutine decisions by conducting marketing research.
2. **What kinds of information go into a marketing information system?**
   A marketing information system comprises an internal accounting system, a marketing intelligence system, and marketing research reports.
3. **What are the steps in the marketing research process?**
   The steps in the marketing research process are problem identification, exploratory investigation, decision on whether to conduct further research, research design, data collection, data interpretation, and problem solution.
4. **What are the basic ways to conduct an exploratory investigation?**
   An exploratory investigation may consist of informal interviews with customers, intermediaries, or staff. These interviews might be focus group interviews. In addition, researchers review the literature for secondary data.
5. **What are some advantages and disadvantages of the basic methods of conducting research?**
   Observation records actual behaviors but does not give reasons for behavior. Experimentation discloses cause and effect relationships but is expensive and can be difficult to control. Surveys are flexible but subject to low response rates and inaccurate answers.

6. **Why do researchers often use samples rather than trying to survey everyone?**
A census is time consuming, costly, and possibly even impossible. Samples are often more accurate because fewer errors are made.
7. **What types of samples are available to researchers?**
Researchers can use probability samples, such as random, stratified, and cluster sampling, or they can use nonprobability samples, such as convenience, judgment, and quota samples.
8. **What is the role of analysis, intuition, and communication in interpreting data?**
Analysis involves reviewing the data and deciding how to organize it and calculate statistics that will yield relevant information. Intuition gives the researcher insight into the implications of the data. Communication skills are necessary to make the results meaningful to management.
9. **Why is marketing research important to organizations?**
Research enables the company to meet the marketing objective of paying attention to customer needs. Greater risks involved in running a modern business make advance information crucial.

Key Terms

census
cluster sampling
convenience sample
data bank (data base)
experimentation
focus group interview
hypothesis
judgment sample
marketing information system (MIS)
marketing research
nonprobability sample
observation
primary data
probability sample
quota sample
random sample
research design
sales analysis
sample
secondary data
stratified sampling
survey research

Discussion Questions

1. What is the difference between a marketing information system and marketing research?
2. Jack Crabmeat of Crabmeat Cable Services has called in a computer consultant, Bea Brilliant, to put the company's sales invoices onto the company's computer. He has called a meeting of Bea; himself; Hal Roe, the company's marketing manager; and Lynette Flax, the accounting manager, to plan how to set up the system.
   At the meeting, Bea says, "I can set up the system to prepare reports in any format you'd like." Jack turns to Hal and asks, "What information would you need from a marketing standpoint?" How

can Hal use the data on the sales invoices as a source of marketing information?

3. What conditions should be present for marketing researchers to work as partners with management?
4. Hospital administrator Jill Waverly telephoned marketing consultant Phil Sunderby. "Phil," she said, "we just aren't filling up our beds like we used to. We need to do a survey and plan a good advertising campaign." In light of what you know about the marketing research process, does Jill seem to be starting at the beginning? How might Phil suggest she go about solving her marketing problem?
5. Why do marketers sometimes decide *not* to proceed beyond the stage of exploratory investigation?
6. Master Mayonnaise Makers USA is planning to introduce its popular brand of mayonnaise in a plastic squirt bottle. The company's marketers estimate that the new container will capture 50 percent of the mayonnaise market. To predict whether the product will succeed in reaching that goal, Master Mayonnaise will conduct marketing research. Suggest how the company could design a study to make this prediction. Give three suggestions: one using observation, one using experimentation, and one using surveys.
7. Deluxe Video Creations is a company that develops and sells video games. The company has plans for a new game, but before spending any more development money, management wants to see whether enough people seem interested in playing it. Ted Tremendous, marketing consultant, has drafted a questionnaire to explore interest in the new game. Trained callers will randomly call students on a local campus. Following are the first three questions. For each question, indicate any shortcomings you see and suggest ways to improve the question.

   a. How many times have you played video games during the past year?
   b. Do you agree that the self-righteous people who castigate video games as being excessively violent just don't understand the many advantages attributable to playing the games, such as developing coordination and decision-making skills?
      [ ] yes [ ] no
   c. Which video game do you prefer?
      (1) Marble Madness
      (2) Dungeons and Dragons
      (3) Centipede

8. Under what conditions might stratified or cluster sampling produce more accurate results than random sampling?
9. Marianne Hitek entered the office of her boss, the vice president of marketing, who started in sales and rose through the ranks. "Marianne!" cried the boss, "We hired you because of your brilliance in statistics, but I can't make any sense of this report of yours. What's the conclusion? What do you recommend?" "The conclusion is at the

end of the report," replied Marianne, pointing to the last sentence: "Conjoint analysis predicts the attribute utilities shown in Table 14, which support the null hypothesis as described on page 3."

What aspect of data interpretation has Marianne failed to provide her boss? Suggest some ways she can improve her report.

Case 5.1
Whirlpool Corporation

Whirlpool

Whirlpool Corporation, a leading manufacturer of major home appliances, has corporate roots that go back to 1911. During the more than 70 years the firm has been making appliances, the variety of consumer products and services has grown dramatically. At the same time, competition for the consumer's dollar has become fierce. Whirlpool has always placed quality first in its products and services.

In an attempt to help understand more about consumers today, Whirlpool commissioned Research and Forecasts to conceive and execute a study that would uncover new information about the desires, expectations, and judgments of the consuming public, with emphasis on—but not limited to—an exploration of quality-related issues. The following material relates to that study.

Overview of Research

As more than a generation of marketing research has demonstrated, different perspectives on the American consumer are much like the proverbial blind men touching different parts of one elephant and coming to radically different conclusions about the animal. *The Whirlpool Report,* however, deals with the broad topic of quality and the American consumer. Rather than detailing specific profiles of markets for particular products or services, it outlines for the "postconsumerist" era what it means today to be a quality consumer. Some of the key questions explored in the research include:

☐ Do Americans feel surrounded by junk and poor quality goods and services, or are they satisfied?

☐ Do Americans think quality is becoming scarce, or do they think the quality of goods and services has improved in recent years?

☐ Do consumers feel they have an adversary relationship with manufacturers and service providers?

☐ Are they more or less demanding about quality than they have been in the past?

Source: Adapted from "America's Search for Quality: The Whirlpool Report on Consumers in the 80's," published by Whirlpool Corporation in 1983.

Research Methodology

A multistage research design was used in conducting this study of American attitudes toward quality in goods and services.

Phase One The first phase consisted of qualitative and background research undertaken to generate hypotheses and develop topic areas for the general public survey stage of the project.

Phase Two The second phase consisted of a series of interviews with 50 representatives of the print and broadcast media from throughout the nation between May 24 and June 18, 1982. These media representatives were specialists in the areas of consumer interest, business and finance, and home/life-style reporting. In these interviews topic areas for the general public survey were discussed at length in an open-ended interview format, and suggestions as to issues of consumer concern were solicited.

Advisory Panel During phase one and phase two of the project, the advice of experts in the consumer relations and consumer research fields was actively solicited through numerous telephone and face-to-face interviews. The research staff invited a number of experts to act as an advisory panel for the general public survey stage of the project.

Phase Three The third phase of the project was a general public survey. Twenty trained interviewers conducted phone interviews for a period of five weeks in late 1982 and early 1983. The interviews were conducted on weeknights, between the hours of 6 p.m. and 10 p.m., and on weekends, between the hours of 10:00 a.m. and 11:30 p.m. The interviews took an average of 34 minutes to complete. In order to ensure that the respondents interviewed represented a random sample of the total U.S. population, at least four callbacks were made to each telephone that had neither yielded a complete interview nor had been disqualified. A final response rate of 63 percent was obtained.

Phase Four, Weighting In order to make valid projections to the entire population of the United States, the sample should match the total U.S. population on key demographic variables. Due to sampling fluctuations, it was necessary to weight the data to match census figures on four characteristics: age, race, gender, and education. The final weighted sample matches census figures very closely. The weighting produced a total weighted sample size of 1,002.

Statistical Analysis The bulk of analyses reported in the text are illustrated with cross-tabulation data. Relationships between variables were confirmed by reference to the chi square and Pearson's R statistics where applicable. Several three-way crosstabs were computed to test further for relationships among variables. The accompanying exhibit shows a few of the research results.

Exhibit
Selected Research Results

	Very Satisfied	Somewhat Satisfied	Just Barely Satisfied	Unsatisfied	Very Unsatisfied
How satisfied are you with the manufactured goods you can purchase in your area? (992 respondents)	33%	52%	10%	3%	2%
How satisfied are you with the services you can get in your area? (998 respondents)	23%	59%	15%	2%	1%
	Significantly Improved	**Somewhat Improved**	**Stayed about the Same**	**Somewhat Deteriorated**	**Significantly Deteriorated**
In general, do you think the quality of goods in America has improved or deteriorated over the last ten years? (998 respondents)	13%	35%	24%	21%	7%
In general, do you think the quality of services in your area has improved or deteriorated over recent years? (979 respondents)	11%	36%	36%	13%	4%

Focal Topics

1. From the perspective of Whirlpool and recipients of the research (other businesses, academia, and the American public), why is this type of research of value?
2. What is your evaluation of the research methodology used in the study?
3. What changes or additions would you recommend in the method of gathering data, in the types of topics explored, and in the data analysis?

Case 5.2
USA TODAY

"*USA TODAY* is coming of age with our millions of curious, intelligent, affluent readers from New York to California who depend on *USA TODAY* for factual, comprehensive reports of top news across the USA and around the world everyday." This statement was on the cover of a special insert in *Advertising Age,* promoting *USA TODAY* to potential advertisers. The insert also stated that *USA TODAY* was coming of age with advertisers in terms of number of pages of advertising.

Source: Material presented here has been adapted from Janet Myers, "Gannett pushes *USA TODAY* as tomorrow's paper." *USA TODAY,* its logo, and associated graphics, are the federally registered trademarks of Gannett Co., Inc. All rights reserved. Reprinted with permission. *Advertising Age,* January 23, 1986, pp. 32+ and from an advertising insert for *USA TODAY* in *Advertising Age.* The original case appeared in *Cases for Analysis in Marketing,* by W. Wayne Talarzyk. Copyright © 1985 by CBS College Publishing. Reprinted by permission of Holt, Rinehart & Winston, Inc.

Product Characteristics

USA TODAY, published by the Gannett Company, was introduced in September 1982. Positioned as "The Nation's Newspaper," the publication was rolled out in different geographic markets over the next two years. As of early 1986, the newspaper was available in all 100 of the USA's top areas of dominant influence (ADIs). Sales are made through newsstands, corner vending machines, and in some markets via home or office delivery. *USA TODAY* also has a "blue chip" sales program in which papers are sold at a discount to airlines, hotels, and schools that redistribute them.

After a year of publication, daily paid circulation reached 1.16 million. A year later it had reached about 1.25 million. In early 1986, *USA TODAY* announced that its circulation rate base (number of copies sold) would move to 1.45 million on March 1. By way of comparison, the circulation of the *New York Daily News* at the start of 1986 was about 1.35 million and that of *The Wall Street Journal* at a little over 1.91 million. The introductory price of *USA TODAY* was 25 cents. During 1984, the price was raised to 35 cents, and in 1985, to 50 cents.

In the advertising insert, the newspaper was described as follows: "*USA TODAY* is different: filled with color and graphics, serious where it should be serious, fun when it's appropriate, and always introducing something new for our readers." The newspaper used many forms of direct reader response in 1985, including reader lotteries and special reader polls.

Selected Marketing Activities

During 1986, *USA TODAY* planned to spend about $4 million to advertise itself to potential readers and advertisers. A variety of media, including television, print, radio, and outdoor were used to advertise the newspaper. That year *USA TODAY* announced it would sponsor the 1987 Major League Baseball All-Star fan balloting in an expansion into sports marketing. A special promotion in the summer of 1985 with General Mills cereals offered consumers a free, six-month subscription. That promotion yielded 450,000 new, but unpaid, subscribers. A significant number of these have since converted to paid subscriptions.

A print advertisement to potential advertisers said in its heading, "A lot of media people are saying *USA TODAY* is neither fish nor fowl." Alongside a sketch of a part fish, part chicken creature were the words "They're right!" The advertisement went on to say that readers viewed the publication as a newspaper, "bold, exciting, colorful, and unique," while many advertisers saw it as a newsmagazine, "bold, exciting, colorful, and unique." Concluding copy said, "The truth is, we don't much care what you call us. Just as long as you call us." The theme line, "The advertising might of *USA TODAY*," appeared at the bottom of the advertisement over the newspaper logo.

Focal Topics

1. What types of research should *USA TODAY* undertake to market itself to potential readers?
2. What types of research would be helpful to market *USA TODAY* to potential advertisers?
3. How might an advertiser in *USA TODAY* measure the effectiveness of its advertising?

Consumer Buying Behavior

Sounding Out the Chapter

In this chapter, you will learn:

1. **Why cultures and subcultures are important to marketers.**
2. **The kinds of groups that can influence buying.**
3. **The order in which human needs arise.**
4. **How people filter information.**
5. **Why marketers are concerned about attitudes and personality.**
6. **Ways in which consumers learn.**
7. **How life-styles influence buyer behavior.**
8. **The stages of the buying process.**

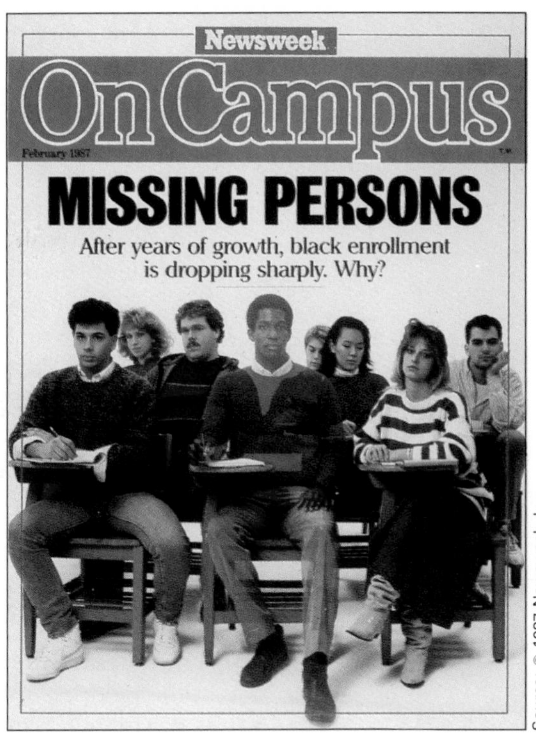

Source: © 1987 Newsweek, Inc.

College-Level Consumption Attracts Marketers

Banks have targeted the monetary needs of college students by offering accounts that combine high interest rates, bounce-free checking, and credit cards linked to savings accounts. Many offer loans designed to meet students' needs.

Campbell Soup Company is studying students' eating habits as it considers repositioning student favorites such as Chunky Soups and Pepperidge Farm cookies. The company is also considering development of more products for microwaves, which are increasingly available to students.

American Express also targets college students. The company "saw early on that [college students] were the future business leaders," reports Diane Shaib, a senior vice president at American Express.

College students spend little time watching TV or reading newspapers, compared to the general population. So publishers are reaching this market through specialized magazines, such as *Dorm, College Woman,* and *Newsweek on Campus.* These magazines carry ads targeted to college students. One publication—*Semester*—boosts circulation by including the official class directory of the schools at which it is distributed. Students need the magazine in order to register for class.

Companies also can obtain help in reaching college students by hiring marketing services that specialize in the college market.

Why would marketers want to target the college market? For one thing, students have discretionary income—in fact, one study shows that college students control half of the discretionary purchasing power in the United States. Their special needs and life-styles lead college students to spend more money per month on discretionary items than the average family of four. Furthermore, college students are at a stage in their lives when they are building brand loyalty. As a result, many marketers see advertising to them as an investment in the future. Finally, they are highly concentrated on college campuses, enabling marketers to target them geographically.

Together, these characteristics of college students make them an attractive group for some marketers. Other segments of the population have different patterns of spending. The differences arise from variations in family structure, values, life-styles, and many other characteristics. This chapter looks at influences on buyer behavior and at ways marketers can put that information to use.

Sources: Marilyn Adler and Geralyn Wiener, "Student Buying Rates High Interest," *Advertising Age,* February 2, 1987, p. S-1; Maureen McFadden, "College Media Lead to Deep Pockets on Campus," *Advertising Age,* February 2, 1987, pp. S-2, S-4–S-5; and Constanza Montana, "New Magazines Try to Target College Market," *The Wall Street Journal,* February 18, 1987, p. 25.

The Scope of Buyer Behavior

Your attitudes and personality influence whether you spend your leisure time skiing, taking in a movie, or attending a party. Your friends and financial resources may affect this decision as well. And these are only some of the influences.

Knowing about these kinds of influences helps the managers of ski resorts, movie theaters, and potato chip manufacturers to plan successful marketing strategies. Therefore, marketers study **buyer behavior.** Buyer behavior is the discipline that provides marketing managers with an understanding of what is behind the decision to spend money, time, and effort on consumption-related items. It probes not only what is exchanged, but also why, where, when, and how often.[1] Without such knowledge, marketers do not know why their products are selling or failing to sell.

Buyer Behavior
Study that provides marketing managers with an understanding of what is behind the decision to spend money, time, and effort on consumption-related items.

Contributions of the Social Sciences

The systematic study of consumer behavior is relatively new. Pioneers in the field have therefore borrowed heavily from other, more established disciplines, particularly the social sciences. The fields that have been of most use to marketers are anthropology, sociology, demography, and psychology. Anthropology studies the culture of a society or part of a society. Sociology studies human behavior as influenced by groups. Demography uses statistics to analyze various population characteristics such as residence, age, education, occupation, and income. Psychology studies the human mind and individual behavior.[2]

Except for psychology, each of these fields treats individuals as part of a group. Every person belongs to several groups. One group membership might include teenager, suburban resident, high-school graduate, American, middle-class, single, and fraternity member. The first three labels (teenager, suburban resident, high-school graduate) are demographic categories and provide marketers with some very useful information. They indicate, for example, that a member of the group is much more likely to buy a stereo than bifocal glasses.

Demographic categories paint a portrait of a group by numbers. The supplied information is sketchy. To add color to the numbers, anthropological data (the label "American") and sociological information (middle-class, fraternity member, and single) must be added. To marketers, these labels indicate, for example, that a group member would probably value leisure time and have the interest and income to fill some of that time with music. Such information would be of great value to a stereo manufacturer.

If there are enough people matching those characteristics, marketers are likely to identify the group as a promising market. It is no mystery, then, why there are often many stores specializing in stereo equipment, records, and cassettes in college towns.

Users and Uses of Consumer Behavior Data

As the chapter on market segmentation points out, few manufacturers can afford to sell to the whole American market. It is simply too vast, and money would be wasted appealing to those who have neither the

Marketing Today 6.1
British Marketer Meets American Culture

When Terence Conran brought his chain of home furnishing shops to the United States, he learned about American culture the hard way. During its first years, the stores consistently lost money.

In England, the original stores sold sleek and functional designs in bold colors on the premise that it is possible to sell furniture and housewares that are inexpensive but not ugly. The store kept prices down by selling unassembled furniture with instructions on how to put it together.

In the United States, the merchandise at Conran's did not always suit American lifestyles and tastes. Observes Pauline Dora, president of the U.S. operation, "You can't just take an English company and transplant it." Now only half of Conran's merchandise duplicates what is sold abroad. A notable difference is in size; Americans prefer bigger beds, chairs, sofas, and glasses.

Another American difference Conran's discovered is the relatively greater importance of advertising in the United States. In England, word-of-mouth reputation promoted the stores. Explains Dora, "In the U.K. you've got a country that is the size of New York State. . . . Here you've got to advertise constantly."

Source: Karen Cook, "The Brits Find Their Niche," *Working Woman,* August 1986, pp. 53–54.

interest nor the income to buy. It is usually more profitable to specialize—to appeal to one group or, at most, a few. But such specialization requires knowledge of buyer categories, what interests them, and how they can be influenced.

In addition to businesses, nonprofit organizations are major users of buyer behavior information, because they must understand demographic trends to plan facilities. Charities must learn what groups in society are most likely to heed appeals. Similarly, hospitals have found that women are a major—and often dissatisfied—part of their market; many hospitals have responded by tailoring their services to appeal more to women. Any organization that requires the support of a group (or the public) can benefit from knowing that group better.[3]

Cultural Influences on Consumer Behavior

Culture

Culture
A people's shared customs, beliefs, values, and artifacts that are transmitted from generation to generation.

Anthropologists study **culture,** which refers to a people's shared customs, beliefs, values, and artifacts (housing, works of art, and so on) that are transmitted from generation to generation. The word *anthropology* brings to mind images of scholars in pith helmets digging up bones and taking notes on the behavior of remote tribes. But those interested in consumer behavior are primarily concerned with the study of contemporary culture. (See Marketing Today 6.1.) As Americans, we share a distinctive culture. One marketer has noted:

Most Americans know how to speak English, handle money, turn on a television set, tie a shoelace, shake hands, write letters, dance a waltz, hold a fork, pay income tax, shop in a supermarket, and drive a car. These seem easy and natural. Yet people from another culture would be confused by these customs, just as we

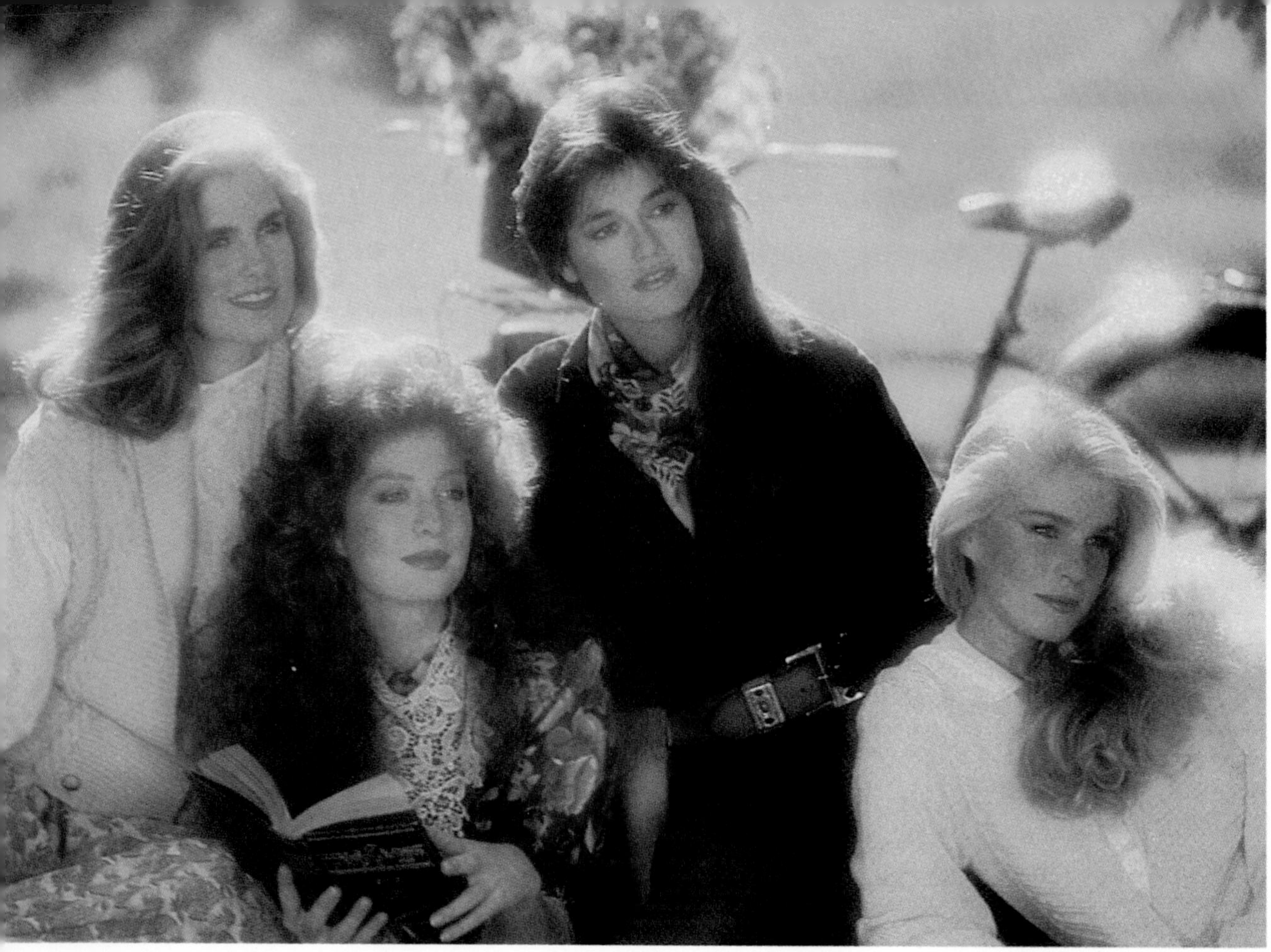

BRING OUT YOUR NATURAL HIGHLIGHTS WITH HÄLSA.

Your hair has its own special glow. Make it come alive with Hälsa.

CHAMOMILE
Warms the glow of ash blonde, light brown or light chestnut hair.

GINGER ROOT
Lights the fire of red, reddish brown or auburn hair.

WALNUT LEAVES
Deepens the natural shine of brown, dark brown or black hair.

MARIGOLD
Brings out golden highlights in natural blonde or lightened hair.

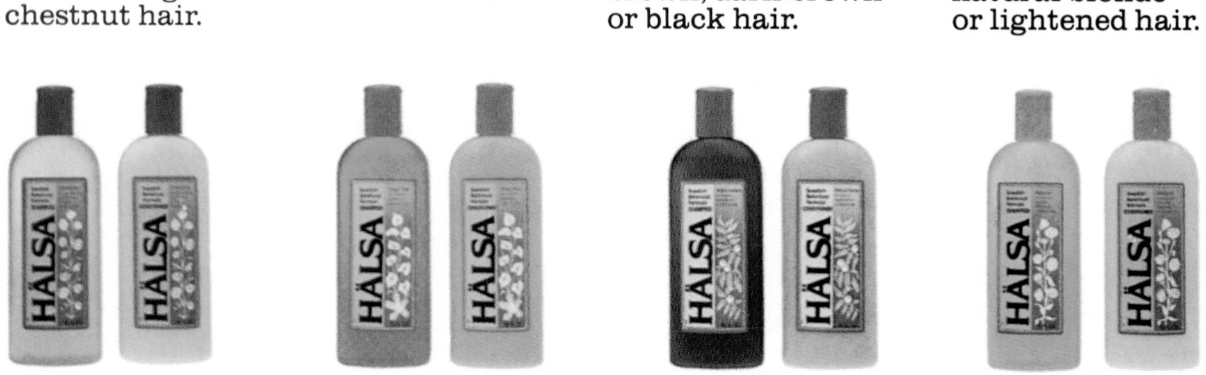

HÄLSA SWEDISH BOTANICAL SHAMPOOS AND CONDITIONERS

would be confused if we saw them rub noses, pierce lips, fast regularly, eat insects, and speak in squeals.[4]

Even if marketers operate only in the American market, they can benefit by a study of culture. Values, an important aspect of culture, help shape what Americans buy. There is some evidence today that American values are changing, and those changes should be of vital concern to marketers.

A good many mistakes have been made by American marketers abroad who ignored cultural differences. For example, Green Giant erred in trying to introduce canned sweet corn to Britain. Unlike Americans, the British have no experience with eating fresh corn and think of it as feed for animals.[5] Cultural differences between nations are explored in the chapter on international marketing.

Cultural values are dynamic, changing in response to pressure both within and outside a society. Many analysts see traditional values losing ground to a new set of values. Although the implications of all these changes cannot be discussed here, a few examples show the far-reaching effects they can have.

A trend toward valuing instant gratification, for example, reverses the long-held belief that the future must be planned for, money set aside, and pleasures put off. It is supported by the trend toward hedonism, the notion that self-fulfillment is found in pleasure, not work. Together the trends could signal an upsurge in the purchase of luxury goods. Marketers of food might also see growth in convenience items, which, though costly, free people for more leisure activities.

The increased tendency to value "experiences" over the possession of material goods is evident in the growth of the travel industry. The airlines, restaurants, gas stations, phone companies, and linen services all profit from this growth. On one day in June, Hertz alone received 60,000 phone calls for car rentals.[6]

Marketers have also been quick to exploit the growing trend toward naturalism. "Natural" products from soft drinks to makeup now flood the market. In addition, clothing is more casual and furniture styles more basic. Figure 6.1 shows an ad emphasizing the "natural" aspect of Halsa Shampoo.

Americans are increasingly concerned about protecting and insulating themselves from the harsh realities of the outside world, according to one consultant, who calls this effort "cocooning." Extreme cocooning involves a quest for a perfect environment in which one can forget the rest of the world. Along with this trend, Americans are seeking comfort, cleanliness, and ease. Those who can afford it have fancy bathroom suites, complete with whirlpools, saunas, bidets, exercise equipment, a stereo–video system, and a refrigerator for champagne and caviar or health snacks and vitamins.[7]

Figure 6.1
Halsa Emphasizes Tie to Nature
Source: Courtesy of S. C. Johnson & Son, Inc. Photograph courtesy of Nancy Brown.

The importance of keeping up with value trends cannot be overestimated. Insofar as anthropology can shed light on changing American values, it is of great use to marketers in planning strategy. It also can be helpful in another way—by describing the behavior of subcultures.

Subcultures

Subculture
Subgroup within a larger culture that has distinctive life-styles, values, norms, and beliefs.

Within the U.S. population there are certain segments with distinctive life-styles, values, norms, and beliefs[8] known as **subcultures.** In American society, subcultures exist based on race, ethnicity, geography, religion, and occupation, among others. Marketers are interested in subcultures because they represent possible target markets.

A major American subculture distinguished by race is the black subculture. With 12 percent of the American population and buying power of $203 billion annually,[9] blacks constitute a large and attractive market. Marketers have found that blacks' demand for many consumer goods—typewriters, air travel, high-priced fishing equipment, and color TVs, among others—is two to four times that of white customers.

Another large subculture is the Hispanic subculture, which in 1987 made up more than 7 percent of the population and had purchasing power of $134 billion.[10] Some marketers break this subculture down into smaller groups, including Mexicans, Puerto Ricans, and Cubans. In general, the Hispanic market is younger, has more children, and is growing faster than the Anglo population.[11] Besides these differences, marketers targeting Hispanics need to consider possible differences in the group's values. For example, PepsiCo prepared billboards proclaiming in Spanish that Pepsi Free "has no caffeine and all the taste" of regular Pepsi. But a Hispanic marketing specialist notes, "Hispanics are not even a tenth as diet and health conscious as the general market."[12]

While the Asian subculture is smaller than the black or Hispanic subcultures, it is an appealing market segment. Figures for 1980 indicate that U.S. Asians had a higher median income and a greater proportion of college-educated adults than the general population. One marketing expert described the values of the U.S. Asian subculture as follows: "They are conservative, traditional, and maintain their native language. They are family oriented and feel a strong need to improve their education."[13] Marketing Today 6.2 describes some efforts to target this subculture.

Not all subcultures are determined on the basis of ethnicity or race. One subculture that has received a great deal of attention from marketers has been labeled "yuppies," for young urban professionals. These are generally the high-earning segment of the baby boom generation who have chosen to live near the amenities of urban life. As a group, yuppies are thought to value consumption of high-quality (and expensive) goods and to place great emphasis on their careers. Figure 6.2 shows an ad targeted to this subculture.

Markets serving religious interests have also been the focus of growing attention from marketers over the past decade. The Christian book publishing industry, for example, reports annual revenues in excess of $400 million, several million Christian record albums are sold each year,

Marketing Today **6.2**

Appealing to Asian-Americans

With their relatively great educational level and spending potential, Asian-Americans were bound to be targeted by insurance companies before long. One leader in this market is Metropolitan Life Insurance Company. When Chinese-Americans celebrated the Year of the Tiger in February 1986, Metropolitan Life wished them well in Chinese—the company's first-ever Asian-language advertisement.

The ad is part of Metropolitan Life's overall strategy to win over Asian-American consumers. The insurance company has assembled a sales force of more than 300 Asian-Americans. It is also considering hiring people fluent in Asian languages to staff a special toll-free phone line for consumer inquiries. "Asian-Americans are our kind of market," explained Robert J. Crimmins, senior vice president, personal insurance sales, "They're family-oriented and solidly educated, and they're looking for financial security."

For others wishing to reach the Asian-American market, a good advertising medium might be the Asian Yellow Pages. Chinese, Japanese, and Vietnamese versions of this directory include non-Asian companies. The publisher recommends that advertisers stress quality, brand names, and length of time in business.

Source: Ronald Alsop, "Firms Translate Sales Pitches to Appeal to Asian-Americans," *The Wall Street Journal,* April 10, 1986, p. 35.

and some apparel manufacturers have had success marketing clothing bearing Christian symbols (such as a fish, cross, or dove).[14]

Social Influences on Consumer Behavior

Although population can be segmented in a variety of ways, not all segments are of equal use to marketers. "Midwesterners," for example, represent a demographic category. But people in this group do not interact with one another on the basis of shared geography, and individual buying behavior is not directly affected by membership in that category. Members of a social group like the family do exchange views or act in ways that may influence what is purchased. Besides the family, the social groups of greatest interest to marketers are social classes, reference groups, and opinion leaders and innovators. Other social factors, such as the current age mix of the population, also affect the goods and services that are in demand.

Social Classes

If asked to identify themselves by **social class,** most Americans would probably respond that they are part of some vague "middle class." Marketers, however, recognize distinctions among social classes, which differ from one another in several ways.

Social Class
Group distinguished by characteristics such as occupation, education, possessions, and values.

Distinguishing the Classes People commonly consider income to be the characteristic that differentiates the classes, but in fact it is a poor measure. A college professor and a factory foreman may both earn $25,000 per year, but most people would agree that the professor has

a r a m i s
An American Hero
aramis
cologne
aramis
The impact never fades
amis Inc., 1986 Suit: Burberrys Ltd.

higher social status. Occupation is the most important basis for determining a person's social class. Other criteria include education, possessions (including type and location of home), and values.

Researchers have tried many methods for distinguishing the social classes, including asking people to rank the social positions of others or to estimate their own position. Commonly used categories are those developed by Lloyd Warner and other sociologists: upper-upper, lower-upper, upper-middle, lower-middle, upper-lower, and lower-lower. The largest of these are the upper-lower class and the lower-middle class. These groups make up the primary market for mass consumer goods. Many marketers target the upper classes, however, because their higher-status occupations often pay well.

Importance to Marketers Certain products are more likely to appeal to one class than another. For example, marketers of adult education courses would probably have more success recruiting among those in the lower-middle class, who are interested in getting ahead, rather than among the lower-upper class, whose members think they already have made it.

Even when members of different classes purchase the same product, the kind and quality of product selected may vary. Consider home furnishings. "Old money" families of the upper-upper class, secure in their fortunes for generations, tend to shun ostentatious displays of wealth. Their homes may be grand but are rarely decorated in the up-to-the-minute styles promoted by glossy magazines. The lower-upper and upper-middle classes, whose money, while substantial, is more recently acquired, tend to favor a more stylish approach to decorating, and are the group most likely to employ the services of an interior decorator. Middle-class families tend to prefer do-it-yourself decorating with good quality items purchased from local department and furniture stores. The lower classes may pay little attention to decorating trends, opting instead for functional, rather than stylish, furnishings.[15]

Differences among classes also can be demonstrated in other marketing areas. For example, the classes have different preferences in where they shop. The lower classes do much of their shopping in neighborhood "mom and pop" stores that give them credit or in discount houses. The middle classes feel "safer" purchasing highly visible goods (like furniture and clothing) in department stores, although they shop in discount houses for appliances and other, less socially risky goods. The upper classes enjoy shopping in prestige stores like Neiman-Marcus or in exclusive "to-the-trade-only" shops.

One other difference that affects marketing is class variation in media habits. The upper and middle classes read more newspapers and magazines that report on news, fashions, and hobbies than the lower

Figure 6.2
Advertisement Targeted to Yuppies
Source: Photographed by Uli Rose for Aramis, Inc.

classes. All classes watch television, but the different groups watch different shows. Advertisers who want to market to a particular class must consider these media habits when placing their messages.[16]

Reference Groups

Reference Group
Group that serves as a model for an individual's behavior and frame of reference for decision making.

Membership Group
Reference group to which a person may belong—for example, family, friends, neighbors.

Aspirational Group
Reference group with which a person may want to be identified.

Dissociative Group
Reference group from which a person may want to dissociate himself or herself.

Marketers have discovered that **reference groups** also strongly influence buying. These are groups that serve as a model for an individual's behavior and as a "frame of reference" for decision making. A reference group may influence a decision to buy in one of three ways:

1. By reason of being a member of the group (called a **membership group**—family, friends, neighbors). You may buy a pair of Reebok aerobics shoes because your friends have them.
2. By reason of wanting to belong (called an **aspirational group**—sports figures, cultural heroes, various occupational categories). A management trainee may purchase an attaché case to look like a successful manager.
3. By reason of not wanting to belong (called a **dissociative group**—lower social classes, cults, recently arrived immigrant groups). A first-generation American student may avoid restaurants reflecting ethnic heritage as a way of dissociating from "Old-World" customs.

Some products can be sold by an appeal to reference groups, and others cannot. Researchers have shown that people tend to seek reference group approval when products are high-risk, that is, when an individual has little previous experience with them, or when they are highly visible in use.[17]

Purchasing usually involves a twofold decision: (1) whether to buy the product at all and, if so, (2) what brand to buy. Reference groups may influence either, neither, or both of these choices.

Reference groups have been shown to have a strong product and brand influence on purchases of cars and color TVs. There seems to be little reference group influence on purchases of such things as canned peaches and soap. Given this information, advertisers for products showing little or no reference group influence may want to stress product features like price and quality. To encourage product purchases demanding strong reference group approval, advertisements might show the kinds of people who use the product.[18]

MasterCard has used a variety of entertainers, such as Jackie Gleason, Lee Marvin, and Grace Jones, in ads promoting the credit card. Presumably, the company hopes that these famous people serve as an aspirational group for many consumers. The sports figures shown in the ad in Figure 6.3 are another aspirational group.

Opinion Leaders and Innovators

While studying reference groups, researchers became curious about the way influence is exerted on members. Members of a group do not generally act as individuals, they found. Rather, certain members act as

Figure 6.3
Sports Figures As an Aspirational Group

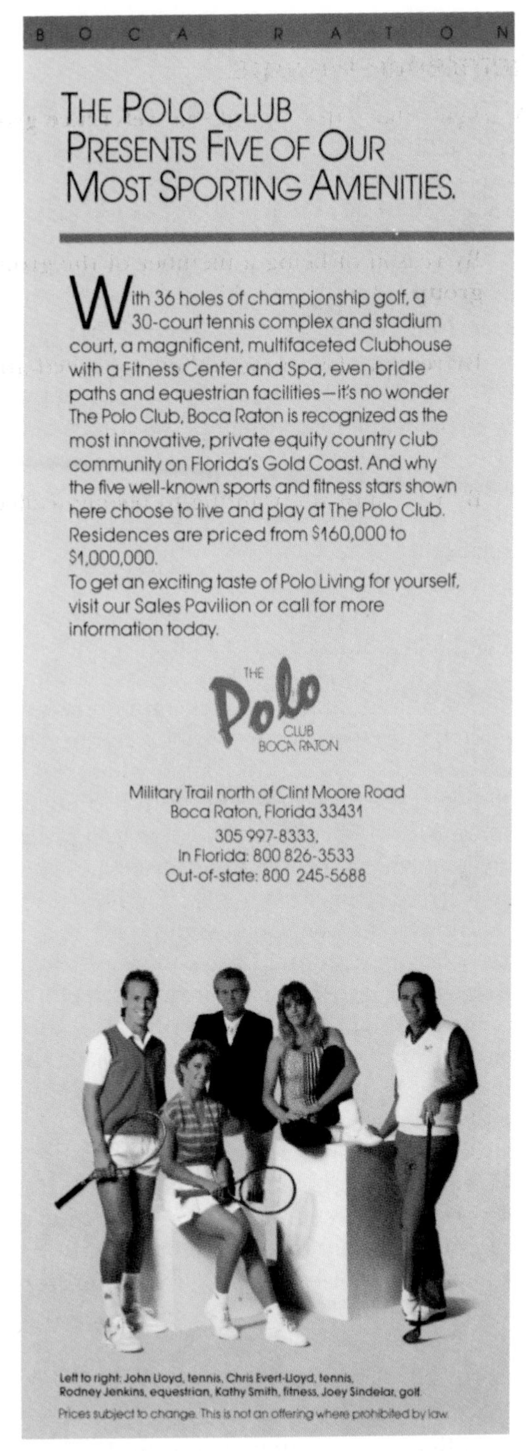

Opinion Leader
Member of a group who is capable of influencing others in it.

Innovator
Person who is first to find out about and use a new product.

influencers. Moreover, information spreads slowly, and not everyone absorbs it or chooses to act on it at the same rate. **Opinion leaders** are those capable of influencing others in a group, and **innovators** are those who are the first to find out about and use new products.

Role of Opinion Leaders People become opinion leaders in a given area because they possess certain characteristics. Opinion leaders have been found to be (1) more interested and better read in the area they influence, (2) more self-confident and sociable, (3) slightly higher in social status, and (4) slightly more innovative.[19]

Study of opinion leaders has shown marketers how important word of mouth can be in spreading product information. At one time, many marketers thought that everyone received information directly from ads or salespeople. Researchers then showed that information travels in a two-step flow of communication: Ads or salespeople supply information first to opinion leaders, who then pass it on to followers.[20]

In some cases, marketers have been able to harness the power of opinion leaders to spread the word. The Cuisinart food processor, for example, gained initial acceptance not by massive advertising but by winning over professional cooks. Sometimes opinion leaders in a given category are hard to identify. In those cases, marketers may try to "create" such leaders. In exchange for a special discount on a pool or encyclopedia, for example, a family may agree to "talk up" the product in its neighborhood.

Role of Innovators Besides opinion leaders, marketers are interested in innovators—the ones who are the first to try something new. Researchers discovered innovators while looking for the way new ideas are adopted. Not everyone is receptive to novelty immediately. In fact, people appear to fall into one of five categories depending upon how soon they adopt new trends: innovators, early adopters, early majority, late majority, and laggards.[21] (See Figure 6.4.)

Innovators (the speedy adopters) and laggards (the last to change) are poles apart in more ways than just their psychological profiles. In comparison with laggards, innovators tend to be younger, wealthier, and more educated, and they have higher-status jobs. They also know more people outside their immediate circle of friends and read more magazines.

For their new products to succeed, marketers must catch the attention of innovators. One way is to advertise in special-interest magazines. Fashion marketers may rely on *Vogue* or *Gentlemen's Quarterly*, for example, and automakers in *Motor Trends* magazine. Innovators may then be seen and imitated by early adopters. Since many opinion leaders come from the class of early adopters, word-of-mouth communication can play an important role.

The Family Group

Did you ever wonder why you use Hellman's mayonnaise rather than Miracle Whip or vice versa? The chances are that you learned to use one or the other while growing up. Your family, in effect, steered you into

Figure 6.4
Characteristics of Adopter Groups

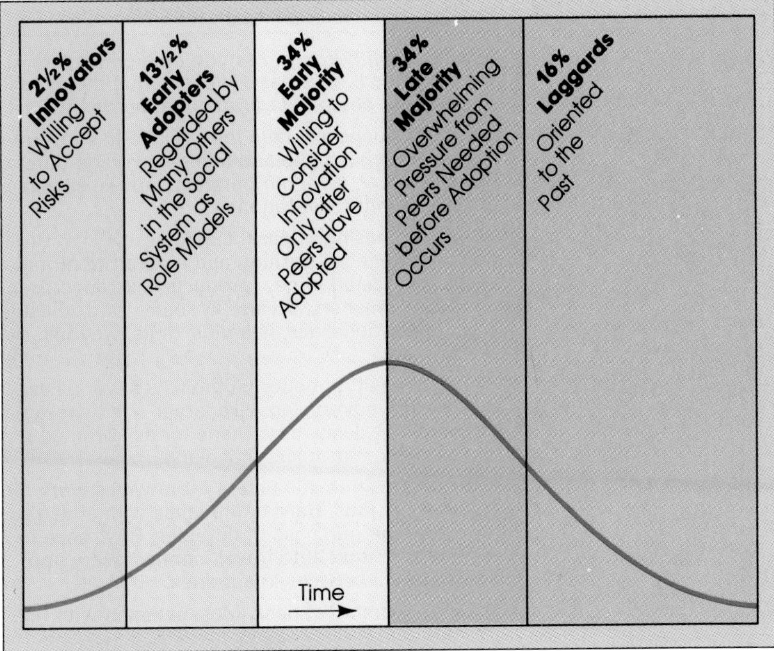

Source: Everett M. Rogers, *Diffusion of Innovations* (New York: Free Press, 1962).

the market for one product rather than the other. Buying behavior is often shaped by the family. Two concepts—the family life cycle and the role of family members—help explain such influence.

Traditional Family Life Cycle The stages of traditional family formation and change constitute the **family life cycle.** These stages start with the unmarried state and continue through the rearing of children and loss of a spouse.

Family Life Cycle
Traditional stages through which families pass, from the unmarried state through child rearing, empty nest, and loss of a spouse.

The family life cycle concept considers four factors that influence buyer behavior: (1) marital status, (2) age of family members, (3) size of family, and (4) work status of the head of household. On the basis of these factors, the family life cycle specifies a series of stages through which families pass and the purchase behavior of families in each phase. Table 6.1 divides the traditional life cycle into nine stages.

Consider two young persons who recently graduated from college, have married, and have begun new jobs. The partners in the new marriage (stage 2 of the life cycle) have a good deal of discretionary income but not a great deal of shopping experience. They will probably concentrate on purchasing moderately priced, basic furniture for an apartment or house, and they may be susceptible to ads or sales pitches that offer advice in an unfamiliar area. In contrast, parents (perhaps in stage 5) already have a furnished home and a great deal of shopping experience. If they are interested in household goods, they are likely to purchase

Table 6.1
An Overview of the Family Life Cycle and Buying Behavior

Stage in Family Life Cycle	Buying or Behavioral Pattern
1. Bachelor stage: Young single people not living at home.	Few financial burdens. Fashion opinion leaders. Recreation-oriented. Buy: basic kitchen equipment, basic furniture, cars, equipment for the mating game, vacations.
2. Newly married couples: Young, no children	Better off financially than they will be in near future. Highest purchase rate and highest average purchase of durables. Buy: cars, refrigerators, stoves, sensible and durable furniture, vacations.
3. Full nest I: Youngest child under six	Home purchasing at peak. Liquid assets low. Dissatisfied with financial position and amount of money saved. Interested in new products. Like advertised products. Buy: washers, dryers, TV, baby food, chest rubs and cough medicines, vitamins, dolls, wagons, sleds, skates.
4. Full nest II: Youngest child six or over	Financial position better. Some wives work. Less influenced by advertising. Like larger-sized packages, multiple-unit deals. Buy: many foods, cleaning materials, bicycles, music lessons, pianos.
5. Full nest III: Older married couples with dependent children	Financial position still better. More wives work. Some children get jobs. Hard to influence with advertising. High average purchase of durables. Buy: new, more tasteful furniture, auto travel, nonnecessary appliances, boats, dental services, magazines.
6. Empty nest I: Older married couples, no children living with them, head in labor force	Home ownership at peak. Most satisfied with financial position and money saved. Interested in travel, recreation, self-education. Make gifts and contributions. Not interested in new products. Buy: vacations, luxuries, home improvements.
7. Empty nest II: Older married couples, no children living at home, head retired	Drastic cut in income. Keep home. Buy: medical appliances, medical care products that aid health, sleep, and digestion.
8. Solitary survivor, in labor force	Income still good but likely to sell home.
9. Solitary survivor, retired	Same medical and product needs as other retired group; drastic cut in income. Special need for attention, affection, and security.

Source: Philip Kotler and Gary Armstrong, *Marketing: An Introduction* (Englewood Cliffs, N. J.: Prentice Hall 1987), p. 157.

better furniture or nonnecessary appliances (such as microwave ovens or food processors) and be guided by their own experience.[22]

Changing Family Patterns The family life-cycle concept has been used in segmenting markets and targeting product and promotional appeals for more than 20 years. During that time, however, changes have occurred that may affect some generalizations. For example, the traditional family group of a working father, a homemaking mother, and one or more children accounted for less than one-fifth of the population as of the beginning of the 1980s.[23] During the first half of the 1980s, the fastest-growing type of household was families headed by men or women without spouses.[24] By the year 2000, the proportion of such households is expected to reach more than 15 percent.[25] While single-parent households may be less financially secure than other households, they represent a growing market for lower-priced goods and functional products, such as used cars, inexpensive clothing and furniture, and fast-food restaurants.

Another type of household that is gaining a larger share of the population is the nonfamily household. Such households consist of persons living alone or with people to whom they are not related. This group includes unmarried couples who are living together. During the 1970s and the first half of the 1980s, the number of nonfamily households grew faster than the number of family households. By the year 2000, nonfamily households are expected to rise from about one-quarter of the total to almost one-third. This group represents a promising market for personal services such as health spas and tennis clubs.

Family Roles The sociological concept of "roles" also has implications for marketing. A **role** refers to a kind of specialization of task. Many families divide household tasks by role: a wife cooks, a child sets the table, and a husband takes out the garbage. Research has shown a similar specialization in buying.

Role
In sociology, a kind of specialization of task. Family roles include those concerning decisions that may be wife-dominated, husband-dominated, or autonomous (either spouse may decide).

Most studies have concentrated on the relative influence of a husband or wife in a particular product category. One study indicated that purchase decisions should be classified as:

1. *Wife-dominated decisions.* Those in which the wife is the most influential in selecting a product in the majority of households (such as food, health care).
2. *Husband-dominated decisions.* Those in which the husband exerts the greatest influence in most households (such as insurance).
3. *Autonomous decisions.* Those in which either spouse may decide, though one may slightly dominate (such as appliances, alcoholic beverages).[26]

More recent studies have shown that roles in purchasing decisions have shifted somewhat over the years. As more women join the work force and contribute to the family income, they are gaining more influence on purchase decisions formerly reserved for men. Marketing Today 6.3 describes the increasing role of women as car buyers. As women have become a greater share of that market, automobile companies have taken a closer look at their buying behavior; Figure 6.5 illustrates one effort to do this. Conversely, as men share more in child-care and housekeeping duties, they are beginning to influence purchasing decisions previously reserved for women.

The role of children in decision making has been studied much less frequently. But anyone who has ever brought a child along on a shopping trip knows that children do have a say. Children apparently have a great deal of influence in the selection of toys and fast-food restaurants (McDonald's spends millions advertising on Saturday morning television). However, when it comes to nutrition, mothers often veto a child's choice that is felt to be unsound.[27] That is why the makers of Cocoa Puffs, a chocolate-flavored cereal, also advertise their product's vitamin content—to overcome mothers' doubts.

Marketing Today 6.3
Women Key to Car Sales

Women are becoming an increasingly important part of the market for new cars. In 1985, females bought almost 40 percent of passenger cars, compared to only 29 percent a decade earlier. By 1990, according to one estimate, women will buy 44 percent of all passenger cars. As a result, women sometimes determine the success of a new model.

Automakers have responded by trying to appeal to this group. Chrysler Corporation, for example, has developed educational brochures and seminars to help dealers and salespeople serve their female customers. The company also developed a guide to financing alternatives for women.

At Ford Motor Company, focus group discussions indicated that women view the automobile dealership as a hostile environment. Another report shows that women feel car advertising misrepresents their views, underestimates their knowledge, and provides them with too little technical information.

Research at Ford suggests that women are practical car buyers, viewing an automobile as a means of transportation more than a statement about life-style. Women are also interested in ease of handling and ease of parking more than in the purely technical aspects of the car.

Source: Alfred King, "Female Buyers Loom Large in Car Sales," *Boston Globe,* April 12, 1986, p. 57.

Teenagers, too, seem to be involved in many shopping decisions. One study found teenage boys responsible for brand decisions on home computers in 49 percent of the homes surveyed. As you learned in Chapter 4, teenagers do an increasing amount of the family's grocery shopping and also spend about $30 billion per year of their own money.[28]

Age Mix Changes

Besides stages in the family life cycle, marketers are interested in how the population breaks down by age. America is an aging society. While the number of teenagers and people in their early twenties will continue to decline through the first half of the 1990s, the number of people over 65 is projected to increase dramatically. Part of the reason for this trend is increased life expectancy.[29]

Already, people over 50 make up about 25 percent of the population, but they have nearly 50 percent of the nation's disposable income. Because people in this age segment have typically finished rearing children and paying for a home, they have money to spend on travel and luxury items. At Your Service 6.1 describes ways the travel industry has attempted to appeal to this attractive market segment. Sears, too, has directed efforts to the over-50 market. Its Mature Outlook Club offers members discounts on goods expected to appeal to this age group. For example, older people buy more than one-third of all gardening tools, so club members receive a 20 percent discount on any garden tool they buy at Sears.[30]

Another significant demographic change for marketers is the aging of the Baby Boomers, those born after World War II. This group has had a dramatic effect on the marketplace at each stage of its life cycle. It

Figure 6.5
Conde Nast Researches the New Female Car Buyer

Conde Nast puts the pieces together
Value seekers—These women want it all. They are aggressive drivers and like cars with great pickup, yet they will watch the price. Japanese name plates score well with them, although they do like Dodges. Most are single, average age 29, working fulltime and have attended college.
Comfort seekers—The oldest purchasing group, these women are very conservative when purchasing an automobile. Most are retired, and few attended college. They try to save money and look for rebates. They prefer larger domestic-cars, including Oldsmobiles and Buicks
Driving enthusiasts—Life in the fast lane: These women like sports and gambling, and are keenly interested in their cars. They are single, 30-35 and prefer American performance cars such as Pontiacs, Chevys and Dodges.
Affluent luxury seekers—With household incomes $20,000 higher than the average, these women are the big spenders. They will not hesitate to spend money on an expensive European import. Most are married and work fulltime in a professional position. Average age is 41. They don't buy as many American cars as Detroit could wish.
Voluntary minimalists—These women choose to spend as little time as possible thinking about cars. Most are married, well-educated, white-collar workers with an average age of 40. They prefer Chevys, Fords, Plymouths and AMCs.
Budget-minded—These consumers are family-minded homemakers. Their average age is 43 and very few have attended college. If they work, they hold clerical or factory positions. They love American cars—Fords, Chevys and Oldsmobiles—and stay away from foreign models.
MARKET
Ellis
Source: 1986 Conde Nast Report

Source: Christy Ellis.

At Your Service 6.1
Over-50s Are on the Road

The travel industry is discovering customers over 50. Several airlines have formed travel clubs for older passengers. The clubs offer fare discounts, with no limitations on flight times or destinations. Eastern Airlines and TWA are also offering their older travelers passes for a year of travel.

Hotels, too, are interested in the over-50 market. At Marriott Corporation, a promotion called "Leisurelife" provides room discounts of 50 percent and restaurant discounts of 25 percent to guests over age 62. Quality Inns International is offering "Prime Time" discounts. Hotels see attracting retired travelers as a way to fill rooms during normally slow seasons.

Tour operators are diversifying their offerings to attract repeat business. One of the first companies to rediscover the older market is Insight International. John R. Peckham, the company's North American president, observes, "This is an adventurous, well-heeled group." Insight International has even redesigned its brochures to show more gray hair and glasses.

Source: Courtesy of Insight International Tours.

Source: Linda Lehrer, "More Marketers Seek to Target People over 50," *The Wall Street Journal*, February 18, 1986, p. 35.

initially created an enormous market for everything from tricycles to books by Dr. Spock. As teens, the Baby Boomers purchased records, fast foods, and used cars in vast numbers. As young adults, they created boom markets in stereo equipment, sports cars, and sportswear. As we noted earlier, in the 1980s this group came into its peak buying years: ages 35 to 44. The 35- to 44-year-old segment is expected to reach its peak in the year 2000. The 25- to 34-year-old group is expected to reach its peak ten years before that.[31] Marketers using traditional life-cycle projections can expect this large group of people to be in the "full nest" stages when they make heavy purchases of appliances, food, furniture, and toys, as well as when they purchase services ranging from dental care to piano lessons.

Metropolitan Home magazine tailored itself to fit the changing needs of this generation. In the 1970s, as the Baby Boomers left home and set up their first independent households, the magazine was called *Apartment Life*. As the group married and entered its house-buying years, the magazine changed its name and editorial content to suit its subscribers. It now promotes itself as the magazine "Where the most potent generation in history finds its style."

Psychological Influences on Consumer Behavior

Up to now, we have concentrated on the kinds of things that influence a consumer as part of a group. But marketers know that individuals are unique and their behavior can only partially be explained by such factors as age, social class, and family role. Consequently, marketers use many concepts borrowed from psychology to explain what goes on in a consumer's mind during the buying-decision process.

The consumer's mind is often referred to as a "black box" because what goes on inside is largely hidden from market researchers. Two men, who seem very much alike, walk into a supermarket. One picks up a frozen TV dinner and the other heads for the fresh meat and produce sections. Why? The answer lies in the workings of their individual black boxes.

Motivation, perception, attitudes, personality, and learning are concepts familiar to psychologists that marketers have also found of enormous value.

Motivation

Human behavior is complex, and the phenomenon of motivation is one of its most perplexing aspects. Psychologists define **motivation** as an inner state that activates or moves people toward goals. To be motivated, individuals must feel pushed by an inner need or driving force, but they must also feel pulled toward a goal outside themselves.

Motivation
Inner state that activates or moves people toward goals.

Marketers are interested in discovering what motivates people to buy everything from chocolate chip cookies to condominiums, and in influencing people to meet needs with the marketers' products. Needs must be understood if marketing goals are to be correctly established. Psychologists have shown marketers that needs can be classified and that people are often unconscious of the needs that motivate them.

Maslow's Hierarchy A number of psychologists have proposed lists of needs considered basic to all humans. Abraham Maslow was the first to suggest a **need hierarchy,** or order in which human needs arise. Maslow proposed five basic levels of motivating needs and believed that when one need is at least partially satisfied, the need at the next highest level arises (Figure 6.6).[32]

Need Hierarchy
Theory of Abraham Maslow that there is an order in which human needs arise. When one need is at least partially satisfied, the need at the next highest level arises.

The first two levels of need are physical in nature. The most basic need is for the necessities of life—food, clothing, and shelter. Only when the need for these is partially satisfied do humans start feeling the need for physical safety, perhaps to protect the things gathered to fulfill the first need.

The next three levels are psychological. The need for love, affection, and belonging arises first. When people are secure with family and friends, they may then seek to enhance their own self-esteem, or sense of personal worth. Some try to do this by achievement (on the job, at a hobby), while others direct the need outward in search of prestige and recognition by others (collecting status symbols). After achieving some sense of personal worth, they may then feel the need for something even higher—to become fully developed as a human. This need may be satisfied by such activities as learning to play the piano, traveling, reading, or even running in a marathon.

Figure 6.6
Maslow's Hierarchy of Needs

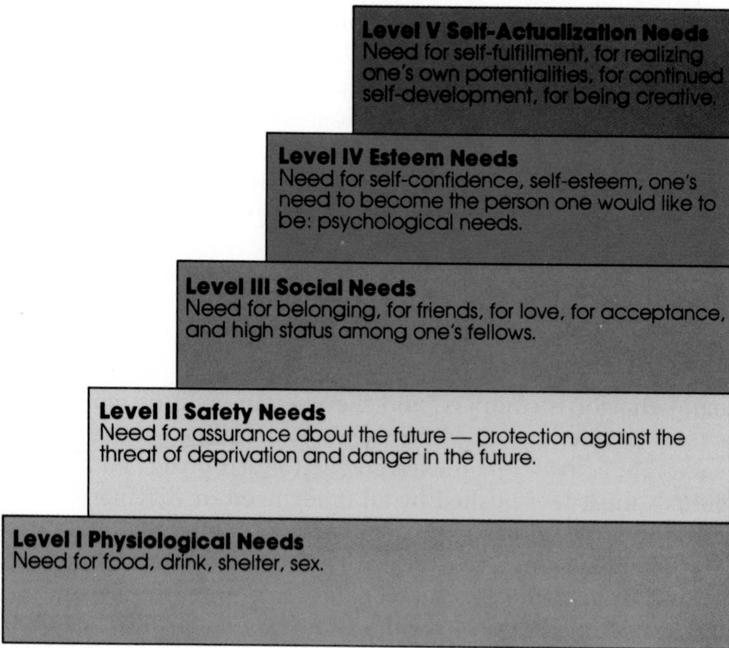

Level V Self-Actualization Needs
Need for self-fulfillment, for realizing one's own potentialities, for continued self-development, for being creative.
Level IV Esteem Needs
Need for self-confidence, self-esteem, one's need to become the person one would like to be: psychological needs.
Level III Social Needs
Need for belonging, for friends, for love, for acceptance, and high status among one's fellows.
Level II Safety Needs
Need for assurance about the future — protection against the threat of deprivation and danger in the future.
Level I Physiological Needs
Need for food, drink, shelter, sex.

Significance to Marketers Maslow's hierarchy is useful to marketing strategists in a number of ways. Understanding motives gives clues to the appropriate design of products. For example, a coat aimed at the low-income consumer who is concerned with satisfying basic physical needs would be designed differently from a coat for the high-income consumer who probably dresses for prestige and social status.

Some goods and services can be marketed only in societies that have reached a level at which physical needs are satisfied and psychological needs can be indulged. In a relatively affluent society like the United States, needs for affiliation, esteem, and self-actualization tend to dominate consumer behavior.[33]

Perception

Perception
Process by which an individual becomes aware of the environment and interprets it so that it fits into his or her frame of reference.

An individual will buy a product if motivated by a need. But to buy a specific product, the person must be aware of it, and that is where perception becomes important. **Perception** has been defined as the process by which an individual becomes aware of the environment and interprets it so that it fits into a frame of reference.[34] This definition recognizes that perception involves both an objective component (information brought by the sense of sight, hearing, touch, smell, and taste) and a subjective element (interpretation, in light of a person's experience).

The subjective component explains why people perceive things that are objectively the same as different. Researchers using blind taste tests, for example, have shown that most people cannot tell the difference between various colas. Tests of cigarettes and beer have produced similar results. Yet many people are loyal to one product or another and insist that these products are superior to others.

People tend to read their subjective feelings into a product, insisting qualities are "there" for everyone to see. Marketers, of course, play a role in encouraging such interpretations. When products are indistinguishable to the senses, marketers try to differentiate them by packaging, advertising, and other marketing tools.

Selective Exposure Every day you are barraged with information about goods and services. If you drive to work or school, you may hear ads on the radio or see billboards and signs along the road. If you take public transportation, you may see signs inside your train or bus, as well as advertisements in the magazine or newspaper you are reading. When you watch television in the evening, you see more ads. If you tried to pay attention to all of this information, you would probably be overwhelmed.

Consequently, people use a process called **selective exposure** to filter out information in which they are not interested. For example, if you don't drink coffee and are planning to buy a stereo, you probably would flip past the coffee ads in a magazine and stop to pore over the stereo ads.

Selective Exposure
Process of filtering out information that is not of interest.

Selective Perception People also filter out information that conflicts with their ideas and beliefs. This is called **selective perception.** For example, if you believe that compact disks are overrated but decide to ask the stereo dealer about them anyway, you probably will pay less attention to the positive attributes he cites than to the negative ones.

Selective Perception
Process of filtering out or modifying information that conflicts with one's ideas or beliefs.

Selective Retention Finally, people have a selective memory filter that causes them to remember mainly information that supports their ideas and beliefs. Filtering conflicting information from our memory is called **selective retention.** When you tell your friends about your conversation with the stereo dealer, you probably will remember only the dealer's arguments against buying a compact disk player.

Selective Retention
Memory of only what supports one's ideas or beliefs.

Implications for Marketers Over the years, marketing managers have devised strategies to bypass the consumer's mental filters. Advertisers in particular have succeeded somewhat in penetrating the attention barrier.

Repeating messages has been found to work both in increasing awareness and in reducing forgetfulness. Ralston-Purina, for example, uses cats in TV commercials to repeat again and again the brand name of its cat food Meow Mix.[35]

Advertisers have other techniques for penetrating perceptual barriers. Breaking with expectations can cause people to take notice. When Joe Namath pulled Hanes Beauty Mist pantyhose over his legs and gnarled knees, people noticed.

Attitudes

Attitude
State that includes a person's beliefs about and feelings toward some object, combined with a tendency to behave in a certain way with respect to that object.

Each one of us holds attitudes that affect our buying behavior. An **attitude** is a state that includes a person's beliefs about and feelings toward some object, coupled with a tendency to behave in a certain way with respect to that object.[36] Of particular interest to marketers are attitudes that include a predisposition to buy the marketer's product.

Marketers are very concerned about consumers' attitudes toward their products, since favorable attitudes often lead to higher usage rates and unfavorable ones are difficult to change.

Attitude Scale
Technique for measuring consumer attitudes that poses statements about which respondents are asked to indicate the intensity of their agreement or disagreement.

Attitude Measurement Marketers use several techniques to measure attitudes. Probably the most widely used method is the **attitude scale.** In this technique, consumers are asked to indicate the intensity of their agreement or disagreement with certain statements posed by the researcher. For example, a researcher might state, "Cigar smoke is offensive." Consumers would then respond either "strongly agree," "agree," "no opinion," "disagree," or "strongly disagree." (This set of choices is called the Likert scale.) Researchers would then tally the answers to get an indication of the strength of consumer opinions.

Changing Attitudes Reversing a negative attitude is perhaps the marketer's most difficult job. Sometimes it is impossible, and a product may have to be scrapped. When change is possible, promotion often plays a large part in the process.

In the face of declining coffee sales, for example, rivals General Foods and Procter & Gamble put aside their competitive tactics to support a $20 million campaign to promote coffee drinking to 18- to 34-year-olds. After years of commercials featuring Robert Young, the Pepsi Generation associated coffee drinking with being old and sedentary. The new campaign featured celebrities such as comedienne Jane Curtin and author Kurt Vonnegut drinking coffee at their jobs. In each case, coffee was portrayed as part of achieving goals, especially in creative fields. Whether the promotion will sell coffee is another question. The beer and soft-drink industries spend $700 million annually pitching their products to the same audience.[37]

Personality

Personality
Sum of characteristics that make a person what he or she is and distinguish each individual from every other individual.

Personality is one of those terms that everyone seems to understand, but few can define. For our purposes, **personality** is the sum of characteristics that make the person what he or she is and distinguish each individual from every other individual.[38] It is a broader concept than those discussed thus far and may even be said to include them.

Marketers are interested in the connection between an individual's personality and product or store choice. Most of the attempts to relate personality to products or store type have tried to link certain personality traits with the heavy use or loyal buying of a product.

Researchers select traits they feel may influence choice of the product in question. They then conduct studies to see if the hypothesized

Figure 6.7
The Learning Process

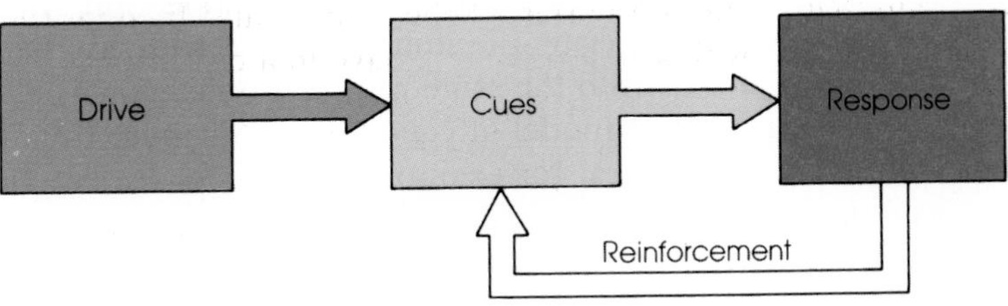

relationship exists. The results have been somewhat promising. By using this method, Anheuser-Busch, brewer of Budweiser, Michelob, and Busch beers, has been able to isolate four distinct personality types who drink beer. One of the groups identified was social drinkers, generally young people who tend to drink with friends on weekends or vacations. The company used this information to design ads for Michelob, the brand whose central target is the social drinker. In TV commercials, friends are shown gathering together and in the background the words "Weekends are made for Michelob" are heard. Anheuser-Busch reported increased sales for Michelob beer.[39]

Learning

Learning
Any change in an individual's response or behavior resulting from practice, experience, or mental association.

Learning, like personality, is a concept that underlies several others that have been discussed. It is defined as any change in an individual's response or behavior resulting from practice, experience, or mental association.[40]

Studies have shown that learning usually involves three basic steps: drive, cues, and response.[41] (See Figure 6.7.) A "drive" is the force that motivates an individual. Hunger, for example, is a particularly powerful drive. If a hungry person sees a sign for a pizza shop—a cue—the person might satisfy the drive by buying a pizza—the response. If the person likes the pizza, the response is reinforced. Hence, the next time the person is hungry, he or she might choose to seek out a pizza shop, and the cycle would begin again. Of course, the person may not like the pizza and may ignore pizza signs and look instead for a place to buy a hamburger.

Marketers can take a lesson from this cycle. Often they have only one opportunity to demonstrate a product to a consumer. If the product is good and satisfies the person, they may have a customer for life. But if a product is poor or fails to live up to expectations created by its advertising, a marketer may not get a second chance.

Theory of Conditioned Learning
View holding that learning takes place by association.

There are many theories about how learning takes place. Two are particularly helpful to marketers who want to influence consumer behavior. Ivan Pavlov's famous experiments with dogs led to the **theory of conditioned learning,** which holds that learning takes place by association. The

Russian psychologist presented hungry dogs with food while a bell rang in the background. Invariably, the dogs salivated. After several trials, the food was omitted; only the ringing bell was heard, but the dogs still salivated. The dogs had learned to associate one stimulus (food) with another (the bell's sound) and to link both to the same response (salivation).

Advertisers often use the model of conditioned learning. In a long-running commercial for Nestea, for example, consumers are taught to associate iced tea with a cooling plunge in a pool on a hot day. When warm weather arrives, the commercial implies, Nestea is a good substitute for a cool dive. The surge of iced-tea sales in the summer points to the effectiveness of the simple association.

Theory of Instrumental Learning
View that people learn to act in a certain way when some responses are rewarded (or reinforced) and others are punished.

Although often confused with conditioned learning, the **theory of instrumental learning** works with the response rather than the stimulus. This theory maintains that people learn to act in a certain way when some of their responses are rewarded (or reinforced) and others are punished. Reward strengthens the link between stimulus and response and increases the chances that the response will be repeated.

The instrumental model of learning is also valuable to marketers. Companies launching new food products often include a cents-off coupon in the package. They hope an early encouragement of repeat business will shape buying habits that will continue once the price incentive stops.

Applications of Learning Principles Over the years, a large body of data about conditioned and instrumental learning has developed. Principles of practical value to marketers include:

1. *Learning cannot be conditioned or reinforced in the absence of a felt need.* Consumers are not robots. They learn best when they are experiencing an intense need. No amount of ads for Nestea in the wintertime could increase sales significantly because consumers are not motivated by a physical need for cooling. Similarly, if a product is terrible, no amount of couponing will spur sales.
2. *Learning is fastest and most complete when people are actively involved.* Department stores often use demonstrations at cosmetic counters to involve consumers in a trial of their products. Advertising cannot involve consumers physically, but it can engage their minds and emotions. Jingles are an attempt to get people to carry the message away with them by repeating the song.
3. *People learn to generalize more easily than they learn to discriminate.* Marketers find it easier to teach consumers to transfer what they already know to a new situation. That is why many new products are introduced under the same brand name as an old product. For example, Dannon retained its brand name for a line of frozen yogurt products because consumers would be able to transfer the quality reputation of the original to the new product.

The ease with which people generalize their learning also explains why successful new products are widely imitated. Other companies quickly followed Dannon into the frozen yogurt market hoping that consumers would generalize favorable feelings from the product they already knew to other brands.[42]

Life-Styles

Some of the influences on buyer behavior that you have been reading about—attitudes, personality, and group characteristics—are related to consumers' life-styles. As you learned in Chapter 4, a person's life-style consists of his or her pattern of living as expressed in activities, interests, and opinions. Marketers are interested in life-styles because consumers tend to buy goods and services that are compatible with or appeal to their life-styles.

A major scheme for classifying according to life-style is the Stanford Research Institute's Value and Life-Styles (VALS) program.[43] This system classifies American adults as integrated, achievers, emulators, belongers, societally conscious, experientials, I-am-me's, and need-driven. Each group behaves differently in the marketplace.

People who are classified as integrated value maturity, individualism, tolerance, and a world view. Their buying styles focus on ecology, quality, esthetics, uniqueness, and high standards. Achievers are leaders in business, professions, and government. They value efficiency, fame, status, comfort, and materialism; as buyers, they look for luxury and high technology. Emulators strive to attain the life-style of achievers; they are ambitious, upwardly mobile, status-conscious, and competitive. They look for products that are conspicuous and fashionable. Belongers are traditional, conservative, and home-centered. They look for popular products and brand names.

People who are societally conscious support social causes and are attracted to simple living. As buyers, they look for conservation and authenticity. Experientials value direct experience and vigorous involvement; they are heavy consumers of products that involve crafts and sports. I-am-me's are dramatic, self-expressive, impulsive, and individualistic. As consumers, they tend to favor products that are faddish and striking.

Sustainers are struggling to survive, and they value instant gratification. They buy to satisfy basic needs and shop at local outlets. Survivors are typically older and poor; they value security and are authoritarian, rigid, and followers. They are cautious shoppers, seeking low price, familiar brand, guarantees, and reassurances.

Because consumers make different buying decisions based on their life-styles, marketers can use a classification such as this to tailor a product, advertising campaign, or distribution system to reach a certain segment of the population. For example, experientials might be more inclined to buy a car that is fun to drive, whereas emulators would be more attracted to a car that is associated with high status.

Consumer Buying: A Dynamic View

Previous chapters have shown, in a sense, still photos of the influence of various groups on purchase behavior and the inner mechanisms of the consumers's mind. But buying is an activity—a dynamic process. To understand it, the still shots must be spliced to make a motion picture.

Figure 6.8
A Model of Consumer Problem Solving

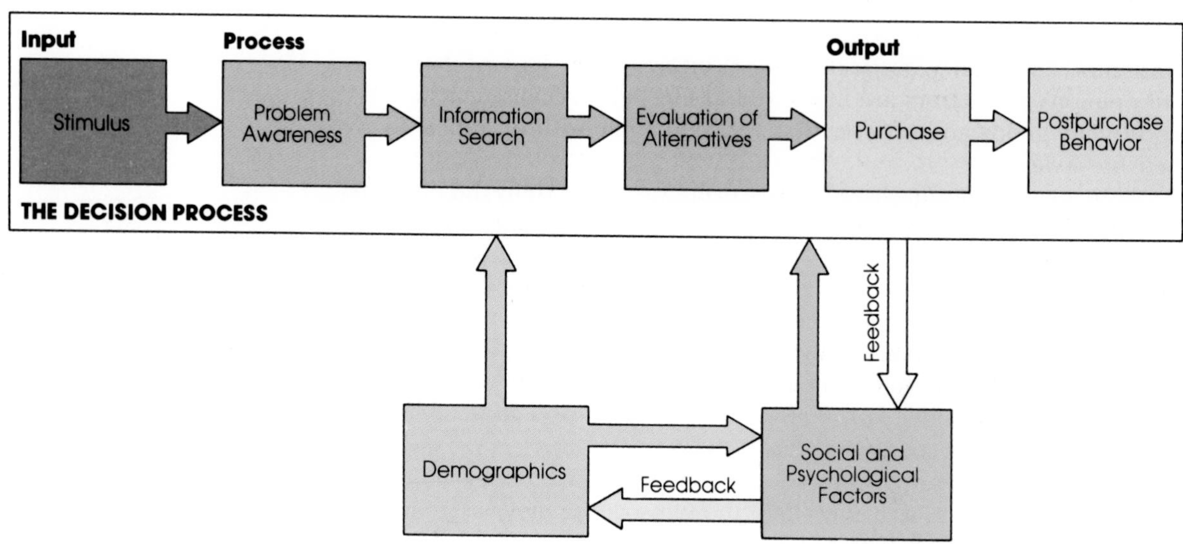

Researchers have proposed various models, or ways of representing how concepts from the social sciences fit together to describe consumer behavior. Most of the models recognize that buying involves problem solving. The problems vary in difficulty. For example, people put more time and effort into buying a car than purchasing a quart of milk. Whether the item is expensive and seldom purchased or cheap and bought frequently, some problem solving is involved.

Figure 6.8 presents one model of consumer problem solving. The model shows that buying involves three stages—input, processing, and output.[44]

Input

Input
Facts not in a consumer's control that may affect decisions to buy.

Input consists of all those facts not in the consumer's control that may affect a decision to buy. Any element of a firm's marketing mix (such as a special warranty, a newspaper ad, a sale, or the opening of a new outlet) may influence a person to think about buying.

Equally influential as a spur to buying is the input a consumer receives from social or cultural groups. The comment of a friend considered an opinion leader, the example of reference group members, or usage by a family member exposes an individual to products he or she might consider buying.

Processing

Inputs will have no effect unless the consumer chooses to act on them. Generally, action is triggered by recognition of a problem—an unsatisfied need.

Consider a hypothetical problem. Suppose that after attending a party at a friend's house, you decide to have a party. But a good party requires music, and you have no stereo. You have a social need (in Maslow's words) that you think can be satisfied by purchasing a stereo.

At this point, you may begin an active search for more information. The process of selective exposure lets in some of the information previously screened out. Ads for Sony, Panasonic, and Technics products now seem to appear everywhere. To learn how to evaluate these brands, you may look for more objective information (such as from *Consumer Reports*) or seek out the opinion of family and friends. (If the purchase had been of a more routine item like a record, you might have eliminated much of this prepurchase search and relied solely on past experience.)

In the next stage of problem solving, the alternatives must be evaluated. The criteria used in evaluating products vary. In the case of a stereo, you may want to consider sound quality, styling, brand name reputation, and cost. To decide which qualities have the most weight, you may fall back on previously formed attitudes. For example, you may prefer to pay a high cost for goods that will last a long time. Personality may also influence the evaluation. Recall that if you lack self-confidence, you may shop at a department store and look for well-known brands.

At the end of the evaluation stage, you are ready to buy. However, a purchase is not always made at this point. If you decide to give the most weight to price, for instance, you may have to wait until you have enough money to buy an expensive model or until the store you frequent has a sale.

Output

Output
Actual purchase and post-purchase evaluation by a consumer.

The model shows that **output** consists of the actual purchase and post-purchase evaluation.

In the case of new food or drug products, consumers are often encouraged to buy with an offer of a free or inexpensive "trial" package. In the case of the stereo, no such trial period is possible. The decision to purchase is equivalent to a full commitment to the product, and that is why, after buying major products, people often feel anxious about their decisions.

You may turn to friends for assurance that you made the right choice. You will probably also rely on your own judgment to evaluate the product. In both cases, instrumental learning is involved. Every time the stereo receives a compliment or performs up to par, your initial decision to purchase is reinforced or rewarded. What you learn will become part of your experience and serve to influence future decisions.

Much of what has been said here about buying by consumers applies to industrial purchases as well. The next chapter explores the similarities and differences between industrial and consumer buying.

Chapter Replay

1. **Why are cultures and subcultures important to marketers?**
The values of consumers' cultures and subcultures help shape what they buy. Marketers can look for trends in values that offer marketing opportunities.

2. **What kinds of groups can influence buying?**
The kinds of groups that can influence buying include social classes, reference groups (especially innovators and opinion leaders in these groups), the family, and age groups.

3. **In what order do human needs arise?**
According to Maslow's need hierarchy, physiological needs emerge first, then safety needs, social needs, esteem needs, and self-actualization needs.

4. **How do people filter information?**
People use selective exposure to filter out information they are not interested in. When they listen to a message, they use selective perception to filter out information that conflicts with their ideas and beliefs. They also tend to forget conflicting information; this is called selective retention.

5. **Why are marketers concerned about attitudes and personality?**
Marketers are concerned about attitudes because favorable attitudes often lead to higher usage rates, and unfavorable attitudes are difficult to change. Marketers are concerned about personality because certain traits may influence the choice of a particular product.

6. **What are two ways in which consumers learn?**
The theory of conditioned learning holds that learning takes place by association. Consumers may learn to associate a product with something pleasant and therefore learn to like the product. The theory of instrumental learning holds that people learn to act a certain way when their responses are rewarded, for example, through a product that delivers desired benefits.

7. **How do life-styles influence buyer behavior?**
Consumers tend to buy goods and services that are compatible with or appeal to their life-styles.

8. **What are the stages of the buying process?**
The stages of the buying process are input (stimulus), process (problem awareness, information search, and evaluation of alternatives), and output (purchase and postpurchase behavior).

Key Terms

aspirational group
attitude
attitude scale
buyer behavior
culture
dissociative group
family life cycle
innovator
input
learning

membership group
motivation
need hierarchy
opinion leader
output
perception
personality
reference group
role
selective exposure
selective perception
selective retention
social class
subculture
theory of conditioned learning
theory of instrumental learning

Discussion Questions

1. What are some current trends in American cultural values? If you can think of some trends not identified in the chapter, describe these as well.
2. What characteristics differentiate the social classes? John and Jake both got jobs within a week of graduating from high school. John went to work in a factory for $5 an hour and moved into an apartment with a friend. Jake became a bank teller at $4 an hour and saved money by living at home so that he could go to college in the evening. Does the difference in wages mean that John has higher social status than Jake? Why, or why not?
3. What is a reference group? What kinds of products can be sold by an appeal to a reference group?
4. How does the family shape buying behavior? How do marketers use this information?
5. When Terry Travis opened Terry's Tune-Up Shop last September, he had flyers distributed to all the homes in the neighborhood. The announcement read: "Terry's Tune-Up Shop Now Open on Main Street. Come in and get your car tuned up today!" During the next few weeks, business was so slow that Terry made phone calls to local homes to ask people whether they had seen the flyers or heard of his business. To Terry's dismay, most people could not recall seeing or hearing anything about Terry's Tune-Up Shop.

   How can you explain this situation in terms of perception? How might Terry overcome the perception problem?
6. "Above all, be polite to our customers," restaurant manager Myrna Byrd lectured the serving staff. "We can't afford rudeness here. If you are surly to a customer, we may never see that customer again."

   How does learning theory support Myrna's concern? How does your understanding of attitudes support her concern?
7. What personality type might be most interested in each of the following products?

   a. Ski equipment
   b. An obviously expensive home entertainment system
   c. A membership in a consumerist group

8. How do marketers try to influence a buyer's choice during the input, processing, and output stages of the buying process?

Case 6.1 California Beef Council (C)

The California Beef Council (CBC) supports and works with the National Livestock and Meat Board in developing marketing plans for beef. As a result, the CBC was very interested in a Meat Board report on the values and life-styles of Americans and their meat consumption. The following material summarizes the report.

Today's Consuming American

The life-style of today's consumer is dramatically different from that of his or her parents. Consumers today watch more television, for example, eat away from home more often, have fewer children, and spend less of their overall budgets on food and red meat.

The U.S. Department of Agriculture says that on a retail basis, the average consumer ate approximately 145.5 pounds of red meat in 1981, with average consumers spending about 3.3 percent of their total disposable income ($291.25) on meat. Those figures compare with 135.9 pounds and 4.2 percent of the income in 1965.

Those figures only tell half the story, however. Although they are effective in describing something about levels of production and the general outline of demand, they do not tell much about the people who are buying meat. The marketplace is changing rapidly, and the consumer of today may not have the same needs and wants as the consumer of yesterday.

VALS Research

One of the most recent research projects trying to identify and categorize attitudes among the different segments of our population is being conducted at the Stanford Research Institute in California. The project is called VALS—Values and Life-Styles—and tries to go beyond demographic statistics to describe specific attitudes and traits exhibited by different parts of American society. These traits can give marketers a better idea of the needs and wants of the audience they are trying to reach.

In effect, VALS breaks down the nation's adult buying population into eight segments, analyzing the character of each. VALS gathered data through extensive interviews with consumers around the country, dealing with the economic, social, and emotional makeup of the individ-

Source: Adapted from an article in *Meat Board Reports,* January 1983, published by the National Livestock and Meat Board.

ual. Instead of measuring a person's direct attitude about a specific product, VALS tries to get an understanding of people's attitudes toward life in general—and why they make the decisions they do.

The largest segment of the American society identified by VALS research is the "Belongers," or those people who are patriotic, stable, sentimental traditionalists of any age, basically content with their lives. Belongers represent about one-third of the American population, according to the research. Another quarter of the population consists of "Achievers," who are prosperous and middle-aged materialists. Young adults who are ambitiously trying to break into the "Achievers" group are known as "Emulators," and represent about 10 percent of the population.

Another 9 percent fall into the "Societally Conscious" group, which is composed of mission-oriented people who like causes and are usually affluent and well educated. The people in this group are sometimes considered to be the opposite of those who are "Achievers." Seven percent of the population are "Sustainers," who have a hard time making ends meet. They are often minorities, have little education, and are, on average, young. An equal number of people are considered "Experiential," or highly educated younger people with good incomes who are directed toward "inner growth."

Experimental, fiercely individualistic young people belong to the "I-Am-Me" group, which includes 5 percent of the U.S. population. This group is composed of persons who are usually single and who are faddish and often outlandish. The final group is made up of people who are old and poor, with little optimism about the future. They are the "Survivors," who make up about 4 percent of the population. Many are female, according to the research, with little income and little education.

Because they are poor, Survivors and Sustainers are considered to be need-driven, with little actual choice as to the products and services they buy. Belongers, Emulators, and Achievers are considered to be the mainstream of society and "outer driven." They conduct their lives in response to real or imagined signals from others within society. The other segments—I-Am-Me, Experiential, and Societally Conscious—are considered "inner directed" because they conduct their lives in accordance with inner needs and desires rather than in accord with values received from others.

VALS Research and the Meat Industry

By finding out which groups eat meat products most frequently, the meat industry can determine the general attitudes held by consumers buying their products. For example, as shown in the Exhibit, beef and pork are, in general, consumed more than average by the outer-directed group, while lamb and veal are more commonly consumed by the Achievers and inner-directed group. By matching the characteristics of the products with the characteristics of the consumers being reached, a more clear understanding emerges of how the product fits into the marketplace.

Exhibit

	Total Adults (%)	Meat Eaten by VALS Group in Last 7 Days				
		Beef (Index)	Bacon (Index)	Pork (Index)	Lamb (Index)	Veal (Index)
Need-Driven						
Survivors	3.9	64	74	67	21	41
Sustainers	7.1	77	96	87	54	97
Outer-Directed						
Belongers	38.6	98	104	101	96	92
Emulators	8.1	102	106	104	62	64
Achievers	21.4	115	105	114	125	124
Inner-Directed						
I-Am-Me	3.1	90	87	84	174	123
Experiential	6.1	95	92	80	36	130
Societally Conscious	11.8	109	93	100	160	105
Total percentage who ate this meat last seven days		72.8	55.6	47.7	4.6	4.9

But matching these characteristics also raises some questions that the meat industry needs to consider. How important are each of the segments in relation to the other segments? Where should the different messages be targeted for maximum effectiveness? How much importance should the industry place on economic considerations as opposed to consumer nutritional or quality perceptions of meat products?

Focal Topics

1. What is your general evaluation of VALS research as a way of studying consumer markets?
2. In what ways can the VALS information be used to develop a marketing plan for beef?
3. What other types of consumer information would you like to have to help develop a beef marketing plan?

Case 6.2
M & M Products, Inc.

In 1973, two young black pharmacists named Cornell McBride and Therman McKenzie each invested $250 and went into business marketing a hair spray for black men that would keep their hair soft. The two

Source: Adapted from Mill Roseman, "The Black Consumer Market: Problem or Opportunity," *Madison Avenue,* May 1983, pp. 66–70; Sarah Lum, "Ethnic Hair Care—A Growing Market," *Madison Avenue,* May 1983, p. 72; and Ezra K. Davidson, "Success of Hair Care Company Illustrates Progress of Black-Owned Businesses in the U.S.," *The Wall Street Journal,* September 15, 1983, p. 29ff.

men developed the spray while studying pharmacy in Atlanta. After graduation, they worked during the day for a large drugstore chain and spent their evenings taking business courses and preparing to run their own company. In 1983, the company they started and still own had become the 11th largest black business in the United States, according to *Black Enterprise* magazine. Sales in 1983 reached $47.3 million.

Black Hair-Care Market

From all dimensions, the statistics for blacks in the United States are impressive. Blacks represent about 12 percent of the total population, with aggregate income estimated between $140 and $160 billion. With allowances for the generally recognized income differentials, on a per-capita basis it is a fair assumption that blacks represent at least 8 percent of all the dollars spent on consumer goods and services. In addition, all indications point to a disproportion in the way black consumers spend their dollars. In many categories, their expenditures significantly exceed the proportion of income devoted by consumers in general.

It is estimated that blacks use about 36 percent of the hair-care products sold in the United States. The general hair-care market has been growing at a rate of less than 5 percent annually, while the rate of growth for ethnic hair-care products is rising at an annual increase of 15 to 20 percent, according to the American Health and Beauty Aids Institute, a 15-member association representing minority-owned hair-care and cosmetics companies.

During 1982, the health and beauty aids market in the United States was estimated at $10 billion. Blacks accounted for some $2 billion in that market, with more than $800 million being spent on ethnic products. It is estimated that blacks spend three-and-a-half to five times as much as whites on health and beauty aids, making the black market the fastest-growing segment of the industry.

Product Offerings

Madame C. J. Walker is generally credited with starting the black hair-care market in the early part of this century. She developed products aimed at straightening the hair of black women, who often viewed their hair as a symbol of slavery and viewed straight hair as a sign of privilege. Mrs. Walker, the daughter of slaves, was so successful that she is considered the first black woman millionaire.

George E. Johnson, president of Johnson Products, is generally considered the founder of the present-day, black hair-care industry. He founded his company in the 1950s with a line of hair-care products named Ultra Sheen. Within the next 20 years, more than 100 black-owned hair-care companies followed Mr. Johnson into the marketplace. Today, three of the 12 largest companies in *Black Enterprises'* ranking of the 100 largest black-owned businesses are in the hair-care field.

There are six basic product categories in the black hair-care market: conditioners and hair dress products, comb-easy conditioner lotions, blow-out and creme relaxers, hair sprays for sheen and aerosol products, perm products and permanent curl kits, and curl activators. Of these, the current hottest category is the permanent curl (or cold wave) treatment introduced by Jhirmack to the professional market in 1978. It was brought to the retail market in 1980.

M & M Products

Working in the basement of his three-room home, Mr. McBride and his partner, Mr. McKenzie, mixed the first batch of their hair spray in a 55-gallon drum and stirred it with a pool cue. Their families helped them mix and bottle the spray, which was marketed under the brand name Sta-Sof-Fro. In the summer of 1974, a year after founding their company, both quit their jobs to devote full time to the business.

In the beginning, the two marketed the product themselves. Larger retailers were skeptical, so they focused on small stores, making deliveries in their own cars. The product caught on, and the big retailers became interested in carrying the product. In 1977, four years after its founding, M & M Products reached annual sales of more than $1 million.

Around 1978, the "curl" style for blacks became popular—the first major change in hair styles for blacks since the Afro began in the late 1960s. M & M Products again recognized the need for specialized products and began to add to their growing array of consumer offerings. By 1983, the company was marketing 65 hair-care products with sales in Canada, Europe, Africa, and the Caribbean, as well as in the United States. The company employs 400 people, most of them black, and spends nearly $4 million a year on advertising.

Focal Topics

1. What consumer behavior concepts do you feel are appropriate to consider in the marketing of hair-care products to all market segments?
2. How might these concepts apply differently to M & M Products' consumers compared with other consumer groups?
3. What types of marketing research would be helpful for M & M Products to better understand its consumers?

7 Organizational Buying Behavior

Sounding Out the Chapter

In this chapter, you will learn:

1. How the industrial market is important to the U.S. economy.
2. Differences between the industrial and consumer markets.
3. Major classes of industrial products.
4. The nature of demand in the industrial sector.
5. What influences buyer behavior in the industrial sector.
6. Types of buying decisions in the industrial sector.
7. Principal roles in industrial buying situations.
8. Why some companies lease rather than buy certain products.

Source: Courtesy of Alaska Seafood Marketing Institute.

Selling Seafood to Restaurants

While restaurants are advertising for your business, other marketers are advertising to the restaurants. One of these advertisers is the Alaska Seafood Marketing Institute (ASMI), an organization jointly sponsored by the State of Alaska and the state's seafood industry. The ASMI has run ads for "the hottest steak in America" (Alaska salmon steaks) and "All-American cod." The advertisements appear in specialized magazines such as *Restaurants and Institutions, Restaurant Business, Foodservice Product News,* and *Restaurant Hospitality.*

Some of the criteria restaurants use in choosing foods differ from those that families use. For example, a restaurant owner is interested in preparing dishes that can be sold at a profit. The ASMI targeted this objective in its holiday advertising for king crab. The ads compared king crab to lobster, its major competitor in the marketplace for elegant shellfish. The message was that restaurateurs could buy king crab for less than lobster and that lobster is more work to prepare. The implication: Higher profits result from serving king crab.

Another campaign promoted Alaska seafood generally. A series of advertisements featured the "Northern Lites"—Alaska's high-protein, vitamin- and mineral-rich seafoods, which are low in saturated fat. Because it is more difficult to target such advertisements to a specific market segment, such as white-tablecloth restaurants, these ads usually run only in magazines that reach the seafood industry.

Besides advertising, the ASMI promotes Alaska seafood at trade shows and provides stories, information, and photographs to publications for the food service industry. An appealing recipe might encourage a chef at a restaurant to begin serving Alaska seafood. The ASMI also provides such information to consumer publications; increased consumer demand would encourage restaurants to order more seafood.

Marketing to restaurants uses many of the same techniques as marketing to consumers, but organizations do not always make buying decisions in the same way consumers do. Marketers to organizations therefore must understand organizational buying behavior. This chapter looks at the industrial market and describes how organizational purchasing decisions are made.

Source: Alaska Seafood Marketing Institute, *Annual Report,* Juneau, Alaska, 1986.

Figure 7.1
Selected Suppliers of Component Parts for a Ford Automobile

Source: Data from "Are U.S. Cars Really Getting Better?" *U.S. News & World Report*, August 29, 1983, p. 57.

As buyers of consumer goods, we are often only dimly aware of the bustle of purchasing activity that preceded an item's appearance in the local supermarket, shopping mall, or dealer's showroom. Consider, for example, the many buying decisions that went into assembling the components of the family car: one company supplied the glass for the windows, another the steel for the body, still others the carpeting for the floors, the vinyl for the seats, the bulbs for the lights, and the locks for the doors. (See Figure 7.1.) Even before these parts could be purchased, however, they too had to be manufactured, necessitating even more buying decisions. The steelmakers bought barges of iron ore, the vinyl manufacturers purchased trucks of petroleum products, and the glass producers shopped around for a good price on silicon. In addition, manufacturing equipment had to be purchased to turn these raw materials into finished goods.

Besides the obvious products used in manufacturing, consider the many other supplies a company needs to buy in order to function: soap

Table 7.1
Number and Kinds of Organizational Buyers

Services	5,374,000
Agriculture, forestry, and fisheries	518,000
Retailers	2,849,000
Finance, insurance, and real estate	2,150,000
Construction	1,551,000
Wholesalers	590,000
Manufacturers	531,000
Governmental units	82,000
Others	983,000
Total	14,628,000

Source: *Statistical Abstract of the United States,* 1986.

for workers' hands, cardboard cartons for shipping, office forms for invoices, and filters for the coffee machine. Depending on the company, it may have purchased anything from paper clips to a Lear jet to enable it finally to manufacture that car in the driveway. From the first crude lump of iron ore to the final squirt of rustproofing, someone in the industrial sector had to make a buying decision.

What Is the Industrial Market?

The **industrial market** is composed of businesses (manufacturers, wholesalers, and retailers), governments (federal, state, and local), and organizations (universities, hospitals, nursing homes, and others) that buy products and services for resale or for use in producing other products and services.

Industrial Market
Businesses, governments, and organizations that buy goods and services for resale or for use in producing other goods and services.

This market is much larger than the consumer market. More than 14 million different industrial buying organizations (see Table 7.1), which employ more than 113 million workers, generate an annual income of more than three trillion dollars![1]

Industrial marketing accounts for well over half the economic activity in the United States and Canada, and more than half of all business school graduates enter industrial product or service firms.[2] Given these figures, it becomes clear how important it is to include this vast range of activity in our study of marketing.

Differences between Consumer and Industrial Markets

While many of the issues discussed concerning consumer buying behavior also hold true for the industrial market, there are some important differences between the two markets.

Fewer Buyers

The scope of industrial buying is vast, but it is startling to realize how few buyers actually account for the enormous sums. In 1982, there were fewer than half a million manufacturing firms in the United States. Yet these firms spent over $1 *trillion* for materials.[3]

These numbers are not so surprising when one considers that a company such as Boeing need only sell a few jumbo jets, worth a few million dollars each, to a handful of customers in order to have a profitable year. By contrast, McDonald's must sell a few million hamburgers to a few million people to do as well.

Geographical Concentration

Not only are there fewer buyers in the industrial market, but their numbers are greatly concentrated in certain areas of the country. Manufacturing industries in eight states—California, Illinois, Texas, Ohio, Pennsylvania, Michigan, New York, and New Jersey—accounted for half of total U.S. shipments in 1985.[4] Among nonmanufacturing industries, the top ten states in 1985 were Texas, California, New York, Illinois, Pennsylvania, Ohio, Michigan, Florida, New Jersey, and Massachusetts. These states accounted for over half of 1985 receipts to nonmanufacturing industries.[5]

This concentration of activity has important implications for marketers. Companies that sell to the industrial sector can effectively concentrate their efforts in areas of high market potential. Often companies will locate a full-time personal sales force in these markets. In addition, they may locate distribution facilities in large-volume areas so that major customers can be assured speedy delivery.[6]

Nature of Demand

Another important difference between industrial and consumer markets is the nature of the demand for goods. The demand for products in the consumer market is direct: if consumers want houses, they buy houses, and the number can be easily measured. But demand in the industrial market is not so simple. If consumers buy houses, builders buy plumbing supplies, lumber, roofing shingles, and nails. If consumers stop buying, the need for all these goods may decrease. Thus, the demand for industrial products is a derived demand—it depends ultimately on how much consumers are willing to buy.

Industrial marketers therefore watch changes in consumer buying patterns carefully. Economic factors, changes in consumer tastes, or new government regulations all have important effects on industrial markets. For example, when the military cuts spending, Lockheed may have less business. Or when consumers demand better gasoline mileage, automakers buy lighter materials to use in making cars.

Figure 7.2
Classification of Industrial Goods

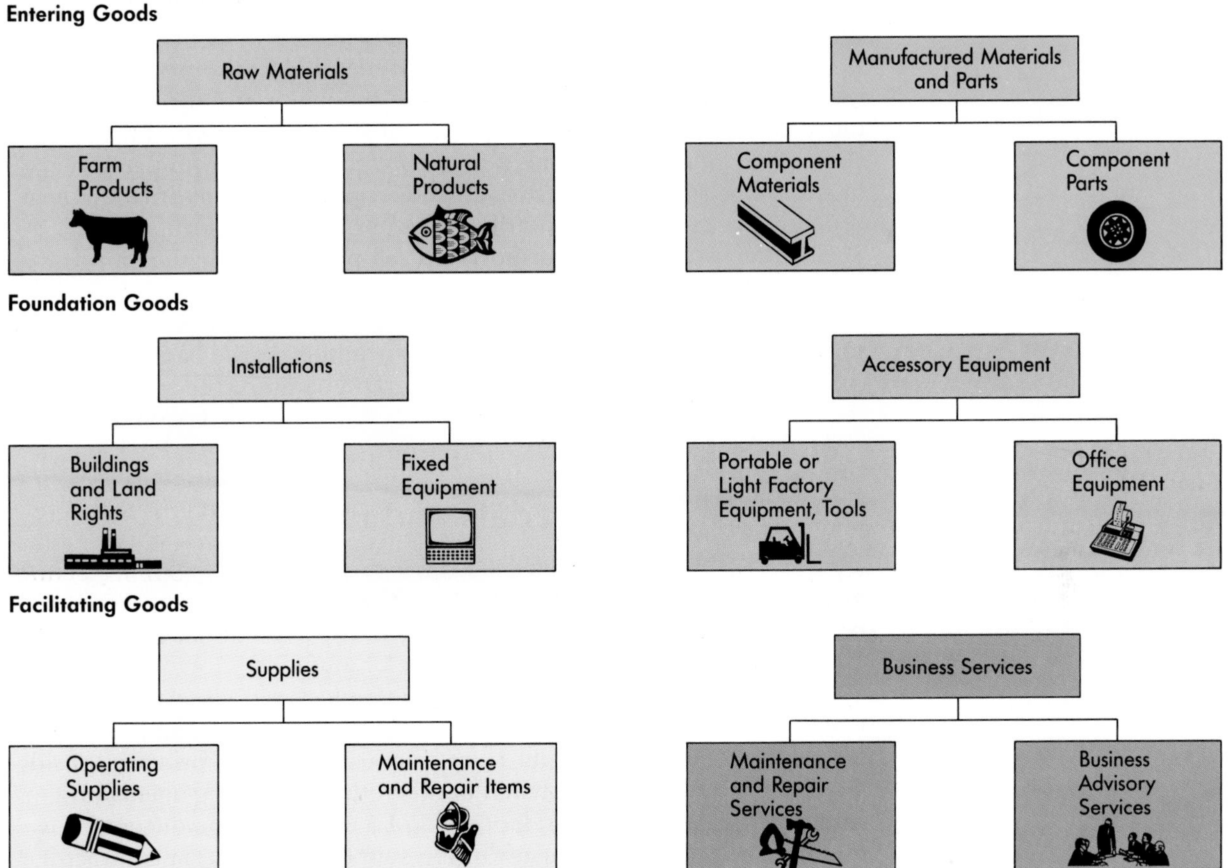

Source: Philip Kotler, *Marketing Management: Analysis, Planning, and Control,* 4th ed., © 1980, p. 172. Adapted by permission of Prentice-Hall, Inc., Englewood Cliffs, N.J.

Industrial Products and the Marketing Mix

Another difference between consumer and industrial markets rests in the kinds of products that each buys. An earlier example showed that automotive manufacturers need everything from sheet metal to paper clips to get a car to a dealer's showroom. While companies may buy large quantities of each of these products, the way in which each company acquires them may be quite different.

Planning a marketing strategy for the tens of thousands of industrial products sold would be impractical without some way of classifying them. One of the most practical classification systems is based on their use. There are six major classes: (1) raw materials, (2) manufactured materials and parts, (3) installations, (4) accessory equipment, (5) supplies, and (6) business services. (See Figure 7.2.)

Raw Materials

Raw Material
Natural resource such as crude oil or a cultivated product such as wheat used in the production of finished products.

All manufactured products are composed of **raw materials,** which are natural resources such as crude oil, iron ore, and other minerals, or cultivated products such as wheat, cotton, and timber. Raw materials can be very important to food processors like General Mills. Consequently, the initial buying of raw materials may be in the hands of a top executive, though the regular purchase thereafter can be handled by company purchasing agents. Raw materials may be bought directly from producers, or they may be purchased through cooperatives like Sunkist (which markets oranges grown on numerous farms) or through distributors like Shell and Exxon (which transport and sell petroleum for the oil-producing nations of the world).

The price of raw materials rarely varies from producer to producer, so purchasing agents often make up their minds on the basis of who can supply a steady flow of quality material. To guarantee the supply, agents may negotiate long-term contracts, or they may buy from many suppliers.

Manufactured Materials and Parts

Manufactured Materials (Manufactured Parts)
Industrial goods that have in some way been shaped or finished and are incorporated into another product.

Goods that have in some way been shaped or finished and incorporated into another product are known as **manufactured materials,** or **manufactured parts.** As shown in Figure 7.1, such parts and materials are especially important to the manufacture of automobiles.

The marketing strategy for selling manufactured parts and materials is similar to that for selling raw materials. In both cases, purchases are frequent, and a steady supply—not price—is often the primary consideration. Contracts are negotiated between the purchasing agents of a company and the sales representatives of a supplier. One difference is that design considerations can win the supplier a long-term contract if the supplier can promise to build to the specifications requested by the buyer.

Installations

Installation
Large, expensive, industrial product necessary for the production of final products but not a part of those goods—for example, industrial plants and major equipment.

Large, expensive goods necessary for the production of final products, although they do not become a part of those products, are known as **installations.** Factory sites, such as the automobile plants of Detroit, and major equipment, such as machine tools, fall into this category.

The purchase of installations is a major decision, and sales negotiations usually take place over long periods of time. The top personnel of the buyer company and the technical experts and high officials of the selling company often conduct negotiations for installations. Thus, when Volkswagen decided to purchase a factory site in the United States, top-level executives for Volkswagen deliberated with state officials, experts, and upper management of the Chrysler Corporation before deciding on a former Chrysler facility at New Stanton, Pennsylvania.[7] Negotiations over major equipment can last equally as long because machinery sometimes has to be made to engineering and production specifications. The final decision to buy is usually made less on price than on the installation's expected performance. Obviously, a relatively cheap computer that keeps breaking down would prove a very expensive item for a company. Because price is not often the major consideration, sellers must attract buyers in other ways, such as providing leasing or rental arrangements and service guarantees. IBM business computer equipment, for example, may require too much capital for a small company to buy outright and may be too complex to be maintained by the company's personnel. Therefore, IBM often rents equipment to companies and sends in technicians to set up a system for a client.

Accessory Equipment

Like major equipment, **accessory equipment** does not become part of the final product, although it is necessary to the final product's manufacture. Included in this category are hardware of all sorts, such as hand tools and drills, and office equipment, such as typewriters and adding machines.

Accessory Equipment
Less expensive industrial product necessary to the final product's manufacture though not part of it—for example, hand tools and office equipment.

Because accessory equipment is less expensive and needs replacement or parts on a regular basis, responsibility for purchase is generally given to a company purchasing agent who specializes in equipment and can follow up on any purchases. Companies that manufacture accessory equipment may depend upon **industrial distributors,** wholesalers who sell to the industrial market, to sell their products. To supplement the efforts of the wholesalers, manufacturers sometimes advertise equipment in such trade magazines as *Industrial Equipment News* and *Plant Engineering*. Purchasing agents generally shop around for the best price, so extras like rental arrangements and service guarantees can be important. Figure 7.3 shows an example of an advertisement for this type of product.

Industrial Distributor
Wholesaler who sells to the industrial market.

Supplies

Products needed for the maintenance or repair of equipment or for the operation of a business are classified as **supplies.** Light bulbs, lubricating oil, paper clips, and adding machine tape may not be part of a finished product, but they are often essential to its manufacture or sale.

Supplies
Industrial products needed for the maintenance or repair of equipment or for the operation of a business.

Supplies are regularly used up and must be purchased constantly. Purchasing departments have informal or contractual supplying arrangements with wholesale intermediaries. Computer systems greatly reduce reordering chores that were once done by clerks. When supplies are first purchased, price is the primary consideration, and price competition among wholesalers for a contract can be fierce. Thereafter, price may play a relatively insignificant role, since purchasers are unwilling to spend time searching out bargains for small, inexpensive items. For the seller, therefore, the basic strategy is to get in early and maintain good relationships.

Business Services

Organizations often turn to specialists outside the firm to perform specific functions. Services may include maintenance and repair support (e.g., window cleaning, copier repair) or advisory support (e.g., management

FRY, FRY, FRY AGAIN

Save money by making fat last longer with Keating's Instant Recovery 14" Gas Fryer.

The Keating Trump Special is a low-temperature specialist. It lets you fry at temperatures from 325°F to 335°F, so you can turn out portion after portion without fat breakdown.

A patented temperature control system is so precise it keeps fat within two degrees of any temperature you set between 250°F and 350°F.

With high-input burners, another patented feature, the Trump Special preheats in less than seven minutes and recovers temperature instantly, even under the heaviest load conditions.

What's more, a full range of signals and controls makes perfect frying almost automatic, even for a beginner. The front drain design permits ease of filtering. And, pilotless ignition makes this energy-efficient gas fryer even more efficient.

KEATING OF CHICAGO, INC.®

To learn all the benefits of this Keating gas fryer contact:
Keating of Chicago, Inc.,
715 So. 25th Avenue,
Bellwood, Illinois 60104;
(312) 544-6500.

Gas. America's best energy value.

When you compare the costs and benefits of all energies, natural gas continues to be your best value.

CALL F.I.R.S.T. ITEM # 53

At Your Service 7.1
Temporary Employees, New Employees, Transferred Employees

The Dunhill Personnel System provides business services in a variety of ways, including temporary help, searches for new employees, and employee relocation.

Dunhill Temporary Systems provides temporary help to business. This is a service that many businesses are turning to these days. The Department of Commerce reports that temporary help services are one of the nation's fastest-growing industries. Dunhill Temporary Systems meets this demand with a network of franchises serving local markets. A computerized accounting system enables the franchisees to promote their ability to provide individualized billing.

The Dunhill Personnel System also offers franchises to those who want to provide personnel recruitment services. These services include senior- and middle-management search, technical recruiting, and office personnel. In addition, the company offers a Relocation Management Program, which includes selling a transferred employee's home and helping him or her find a new home. The relocation service also arranges for the employee's move to the new location.

Source: Brochures from Dunhill Personnel System, Inc., including "A Dunhill Personnel Franchise," "A Dunhill Temporary Systems Franchise," and "The Dunhill International Search & Relocation Program."

consulting, legal counsel, advertising, and public relations services).[8] At Your Service 7.1 describes a company that provides personnel services.

Industrial Demand

Derived Demand

As discussed earlier, one of the essential differences between industrial and consumer marketing is that in industry, demand for a product is based on what a buying organization's customers want—**derived demand**—not what the organization itself wants. Because consumers ultimately determine industrial demand, occasionally an industrial marketer will develop a campaign directed at a product's final buyer. An ad for potatoes (see Figure 7.4), for example, mentions no specific brand or store. The industry group paying for the ad is mentioned only in a footnote at the bottom of the ad. The advertisement simply seeks to encourage consumers to eat potatoes even if they are on a diet. In response to consumer demand for potatoes, grocery store and restaurant managers will buy more of this vegetable. Similarly, an ad for canned food (see Figure 7.5) encourages consumer demand for this form of packaging.

Derived Demand
Demand by industrial users that depends on consumer demand for the finished product.

Fluctuating Demand

Because demand in the industrial sector is derived from consumer preferences, it may fluctuate widely in response to changing economic conditions or when consumer tastes change. Since **fluctuating demand**

Fluctuating Demand
Demand in the industrial sector that may vary widely in response to changing economic conditions or changes in consumer tastes.

Figure 7.3
Advertisement for an Industrial Market

Can you recognize America's favorite diet food?

A potato is one diet food that's hard to disguise.

Because no matter how you dress it up, it's still full of things that are good for you. Without the things that aren't.

A medium-sized potato,* for example, has only about 110 calories — fewer than a cup of yogurt. Or a six-ounce serving of cottage cheese. Or even a green salad with dressing.

And a potato is 99.9% fat free. And 100% cholesterol free.

Plus, potatoes are packed with nutrients your body needs. Like Vitamin C, iron, fiber and hard-to-find Vitamin B_6. All at pennies per serving.

So when planning your next menu, remember. The diet food you've been looking for is right under your nose.

Potatoes. America's Favorite Vegetable.

*150 grams, round type, boiled in skin. Source: "Nutrition Labeling, Tools For Its Use," USDA Bulletin No. 382. 1983–84 National Consumption Study. © 1984 The Potato Board

Figure 7.5
Advertisement from the Canned Food Information Council

IN THE YEAR 3000, FOOD WILL
COME IN AMAZING CONTAINERS THAT
SAVE NUTRIENTS, FRESHNESS AND TIME.
IT WILL BE FOOD IN CANS.
The question isn't when canned foods began. It's when you discover them. Canned foods are convenient. Time-saving. Versatile. Healthy. And good. They go into everything from salsa to soufflés. And from baby peas to pineapple rings, they can be very impressive. Who says you have to be new to be very, very modern.
CANNED FOOD
INFORMATION COUNCIL

Source: Courtesy of National Food Processors Association.

influences not only inventory levels and warehousing needs, but also has serious effects on production, many industrial marketers have diversified their product lines.

Joint Demand

In some cases, demand for one product will be affected by the availability of another product with which it is used. This is called **joint demand.** For example, record manufacturers need vinyl for records and card-

Joint Demand
Market condition when demand for one product will be affected by the availability of another product with which it is used.

Figure 7.4
Advertisement from the Potato Board
Source: Courtesy of The National Potato Board.

board for slip cases. If petroleum shortages affect the supply of vinyl, resulting in diminished record production, then industrial buyers may cut back on the amount of cardboard they purchase.

Inelastic Demand

Inelastic Demand
Demand that remains relatively constant despite price changes.

Although demand for a manufactured product may be seriously affected by changes in the consumer market, within the industrial market, demand remains relatively constant despite price changes. This is known as **inelastic demand.** Since most industrial products are composed of many parts, price increases on one or two of the parts may result in a slightly higher cost to the consumer but will not seriously affect how much of that item a manufacturer purchases. If consumer demand for products containing NutraSweet remains high, manufacturers will continue to buy it instead of saccharin despite the product's higher cost.

Buying Behavior in Industrial Markets

In many ways, the industrial buying process is similar to that of families. For everyday items (e.g., ketchup or paper clips), one member may routinely buy a preferred brand. On the other hand, major decisions—a new refrigerator or computer installation—may involve a lengthy search for information and long deliberations over size, price, and features among a family or organization's decision makers.

Just as marketers must understand what influences consumer buying behavior, they also must recognize the factors that affect buying decisions within an organization.

Criteria for Industrial Purchases

Because businesses are motivated by profit considerations and governments and institutions must be accountable for their budgeted expenses, economic considerations such as price, quality, features, and service are often the primary considerations of industrial buyers. Unfortunately for marketers, various members of the buying organization may place different emphasis on these factors. A company's engineers, for example, may stress quality, and the purchasing agent may value maximum price economy. The weight of each of these factors and the influence of each participant may vary with the organization and the type of product being considered.[9] The challenge for marketers is to determine who among the participants has the final say—and what that person values most.

Continuity of supply is also an important consideration for an industrial marketer. Because interruption in the flow of materials can bring the production process to a grinding halt, industrial buyers are often reluctant to rely on a single source for supplies. This is especially true when there are few alternative suppliers.[10]

Marketing Today 7.1
What Hidden Forces Motivate the Machine Tool Buyer?

Can marketers use psychographic research in industrial advertising and sales? One of the few attempts to answer that question was a study of 200 industrial buyers done by psychologist Bruce J. Morrison.

Morrison studied four groups of industrial buyers: managers, purchasing agents, design engineers, and production engineers. Each group, he found, had distinct personality traits that influenced the way in which they perceived advertising and selling appeals.

Design and production engineers, for example, tend to have low anxiety levels and a sense of personal control over their environments. They prefer advertising that shows solutions to problems and specific engineering information.

Managers and purchasing agents tend to be more anxious than engineers and feel controlled by their environment. They also tend to have authoritarian personalities.

The best way to reach managers, Morrison suggests, is to design advertising around "modern, aggressive, idea presentations—the big picture approach." Managers are anxious to succeed and willing to take risks to move their companies ahead.

Purchasing agents, on the other hand, like facts and figures and are fond of wheeling and dealing. Morrison found that purchasing agents are "subjective fellows striving for status." Ads geared to them should stress quality, reliability, delivery, and company image.

Based on this information, Elco Industries, Inc., a manufacturer of specialty metal components, felt confident that its advertising strategy was on target. Advertising directed at design engineers, for example, stressed the full range of capabilities of Elco's custom-engineered metal components.

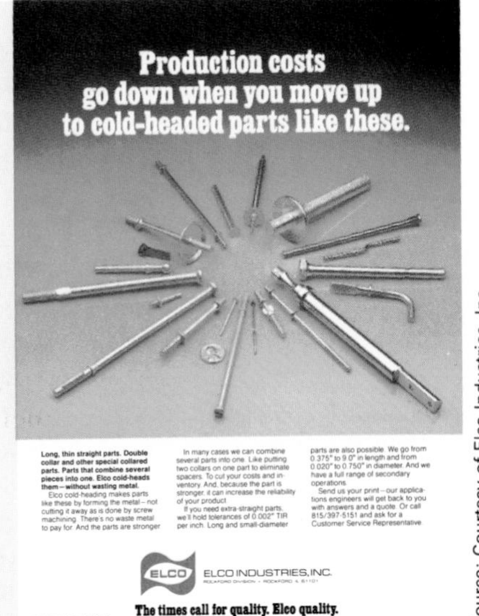

Source: Courtesy of Elco Industries, Inc.

When the company advertised the same product to purchasing agents, however, it emphasized delivery, quality, reliability, and company image.

Sources: "Know the Buyer Better," film by B. J. Morrison, and Marianne Paskowski, "Psycho-Marketing," *Industrial Marketing*, July 1981, pp. 41–42.

Emotional Influences on Buying Behavior

Although industrial buying decisions are often less whimsical than those in consumer markets, they are not necessarily free from emotional influences. Human beings, with all their strengths, faults, and frailties, still make the big decisions. (See Marketing Today 7.1.)

The same needs for esteem, affiliation, and security that were explored in Chapter 6 are also at work in the industrial marketplace. In business, a buyer may be motivated by a desire for status within the organization, a promotion, or a salary increase. Industrial salespeople need to understand this reward system in order to compete effectively with other suppliers.[11]

In one case, a manufacturer of sophisticated graphics computers was puzzled by its unimpressive record in selling to large potential customers. Instead of following the industry practice of quoting high list prices and giving generous discounts for quantity purchases during negotiations with buyers, this company had simply offered the lowest net prices in the industry. Sales had failed to materialize. The reason? Purchasing agents and their bosses evaluated their performance on how much of a price break they had managed to negotiate from suppliers, not on the net price actually paid.[12]

Fear plays a role, too. A purchasing agent may be insecure because of uncertainty about decisions, about status within a firm, about executive approval, and about job security.[13]

Many analysts attribute IBM's success in selling personal computers to industry at least partially to this factor. With more than 150 different computer manufacturers pounding on corporate doors, many purchasing agents began suffering "option shock." As a result, for many, "the low-risk decision was to buy IBM."[14]

Friendship may also influence buying decisions. While many companies require competitive bids on purchases, a buyer may work closely with a friend to ensure the friend's competitiveness on price and product specifications.[15]

Industrial marketers who recognize the various emotional factors that influence buyers may be able to design strategies that can subtly address the unspoken issues in a purchasing decision.

The Importance of Personal Selling

In the industrial market, personal selling is much more important than advertising. The opposite is often true for the consumer market. Another distinction is that intermediaries are seldom used in the exchange of goods between supplier and industrial buyer. Because large industrial purchases often rest on the skill and quality of a company's sales force, the larger firms often spend substantial amounts of time and money training their salespeople. Table 7.2 shows the results of a poll in which 300 purchasing managers were asked to identify what characteristics they liked—and disliked—in salespeople.

Many firms find that an efficient way to generate high-quality sales leads is to attend trade shows of the industries they serve. Trade show selling is less expensive than paying visits to buyers and often requires fewer follow-up calls. Furthermore, the visitors to a trade show tend to be well motivated to buy. The results for marketers can be impressive. For example, Acco International, manufacturer of a full line of office products, has made trade shows the focus of its marketing strategy. During one three-day show, the company wrote $700,000 in sales.

Continuing Contact between Buyer and Seller

Unlike consumer markets, buyers and sellers in the industrial sector often build relationships that span years. This is partly the result of fewer buyers for a given industrial product. In addition, sellers may extend credit to buyers for large purchases and provide follow-up service and technical assistance for their products.

Often two industries are so inextricably bound together that the vitality of one is closely tied to the other. Depending on the industries, there may even be trade possibilities between them. In such cases, they may choose to make an arrangement between them based on **reciprocity**.

Reciprocity
In industrial marketing, the relationship between buyer and seller that influences purchasing decisions rather than economic or performance factors.

Table 7.2
Buyers Rate Salespersons: Likes and Dislikes

What Buyers Like	What Buyers Dislike
Thoroughness and follow-through	Hard-selling, high-pressure tactics
Complete product knowledge	Talking too long about unrelated matters
Willingness to pursue the best interests of the buyer within the supplier firm	Exhibiting little interest in meeting the buyer's "real needs"
Sound market knowledge and willingness to keep the buyer informed	

Source: Based on a survey of 300 purchasing managers conducted by *Purchasing* magazine and reported in Larry Giunipero and Gary Zenz, "Impact of Purchasing Trends on Industrial Marketers," *Industrial Marketing Management*, February 1982, pp. 17–23.

Such an arrangement may be stated as, "I'll buy from you if you buy from me." A relationship involves reciprocity when the buyer-seller arrangement, rather than economic or performance factors, influences the purchase decision.[16]

The Justice Department and the Federal Trade Commission frown on reciprocal agreements that are anticompetitive, but such arrangements are legal as long as they do not involve coercion or seriously limit the competition in that industry.

Types of Buying Decisions

Industrial buyers make decisions differently, depending on whether the purchase is routine or complex. To better understand these buying decisions, marketers classify them into three types: the straight rebuy, the modified rebuy, and the new task.[17]

Straight Rebuy A **straight rebuy** involves reordering something without any modifications. Electric service is an extreme example; few organizations shop around for a supplier. Office supplies also are routine purchases. Typically, a purchasing department handles straight rebuys. Suppliers try to maintain quality and may propose that the organization use an automatic reordering system.

Straight Rebuy
Repurchase without any modifications to the product, terms, or suppliers.

Modified Rebuy A repurchase in which the buyer wants to modify product specifications, prices, terms, or suppliers is called a **modified rebuy.** Employees other than purchasing agents may take part in such decisions. Companies that wish to become suppliers try to make a better offer than current suppliers. Current suppliers must work harder to keep the business.

Modified Rebuy
Repurchase in which the buyer wants to modify product specifications, prices, terms, or suppliers.

New Task A **new task** involves buying a product or service for the first time. If the cost and risk are great, many people may participate in making the decision. Machinery and computer systems are often purchased this way. Marketers in this situation may have to supply a great deal of expertise and make a favorable impression on a number of decision makers.

New Task
Purchase of a good or service for the first time.

A Profile of Industrial Buyers

Buying Center
Group involved in purchasing for an industrial market.

User
Member of a buying center who works with the products purchased.

Buyer
Person, often called purchasing agent, with the formal responsibility of placing orders.

Influencer
One who can affect the decision process by assisting in evaluating alternative products.

Decider
Manager with authority to make the final choice.

Gatekeeper
Organizational member who controls the flow of information into the buying center.

Those who have studied the industrial buying process refer to the group of people who are involved in purchasing for an industrial market as the **buying center.** The members of a buying center, like the members of a family, tend to assume certain roles. According to one system of classification, the five principal roles in industrial buying situations are:

1. **Users**—those in the organization who work with the products purchased.
2. **Buyers**—individuals, often called purchasing agents, with the formal responsibility of placing orders.
3. **Influencers**—those who can affect the decision process by assisting in evaluating alternative products.
4. **Deciders**—managers with the authority to make the final choice.
5. **Gatekeepers**—organizational members who control the flow of information into the buying center.[18]

Sometimes an individual may assume more than one of these roles. For example, for relatively routine buys such as the ordering of office paper supplies, the purchasing agent may have full authority to buy without consulting others, in effect becoming gatekeeper, influencer, decider, and buyer.

Many purchases are much more complicated than a simple reorder. This is why other people are called in to consult or decide. Consider what might happen if a firm decides to order new carpeting for an office. Along the way, a variety of people take on the roles described above, but only two decisions are being made—the decision about whether to purchase at all and the choice of what to purchase.

The role of gatekeeper for the first decision may be played by the company receptionist, who makes others aware of the need. Various divisional heads may influence the decision to act on the receptionist's suggestion, but the plant manager may be the person who makes the final decision.

Once the decision to purchase is made, a whole different set of people becomes involved. The gatekeeper this time may be the supplier who selects the sample to be shown. Engineers and a secretary may act as influencers in viewing the samples and giving opinions on the durability and beauty of the selections. Ultimately, the chief factory engineer and company co-owner may make the final selection. In a decision such as this, the purchasing agent may play only the minor role of buyer or order taker.

Distinguishing the persons in a buying center and the roles they play is crucial to making a sale. If the salesperson in the carpet decision (the supplier) had assumed that the purchasing agent had full authority in the buying decision, he or she would have wasted time trying to sell to someone whose decision power in the case at hand was minimal. In fact, while the composition of a buying center would be different for a new computer than for new carpeting, research has shown that for many buying decisions key influencers are outside the purchasing department. Many firms conduct extensive marketing research to identify buyer

At Your Service 7.2
A Leasing Alternative

Source: Courtesy of Kayser Leasing.

Located in the Midwest, Kayser Leasing leases cars and trucks to a variety of companies. Because Kayser purchases thousands of vehicles each year, it can obtain them at a lower price than if the client bought them from a local dealership. The company uses a computer system to order the vehicles directly from the manufacturer. They are then shipped to a dealer as close as possible to the driver's home or office.

Kayser's services include a national account purchasing program, which offers savings on the purchase of tires, batteries, and minor maintenance, and a preventative maintenance program, which uses a coupon book to ensure that each driver has maintenance performed at prescribed intervals.

The company tailors its leases to the client's needs. Its net lease program provides a vehicle for a fixed duration with a mileage limitation. Its finance lease allows the client to decide when to terminate the lease. The company has also offered leases designed to minimize clients' taxes. In addition, Kayser offers programs that provide clients with information for operating their fleets most efficiently.

Explains Ray Stalowski, who runs Kayser Leasing, "Vehicle costs have increased so drastically during the last several years that companies just don't want to tie up huge amounts of capital in their fleet. Leasing gives companies a choice."

Source: "Kayser's on a Roll," *The Associates Magazine* (Associates Corporation of North America, Dallas, Texas), Summer 1986, pp. 8–11.

roles. The research guides them in tailoring a sales message that addresses the concerns of each participant.[19]

By anticipating the needs of each department involved in the decision and developing a strategy that takes individual concerns into account, a marketer can greatly increase the chances of closing a sale.

Leasing versus Buying

A growing pattern in industrial buying behavior is to lease products instead of buying them. (See At Your Service 7.2.) Organizations may sign leases for products as diverse as data-processing equipment, delivery trucks, and machine tools.

Among the benefits of leasing rather than buying are that the user has money free for other uses, and that lessors often service the products they lease. Companies that lease may also enjoy tax advantages, including deductibility of rental expense. For companies that use equipment only part of the year, leasing can be particularly attractive.

Chapter Replay

1. **How is the industrial market important to the U.S. economy?**
The industrial market is much larger than the consumer market. Industrial marketing accounts for well over half the economic activity in the United States.

2. **What are some differences between the industrial and consumer markets?**
The industrial market contains relatively few buyers, and their numbers are geographically concentrated. Demand in the consumer market is direct, but demand in the industrial market is indirectly influenced by consumer demand.

3. **What are the major classes of industrial products?**
The major classes of industrial products are raw materials, manufactured materials and parts, installations, accessory equipment, supplies, and business services.

4. **What is the nature of demand in the industrial sector?**
Demand in the industrial sector is derived, fluctuating, and inelastic. Also, in some cases demand for one product is affected by the availability of another product with which it is used.

5. **What influences buyer behavior in the industrial sector?**
Industrial buying behavior is affected by economic considerations and emotional factors. Personal selling is very important in the industrial market, with buyers and sellers typically maintaining long-term relationships.

6. **What types of buying decisions are made in the industrial sector?**
Buying decisions in the industrial sector include straight rebuys, modified rebuys, and new tasks.

7. **What are the principal roles in industrial buying situations?**
The principal roles are users, buyers, influencers, deciders, and gatekeepers.

8. **Why do some companies lease rather than buy certain products?**
Leasing frees up money for other uses. Suppliers of leased products often service what they lease. Companies that lease may also benefit from tax advantages, including deductibility of rental expense. Companies that use equipment for only part of the year can pay for it only when they need it.

Key Terms

accessory equipment
buyer
buying center
decider
derived demand
fluctuating demand
gatekeeper
industrial distributor
industrial market
inelastic demand
influencer
installation
joint demand
manufactured materials (manufactured parts)
modified rebuy
new task
raw material
reciprocity
straight rebuy
supplies
user

Discussion Questions

1. What are three major differences between consumer and industrial markets?
2. Give an example of each of the following categories of industrial products.
   a. Raw materials
   b. Manufactured parts
   c. Installations
   d. Accessory equipment
   e. Supplies
   f. Business services
3. What is "inelastic demand"? Why is industrial demand relatively inelastic?
4. Bernice Bliss is a sales representative for Industrial Janitorial Service, Inc. In preparing to sell her company's services to a potentially large client, she has decided to list the factors that might influence the customer's decision to buy. What criteria could Bernice put on her list?
5. Tim Treemont is a sales representative for Perfect Packaging Products (PPP). He likes to use a friendly approach, so when he called on Rob Freemont of Yummy Foods, he spent 20 minutes discussing the past World Series. When Tim turned the subject to the previous year's World Series, Rob looked agitated and exclaimed, "I thought you wanted to talk about why we should start putting our chocolate frosting in aerosol cans." "That's right," replied Tim quickly, "Listen, I'll give you a deal on your first 500. Trust me; it'll be the best move you ever made. Can I count on your order?"

   Why do you think Tim didn't get the sale? What traits do buyers like in a salesperson?

6. Describe the three types of buying decisions. Which type of decision is likely to involve the greatest number of decision makers?
7. Eileen Green, secretary, reported to her boss, Sue Blue, that the service rep had told her that fixing her typewriter any more was probably hopeless because it was so old. "Well," replied Sue, "get some information on typewriters, narrow your choice to one or two, and then show me what you found."

   Eileen looked through a couple of catalogs she got from the company's purchasing agent. She also called her friend, Jack Black, to discuss how he liked his new electronic typewriter. The next day she described her first choice to Sue. Sue approved Eileen's choice, and Eileen requested the purchasing agent to order the typewriter.

   In this scenario, who played each of the roles as members of the buying center? How could a marketer have influenced the buying decision?
8. Why might a company prefer to lease its sales representatives' cars rather than own them?

Case 7.1 Jefferson Manufacturing

One of the major components of Jefferson Manufacturing is its rivet division. In recent years, the overall demand for rivets has declined as other fastening systems have replaced them. Rivets, however, still remain the best buy for their strength-to-weight ratio, ease of application compared to welding, and speed compared to nuts and bolts. Adhesives have replaced them in some applications in appliances and automobiles. Welding, however, is providing more competitive pressure than adhesives.

Markets for Rivets

The four key markets for rivets are construction, aircraft, automotive, and consumer. In the automotive industry, rivets have been selectively used to assemble certain interior parts. Unibody construction with automotive welding has virtually eliminated rivets from other autombile assembly processes. Rivets one-to-two inches in diameter and four-to-six inches in length are used to fasten structural steel in high-rise construction. Since the early 1970s, this market has been declining as rivets have been replaced by welding and high-performance steel bolts.

Because aircrafts are formed from smaller sections of plates or frames, rivets are used to hold the structures together. The number of rivets per aircraft has not changed, but the number of aircraft produced has declined since its peak in the late 1960s and early 1970s. There is

Source: Much of the material in this case was developed by Jim Staneluis. Appreciation is expressed to him for his assistance and cooperation.

Exhibit

	Annual Sales by Type of Account (In Millions of Dollars)			
	1984	1983	1982	1981
Consumer Markets				
Retail stores	1.23	1.51	1.64	1.52
Construction contractors	7.45	6.92	7.59	8.12
Welding shops	1.01	1.39	1.45	1.51
	$ 9.69	$ 9.82	$10.68	$11.15
Industrial Markets				
Aircraft	3.47	3.59	3.91	4.31
Automotive	2.98	2.80	2.70	2.95
Others	3.75	3.97	4.52	4.91
	$10.20	$10.36	$11.13	$12.17

strong pressure from structural adhesive companies and a high interest by aerospace engineers to replace rivets. If an aircraft could be fabricated with adhesive, its cost could be reduced by as much as 20 percent, largely because of labor savings.

At the consumer level, sales are primarily to do-it-yourselfers, various types of assembly contractors in the construction business, and welding shops. A pop rivet system sold to these customers is used with a gun that compresses the rivet in one step. Small contractors and shops find the pop rivet system a definite time saver. Most of the customers purchase rivets and guns from distributors that service them with other tools, primarily with imported products from the Far East.

Jefferson's Marketing

A customer survey indicates that the Rivet Division of Jefferson Manufacturing has an image of a high-quality supplier who meets delivery schedules on time and is, in general, a good company with which to do business. The division also has a fine reputation for the degree of technical services it provides customers. As shown in the exhibit, however, total sales have been declining in recent years.

The consumer side of the rivet market is serviced by 50 salespeople calling on hardware stores, lumber yards, large chains, discount stores, contractors, and manufacturers. The total market is divided into 5 regions and 25 sales territories and involves almost 20,000 individual accounts. Because the product here is used by contractors and small manufacturing firms, some technical service is provided via telephone using an 800 toll-free number. Advertising for the consumer side of the business is through trade journals, along with special promotions involving prizes and trips for dealers.

Ten application engineers work as the field sales force and five technical service people in the home office provide marketing activities for the industrial side of the rivet business. Three of the engineers are in San Francisco and handle the aircraft companies, and three more are in the Detroit area to help service the automotive industry. The other four engineers cover the balance of the country.

The process of selling means calling on the research and development groups of existing and potential accounts every few weeks to help identify new applications for rivets and ways in which current applications might be improved. The emphasis of the marketing effort on the industrial side is to manage programs that introduce new products to keep up with the changes in fastening technology plus specific changes in the technology of the automotive and aircraft industries. The industrial group also has a number of accounts in the appliance industry.

Focal Topics

1. What recommendations do you have for Jefferson Manufacturing in the area of applying market segmentation strategies to the rivet market?
2. Discuss the techniques that the firm could use to forecast its rivet sales for 1985 and 1989.
3. Given the information in the case, what is your best estimate for Jefferson's 1985 rivet sales?

Case 7.2 California Beef Council (D)

As part of its overall marketing plan, the California Beef Council (CBC) has a mission "to build upon proven successes of the 1986 food service program and to further enhance the credibility of the CBC as a viable and reliable organization serving the food service industry."

A specific objective relating to the achievement of this mission is "To encourage and support the additional sales of beef to operators by providing them with well-targeted, timely information." The following information describes the "whys" and "hows" of four activities related to this objective.

Recipe Development and Distribution

Why: CBC and National Restaurant Association research shows that recipes, menu suggestions, and product-handling suggestions are among the most useful information tools provided to food service operators. For four years, the CBC has created recipe and information cards that have been widely distributed and favorably received by the industry.

Source: Adapted from the California Beef Council's 1987 Marketing Plan.

This information has been used to create new menu items and to train students and industry personnel.

How: Develop a new brochure featuring beef menu ideas and beef usage/handling tips that would support the national campaign. The brochure could contain recipes for all meal periods plus additional suggestions for menu and merchandising possibilities. The brochure would continue the "light and healthy" theme of the national campaign. Clean, clear, and simple photography would follow the established "look" CBC has achieved.

Recipe Cards

Why: Through its public relations program, CBC has developed many recipes that have not been printed in recipe card format. Because of the popularity of these placements, the recipes could be printed in standard format for distribution at trade shows and through announcements in trade journals. These also make excellent "leave-behinds" for packer/purveyor salespeople.

How: Use existing recipes to produce simple, standard-format recipe cards that would complement public relations placements, and display photographs on the CBC booth at trade shows.

School Food Service

Why: Because of the amount of donated beef to the school food service system, CBC can provide this sector of the industry with information to assist in the proper utilization of this product.

How: Provide timely and pertinent information to members of the American School Food Service Association, especially information on the industry and how to use beef in low-fat, low-sodium entrees. Assist the National Cancer Institute with its pilot project school lunch program in California.

Food Service Operator Seminars

Why: From pilot project work conducted in 1986, CBC ascertained that there is a need to educate those on the operator level about beef. The project was conducted in the in-plant (noncommercial) environment with success. CBC plans to build upon this success in 1987.

How: Cooperate with major corporations in the industrial sector of the economy and with other commodity organizations throughout the country. Publicize the programs through the corporate network to gain further support. Conduct actual "hands-on" experience for those attending the various sessions. Possibly create a workbook about conducting this type of workshop for distribution to other beef councils.

Focal Topics

1. How is the behavior of organizational buyers such as restaurants and schools different from that of household consumers when it comes to products like beef?
2. What is your overall evaluation of CBC's plans to help some organizational buyers?
3. What other marketing strategies would you recommend to better serve food service buyers?

Case for Part Two

Jolt Cola

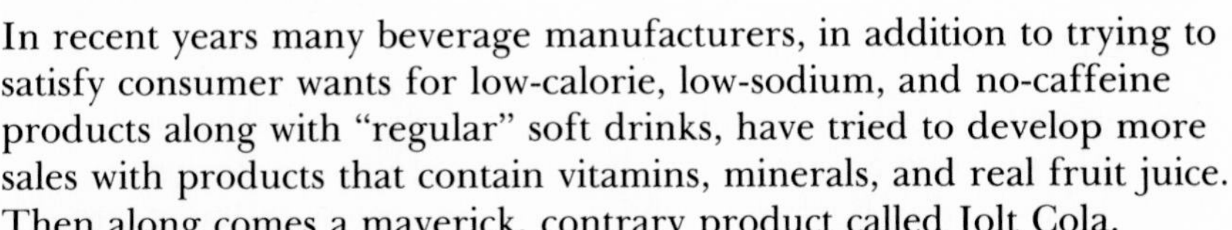

In recent years many beverage manufacturers, in addition to trying to satisfy consumer wants for low-calorie, low-sodium, and no-caffeine products along with "regular" soft drinks, have tried to develop more sales with products that contain vitamins, minerals, and real fruit juice. Then along comes a maverick, contrary product called Jolt Cola.

Jolt offers "all the sugar and twice the caffeine" of mainline colas. Developers of the product state, "Our product is naughty and bold, and we don't mind that image." The label carries the claim, "Inspired by the Need for a Better-Tasting Soft Drink!"

The Soft-Drink Industry

Americans are drinking more soft drinks than ever before. According to *Beverage World,* consumption reached 43 gallons per capita in 1985 compared to 37 gallons in 1981. Viewed somewhat differently, the average American consumed 500 12-ounce units of soft drinks in 1985, according to the National Soft Drink Association, with consumption growing at about 7 percent annually.

One percentage point in the soft-drink industry translates into an average of $300 million. Other trends and information on the industry include:

- Coca-Cola, with all of its products, has 38.6 percent of the market, while Pepsi-Cola products account for some 27.4 percent.
- Dr Pepper brands and Seven-Up brands account for 7.1 percent and 6.3 percent, respectively.
- Brand Pepsi (with 17.4 percent) moved into the number-one brand spot by default because of the splitting of former number-one Coke with Classic (14.2 percent) and regular or new Coke (7.0 percent), a multibrand strategy that whether planned or not gave Coca-Cola a higher corporate share. Diet Coke has 6.7 percent and Cherry Coke has 1.6 percent. Pepsi-Cola's Slice brands have achieved a 2.1 percent share with about 60 percent national distribution.

Source: Material presented here has been adapted from Stephen W. Bell, "Jolt offers 'all the sugar, twice the caffeine'," *The Columbus Dispatch,* September 9, 1986, p. 2F; Richard W. Stevenson, "Jolt Cola's Contrary Strategy," *The New York Times,* August 20, 1986, p. D19; "100 Leading National Advertisers," *Advertising Age,* September 4, 1986, pp. 66+; and other related materials. Logo courtesy of The Jolt Company, Inc.

- ☐ At least six companies have rolled out or announced plans for 14 soft drinks with "value-added" ingredients such as fruit juice or vitamins and minerals. Examples of these brands include Pepsi's Slice, Del Monte's Diet Sunkist Plus, Squirt's Diet Squirt Plus, Crush's Crush with Juice, Coca-Cola's Minute Maid sodas with vitamins C and B-6 and folic acid added, and Coca-Cola's Tab with calcium.

Development of Jolt

C. J. Rapp and his father, Joseph F. Rapp, Jr., who retired in 1985 after 40 years of operating a Canada Dry bottling operation in Rochester, New York, decided to buck the trend of less sugar, less caffeine, and fruit juice and vitamin additions to soft drinks. The Rapps invested $100,000 and spent six years testing 114 formulas before arriving at the one they liked for Jolt.

Jolt has 5.9 milligrams of caffeine per fluid ounce, which is just less than the 6.0 milligrams allowed by the U.S. Food and Drug Administration. The level of caffeine in Jolt is about twice the amount in leading soft drinks but only one-fifth the amount in regular coffee. The product's sugar content is just slightly higher than other sugared colas. The only difference is that Jolt is made with 100 percent sugar compared to the less expensive corn syrup sweetener that is used by the rest of the soft-drink industry.

In personal interviews, C. J. Rapp has stated, "Soft drinks were never really created for people who wanted to lose weight. What the big companies did was try to gain soft-drink consumers that otherwise were not. In our opinion, what they did was they abandoned those that had been drinking soft drinks for years." He also said, "Soft drinks were created for sheer enjoyment and pleasure, but the industry has become awfully serious. They've saturated the negative selling aspects, and they've drastically changed their products. We're trying to bring back the fun."

Industry Response

A spokesman for Pepsico Inc., Stuart Ross, said that today's Pepsi tastes the same as it did 15 or 20 years ago. He added, "Soft drinks today are so popular, there's a niche for everyone." Ronald Coleman, a Coca-Cola spokesman said, "We've been in the business for 100 years; we're the world's most popular drink, and I think that speaks for itself."

The National Action Health Letter, a publication of the Center for Science in the Public Interest in Washington, D.C., has assailed the product as unhealthy because of its caffeine content. The organization nominated Mr. Rapp for a "personal niche in the nutrition hall of shame."

Jesse Meyers, editor and publisher of *Beverage Digest,* commented on Jolt by saying, "The hallmark of the soft-drink industry from word one has been innovation. Word two has been filling a market niche. The industry has seen fragmenting over the last few years . . . so they certainly have a shot at a market."

Future Directions

Jolt is seeking a national market by signing up franchised bottlers and distributors. The company is planning on spending more than $1 million in introducing advertising nationally as the product begins appearing in more areas. The company is confident that it can obtain a 2 percent share of the market where Jolt Cola is available. The objective is to achieve a 4 percent share.

Many consumers have tried the brand either out of curiosity or because the product appeals to them. C. J. Rapp realizes that Jolt's real challenge is to sustain its momentum and grow into more than just a novelty.

Focal Topics

1. In your opinion, why has the soft-drink industry become so segmented in recent years?
2. What market segmentation strategy would you use to position Jolt?
3. What problems would you anticipate in trying to get distributors and retailers to carry Jolt?
4. What types of marketing research would be helpful to Jolt at this time?
5. What overall marketing strategy would you recommend to Jolt management at this time?

Part Three

Product and Pricing Strategy

8 Product and Service Concepts

□ Sounding Out the Chapter

In this chapter, you will learn:

1. Why new-product development is risky.
2. Three dimensions of products.
3. How consumer products are classified.
4. How industrial products are classified.
5. Some pros and cons of branding.
6. Issues marketers face in planning for branding.
7. Advantages of nationally branded, private label, and generic products.
8. Characteristics of services that distinguish them from goods.
9. Special issues that arise in the marketing of services.

Lauren Respects the Past but Has a Flair for the Present

Polo matches in Palm Beach. A safari in Kenya. Tea in a London hotel. A life of hand-tailored clothes, manor houses, sports cars, fine horses, manicured lawns. These are the images conjured up by the name Ralph Lauren.

Ralph Lauren has built a sportswear empire based on selling what his advertising calls "originality, but always with integrity and a respect for tradition." His products are comfortable, durable, and elegant, and not too shocking. They are designed to appeal to those who think fashion is too faddish but traditional business clothing is dull.

While Ralph Lauren's most famous item may be his Polo shirt, his products extend to an entire line of menswear with the Polo label, another called Chaps, a line of womenswear, clothing for boys and girls, fragrances, luggage, eyeglasses, handbags, and home furnishings. What the products have in common is a link to classic design. Describing his sources of inspiration, Lauren says, "I love jeans, cowboy boots, tweed jackets, pinstripe suits, old race cars, Porsches, Indian blankets, and baskets."

All these tasteful products come at a price. But many consumers are willing to pay a high price for the prestige that accompanies the Ralph Lauren name. In particular, the image of prestige attracts upwardly mobile consumers who want to display their success.

Lauren reinforces the image of his products in the way he displays them. His Madison Avenue store features hand-carved mahogany woodwork, custom-forged brass trim, Oriental rugs, orchids, saddles, trophies, and other paraphernalia. A side table in a Lauren display contains rows of framed pictures evoking comfortable, traditional surroundings.

All this image making is intended to generate an appeal for the many products that bear the Lauren name. Someone who likes the feel of a Lauren blazer might want to carry that image further with a suitcase or sofa. So far, the strategy seems to be working. Between 1981 and 1986, sales rose fourfold.

Selling a variety of products linked by a brand name such as Polo or Ralph Lauren is only one of the strategies marketers can adopt. Other marketers find advantages in lower-cost approaches that enable them to charge lower prices. This chapter describes some of these choices. It also looks at some of the special issues that arise in marketing to industrial buyers and in marketing services.

Source: Stephen Koepp, "Selling a Dream of Elegance and the Good Life," *Time,* September 1, 1986, pp. 54–61.

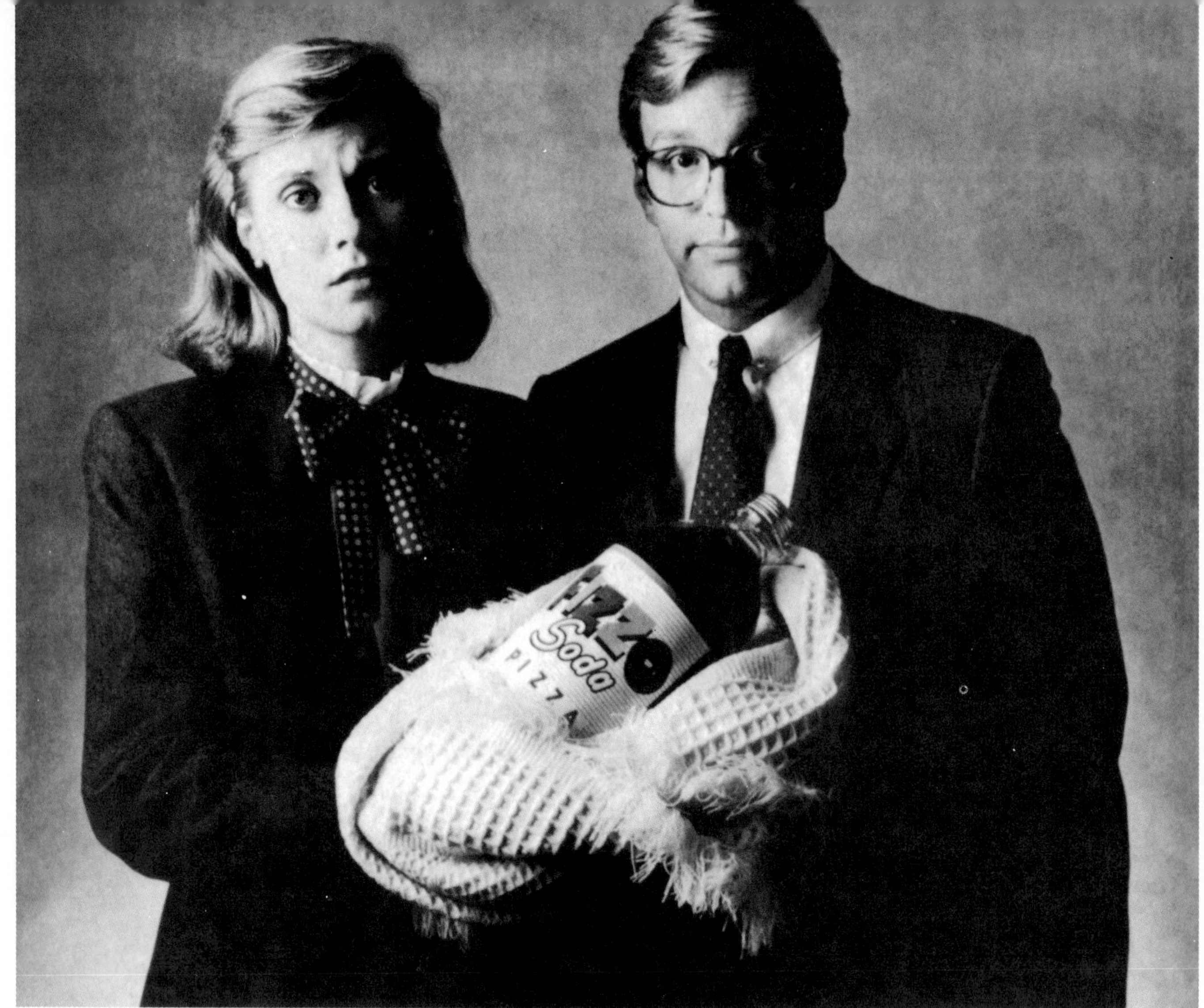

HELP PREVENT UNWANTED PRODUCTS.

There's nothing sadder than a product that hasn't found a home in the marketplace.

Nothing more disappointing than an idea that's ill conceived, badly delivered and poorly evaluated.

But saddest of all is the fact that most unwanted products need never happen.

At Yankelovich Clancy Shulman, we know how to prevent those big marketing mistakes.

Our "state-of-the-science" models are designed to do just that. To give you the kind of information you need for successful marketing action.

At every stage of product development—from target selection to product positioning and configuration all the way to actual test market—our Litmus™ and strategic models work to put you in touch with the answers critical to the decisions you have to make.

And because they're geared toward product success, the answers they provide are the *optimal* ones for your product and marketing plan. The kind of answers no one else can give.

So before you go too far in product development, talk to our Senior Vice President for Marketing, Mr. Watts Wacker, at (203) 227-2700.

He'll show you how we can help turn the arrival of your next new product into a truly joyous event.

Yankelovich Clancy Shulman

Marketing Intelligence℠

Eight Wright Street Westport Connecticut 06880

Defining a Product

What do a cheese-of-the-month club, an album by the Police, a Dallas Cowboys' football game, a rerun of MASH, a dog-walking service, and a flight on the Concorde have in common?

They are all **products.** A product is anything that can be offered to a market for attention, acquisition, use, or consumption that might satisfy a want or need. It includes physical objects, services, persons, places, organizations, and ideas.[1] Physical objects offered in the marketplace are as diverse as record albums and machine tools. Services, too, are varied, including haircuts and legal assistance. Persons include the performers and athletes you pay to watch. Places include where people choose to vacation or set up a new business. When you buy a membership in an organization, such as the Smithsonian Institution, that organization is a product. Ideas offered to the marketplace include antismoking messages.

Products
Anything that can be offered to a market for attention, acquisition, use, or consumption that might satisfy a want or need.

In today's world, developing new products is difficult and expensive. Marketers must find a niche in an ever-changing marketplace. Government agencies check many aspects of the marketing mix, including contents, claims to effectiveness, and possible side effects of packaging material. Competitors are working on innovations of their own. For product managers to navigate these shoals, they must find ways of getting the public to notice their products amid shouts of competitors all promoting better, faster-acting, new, and improved products.

As shown in Chapter 5, it can cost enormous amounts of money to launch a new product nationally. Nonetheless, in recent years new-product introductions in the U.S. alone have increased to the rate of nearly 150 per month. This furious pace continues even though, according to one industry source, only a hundred or fewer new products a year top a million dollars in sales in their first twelve months.[2] In spite of this daunting record, few companies can afford to rest on their previous successes. Some marketing experts have responded to the difficulty and expense of new-product development by creating specialized services that help companies with this task. (See Figure 8.1.)

In just one month at the end of 1986, announcements of new products included Malibu and Capri brands of cigarettes; Windex heavy-duty bathroom and kitchen cleaner; a peach variety of California Cooler; Eat 'N Lose, a blend of fiber and minerals designed to be sprinkled on food; Sun Country Classic, a drier-tasting wine cooler; liquid Clorox 2 bleach; Masterpiece premium barbecue sauce; Salon Selectives, a hair-care line; Juicy Flavors, a line of soft drinks; Bartles & Jaymes blush wine cooler; Ice Cream Cones ready-to-eat cereal in vanilla and chocolate-chip flavors; Cherry 7-Up; Celestial Seasonings dry salad dressing mixes; Nestlé Toll House Mint-Chocolate Morsels; Toselli nonalcoholic sparkling spumante (wine); Folgers Coffee Singles and Martinson Microwave Bags,

Figure 8.1
Ad for a Company Specializing in New-Product Development Market Research

single-serving coffee bags for use in a microwave oven or with boiling water; O.N.E. nutritional-style dog food; peach-flavored Mix & Eat Cream of Wheat hot cereal; Colorado Crystal sparkling water; Extra-Strength Aim toothpaste (with extra fluoride); and Concentrin, a liquid cough remedy contained in a soft gelatin capsule.[3] It will be interesting to see which of these products succeed.

Clearly, new-product development is critical to any company's success. This chapter explores some of the decisions marketers must make as they transform a new product from an idea in someone's mind to an item in a consumer's shopping cart.

Three Dimensions of Products

Products serve human needs in various dimensions. We may think of a product as being similar to an apple. It has several layers, each of which contributes to the total product image. At the heart, or core, of the apple is the basic need-satisfying aspect or benefit of the product or service. It answers the question, "What problem does this product solve?" Passengers flying to Paris on the Concorde, for example, are not simply seeking transportation. Many other airlines offer that service for less. In fact, according to officials at Air France, Concorde passengers are not even primarily interested in luxurious surroundings and service. After all, for a fare significantly less than that of the Concorde, passengers flying first class on a regular wide-bodied Air France 747 have much more leg room and comparable amenities. What Concorde passengers are chiefly buying is *speed.* In the fast-paced world of international business, those few hours gained are often worth the premium price. When developing a product, a marketer must always ask, "What is it that people are *really* buying when they purchase this product or service?" The answer will affect the other dimensions of the product.

Once the basic benefit offered by the product or service is defined, a product planner can begin developing physical or functional features of a product. Disposable diapers, toothpaste, sports cars, and running shoes are all tangible products. They all include physical characteristics such as packaging, product features, and distinctive styling. They may also include a brand name that may give the product additional value because of the manufacturer's reputation for quality or because of an image created through advertising.

Additional benefits and services often added to a product make up the outer skin of the apple. These may include after-sale service (such as a warranty on a new car), installation, credit, or delivery. For example, fast home delivery has enabled Domino's Pizza to grow rapidly. Domino's successfully competes with other sellers of fast food by promoting the convenience of having the meal delivered.[4] (See Figure 8.2.)

Many products or services that are otherwise indistinguishable physically become preferred products of consumers because of these added features. For example, tax consultants perform essentially the same service, but H&R Block has captured an important share of the market by offering extras such as free estimates of the cost of preparing forms and

Figure 8.2
Domino's Popularity Is Due in Large Part to Fast Home Delivery

Source: Photo © 1987 Phyllis Woloshin.

back-up assistance in case of an Internal Revenue Service audit. Product managers who ignore this dimension in defining a product miss an important marketing opportunity.

Marketing by Product Types

The 3M Company—Minnesota Mining and Manufacturing—sells more than 27,000 products ranging from Scotch tape to copying machines and Scotchguard fabrics. Each of these products requires a different marketing strategy. Scotch tape is sold through many small outlets, such as grocery and stationery stores, and is promoted through advertising. Copying machines are sold through office machine stores staffed by personnel who carry on the main sales effort. Scotchguard fabrics are sold to upholsterers, furniture factories, and clothing manufacturers through sales representatives of the 3M Company.

If 3M's marketing managers had to devise separate strategies for each of the 27,000 products, their task would be time consuming, if not impossible. Fortunately, their job has been simplified because it is possible to group products into categories according to the markets served and to develop generalizations about products in each category.

As discussed in Chapter 7, industrial products are goods bought by an organization's purchasing agents, or by intermediaries, to make other goods, to resell them, or to carry on some other exchange-related ac-

Consumer Products
Goods sold to individuals or households for their personal use.

tivity. Scotchguard fabric, IBM computers, and GMC trucks are industrial products. By contrast, **consumer products** are those goods sold to individuals or households for their personal use. Scotch tape, Kellogg's Rice Krispies, and Sony Walkmans are familiar examples.

Some goods can be classified as either consumer or industrial products. A GE light bulb can be used in a home, office, or factory. But a marketing manager would vary product strategy according to the market for which the product is destined. Each of these two broad classes of products can be further divided into groups whose shared characteristics lend themselves to similar marketing strategies.

Consumer Products

Although there is no reliable estimate of the number of consumer products available, it is known that the average retail grocery store contains between 7,000 and 10,000 different items. It is safe to say, then, that consumer products number in the hundreds of thousands. Effective market planning requires a system for classifying the vast number of consumer products.

Since consumers buy goods and services not only for their functional value but also to satisfy a variety of emotional needs, a classification system based on use would be of little value. Consumer products are usually grouped according to the manner in which consumers buy them: convenience goods, shopping goods, or specialty goods. A closer look will show why each requires a different marketing strategy.

Convenience Goods
Products that individuals buy quickly and often.

Staple Items
Products bought through habit—for example, milk.

Impulse Items
Products bought on the spur of the moment.

Emergency Items
Products bought when an unexpected need arises.

Convenience Goods Products that individuals buy quickly and often are **convenience goods.** Candy, drug products, food, snacks, cigarettes, and almost any ordinary household item may be included in this category. Such products may be **staple items** bought through habit (such as milk), **impulse items** bought on the spur of the moment (a copy of *People* magazine bought while standing in the checkout line with a bottle of milk), or **emergency items** bought when an unexpected need arises (a bag of rock salt bought when one discovers it has begun snowing while standing in the line with a bottle of milk reading *People*).

Ordinarily, convenience goods are low priced. Because these items cost so little, few people will bother to shop around for them. The tobacco industry, for example, has discovered that people will rarely go more than a block or two to pick up a pack of cigarettes. Consequently, they must supply many retail outlets—including food stores, candy stores, taverns, gasoline stations, vending machines, and drugstores—with their products.

Although consumers will not make a special effort to purchase a convenience good, they can be persuaded to buy a particular manufacturer's product regularly. This is done by building a brand name for a product and advertising the brand heavily. Procter & Gamble, probably the foremost user of this tactic, ranks first in the selling of detergent (Tide), shampoo (Head and Shoulders), and toothpaste (Crest). Other successful brand names include Kraft cheese, Scotch tape, and Kleenex tissues. Retailers sometimes draw customers to their stores by marking down the price of such widely advertised, popular convenience goods. Such marked-down goods are often referred to as "loss leaders" because store owners may take a loss on those items in exchange for the many additional customers drawn into the store by the low price.

Convenience goods are the fastest-growing category of consumer goods. This is due in part to the increase in the number of working wives and mothers who no longer have the time to comparison shop. In addition, more goods are now considered convenience goods by consumers. Even drugstores now stock such items as radios and wristwatches in addition to cheaper, small items traditionally classified as convenience goods.

Shopping Goods Products that individuals buy only after making comparisons in competing stores are known as **shopping goods.** If the basis of comparison is price, those products are known as **homogeneous shopping goods,** because consumers see them as essentially the same except for price. For example, one would probably shop around for a desk lamp on the basis of price. If the basis of comparison is quality or style, the products are called **heterogeneous shopping goods.** Shoppers looking for a dress or suit would probably go from store to store until they hit upon an appealing style.

Shopping Goods
Products that a consumer buys only after making comparisons among competing stores.

Homogeneous Shopping Goods
Products that a consumer buys only after making price comparisons among sellers—consumers see them as essentially the same.

Heterogeneous Shopping Goods
Products that a consumer will buy only after making a comparison of the style or quality of brands—for example, a dress or suit.

Shopping goods are usually more expensive than convenience goods. Because consumers are willing to make an effort to locate these more expensive goods, manufacturers need fewer stores in which to sell their products. Some manufacturers (Magnavox, for example) sell their merchandise mainly through major department stores. Stores carrying shopping goods are often clustered together, a pattern different from that of stores selling convenience goods. Rarely are two supermarkets on the same block, but a row of shoe stores or automobile dealers is not uncommon. (See Figure 8.3.) Clustering makes comparison shopping easier.

Advertising can be important in the case of shopping goods, especially to lure customers into stores where the goods are sold. But at the point of purchase, the most important means of promotion is the personal selling effort of salespeople. Appliance manufacturers recognize this point and frequently offer salespeople bonuses to reward sales of their brands.[5]

Specialty Goods **Specialty goods** are so named because consumers are willing to make a special effort to obtain them. Included in this category are such items as Ray-Ban sunglasses, Gucci handbags, Porsche sports cars, gourmet coffee, and Rolex watches. Specialty-goods buyers differ from shopping-goods buyers in that the former know what they are looking for and have a particular brand in mind. They are unwilling to settle for substitutes and will go out of their way to find an outlet handling the product.

Specialty Goods
Products that a consumer is willing to make a special effort to obtain.

Specialty goods are usually high priced. But because they are so highly valued by the consumers who seek them, few sales outlets need to carry such items.

Figure 8.3
A Cluster of Auto Dealers

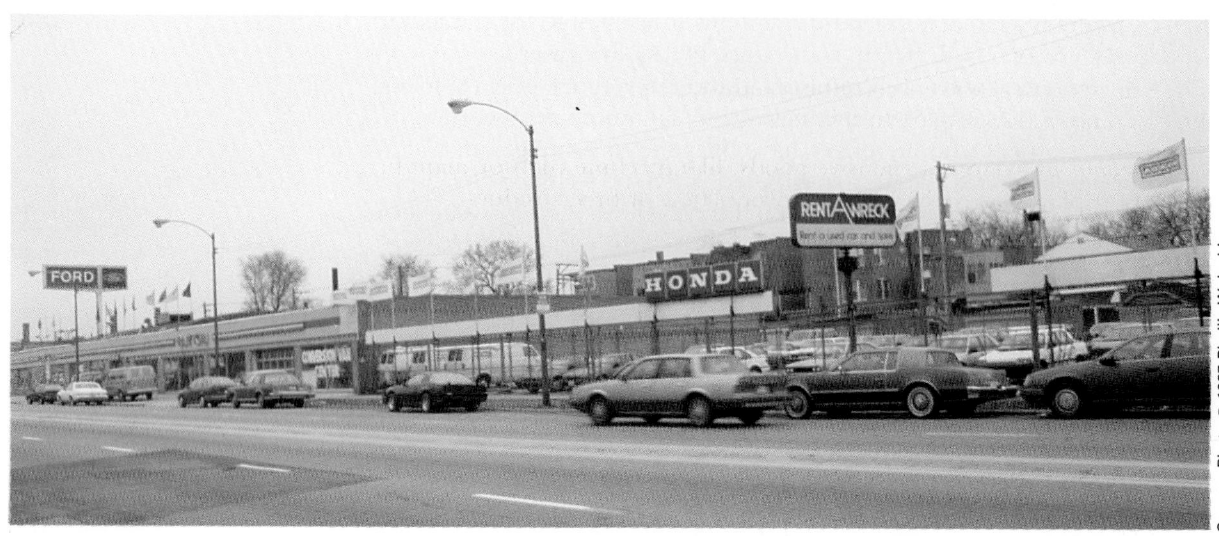

Source: Photo © 1987 Phyllis Woloshin.

Specialty goods are a growing category of products. Many Americans have more leisure time and are willing to spend more on such goods. Hobbyists are typical shoppers for specialty goods. Coin collectors, for instance, will make a special effort to find a 1906 buffalo-head nickel. People who enjoy gourmet cooking may travel a substantial distance to find a store that carries fresh basil or a particular brand of copper skillet.

Limitations of Consumer Product Classification As noted earlier, a particular product can be classified as a consumer or an industrial product depending on its use. Similarly, within the consumer product category, a particular good may be a convenience, shopping, or specialty good depending on the buying habits of a certain shopper. A student living on a tight budget may feel obliged to shop around for an occasional steak dinner. But high-income families may treat it as a convenience good, settling on a Porterhouse steak when they need a quick dinner. A consumer interested in taking snapshots of the family might shop around for a camera, while a tourist who discovered she had left her camera at home might buy a disposable camera (a convenience good). A serious amateur photographer might insist on a high-quality Nikon (a specialty good).

The categories are not neatly marked off from one another. The more effort consumers are willing to expend to obtain it, the more a product resembles a shopping or specialty good. For the product manager, of course, the important point is how the *majority* of buyers view the company's product. This information is integral to the marketing approach—selecting target markets and drawing up policies on price, promotion, and distribution.[6]

Industrial Products

The most practical way of classifying industrial products is by their use. The six major classes of industrial products are:

1. *Installations*—large, expensive goods, like machine tools or manufacturing plants, necessary for the production of final products.
2. *Accessory equipment*—smaller items, such as tools and typewriters, that do not become part of the final product but are necessary for its manufacture.
3. *Raw materials*—natural resources, such as crude oil and iron ore, or cultivated products, such as wheat or cotton, that become part of the final product.
4. *Manufactured materials and parts*—finished items, such as headlights or buttons, that are incorporated into the final product.
5. *Supplies*—those items needed to operate a business but not part of the final product. Supplies are sometimes called MRO items because they can be divided into three categories: (1) maintenance items, (2) repair items, and (3) operating supplies.
6. *Business services*—specific functions, such as copier repair and legal counsel, performed by specialists outside the firm.

While industrial products are not customarily classified into convenience, shopping, and specialty goods, many of the same principles apply. In an industrial buying decision, "staple" items such as office supplies may be solely the responsibility of an office manager or purchasing agent; in highly automated offices, they may be ordered by one computer "talking" to another. "Specialty goods," such as major new pieces of machinery, may require months of planning and negotiations, in which large numbers of people have input. Each of these categories of products requires a specialized type of marketing strategy.

The Question of Branding

A major decision, particularly for consumer goods manufacturers, is whether to produce a product with a recognizable brand name or market the product without such identification. The various terms marketers use when discussing branding are defined in Figure 8.4.

The practice of attaching a brand name or symbol to a product is very old. Some say it began when ancient Greek artists etched their names in sculptures. Branding became commercially significant in the Middle Ages when guilds (the precursors of unions) required handcrafters to put their mark on the goods they made. The guilds did this for two reasons: to be able to trace poor workmanship and to limit output and thereby prevent prices from falling. The practice faded at the end of the Middle Ages but was revived a century ago with the start of mass

Figure 8.4
The Terminology of Branding

Trademark
A name, term, sign, symbol, design, or some combination used to identify the products of one firm and to differentiate them from competitors' products. The golden-arch symbol and the word *McDonalds* in its distinctive typeface combine to identify a certain brand of fast-food restaurant.

Logo courtesy of McDonald's Corporation

Brand Name
The most common form of trademark is the brand name that can be expressed verbally, including letters, words, and numbers. Atari, Ultima II, and RC Cola are examples.

Brand Mark
The part of the brand that can be recognized but not spoken. It may consist of symbols, designs, or distinctive lettering or colors. Coca-Cola's red and white colors and script lettering are recognized worldwide. The Playboy bunny, Ralph Lauren's polo player, and the symbol "Dryden" on the spine of this book are all brand marks.

Trademark Rights
A brand name, slogan, or fanciful design becomes a trademark with use in connection with a product or commercial service. The trademark created and used is sometimes referred to as a "common law" trademark, but it is a valid, protectible trademark nonetheless. Registration of a mark in the U.S. Patent and Trademark Office gives the owner of a mark important procedural rights. *Xerox*, a coined word, is a trademark of the Xerox Corporation to identify its copiers and other equipment. The title *Realtor* is a trademark of the National Association of Realtors. A trademark protects a company's exclusive rights to use a brand name and/or brand mark.

Logo courtesy of the Xerox Corporation

Source: Committee on Definitions, *Marketing Definitions: A Glossary of Marketing Terms* (Chicago: American Marketing Association, 1960), pp. 9–10.

production. Some hundred-year-old brand names are still around, including Ivory soap, Quaker Oats, and Vaseline.

Branding Pros and Cons

Branding has clearly caught on since its reintroduction a century ago. Nearly all consumer products today are branded, and even some industrial products (Mack trucks, NutraSweet aspartame, IBM computers) carry brand names. A decade ago, marketers believed that shopping goods such as women's ready-to-wear apparel could not be branded. They assumed that women bought dresses because of fit or styling that could not be duplicated by other dresses sold under the same brand name.

Today, apparel manufacturers—as well as manufacturers in a wide variety of other industries—practice a kind of branding called **licensing.** Licensing is a process by which designer or character names or identities are leased to businesses for use on their products in exchange for royalties. Millions of consumers now seek out jeans, sportswear, sunglasses, wallets, handbags, and other items bearing the brand names of fashion designers such as Norma Kamali, Calvin Klein, or Perry Ellis.

Licensing
Process by which designer or character names or identities are leased to businesses for use on their products in exchange for royalties.

Why do businesses favor branding? Primarily because it permits a company to distinguish its products from those of others. The company does not have to compete with others directly on the basis of price. Many consumers buy Coca-Cola even when cheaper substitutes are readily available because they have built up a certain loyalty to the brand.

Another important reason for using a brand name is the value it creates and lends to other products the company produces (called the company's product line). For example, after watching its profits plunge along with the U.S. birth rate, Binney & Smith, the manufacturer of Crayola crayons, revamped its marketing strategy. It created a consistent "family" look for the other products in its line by using the familiar yellow and green graphics that distinguish its crayon boxes. As a result, many products, particularly felt marker pens, showed dramatic sales increases.[7]

The transfer of goodwill from one product in a company's line to another is known as the **halo effect.** Ralph Lauren benefits from the halo effect in selling its broad range of products. Similarly, Benetton is planning a fragrance, cosmetics, and skin-care items in the hope that consumers who like its apparel will be attracted to these items as well.[8] Marketing Today 8.1 describes how Swatch USA is also trying to take advantage of the halo effect.

Halo Effect
Transfer of goodwill from one product in a company's line to another.

Consumer groups sometimes complain that branding is detrimental to their interests. Establishing a brand name involves heavy advertising costs that are inevitably passed on to consumers. Marketers counter that while establishing a brand name is expensive, consumers do benefit from the practice. They are guaranteed consistent quality because brand-name companies have a reputation to maintain. Moreover, brand-name merchandise allows a consumer to comparison shop for value. Cuisinart food processors, for instance, are the same everywhere they are sold, so

Marketing Today 8.1
Swatch Shops: Going for the Halo Effect

Swatch USA built its initial success on a hot product gimmick; it sells cheap watches at a high markup. The watches feature bright colors, geometric designs, and a $30 price tag. Between 1983 and 1985, retail sales of the watches soared from $3 million to more than $150 million. The watches sell because they are fun.

The company hopes to expand its business based on the image of its watches. It is putting its brand name on sweatshirts, T-shirts, umbrellas, and sunglasses. These products incorporate the same graphics that attracted consumers to the watches. They are to be sold in Swatch Shops located in a few specialty stores, such as The Limited, and department stores, such as Bloomingdale's.

Swatch hopes to attract young consumers who want status but lack the means to afford it. This market can be fickle, but the company has high hopes.

Source: Matthew Heller, "Swatch Switches," *Forbes*, January 27, 1986, pp. 86–87.

potential buyers can compare prices in various stores. Further, some branded products are perceived as conferring status or prestige.

Despite advantages for both the seller and the buyer, some companies decide not to seek national brand awareness for their products. The cost of promoting a national brand may be too great for them. Or they may deal in a standardized product (such as lettuce or nails) that does not readily lend itself to differentiation and brand recognition. Sometimes branding can limit marketing opportunities. Estée Lauder, for example, ordinarily keeps its cosmetics out of discount stores because it wishes to maintain a quality image for the brand.

Planning for Branding

If a company's product is unique and it has the resources to promote the product, the advantages of branding far outweigh the disadvantages. Once the decision to brand has been made, two other important questions must be answered: What type of brand should be used? What name should the product carry?

Brand Type Marketers generally distinguish two types of brands. A **family brand** covers many products under one brand name. For example, the name Heinz is used for ketchup and soups as well as for baked beans, pickles, and relishes. By contrast, some companies treat their products as **individual brands,** giving each product a distinct name. General Mills, for example, produces Gold Medal flour, Nature Valley granola bars, Cocoa Puffs, Chef Saluto pizza, Wheaties, Bisquick, and Betty Crocker cake mixes.

Family Brand
Brand that covers many products under one brand name.

Individual Brand
Distinct name given to each product a company produces.

Family brand names are commonly used when products are essentially similar or sold in the same market. The Heinz products cited are obviously related and might be bought together. Products sharing the same brand name also share promotional costs, thus cutting down on that expense. Moreover, new products can take advantage of the halo effect.

Sometimes a company produces products that are essentially dissimilar, so no halo effect could occur. Allegis Corporation's Hertz rental cars, United Airlines, and Westin hotels may be examples of such products. Another example is the Coca-Cola Company, which uses the Columbia Pictures name on its movies and video services.

Occasionally, one product may actually detract from the sales of another if marketed under the same name. Consumers would probably just as soon not know that the company that produces Purina Cat Chow also makes Rice Chex. Markets, too, may be so dissimilar that individual brand names are essential. Chevrolet and Cadillac, both produced by General Motors, appeal to very different market segments.

Some companies promote individual brands that compete with one another. Procter & Gamble produces two toothpastes under individual brand names—Crest and Gleem. Marketers call this tactic a **multiple brand strategy.** Procter & Gamble maintains that this policy promotes efficiency within the company by encouraging competition between individual brand managers. Also, since there is competition for supermarket space among companies, P&G thus keeps its competitor (Colgate-Palmolive) from having more room to display its products. And, if consumers decide to switch from Crest, they might switch to Gleem, thus retaining sales for P&G. Finally, a multiple brand strategy increases a firm's total market share.

Multiple Brand Strategy
Corporate practice of promoting individual brands that compete with one another.

Naming a Brand For a company that decides on an individual brand name, the next problem is to find a distinctive name around which to build a marketing program. While many companies continue to pick names based on brainstorming sessions, employee contests, or bosses' inspiration, some analysts believe that such unscientific methods pose great risks. Marketing Today 8.2 describes other approaches. Some of

Marketing Today 8.2
A Computer Company Gets a Name

As head of a computer company, Ben Rosen wanted his new product to have widespread recognition. For help he turned to NameLab, a company that specializes in coming up with names for products and organizations.

Ira Bachrach, president of NameLab, scheduled meetings with the computer company's officials to determine what they wanted their product's name to project. They wanted a new word that indicated "small integral object which is a computer."

Next, NameLab's computer sifted through a list of 6,200 morphemes (the smallest meaningful element of a word). The computer prepared a list of every word combination possible using morphemes that suggested small objects and computers. The potential choices included Cortex, Cognipak, Suntek, and Compod. None of these sounded quite right.

Eventually, the computer company and NameLab personnel agreed on "com," which suggested a computer, and "pac," which indicates smallness. To make the printed name more visible, they changed the final "c" to a "q." The company had a name: Compaq Computer Corporation.

Source: Mike Sheridan, "Naming Names," *Sky,* November 1986, pp. 11–12+.

the things a company must keep in mind when choosing a brand name are:

- ☐ The name should be easy to pronounce, recognize, and remember.
- ☐ The name should have impact.
- ☐ The name should be relevant and suggest product benefits.
- ☐ The name should suggest positive images to the consumer.
- ☐ The name should be appropriate to the product category.
- ☐ The name should be available for use.

Many firms fight legal battles to defend their names from encroachers. The Coca-Cola Company has set a record for persistence in defense of a brand name. Coke, the product's trademark, is clearly identified as a registered name by both the word "trademark" and the symbol ® whenever it appears. Typically, the company will initiate 50 cases a year against soft-drink firms who use the name Coke. In addition, the firm sends warning letters to print media when Coke is not capitalized or is used in the possessive form.

Apart from the harmful impression left by the misuse of brand names, companies seek to protect their trademarks because they can lose legal protection and market share if the name comes into common use. Such names as cellophane, thermos, aspirin, escalator, yo-yo, and ping-pong can now be used by any company today because the companies that once owned those names allowed them through usage to become common words describing a product class.

Parker Brothers lost the trademark to its game Monopoly. The United States Supreme Court ruled that it had become the generic term denoting a kind of game. That decision cleared the way for a San Francisco State University professor to market a game called Anti-Monopoly. Many analysts expect that the court's action in this case will result in more companies protecting their trademarks by carefully distinguishing the product's brand name from its generic name.[9]

The Battle of the Brands

The term *brand* has been used here mainly in connection with those branded items distributed by national manufacturers. Such items are called **national brands.** In addition, there are products sold under the name of a retailer or wholesale intermediary called **private** (or **distributor**) **brands.** Some private brands have a national reputation even though they are not promoted by a national manufacturer. Perhaps the best known retailer-produced private brands are those of Sears (Kenmore, Craftsman, and Die-Hard) and A&P (Ann Page bread and Eight O'Clock coffee).

National Brand
Branded item distributed by national manufacturers.

Private (Distributor) Brand
Product sold under the name of a retailer or wholesale intermediary.

The "battle of the brands" refers to the competition that exists between owners of national and private brands to win retail outlet shelf space and consumer loyalty.[10] The competition is intense. In 1985, about seven new products were introduced each day, compared to only three a day in 1980.[11]

"House," or private brands, often mimic the formula, specifications, and taste of national brands. In many cases, even the shape of the container and the label imitate the better-known national brand. One obvious advantage that private brands have over national brands is that they are generally less expensive. Because most private brands are not advertised nationally, they can be marketed more cheaply.

The consumer appeal of private brands is matched by their appeal to retailers and wholesalers. Many store owners maintain that such brands allow them greater freedom to sell what they and their customers need. Selling private brands, moreover, allows intermediaries to build up a faithful clientele that prefers such brands. Finally, intermediaries prefer private brands because they earn higher markups on them.

Manufacturers may oppose private brands because they believe their quality is inferior. They also maintain that it is nationally advertised products, not private brands, that tend to bring customers into stores. Despite their objections to private brands, many manufacturers of nationally advertised merchandise also produce private-brand products for retailers. For example, Firestone produces tires for Montgomery Ward under the store's brand name and Ward sells them at competitive prices, and Sears' Kenmore washers and dryers are manufactured by Whirlpool.

Because of their advantages for both consumers and retailers, private brands appear to be gaining in the battle of the brands. Thirty years ago, most Americans bought national brands. According to the National Retail Merchants' Association, private brands account for 60 percent of the annual sales of department stores. They also represent an important share of the grocery business—as much as 16 percent of total sales and up to 35 percent in other categories.[12]

Some supermarkets hope to increase profits by offering an even cheaper alternative to private brands—**generic,** or no-name, **products.**

Generic Product
Product that is unbranded and marketed with minimal advertising.

Table 8.1
Price Comparison of Generic, Private Label, and Nationally Branded Products

Item	Size	National Brand	Private Label	Generic Product
Peanut butter	18 oz.	$2.06	$1.63	$1.23
Tea bags	100	1.99	1.29	.99
Applesauce	25 oz.	.95	.55	.49
Sandwich bags	150	1.12	.89	.69
Strawberry preserves	32 oz.	2.56	2.37	1.51
Crushed pineapple	20 oz.	.79	.75	.59
Facial tissues	175	.96	.69	.55
Orange drink	46 oz.	.68	.54	.49

These are unbranded goods that receive little advertising and may be slightly lower-grade. Since they are usually sold in plain white packages with black lettering, they are also referred to as "no-frills" goods. According to supermarkets that carry the goods, the lower grades, plain packaging, and lack of advertising allow them to sell the products for 15 to 40 percent less than national and private brands.[13]

When generic products were first introduced in 1977, certain national manufacturers predicted that they would be nothing more than a fad. In recent years the growth of generics has leveled off, but they still command about an overall 2 percent market share in supermarkets. Although generics command only a small share of the grocery business, many stores claim they will continue to carry them in order to offer consumers a three-tier price choice. (See Table 8.1 and Figure 8.5.)

Some marketing experts have suggested that a significant market segment may comprise buyers who have a "generic mentality"—that is, they want products that offer simple, basic value. Buyers of generic grocery products tend to be price-conscious members of middle-income, large households.[14]

In the hotly contested area of prescription drugs, the total market for generic equivalents is expected to reach $8 billion by 1990. One success story is Zenith Laboratories, whose sales of generic drugs soared 115 percent from 1984 to 1985.[15]

Brand-name manufacturers maintain that drug products are not always interchangeable. They say generic drugs may vary in the speed at which they are released into the body or in their capacity to produce side effects. Nonetheless, this segment of the market is likely to remain strong, thanks in part to a 1984 federal law easing approval for generics and an increasing number of state laws encouraging pharmacists to substitute generic drugs for brand-name medications when appropriate. A case in point is diazepam, the generic equivalent of Valium. In diazepam's first year on the market, Valium's share fell from 100 to 50 percent.[16]

Figure 8.5
Generic, National, and Private Brands of Peanut Butter and Jelly

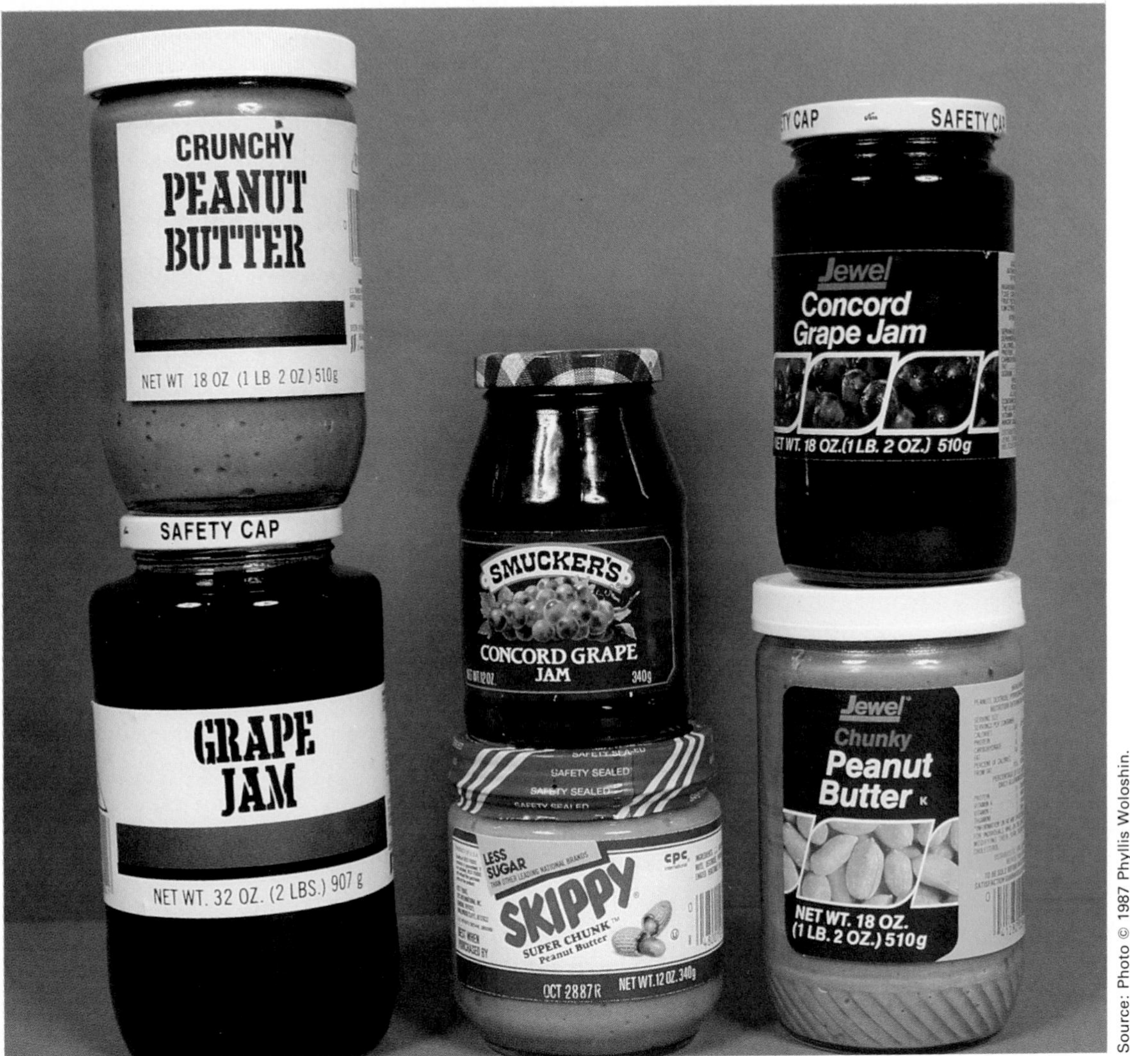

Source: Photo © 1987 Phyllis Woloshin.

Marketing Services

Most of the products discussed so far in this chapter have been tangible items. Products also include services: financial advice, sales services at a store, a taxicab ride, research assistance from a librarian, and entertainment by a singer. Together, services are a large and growing part of the U.S. economy.

The Goods-Services Continuum

When you pay for legal advice, it is clear that your product is intangible—a service. But when you pay for dinner at a restaurant, you are buying something to eat along with the service and something to drink along with the atmosphere. Thus, some products are clearly goods or services, while others fall somewhere in between.

One way to describe the nature of products is to place them on a continuum. At one end are products that are purely tangible; at the other end are purely intangible products. In general, the products on the continuum fall into four major categories of offerings:[17]

1. *A pure tangible good.* Masking tape, margarine, mothballs, and mousetraps are all such goods; no services accompany the product.
2. *A tangible good with accompanying services.* Toaster ovens, calculators, home computers, and microwave ovens usually come with warranties. They may also come with users' manuals, cookbooks, and maintenance tips. Automobile manufacturers offer many customer services with their products. In fact, promoting the quality of a company's postpurchase service has recently become an important aspect of the marketing strategy.
3. *A major service with accompanying minor goods and services.* On an airline flight, a passenger usually accumulates a variety of minor items in addition to the major item (transportation). A trip on the Concorde might net one a rose, an in-flight magazine, a direct-mail catalog of Concorde-inspired accessories, and other items. The airline may also offer additional amenities: earphones for the stereo system, a wheelchair for the disabled, or help in securing a limousine on arrival.
4. *A pure service.* A doctor's advice, a trip to the movies, or a haircut are pure services. Penicillin, popcorn, or shampoo would be additional product purchases.

Characteristics of Services

Four characteristics are unique to services and influence the way they are marketed: intangibility, perishability, simultaneous consumption and production, and lack of control.[18]

Intangibility A service is intangible—a deed, a performance, or an effort. This is true even if providing the service requires equipment. For example, a landscaping service must purchase lawn mowers to do the job, but the company's customers are buying efforts at lawn beautification, not the lawn mowers. Similarly, a bank that offers checking account services may buy automatic teller machines to help it deliver those services more economically.

Perishability Sellers of tangible goods can generally stock some inventory to meet demand during peak periods or order less when sales are slower. For services, however, there is no inventory. This makes it especially important for services providers to anticipate and respond to changing levels of demand.

Perishability of their product has been an issue for many colleges and universities as the 18- to 22-year-old population has shrunk. The schools simply cannot put their faculty into cold storage and wait for the environment to change. In Lexington, Kentucky, Transylvania University has responded by each year offering 25 full four-year scholarships to National Merit Scholars. Not only has enrollment improved, but the scholarship winners have inspired faculty and fellow students to work harder, possibly improving the academic climate for everyone.[19]

Simultaneous Consumption and Production Sadly enough, you simply cannot get your cavities filled unless you accompany your teeth to the dentist. You also cannot be transported to Paris unless you show up at the dock or the airport. Services are used at the same time that they are produced. This typically puts the supplier of services into close contact with customers.

It also means that customers cannot test products before they buy them. As a result, consumers of services tend to perceive relatively greater risk when they are shopping for a service. They rely more heavily on the recommendations of others.[20] Amica Mutual Insurance, for example, has prospered by focusing on good service and letting referrals substitute for advertising.[21]

Lack of Control To maintain a standard of high quality, makers of tangible goods can discard defective products before they reach the consumer. The quality of service delivered is harder to control. On an airplane, a passenger's flight may be ruined by a thunderstorm or an irritable flight attendant. Such experiences can alter a passenger's perception of an entire airline.

Marketers of services try to compensate by controlling where they can. Some companies go to great lengths to standardize their services. It is no coincidence that McDonald's restaurants are nearly identical whether they are in Maine or California. Another approach to control is to invest in high-quality employees. For example, Nordstrom department stores pay their sales clerks about 20 percent more than the clerks of competitors. Nordstrom trains them thoroughly and encourages them to do almost anything within reason to satisfy customers. The store also has a policy of replacing any item on demand.[22]

Marketing Strategy Decisions

To market services effectively, a company must perform many of the same basic functions it would do if its product were a tangible good, but often with significant differences. (See At Your Service 8.1.) For example, a service company must analyze the market to determine consumer needs and preferences, but it must also consider whether the concept it has in mind will be understandable and attractive to consumers. Often, this must be accomplished without the same kinds of test marketing and marketing research that usually accompany new product introductions.

A service provider must also analyze its abilities to deliver the service. If a restaurant has limited seating, for example, it could do itself more harm than good by mounting a large promotional effort that might generate demand it could not satisfy.

At Your Service 8.1
Chicago Parking Garages Get Exciting

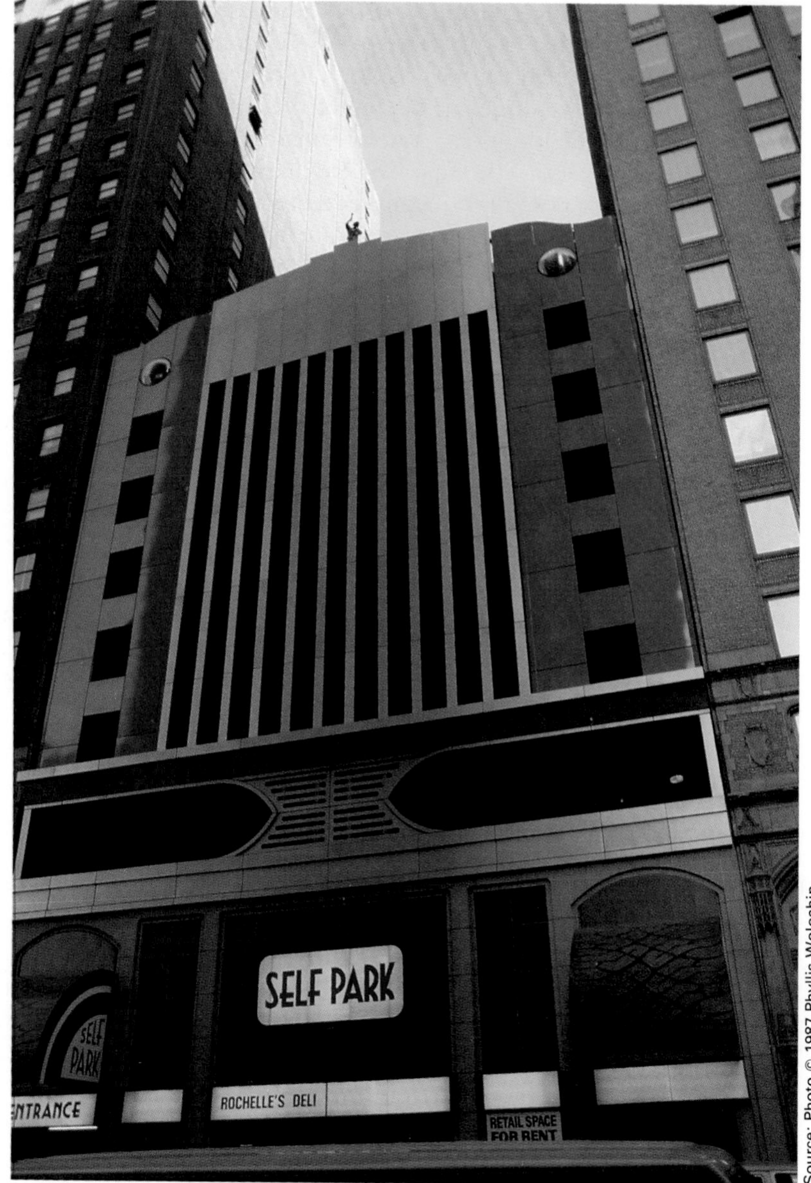

Source: Photo © 1987 Phyllis Woloshin.

Chicago developer Ronald B. Grais has a philosophy about parking: "If you want to excite people about being downtown, you've got to make the entire experience pleasant. It doesn't matter how good the shopping or the restaurants or the theaters are, the first thing people do is park."

To make that first experience a pleasant one, Grais has opened a downtown parking garage designed by an award-winning architect. Its facade is designed in the shape of a classic touring car's front end. And at the sidewalk level is a retail tenant.

Retail space is also a feature of two other Chicago parking garages developed by Grais. And the garages have themes as well. In one garage, each floor has a visual and musical theme of a different U.S. city. The other garage is the "Theater District" garage, where each deck is named after a well-known Broadway musical and the title song from each show is playing on the appropriate level.

Explains the operator of one of the garages, "We have added a new dimension—ambience—in parking."

Source: F. K. Plous, Jr., "City's Parking Garages Losing Mundane Image," *Crain's Chicago Business,* August 25, 1986, pp. T8–T9.

In addition, a service company must analyze the competition. This process is also trickier for services than it is for products. The competition is not just other service businesses, but what people can do for themselves. A person who wants a well-kept lawn, for instance, can do it alone, see that the family's children do it, or hire a lawn service. Service industries must keep consumers' options in mind when designing a marketing strategy.

Once a market analysis is completed, a service company must identify the market segments it wants to reach and investigate ways to reach them. Because services may mean different things to different people, more initial research may be required to determine how the public really views a proposed service. Service marketers must rely more heavily than product marketers on the tools and skills of psychology, sociology, and other behavioral sciences to uncover the public's perception of their offering and to determine how those markets might be segmented.[23]

Finally, because a service is essentially abstract, it becomes very important to pay attention to the tangible elements surrounding the service. In a restaurant, this may include making sure the tablecloth is spotless, the restrooms immaculate, the menus attractively printed, and the bar well stocked. It may also extend to dismissing a surly bus boy or recooking a dissatisfied customer's steak.

To the extent possible, management of the physical environment should be one of a service marketer's highest priorities. For example, Big Sam's hair salons, which call themselves "the hair club," use the atmosphere of the salons to appeal to their target market: people in their teens and twenties. The salon's design blends Art Deco with mirrors, chrome, and bright colors. (See Figure 8.6.) The stylists wear casual clothing, and popular music is played loud—all to make the young customers feel at home.[24]

In a similar fashion, even the quality of a firm's letterhead may influence a consumer's perception of the company's service. A cheaply duplicated, nonpersonalized letter contradicts any words about service quality in the text.

Special attention should also be paid to creating advertising and promotion that gives the service a concrete image in the public's mind. Merrill Lynch's herd of bulls is a clear, visible symbol for its abstract financial services.

A service's price often determines how people perceive its quality. Because comparison shopping is often difficult, customers will pay what they think the service is worth. Thus, pricing in many service businesses is based on whatever the market will bear. Rarely, for example, will you hear businesspeople boast that they have just hired the cheapest consultant available.[25]

As the service industry becomes more competitive, more companies are offering guarantees as a way to differentiate themselves from the competition. Certain services, such as those offered by hairdressers, are so personal that guarantees of satisfaction would be difficult to fulfill, but others, among them Federal Express—and even the U.S. Post Office—are now willing to guarantee fulfillment, such as overnight delivery of a package or letter.

The service sector accounts for two-thirds of the U.S. gross national product, and three of four nonfarm jobs.[26] As this sector of the economy continues to grow, marketers will be increasingly expected to respond to the unique challenges posed by service marketing.

Figure 8.6
Big Sam's Uses Ambiance to Attract Its Target Market

Source: Courtesy of S. M. R. Enterprises, Inc., Memphis, Tennessee.

Chapter Replay

1. **Why is new-product development risky?**
   Customer needs, government regulations, and competitor offerings continually change. Launching a new product can be enormously expensive. One marketer's new products must compete for attention with many other new offerings.
2. **What are three dimensions of products?**
   Three dimensions of products are a basic benefit, physical or functional features, and additional benefits or services.
3. **How are consumer products classified?**
   Consumer products may be (a) convenience goods, which include staple items, impulse items, and emergency items; (b) shopping

goods, which may be homogeneous or heterogeneous; or (c) specialty goods.

4. **How are industrial products classified?**
   Industrial products may be installations, accessory equipment, raw materials, component parts or materials, or supplies.
5. **What are some pros and cons of branding?**
   Branding permits a business to distinguish its products from those of others so that it does not have to compete directly on the basis of price. Brand names lend value to other products the company produces and guarantee consistent quality. Consumer groups sometimes complain that branding is detrimental to their interests because the costs are passed on to consumers.
6. **What issues do marketers face in planning for branding?**
   The marketer must decide whether to use a family brand or individual brands, including, possibly, a multiple brand strategy. The company also must find a distinctive brand name around which to build the marketing program.
7. **What are some advantages of nationally branded, private label, and generic products?**
   Nationally branded products, according to their manufacturers, bring people into stores and are of higher quality. Private label products resemble national brands but at a lower cost. According to store owners, they allow stores to stock what customers want and to build up a faithful clientele. Generic products are the least expensive.
8. **What characteristics of services distinguish them from goods?**
   Services are intangible, perishable, simultaneously consumed and produced, and difficult for marketers to control.
9. **What special issues arise in marketing services?**
   Some concepts may be difficult for consumers to understand. Providers must have the capacity to deliver the product. The competition for services includes customers who can provide the service themselves. Service providers may find it more difficult to uncover public perceptions and to segment the market. Marketers must pay special attention to the tangible elements surrounding the service and to the promotional message. Difficulty in comparison shopping may affect how consumers view a service's price.

Key Terms

consumer products
convenience goods
emergency items
family brand
generic product
halo effect
heterogeneous shopping goods
homogeneous shopping goods
impulse items
individual brand
licensing
multiple brand strategy
national brand
private (distributor) brand
product
shopping goods
specialty goods
staple items

Discussion Questions

1. Products may be thought of as having three dimensions. Read the following scenario and identify which features of the product purchased fall into each of these three dimensions.

   Marianne Matrix wanted to spend less time writing term papers, so she bought a word-processing software package for her personal computer. Included with the diskette containing the software was an instruction manual. On the first page of the manual, Marianne found the phone number of a toll-free hotline for customer questions.

2. Identify each of the following as a convenience good, a shopping good, or a specialty good. For convenience goods, state whether they are staple, impulse, or emergency items. State whether shopping goods are homogeneous or heterogeneous.

   a. The boots Marge bought when they were on sale.
   b. The bottle of aspirin Jim bought when his head began to ache.
   c. The rare Bordeaux wine Alicia bought for a special dinner she was planning.
   d. The newspaper Philip bought when the headline caught his eye.

3. What is the difference between a brand and a trademark?
4. What are some advantages of using branding? Why do some consumer groups object to the practice? Why do some companies choose not to use branding?
5. Under what circumstances would a company use a family brand? Under what circumstances would it use individual brands?
6. In the Sears catalog, microwave ovens, refrigerators, and vacuum cleaners carry the brand name Kenmore; tool chests, hammers, tractors, and ladders carry the name Craftsman. What type of brands are these? What benefits does Sears derive from selling such brands?
7. Marge McClain is a real estate broker; her product is the service of bringing together buyers and sellers of real estate. Explain why her product can be described as perishable. How might the perishability of Marge's product affect the way she markets it?
8. Last March, Max Mustard decided to open a generic tax preparation company. He thought that a lot of people would want to cut costs, especially considering how painful it is to pay taxes anyway. So Max signed a lease for a plain storefront office, bought a couple of chairs and a second-hand steel desk, and moved in. His only advertising was a black-and-white sign that read in plain block letters, "Tax Preparer, Cheap. Open 8 a.m. to 4 p.m."

   Based on what you have read about marketing services, why do you think Max's business failed?

9. Because a service is intangible, marketers need to pay attention to the tangible elements surrounding the service. What tangible elements do you look for when selecting a restaurant?

Case 8.1
Cheryl's Cookies

Cheryl's Cookies

Cheryl's Cookies enters 1986 with plans to open 2 to 5 stores during the year and to position itself not just as a place to buy a cookie or brownie, but also as a gift shop. In a little over four years since the firm was founded, Cheryl's has grown from a single shop to a mininetwork of stores in Ohio, Indiana, Pennsylvania, Missouri, and New Jersey. The company would like to have 100 stores open by 1990.

Company Background

People in Bellevue, Ohio, probably best remember Cheryl Krueger as the little farm girl who made cookies for various church groups. As the eldest of three children, Krueger was always baking. The aroma of cookies, cakes, brownies, and other baked goods always seemed to fill the family home.

A 1974 graduate of Bowling Green University, Krueger gained some of her early business experience as a buyer for Burdines, one of the Federated stores, and The Limited, based in Columbus. "Through my travels I saw David's Cookies and Mrs. Fields' Cookies, which operate on both coasts," she said. "We lived on a farm when I was a child, and I was always baking things at home. I thought it would be great to bring something like David's or Mrs. Fields' to Columbus." At first, Krueger weighed the advantages and disadvantages of bringing one of those franchised operations to Columbus. "But, it would always be their store, and I didn't really want that," she said.

The first Cheryl's Cookies was opened in September 1981. In January of the next year, the second store was opened. Sales for 1982 reached $250,000. By the end of 1985, the company had 14 stores with total sales of $2.5 million. Krueger estimated average monthly sales at about 280,000 cookies with around quadruple that to 1.2 million during the 1985 Christmas season. Overall, the company has some 130 to 150 full- and part-time employees. Krueger estimates that sales from 15 to 18 units will top $4 million during 1986.

Product Description

The stores feature about ten varieties of cookies, including chocolate chip and chocolate chunk, peanut butter, oatmeal, macadamia coconut, oatmeal raisin, white chocolate pecan, and others. Through product development, Krueger keeps the assortment current with demands of the consumers. She is currently developing her line of brownies by adding more chips and switching varieties of pecans, finding that the brownies sell better than chocolate chunk cookies. When Cheryl's first

Source: This case has been edited from an earlier one that appeared in *Cases and Exercises in Marketing*, by W. Wayne Talarzyk. Copyright © 1987 by CBS College Publishing. Logo courtesy of Cheryl's Cookies.

started, the cookies were priced at $4 per pound. Today they sell for $4.95 per pound compared to competitors' prices that range up to $6.95 per pound.

In addition to over-the-counter business, Cheryl's operates a good-sized mail-order service, especially around Christmas. Orders can be placed at the store or by phone, charged to Visa or MasterCard, if preferred, and mailed anywhere in the continental United States. Cheryl's also has a corporate gift service that assists organizations in arranging gifts for corporations, fund-raisers, or any group purchase. Discounts for quantity purchases are available. In some of Cheryl's market areas, the firm's delivery service will deliver free of charge orders of $3 or more in designated downtown areas.

Cheryl's has recently introduced several new cookie packages, as well as packages that combine cookies with nonedible items like oven mittens and coffee mugs. Cheryl's offers three different sizes of cookie tins and two sizes of gift boxes. Four sizes of "gourmet dessert baskets" have been created and are priced from $39 to $75 each. In addition to brownies or cookies, the baskets contain such items as dessert sauces, gourmet coffee, imported chocolates, nuts, napkins, kitchen mittens, and coffee mugs.

Additional Information

All of Cheryl's cookie and brownie dough is prepared in Columbus and shipped frozen in 30-pound boxes via the company's own refrigerated trucks. "We're trying to have control of a highly perishable product," Krueger explains. Each location gets a four-week inventory per trip. The dough is thawed and baked as needed in each store. The centralized preparation enables the company to ensure consistent quality. There is no difference in taste between cookies baked from fresh or frozen raw dough.

To help use the additional retail space, the firm is introducing some gourmet innovations. For example, at the Columbus store, the firm is testing new ideas like muffins, croissants, and freshly squeezed orange juice in the morning, and different kinds of coffee. The store opens at 7 a.m. to capture the didn't-have-time-for-breakfast trade Monday through Friday. If there is a special evening event in the downtown area, the store will stay open for after-theater customers. For this group there will be espresso, cappuccino, and perhaps some gourmet desserts. Unlike the other Cheryl's Cookies, this store has tables at which to sit.

Focal Topics

1. What is the "real business" of Cheryl's Cookies? What do you see as the marketing problems it is likely to face in the future?
2. What are the benefits sought in a product like Cheryl's Cookies by each of the following market segments: (a) consumer (personal use), (b) consumer (gift-giving), and (c) organization (gift-giving)?
3. What recommendations do you have for Cheryl's in terms of the firm's product and service offering?

Case 8.2
Geo. A. Hormel & Company

Geo. A. Hormel & Company, founded by George A. Hormel in 1891 in Austin, Minnesota, is a federally inspected food processor engaged in the processing of livestock into meat and meat products, the production of a variety of prepared foods (both meat and nonmeat), and the marketing of these products throughout the United States.

Overview of Products

The principal products of the company are meat and meat products, which are sold fresh, frozen, cured, smoked, cooked, and canned. The products of the Meat Products Group include fresh and frozen meats, sausages, hams, wieners, and bacon. The Prepared Foods Group products include canned luncheon meats, stews, chilies, hash, and meat spreads.

The company's products are sold in all 50 states by sales representatives who operate in assigned territories that are coordinated from district sales offices located in most of the larger U.S. cities, and by brokers and distributors who handle carload lot sales.

Numerous trademarks are important to the company's business, including Hormel, SPAM, Dinty Moore, Mary Kitchen, Cure 81, Curemaster, Black Label, Di Lusso, Little Sizzlers, Wranglers, Light & Lean, Super Select, Rosa, Homeland, Range Brand, Frank 'N Stuff, and Broiled & Browned.

Prepared Foods Group

New Products To strengthen its leadership position, the company introduced two new products—Hormel chili with beans (reduced salt) and Hormel chunky chili—nationally during the year. Twenty-five percent of the salt has been removed from Hormel chili with beans. This specialty product, which meets tailored consumer tastes for reduced sodium content in their diets, is an example of niche marketing, or providing innovative and distinct products for specialized market segments. Hormel chunky chili is a premium product formulated specifically to attract new users to the category.

New-product activity in 1985 was highlighted by the introduction of CountrySide salads, four distinct varieties of fully-prepared salads freshly packed in a new, modern-looking plastic container. This new line takes full advantage of the growing consumer trend toward more nutritious, healthful, and lighter meals that feature fresh foods and vegetables. Recent changes in life-styles and the accelerated pace of daily life have created a need for convenient, fully prepared side dishes, either to complement a

Source: Adapted from Geo. A. Hormel & Company's *1985 Annual Report.* Logo courtesy of Geo. A. Hormel & Company.

main course or as meals in themselves. CountrySide salads were developed with these contemporary consumers in mind.

The newest additions to the family of Short Orders individually canned servings are Dinty Moore chicken stew and Hormel scalloped potatoes and pepperoni. Twenty-four items comprise the extensive array of single-portion meat and meat/pasta products offered under the Hormel, Dinty Moore, and Mary Kitchen brand names to the retail, vending, and mobile catering trade.

SPAM Luncheon Meat Increasingly, new products are vital to growth in the food industry. Balance must be kept, however, between established and new products.

The most notable example is SPAM luncheon meat. This flagship product posted a record-high 73 percent of all canned luncheon meat sales and gained 3 percent in volume during 1985, even though the category itself was declining. The base of this overwhelming popularity stems from the 50 million Americans who regularly purchase SPAM luncheon meat. To reinforce the brand's popularity with established consumers and to attract nonusers to the category, extensive advertising and promotional activities were launched. The most exciting element was the "Instant Winner" game, whereby $100,000 was awarded to consumers who found a secret slogan printed beneath the lid of specially marked SPAM luncheon meat cans. At a cost of $1.5 million, this promotion was the largest single merchandising effort ever undertaken by Hormel.

Research studies determined that SPAM luncheon meat sales have a very high index in Hispanic markets. As a result, Hormel began running a series of Spanish radio commercials in selected markets with high Hispanic populations.

In a program aimed at modernizing SPAM luncheon meat to make it more compatible with today's fast-paced, nutritionally oriented lifestyles, several new product improvements and line extensions are under consideration.

Focal Topics

1. What is your evaluation of Hormel's product strategy?
2. Do you think that more prominent use of the Hormel name should be made, such as Hormel's Dinty Moore beef stew or Hormel's CountrySide salads? Why, or why not?
3. What would you do if you were the brand manager for SPAM?

9 Product Development and Strategy

Sounding Out the Chapter

In this chapter, you will learn:

1. What makes a product new.
2. The stages of a product's life cycle.
3. What is involved in the incubation of a new product.
4. How companies delegate responsibility for developing new products.
5. How marketing proceeds during the introduction of a new product.
6. How marketers take advantage of the growth phase.
7. The marketing emphasis during a product's maturity.
8. How marketers manage the decline phase of the product life cycle.

Source: © 1986 Jeff Slocumb/The Picture Group, Inc.

Test Audiences Vote for Happy Endings

If you saw the movie *Risky Business,* you might have envied the way that Joel Goodsen (Tom Cruise) seemed to have it all. Joel gets a practical experience in free enterprise when a young hooker named Lana (Rebecca De Mornay) helps him turn his parents' fancy suburban home into a bordello for a night. After that big party and an unorthodox college interview, he gets into Princeton. He feels great.

The movie's author isn't so happy. The ending you saw is not the original one Paul Brickman wrote for *Risky Business.* In the original ending, Joel Goodsen doesn't get into Princeton, he and Lana don't walk off into a starry night, and when Joel describes his money-making scheme at the end of the movie, his voice is grim.

Why the change? Movie makers conduct audience research, and this research shows that moviegoers want the story to make them feel good. Hollywood has found that there's more money to be made in a happy ending. In the case of *Risky Business,* test audiences watched the movie with the original ending and with the happier ending that was ultimately used. The test audiences preferred the version that didn't teach a lesson.

Test audiences also influenced the ending of *Pretty in Pink.* The first version had Andie (Molly Ringwald) attend the prom with her faithful pal Duckie (Jon Cryer). In the final version, however, she ends up with handsome, preppie Blaine. The paperback novelization of the movie uses the original ending.

Another movie influenced by test audiences was *First Blood.* Three endings were planned for the movie: the original ending, in which Rambo dies at the end; one in which he is wounded and carried off in a stretcher; and one in which he breaks down and is led away crying uncontrollably. Of these endings, two were filmed, and the one in which Rambo is carried off was not. Test audiences saw the two versions, but their preferences for the endings were split 50-50. The final decision—to let Rambo live—enabled the subsequent filming of *Rambo: First Blood Part II* and *Rambo III.* Says director Ted Kotcheff, "It's a good thing we didn't kill him. Everybody would be a lot poorer."

Planning and selling new movies and other new products is a complex process. Marketers want to develop products that will have a strong and enduring appeal. This chapter describes the development of new products, as well as strategies for marketing them as their popularity grows, matures, and declines.

Source: Pat H. Broeske, "Hollywood's Change of Art," *Rolling Stone,* February 12, 1987, pp. 24+.

Americans have always been fascinated with newness. From the New Deal to New Wave, U.S. native optimism is rekindled at the idea of a fresh beginning.

American businesspeople share this fascination with novelty. Many companies invest heavily in the development of new products. As a result, a 1981 study predicted that new products would account for one-third of U.S. companies' profits in the 1980s.[1]

A case in point is 3M Company, where products less than five years old account for one-quarter of the company's sales.[2] According to Robert Adams, 3M's senior vice president of technical services, management considers just about anything related to coated products to be a possible 3M line. This tradition dates back to the 1950s, when one of the company's technicians thought of making an extra-wide sheet of adhesive that could be used as a drape during surgery. Today, the technician is 3M's chairman of the board, and health-care products and services account for a significant part of the company's sales. One of the company's best known innovations of the 1980s is Post-It notes, developed as a result of research into a new type of adhesive.

3M actively encourages innovation within the company. Salespeople try to obtain one-fourth of their revenue from items that were not in the product line the year before. Engineers are encouraged to spend 15 percent of their time working on new ideas of their own. In this way, 3M encourages **intrapreneurship**—entrepreneurial activity within an organization.[3] 3M hopes that its intrapreneurs will enable the company to continue bringing out successful new products.

Intrapreneurship
Entrepreneurial activity within an organization.

New Products

What is a new product? According to the Federal Trade Commission, a company can call its product "new" for up to six months after it enters regular distribution. In planning a marketing strategy, however, companies need a broader definition of newness.

New Product
Good or service new to the company producing it.

In general, a **new product** is a good or service new to the company producing it. This may include a technological breakthrough, such as digital audio tape machines. Or it may be merely an existing product to which the company has made major or minor revisions, such as Pillsbury's calcium-enriched flour.

When the new product has a different function than existing products, marketers must not only tell consumers that the product exists, they must also educate them about the use of the product. For example, the managers of the first tanning salons had to generate publicity about what was involved in visiting a tanning salon. Then they could encourage customers to visit their particular establishment.

More commonly, a new product is an improvement on an existing product. A product improvement can be a relatively minor change in packaging, formula, or design. For example, when consumers indicated concern about meeting their calcium requirements, Breyers printed "High in Calcium" on its yogurt cartons. Pillsbury added calcium to its

Figure 9.1
Product Life Cycle

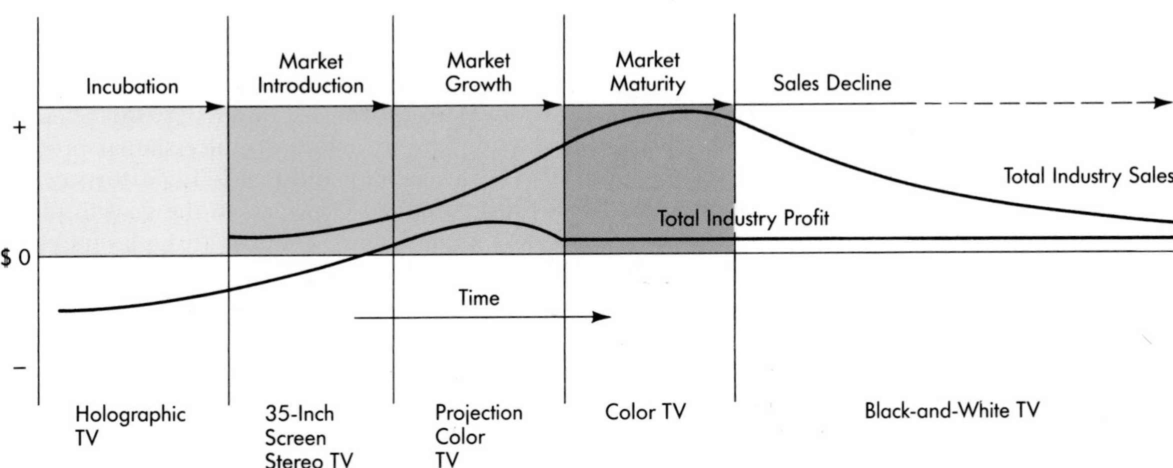

flour and indicated this fact on its package.[4] A product improvement can also be a major change in the product itself, such as the development of disposable cameras.

Improvements on a product already manufactured by a company qualify as new when they involve a shift in the firm's marketing effort. For example, even though the "High in Calcium" message on a carton of yogurt does not change what is inside the carton, the company has changed part of the total marketing mix (in this case, promotion).

To maintain a competitive edge, companies invest much time and effort in improving upon and developing new products. These investments are necessary to the firm's survival. To understand why, we must investigate the concept of the product life cycle.

The Product Life Cycle

William Shakespeare spoke of the seven ages of man from birth to death. Like humans, products also pass through several phases. The **product life cycle** is composed of five phases: (1) incubation, (2) introduction, (3) growth, (4) maturity, and (5) decline. Figure 9.1 depicts the product life cycle in terms of the sales and profit of a typical product. It also gives examples of a product at each phase of the cycle.

Product Life Cycle
Five phases through which a product passes: (1) incubation, (2) introduction, (3) growth, (4) maturity, and (5) decline.

In the **incubation phase,** a company conceives, develops, and tests a product before bringing it to the marketplace. Figure 9.1 shows the profit line sinking below the axis because research and development drain money from the company. For example, companies working on development of holographic television are not yet bringing in any money for this product.

Incubation Phase
Stage of product life cycle during which a product is conceived, developed, and tested.

Introductory Phase
Stage of product life cycle during which a company brings a new product to the marketplace.

After testing, a product enters the **introductory phase,** during which a company brings the new product to the marketplace. Sales begin to build as potential buyers learn of the product from advertising. But profits are still generally low because the company must recoup some of its losses incurred in developing the product. Thirty-five-inch screen stereo TVs represent a product at this stage of the life cycle.

Growth Phase
Stage of product life cycle during which product availability and marketing efforts expand and sales and profits surge upward.

As buyer interest expands, a product moves into its **growth phase.** Other firms, sensing a marketing opportunity, introduce similar products at this phase. Both product availability and marketing efforts expand, and sales and profits surge upward. Products in the growth phase include nonaspirin pain killers, granola bars, compact disk players, health clubs, and financial planning. In Figure 9.1, projection color TV illustrates a product in this stage of relatively rapid growth and high profits.

Maturity Phase
Stage of product life cycle during which the number of buyers continues to grow, but more slowly, until sales level off.

In the **maturity phase,** the number of buyers continues to grow, but more slowly, until a leveling-off occurs. So many competitors have entered the field that supply exceeds demand. Competition becomes more fierce, money is spent to lure customers from one brand to another, and profits may begin to decline. Most products now on the market are in this phase of the life cycle. Color televisions are at this stage. Similarly, owners of video stores have struggled to keep up in a maturing market. (See At Your Service 9.1.)

Decline Phase
Stage of product life cycle during which products start losing a significant number of customers without replacing them.

When products start losing a significant number of customers without replacing them, they enter the **decline phase.** Both sales and profits drop steadily, and new products begin to take the place of declining products. Black-and-white televisions are an endangered species since the introduction of color television. And you probably don't ever have to worry about learning how to use a slide rule now that pocket calculators are so inexpensive. Producers of slide rules must turn to other products.

Length of the Product Life Cycle

In diagrams of product life cycles, the vertical axis indicates the dollar amount of sales and profit and the horizontal axis shows the amount of time for each phase. In general, it is much easier to specify sales and profits than time span because the length of the product life cycle varies greatly from product to product. Generalizations are risky, though some have been made.[5]

One study has found a 40-year life cycle for many industrial products. For grocery products, the product life cycle may be as short as 12 to 18 months. For most types of products, because of the increasing pace of technological innovations and the rapid rate at which new products are being introduced, the life cycle is shrinking.[6]

Fad
Product with a short life cycle, usually no more than two years.

Some products, called **fads,** have extremely short life cycles, usually no more than two years. Fads have shorter lives because they do not require much development time and they usually skip the maturity phase. Pet Rocks, Silly Putty, Hula Hoops, Rubik's Cubes, and Wacky Wallwalkers were all products extremely popular for short periods of time and then settled to the bottoms of toy boxes where they languished until exhumed for yard sales.

At Your Service 9.1
Video Store Wars

Source: Photo © 1987 Phyllis Woloshin.

During the early 1980s, the videocassette rental business was hot. Such a business was relatively easy to operate and relatively inexpensive to enter, and customer demand for home videos was booming. Many new businesses opened during that time, and, as a result, the competition has become stiff. Today, owners of video stores are competing with video rental services at car washes, grocery stores, and even in vending machines that accept credit cards. In addition, video superstores stock as many as 10,000 movies, compared to 2,000 titles in a typical neighborhood shop.

The owners of small rental shops are having a particularly difficult time competing against giant chains such as K mart, Wal-Mart, and Waldenbooks. The competition has cut prices by 50 percent or more. Because the big chains can get quantity discounts, the competition is especially hard on the small shops.

While many mom-and-pop operations are closing down, others are trying to find a niche in the market. Some offer more personal service. Others, such as Video Adventure, of Evanston, Illinois, attract an upscale clientele with foreign titles and movies featuring dance and opera.

Source: Stephen Koepp, "Clash of the Video Merchants," *Time,* November 17, 1986, p. 74.

Importance of the Product Life Cycle

Although it is extremely difficult to predict when the sales and profit of a particular product will peak, the life-cycle concept is a useful tool for marketing managers. Earlier we indicated that companies must continuously create new products and recreate the image of their older products. The life-cycle concept explains why.

The product life cycle reminds management that sooner or later a product will die. If a business is to be an ongoing concern, it must develop new products or improve on those already established. Microwave ovens, for example, will probably replace many gas and electric ranges within the next 20 years, just as color televisions have now replaced most black-and-white sets. Appliance manufacturers that have not already entered the microwave market may be too late and may have to drop out of the market for stoves altogether.

The product life cycle also indicates that a firm's products must compete with the products of other companies for consumer attention. By knowing the phase through which a particular product passes, marketers can plan a strategy to meet that competition. A declining product may have to be replaced; a mature product may simply need more advertising. In the remainder of this chapter, we will investigate each phase of the product life cycle.

The Incubation Phase

Even the simplest products require a large amount of work. An example is the development of dust-free Kitty Litter. To maintain its leadership in the market for cat litter in the face of competition from Clorox, Lowe Industries, the makers of Kitty Litter, decided to try to make a product with less dust. First, Lowe Industries developed a machine that used vacuum vents to shake the dust out of the litter before packaging. The device didn't work; more dust was generated during shipping.

So the company quadrupled its research and development spending from $1 million to $4 million. Months passed, the researchers kept sending the marketing committee dust-free products, and the committee kept sending them back. Meanwhile, Clorox's Fresh Step was gaining on Kitty Litter. Finally, two years later, Lowe Industries had developed a successful dust-control additive. The company introduced 99 percent dust-free versions of its two products, Kitty Litter and Tidy Cat 3.[7]

This example shows that the incubation of a product involves several important steps. First, a product idea must be conceived. Next, the idea must be developed; it must be shown to be feasible technically and from a business perspective. Finally, marketers must demonstrate in some way that the public will buy it. The process is the same whether the product is a television show, a new toy, or a college textbook.

To keep up with today's rapid pace of product development, many companies are seeking ways to bring out new products faster than before. Some marketing experts suggest replacing the traditional sequential approach with a holistic approach. In this approach, product development is the responsibility of a team of people with many areas of expertise, such as marketing or research and development. The team members share information throughout the development process, revising plans as research and testing increase their information. Canon, for example, developed its Sure Shot camera using this approach.[8]

Conception

According to one marketing wit, the "perfect product" is one that is (1) cheaper than any possible competitor's product, (2) nonreusable, and (3) guaranteed to be habit forming. Needless to say, perfect products are scarce. Companies generally settle for far less in their search for new product ideas. They look mainly for ideas that seem technically feasible.

Where do technically feasible product ideas originate? They can come from almost any source. In general, however, companies usually derive new product ideas from one of three sources: (1) their work force, (2) customers, or (3) competitors.

Company Work Force Many firms maintain research and development departments that look for product ideas related to the technology the company has already developed. The Du Pont Company, which specializes in synthetic materials such as nylon, plastics, and polyesters, is an outstanding example. Another is Eastman Kodak, which has more than 600 Ph.D.s on its staff who turn out thousands of scientific papers each year.

Not all product ideas originate with a company's research staff. For example, an assembly-line worker for the Lewyt Company, a manufacturer of industrial cleaners, came up with the idea for a home vacuum cleaner. One of Pillsbury's greatest successes, Crisp Crust Pizza, was based on an old family recipe of a company vice president.

Customers Feedback from customers is also an important source of new product ideas. Sometimes companies send out questionnaires or set up interviews to ask customers for their complaints or suggestions. As a result of questioning more than 2,000 people, for example, Gillette discovered consumer demand for a roll-on deodorant that goes on dry. The product, Dry Idea, was launched a few years later.[9] Consumers' complaints about having to run down to their washing machines at the rinse cycle to pour in fabric softener led Procter & Gamble to develop Bounce, a rayon softener sheet that goes in the dryer.[10]

Competitors Perhaps the major source of product ideas for a company is the new products of competitors. Copying competitors' ideas can save a company a great deal in research and development costs; by looking at competitors' results, marketers can gauge what works and what doesn't. It can also save the imitating company the expense of building initial demand. For example, Ed Lowe came up with the idea of labeling 10-pound bags of dirt Kitty Litter and selling them in pet stores and supermarkets. Once this idea became practical, Clorox moved into the market with a similar but improved product.[11]

One of the most publicized cases of all times was that of the stainless steel blade. The Wilkinson Sword Company, manufacturer of swords and garden tools, produced a small quantity of stainless steel razor blades for the U.S. market and sold them through garden shops. There was an immediate demand for the blades because of their superiority over those then on the market. The Wilkinson Company did not have the production capacity to keep up with demand, so the Gillette Company jumped into the market. Gillette soon surpassed Wilkinson in production and thereafter retained the largest share of the market.

Development

A company must sift through ideas that flow in, gear up for production, and conceive a workable marketing program for each new product. This is the second step of the incubation phase—development.

Organizational Arrangements Almost all company departments—research and development, finance, marketing, and production—have some say in new-product development. Many large and medium-size companies with diverse products have found that assigning their marketing managers the duty of coordinating input from many other departments becomes too burdensome. They cannot efficiently handle both new product development and the management of existing products, which is their primary responsibility. Some firms have tried to resolve this dilemma by creating the post of new product manager. In practice, however, this arrangement also has serious drawbacks. New product managers rarely have authority over members of other departments, so they must rely on persuasion to implement their decisions.

Many companies now delegate responsibility for new product decisions to a group rather than an individual. Three types of groups have been used:

New Product Committee Group of top-level executives and representatives of several departments that meets regularly to consider new products.

1. The **new product committee.** This group is composed of top-level executives and representatives of several departments. At the Gerber Company, for example, the board chairman, president, vice president, and other officers representing diverse interests meet once a month to consider new-product ideas.[12] Their high standing in the company guarantees that disputes over authority will seldom arise.

   This type of organization usually serves a company well when only a few product ideas must be considered. The major disadvantage of the new product committee is that, since it meets only occasionally, it cannot handle a large volume of ideas efficiently. Meeting more frequently would be a costly use of time for a company's highest-paid executives.

New Product Department Permanent committee that works on new product ideas on a day-to-day basis.

2. The **new product department.** This form of organization is, in effect, a permanent committee that works on new product ideas on a day-to-day basis. It is usually responsible directly to the chief operating officer and is staffed with researchers and experts in production, marketing, and finance to avoid conflict over authority. Both General Mills and S. C. Johnson and Company (makers of household waxes) employ this type of organization for product development.

   The new product department solves the problem of working with many new product ideas, but it has one major drawback: The department's responsibility for the product usually ends after test marketing. The product's success after that may depend on a product manager who does not fully understand the potential of the product.

New Product Venture Team Group that usually assumes total responsibility for a new product from conception through decline.

3. The **new product venture team.** Like new product departments, venture teams are staffed by experts from various fields. The small team of employees that begins a project grows as the project progresses. Unlike new product departments, however, venture teams usually assume total responsibility for a new product from its conception through its decline. Another distinction is that venture teams often operate apart from the firm's headquarters. The venture team has several advantages. One is that it inspires an enthusiastic team spirit. In addition, it encourages greater creativity, speed, and flexibility. Studies have shown, however, that the venture team concept is not the ideal solution it once appeared to be. Venture teams have

been accused of being too expensive and unproductive, and of developing ventures too unrelated to existing business capabilities.[13]

The Developmental Process Product committees, product departments, and venture teams perform three important functions during the developmental process: screening, business analysis, and planning for the production and marketing of the product.

Screening refers to the first attempt to separate those ideas worth pursuing from those that are not. If properly done, screening can save companies time and money. But firms often make two types of errors in the screening process.[14]

Screening
First attempt to separate ideas worth pursuing from those that are not.

Sometimes companies commit DROP-errors, which occur when potentially profitable ideas are eliminated. Lack of vision is the most common cause of DROP-errors. Eastman Kodak, for example, dismissed Edwin Land's self-developing camera as "a toy with limited commercial appeal." Kodak then spent years trying to regain the significant share of the amateur photography market it lost to Polaroid. Almost every publishing company has a list of books it has rejected that later went on to become enormous hits. George Orwell's *Animal Farm* was rejected by many publishers who complained either that its writing was "too cerebral" or that the pigs in the book were "offensive characters."[15]

By contrast, some companies commit GO-errors in screening. They let poor ideas proceed. The Ford Motor Company's Edsel was one of the costliest new product failures in history. The car was introduced in 1957 and discontinued by 1959. Ford lost $350 million on the project.

Often companies develop products that are not complete failures, but are not successful enough to continue producing. Some products may cover their costs, but make no profit. Others may earn a profit, but one that is smaller than a company's normal rate of return.

Marketers estimate that as many as 70 percent of the new consumer products that enter the marketplace fail. Obviously, many of these failures could have been prevented by eliminating poor ideas from the start.

How are poor ideas detected? One way is to subject them to careful **business analysis,** which involves estimating the future sales and profit potential of the new product. Most firms, before seriously entertaining a new product idea, have certain criteria that must be met. For example, one major oil company insists that all new product ideas return 20 percent of the cost of investment by the second year. In addition, the firm insists that this return on investment must increase to a minimum of 30 percent by the fifth year.

Business Analysis
Process of estimating future sales and profit potential of a new product.

After management has demonstrated a product's financial feasibility, it must convert the product idea into an actual physical product. That task involves the cooperation of experts in both production and marketing. If a product is complex, engineers may develop a model first and take the product through a limited production run. Even with such precautions, "bugs" may show up in the product.

While production managers work out the physical dimensions of the product, marketing managers develop the image of the product. Branding and packaging decisions must be made at this time, as well as decisions regarding pricing, promotion, and distribution. Just as flaws in the physical product may show up despite careful planning, so too can flaws in the marketing program. Because of this possibility, market planners have developed a kind of dry run for the product, the next step in the incubation phase.

Test Marketing

Test Marketing
Testing products by marketing them through retail outlets under controlled conditions in selected cities.

Most major firms test their products in some way before launching a full-scale marketing effort. In large companies with sophisticated electronic hardware, computers may simulate market conditions to determine consumer demand. More commonly, firms may do in-home testing, during which potential buyers use the products and then evaluate them on a questionnaire. Or they may test their products by marketing them through retail outlets under controlled conditions in selected cities—a process called **test marketing.**

Test marketing is not practical for all products. For example, it would be difficult for an automaker to produce a car before introducing it because of the tremendous cost of the operation. But for technically simple products, especially those that represent a major product innovation, test marketing is a good idea. It can save a company a multimillion dollar loss by uncovering errors in the marketing program. Green Giant, for example, once thought they had a sure winner in Oven Crock baked beans, which came already sweetened in the can. In blind taste tests, people loved them. But the beans bombed in a test market. Research later showed that people who ate heavily flavored baked beans added their own seasonings to the bland variety and did not want anybody doing it for them.[16]

Test marketing presents some difficulties, however. The most severe problem is that it informs competitors of a company's new product. The competitor can then jump into the market without a similar investment of time and money.

General Foods, for example, spent more than $600,000 to test its fruit-filled waffles, Toast'em Popups, in the 1960s. Immediately after General Foods finished testing, Kellogg introduced its own line of toasted waffles, Pop Tarts. Kellogg skipped the testing, but Pop Tarts reached first-place standing in the market. Marketing people believe that Kellogg decided to make Pop Tarts only after seeing the success of General Foods' test.[17]

Another serious drawback to test marketing is that it sometimes produces what is referred to as the "laboratory effect." Those in charge of the testing programs usually pay very close attention to details in the test market. Displays are fully stocked, price tickets are prominently displayed, and all decals and banners are positioned advantageously. In effect, test marketing managers create an unreal situation. When the product is actually marketed, it will never receive the same amount of attention from the retailer.

In addition, new product managers, eager to get their products distributed nationally, have been known to bias factors (such as test-city location) in their product's favor. People in the South, for example, generally buy more biscuits than consumers in other areas of the country. Test marketing a new biscuit mix in Savannah would probably yield results that could not be duplicated nationally.[18]

Test marketing, then, provides no guarantee of product success. In fact, a product that survives test marketing may have just a 50-50 chance of becoming a commercial success. Faulty test marketing partly accounts for that failure rate. Another important factor is the strategy employed after the incubation phase to bring the product to the consumer's attention and to keep attention focused on it. One way to do this is to develop an effective product positioning strategy.

Product Positioning

Regular readers of *Rolling Stone* may have noticed a change in the magazine a few years ago. The counterculture publication, which documented the latest trends on the rock music scene, suddenly seemed to change. The magazine's format was streamlined, its graphics updated, and the paper on which it was printed was of a different quality. More importantly, its editorial coverage changed. The space devoted to music was cut back, and there was more talk of politics and entertainment. The magazine was clearly being redesigned to meet the needs of a changing market.[19] Marketers would say that the product had been repositioned.

A **product's position** is the image that a product has in consumers' minds, especially in relation to competing products. **Product positioning** refers to the decisions marketers make to create or maintain a certain product concept in consumers' minds.[20]

Product Position
Image that a product has in consumers' minds, especially in relation to competing products.

Product Positioning
Decisions marketers make to create or maintain a certain product concept in consumers' minds.

Product positioning is a natural outgrowth of market segmentation. Once a market segment has been identified and its characteristics understood, marketers may decide to position the product to appeal to the specific wants and needs of a particular segment. If that target market changes, the product may need to be redesigned to keep up with the market's new needs and interests. In the case of *Rolling Stone,* the magazine's editors found that their target market had aged and had become wealthier and more conservative in their music tastes. The company pointed out this change to potential advertisers by using a series of ads comparing the image of typical *Rolling Stone* readers with the reality. (See Figure 9.2.)

But as *Rolling Stone* evolved into a publication with a different orientation, it left a gap in the marketplace. That position was soon filled by *Rockbill,* a new magazine whose intent was to cover the new music for the consumers who are 18 to 34.

Products can be positioned in two ways. Marketers may choose to position the products in head-to-head competition with the industry leader. This strategy may be effective if the product's performance characteristics are similar to those of its competitors, but its price is lower. Automobile manufacturers are particularly fond of this strategy, since cars can be compared on the basis of so many different features. In ads for the Thunderbird Turbo Coupe, for example, Ford boasts that its car

Figure 9.2
Advertisement from *Rolling Stone's* Perception/Reality Campaign

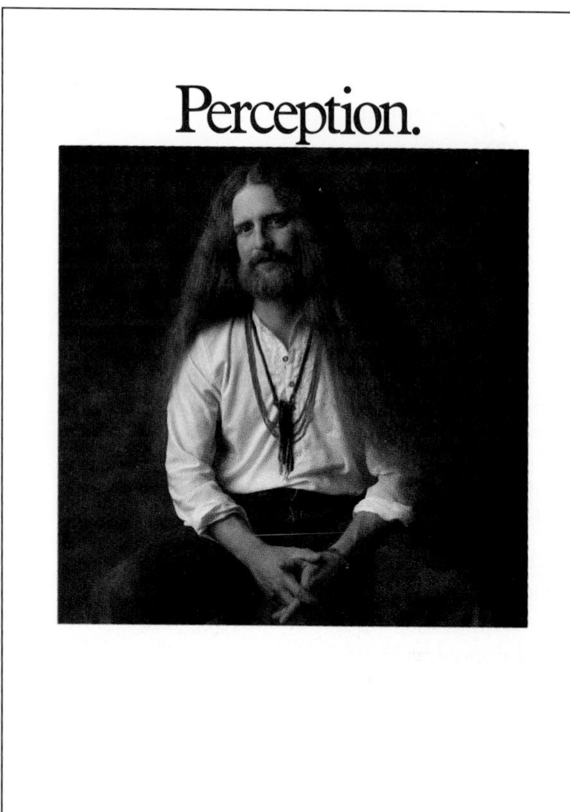

Source: *Rolling Stone*, 1986, Straight Arrow Publishers, Inc. © 1986. All Rights Reserved. Reprinted by permission. Agency: Fallon McElligott.

surpasses the BMW 633 CSi in handling but not in price. And ads for Volkswagen claim, "German engineering is either expensive or Volkswagen."

If a product's performance characteristics are superior to those of the competition, a marketer may choose a head-on position even if the product's price is higher. For example, in its advertising for running shoes, Puma USA promotes its 40 years of experience: "New shoes are introduced almost daily. They come from companies that have experience . . . in just about every activity except performance walking."[21]

Not all marketers wish to position their products against the competition, however. If a product's characteristics do not differ substantially from those of competitors, marketers may seek another positioning strategy. Thus, when makers of athletic shoes began to target the market for walking shoes, Lowell Shoe, maker of more conservatively styled "comfort shoes," chose to focus on a different market segment. "There are 60-year-old grannies wearing Reeboks," explained Lowell's marketing director, "but they'd rather be wearing a traditional shoe." And, after

Figure 9.3
Perceptual Map—Brand Images

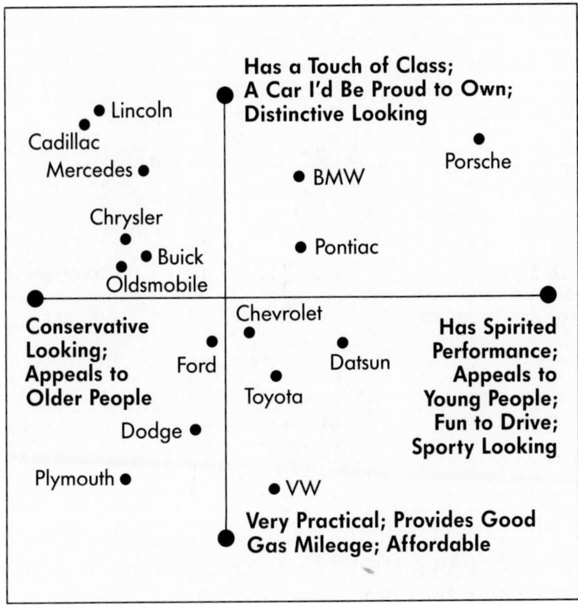

Source: John Koten, "Car Makers Use 'Image' Map as Tool to Position Products," *The Wall Street Journal,* March 22, 1984.

seeing its drawing appeal eroded by Atlantic City, the Las Vegas Convention Authority began to tout its city as "The Resort Bargain of the World."

Companies that have several similar products may also wish to position a new product so that it does not erode sales, or **cannibalize,** those of earlier brands. Pepsi Free, Pepsi Cola's caffeine-free cola, for example, has been considered only a qualified success, since most of its sales have come at the expense of regular or Diet Pepsi. Typically, manufacturers differentiate brands on the basis of size, features, quality level, or price.

Cannibalization
Process by which a company's new product takes sales away from existing products in the same company's line.

To decide how to position a product, marketers sometimes use a map such as the one shown for automobiles in Figure 9.3. Chrysler Corporation uses this map to determine whether consumers see its cars as relatively stylish or practical and relatively appealing to young or old drivers. In other industries, marketers may map whatever characteristics are relevant to their products. Based on the information in the map, marketers may decide to revise their choice of target markets or their marketing mix.

Once a positioning strategy has been determined, marketers use the various elements of the marketing mix to reinforce that product's image in consumers' minds. The success of a positioning strategy can be evaluated by several tests (discussed in Chapter 15). If the product's position has failed to make an impact on consumers, marketers may choose to

Table 9.1
Marketing Strategy over the Life Cycle

	Price	Promotion	Placement	Product Changes
Introduction	High, to recover development costs; or low, to capture large market share	Heavy, emphasizing information on product benefits	Generally, many outlets to assure wide public access; however, access to outlets may be limited	None
Growth	As high as possible, because consumer demand is high	Heavy, emphasizing brand name to win consumer loyalty	Additional outlets	New sizes, packages, and styling features; service extras
Maturity	Lower, to draw remaining potential customers	Heavy, emphasizing superiority over competitors and reminding consumers of benefits	Additional outlets	New uses, new users, flanker products, major modifications
Decline	Low, to liquidate inventory quickly	Moderate, discouraging product use	Decreasing number of outlets	Major modifications, if not already made

reposition it. This strategy should be used with caution, however, since an inconsistent positioning strategy can create consumer confusion.

Following positioning decisions—the last stage in the incubation phase—a product is ready to be launched. Each phase of the product life cycle requires a different marketing strategy. The remainder of this chapter focuses on effective strategies for the other phases. Table 9.1 summarizes the basic strategy for each phase.

The Introductory Phase

Risks are highest during the introductory phase when a product first becomes available nationally. Marketing managers' aims during this phase are really twofold: (1) to make the general public aware of the product's benefits and (2) to recover some of the costs incurred during the incubation phase. To accomplish these objectives, managers must work with the elements of the marketing mix—product, price, promotion, and placement.

Marketing Mix Strategy

Product Often when a product is first introduced, it will be available in limited quantities, reflecting a manufacturer's reluctance to invest substantial sums in production equipment until there is evidence that enough of a demand for the product exists to warrant such an expenditure. In the food industry, a company may even contract with another company to produce the product initially. If sales go well, the sponsoring company may then decide to invest in the necessary equipment.[22]

Price A firm may charge a very high price in the introductory phase or price the new product extremely low. When videocassette recorders first came on the market, they were expensive (about $1,500), but they have been coming down in price ever since. Bic disposable razors were first marketed at practically a giveaway price (25 cents). High-technology products are priced high initially to recover developmental costs quickly. Low-technology, convenience products are priced low to capture a large market share as quickly as possible.

Promotion A company seldom makes a substantial profit when introducing a product, because the company must spend huge amounts on promotion to inform the public of the product's virtues. Many analysts believe that home computer marketers missed this first step when they introduced the machines. Initial advertising, they say, stressed RAM, keyboards, and screen resolution. The problem was that people did not know what to do with a computer. By the time the industry stepped back and addressed the more important issue of product benefits, several companies had already filed for bankruptcy.[23]

Placement The manufacturer must also convince retailers and wholesalers of the merits of carrying the product. The placement (or distribution) strategy for most new products, with the exception of specialty goods, is to find as many outlets as possible. Thus, much of the promotion and advertising at this stage is aimed at the reseller market. Manufacturers may promise intermediaries high profit margins or special sales aids.

A product priced correctly, promoted heavily, and distributed widely can still fail because of improper timing. Timing is crucial in the introductory phase.

With careful attention to the marketing mix and proper timing, some of the risks of new product introduction can be reduced. A product that survives introduction stands a good chance for rapid sales growth in the next phase.

The Growth Phase

The growth phase is sometimes referred to as the market acceptance phase. The product may have gained a reputation by word of mouth. New customers raise the level of sales, though not necessarily the firm's market share (since other firms' sales may be growing more rapidly). In general, profits start to take off, but rising profit is a mixed blessing, since it attracts more competition. Marketing managers must adjust the elements of the marketing mix to the new competitive situation. They must also begin the process of recreating the product, that is, adding features to distinguish it from others.

Marketing Mix Strategy

Product In the growth phase, a firm must begin to increase the desirability of its product to counteract competition. It can do so by making minor product modifications that would strengthen its position or broaden its appeal.

Product Modifications Radical product changes in the growth phase would be unwise because they would confuse the public. But minor changes can help give the product a unique image in the consumer's mind. The most common types of minor modifications are:

1. *The addition of new sizes.* When Pepsi-Cola introduced its new soft drink, Pepsi Light, it offered only individual cans and bottles. When sales started growing, it introduced larger sizes.
2. *The introduction of new packages.* In the growth stage of Head and Shoulders shampoo, Procter & Gamble offered the product in unbreakable plastic bottles, plastic tubes, and jars to satisfy consumer preferences.
3. *The addition of new product features and models.* In the growth phase of the life cycle of blow dryers, Gillette added a swivel handle to its stylers.

Price As greater production leads to cost savings, marketers may lower an initial high price, which may also be an effective way of discouraging potential competitors. On the other hand, if the product's initial price was low, marketers may choose to raise it to take advantage of heavy consumer demand.

Promotion The major change in marketing strategy occurs in the product's promotion. Expenditures for advertising are likely to remain high, but the content of messages changes. The emphasis shifts from informing consumers of a product's benefits to persuading them to buy and to continue purchasing a particular brand. Thus, in the early 1970s, most advertising for microwave ovens stressed the product's cooking speed and tried to dispel fears of potential dangers from high-frequency waves. Today, manufacturers build advertisements around such slogans as "Litton . . . Changing the way America cooks" and "If it isn't an Amana, it isn't a radar range." These slogans build brand recognition among consumers.

Placement As demand for the product increases, marketers may continue to expand the number of distribution outlets. As competitors enter the market, a company may want to pay particular attention to keeping dealers happy by ensuring prompt delivery of merchandise, allowing credit for damaged goods, or making service adjustments. To forestall competition, managers may try to persuade retailers to sell only their products.

The Maturity Phase

The maturity phase is sometimes referred to as the saturation point in a product's marketing because most potential buyers have already adopted the product. Sales growth continues very slowly, if at all, during this phase, so new, competing products do not enter the market. The competition is set. A few companies generally divide the market among themselves. Market share, not sales, is the key figure to watch. The only way marketing managers of mature products can succeed is to capture a larger share of the market by luring customers away from competitors.

Figure 9.4
Hypothetical Life Cycle

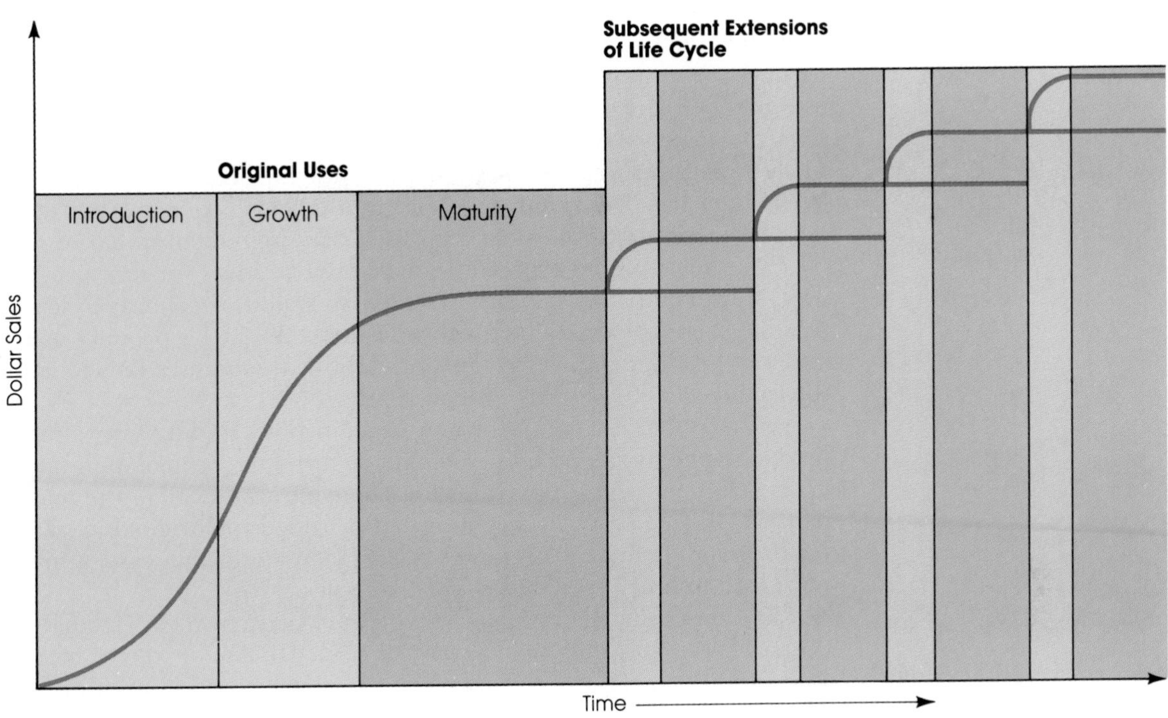

Source: Adapted from Theodore Levitt, *Marketing for Business Growth,* 2nd ed. (New York: McGraw-Hill, 1974), p. 163.

To accomplish this, managers again adjust the elements of the marketing mix. They must also rework the consumer's image of the product.

Marketing Mix Strategy

Product Theodore Levitt has shown how the life cycle of mature products can be extended almost indefinitely by reworking the product. He cites the example of Du Pont's nylon.[24] The product was used primarily by the military in the 1940s for parachutes and ropes. After World War II, military use of the product fell off sharply. Du Pont then entered the consumer textile market. The company convinced women to switch from silk to nylon stockings. It later expanded the market by persuading teenagers to wear nylons, then further increased sales by introducing stretch socks, nylon rugs, tires, and many other nylon-based products. The effect on the life cycle is illustrated in Figure 9.4.

The Du Pont experience shows some of the ways in which managers can increase a product's market share by reworking its image. The four most common methods are (1) to find new uses for the product; (2) to discover new users; (3) to add flanker, or related, products to the company line; and (4) to make major product modifications.

New Uses From the standpoint of a marketing manager, the best way to keep a mature product's sales growing is to convince consumers of the product's versatility. Du Pont developed a variety of products made from nylon. Doing so required a major effort by its research department, but finding new product uses need not be costly at all. New uses for food and other convenience products are relatively easy to find. Orange growers have conducted a major advertising campaign to persuade Americans that "orange juice isn't just for breakfast anymore." Arm & Hammer has persuaded the public to use baking soda as a refrigerator deodorant and drain cleaner as well as an ingredient in baked goods.

Consumers are an especially good source of ideas for new product uses. Many companies conduct research and sponsor contests to learn of possible product extensions from consumers. Bisquick's product manager ran a golden-anniversary recipe club for the brand's fans to launch the baking mix into its second half-century.[25]

New Users The search for new users involves finding unexplored market segments. As noted in Chapter 7, through segmentation managers develop marketing programs for subgroups rather than the mass market. As time passes, subgroups that provided the original markets for the product may offer no new sales potential. In that case, a firm must look to other segments to increase sales.

The most radical shift in markets occurs when a firm goes from the industrial to the consumer market, or vice versa. Du Pont made the move when it shifted production from nylon parachutes to nylon stockings. The move is radical because it involves entirely new methods of distribution, promotion, and pricing. A firm rarely drops out of one market altogether. Instead, it operates in both until one shows itself to be more profitable. Arm & Hammer, for example, also sells baking soda to commercial bakers and to the manufacturers of deodorants and powders.

More frequently, a firm looks for a new subgroup of buyers within the consumer or industrial market. For example, Dannon yogurt, which was positioned as a diet food in the 1950s, expanded its market in the 1980s by promoting yogurt as a wholesome food for people interested in keeping fit, with or without dieting. Its advertising campaign, "Get a Dannon Body," never mentioned the word "diet."[26] Two hospitals in Arizona have found a new market for their food: consumers outside the hospital. Building on their expertise in meeting special dietary requirements, the hospitals sell "Oven Ready Classics," frozen meals low in calories, sodium, and cholesterol.[27]

Flanker Product
Item related to an already established product and bearing the same brand name.

Flanker Products Items related to an already established product and bearing the same brand name are termed **flanker products.** Pepsodent toothbrushes are a flanker product to Pepsodent toothpaste. Marketing managers sometimes succeed in boosting sales of a mature product by the introduction of other use-related products. For example, Clairol's main product is hair coloring. In recent years, Clairol has added a number of other products, including conditioners, shampoos, and hair dryers. These flanker products support sales of the main product by encouraging home hair care.

Flanker products sometimes serve as cheap giveaways to encourage the sale of the more profitable mature item. For years the Gillette Company has sold razors at comparatively low prices in the hope of hooking customers into coming back for profitable blades. Some computer manufacturers have extended that concept to their own markets.

Major Modifications Many companies wait until products show definite signs of decline before introducing major product changes. They do this because they fear that a modified product will cut deeply into the sales of the old product before the latter is ready to be retired.[28] Most marketing experts, however, think such a policy is a mistake. The problem with a don't-rock-the-boat approach to product improvement is that changes in the market are inevitable, and the penalty for being second with an innovation is a permanent loss of customers.

The steel industry's experience with canning shows how disastrous delay can be. The industry thought that no one could challenge its dominant position in canning and failed to improve its basic product. Aluminum and plastic manufacturers then entered the field with a lighter can that was easier to ship. The steel industry was then forced to develop a lighter product, but it never succeeded in winning back lost markets.[29]

Major product improvements should be planned well in advance of a product's decline. The introduction of an improved product may indeed cut into the sales of an already established product, but it is far better for a company to lose ground to itself than to an innovative competitor. The makers of Coca-Cola, for example, hope that the combination of Classic Coke and regular Coke will maintain their position as the number one cola.

Price Because of intense competitive pressures at this point in the life cycle, marketing managers often lower the price of their products. The lower price draws the remaining potential buyers who could not previously afford the product. For example, color TV sets now outsell black-and-white models because the color sets are less expensive than ever before. Sometimes marketing managers deliberately engage in price wars to draw away consumers from other brands. In the short run, this can be an effective technique, but in the long run it usually fails because competitors retaliate.

Promotion Instead of competing directly with other companies on the basis of price, most marketing managers prefer to compete indirectly through new promotional programs. Advertising may feature competing products and show their supposed faults. This technique is known as "comparative advertising." Much of the advertising in the maturity phase is also geared to reminding customers of product benefits in order to keep them loyal users of a brand.

Placement Firms also compete indirectly by trying to place products in more outlets than competitors. Food producers may offer supermarket owners more services in exchange for more display space. Appliance manufacturers may offer their products in discount stores to appeal to a wider segment of the market.

The Decline Phase

All products eventually outlive their usefulness. The telltale signs are poor sales performance and profit declines that cannot be traced to a slump in the industry. There may be many reasons for the decline. Con-

Marketing Today 9.1
Corning Cookware: Premature Decline?

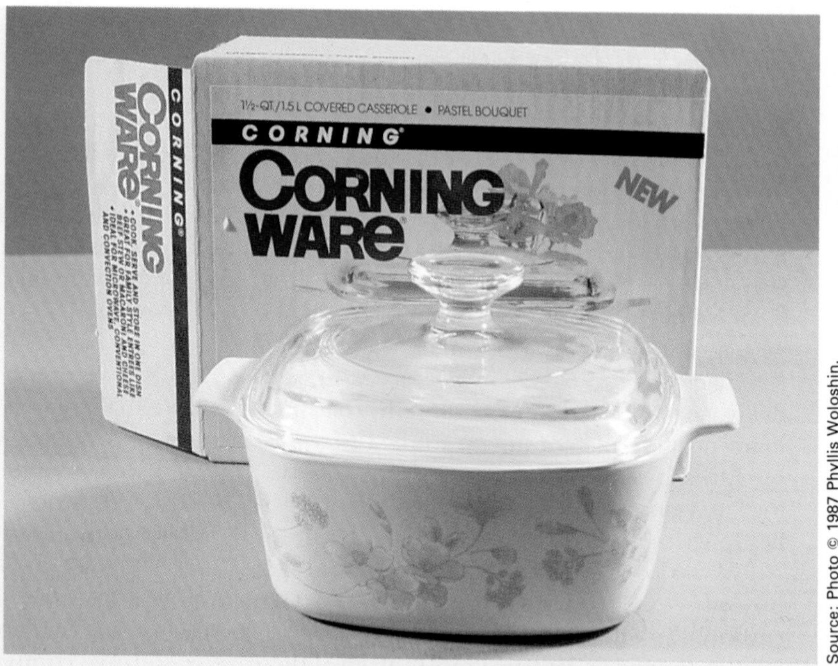

Source: Photo © 1987 Phyllis Woloshin.

For generations, consumer demand for Corning Glass Works' bowls, casserole dishes, and dinnerware was so strong that Corning's management seemed to think it had a perpetual franchise in America's kitchens. But the company was wrong.

First, the company failed to see the attraction of lower-cost but good-quality imports from Japan and Taiwan. Consumers found that they could get an equivalent foreign-made set of dinnerware for half the price of Corning's product. Many of the imports were more stylish as well. In 1982, Corning was selling dinnerware that had been designed in the early 1970s.

Furthermore, Corning had managed to overlook the boom in microwave cooking. Even though Corning's products are suitable for use in a microwave oven, the company didn't get around to informing consumers of this until early in 1985. And Corning failed to introduce a product line specifically targeted for microwave users until 1985. While competitors were profiting from microwave cookware, Corning was losing share.

While Corning has embarked on a strategy to regain share, it is finding that losing business is easier than regaining it.

Source: Jeffrey A. Trachtenberg, "Too Little, Too Late," *Forbes,* March 24, 1986, pp. 172–173.

sumers may simply be tired of the product. A competitor may introduce a superior product. Or the company itself may have wisely implemented a major product improvement that makes a particular product outmoded. Whatever the reason, management must face the problems of eliminating one of their offerings. (See Marketing Today 9.1.)

The decision to withdraw a product can be difficult, especially if the product has had a long life cycle. Internally, the company faces the problem of managerial resistance to the withdrawal of an old favorite and employee demoralization at the prospect of job loss. This happened, for example, when Westinghouse decided to discontinue production of most major appliances. A firm's external relations may also be negatively affected by product elimination. When RCA announced its withdrawal from the manufacture of computers, the company generated ill will among customers, who wondered who would service the equipment in which they had invested millions.

Despite such problems, if a company decides after analysis that a product is no longer profitable, it must make plans for the product's elimination. A change in the marketing mix will again be necessary to accomplish this new goal.

Marketing Mix Strategy

Product At this point in the life cycle, many of the product's original competitors may have dropped out of the market or introduced products that are so similar that consumers fail to distinguish between them. A product now need not be available in all sizes, colors, and styles. A company may continue producing only models or styles that retain a certain level of demand.

Price The main objective of the decline stage is to gain as much profit as possible. Since demand for the product is declining, however, prices cannot be raised. During decline, a product's price usually reaches a low point so that the company can liquidate its stock as quickly as possible.

Promotion Relations with the public may suffer unless customers are prepared for the prospect of the product's eventual elimination. Promotion can help ease the shock. Marketers have developed a special type of promotion, called **demarketing,** to persuade the public that there are valid economic reasons for withdrawing the product. Demarketing is especially important for concerns such as telephone, gas, and electricity companies, which are eager to maintain customer goodwill. Thus, when American Telephone & Telegraph decided that it could no longer afford the expense of a large staff of operators to handle long-distance calls, it sponsored a series of educational commercials. The ads stressed that it was cheaper to dial a long-distance call directly.

Demarketing
Promotion aimed at persuading the public that there are valid economic reasons for withdrawing a product.

Placement To keep profits at an acceptable level, costs must be cut. This usually involves cutting back on the number of intermediaries who handle the product. Retail outlets that are unprofitable must be phased out.[30] Sometimes a new marketing channel, such as a factory outlet, will be used to liquidate the remaining inventory of an obsolete product. As the product becomes harder to find, it may become a specialty item and loyal users will seek out dealers who still carry it.[31]

The decision to lower prices, eliminate distributors, and promote the idea of the product's elimination should be made only after careful analysis of the product's future in the marketplace. Some product managers have later regretted their decision to kill a product. *Life* magazine, Ipana toothpaste, and even the television program "Cagney and Lacey" have all made successful comebacks after being withdrawn from the market. Product management in the decline phase is a balancing act. Managers must have the courage to pull the plug on an obviously ailing product and the perception to see when the reports of a product's demise have been greatly exaggerated.

Chapter Replay

1. **What makes a product new?**
A new product is a good or service new to its producer; its newness may result from a technological breakthrough or from major or minor modifications.

2. **What are the stages of a product's life cycle?**
The product life cycle consists of incubation, introduction, growth, maturity, and decline.

3. **What is involved in the incubation of a new product?**
In the incubation phase, new product ideas are proposed, and the better ones are developed and produced. Often a new product is test marketed before it is made widely available. A product positioning strategy is also usually developed at this stage.

4. **How do companies delegate responsibility for developing new products?**
Input comes from almost all company departments, including research and development, finance, marketing, and production. Many companies delegate responsibility for new product decisions to a group. Such a group may be a new product committee, a new product department, or a new product venture team.

5. **How does marketing proceed during the introduction of a new product?**
In the introductory phase, managers may set high or low prices, seek out as many distributors as possible, and spend heavily on promotion to acquaint the public with the product.

6. **How do marketers take advantage of the growth phase?**
In the growth phase, marketers begin improving and expanding upon the product and use promotion to build brand recognition and preference.

7. **What is the marketing emphasis during a product's maturity?**
In the maturity phase, marketers focus on winning market share by making major product improvements and by increasing promotion and distribution channels.

8. **How do marketers manage the decline phase of the product life cycle?**
In a product's decline phase, marketers reduce the number of styles and models of a product, eliminate distributors, cut prices, and may even demarket the product.

Key Terms

business analysis
cannibalization
decline phase
demarketing
fad
flanker product
growth phase
incubation phase
intrapreneurship
introductory phase
maturity phase
new product
new product committee
new product department
new product venture team
product life cycle
product position
product positioning
screening
test marketing

Discussion Questions

1. When Dairy Delights Company came out with a line of sugar-free, calcium-enriched ice cream, its cartons carried the message, "New! You'll Love This Stuff!" According to the Federal Trade Commission, how long can Dairy Delights call its new product new? From a marketing perspective, when do changes to a product make the product "new"?
2. Describe the stages of the product life cycle. Why is this cycle important to marketers?
3. Which stage of the product life cycle is generally most profitable? During which stage are sales likely to peak? Why don't sales and profits peak at the same time?
4. Marge Watercress owns the Sleepy Time Motel. When two new motels started going up just down the street from hers, Marge realized that she would have to offer something extra, or the competition would take away all her profits. Where can Marge get suggestions for new services to offer?
5. Distinguish the following: new product committee, new product department, new product venture team.
6. Would it make more sense to test market a dishwasher or a new kind of candy bar? An improved version of a cassette tape or a revolutionary new detergent that washes clothes without water?
7. What is a product's position? In the map in Figure 9.3, identify a car that is positioned to appeal to young drivers who are willing to spend extra for style and status. Identify a make that is positioned to appeal to conservative drivers who value economy.
8. During a product's introductory phase, what do marketers typically emphasize in their promotional messages? What do they emphasize during the growth phase?
9. Belweather Savings and Loan Association operates in a mature market. To enhance its opportunities in this market, the S&L has hired a marketing manager. What general strategies might the marketing manager suggest for winning market share?
10. What is demarketing? When might a company want to use such a strategy?

Case 9.1
International Dairy Queen Inc.

"It's certainly the biggest thing that has happened to Dairy Queen in the last 25 years," according to Harris Cooper, International Dairy Queen's president and chief executive. He was referring to Dairy Queen's Bliz-

Sources: International Dairy Queen Inc.'s *1985 Annual Report,* and Stephen Phillips, "Dairy Queen's Blizzard Is Hot," *New York Times,* Business Section, August 31, 1986. Logo and additional information courtesy of International Dairy Queen, Inc.

zard, a new, flavored, frozen dairy dessert product introduced in the spring of 1985. Company sales in 1985 were $159.1 million, compared to $132.3 million in 1984, and net income increased to $9.7 million from $7.7 million. Much of these increases were attributed to the introduction of the Blizzard.

Company Background

In 1938, near Moline, Illinois, J. F. McCullough and his son Alex developed the product millions have come to know as "Dairy Queen" soft serve. The McCulloughs' innovation was the beginning of what was to become a system of more than 4,900 Dairy Queen and Dairy Queen/Brazier stores in the United States, Canada, and 12 other countries.

The McCulloughs made an arrangement with Sherb Noble, owner of an ice cream retail shop in Kankakee, Illinois, to test their new product in his store. Noble held an "All You Can Eat for 10¢" sale, and more than 1,600 people lined up to try the new treat. Based on this success, the McCulloughs knew they had an exciting business opportunity.

The first Dairy Queen store opened in Joliet, Illinois, in 1940 and was owned by Sherb Noble. Early growth of the system progressed through a network of territory operators, individuals who have been granted territory rights to develop Dairy Queen stores in a specified geographic area. In 1962, several territory operators pooled their assets and formed International Dairy Queen, Inc. and its wholly-owned subsidiary, American Dairy Queen Corporation. In 1968, the Dairy Queen system adopted a new food system, the Brazier system, which teamed soft serve treats with a hot food line consisting of hot dogs and hamburgers. One of the system's goals is to continually live up to the slogan, "We Treat You Right!" and to offer customers uniform quality, value, service, and cleanliness.

Product Description

The Blizzard consists of Dairy Queen soft serve ice cream blended with a variety of cookies, fruit, and nationally branded candy and cookies (such as Snickers, Butterfinger, Heath bars, and Hydrox cookies). No milk is added. It is blended in seconds in a $500 machine called the Blizzard Blender. Served with a spoon rather than a straw, the Blizzard comes in some 35 flavors.

According to Dairy Queen, the butterfat content of the Blizzard is 5 percent, compared with 10 to 12 percent for many ice creams and 15 percent for premium ice creams. This allows Dairy Queen to sell the Blizzard for a lower price—$1.29 for 12 ounces and $1.99 for 21 ounces.

Dairy Queen officials credit Samuel J. Temperato, a franchise holder of 67 Diary Queens in the St. Louis area, with developing the Blizzard. Although Temperato agrees to having introduced the Blizzard to Dairy Queen officials, he says that credit for the invention should go to Ted Drewes, Jr., also of St. Louis and associated with two frozen custard stores.

According to Dairy Queen, the success of the Blizzard has been spectacular. At the end of 1985, over 80 percent of all Dairy Queen stores in the United States and Canada had included this product in their line of frozen dairy desserts. Interest in the Blizzard generated increased consumer visits to Dairy Queen stores, which favorably impacted other product sales.

One stock analyst called the Blizzard a "signature item." He added that if Dairy Queen can introduce new flavors, the Blizzard can be as long-lasting as the ice cream cone. Company officials stated that "The successful and quick introduction of the Blizzard reflects the strength of the Dairy Queen system." The organization plans to ". . . take advantage of other opportunities to expand the company's business and profitability."

Focal Topics

1. Discuss other ways in which Dairy Queen might build on the success of the blizzard.
2. Based on the information in this chapter, discuss ways in which Dairy Queen might engage in new product development.
3. Discuss other product strategies that could be used to strengthen the Dairy Queen system.

Case 9.2
Newman's Own, Inc.

Paul Newman's lines of spaghetti sauce, salad dressing, and gourmet popcorn have been major successes since his company, Newman's Own, Inc., was formed in 1982. It is estimated that as of 1986, Newman's spaghetti sauce had about 1.6 percent of the market, his salad dressing had a 3 percent share of the market, and his gourmet popcorn may have owned as much as 10 percent of the market. Most recently the company has introduced microwave popcorn and lemonade.

Company Background

Newman's Own, Inc. started as a lark when Newman and his friend, author A. E. Hotchner, decided to market the homemade salad dressing Newman gave his friends each Christmas. The product was marketed locally in Connecticut under the Newman's Own label. In a few months, requests for the product were being received from throughout the country. A chance meeting with a food broker led to national distribution.

Source: Materials presented here have been adapted from "Paul Newman is packing 'em in at the supermarket," *Business Week,* November 4, 1985, p. 38, and a product review in *Consumer Reports,* October 1985, p. 630. This case originally appeared in *Cases and Exercises in Marketing,* by W. Wayne Talarzyk. Copyright © by CBS College Publishing. Reprinted by permission of Holt, Rinehart and Winston, Inc. Logo courtesy of Newman's Own, Inc.

Newman's Own products are now sold in about 80 percent of the supermarket chains in the United States.

In 1983, the company introduced its Industrial Strength Venetian Spaghetti Sauce. Newman explained that he chose that name because he thought it signified that the sauce was "the real thing." Later the company brought out its gourmet popcorn.

At the outset, the two partners never expected to make any money. After a year of phenomenal success, they decided to give away the profits. So far the company has given away over $7 million to some 200 groups including the Sloan-Kettering Center for Cancer Research, Catholic Relief for Ethiopia, and Recording for the Blind. Overall, about 20 percent of the price of a jar of Newman's spaghetti sauce goes to charity.

Marketing Strategy

When they first started the company, the partners sought marketing advice. After receiving estimates of $500,000 for test marketing and a probable loss of $1 million in the first year, they decided to go it on their own. Each partner put up $20,000 to set up the company and had his investment back in six weeks.

The company's sales philosophy can probably best be described by a small banner that reportedly hangs above a ping-pong table in the three-room corporate headquarters furnished with patio furniture: " 'If we ever have a plan, we're screwed'—Paul Newman to himself at the Stork Club urinal, 1983." The company does not advertise and only occasionally distributes coupons.

Newman's smiling face does appear on the label of each product. He has explained the products' success by saying that people first try the products because of his name, but because they are good food, customers buy again. The label on the spaghetti sauce states: "La stella della salse e la salsa delle stelle." Translated, that means "The star of the sauces, the sauce of the stars."

Focal Topics

1. From a marketing perspective, how would you explain the success of Newman's Own?
2. In what ways might marketing be of help to the company?
3. What sort of marketing strategy would you recommend for Newman's Own?

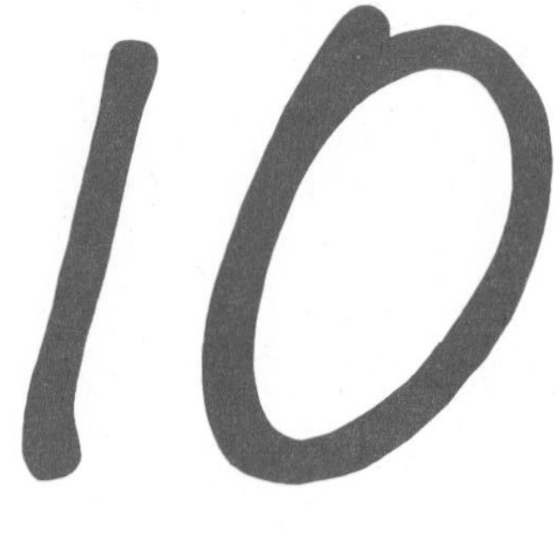

Pricing Concepts and Practices

Sounding Out the Chapter

In this chapter, you will learn:

1. Basic considerations consumers and businesses weigh in accepting a price.
2. Typical steps involved in price setting.
3. Objectives companies try to achieve in price setting.
4. General characteristics of demand.
5. Types of costs sellers must cover.
6. Some pricing policies companies might choose.
7. Methods companies use to set prices.
8. Kinds of discounts a company might offer.
9. How companies can adjust for location in setting prices.
10. How companies can adjust prices to meet consumer expectations.

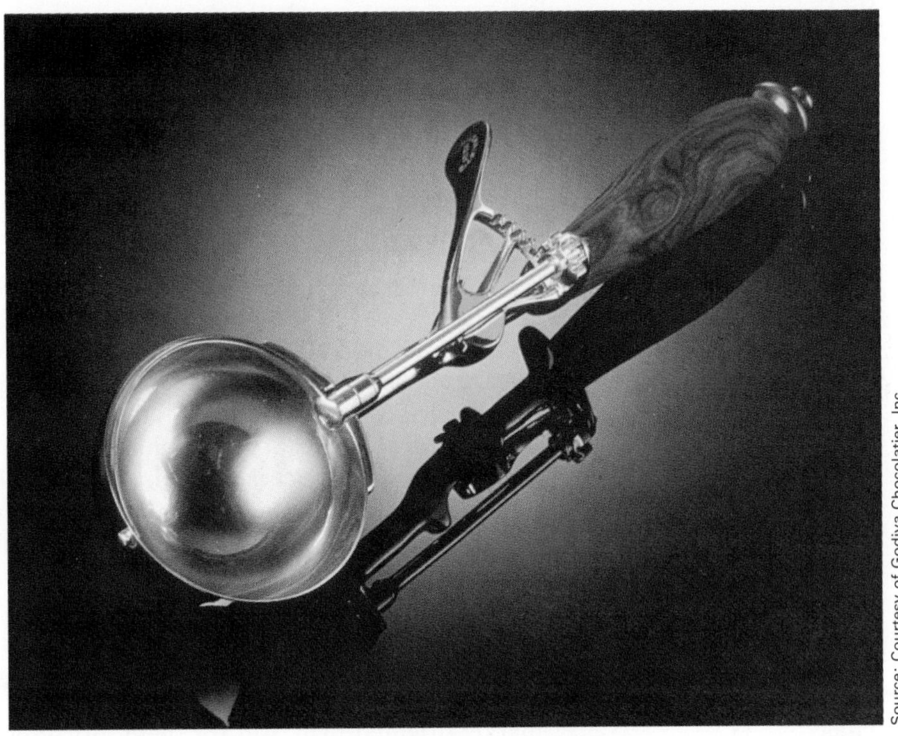

Source: Courtesy of Godiva Chocolatier, Inc.

Sweet Satisfaction at a Premium Price

Back in 1960, ice cream was pretty much all the same. Despite marketing research that showed consumers considered quality more important than price, dairies continued to churn out inexpensive half-gallons of ice cream as a sideline to the milk business. Then Reuben and Rose Mattus changed all that.

The Mattuses developed a premium-quality ice cream and invented the foreign-sounding name Häagen-Dazs. They sold their ice cream in small gourmet shops in New York for the then-outrageous price of 75 cents a pint. Despite the high price and minimal promotion their ice cream was a hit. Says Reuben Mattus, "The only problem we ever had with Häagen-Dazs was keeping up with demand."

Today, Häagen-Dazs sells for $1.65 a pint. In addition, consumers can choose from many other superpremium brands, including Alpen-Zauber, Frusen Glädjé, and Ben & Jerry's. That's not to mention the ice cream sold by Godiva, the famous candy maker, which commands a steep $3.75 a pint.

In California, ice cream lovers are lining up to spend $1.50 a *scoop* for Robin Rose ice cream. The price is justified by the quality: Robin Rose ice cream averages 20 percent butterfat, compared to 14 to 16 percent for Häagen-Dazs. The factory cuts up its own fresh fruit and nuts and buys raspberry puree from an Oregon supplier for a sky-high $120 a gallon. Costs for prime-quality cream, nuts, and other ingredients often come to half the product's retail price. In fact, the best-selling flavor, Raspberry Chocolate Truffle, is so expensive to make that the company sells the flavor for less than its cost as a way to attract customers.

High prices on superpremium ice cream don't seem to deter customers. While sales of regular ice cream were projected to grow at not much more than half a percentage point a year from 1985 to 1990, sales of the superpremium brands were expected to grow by 13 percent a year to more than $3 billion.

As the example of ice cream illustrates, determining a price for a product is more complicated than setting it as low as possible to attract buyers. This chapter explores some of the choices companies make in setting prices for their products.

Sources: Michelle Bekey, "Empire Building with Ice Cream," *Working Woman,* August 1986, pp. 37–39; Lynne Morgan Sullivan, "Ice Cream's Cold Wars," *Sky,* August 1985, pp. 40–42+.

Basic Considerations in Price Setting

You are a price setter, though you may never have thought of yourself in those terms. As a consumer, you set prices by deciding what you are willing to pay for something and then finding a seller who agrees with that estimation. Of course, finding the point of agreement—the right price—is complicated by many subjective factors.

Have you ever passed up an item in the supermarket because it was 10 cents more than you expected, but spent an entire week's budget getting scarce tickets to a concert? Why was one not worth the extra dime, but the other worth purchasing at any price? To a buyer, price reflects the value of the total product, which includes both tangible and intangible benefits. The concert tickets had more **utility,** or want-satisfying power, than the supermarket product and were therefore worth the extra sacrifice of money. Similarly, customers willing to spend $1.50 a scoop for Robin Rose's ice cream may be satisfying a variety of needs: taste, status, or simply the thrill of wild extravagance on an affordable scale.

Utility
Want-satisfying power of goods or services.

Businesspeople see prices from a different perspective. They cannot ignore the want-satisfaction dimension, especially if they belong to a market-oriented firm. But for them, price represents **profit**—what is left over after expenses are deducted from revenue (income). Like consumers, businesspeople too must weigh many factors before arriving at the "right price."

Profit
What is left over after expenses are deducted from revenue (income).

In the late 1970s, for example, the major American automakers decided to lower the prices of some cars on the West Coast and raise the prices of large cars throughout the country. They made these decisions for several reasons. Lower prices on compact cars on the West Coast seemed necessary because the auto market there was particularly oversupplied, especially with Japanese imports. The decision to raise the price of big cars stemmed from government rules regarding gas mileage. Manufacturers had been forced to make cars smaller and lighter to get better mileage. But smaller cars did not produce as much profit as did the big gas guzzlers. To offset decreased profit from smaller models, companies made big cars more expensive. They also began offering luxury small cars—compacts with many options—to boost profits.

This example and that of the gourmet ice cream illustrate several important pricing factors. In setting prices, firms must consider: (1) buyer demand; (2) supply and costs; (3) competition; (4) government regulation; and (5) other elements of the marketing mix. Before we discuss these factors, consider first who in a firm is responsible for setting prices.

Who Sets Prices?

Because so many factors must be considered, a number of specialists participate in setting prices. Marketing managers play an especially important role. Aside from estimating marketing costs, they may also coordinate information from other department heads. The controller and production engineer supply cost estimates. The company's attorney and public relations head indicate possible legal and consumer reactions to a

Figure 10.1
The Price-Setting Process

proposed price. The economist collects information on how demand will fluctuate in response to various price levels.

In highly centralized companies like General Motors, this information is then given to top executives who make the major pricing decisions. In companies like Du Pont, with many large product divisions, price decision making may be more decentralized.

Top management makes the major decisions, and lower-level employees carry out, or administer, the prices. The latter often have a great deal of freedom in the prices they quote. For example, a clothing manufacturer's sales representative may be allowed to negotiate a price (within the limits of the Robinson-Patman Act) with retailers.

Recent studies have shown that pricing is the main source of concern for many top marketing officers in a highly competitive environment, surpassing such obvious areas of anxiety as new product introduction and the competition provided by rapidly changing technology.[1] Price is the only element in the marketing mix that produces revenue; the other elements represent costs.[2] As price is the one variable in the mix that can be changed quickly, it becomes increasingly important that a company's price setters be sensitive to changes in the marketplace.

The Price-Setting Process

The process of setting a price may be compared to the way a sculptor makes a statue. First, the broad outlines appear, and then details are added. The broad outlines are the responsibility of top managers. Their tasks are twofold: (1) to state the company's pricing objectives and policies and (2) to translate these goals into specific prices. Salespeople and others then adjust prices in specific competitive situations. Figure 10.1 shows the main steps most companies follow when setting prices. This pattern is far from rigid. While certain factors—such as fixed costs and competitors' prices—are usually taken into consideration, setting a final price is often somewhere between an art and a "best guess." Herbert Denenberg, former state insurance commissioner in Pennsylvania, has observed, "Everybody thinks people go about pricing scientifically. But very often the process is incredibly arbitrary."[3]

While in practice price setting may not adhere to neat formulas, this chapter explores the various factors that most marketers weigh when determining a price.

Step One: Set Pricing Objectives

As Chapter 2 pointed out, most organizations formulate marketing objectives before devising a marketing program. These objectives give the firm direction, but in themselves are not sufficient. Marketing managers should also specify related objectives for each of the four "Ps."

Setting objectives is an especially important step in the area of pricing. Products have failed because managers have neglected to state clearly how pricing should work to support a marketing objective. For example, a food processing firm once set as a marketing objective the production of goods of superior quality. A new product, mustard, was packaged in a crock jar to convey a quality image. But the product failed in test marketing. Its price—49 cents—was the same as that for ordinary mustard. When the price was raised to $1, it finally succeeded in winning consumer acceptance as a quality product.[4] While there is some evidence that high price does not correspond to high quality, consumers do tend to perceive such a relationship.[5] Management could have avoided the initial trouble by specifying pricing objectives consistent with the overall marketing objectives.

Pricing Objectives
Long-range goals that managers wish to pursue in their pricing decisions.

Pricing objectives are the long-range goals that managers wish to pursue in their pricing decisions. Most pricing objectives can be grouped into categories relating to profit, sales, maintaining the status quo, or pursuing social goals.

Profit-Related Goals

Profits are important to a business. They show that a company is doing something right because revenues (money taken in) exceed costs (money paid out).

Economists say that the main objective of business firms is to maximize profits. According to this view, it pays for a company to raise its price just to the point at which a decline in sales begins to have a negative effect on revenue. For example, when Hershey raised the price of its candy bars from 15 to 20 cents, the price hike was a wise move that helped Hershey maximize profits. Sales dropped (that is, fewer people bought at the higher price), but profits remained the same or were slightly better. Why? To make $30 at 15 cents an item, Hershey had to sell 200 candy bars; but at 20 cents, they had to sell only 150. As long as the firm sells at least 151 bars at 20 cents, it is better off than selling 200 bars at 15 cents, according to this analysis.

Although profit maximization makes sense economically, it is a difficult objective to pursue. It requires a knowledge of how much demand will fall in response to price increases, and that is difficult to predict. Also, a firm may find it worthwhile not to maximize profits in the short run as a strategy to gain a large and loyal clientele.

Target Rate of Return
Goal stated as a certain percentage of return on sales or investment.

For these reasons, many firms reject profit maximization as an explicit goal. Instead, they speak of gaining a "satisfactory" profit, or a "fair rate of return." The specific level of profits pursued may be expressed as a **target rate of return.** The target is stated as a certain percentage of return on sales or investment. When firms fail to meet their targets, they

Figure 10.2
Strategic Planning for Price

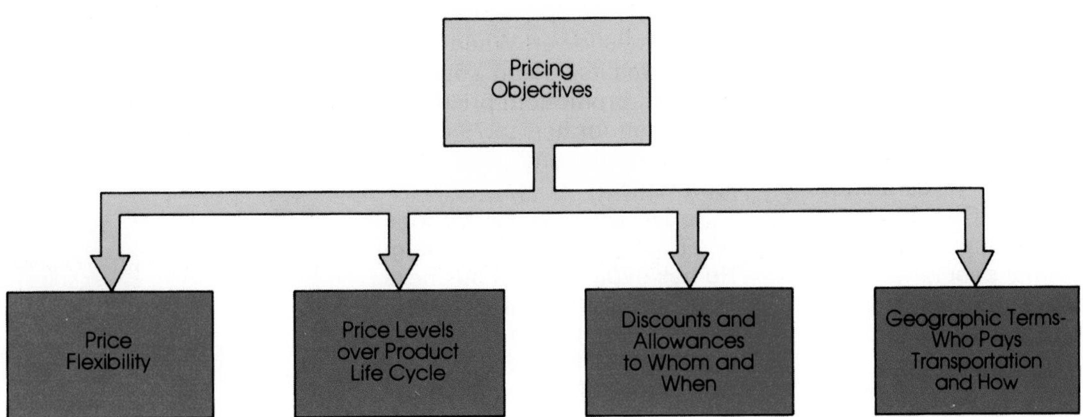

have some measure of by how much they failed and can take steps to improve their profit. Figure 10.2 shows strategic planning for price.

Sales-Related Goals

At one time, many firms preferred to state their pricing goals in terms of maximizing sales, not profits. The theory was that high sales inevitably led to high profits. But if the costs of doing business increase more rapidly than sales, profits will decline.

Today, when businesses tie their pricing objectives to sales, they do so more indirectly. A common pricing objective is to increase market share (a company's sales in relation to those of its competitors). A case in point is the competition in the home computer market during the early 1980s. Texas Instruments tried to gain market share from Atari, Commodore, and Mattel by dropping the price for its 99/4A computer from $950 to $199. Sales soared, and TI took another $50 off the price. But Commodore cut the price of its competing model to $99 and began outselling TI ten to one. TI again cut its price to match Commodore, but its profits had evaporated. In 1983, TI pulled out of the home computer market after sustaining losses of half a billion dollars.[6]

Studies have generally correlated large market share with bigger profits. Consequently, firms continue to pursue market share as an objective. At Your Service 10.1 describes how a dry-cleaning business has pursued such a strategy.

Status Quo Objectives

These objectives can take two distinct directions. In one sense, firms that maintain a status quo pricing objective merely reflect management's keen interest in avoiding the type of pricing battle in which Texas

At Your Service 10.1
One Place That Won't Take You to the Cleaners

At Clean 'N Press of Phoenix, Arizona, customers can have any garment dry cleaned for only 99 cents. On the opening day of the company's first outlet, so many people were lured by the low price that most of them had to wait at least half an hour.

"I never thought people would wait in line for *dry cleaning,*" says owner Robert Gottschalk. His stores provide the same services as other dry cleaners but at prices two to three times lower. When the chain runs its "Clean Your Closets" promotion, prices drop even further, to 79 cents per garment—and the cleaning load triples.

So far, Gottschalk is optimistic about his low-price strategy. He has expanded his business from one store to nine and plans to open more franchises around the United States. Says Gottschalk, "Discount pricing is powerful."

Source: Courtesy of Clean 'N Press.

Source: Laurie Freeman, "In Arizona, They'll Stand in Line to Be Taken to the Cleaners," *Advertising Age,* July 21, 1986, p. 44.

Instruments found itself. Usually a firm in such a situation finds it is dealing with a market that is not growing. It presumes that an aggressive policy will take market share from competitors and provoke an instantaneous reaction.

By contrast, a firm can maintain a status quo pricing policy but at the same time focus on an aggressive marketing policy that does not include price. Franchises such as Midas Muffler or AAMCO Transmission, for example, emphasize their warranties, numerous outlets, and large selection of replacement parts for both domestic and foreign autos. Both firms combine these offerings with a strong advertising program. In this case, these firms may choose to emphasize, in an aggressive manner, one or more of the four "Ps" other than price.

Social Objectives

A number of pricing objectives relate to social goals. Examples include being regarded as fair by customers or trustworthy by rivals. A fair price wins customer loyalty. Repeat sales may ultimately be more profitable than a highly lucrative one-time sale. Similarly, gaining a reputation as trustworthy among rivals may pay off in the long run by avoiding market share squabbles that damage the profits of all concerned.

Social considerations are very important in setting prices for some service businesses and for many nonprofit organizations. Many health clinics, for example, set fees by the ability of their patients to pay. Universities subsidize the price that many students pay for their education by offering scholarships. More is said about these pricing situations on page 567.

Figure 10.3
Demand Curve Showing Hypothetical Demand

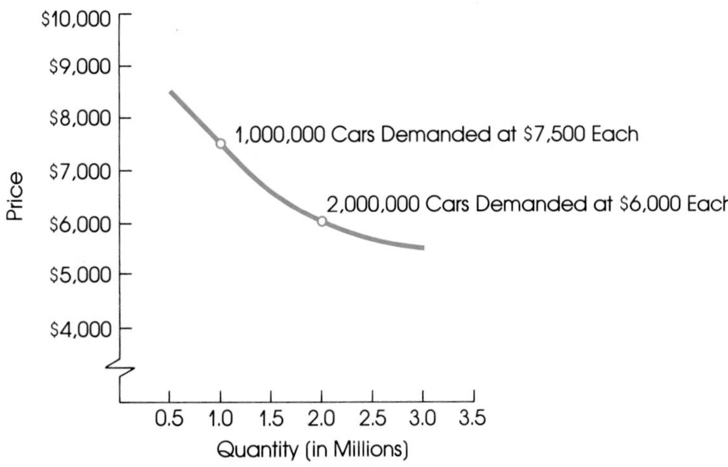

Step Two: Estimate Buyer Demand

The price a firm may charge for a product depends to a large extent on demand. At the beginning of the chapter we noted that automakers lowered prices on the West Coast because demand decreased. The car manufacturers' response illustrates the **law of demand,** which states that, in general, more goods are sold at a lower price than a higher one. The law of demand holds true only if buyers have a genuine need for a product and the income to satisfy that need. Thus, no matter how low the price of microwave ovens in the Brazilian jungle, demand is not likely to increase. Few homes have electricity or the discretionary income to justify the purchase.

Law of Demand
Economic rule that states more goods generally are sold at a lower price than at a higher one.

Figure 10.3 illustrates the law of demand. It shows some prices at which a hypothetical automobile manufacturer might offer one of its models and the number of cars people might buy at those prices. For example, at $7,500, people would be willing to buy one million of these cars. If the company lowered the price to $6,000, it could sell twice as many cars. Because the number of cars purchased increases as prices decrease, the demand curve slopes downward as it moves to the right. Most demand curves follow a similar pattern.

Marketing managers are not just concerned with the absolute level of demand at each price. They also want to know about the **elasticity of demand**—how fast demand changes in response to price changes. In some cases, the quantity demanded changes very little or not at all when price changes. For example, if a person needs a drug for which there is no substitute, a price increase will not affect demand. In other cases, demand fluctuates a good deal in response to price changes. The market for compact disk players has been growing steadily since the price has

Elasticity of Demand
Rate at which demand changes in response to price changes.

spiraled downward. Despite price cuts, manufacturers have increased total revenue.

Chapter 7 discussed demand inelasticity in industrial markets. Variations in a product's price cause relatively little change in demand for the product, because a company buys numerous products for use in producing a good or service. If, for example, car manufacturers have to pay more for upholstery, they can raise the price of cars a little, or they can cut other costs involved in making cars. In either case, the change in the price of upholstery will not have much influence on how much of it the automaker buys. This means that if the upholstery company increases its prices, its revenues also will increase. In general, demand is **inelastic** if an increase in price also increases total revenue or a decrease in price decreases total revenue.

Inelastic Demand
Relationship that holds between price and revenue if total revenue increases with price rises or declines with price cuts.

Elastic Demand
Relationship that holds between price and revenue if total revenue increases with a price drop or decreases with a price rise.

In contrast, **elastic demand** means that a decrease in price will increase the seller's revenues, while a price increase will decrease revenues. Compact disk players are an example of demand elasticity. When the manufacturers of CD players reduced prices, demand rose; the lower price actually increased revenues. Elastic demand can also work in the opposite direction. If tuition at a given school were to double suddenly, many of its students might look for a less expensive alternative. Just as stretching an elastic band causes a pull in opposite directions, so elastic demand causes price and total revenue to move in opposite directions.

In general, the more substitutes for a product, the more elastic is its demand, and vice versa. If frost wipes out an orange crop, causing prices of juice to double, consumers might switch to grape, apple, or cranberry juice until orange juice prices come down again. But the demand for pro football tickets has not fallen off despite price hikes because there are no close substitutes. Keep in mind, however, that demand is inelastic only over a certain range. If a football fan had to pay a very steep increase, demand for such tickets would no doubt start falling off.

Step Three: Calculate Costs

Demand is only one of the factors that affect price. Equally important are costs, or how much money producers need to pay out to supply goods or services. Virtually every consumer in the United States would be willing to buy a car at $100. However, no manufacturer could supply them at that price because of the costs of steel, labor, machinery, and other elements.

In general, supply curves are mirror images of demand curves. They slope upward as they move to the right. The supply curve for the prices in Figure 10.3 may look like that in Figure 10.4. Figure 10.4 shows that at a price below $5,000, few cars would be produced because costs would be prohibitive. But at prices above that figure, the number of cars produced steadily increases. At higher price levels, more and more car manufacturers can cover their costs and make a profit.

Costs set a floor on how much will be offered for sale. Producers must cover them over the long run, or they will not market a product. Marketers are concerned with two types of costs—fixed and variable.

Figure 10.4
Supply Curve Showing Hypothetical Supply

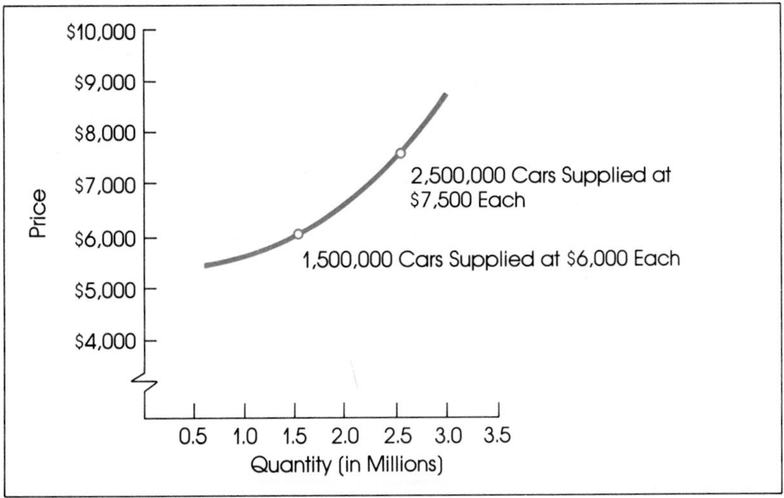

Fixed Costs
Costs that do not vary with a firm's output; also called overhead.

Variable Costs
Costs that increase or decrease with the amount of output.

Fixed costs are those that do not vary with a firm's output. Also referred to as "overhead," these costs include all contractual payments (such as interest, rent, and associated property taxes) and executive and clerical wages. A firm must pay property taxes or make mortgage payments on its facility regardless of whether there is any output.

Variable costs, as the name implies, are costs that increase or decrease with the amount of output. Examples include direct labor costs and the costs of materials and utilities used in the production of goods or services. A restaurant owner who wants to increase business by staying open later will have to buy more food and pay staff for working longer hours (or hire more people). These costs are variable because they change with the number of customers served.

In the long run, businesses must cover all their costs in setting prices or face bankruptcy. As Marketing Today 10.1 illustrates, this is sometimes difficult to do. Besides setting prices high enough, businesses can look for ways to keep their costs under control. To keep up with competitors, most companies try to do both.

Step Four: Analyze Competitors' Prices

Ideally, companies set prices based on the interaction of supply and demand. Digital watches provide a good example of how action in the marketplace influences price setting. In the early 1970s, digital watches sold for more than $2,000. Many companies, seeing a profit opportunity, began producing the watches. As demand for the product increased, supply also increased because more companies entered the field. In the face of increased competition, price cutting began in earnest. The price

Marketing Today **10.1**

Keeping Costs below Profits Is a Struggle for Some

Between 1981 and 1985, costs in the tire industry rose 4 percent, but the prices charged by tire companies *declined* 7 percent. Because buyers are willing to switch among brands of tires, one company cannot charge a higher price than other companies selling similar tires.

To earn a profit in this difficult environment, Firestone has tried cutting costs wherever it can. The company has closed aging plants and slashed the number of sizes and brands of Firestone tires. The company also sold off a profitable polyvinyl chloride resins business when it appeared that the business would never become a force in the industry. And Firestone executives have pruned management ranks and reduced the number of employees almost by half. Despite these efforts, Firestone ended its 1986 fiscal year with a profit considered paltry for its revenues.

Stiff competition has forced Firestone to pass its savings along to customers. Many other producers of commodities—products such as steel and semiconductors that seem indistinguishable from one maker to another—have experienced this problem during the 1980s.

Source: Ralph E. Winter, "Many Companies Find They Can't Pass Along Rising Costs to Buyers," *The Wall Street Journal,* April 28, 1986, pp. 1, 19.

slipped to below $10. Many companies dropped out of the market because they could not produce at the low cost required.

The digital watch market in the early 1970s exemplifies the workings of pure, or perfect, competition. As noted in Chapter 3, pure competition exists when there are many sellers, no seller dominates the others, and the products sold are interchangeable. In pure competition, any increase in supply results in lowered prices until supply just equals demand. Similarly, increases in demand call forth new suppliers who cover the demand. (Supply and demand reach an "equilibrium point.")

Today, most firms operate in markets in which imperfect competition is the rule. In some cases monopolies exist—one seller has absolute control over the price. More often, firms operate as oligopolies or partial monopolies. An oligopoly, as noted earlier, is a market controlled by a few firms that tend to set similar prices and make entry by other firms difficult. The five largest cereal companies (Kellogg, General Mills, General Foods, Ralston-Purina, and Quaker) produce most of the cereals consumed in the United States and market them at similar prices. In the case of partial monopolies (or more commonly, monopolistic competition), there may be many sellers, and entry into the market may be easy. However, the sellers have more control over the market than under pure competition, and they rarely engage in direct price competition. Most businesses are characterized by this form of competition.

Firms can avoid price competition in partially monopolistic markets because they are able to make their products distinctive in the eyes of consumers. Hewlett-Packard can charge a premium price for its calculators because its models offer special features, the company has a quality reputation, and the target market is mainly professionals who are relatively insensitive to price. Advertising is another way to establish a unique product image and avoid direct price competition. Recall from Chapter 2 that this tactic establishes a "differential advantage."

Thus, a company may or may not have to pay attention to a competitor's pricing, depending on the structure of the market. Today, however, even industries with very few domestic competitors are being forced to look at price as a competitive tool as foreign competition becomes more intense.

Step Five: Select a Pricing Policy

Pricing policies are more specific than objectives and deal with situations in the future that generally recur.[7] A firm whose dominant pricing objective is to maintain an established prestige image may make it a policy to offer goods for sale at only one suggested retail price. Unlike objectives, pricing policies may not be stated explicitly, but they are generally known throughout the organization.

Pricing Policies
Pricing plans for dealing with situations in the future that generally occur.

Three important policy-making issues are: (1) whether to offer a product at a single price or many different prices; (2) whether to price at, above, or below the market; and (3) how to price a new product. Government regulations regarding pricing policies must also be considered.

One Price or Many?

Before the beginning of the century, almost all prices were determined by bargaining. In some open-air markets today, one can still haggle with sellers to get a "price." But, for the most part, shoppers are likely to trade in stores with a **one-price policy.** They offer goods purchased at the same time and in the same quantity at a single price to all.

One-Price Policy
Policy of offering goods purchased at the same time and in the same quantity at a single price to all.

George Fox, founder of the Quakers, is credited with first advocating this policy. He believed that bargaining created opportunities for deception, which violated his religious principles.[8] His policy has been adopted not only by retailers, but also by many manufacturers. The major advantages of the one-price policy are that it simplifies transactions, creates customer trust, and simplifies bookkeeping and forecasts of earnings. One disadvantage is that once a price becomes well known, competitors may try to undercut it.

A **variable-price policy** allows special prices for different customers. It is often followed in pricing expensive consumer shopping goods or industrial products. No two customers are likely to pay the same price for a new car or a new home. Automobile salespeople try to assess each buyer's desire to own a particular model. Some customers are ready to bargain for days, while others cannot be bothered. The salespeople use this information to make the sale at the highest price they can.[9]

Variable-Price Policy
Policy that allows special prices for different customers.

The major advantage of variable pricing is its flexibility. Sometimes only a little negotiation will result in a major sale. The chief limitation is government regulation against price discrimination.

Heeding Government Regulations The government has a powerful impact on pricing. One example of its indirect influence is gas-mileage regulations, which have influenced automotive prices. Government also affects pricing directly, primarily by forbidding certain practices. The Robinson-Patman Act forbids the sale of identical products to different customers at different prices except under certain specified conditions. The Sherman and Clayton acts forbid price collusion, and the Federal Trade Commission Act and the Wheeler-Lea Act both forbid deceptive advertising of price.

Price Collusion
Joint fixing of prices by competitors.

The government has been particularly active recently in enforcing laws against **price collusion,** or the joint fixing of prices by competitors. In the government's view, price collusion lessens competition and harms consumers. Therefore, it has strengthened antitrust laws by:

1. *Making price collusion a criminal violation.* Corporate managers may be fined and imprisoned if convicted. Not long ago, 11 officers of firms in the electrical wire industry were convicted, imprisoned for terms of one to three months, and personally fined $200,000. Fines for price fixing in the paper industry have been more than $500 million.[10]
2. *Extending the definition of price collusion.* Price fixing may occur even when there is no formal agreement among executives. General Electric has been accused of price fixing for publicly announcing a price hike with the intent, according to the government, of influencing Westinghouse and other competitors to follow suit.[11]
3. *Allowing states to sue corporations for damages.* Seven states filed price-fixing suits against the major oil companies for damages against their citizens resulting from the oil price hikes of 1973–1974.[12]

In addition to guarding against price collusion, the government watches for cases of price deception and price discrimination.

Bait Pricing
Illegal practice of advertising a "special" at a cut-rate price with no intention to sell at the price advertised.

Price Discrimination
Price cuts that are not offered equally to every buyer.

Price deception involves any false advertising of prices. An example is **bait pricing,** whereby a seller advertises a "special" but has no intention of selling it. At one time, the government complained that Sears was following that policy in advertising home appliances. Consumers, lured to the store by bargain prices, were discouraged from buying the specials and talked into purchasing higher-priced appliances.[13]

The issues surrounding **price discrimination** are complex. Basically, the government outlaws price cuts that are not offered equally to every buyer.

Price At, Above, or Below the Market?

In devising a pricing policy, firms have three choices with respect to a competitor's price: they can meet it, undercut the going rate, or price at a higher level.

In the past, meeting a competitor's price was very common in oligopolistic industries such as steel, automobiles, and oil. Products were very similar and competitors' prices were well known. Any variations set off price wars that lowered profits for all. To avoid the charge of price collusion in such industries, one company usually assumed the role of **price leader,** setting a price that other companies matched. In the steel industry, for example, a price rise announcement by U.S. Steel usually led to similar announcements by other companies. Although price leadership discouraged active price competition, in a way it protected smaller firms by guaranteeing a price at which they could compete. (Leadership pricing is therefore often called "umbrella pricing.")

Price Leader
Dominant member of an industry that announces pricing policies other companies often follow.

All this has changed in today's competitive market. For one thing, the government's extended definition of price collusion throws into question the concept of price leadership. For another, a recession early in the 1980s meant slower sales and a consequent emphasis on price variations to encourage buying. According to one expert, a firm "should either price above or below the competition—anything to set it apart."[14]

Pricing below the market has become common. For example, small steel companies have cut prices independently of the traditional price leaders.

Pricing above the market is an effective alternative, provided a firm can distinguish its offering in some way. First-run movie houses often charge a premium price. Some convenience supermarkets, such as 7-Eleven, can charge higher prices because they offer round-the-clock shopping. Brooks Brothers shirts are more expensive because the name is associated with superior quality. Godiva could charge—and receive—a premium price for its ice cream because its chocolates had already established the company as a producer of prestige products. (See Figure 10.5.) An identical ice cream by Sealtest probably would not command the same price.

Price hikes have actually increased demand, contrary to the law of demand. In the case of deteriorating sales, Fleischmann's raised the price of its gin $1 a bottle. Sales picked up dramatically.[15] Many customers associate high price with quality, although the relationship does not always exist. One researcher found that there was a positive relationship between price and quality for only 51 percent of the products analyzed. For 14 percent of the products, higher prices actually meant poorer quality. Some of the product categories for which consumers paid more and received less were electric hair dryers, eight-track tape decks, microwave ovens, and electric blankets.[16]

Despite such evidence, many buyers still rely on price as a guide, especially for intangible services. Most consumers, for example, find it difficult to distinguish a poorly prepared tax return from a well-prepared one, or to judge whether one lawyer or physician is better than another. Because criteria to guide the purchase of services are often lacking, people tend to judge on the basis of fees charged.[17] Just as with goods, though, price is not always a reliable guide to quality. As long as people think such a relationship exists, however, pricing above the market will continue to be used by marketers of goods and services.

Figure 10.5
A Prestige Product at a Premium Price

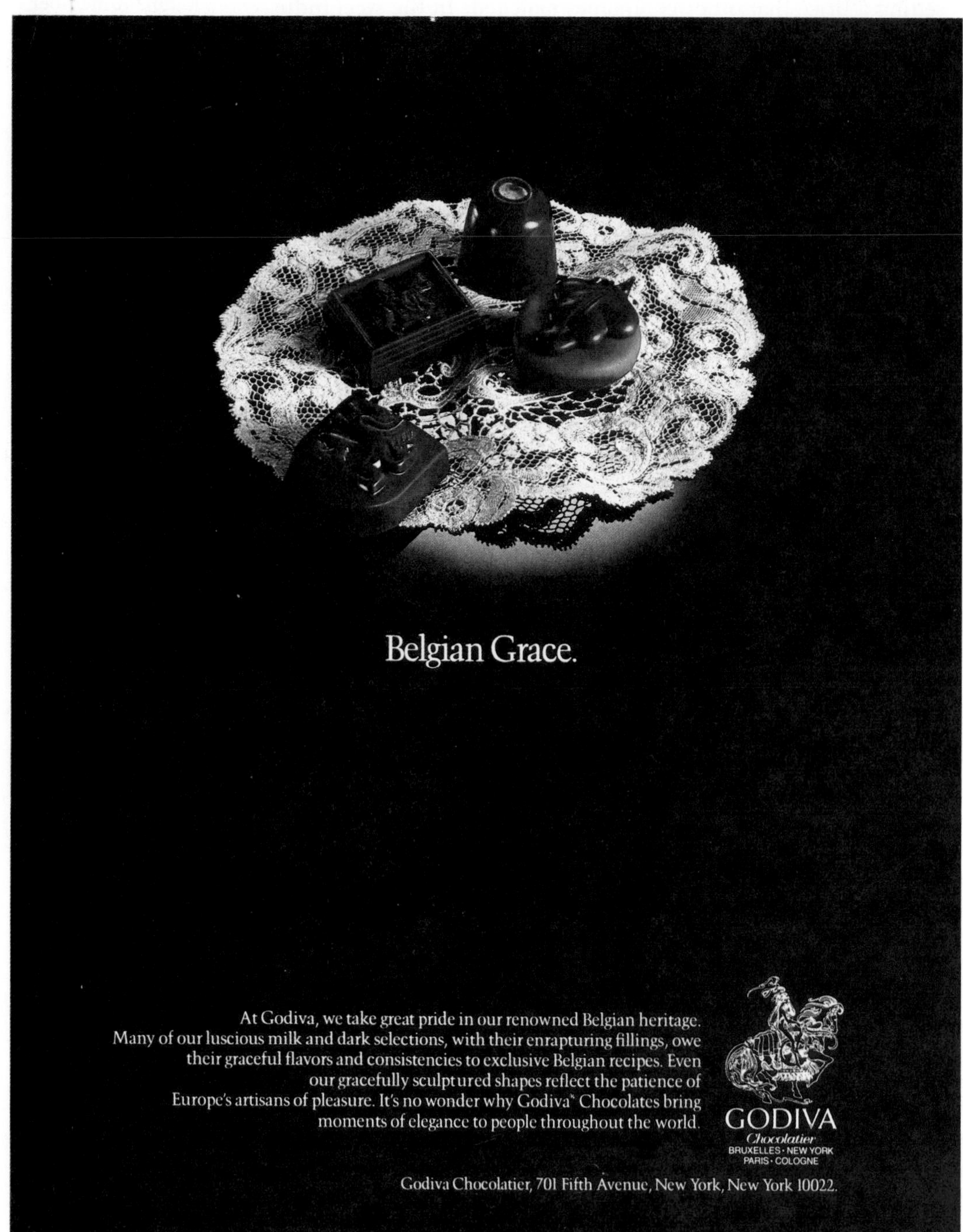

Source: Courtesy of Godiva Chocolatier, Inc.

Price New Products High or Low?

The previous chapter noted that new products are often priced high, and their price is gradually lowered as they mature. This pricing policy is referred to as **skimming.** The cream of the profit is "skimmed off" at the very beginning.

Skimming
Pricing policy under which new products are often priced high, and their price is gradually lowered as they mature.

Sony routinely follows this policy. The company claims to have the largest engineering staff in the consumer electronics industry. It also maintains that only 1 product in 20 that are developed ever becomes commercial. To support this costly process, the company "sells the first run at the highest price [it] can get without pricing itself out of the market," according to one Sony vice president.[18]

Skimming has three advantages. First, it allows a firm to recover its initial investment quickly. Second, it gives the company a chance to work out flaws in production before having to meet maximum demand. Third, by establishing an initial high-quality image, skimming leaves consumers with the impression that they are getting a good buy when prices go down. The chief disadvantage is that the high price exposes the product to cut-rate imitators.

Occasionally, to prevent competitors from rushing in, a company will follow a **penetration pricing** policy. The initial price for a new product will be very low to achieve the largest possible market share quickly. Penetration pricing is very popular among retailers, who may offer special low prices at a "grand opening." Their purpose is to build traffic and store loyalty. Manufacturers who expect costs to go down as production increases may also follow this policy. For example, transistor manufacturers foresaw that the most profitable course was in mass production and set an initial low price to stimulate the largest possible demand quickly.

Penetration Pricing
Policy of setting initial price for a new product very low in order to achieve the largest possible market share quickly.

Penetration pricing may discourage competitors from entering a market and builds brand loyalty. But there is one problem. Demand may build so quickly that a firm may be unable to keep up.[19]

Step Six: Determine Price-Setting Methods

Objectives and policies serve as a framework for determining prices. Table 10.1 provides three examples of how objectives and policies mesh to form a pricing structure. Working within this framework, an organization's price setters apply various methods to arrive at a basic price. If the price will be variable, the basic price will serve as a point of departure for negotiating with a buyer.

Price-setting methods vary from firm to firm just at objectives and policies do. Some are simple to apply and are used mainly by firms with status quo objectives. Others may require a computer to determine costs and to analyze statistical data regarding demand. The latter methods are more likely to be used by large, multiproduct companies with aggressive objectives. Three methods are discussed here. The first two—cost-plus and markup—determine price solely on the basis of costs. The third—breakeven analysis—can be used in combination with demand projections to arrive at a price figure.

Table 10.1
Possible Combinations of Pricing Objectives and Policies

Objective	Policy	Advantages	Disadvantages
Maximize short-term profit	Skimming Pricing above the market	Provides funds quickly to cover costs Limits demand until production is ready Suggests higher value in buyers' minds	Attracts competition Discourages some buyers from trying the product
Stabilize prices	Pricing with the market	Requires less analysis and research Causes no competitive ill will	Limits flexibility
Increase market share	Penetration pricing Pricing below the market	Discourages competitive inroads Allows maximum exposure in minimum time	May create more business than production capacity can handle Requires significant investment Small errors may result in large losses

Cost-Plus Pricing

Cost-Plus Pricing
Policy of setting prices by totaling costs and adding a margin of profit.

Firms that use **cost-plus pricing** set prices by totaling their costs and adding a margin of profit. This method is used by contractors, public utilities, most service businesses (such as exterminators or restaurants), and by companies whose objective is to secure a target rate of return. In all of these cases, certain conditions prevail:

- ☐ Cost figures—but not demand figures—are relatively easy to secure.
- ☐ The firm seeks a fair rate of return, rather than maximum profits.
- ☐ Price competition within the industry may not be very keen.

Cost-plus pricing may be a poor method when rapid inflation is expected. Costs may rise so fast that a fixed rate of return on investment or a rigid markup may be insufficient to guarantee a profit.

A simple case, showing how costs enter into target return pricing, will demonstrate how cost-plus pricing works. Suppose a company produces only one product—an alarm clock. It will first determine how many clocks it can expect to produce in a year's time and the total costs of that output. Those figures may be 100,000 alarm clocks at a cost of $1 million. The company may hope to reach a target of 20 percent profit over costs (a figure arrived at by looking at industry averages, the company's past profit performance, or some combination thereof). If so, it will calculate 20 percent of $1 million (or $200,000) and add that to its total cost figure.[20] The result ($1.2 million) represents what the firm must take in to operate at its desired level of profit. At 100,000 units, each alarm clock must be priced at $12 ($1,200,000 ÷ 100,000 units) to achieve that target rate of return.

Some Complications Under the assumptions made in the clock example, cost-plus pricing is simple to apply. In the real world, however, the costs that serve as the basis for price setting are not always easy to specify. For instance, if the clock company manufactures many products—electric as well as mechanical alarm clocks, pocket watches, and wristwatches—total costs for each can be difficult to figure. Remember that total costs are made up of variable costs (labor, materials, etc.) and fixed costs (overhead costs such as insurance, salaries). If the factory is producing all four products at once, determining the fixed overhead costs for each is a problem. If the company's president is making $95,000, for example, how much of that should be assigned to the making of alarm clocks as opposed to wristwatches? Companies usually have formulas for assigning fixed costs, but the figure can be arbitrary. However, that figure directly affects the final price of each product.

Another complication in cost-plus pricing is that companies occasionally produce a product even though they cannot cover *all* their costs in doing so. The theory is that as long as a company will run up fixed costs, whether it is manufacturing or not, it may as well produce any good that covers variable costs and contributes even a small amount to paying overhead.

Assume a company manufactures three products—tennis rackets, squash rackets, and skis. Only the first two items are profitable. The skis are unprofitable because they cost $50.40 to make ($36 in variable and $14.40 in fixed costs), but they sell for only $40. However, the company may decide to continue producing them because the $40 is enough to cover variable costs and make a contribution of $4 to fixed costs or overhead ($40 price; $36 variable cost). The assumption here is that ending the manufacture of skis will free no additional resources for the production of tennis or squash rackets.

This special type of cost-plus pricing, which allows companies to produce unprofitable items to cover variable costs, is referred to as **contribution,** or **incremental, pricing.** Airlines use this method of arriving at prices when they offer half-price fares at off-peak hours. Rarely do they cover all costs on such flights. However, merely keeping a plane in a hangar adds to costs. Therefore, they will offer the flight as long as they can cover the costs of fuel, flight crew, and other variable costs.[21]

Contribution (Incremental) Pricing
Special type of cost-plus pricing that allows companies to produce unprofitable items to cover variable costs.

The airlines have encountered some problems in following this pricing method, however. Selling at lower prices in off-peak hours has drained some customers from full-fare flights in peak hours. In effect, the airlines may be merely shuffling customers about rather than gaining new customers by offering lower fares. During the first years of airline deregulation, from 1978 through 1984, the proportion of airline passengers using discount fares rose from 33 percent to more than 80 percent. Profits suffer from contribution pricing as long as markets cannot be kept isolated.[22]

Other problems with contribution pricing and cost-plus pricing will be considered after looking at another pricing method based on costs.

Markup
Difference between the cost of an item and its selling price.

Markup Pricing

Markup has traditionally been defined as the difference between the cost of an item and its selling price. In modern merchandising, firms generally express this difference as a percentage—the **markup percentage.**

Markup Percentage
Markup expressed as a percentage.

If, for example, an item costs a firm $50 and is sold for $75, the markup is $25; the markup percentage is 33⅓ of the selling price. The markup percentage has two purposes. It must cover all the expenses of the firm, including the cost of the item and the cost of selling it to the public. It must also contain an allowance for planned profit.

Figuring a Markup Percentage A markup percentage is usually expressed in terms of the retail selling price. To determine the markup percentage of the retail price, divide the markup by the selling price. For example, a paperback that sells for $3.00 and costs $2.25 per copy to make has a markup of $.75, or 25 percent of the retail price:

$$\text{Markup Percentage} = \frac{\text{Markup}}{\text{Selling Price}}$$

$$= \$.75/\$3.00$$

$$= 25 \text{ percent.}$$

Sometimes the markup is figured as a percentage of the cost to make the item, rather than as a percentage of the retail price. In the preceding example, the markup would be 33⅓ percent:

$$\text{Markup Percentage} = \frac{\text{Markup}}{\text{Cost}}$$

$$= \$.75/\$2.25$$

$$= 33\tfrac{1}{3} \text{ percent.}$$

Whether a firm uses retail price or cost as the base depends on its accounting procedures. The accounting procedures, in turn, depend on the type of merchandise sold. In general, the cost base is used by stores that sell a limited variety of merchandise, such as furniture stores, and those that have a wide range of markup percentages, such as jewelry shops. In any case, a marketing manager should be familiar with both methods of determining markups to set prices.[23]

Choosing a Markup Rate Unlike manufacturers, wholesalers and retailers seldom attempt to determine fixed and variable costs for each product they sell before setting a price. The reason is simple. A large department store may carry more than 100,000 items. It would be almost impossible to determine such costs for each item. Instead, such businesses use an **average markup,** that is, the same markup percentage is used for each item in a given product line. Hats may have a high average markup (such as 50 percent), whereas books may be marked up only 20 percent. Different types of stores also have different markups. The same bottle of aspirin may be found at widely varying retail prices depending on whether it is being sold in a small convenience store or a large discount drugstore chain.

Average Markup
Single percentage used to determine the selling price of each item in a given product line.

Why do some categories of goods carry higher markups than others? One reason is **turnover,** the number of times average inventory is sold during a given period.[24] Generally, the slower an item moves off the shelf, the higher its markup. A slow-moving item, such as a high-priced necklace, occupies the same selling space and requires the same investment as a fast-selling item such as a book. Thus a higher markup is required on jewelry if it is to contribute an equivalent share to profit. In stores carrying a homogeneous assortment of merchandise, the rate of turnover can also be expressed as an average. For example, if a firm's average inventory is $10,000, and sales for a month (or some other specific time period) amount to $30,000, the turnover is three. A furniture store with a turnover of three times a year, therefore, must make more profit on each item than a grocery store with a turnover of thirty times a year.[25]

Turnover
Number of times average inventory is sold during a given period.

Other factors also influence the markup rate. The price level of competition is important. Most intermediaries are aware of what their competitors charge and adjust their markups accordingly.

Markups that vary with competition and other factors are termed "flexible." A cake that normally sells for $1.79 may go for $1.59 on Saturday and $1.99 on Wednesday. Saturday specials are meant to attract price-conscious customers. When an item is priced below cost to attract customers, it is called a **loss leader.** A slightly higher than normal markup for other items or for the same item on a slow day makes up for the loss. The trend among businesses that use markup pricing is to treat the average percentage of markup as a guide only, not as a rigid formula.

Loss Leader
Item priced below cost to attract customers.

Evaluation of Cost-Plus and Markup Pricing

The chief merit of setting prices on the basis of costs is that the method is convenient. The technique is also easy to apply, even by an unskilled business owner.[26] Buying a product for a dollar and selling it for two dollars is a tempting way to price a firm's products.

Despite its advantages to users, pricing based solely on costs is flawed. Cost-based pricing fails to recognize that there is a two-way relationship between costs and price. The law of demand states that more goods are sold at lower prices. It is also true that the more goods produced and sold, the less the cost of production. It follows that if prices are lower, more goods will be sold, and thus costs should be lower. Price indirectly affects cost.

In effect, both cost-plus and markup pricing ignore demand. Basing a high price on high costs is wrong if costs can be lowered by increasing demand through lowering the price. Marketers, therefore, often use another method of pricing, breakeven analysis, which attempts to consider both demand and costs.

Breakeven Plus Demand Pricing

Breakeven analysis is a way for price setters to determine what will happen to profits at various price levels. It, too, is cost based and, when used alone, suffers from the same weaknesses as other pricing methods.

Breakeven Analysis
Way for price setters to determine what will happen to profits at various price levels.

Figure 10.6
Charting the Fixed Costs of Business

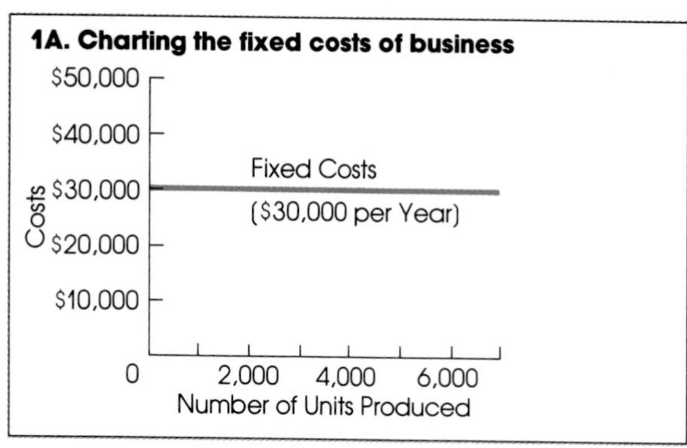

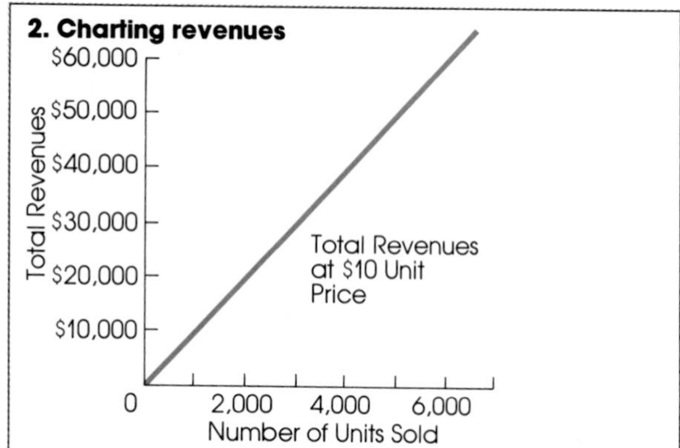

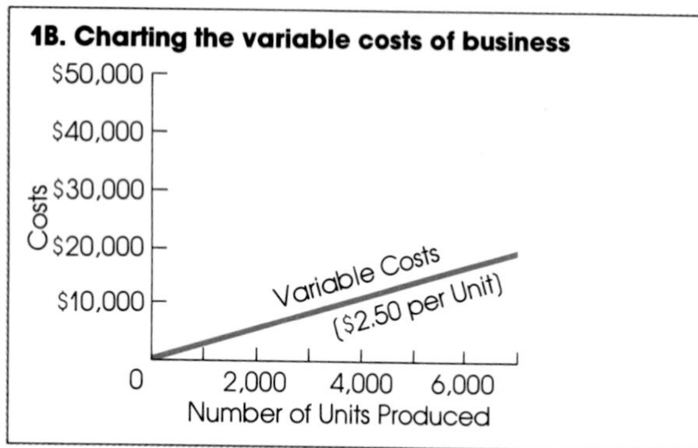

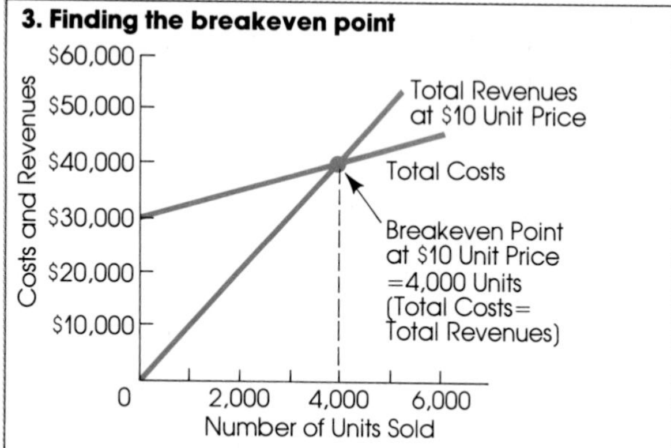

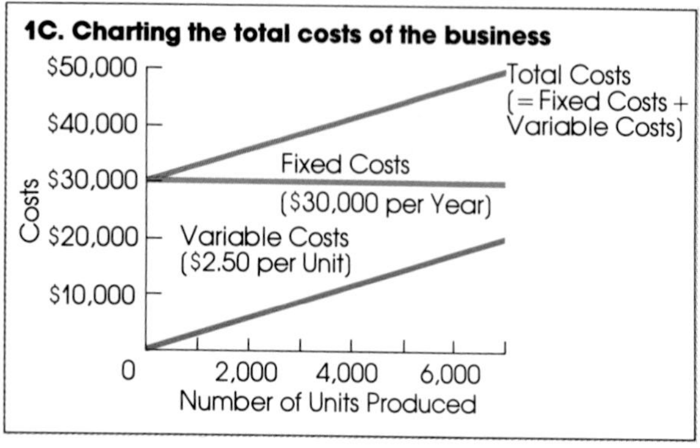

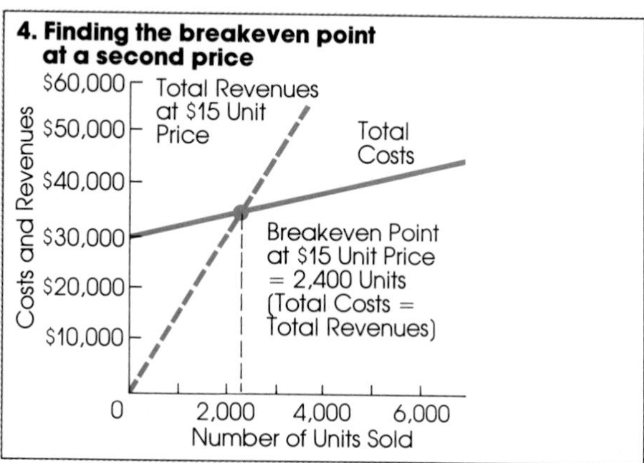

Source: David J. Rachman and Michael Mescon, *Business Today* (New York: Random House, 1982), p. 288. Reprinted with permission by Random House.

Figure 10.6 (Continued)

One of the basic questions all businesspeople need to answer is, "How many units of my product (or service) will I have to sell in order to break even—that is, to cover costs?" And, of course, the question that goes along with that one is, "How many units will I have to sell in order to make a reasonable profit?" If you don't have a basic estimate of these two figures, you may be out of business before you know it.

The best way to attack these questions is through a method known as breakeven analysis. Here's how it's done.

1. Charting the costs of the business We have seen that marketing managers have to take two different kinds of costs into consideration: fixed costs (rent, taxes, etc.) and variable costs (supplies, labor). In a small beauty salon, for example, fixed costs might amount to $30,000 a year. Variable costs, such as labor and shampoo for one haircut (with wash and set) might be $2.50. So 10 units would cost $25, 20 units would cost $50, and so on.

To figure out the total costs of operating the business, simply add the variable costs to the fixed costs. Total costs increase with the number of units produced.

2. Charting revenues The next step is to chart the revenues, or payments, the company will receive as it sells more and more units at the price the manager plans to charge. If the beauty salon charges $10 per haircut, its revenues are $1,000 for 100 units, $2,000 for 200 units, and so on.

3. Finding the breakeven point Next, we put the two graphs together, to show costs *and* revenues. Notice that there is a point at which the line representing revenues crosses and goes over the line representing costs. This point is the **breakeven** point—*the point at which revenues will just cover costs.* Now, to find the number of units the business must sell to reach the breakeven point, just look along the "number of units produced" line at the bottom. Any additional units sold will produce profit for your business.

4. Finding the breakeven point at a second price What if you charge a higher price for your product or service? You will break even after selling a smaller number of units. To find out exactly how many units you will have to sell to break even at your second price, simply repeat steps 2 and 3 using the second price. Here, we have charted revenues and breakeven point at a unit price of $15.

Making a final decision on a price Clearly, each of the two prices offers you certain advantages. The higher price, which allows you to break even after selling fewer units, may be attractive if you suspect that the market for your product or service is limited in your geographic area. At the lower price, you will have to sell more units, but your price may bring in more customers. Which price do you decide on? Here you have to make an "educated guess" about your customers and your product.

However, it is possible to combine figures obtained from breakeven analysis with demand estimates, thereby avoiding the difficulty mentioned earlier. Figure 10.6 explains how breakeven analysis is figured.

Step Seven: Decide on a Final Price

By applying the techniques described earlier, firms arrive at a **list price,** the selling price quoted to buyers. However, as anyone who has ever bought a new car knows, the price is often negotiable. In general, prices may be modified in response to consumer expectations, or they may be adjusted to gain wholesaler or retailer cooperation.

List Price
Selling price quoted to buyers.

Discounts

Discounts are deductions made from the list price and offered to wholesalers and retailers. Discounts come in many forms. Some are special promotional allowances, like free advertising to gain dealer support (see

Discount
Deduction made from the list price and offered to wholesalers and retailers.

Chapter 15). Others—trade, cash, quantity, and seasonal discounts—mean a reduced purchase price. In theory, discounts are simply cost savings realized by manufacturers and passed on to intermediaries. In practice, they may be special treatment offered to big dealers because of their size. The Robinson-Patman Act attempts to curb unfair discounting practices.

Trade Discount
Reduction to "the trade" (wholesalers and retailers) from list price.

Trade Discounts Manufacturers offer **trade discounts,** reductions from list price to "the trade" (wholesalers and retailers), in return for services performed. For example, Birdseye's wholesalers save the manufacturer the trouble of dealing with the many small grocers who carry the brand. In exchange, the wholesalers, and their retail customers who also perform services for the manufacturer, buy at lower prices.

A typical manufacturer's price quotation to the trade is "list $10 less 30 percent less 10 percent." The price to the wholesaler and retailer is calculated as follows:

$10.00	
−3.00	(30 percent)
7.00	
− .70	(10 percent)
$ 6.30	

The wholesaler pays $6.30 and sells to the retailer for $7, who in turn sells to the consumer for $10.

Discounts to the wholesaler and retailer vary according to the function they perform and their profit needs. Retailers, because they perform more functions than wholesalers, tend to require most of the discount. In this example, more than 80 percent of the $3.70 trade discount is given to the retailer.

The Robinson-Patman Act makes clear that discounts offered to one reseller must be made available to all similar resellers. But some difficulty has arisen in interpreting the act. Some retailers (such as large chain stores) perform wholesaler tasks such as storage and transportation. Should they be given the wholesaler's as well as the retailer's discount? In general, the courts have said yes, provided smaller firms are offered proportional discounts.

Cash Discount
Reduction from list price made for early payment.

Cash Discounts Reductions from list price made for early payment are called **cash discounts.** A typical cash discount is "2/10, net 30." In this case, the buyer may deduct 2 percent for paying within 10 days of billing, or may pay in full in 30 days. Both the buyer and the seller benefit from cash discounts. A savings of 2 percent on a regular basis can add up for the buyer, and early payment means more cash on hand for the seller. No legal problems arise in offering cash discounts as long as all buyers have an equal opportunity to save. The practice is widespread in business transactions.

At the retail level, cash discounts are a small but growing trend. Many gasoline stations offer customers discounts for paying cash. This policy saves the dealer and oil company the cost of financing credit and allows the dealer to compete with private-brand dealers who rarely accept credit cards.

Quantity Discounts Manufacturers sometimes offer **quantity discounts,** a reduction in list price to intermediaries for buying in large volume. Large purchases save the manufacturer money. Less inventory must be stored, and it costs less to do the paperwork for one large order than several smaller ones. Sometimes these savings are passed on to consumers. One merchant in New York, for example, sells Ted Lapidus silk ties for $6.99. (The same tie in the swank Ted Lapidus boutique on Fifth Avenue sells for $55.) How does the merchant do it and still make a profit? "I buy in huge quantities and I pay immediately," the merchant says.[27]

Quantity Discount Reduction in list price to intermediaries for buying in large volume.

There are two types of quantity discounts. **Noncumulative discounts** are one-time reductions for larger-than-usual orders. (Group fares on airlines are a form of noncumulative discount for consumers.) **Cumulative discounts** permit a customer to total up consecutive orders to qualify for the discount. Manufacturers encourage the use of cumulative discounts because it tends to tie buyers to them in the hope of securing a discount.

Noncumulative Discount One-time reduction for larger-than-usual order.

Cumulative Discount Policy that permits a customer to total up consecutive orders to qualify for the discount.

Quantity discounts are legal as long as the manufacturer can prove that costs are reduced by selling in quantity. Savings are much harder to prove in the case of cumulative discounts because consecutive orders do not lower storage or order-processing costs. Manufacturers may claim that they offer such discounts in good faith to meet an equally low price of a competitor. The courts have upheld this defense.[28]

Seasonal Discounts Manufacturers of boats, air conditioners, or other such goods offer **seasonal discounts,** cash savings for buying out of season. Airlines, hotels, and other service businesses may also offer seasonal discounts for out-of-season periods. The special price helps spread production (or usage of facilities) throughout the year, which can mean savings for the seller as well as the buyer. For example, a retailer who buys a boat in the winter allows the manufacturer to reduce storage costs rather than borrow money at high interest to finance the inventory.

Seasonal Discount Special price for buying out of season.

Seasonal discounts may come in the form of extended payments. Purchases made in December may not have to be paid for until May, which represents a kind of cash advance to the buyer. Seasonal discounts are legal—provided they are offered equally to all.

Geographical Adjustments

Prices may also have to be adjusted upward or downward, depending on who picks up the transportation tab. Consumers who have shopped in a furniture warehouse know how much prices may differ when the transportation charge is an option. Transportation fees are an important factor in pricing bulky goods like machinery or goods that must travel a long distance. Several alternative price strategies are available to sellers.

F.O.B. Pricing Practice of having the buyer choose and pay for transportation from the time goods are loaded on a carrier ("free on board"). The buyer takes title at that time.

F.O.B. Pricing Manufacturers who send goods F.O.B. ("free on board") follow one of two policies—F.O.B. destination or F.O.B. origin. In the first policy, the manufacturer pays freight to the destination. Title and responsibility for the shipment do not pass until the merchandise reaches the buyer. Buyers, of course, prefer the F.O.B. destination terms.

More common terms, however, are F.O.B. origin—the buyer pays for transportation and takes title to the goods from the time they are loaded on board a carrier. The recipient then pays for the freight and makes any claims for goods damaged in transit. Cars and other heavy goods are shipped this way.

Strategically, the choice of destination or origin pricing policies can greatly affect the manufacturer's market range. For example, manufacturers who ship F.O.B. origin may find that buyers will tend to deal with local vendors in order to save freight costs. When freight costs are a large fraction of the final selling price, this may be an important consideration for the buyer of the product.

Uniform-Delivery Pricing For national marketers, one way to compete with local producers is to quote a single price to all sellers regardless of location. Such **uniform-delivery pricing** works by averaging the transportation charges of all buyers and adding that figure to the selling price. Buyers feel that they are getting shipments "free" because they are not aware of transportation costs; however, a Boston buyer is actually subsidizing a Los Angeles buyer if they both purchase from a New York seller. The Post Office engages in uniform-delivery pricing of letters, which is why the practice is sometimes called "postage-stamp" pricing. In business, the practice is followed when transportation is only a small part of the price of goods.

Uniform-Delivery Pricing
Practice of quoting a single price to all sellers regardless of location, reached by averaging the transportation charges of all buyers and adding that figure to the selling price.

Zone-Delivery Pricing A variation of uniform delivery is **zone-delivery pricing.** Manufacturers divide the country or their market into two or more zones, charging the same rate within a zone but different rates among zones. The closer a zone to the manufacturer, the lower the price.

Zone-Delivery Pricing
Policy under which sellers divide the country or market into two or more zones, charging the same rate within a zone but different rates among zones.

Food manufacturers tend to use zone pricing. One manufacturer, for example, divides the United States into three major zones, selling to supermarkets in each zone at a similar price. The different prices among zones are based on the cost of transportation and handling. Advertisements occasionally feature the line "slightly higher west (or east) of the Mississippi." The practice may be unfair to buyers who are just on the edge of another (cheaper) zone. Like uniform delivery, zone pricing is allowable under the Robinson-Patman Act, even though some buyers end up subsidizing others.

Basing-Point Pricing Some sellers practice **basing-point pricing,** calculating freight charges not from their factories, but from a city or cities designated by members of their industry. For example, all transportation charges for steel used to be calculated from Pittsburgh, even though the steel was often produced elsewhere.

Basing-Point Pricing
Policy of calculating freight charges not from their factories but from a city or cities designated by members of an industry.

Unfairness results when sellers in Chicago, Pittsburgh, and Birmingham all quote the same freight charge to a buyer in Minneapolis. The buyer receives delivery from Chicago but is charged for freight from the basing point in Pittsburgh.

In most instances, basing-point pricing works to the advantage of sellers, who gain from "phantom freight rates" (charges for travel that never actually occurred). Basing-point systems also tend to rely on a kind of price collusion among the members of an industry. For these reasons, the government has declared several such plans illegal.

Consumer-Related Price Adjustments

Discounting and geographical adjustments affect the prices paid by intermediaries, but sometimes prices must also be modified to meet consumer expectations. The same person who thinks $3.95 is too much to pay for a paperback novel may think $3.75 is acceptable for a pint of Godiva ice cream. To appeal to consumer preconceptions or needs, price setters use several forms of so-called "psychological pricing."

Price Lining Kodak introduced its Ektra pocket cameras at prices of $19.95, $27.95, and $44.95. This practice is an example of **price lining,** grouping merchandise into classes by means of price. Retailers often use the same tactic in pricing the goods they sell.

Price Lining
Practice of grouping merchandise into classes by means of price.

According to its users, price lining simplifies decision making for consumers. For example, if standard markups on cost are used, two ties may be priced at $3.39 and $3.85. The range is not wide enough to indicate a difference in quality, so consumers may become confused. By pricing one at $3 and the other at $5, a retailer can establish clear lines of distinction.

Price lining also benefits sellers. It simplifies accounting procedures by reducing the number of prices. Also, retailers do not have to train clerks to deal with quality differences among a wide variety of prices.

One drawback is that price lining may limit the kinds of merchandise a retailer can carry. When a manufacturer's costs go up, so does the price to retailers. A retailer who wants to maintain current price lines may have to look elsewhere for suppliers. However, if a retailer is large enough (like the Sears chain), a manufacturer may tailor its output to match the retailer's price lines.

Customary Pricing Some types of products must be priced at a certain level or consumer demand drops off rapidly. Such **customary pricing** is common for small-valued items such as candy bars, gumballs, and newspapers. When manufacturers become locked into customary prices, they may try to adapt by changing the size or quality of their products.

Customary Pricing
Pricing some types of products—usually small-value items—at a certain level to avert consumer resistance at higher levels.

Candy manufacturers have become ingenious at this. From 1949 to 1983, Hershey changed the price of its standard milk chocolate bar only seven times, gradually raising it from 5¢ to 35¢. During the same time, the weight of the candy bar was altered 32 times within a range of ¾ and 1⅞ ounces. In general, the size of the candy bar at a given price gradually declined. Eventually a larger candy bar would be introduced at a higher price.[29]

Some producers redo the packaging rather than the product itself. Aluminum cans have fallen 35 percent in weight since the 1960s and have become much thinner-walled.[30] The change in packaging may also involve a switch in materials, such as replacing glass bottles with plastic ones or with aseptic packages (which are, in effect, paper bottles; see Figure 10.7).

Figure 10.7
Aseptic Packaging Is Gaining Popularity

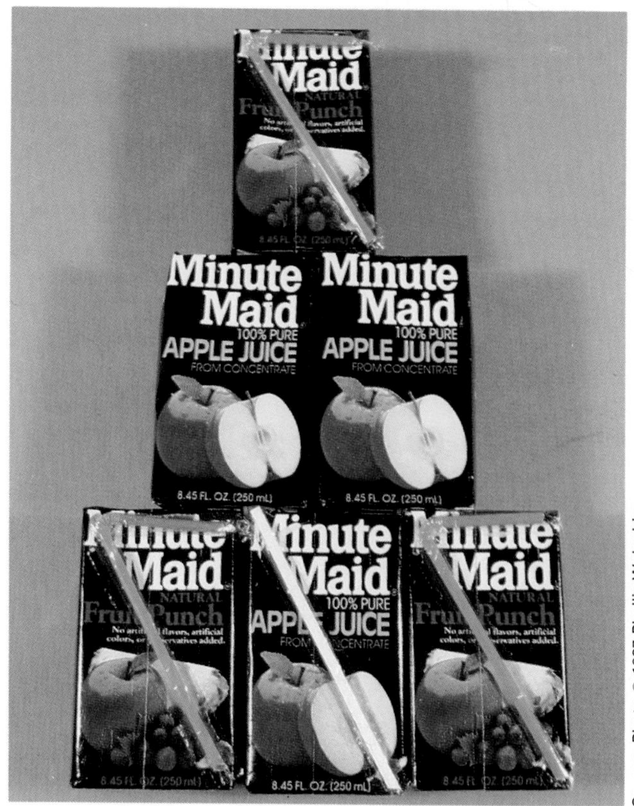

Source: Photo © 1987 Phyllis Woloshin.

Manufacturers insist they are not trying to deceive consumers or to squeeze more profit from the items they sell. Inflation drives up their costs. As long as buyers insist on certain prices, the temptation to pare quantity and quality will remain.

Odd Pricing Prices are sometimes adjusted to end with an odd number (1, 3, 5, 7, 9) or just under a round number (98, 99). This practice, called **odd pricing,** is common among retailers. One study showed that most retail ads contained such prices.[31]

Odd Pricing
Retail practice of adjusting prices to end with an odd number or just under a round number (for example, $7.99).

The custom started years ago among retailers. To prevent clerks from pocketing money from a sale, retailers set odd prices, which forced salespeople to ring up a sale to get change. The practice continues today because most retailers believe that consumers do not round off to the next highest dollar figure and thus think they are getting a bargain. Marketers using odd prices assume they have a jagged demand curve—slightly higher prices reduce the quantity demanded. (See Figure 10.8.) There is little experimental evidence to prove or disprove this assumption. In fact, some merchants think that customers are no longer fooled

Figure 10.8
Demand Curve when Psychological Pricing Is Appropriate

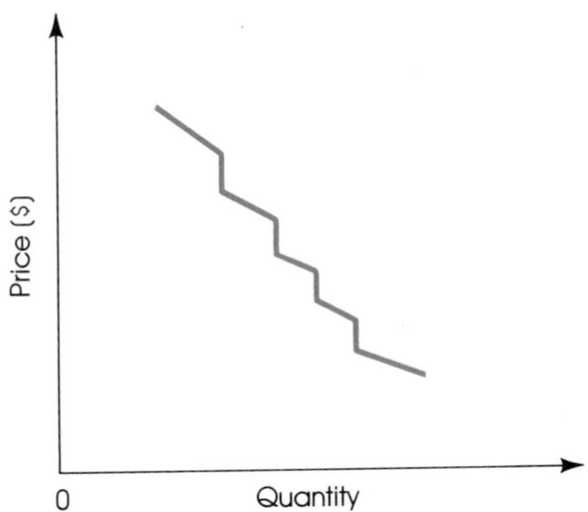

by prices ending in .99 or .98, so they set even stranger prices. A factory outlet in St. Louis, for example, prices its jeans at $9.86. Why the 86 cents? "When people see $9.99 they say, 'That's $10,' " says the sales manager. "But $9.86 isn't $10. It's just psychological."[32]

Conversely, many merchants have adopted an opposite but related tactic to give the impression of quantity or luxury. To connote this image, a quality store may price its offerings at even dollar figures. For this reason, a diamond ring may be priced at $3,000 rather than $2,999. Whether either approach has the desired effect is a topic for further research.

Chapter Replay

1. **What basic considerations do consumers and businesses weigh in accepting a price?**
   Consumers weigh the utility of a product to them. Businesses consider a variety of objective factors, including demand, supply, costs, competition, government rules, and other elements of the marketing mix.
2. **What steps are typically involved in price setting?**
   In the price-setting process, management sets pricing objectives, estimates buyer demand, calculates costs, analyzes competitors' prices, selects a pricing policy, determines price-setting methods, and decides on a final price.
3. **What objectives do companies try to achieve in price setting?**
   Pricing objectives may include achieving a certain level of profits or sales or a certain market share. They may also include maintaining the status quo and achieving social objectives, such as being regarded as fair or trustworthy.

4. **What are some general characteristics of demand?**
   Demand for a good generally increases as the price falls. In addition, demand may be inelastic (if an increase in price increases the seller's total revenue) or elastic (if an increase in price decreases the seller's total revenue).
5. **What types of costs must sellers cover?**
   Sellers must cover fixed costs, which do not vary with the firm's output, as well as variable costs, which do vary with output.
6. **What are some pricing policies companies might choose?**
   A firm must decide whether to charge one price or several; whether to price at, above, or below the competition; and whether to price new products high or low.
7. **What methods do companies use to set prices?**
   A firm may choose from a variety of price-setting methods, including cost-plus pricing, markup pricing, and breakeven plus demand pricing.
8. **What kinds of discounts might a company offer?**
   A manufacturer might offer wholesalers and retailers trade discounts in return for services performed. Reductions for early payment are called cash discounts. Manufacturers may offer intermediaries quantity discounts, which may be cumulative or noncumulative. Companies may also offer seasonal discounts for products used primarily during certain times of the year.
9. **How can companies adjust for location in setting prices?**
   Companies can use various price strategies, including F.O.B. pricing, uniform-delivery pricing, zone-delivery pricing, and basing-point pricing.
10. **How can companies adjust prices to meet consumer expectations?**
    Companies can appeal to consumer preconceptions or needs by using psychological pricing. This may take the form of price lining, customary pricing, or odd pricing.

Key Terms

average markup
bait pricing
basing-point pricing
breakeven analysis
cash discount
contribution (incremental) pricing
cost-plus pricing
cumulative discount
customary pricing
discount
elastic demand
elasticity of demand
F.O.B. pricing
fixed costs
inelastic demand
law of demand
list price
loss leader
markup
markup percentage
noncumulative discount
odd pricing
one-price policy
penetration pricing
price collusion
price discrimination

price leader
price lining
pricing objectives
pricing policies
profit
quantity discount
seasonal discount
skimming
target rate of return
trade discount
turnover
uniform-delivery pricing
utility
variable costs
variable-price policy
zone-delivery pricing

Discussion Questions

1. Who helps set a company's prices? What role do these people play in the price-setting process?
2. Roger Stonewall is a salesperson at Jake's Furniture Outlet. One day he complained to Jake, "If you would lower the price of these chairs, I could sure sell a lot more of them." What are some disadvantages of Roger's pricing objective? What other kinds of pricing objectives can a business pursue?
3. When the Olympia movie theater doubled the price of chocolate-covered raisins, sales fell so much that the theater actually made less money. When the dentist down the street from the Olympia raised her fees, her patient load declined somewhat, but her revenues increased. Other things being equal, what can you infer about the elasticity of demand for chocolate-covered raisins compared with the elasticity of demand for dental care?
4. While he was looking in the newspaper for a summer job, Ray Montana found an ad for delivering phone books. He called and learned that he would have to provide his own car and would be paid a fixed amount for each address to which he delivered a phone book. Ray does not own a car, but his friend Jay will sell him one for $500. What fixed and variable expenses must Ray cover before he can make a profit on this undertaking?
5. What pricing practices are forbidden by law? Describe these practices.
6. Deluxe Software Inc. is planning to introduce a new tax-planning package. What pricing policies might Deluxe use for this new product? Which do you recommend? Why?
7. Under what conditions might a company use cost-plus pricing?
8. At Martha's Bargain World, the markup on a pair of pants is 40 percent. Shoppers at Martha's can buy one brand of pants for $20. What did the store pay for the pants?
9. What is the difference between a trade discount and a quantity discount?
10. Classic Catalog Creations advertises that it ships its handwoven rugs "anywhere in the United States at no additional charge." Is the shipping really free?

Wondrous Office Furniture has a different policy. It ships desks and file cabinets to offices throughout the East Coast. Its terms are F.O.B. origin. What does this mean?

Franklin International

Case 10.1 Franklin International (B)

In addition to producing plastic bottles for other divisions of Franklin International, the Plastic Division is an extrusion blow molder and decorator of plastic containers primarily for the health and beauty-aid market. The division has one Hayssen and five Bekum blow-molding machines, operating 24 hours a day, seven days a week. The division is capable of producing plastic containers out of high-density polyethylene (HDPE) or polyvinylchlorine (PVC). Customers of the division can buy a completely finished product since the division has equipment to silk screen, hot stamp, or use the Therimage process to decorate and print information on the plastic containers.

Division Promotion

The following information from a promotional brochure for the division describes its marketing offer:

The Franklin Plastic Container Division is a very specialized custom manufacturer, providing packaging services to cosmetic, drug, and industrial marketers. From one manufacturing location, both containers and decorative requirements are produced in response to specific orders. A collection of standard and custom plastic container configurations and sizes is in continuous production for promotional packaging and market testing of your products. From this standard collection, Franklin provides custom-labeled containers within very short leadtimes.

Franklin creative structural and graphic design services can also produce unique container shapes and decoration to coordinate with your national distribution requirements. Here, Franklin offers a practical range of production options: single and multiple color silkscreening, hot stamp decoration in metallic colors, and economical multi-colored preprinted Therimage labeling for long production runs. And personal service is part of the Franklin tradition of product excellence in doing business.

Market Segments

There are two product/market segments of the business: private label and national brand. The national brand segment consists of products or a family of related products that go into a well-defined and unified market. National brand accounts consist of nine products, all of which are within Franklin's effective freight area. Products are custom blow molded in sizes ranging from 10½-ounce to 64-ounce containers with various decorating applications. As a result of R & D, quality, and service, more specialty blow molding and new business can be expected in the future.

The private label segment of business consists of products that are close in image to the national brands and also offer a no-frills package emphasizing low prices. Private label accounts consist of 13 products. The division has been able to utilize the distribution department to be cost effective in freight. Stock molds are required to run this segment of the business. Sizes range from 8 to 32 ounces with various decorating applications. Because of multiple cavity molds in HDPE, a larger stock line of containers, and conversion to PVC, increased volumes are expected in the future.

Therimage Decorating

One process of imprinting and decorating plastic containers is Therimage. Multicolored preprinted labels are applied to the containers with special equipment involving heat and a cooling-down process. As part of its marketing planning, management was reviewing pricing procedures and strategies for the Therimage process.

Fixed costs of running the Therimage equipment, such as salaries, indirect labor, fringes, depreciation, taxes, and transfer costs were estimated at $107,000 per year. Various costs for the process, over and above the cost of the bottle, such as direct labor, fringes, materials, utilities, and supplies, were estimated to be $16 per 1,000 bottles printed. Allowing for set-up time, maintenance, and other operating factors, it was estimated that the Therimage process could print up to 20 million containers per year. In checking with prices charged by competitors, division management found that the range was from a low of $17 to as much as $25–$30 per thousand bottles printed.

Focal Topics

1. What issues and pricing alternatives should Franklin take into account in pricing its plastic containers?
2. Why do you think Therimage prices range from $17 to more than $25 per thousand bottles printed?
3. On average, what prices do you think Franklin should charge for Therimage printing on plastic containers?

Case 10.2
Hewlett Enterprises (A)

CO

It all began on a cold winter night in a medium-size town in Wisconsin. Scott and Trish Hewlett were playing one of their favorite board games with their two children—Andy, who was 14 years old, and Rosy, who was 12. The family had always enjoyed playing board games together; Scott and Trish both came from families for whom board games and weekends were synonymous. Scott claimed that when he was about 10 his family once started a Monopoly game on a Friday evening that he did not finally win until 10 p.m. on Sunday evening.

Problem or Opportunity

For years Scott had talked about developing and marketing his own board game. He had even sketched out a few ideas and discussed them with other board game fans. As Andy won the game on that winter evening, he remarked: "Dad, maybe you ought to invent your own game, with your own rules. Then you might have a better chance of winning." The whole family laughed, but little did they realize that future events would lead to such an activity.

With a degree in chemical engineering, Scott had worked for 15 years as a laboratory researcher for a local adhesive manufacturing firm. A few days after his son's suggestion, Scott found himself out of a job for the first time since college. The company he worked for had lost a major private-label adhesive account, and layoffs became necessary. Although his employer was reluctant to lay him off, even temporarily, Scott was let go. A family meeting was held that evening.

There were not many opportunities for Scott in town, given his rather specialized experience. He would receive unemployment compensation, which would help ease the loss of his job somewhat, and Trish still had her part-time position as a special-education instructor with the local school system. The family would be able to get by for a while, but eventually something would have to be done. It was Rosy who came up with the obvious suggestion: Why not take this time to develop one of her father's board game ideas?

Making It

Scott had spent the most time on a game idea in which players would move around a board filled with businesses and life situations. The first person to land on one of the businesses could buy it and then collect payments from other players who subsequently landed on it. The business could be expanded by "building branch locations," which meant that players would have to pay more if they landed on a business with one or more "branches." Each time players moved completely around the board, they received a "salary" of $7,000.

The objective of the game was straightforward—avoid going bankrupt. The payments from people who landed on your business and the salary received from going around the board would be enough, one hoped, to cover expenses as one landed on opponents' businesses. There was one other dimension to the game—life opportunities and problems. Not all spaces on the board had businesses; some contained other activities such as investments ($500 paid to the person landing on the space), contests ("You just won $300"), medical expenses ("You owe $200"), and college tuition ("You owe $100").

Exhibit
Estimated Costs for Producing 1,000 Games

Play money	$140
Plastic pieces	325
Game boards	815
Deeds	115
Situation cards	120
Instruction sheets	45
Dice	110
Boxes	735

Scott decided to name the game MAKING IT. The idea was that the winners made it in life; the losers did not make it and went bankrupt. Summing the total points on two dice determined how many spaces a player would move each turn. If doubles were thrown, the player would select a card from the Life's Little Situations piles. Those cards instruct the player to do such things as: "Your faucet leaks, call the plumber and pay $200," "Your United Way pledge is due, pay $100," "You won an athletic scholarship, take $500," and "You received an income tax refund, take $300."

Pricing Considerations

In its final form the game consisted of a full-color playing sheet attached to a folded cardboard backing, 500 pieces of play money, deed cards for the 25 businesses, 50 small plastic pieces for "branches," 6 different player pieces, two dice, and 50 Life's Little Situations cards. A sheet of playing instructions and a box to hold all of the game items completed the package. Scott was now faced with the problem of what price to charge for MAKING IT.

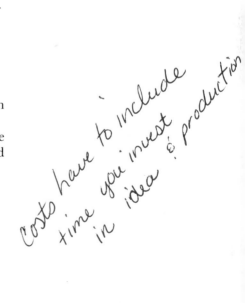

Initially, Scott decided that he would do the selling himself and call on local retail stores to get them to carry the game. Obviously, he was concerned about how many sets of the game to produce at the outset, but he realized that economies of scale are such that to produce just a few would be almost as expensive as to produce a thousand. After talking with several printers, plastic companies, and other suppliers, he came up with the numbers in the exhibit. Several of the people he talked with indicated that they were giving him very special prices in the hope that the game would catch on and that larger orders would come in the future.

Focal Topics

1. What basic pricing strategies could Scott use in establishing his price for MAKING IT?
2. What other "expenses" beyond manufacturing costs should Scott consider?
3. What price do you recommend that Scott charge retailers for MAKING IT? Please support your recommendations.

Case for Part Three

K mart Corporation

In October 1985, K mart Apparel, the clothing division of K mart Corporation, introduced the Jaclyn Smith signature line in 500 K mart stores across the country. The new line is part of an overall merchandising strategy of the retailer that began in 1980 when Bernard M. Fauber became company chairman. The collection was designed to fit into the new image K mart is attempting to develop through its five-year refurbishing and new merchandising plans. The objective is to continue to present a balance of quality merchandise at reasonable prices.

K mart and Apparel

K mart's overall merchandising strategy was modified in the early 1980s to seek out the more discriminating shopper by providing better-quality merchandise. The objective was to accomplish this while still building on the firm's reputation as the nation's lowest-priced general merchandise retailer.

Before the strategy was implemented, K mart stores devoted approximately 30 percent of their floor space to apparel sales, but netted only 20 to 22 percent of their overall business from that line. While size of store displays has not changed, traffic patterns and merchandise selection have been improved to reflect the varied tastes of shoppers. K mart began merchandising better quality apparel three years ago when Names for Less was introduced.

Joseph Antonini, senior vice president of K mart Corporation and president of K mart Apparel, said, however, that merchandise is now placed in stores where it is most popular, not throughout the company's stores. Climate, income, and the personal tastes of shoppers affect the placement of merchandise.

Jaclyn Smith and K mart Apparel have joined forces to bring stylish, moderately priced clothing to American women with two major Jaclyn Smith collections, one in sportswear and the other in maternity. The sportswear line was introduced into 1,400 of the company's 2,100 stores in the summer of 1985. Skirts, trousers, and blouses made of natural and man-made fibers can be mixed for versatility and worn year-around. The merchandise is priced from $16.97 to $24.97.

"I like to have lots of different looks to suit my changing moods and demands of my active life-style," explained Ms. Smith. "The glamorous clothes that I wear on television are just not practical for my off-camera

Source: This case has been edited from an earlier case appearing in *Cases and Exercises in Marketing* by W. Wayne Talarzyk, pp. 107+. Copyright © 1987 by CBS College Publishing. Reprinted by permission of Holt, Rinehart, & Winston, Inc.

life. When I spend time with my son, Gaston, and my daughter, Spencer Margaret, I want to wear clothes that are comfortable yet stylish."

K mart hopes the Jaclyn Smith line and K mart's reputation for reasonable prices will attract women who would not ordinarily consider K mart for clothes. The objective is to improve its apparel and attract the upscale, yet cost-conscious consumer. "Jaclyn Smith's name will help K mart get that message to our customers," said Antonini. "People realize that if Jaclyn Smith puts her name on something, the clothes will be of high quality."

"The Jaclyn Smith line reflects her style and good taste," Antonini said. "The line caters to the varied life-styles of today's woman—working woman, mother, sports enthusiast, and homemaker." "I believe that we can design a wardrobe that is versatile and affordable," said Ms. Smith. "Because today's women have so little time to shop, they can appreciate clothes that are easily mixed and matched."

The Maternity Collection

"There is a tremendous need for fashionable, yet affordable maternity clothing," said Antonini. "K mart is taking a leading role by offering women maternity wardrobing that is comfortable, stylish, and reasonably priced." Antonini added that this is the first time a celebrity has signed his or her name to a line of maternity clothing that has been designed especially for a mass merchandise retailer.

As a busy actress and expectant mother, Ms. Smith is only too aware of the fashion problems pregnancy creates.

The proverbial "tent dress" is, quite simply, too limiting for the woman who wants to feel fashionable and beautiful during her pregnancy. I realized just how frustrating these limitations can be while pregnant with my son, Gaston. When I was expecting my first child, I found it difficult to find well-made maternity outfits. My new signature line will help women dress stylishly during the most important time of their lives.

The maternity collection, as described in the Exhibit, consists of 38 coordinated separates available in sizes 6 to 16 and priced reasonably from $15.97 to $20.97. Natural fibers and synthetics make up this collection, allowing transitional wear from season to season. "A woman's pregnancy usually spans two seasons. However, most women can't afford to buy maternity clothes for both warm and colder temperatures," says Smith. Jaclyn Smith's maternity fashions combine softly tailored separates with casual sportswear. Color coordinated wovens and knits offer an array of wardrobe options in solids, bold stripes, and stylish cabbage rose prints. The pieces include oversized shirts, blouse-knit tops, adjustable pants, and fashionable rib-knit tube skirts.

The following statements reflect some of Ms. Smith's attitudes toward maternity fashions:

My maternity signature collection will help women dress stylishly during the most important time of their lives.

Exhibit

K mart/Jaclyn Smith Maternity Collection Fact Sheet

Debut	The Jaclyn Smith signature maternity collection will consist of coordinated separates designed for the varied life-styles of today's expectant mother. The maternity collection will debut on October 11, 1985, in 500 K mart stores throughout the country.
Clothing	The 38 coordinated separates in sizes 6 to 16 will consist of the following: Oversized tops Boat-neck knit tops Chelsea-collared tops with contrasting bow ties Adjustable snap pants Softly ribbed knit skirts
Styling	The maternity line is fashionable and updated, featuring the quality workmanship women expect in a wardrobe. Designed to be mixed and matched, the collection features casual looks. Quality detailing such as band-bottom tops; solids, stripes, and floral prints; bow ties; mandarin collars; and button shoulder treatments complete the high-quality look of the collection.
Fabrics	The selected fabrics allow for comfort as well as fine styling: Polyester/cotton blending Soft, silky satinessa fabrics Woven stretch twill Cotton double knit
Colors	There is a selection of the soft tones of pastels—pink, powder blue, maize, and grey, as well as a wide assortment of bright tones—black, red, ivory, hot pink, turquoise, and yellow.
Price	The separates are reasonably priced from $15.97 to $20.97.
Jaclyn Smith Involvement	The wardrobe, designed under the creative eye of Jaclyn Smith, is consistent with her elegant, yet down-to-earth style. Jaclyn Smith's involvement spans all aspects of clothing design from the approval of sketches to fabric selection.
K mart's New Marketing Strategy	K mart is spending more than $2.2 billion over the next five years to refurbish its stores. K mart will carry more quality name brands and a wider selection of merchandise and establish a more convenient and pleasant atmosphere.
K mart Background	K mart is the world's second largest retailer with more than $21.1 billion in annual sales. The 2,100 K mart stores in the United States, Canada, and Puerto Rico sell merchandise ranging from apparel and personal goods to housewares.

I like the flexibility of many pieces. This helps to create a maternity wardrobe that easily works together.

There is no reason why maternity clothes can't be attractive, current, and affordable.

The Jaclyn Smith maternity collection is adaptable and functional because we created it that way.

A woman wants to look attractive and feel comfortable, especially when expecting a child.

When I was expecting my first child, I found it difficult to find well-made maternity outfits at reasonable prices.

Focal Topics

1. What do you see as the basic marketing problems facing K mart in connection with the Jaclyn Smith Maternity Collection?
2. What types of marketing research would be helpful to K mart in marketing the maternity collection?
3. What kinds of product extensions and product expansions should K mart consider for the Jaclyn Smith Collection?
4. What are the relative advantages and disadvantages in using celebrity product strategies?
5. Do you think it was wise for K mart to develop and market the maternity collection? Please support your recommendations.

Part Four

Placement Strategy

11

Channels and Wholesaling

Sounding Out the Chapter

In this chapter, you will learn:

1. How marketers make a product available to users.
2. How intermediaries serve consumers and producers.
3. The decisions marketers make in designing marketing channels.
4. What marketers consider in deciding on a channel length.
5. Reasons some companies use multiple marketing channels.
6. The basic kinds of channel members.
7. A firm's choices for how much market exposure a product should have.
8. How conflict in channels is controlled.
9. Why organizations create vertical marketing systems.

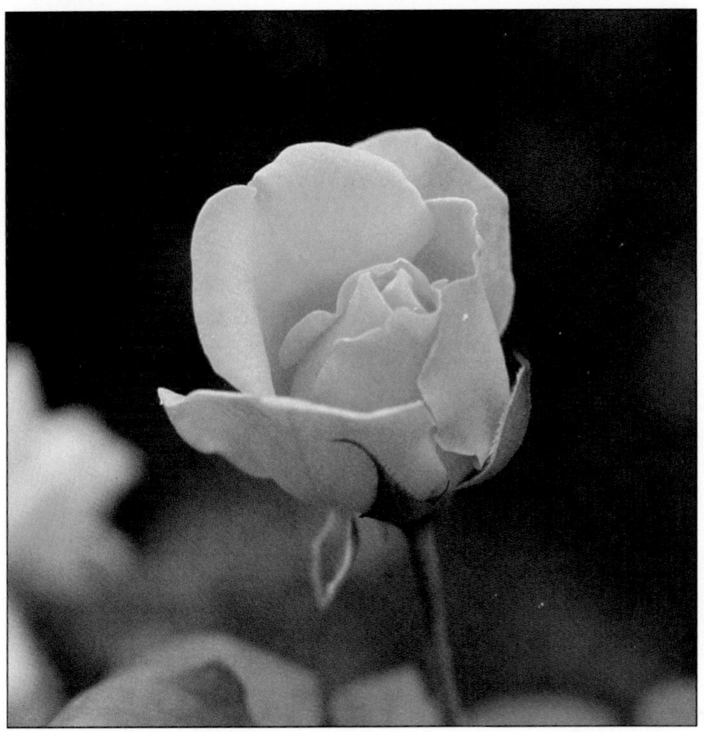
Source: Courtesy of Wes Young, Dallas, Texas.

A Floral Odyssey

It's the dead of winter in Hanover, New Hampshire. Temperatures have hovered in the subzero range for a week. Nathaniel Yanqui, a business major at Dartmouth, is trying to think of a way to impress a new friend he met from Colby-Sawyer College, down the road a bit in New London. Nat knows that Peggy Sue, a native of Galveston, Texas, has not been too happy lately. In fact, she has been wondering what crazy impulse ever led her to leave the sunny Gulf Coast for this frozen turf. Suddenly, an idea hits Nat. How about a bouquet of yellow roses for the homesick Texan? After a long night at the library studying for an upcoming marketing exam, Nat calls 1-800-FLOWERS, a round-the-clock, toll-free, floral wire service, and orders a dozen roses sent to Peggy Sue's dorm. The order is relayed to a participating local florist, and an amazing odyssey begins.

Nat's "Texas roses" may well begin their journey in Israel. Israel, which produces in the range of $100 million in flowers annually, has become a formidable force in the American market for cut flowers. The Israelis regularly load jumbo jets full of flowers bound for Aalsmeer, a tiny Dutch town that is the flower capital of the world. In Aalsmeer, brokers watch while as many as 10 million blossoms—daffodils from Great Britain, carnations from Kenya, tulips and freesia from Holland, orchids from Singapore, and roses and gladioli from Israel—are put up for auction. By 10 a.m. the day's trading is done, and the flowers are flown to florist shops and flower stalls in Stockholm, Paris, New York, and in the case of Nat's roses, to the flower exchange in Boston.

"It's a cut-throat business," one wholesaler says. "I don't want to say 18 cents too loudly because my next-door neighbor might hear me and give them to the customer for 16 cents. So you whisper."

With Nat's order in mind, a florist from New Hampshire strikes a deal for a lot of roses. By that afternoon, the yellow roses of "Texas" are opening their buds in a New Hampshire college dorm—as the temperature outside slips to a frosty −10°.

Getting a product to a consumer is not always this complex. The process may be as simple as opening a laundromat at a well-traveled intersection and posting the facility's hours in the window. Be it complex or simple, however, every product must follow some path from the producer to the consumer. This chapter discusses some of the decisions marketers make in planning for and managing such paths.

Sources: Russell Leavitt, "Billions in Blossoms," *Fortune,* May 18, 1981, pp. 68–75; Barbara Bradley, "Nationwide Phone Setup Peddles Hearts and FLOWERS," *The Christian Science Monitor,* February 14, 1983, p. 11; Peter Sleeper, "Though the Aroma's Sweet, the Atmosphere is Business," *The Boston Sunday Globe,* December 11, 1983, pp. 33, 55; and "Carnations from Kenya," *Forbes,* November 15, 1977, pp. 115–116.

Placing goods and services where they are needed and when they are wanted is the subject of the next three chapters. Marketers call this activity **distribution.** Consumers take distribution for granted because what they need is usually readily available. It is no longer unusual to find mangoes, fresh strawberries, or even roses in the local supermarket when outside there is a foot of snow on the ground. Few consumers think twice about the complex route Japanese television sets, Brazilian boots, or New Zealand lamb chops take to reach shops in a U.S. town.

Distribution
Activity directed toward placing goods and services where they are needed and when they are wanted.

What Is a Marketing Channel?

The people and organizations involved in making a product available to a user form a **marketing,** or **distribution, channel.** This channel enables the user to acquire ownership of the product. Apples, for example, follow a marketing channel from apple growers to apple eaters.

Marketing (Distribution) Channel
The people and organizations involved in making a product available to a user.

Even services have marketing channels. Barbers need a place to provide haircuts in a location accessible to people with hair. Airlines use travel agencies to sell tickets to passengers. Banks often enlist local retailers to help market their credit cards.[1]

A marketing channel, therefore, requires at minimum a seller and a buyer. The buyer may be a consumer or an industrial user. The basic transaction in a simple marketing channel is the exchange of ownership, or title, of goods. Many times the physical movement of goods, such as the transportation of the flowers, is also involved, but it is not necessary.

Typically, a marketing channel includes, besides buyers and sellers, various intermediaries. As the opening example points out, there are two types of intermediaries—retailers and wholesaling intermediaries. **Retailers** sell directly to consumers. **Wholesaling intermediaries,** on the other hand, do most of their selling to retailers, other wholesaling intermediaries, or industrial users, rather than consumers. Sometimes the distinction between wholesaling intermediaries and retailers is a bit unclear; for example, a consumer may buy eyeglasses, furniture, or auto parts from a wholesale establishment. Generally speaking, however, retailers exist to serve consumers, and wholesaling intermediaries sell only to other sellers.

Retailer
Intermediary who sells directly to consumers.

Wholesale Intermediary
Link that sells to retailers, other wholesaling intermediaries, or industrial users.

Are Wholesale and Retail Intermediaries Useful?

From time to time, a public cry goes up to "eliminate the middleman." When the price of coffee skyrocketed in the mid-1970s because of crop failures in Latin America, middlemen were accused of making a bad situation worse by raising their prices. The basis for such views is not hard to understand. Goods that go through marketing channels are in no way physically changed as they pass through several intermediaries, and yet these intermediaries add to the cost. As Figure 11.1 shows, transportation, wholesaling, and retailing costs add 76 cents—or 34 percent—to the cost of a pound of beef. For many nonfood items, distribution costs are even higher. More than 40 percent of the price of a record album,

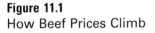

Figure 11.1
How Beef Prices Climb

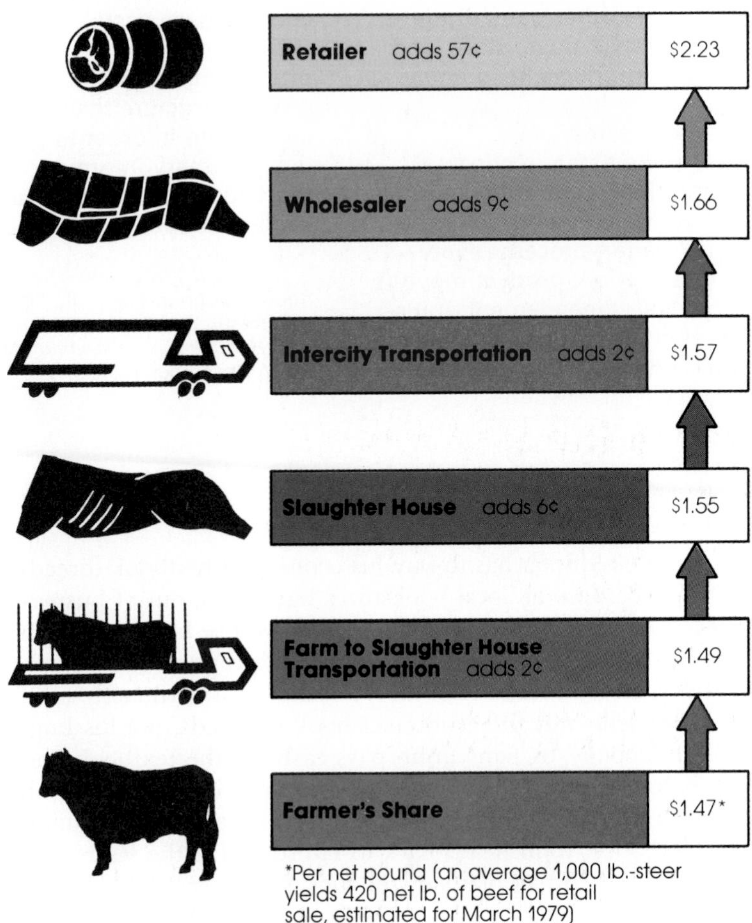

Source: "Meat Bites Back." Reprinted by permission from *Time,* April 23, 1979, p. 62.

for example, goes directly to intermediaries. This means that businesses must keep a watchful eye on distribution costs. (See Marketing Today 11.1.)

Are such high distribution costs justified? Wholesale and retail intermediaries say yes because of the important functions they perform for both consumers and producers.

How Intermediaries Serve Consumers

If intermediaries did not exist and it was necessary to purchase all goods and services directly from the producer, consumers would have to give up a great deal of what they have come to expect. Consider a hypotheti-

Marketing Today **11.1**

Keeping a Lid on Distribution Costs

Companies often find it relatively easy to let distribution costs grow. After all, the distributor can pass along the cost. However, marketers must beware of this attitude, because somewhere a competitor is generally eager to take away business by being more efficient and charging less for a product. This issue is especially important for companies that sell nationwide. Few companies in other parts of the world must move, store, and handle products in so many dispersed locations as in the United States.

The first step in effectively controlling distribution costs is to evaluate every step in the distribution process: every labor motion, product movement, storage element, transportation cost, and administrative process. Once management has assigned costs to each of these elements, the company can look for ways to control these costs.

The process can be complex; often companies find they must restructure their accounting system in order to process the necessary information. But the effort may be necessary to keep a company profitable.

Source: John J. Tracy, Jr., "Cost Controls in Distribution Badly Needed," *Handling and Shipping Management*, December 1985, p. 9.

cal case: John Goldfinch has to buy his economics textbook directly from the publisher because all local bookstores have gone out of business.

Unless John lives near Hinsdale, Illinois, where his publisher is located, he has to fly, drive, or take a train to Chicago. Then he has to make his way to Hinsdale to see the publisher. Unfortunately for John, this publisher sells only the economics book he needs, not his English textbook, notebooks, or pens. John pays cash for the textbook, then heads back to campus. When he arrives, he finds out that the economics professor forgot that the class should have purchased study guides to go with the textbooks. John heads back to Hinsdale for the study guide.

John had to perform many of the jobs that intermediaries usually assume. Marketing intermediaries, particularly retailers, serve consumers by:

1. Bringing together a wide assortment of goods. A typical college bookstore sells textbooks for all classes, other books of interest to students, notebooks, pens, and other supplies.
2. Placing that assortment in a convenient (that is, time-saving) location. College bookstores are located on or near the campus they serve.
3. Providing credit, and therefore the use of goods or services at the time they are needed. If John had not had the cash to buy his books, most stores would have let him charge them with a credit card.
4. Offering money-saving services (such as delivery, alterations, sales help, and so on). A college bookstore could have special-ordered the study guides the professor had forgotten about.
5. Giving consumers the desired product in the desired quantity. If John had been shopping for tomatoes instead of a book, he might have had to buy a bushel instead of the two or three he wanted.

Figure 11.2
How Intermediaries Simplify Transactions

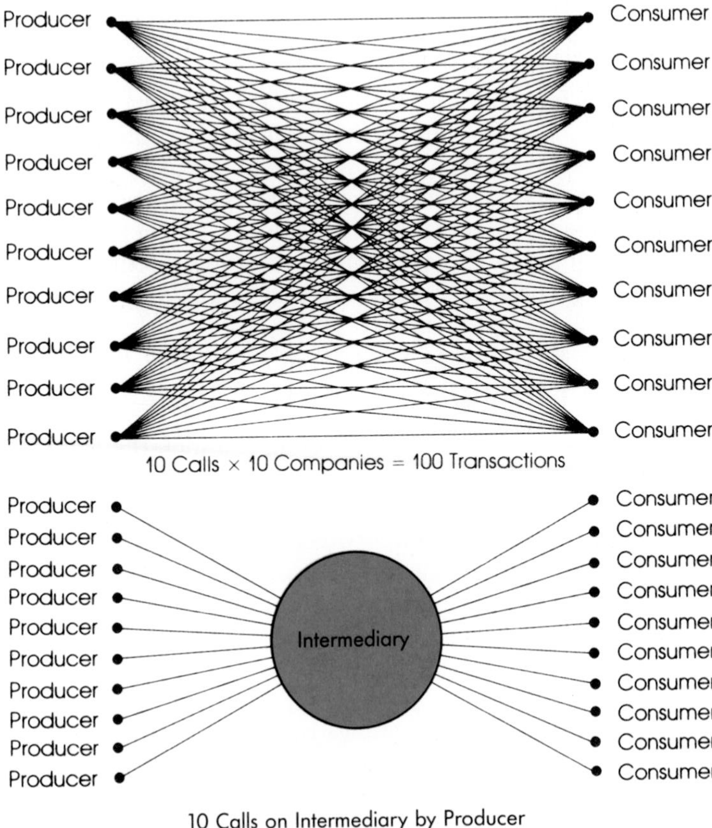

How Intermediaries Serve Producers

Producers as well as consumers benefit from the existence of intermediaries. First, wholesaling intermediaries and retailers help simplify contacts between producers and consumers. As Figure 11.2 shows, if 10 manufacturers or producers of services wanted to contact just 10 consumers, it would require 100 visits—and possibly 100 shipments—with all the paperwork and expense that they entail. By using just 1 intermediary, the total number of transactions is cut to 20. The 10 producers make only 1 visit apiece, a large saving, and after that the task of selling belongs to the intermediary. After a channel is well established, another simplification occurs. Reordering by the intermediary becomes automatic, eliminating repeat calls by the producer.

Intermediaries also help producers financially. In some cases, they save manufacturers the cost of carrying inventory in warehouses, thus freeing up funds for manufacturers, which can be used for other business purposes. Some intermediaries finance the operations of producers of seasonal goods, such as air conditioners or skis, by ordering and paying for goods during slack times. Finally, intermediaries who purchase goods relieve manufacturers of some of the financial risk they might suffer if their goods did not sell. When Evel Knievel toys did not sell well because of adverse publicity for the daredevil motorcyclist, department and discount stores that stocked toys shared the loss with the manufacturer.

One other function that intermediaries perform for producers is the communication of marketing information. Cities with convention bureaus often serve as intermediaries for the hotel industry. They solicit convention business and then let industry members know that a group will be in town so hotels can make arrangements. Retailers offer the same service to manufacturers (and wholesaling intermediaries to retailers) by letting them know what items are selling well.

The Transfer Principle

Transfer Principle
Principle that all functions of the marketing channel are vital and when not performed by one channel member must be taken over by another.

In dealings between members of a marketing channel, the **transfer principle** holds. That principle states that all of the functions of the marketing channel are vital and when not performed by one channel member must be taken over by another. In a two-channel system involving just a producer and a buyer, the producer absorbs some functions (such as financing or providing marketing information) and passes on others to buyers (such as transporting goods or providing services for themselves). The use of one or more intermediaries allows the burdens to be shared by more parties.

Not all organizations take advantage of opportunities to bring in intermediaries and shift various burdens to them. Why? The answer is that the producer sacrifices control to the intermediary. Such risks are evident in the case of Robin Rose of Robin Rose Ice Cream & Chocolate. For a one-time fee, Rose sells licensees the right to serve Robin Rose ice cream. The licensees buy ice cream from Rose at wholesale and are obligated to follow sound business practices and feature a full line of Robin Rose products. Aside from these requirements, says Rose, "They don't have to do things my way." As a result of the loosely structured agreement, licensees can set their own prices, and they have so far opted to charge less than Rose does in the store she owns herself.[2]

The major tasks facing marketers specializing in distribution are to design marketing channels that ensure goods reach a market efficiently and to manage problems that arise within the channels.

Designing Marketing Channels

Why does Revlon sell its products through retail stores, while Avon sells directly door to door? Why can you buy a Firestone tire in an auto supply store and the same tire, under a different brand name, in a Montgomery Ward store? Why can Hanes panty hose be found only in department stores, while L'Eggs are available in almost every supermarket and drugstore? The answer to all of these questions is that marketers have made certain decisions about the way a product can best be distributed. The manufacturer usually has the major say in these decisions, but, as we shall see later, other channel members are having an increasing say today. The four principal decisions concerning channels are:

1. **Channel length:** whether to use wholesaling intermediaries, retailers, or some combination.
2. **Channel number:** how many different marketing channels to employ.
3. **Channel member types:** what kinds of wholesaling intermediaries and retailers to bring in.
4. **Channel width:** how many outlets or individual firms to employ at each level of the channel.

None of these decisions can be made without considering the other elements of the marketing mix. For example, the W. A. Sheaffer Company manufactures two lines of pens—an expensive, high-quality line and a cheaper line to compete with throwaway ballpoints. Product and price considerations make it necessary to sell the more expensive line through department, jewelry, and gift stores; the other line must be sold, via wholesalers, to variety stores, outlets, and drugstores. A closer look at the four principal channel decisions will make clear that product and price are not the only factors that determine how a product will be distributed.

Channel Length
Number of links (intermediary types) in a particular marketing chain.

Channel Number
Quantity of different marketing channels to use in order to reach buyers.

Channel Member Type
Kind of wholesaling intermediaries and retailers in a marketing channel.

Channel Width
Number of outlets or individual firms to employ at each level in a channel.

Channel Length

There are important differences between the channels of distribution used for consumer and industrial products. Figure 11.3 displays the typical channels involved in the distribution of each of these.

Channels for Consumer Goods Consumer goods commonly go through a four-link channel employing both wholesalers and retailers. Almost all convenience goods—including food, tobacco, and nonprescription drugs—come through such a channel. Liggett and Meyers, for example, uses wholesaling intermediaries to distribute its cigarettes to the thousands of candy and grocery stores, newsstands, and vending machines that carry them. The same wholesalers also distribute other firms' cigarettes, saving retailers the bother of having to deal with sales representatives from each company.

Occasionally, consumer products go through a five-link channel when retailers are supplied by two wholesale links, only one of which takes title to the goods. For example, Birdseye frozen foods are first handled by a food broker whose job is to find other wholesale buyers for the products. Brokers specialize in selling to other intermediaries who transport and warehouse the goods.

Another important channel is the three-link consumer channel that uses only retailers. Automobiles are sold through this channel arrangement because dealers also provide service. Clothing and other goods that

Figure 11.3
Marketing Channels Used in Consumer and Industrial Markets

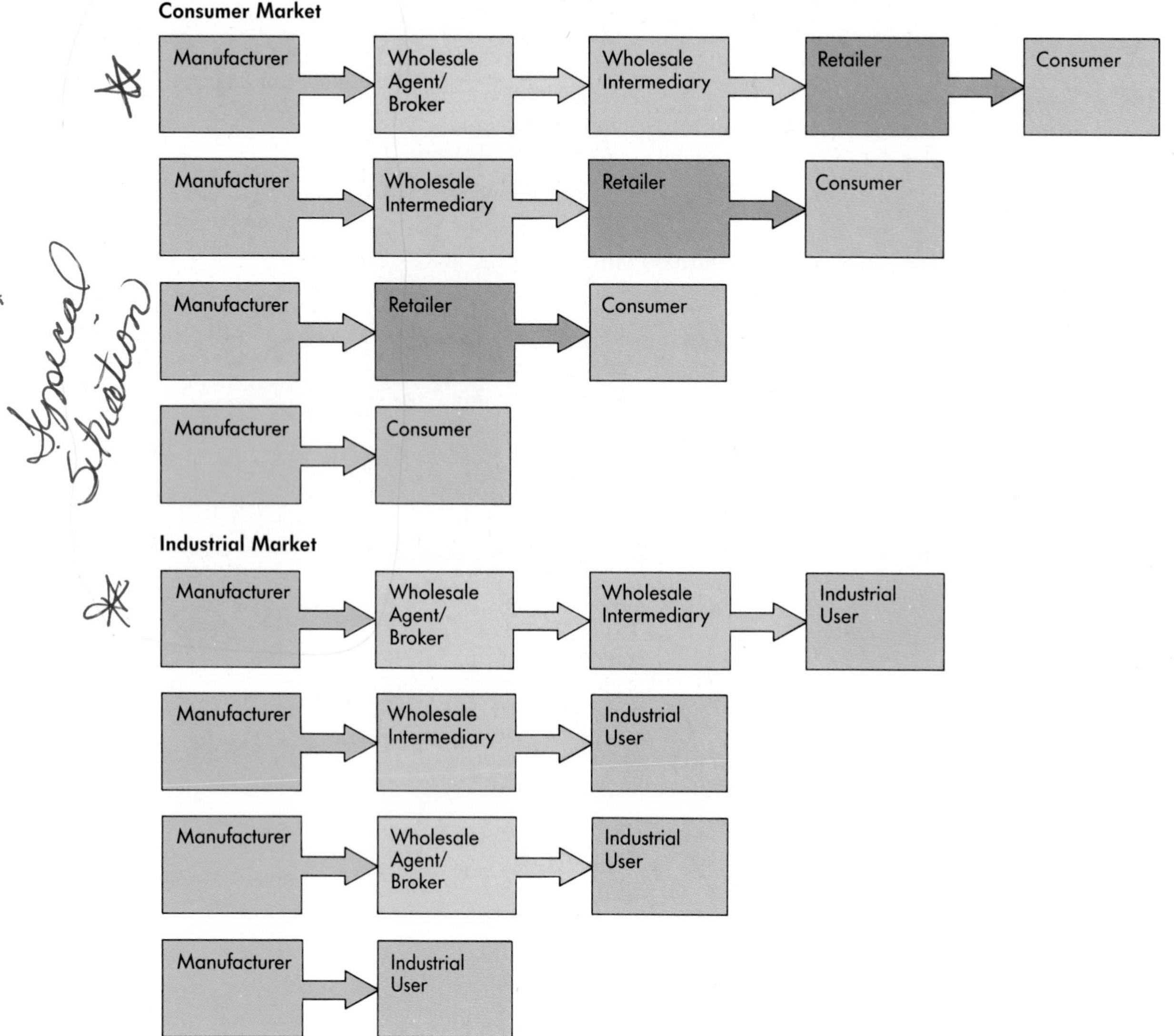

Source: Adapted from Richard R. Still, Edward W. Cundiff, and Norman A. P. Govoni, *Sales Management: Decision, Policies, and Cases,* 3rd ed. (Englewood Cliffs, N.J.: Prentice-Hall, 1976), p. 44.

may quickly go out of fashion also require this short channel. Marketing Today 11.2 describes how Esprit is making this channel even shorter.

An increasingly popular route delivers goods directly from the producer to the consumer. Companies selling door to door (Avon, Electrolux) use this channel arrangement. Direct selling is also characteristic of manufacturers with factory outlets and small businesses such as bakeries. In addition, almost all banks, insurance companies, and other sellers of services deal directly with the consumer, although that is changing. For example, banks now use employers as intermediaries for the direct de-

Marketing Today 11.2
Esprit Hopes for Growth from Shortened Channels

Source: Courtesy of Esprit De Corp.

With sales growth slowing in department stores and popularity rising for specialty stores, fashion maker Esprit De Corp. is hoping to benefit from a change in its distribution channels. States CEO Doug Tompkins: "Because company-owned stores or strictly controlled franchises do such a superior job of presenting sportswear collections, there is interest and enthusiasm to expand these programs."

Saying that Esprit is "cutting out department stores" would oversimplify the situation because many, and perhaps most, of Esprit's large accounts are department stores which have invested heavily and faithfully in specially fixtured Esprit shops within their stores, and they are doing an excellent job in presentation. Explains Kurt Barnard, a New York retail consultant, department stores tend to deal "erratically" with vendors and will "cherry pick" a vendor's collection, taking liberties with the product line that could possibly kill it. Esprit's control is in line with the philosophy of the company's chief executive, Doug Tompkins: "No detail is small."

Esprit expects its retailers to follow precise instructions on how to display its clothing. Explains Tompkins, "Retailers do well as merchants, buying and selling, and for that we give them a lot of credit. But . . . who's going to do the best [image] job with our product? Nobody will do it better than us."

Source: Cleveland Horton, "Esprit to Skirt Retail Clients by Setting Up Its Own Stores," *Advertising Age,* January 26, 1987, pp. 12, 65.

posit of employee checks on payday, and insurance companies write insurance through employers or labor unions.[3]

Channels for Industrial Goods Most industrial goods go through fewer channels than consumer goods. In fact, direct selling is by far the most common channel in industrial marketing. Almost all the components of an automobile, for example, are sold directly to car manufacturers. In general, all high-volume transactions between large suppliers and large buyers are direct.

A wholesaler, usually called an "industrial distributor," may be employed when the unit price of a product is small. Premier Industrial Corporation, a Cleveland-based distributor of "thigamajigs"—nuts, bolts, circuit breakers—carries more than 12,000 products which it sells to 50,000 small customers. The company's average order is only $100—and it thrives on accounts that bigger distributors regard as nuisances.[4]

Occasionally, wholesaling intermediaries who do not physically handle or purchase goods may be used instead of industrial distributors or in addition to them. Such intermediaries act as a manufacturer's sales force. Some of them specialize in selling highly technical products, such as large industrial machine tools, that require a lengthy marketing effort. Others work for small manufacturers who cannot afford their own sales force.

Factors Influencing Channel Length The discussion here has hinted at some of the factors that influence the decision on channel length. The specific characteristics of the product, the market, the company, and the environment may all have an impact on whether a short or long channel is appropriate. For example, a company that makes only a few simple, durable, low-priced products (such as screws or paper clips), for which there are many intermediaries, will probably choose to distribute its goods through long channels. Conversely, a company that produces many complex, high-priced products (such as computerized office systems) for a relatively small number of customers will probably favor shorter channels. A few examples may clarify the circumstances that influence the channel length decision.

The characteristics of a product are an important influence. Crest toothpaste, which is a simple, low-priced, standard consumer item that has remained on the market for 25 years, can be sold through a long chain of wholesalers and retailers. It needs no special intermediary effort to reach consumers. By contrast, the machine tool that makes the auto body of a Buick is custom-made, complex, and high-priced, and it may be discarded with the next model change. A direct effort by the sales force of the machine tool maker is needed to sell it. There are consumer goods that resemble the machine tool in characteristics (such as a custom-made Rolls-Royce), and there are industrial goods that resemble Crest toothpaste (such as a wrench). In that case, the consumer good would go through a shorter channel than the industrial good. The products' characteristics would be the determining factor.

Market characteristics also influence channel length. A snack-food company like Nabisco, which markets nationwide, must use wholesalers to reach thousands of grocery stores and vending machines. But another snack-food company, Lance, which concentrates its sales in the more limited market of the Sun Belt states, uses only its own sales force to reach retailers. Oshkosh B'Gosh, makers of work clothes for almost 100 years, was forced to reevaluate its distribution system when its overalls became the rage of the sandbox set. The company's solid denim and "hickory striped" utility clothing had always been distributed in men's and boys' clothing stores, with a few pairs near the lawn mowers and power tools in the basements of department stores. When a mail order house tried including a pair of Oshkosh B'Gosh children's overalls in its Christmas catalog as a novelty item, so many orders poured in that the company began selling through children's clothing stores.[5] Special customer needs might also favor a short channel. For example, the buyers of Xerox machines or snowmobiles expect servicing, which makes long channels inappropriate.

Company characteristics—particularly financial condition and depth of the product line—might influence channel length as well. At IBM, for example, personal selling is a major component of the marketing program. The company earns enough on its sales to support direct marketing costs and has the resources for direct distribution.[6] By contrast, most new companies have neither the money nor the product assortment to follow a similar strategy.

Finally, a variety of environmental considerations help determine channel length. The most important are:

1. *Economics.* Companies caught cash short in a business slump prefer lower-cost independent distributors to a high-cost sales force of their own.
2. *Law.* State laws limiting door-to-door sales, for example, may force some companies to use longer channels to reach customers.
3. *Intermediary availability.* Wholesale intermediaries overburdened with competitors' products may be unable to handle a new product. A more direct route may be required.

Although the factors considered here are treated separately, in practice they must be weighed against one another to determine the proper channel length. Flowers, for example, are perishable and would be expected to go through short channels. Yet, as the opening example shows, flowers are handled by several intermediaries, perhaps because many small florists must be supplied. In this case, a market characteristic outweighs a product factor in the choice of channel length. Because most cases require a weighing of such factors, channel length decisions are complex.

Channel Number

In contrast to the length of a channel, channel number refers to the number of channels an organization uses to sell its products. For example, IBM uses a sales force to make personal calls on large customers. The company also reaches smaller customers by selling through stores such as IBM Product Centers and ComputerLand. Similarly, hotels take reservations directly from consumers, or they may accept reservations made through airlines, tour operators, or travel agents.

Companies might use multiple channels for four basic reasons:[7]

1. They may be selling to entirely different markets. For example, novels are sold to the general trade market through bookstores by way

of wholesale intermediaries and to other markets (such as public libraries) by a more direct route.

2. They may be selling to different market segments. Revlon sells one of its high-priced cosmetics lines (Ultima II) directly to large department stores and its less expensive products through wholesale intermediaries to drugstores.
3. Different geographic regions may require different channels. A Chicago industrial parts manufacturer sells through its own sales force in that city, but it uses wholesale intermediaries in less densely populated areas.
4. Different-size buyers may be reached through different channels. Bethlehem Steel sells to its large-volume buyers directly but advises its smaller buyers to purchase through service centers.

Although using multiple channels may solve a producer's problems, it may also cause conflict by creating competition. For example, local retailers of IBM computers may lose business because IBM allows customers to buy directly from the company.

Channel Member Types

The manufacturer that has chosen one channel or a number of them has already, in a way, selected the type of intermediary to use—whether wholesale, retail, or some combination. But the choice must be further specified because there are many categories of retailers and wholesaling intermediaries. The wide variety of retail outlets is well known. Less familiar, but even more varied than retailers, are the types of wholesaling intermediaries.

Merchant Wholesaler
Independent who buys goods from manufacturers, takes physical possession of them, and sells them to other intermediaries.

Agent
Wholesale intermediary who merely arranges for the buying and selling of goods but never actually acquires ownership or possession of the goods.

Wholly Owned Wholesaler
Distribution arm of manufacturer that sets it up. Can be manufacturers' sales branches or sales offices.

Merchant wholesalers are independents who buy goods from manufacturers, take physical possession of them, and sell them to other intermediaries. By contrast, **agents** (also called brokers and commission merchants) merely arrange for the buying and selling of goods but never actually acquire ownership or physical possession of goods. **Wholly owned wholesalers,** often called manufacturers' sales branches and offices, are, as their name implies, the distribution arm of manufacturers who set them up. The term "wholesaler" is usually reserved for the first and third categories; "wholesaling intermediary," however, covers all three types.

Choosing the right wholesale intermediary from among the various types can be a key decision in the marketing effort. Welch Foods, makers of grape-based products, discovered this in the early 1970s when a major new product nearly failed because of a faulty distribution system.[8] The new product was grape soda. Welch Foods thought it had a good chance in the soft-drink market because its name was well known.

In test marketing, sales of the product were poor despite consumer tests showing that consumers liked it. The reason was that the product was poorly displayed and almost always out of stock. The company discovered that its choice of wholesale distributors was at fault. Welch was distributing its soda as it did its other products—through food brokers,

Figure 11.4
Types of Wholesaling Intermediaries

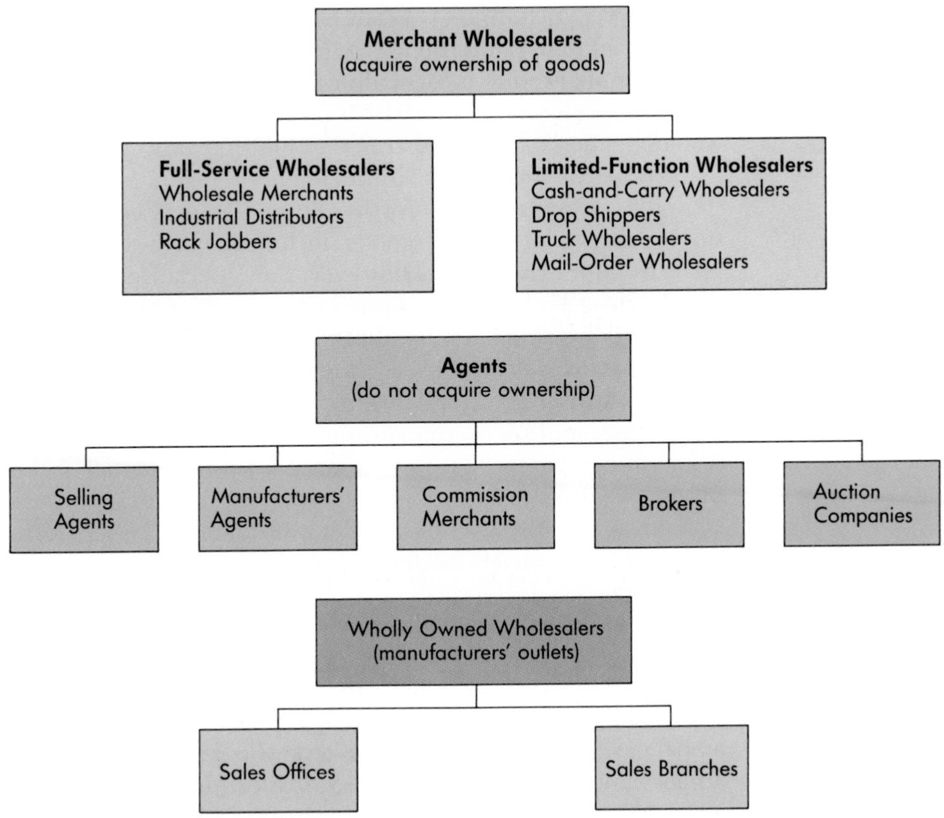

Source: Adapted from Eric N. Berkowitz, Roger A. Kerin, and William Rudelius, *Marketing* (St. Louis, Mo.: Mosby, 1986), p. 356. Reproduced by permission from Times Mirror/Mosby College Publishing.

a special type of wholesaling agent. Those wholesalers delivered only to store warehouses, not directly to the stores themselves, and they checked store shelves only once a month. By contrast, other soft-drink companies hired distributors who delivered directly to the stores several times a week. They claimed the best shelf space in high-traffic areas and did not allow their product to go out of stock.

The Welch case is a good example of how important the right wholesaling intermediary is to sales. Deciding which is right for a product requires knowing how wholesaling intermediaries differ in the functions they perform. The different types of wholesaling intermediaries are illustrated in Figure 11.4.

Full-Service Merchant Wholesalers Of the three categories of wholesalers, merchant wholesalers are the most numerous and account for more than half of all sales by wholesalers. Based on the number of marketing functions they perform, merchant wholesalers are classed as full-service or limited-function wholesalers.

Full-Service Merchant Wholesaler
Wholesale intermediary who performs a wide variety of distribution tasks such as assembly, storage and delivery, and financing, and may provide market information.

Full-service merchant wholesalers perform a wide variety of distribution tasks, including (1) assembling goods from manufacturers, (2) storing and delivering them, (3) financing retailer purchases, and (4) providing marketing information for both manufacturers and retailers. Marketers commonly distinguish three types of full-service wholesalers—wholesale merchants, industrial distributors, and rack jobbers.

Wholesale Merchant
Full-service merchant wholesaler who supplies mainly retailers or institutions.

Wholesale merchants supply mainly retailers and some institutions (hospitals, schools, and so forth). Those that service small department stores carry many lines of goods, including hardware, furniture, and appliances. More commonly, however, they specialize in one line. For example, Drug House, Inc., is one of the country's largest wholesalers of drugs and cosmetics for small retailers.

Industrial Distributor
Wholesaler who sells to the industrial market.

Industrial distributors are the counterparts of wholesale merchants in the industrial market. They are often used to sell small items, such as power tools and workshop equipment. Industrial distributors are best suited to companies that have a large base of potential customers, have a product that is relatively easy to stock, sell in small quantities, and sell to customers at a low level in their organization. IBM and Xerox, for example, use industrial distributors to sell their low-priced copiers and typewriters.[9]

Rack Jobber
Full-service merchant wholesaler who supplies grocery and other retail stores with nonfood items on display racks and who owns the goods and racks.

Rack jobbers emerged in the 1950s as a special category of full-service wholesalers. They supply grocery and other retail stores with nonfood items such as housewares, toys, and health and beauty aids. The racks they set up and supply gave them their name. In a sense, rack jobbers are themselves small retailers who sell from space given them by a merchant. The merchant takes no risk (title belongs to the jobber) and is not billed for unsold goods left on the rack. Yet both merchant and jobber split profits from sales according to a percentage agreed upon ahead of time. (Usually a special cash register key records the sale of such merchandise.) Because retailers risk so little in such an arrangement, they welcome the rack jobbers' business.

Limited-Function Merchant Wholesaler
Merchant wholesaler who provides only a few services for customers.

Limited-Function Merchant Wholesalers Merchant wholesalers who provide only a few services for their customers are in this category. Typically, they extend no credit, and some do not even store or deliver goods, although they all assume ownership or take title. They became popular mainly because full-service wholesalers are expensive, and some manufacturers do not need the full range of services. The four principal types are cash-and-carry wholesalers, drop shippers, truck wholesalers, and mail-order wholesalers.

Cash-and-Carry Wholesaler
Limited-function merchant wholesaler who does not give credit.

The **cash-and-carry wholesaler,** as the name implies, does not give credit. In dealing with such wholesalers, it is customary to pick up the merchandise at their place of business. Traditionally, these firms service small retailers who are constantly in need of fill-in items. Larger stores also use them, however, to cover temporary out-of-stock situations. For example, larger department stores might call on cash-and-carry drug wholesalers to keep the store stocked with the many hundreds of drug items carried in their cosmetic and drug departments. Many of these wholesalers flourish in the grocery field.

In direct contrast to the cash-and-carry wholesalers are the **drop shippers.** They neither maintain warehouses nor carry inventories. They do, however, take title to the goods and are responsible for billing a customer and collecting payment. All orders to the manufacturer are shipped directly to a drop shipper's customer. Drop shippers operate in the lumber, building materials, coal, and other industries in which the costs of hauling and transportation are high in comparison with the final price of the product.

Drop Shipper
Limited-function merchant wholesaler who neither maintains a warehouse nor carries inventories but who takes title to goods and is responsible for billing and collecting payment.

Truck wholesalers perform all the functions of full-service organizations except financing. They may maintain a warehouse, but they operate by selling and making deliveries directly from a truck. Ordinarily, truck wholesalers handle nationally advertised food specialties such as potato chips, bakery products, fruits, vegetables, and many other similar items. Most of these firms call on retailers daily, and usually they demand cash on delivery. Their appeal to manufacturers is great since they aggressively sell a product, but they are expensive because of high overhead costs.

Truck Wholesaler
Limited-function merchant wholesaler who performs all the functions of full-service organizations except financing; operates by selling and making deliveries directly from a truck.

Mail-order wholesalers do not engage in personal selling. Instead, they send catalogs to retail firms or other wholesalers, with instructions on how to order goods. Many of these firms are found in the printing and stationery fields. Although they do not push products actively as truck wholesalers do, they are an attractive distribution alternative because they are relatively inexpensive. Small manufacturers who cannot afford their own catalog get needed market exposure by offering their products, with those of other small manufacturers, in the mail-order wholesaler's catalog.

Mail-Order Wholesaler
Limited-function merchant wholesaler who does not engage in personal selling; sales catalogs are sent to retail firms or other wholesalers.

Agents Unlike full-service and limited-function merchant wholesalers, agents do not take title to goods, and only rarely do they warehouse them. Their principal function is to buy and sell goods for others in return for a commission. Selling agents, manufacturers' agents, commission merchants, brokers, and auction companies are included in this category.

Selling agents handle the entire output of small manufacturers, especially in the textile, canning, and lumber industries. They may combine the outputs of several small manufacturers of the same products and serve as their sales force. Manufacturers are thereby free to concentrate on production while the selling agents take over the marketing functions—including price setting, packaging, advertising, and physical distribution. A manufacturer may find that one problem with selling agents is lack of effort devoted consistently to the selling task. Their loyalty may be divided when they handle competing accounts, as they often do.

Selling Agent
Agent wholesaler who handles marketing for the entire output of small manufacturers.

Manufacturers' agents have far less power because they handle only part of a producer's output. Usually they take over the selling functions in areas that it does not pay manufacturers to cover with their own sales force. Manufacturers' agents may represent several manufacturers of

Manufacturers' Agent
Agent wholesaler who handles marketing in areas a manufacturer chooses not to cover with the manufacturer's own sales force.

Black Opals

Rare black opals, demantoid garnets and sapphires in a circa 1910 setting. You will find this necklace and other antique and period jewelry in our auction of Magnificent Jewelry on October 15 and 16.

For catalogues or more information, please call us at (212) 606-7392. Sotheby's, 1334 York Avenue at 72nd Street, New York, New York 10021.

noncompeting but complementary products, such as roofing, siding, and paint supplies in the building trade or tires, batteries, shock absorbers, and engine parts in automotive supplies.[10]

Commission merchants play an important role in selling the output of small farmers. Unlike most other agents, commission merchants may store the goods they handle until enough is gathered for a sale, though they do not take title to the goods. They are given full power to negotiate price and are paid a commission on the proceeds of the sale.

Commission Merchant
Agent wholesaler who markets the output of small farmers for a commission; may store goods but does not take title.

Brokers are common in fields like real estate and agriculture in which there are mainly buyers and sellers and no central marketplace for exchange. They bring buyers and sellers together, acting on behalf of one or the other. Unlike most other wholesale agents, brokers are used on a one-time basis. After completing a sale, they receive a commission and may or may not act in the future for the party they represented.

Broker
Agent wholesaler who brings buyers and sellers together, acting on behalf of one or the other and used on a one-time basis.

Fast-talking auctioneers who sell tobacco, flowers, or other farm products at a frantic pace have made **auction companies** familiar to most Americans. Artwork, antiques, and other products that vary widely in quality—and thus must be sold individually—are also handled by them. The famous Sotheby's, an international auction house, for example, presided over the sale of a privately owned Gutenberg Bible for $2 million. (See Figure 11.5.) Auction companies often send catalogs to prospective buyers and take bids at the time of the auction. Like brokers, auction companies work on a one-time basis for a commission.

Auction Company
Agent wholesaler that works on a one-time basis for a commission; may send catalogs to prospective buyers and take bids at time of auction.

Wholly Owned Wholesalers Each year, over $250 billion in sales, or one-third of all wholesale business in the United States, passes through the wholly owned wholesale outlets of manufacturers. The outlets may be either sales offices or sales branches.

Sales offices act as a headquarters away from a company's manufacturing plants for the sales force. As a general rule, they do not carry stock. **Sales branches** differ in that in most cases they do carry stock and, more importantly, they act as servicing centers. Sales branches and offices are often used in the sale of farm equipment, electrical and plumbing supplies, elementary school textbooks, and chemicals.

Sales Office
Headquarters for a sales force away from a company's plant.

Sales Branch
A manufacturing firm's service center and stock storehouse.

Channel Width

Besides the length, number, and types of channels to use, marketers must determine the number of wholesalers or retailers to use within each channel. This is called channel width. A manufacturer that has decided to use, say, three different channels must still determine how many wholesalers or retailers to use in each of the channels.

Another way of stating the problem of channel width is: how much market exposure should a product have? A firm has three choices: intensive, exclusive, or selective distribution.

Figure 11.5
Sotheby's Is Famous for Auctioning Unique Items

Intensive Distribution Selling a product through almost all available wholesale or retail outlets.

Intensive Distribution When goods and services are sold through almost all available wholesale or retail outlets, the producer has adopted a strategy of **intensive distribution.** Coca-Cola follows this strategy by using over 1,000 wholesale distributors and about 1.6 million retail outlets. In the consumer market, almost all branded convenience items require intensive distribution because shoppers will switch rather than go out of their way to buy a particular brand. In the industrial market, office supplies, small tools, and all other standardized, low-unit-cost products purchased in quantity are sold this way.

Intensive distribution results in a large volume of sales. But it also costs a great deal—for advertising or maintaining a sales force. Companies using an intensive distribution strategy may find it difficult to motivate intermediaries to sell a particular product more aggressively than a competing item, because intensively distributed items are usually low-value, low-profit ones. Nevertheless, this strategy is more or less essential for items of small unit value.

Exclusive Distribution Selling a product through only one wholesaler or retailer in a given area.

Exclusive Distribution Selling a product through only one wholesaler or retailer in a given area is known as **exclusive distribution.** Hermès handbags are sold through only one or two fine department stores in a city. Automobile and appliance manufacturers also use this strategy in the consumer market. Industrial marketers might use it in distributing expensive installations or special parts.

Exclusive distribution gives intermediaries some incentive to build sales in their assigned territory because they alone will profit. Also, the selection of fine retailers can contribute to the quality image of a product and justify a higher price.

The major problem with this policy is that government often frowns on grants of exclusive territorial rights. The U.S. Supreme Court has held in the past that, with very few exceptions, manufacturers' attempts to control a market through territorial grants or restrictions violates antitrust laws. The Supreme Court seemed to take a different stand in 1977. In a case involving an attempt by Sylvania to prevent expansion by one of its dealers into the territory of another, the Court declared Sylvania's action "reasonable."[11] That ruling means that grants of exclusive territories once title has passed may be legal or illegal, depending on whether they can be justified. Exclusive distributorships are now a gray area, and many companies may want to avoid legal entanglements associated with them.

Selective Distribution Use of more than one but less than all firms that might carry a product.

Selective Distribution To avoid the legal problems of exclusive distribution, many companies follow a **selective distribution** policy. This method involves the use of more than one but less than all the firms that might carry a product. In the consumer market, shopping and specialty goods like appliances and liquor are often distributed selectively. Industrial products such as accessories and parts may also be handled by a limited number of wholesalers.

Manufacturers see three advantages to this method.

1. It costs less than intensive distribution because there are fewer clients to call on.

2. It lessens the possibility of price cutting because competition is less intense.
3. It promotes close cooperation between the selected channel members, who feel that they have an important stake in selling the product.

The last point is very important. There are many sources of friction within channels working against a spirit of cooperation.

Managing Channels: Problems and Solutions

When Royal Viking Line found that promotional mailings to consumers were a more efficient way to find customers for its cruises than going through travel agencies, the company faced a difficult decision. Should Royal Viking risk alienating travel agents by letting them compete with its direct advertising, or should the company find a way to accommodate the travel agents? Royal Viking settled on an arrangement in which it assigns each of its customers to a travel agent who has handled travel arrangements for that customer before or who is located near the customer. The agent receives a 10 percent commission from Royal Viking. Explains John Richards, the marketing vice president, "We need agents to service the customer right up to the point of the customer boarding one of our ships."[12]

The potential for conflict often exists between a manufacturer and its distributors. Conflict arises because channels involve many independent businesses. Sometimes the source of conflict is a simple misunderstanding. Retailers and manufacturers often seem to speak a different language. For example, a Schlitz beer sales rep who talks to a neighborhood tavern owner about "bettering profit margins by increasing promotional outlays" may expect, after a blank stare, outright antagonism.[13] The sales rep might better say, "Charlie, you'll make a lot more money in the long run if you spend a little more money now on telling your customers how satisfying our product is for them."

Besides communication difficulties, conflict can arise because of a genuine disagreement about goals. The intermediary may desire an exclusive territory, for example, while the manufacturer may want to reach as many customers as possible.

Goal conflict may also arise when a manufacturer attempts to introduce a new product version at a higher price. At the wholesale and retail level, new models at higher prices are often not welcome. Intermediaries worry about how they are going to get rid of the old models they now stock or how they can handle new servicing requirements. They anticipate that consumers will resist higher prices, resulting in lost sales.

Not all complaints originate with intermediaries. Manufacturers sometimes feel that other channel members do not put forth a sufficient sales effort. Intermediaries who handle competing products may have neither the time nor the interest to sell one product aggressively. Some companies may even force intermediaries to sign contracts specifying that they cannot handle competing lines. Seven-Up discovered this problem when it began to distribute its caffeine-free cola, Like. More than half of the company's independent bottlers also sold Coca-Cola, Pepsi, or Royal Crown, and they were bound by contracts preventing them from selling more than one cola in their territory. As a result, Like could not be added to store shelves in New York City, Boston, Miami, Philadelphia, Atlanta, or Seattle, and the cola failed to capture even 1 percent of the cola market.[14]

Some conflict is desirable because it reveals flaws in a channel system that can be remedied. For example, resistance to a price increase may mean that intermediaries have not been shown how they too can profit. Such faulty communication is a system weakness that can be eliminated. But not all conflict is beneficial. That is why formal means of controlling it have evolved.

The Channel Captain

Channel Captain
Member of a marketing channel with power or ability to set and enforce policy.

Conflict can be controlled to a certain extent if there is one strong member of the channel that has either the power or the leadership ability to set policy. That member is referred to as the **channel captain.**

In the early nineteenth century, the wholesale intermediary was the channel captain.[15] Manufacturers were small producers of only one product, and retailers were widely scattered. They depended on wholesale intermediaries to forge a link between them. Toward the end of that century, however, manufacturers assumed leadership. They had grown larger, were able to mass produce a multiproduct line, and could reach their markets readily because of transportation improvements. Advertising also enhanced their power. Manufacturers could create consumer demand that could force an intermediary to sell their products. For example, no grocery store today can resist stocking Campbell's soup or Kellogg's corn flakes because consumer demand for them is so great.

For the most part, manufacturers still dominate channels. The reason is simple. Generally, the broader the base of a channel member's financial resources, the less it has to share power with other members.

Some retailers, however, are now challenging manufacturer leadership. The chain style of organization (discussed more fully in Chapter 12) has given some retailers enormous economic power. Sears, Ward, and J. C. Penney, for example, now substantially control the sale of replacement batteries and tires. They are able to insist that their private brand name be put on auto parts made by Monroe and Firestone, among others. Many marketers predict that retailers will take over dominance of marketing channels in the way manufacturers once took leadership from wholesale intermediaries.[16]

Coercion and Cooperation in Channels

A channel captain, whether a manufacturer or a retailer, can force its will on other channel members or use methods to win their voluntary cooperation.

Table 11.1
Legal Limitations on a Channel Captain's Coercive Power

1. Exclusive dealing. The requirement by a seller or lessor that its customers sell or lease only its products or at least no products in direct competition with the seller's products. Such a policy is illegal if the requirement substantially lessens competition and is circumscribed by the Clayton and FTC acts.

2. Tying contracts. The requirement by a seller or lessor that its customers take other products in order to obtain a product that they desire. As with exclusive dealing, such a requirement is illegal when it substantially lessens competition. The policy is directly limited by Section 3 of the Clayton Act.

3. Full-line forcing. The requirement by a seller that its customers carry a full line of its products if they are to carry any of them. Such a policy is a variant of tying agreements and is, therefore, subject to similar scrutiny.

4. Resale restrictions. The requirement by a seller that its customers can resell its products only to specified clientele. Such a policy is illegal when competition is substantially lessened and has recently been viewed by the courts as a *per se* violation of the Sherman Act (i.e., almost no circumstances can justify it).

5. Reciprocity. The requirement by a buyer that those from whom he purchases must also be buyers of his products. Such a policy is prohibited by Section 5 of the FTC Act when a substantial amount of commerce is involved and where reciprocity is prevalent and systematized.

6. Price maintenance. The requirement by a seller that a buyer can resell his products only above a specific price or at a stipulated price. Price maintenance (fair trade) laws have been nullified by the repeal of the Miller-Tydings and the McGuire acts. Similar in intent to now obsolete state fair trade laws are unfair practices acts, which regulate the right of resellers to sell below costs or below specified margins.

7. Price discrimination by buyers. The requirement by a buyer that a seller offer him a price lower than that offered or available to his competitors. Such a policy, as well as one involving the establishment of "dummy" brokerage firms, are covered under the Robinson-Patman Act if they substantially lessen competition and under the FTC Act as unfair methods of competition.

8. Refusals to deal. The right of the seller to choose his own customers or to stop serving a given customer. This threat obviously underlies the enforcement of the above-mentioned policies. Although its use is permitted under Section 2a of the Robinson-Patman Act, it is strictly forbidden if it fosters restraint of trade or is employed so as to substantially lessen competition.

Source: Louis W. Stern and Adel I. El-Ansary, *Marketing Channels,* 2nd ed., © 1982. Reprinted by permission of Prentice-Hall, Inc., Englewood Cliffs, New Jersey.

Some of the coercive techniques—and the legal limitations that government puts on their use—are listed in Table 11.1. As the table indicates, the refusal to deal is the ultimate weapon of enforcement. In the Supreme Court case mentioned earlier involving Sylvania, that manufacturer, in effect, refused to deal with the offending retailer by cutting off credit. Retailers may also use forcible tactics. Several chain discount retailers at one time stopped buying from General Electric because they thought GE was giving larger discounts to catalog store owners.

Since most of the practices listed in Table 11.1 have been declared illegal in many circumstances, channel captains must often rely on voluntary cooperation. They may use a variety of techniques to foster such cooperation. One way is to aid resellers in carrying out their tasks by providing advertising materials, training an intermediary's sales force, or giving financial advice to a channel member.[17] Retail channel captains can aid manufacturers by keeping them current on what products consumers are buying.

Another way to encourage cooperation is to show channel members that disputes will be handled fairly. The Carling Brewing Company, for example, arbitrates distributor complaints under a plan that has become a model for others. A panel composed of a Carling representative, a dis-

Figure 11.6
Types of Vertical Marketing Systems

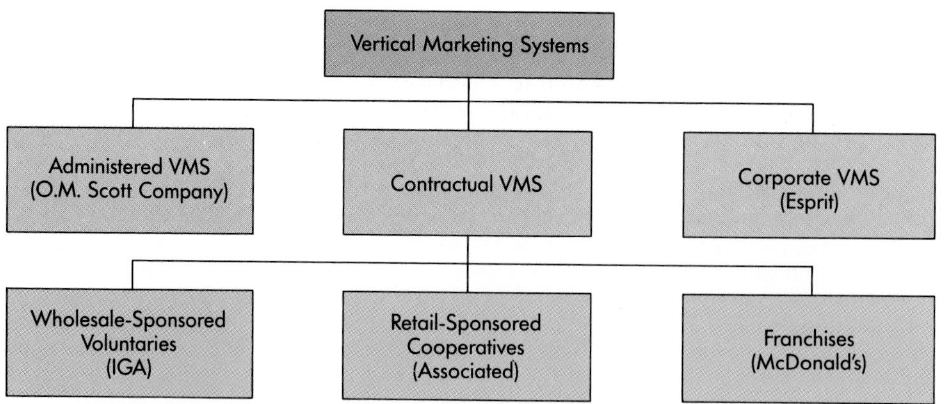

Source: Adapted from Eric N. Berkowitz, Roger A. Kerin, and William Rudelius, *Marketing* (St. Louis, Mo.: Mosby, 1986), p. 360. Reproduced by permission from Times Mirror/Mosby College Publishing.

tributor's representative, and a third party chosen by both work out solutions to disputes.[18]

Vertical Marketing Systems

Vertical Marketing System (VMS)
System in which one channel member owns, controls, or coordinates the operations of other channel members.

Statesmanlike measures to control conflict do not always work. Consequently, more and more firms are trying to guarantee the smooth operation of channels by curbing or eliminating the independence of channel members. When they succeed, the result is a **vertical marketing system (VMS),** in which one channel member owns, controls, or coordinates the operations of other channel members. Besides lessening channel friction, a VMS also saves money. For example, a centralized accounting system may be instituted to eliminate duplication of paperwork on two or more levels.[19]

A vertical marketing system may be administered, corporate, or contractual. These three types of VMS are illustrated in Figure 11.6.

Administered Systems

Administered System
Vertical marketing system in which one member secures agreement from other members of a channel on certain plans concerning price, display, and advertising.

Administered systems are really only one step removed from the channel captain approach of traditional marketing systems. The main difference is that in an **administered system,** such things as what a product will sell for, how it will be displayed, and how much money will be spent on its advertising are included in a detailed plan that the channel leader submits to other members. Usually it is the manufacturer who secures agreement from a retailer that the final say over a product's distribution will be in the manufacturer's hands.

The O. M. Scott Company, which produces lawn products, used an administered system approach when it expanded its sales into department stores and supermarkets. Its program involved a different set of plans, sometimes specified in 50 pages of documents, for every retailer that agreed to handle the firm's products. Retail executives were left little room for independent decisions on when to advertise, when to display the merchandise, or what to charge. The program represented a considerable expense for O.M. Scott, but the company was guaranteed control over quality and price.[20] Similar programs have been developed by Villager clothing and by General Electric in its appliance division.

Corporate Systems

Corporate systems develop when one channel member owns or at least partially owns the business operations of two or more channel levels. There are two ways that such ownership can come about. First, a manufacturer may buy wholesaling or retailing operations and market its products through them. Esprit takes this approach to selling its clothing. Second, and more frequently today, retailers and wholesalers may buy out or buy a controlling interest in manufacturers who supply them. About 50 percent of the merchandise Sears sells comes from such "captive companies." Holiday Inn owns a carpet mill and a furniture manufacturing plant. On the wholesale level, the American Hospital Supply Corporation both distributes and manufactures health-care products.

Corporate System
Vertical marketing system in which one channel member fully or partially owns the business operations of two or more channel levels.

From the retailer's point of view, the major advantages of an integrated corporate system are a lower cost for goods purchased and guaranteed access to supplies. For the manufacturer, the integrated corporate system, as with the administered system, means greater control over price and quality. The major disadvantage is that government is taking a sterner look at vertically integrated companies. For example, the U.S. government required American Telephone and Telegraph to separate its production and marketing arms.

Contractual Systems

Contractual systems are really a middle ground between administered and corporate systems. They involve a formal legal agreement (or contract) between channel members to cooperate on such matters as buying, advertising, accounting practices, and other functions. Members of a contractual system are not owned, but the relationship that exists between them is defined with more legal precision than in administered systems.[21]

Contractual System
Vertical marketing system based on a formal agreement among channel members to cooperate on such matters as buying, advertising, accounting practices, and other functions. Forms are franchises, retail-sponsored cooperatives, and wholesale-sponsored voluntaries.

Contractual systems are familiar to most Americans today under such names as IGA, Associated, and McDonald's. Those companies represent, respectively, three different forms of contractual systems—wholesale-sponsored voluntaries, retail-sponsored cooperatives, and franchises. All three are an important part of retailing today, accounting for about 40 percent of sales to consumers. A detailed description of them is

At Your Service 11.1
A Major Force in the Restaurant Business

It may come as no surprise to you that the number one company in the U.S. restaurant business is McDonald's. But would you have guessed the runner-up? It's Pillsbury Company, a name you may more readily associate with flour and cake mixes.

Pillsbury Company runs six distinct restaurant chains: Burger King, Bennigan's, Steak & Ale, JJ. Muggs (specializing in gourmet hamburgers), Quik Wok, and Bay Street (for seafood). Pillsbury also owns the franchises on Häagen-Dazs ice cream parlors. The company involved itself in the restaurant business as a way to expand into a growing industry while remaining faithful to its goal to keep Pillsbury a food company.

By one measure, however, Pillsbury has a way to go in catching up to McDonald's. While Pillsbury had 1984 sales of $4.6 billion from all the restaurant chains, McDonald's brought in $10 billion from its single chain. Nevertheless, Pillsbury is optimistic, predicting that it will double earnings by 1990.

Source: © 1987 Phyllis Woloshin.

Source: Subrata N. Chakravarty, "Pizzas, Anyone? Hamburgers? Trout Amandine?" *Forbes*, September 9, 1985, pp. 74–75.

given in Chapter 12. For examples of several franchises controlled by Pillsbury, see At Your Service 11.1.

Contractual systems—and in general all vertical marketing systems—are expected to continue to grow in the future. If the trend continues, independent wholesalers and retailers will find it increasingly difficult to survive in the future.

Chapter Replay

1. **How do marketers make a product available to users?**
Marketers use marketing channels, which typically include buyers, sellers, and some combination of retailers and wholesaling intermediaries.
2. **How do intermediaries serve consumers and producers?**
Intermediaries serve consumers by bringing together a wide assortment of goods, placing that assortment in a convenient location, providing credit, offering money-saving services, and giving consumers the desired product in the desired quantity. Intermediaries serve producers by helping to simplify contacts between producers and consumers, by reducing costs or bearing financial risk, and by communicating marketing information.
3. **What decisions do marketers make in designing marketing channels?**
Marketers must select channel length and width. They must decide whether to use a single channel or multiple channels. And they must decide what types of intermediaries to include in the channels they use.

4. **What do marketers consider in deciding on a channel length?**
Marketers consider the specific characteristics of the product, the market, the company, and the environment.

5. **For what reasons do some companies use multiple marketing channels?**
Companies might use multiple channels when they are selling to entirely different markets, different market segments, different geographic regions, or buyers of different sizes.

6. **What are the basic kinds of channel members?**
The basic kinds of channel members are merchant wholesalers, agents, and wholly owned wholesalers. Merchant wholesalers may be full-service or limited-function wholesalers. Agents include selling agents, manufacturers' agents, commission merchants, brokers, and auction companies. Wholly owned wholesalers include sales offices and sales branches.

7. **What are a firm's choices for how much market exposure a product should have?**
A producer can use intensive distribution, selling goods and services through most available outlets; exclusive distribution, selling through a single wholesaler or retailer; or selective distribution, which involves using only some of the firms that might carry the product.

8. **How is conflict in channels controlled?**
If the channel contains a channel captain, that member can control conflict by setting policy. Coercive techniques to achieve control are limited by law, so channel captains often try to encourage cooperation.

9. **Why do organizations create vertical marketing systems?**
By owning, controlling, or coordinating the operations of other channel members, an organization may be able to guarantee the smooth operation of channels. A vertical marketing system may also reduce costs.

Key Terms

administered system
agent
auction company
broker
cash-and-carry wholesaler
channel captain
channel length
channel member type
channel number
channel width
commission merchant
contractual system
corporate system
distribution
drop shipper
exclusive distribution
full-service merchant wholesaler
industrial distributor
intensive distribution
limited-function merchant wholesaler
mail-order wholesaler
manufacturers' agent

marketing (distribution) channel
merchant wholesaler
rack jobber
retailer
sales branch
sales office
selective distribution
selling agent
transfer principle
truck wholesaler
vertical marketing system (VMS)
wholesale merchant
wholesale intermediary
wholly owned wholesaler

Discussion Questions

1. What is the difference between a retailer and a wholesaling intermediary? Can a marketing channel exist without either of these intermediaries?
2. How do intermediaries add value to the products consumers buy?
3. Ron Masters is planning a new business selling his Masterful Chili. He is trying to decide whether to arrange for intermediaries to distribute his chili or to sell it himself from a chili wagon on Main Street. What advantages might the use of intermediaries offer Ron? What are some disadvantages of using intermediaries?
4. Under what circumstances is a marketer likely to prefer a long channel? A short channel?
5. When Renee Fielding decided to start selling her popular accounting software directly to businesses as well as through computer stores, her profits improved. What problem could result from this arrangement? Why should Renee be concerned about that problem?
6. Stuart Participle runs a grocery store. He keeps all the profits from the fish he sells from the frozen food case in the back of the store, but he keeps only a part of the profits from the magazines he sells from the rack near the checkout counter. Nevertheless, Stuart is glad to carry the magazines. Why? What kind of intermediary supplies the magazines to the store?
7. How do agents differ from merchant wholesalers? What is the difference between a selling agent and a manufacturers' agent?
8. Imogene Crumpet sells her hand-painted ties through a few prestigious stores. Imogene's friend Pam Sparks told her, "You could sell a lot more ties if you tried to get them into every store in town." What are some advantages of this recommendation? Why might Imogene be better off with the present arrangement?
9. What are some sources of conflict between manufacturers and distributors? How can conflict be controlled?
10. Ed Strump, owner of Strump Furniture, has decided that he wants to make the marketing channels for selling the company's furniture operate more smoothly. He is investigating ways of using vertical marketing systems for obtaining greater control over the process. What are some ways Ed might do this?

Case 11.1
Easco Corporation

With headquarters in Baltimore, Maryland, and production and distribution facilities throughout the United States, Easco Corporation is engaged in two principal businesses: mechanics' hand tools and extruded aluminum products. This case focuses on the hand-tool segment of the business.

Product Line Overview

Easco, a world leader in the mechanics' hand tool field, is a major producer of sockets and wrenches for both the do-it-yourself (DIY) and professional-user markets. The company is also a leader in the manufacture and distribution of specialty automotive repair and maintenance tools and test and measuring equipment for sale in the automotive aftermarket. Following is the approximate 1983 distribution of Easco's hand tool sales by user type:

Home and auto owner (DIY market)	46%
Professional motor vehicle mechanics	42
Industrial, commercial, and institutional users	12
	100%

Consumer Market

Easco markets tools to the consumer market under the Easco brand name and is the principal supplier of Craftsman brand mechanics' hand tools to Sears, Roebuck and Co. Sales to Sears during 1983 accounted for 66 percent of Easco's hand-tool volume. Easco and Sears work together to promote the hand-tool product line, to improve product displays, and to offer special promotional programs. The company also markets its products under the Master Mechanic™ label through America's largest chain of independent hardware dealers, True Value Hardware stores®. Easco's hand tools are also marketed by Hardware Wholesalers, Inc., one of the largest hardware chains in the United States, with approximately 2,350 member stores. Easco also distributes its tools through many other regional hardware and home-center organizations throughout the United States and Canada.

Professional Auto Mechanics Market

In January 1982, Easco acquired K-D Manufacturing Company, the leader in manufacturing and distributing specialty tools and equipment to professional automotive mechanics. This acquisition provided the company with a significant additional source of products in the hand-tool field and gave the Easco line more potential exposure to the professional segment of the market. K-D distributes its tools to approximately

Source: This case is based on information supplied by Easco Corporation.

1,000 of the largest automotive parts warehouse distributors in the United States and Canada. These distributors in turn sell to approximately 28,000 automotive parts stores in the United States and 3,000 in Canada.

By the end of 1983, more than 200 warehouse distributors and over 3,000 auto parts jobbers had taken on the Easco line. In preparation for the expected expansion of this market, Easco broadened its product line and targeted it for a niche between the more expensive domestic brands and the lower-cost imported products that were being carried by many auto parts stores.

In late 1983, Easco was appointed by the National Automotive Parts Association (NAPA) to become its exclusive supplier of mechanics' hand tools. NAPA is the largest automotive distribution organization in the world, with 73 distribution centers and 6,300 member jobbers throughout the United States. Between Easco's sales to NAPA and K-D brand specialty product sales through other automotive distribution channels, Easco is the largest supplier of mechanics' hand tools to the fixed-location (excluding tool trucks) automotive aftermarket.

Industrial Market

Industrial, commercial, and institutional users make up the third major segment for Easco's mechanics' hand-tool line. Selling prices in this segment tend to be higher, and there is less competition from imported brands. Prior to 1982, Easco made no serious efforts to enter this market. The acquisition of K-D provided the company with the means to do so. During 1982, Easco offered K-D's "Hunter" brand of electronic tools to some of the distributors who serve the industrial market. During 1983, the company considerably expanded its industrial marketing efforts by offering the Easco brand sockets and wrenches as well.

Focal Topics

1. What is your overall evaluation of Easco's channel strategies? Do you see any potential problems?
2. What strategies would you recommend for improving the distribution of Easco's products in the consumer market?
3. What strategies would you recommend for increasing the distribution of Easco's products in the professional and industrial markets?

Case 11.2 Hewlett Enterprises (B)

After six months of attempting to market his board game, MAKING IT, Scott Hewlett was, in fact, not making it. He had great difficulty in developing contacts with the buyers at the major retail stores in his area.

Source: For background information on the company and its product, see Case 10.2, Hewlett Enterprises (A).

Some of the stores were part of large chains and indicated that he would have to work through the home offices. Other buyers said that they were simply too busy to see "another entrepreneur with the world's next great product."

Scott had achieved placement of his game in only three variety stores, two toy stores, and one small department store. Actual retail sales had amounted to only 40 units. The retail selling price varied from $11.95 to $14.95 among the three stores. Scott had sold the games to all the stores at a wholesale price of $6.25. He had also given away almost 50 games as samples to various stores in hopes that they would try the game, like it, and stock it. Another 20 sets of MAKING IT had been given to friends to help get the game played and talked about in the community.

Distribution Issues

From all indications, people who had played MAKING IT enjoyed the game and planned to continue playing it. The retail stores had received no returns, and Scott's friends all said the game looked like a winner to them. But Scott was clearly running out of time. He had invested almost all of his savings in producing 1,000 sets and in expenses of travelling to retail stores. His unemployment benefits would expire soon, and he had few prospects for a job in his town. He had to do something.

Scott began to think about alternative channels of distribution for his game. In talking about some of his ideas with friends and business acquaintances, he assembled the following notes:

- ☐ Maybe the game could be sold directly to the consumer through mail order. Hewlett Enterprises could run advertisements for the game or try to get catalog companies to place MAKING IT in their publications. Hewlett Enterprises could fill the orders in either case or send them directly to the catalog firms and they could stock and ship the game.
- ☐ Try to find a toy distributor who would represent the company and carry MAKING IT as part of its product line.
- ☐ Personally go into the present stores handling the game and give demonstrations to help boost interest in MAKING IT. This gets into the whole area of a variety of types of promotional and personal selling activities that could enhance sales once distribution is achieved.

A Different Approach

As he thought through his options, Scott came up with a smashing new idea. Instead of putting fictitious businesses on the board, why not sell positions to local firms? Hewlett Enterprises would receive additional revenues from selling the spaces, and the firms and organizations involved would receive advertising exposure. This would mean that someone would have to sell the advertisements, that the present inventory of games would be of little value, and that the game would have only local appeal.

But, on the other hand, he could produce specialized games for other markets, maybe even involve some national companies. In addition, if local firms were on the MAKING IT board, they might be willing to help sell the games, perhaps at a lower cost than regular retail stores, since they would be receiving some advertising value from the game.

With these new ideas, Scott began to check around again to see how businesses might respond. Several firms—a bank, a restaurant, and a radio station—showed immediate interest. A couple of larger retailers said they might carry MAKING IT, especially if the game started getting publicity in the community. He now had another option to think about—to get local businesses to help distribute the game, since their advertisements would be on it.

Focal Topics

1. If MAKING IT stays in its present form, what are the relative advantages and disadvantages of alternative channels of distribution open to Hewlett Enterprises?
2. What are the strengths and weaknesses of changing the game by selling advertising on the board?
3. Based on your overall evaluations, what channel of distribution would you recommend to Scott? Please support your recommendation.

Retail Marketing: Structure and Management

Sounding Out the Chapter

In this chapter, you will learn:

1. **The kinds of retailers that emphasize product mix.**
2. **Types of retail establishments that specialize in offering low prices.**
3. **Where retailers locate their stores.**
4. **Ways of retailing without stores.**
5. **Ways of organizing retail establishments.**
6. **How retailers create an image for their store.**
7. **How the wheel-of-retailing theory attempts to explain changes in retailing.**
8. **The life cycle of stores.**

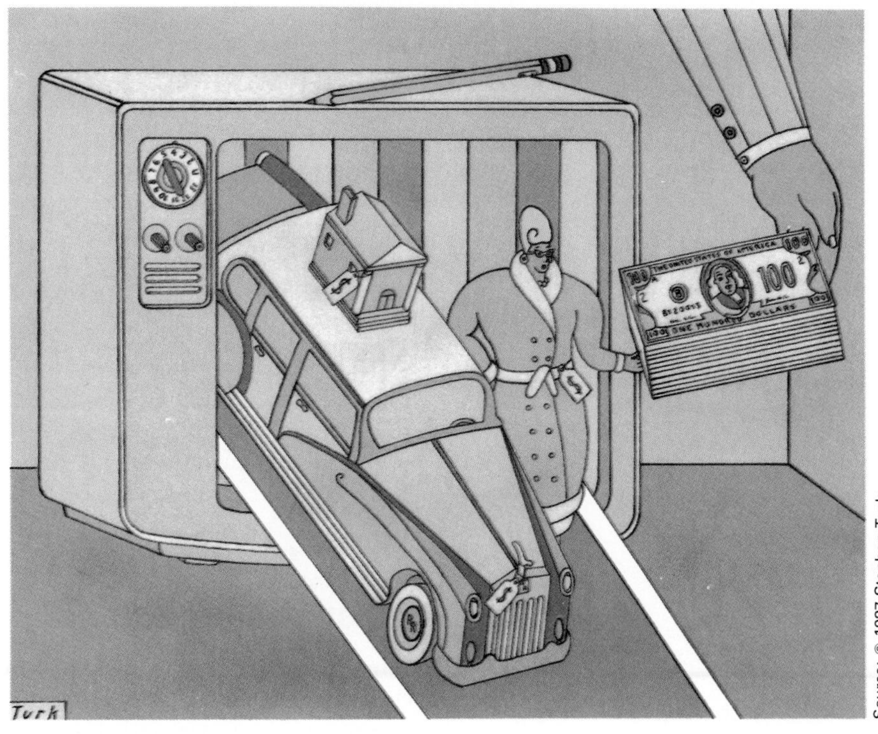

Cable TV Lets Shoppers Buy at Home

Shoppers have long been able to order products through catalogs they receive in the mail. Now shoppers can also shop when they turn on their televisions. Cable networks are bringing shoppers information in various formats. When viewers see a product they want to buy, they call a toll-free number and place their order.

Hanover House produces a live, nightly sales show called "Money Mania," which sells a broad range of Hanover House products and features a computerized bingo game with hourly prizes of $500 to $10,000. The products sold range from women's business suits to appliances like Tea Magic. Another Hanover House show airs in the daytime and features a host/salesperson and educational segments on topics such as exercise equipment and gold prices.

Another venture, called Telshop, offers brand-name merchandise, such as products by Sony and Panasonic, at prices guaranteed to be the lowest anywhere for 30 days. This network also sells vacation packages.

J. C. Penney Company has entered the field with a different format: videotex shopping information. Rather than watching a host describe products, viewers see words and pictures describing the products. This service, called Telaction, allows viewers to select categories such as grocery store, automobile dealer, travel agent, ticket agent, and department store. The viewer uses a touch-tone telephone to enter commands, which are received through the cable hookup. Telaction viewers have been especially favorable about the automobile information. Whereas most advertising for cars focuses on image, the Telaction system provides hard information about the cars.

So far, marketers are pleased with the demographics of home shopping viewers. TV direct-response buyers have more education and a higher income than the U.S. average. The average price paid for a product advertised this way is $40, with some products selling for as much as $700. With this track record, selling on cable television is likely to become increasingly common.

Home shopping programs are only one of the many ways marketers bring products to consumers. Marketers also sell through the mail, over the phone, and in many kinds of stores. All these kinds of selling are forms of retailing. This chapter looks at the development of retail institutions, the organization of retailing today, and some important trends in the retail business.

Sources: Judann Dagnoli, "Penney to Offer Home-Shopping," *Advertising Age,* February 23, 1987, pp. 3, 91; Paul L. Edwards, "Home Shopping Boom Forecast in Study," *Advertising Age,* December 15, 1986, pp. 88, 90; Karrie Jacobs, "Can the Shopping Shows Go Up-Market?" *Adweek,* October 20, 1986, pp. DM2–DM4.

The Scope of Retailing

Nearly half of all American businesses are engaged in retailing. The only thing that those two million firms have in common is that they all sell to the ultimate consumer. Hot-dog carts, Electrolux salespeople, grubby salvage operations, and slick department stores are all part of a vast spectrum of the retail business.

Retailing
All activities involved in selling goods or services directly to final consumers for their personal, nonbusiness use.

Retailing can be said to include all the activities involved in selling goods or services directly to final consumers for their personal, nonbusiness use.[1] Retailers are intermediaries who represent the only contact with the countless distribution channels that make up the national economy. They are the final testing ground for an entire marketing campaign. In a typical year, Americans spend almost half of their after-tax income in retail stores.[2]

The Development of Retailing Institutions

Consumers buy from a variety of retail institutions. Department stores, supermarkets, discount houses, and specialty stores are the kinds of firms that constitute the more traditional retail field. But constant innovations in the industry—the development of catalog showrooms, off-price shopping malls, video-game vending machines, and electronic shopping—continue to make retailing an exciting and fast-paced field.

Because the field changes so rapidly, it has always been difficult to categorize. Traditionally, retailing institutions were grouped into the categories of general merchandisers and limited-line merchandisers. For example, department stores and discounters were considered general merchandisers because they carried many different product lines—clothing, furniture, appliances, and so on. Supermarkets and specialty stores, on the other hand, were thought of as limited-line stores because they carried only one or two lines—food, shoes, or clothing. That classification has lost ground. How does one classify, for example, a drugstore chain, such as Perry, that offers mufflers and shock absorbers? Furthermore, supermarkets may sell pajamas, and department stores sell ice cream and fettucine. This is the era of **scrambled merchandising:** retailers who previously specialized in a particular line now sell many nontraditional lines as well.

Scrambled Merchandising
Practice, by previously specialized retailers, of selling many unrelated lines of goods.

Retail classifications have become untidy. To clarify the marketing aspects of the retailing industry, this discussion focuses on how the various elements of the marketing mix are manipulated to give each retailing firm its unique character. The following sections look at several kinds of businesses:

- ☐ Retailers that emphasize product mix.
- ☐ Retailers that stress price.
- ☐ Retailers that carve out a niche by offering unique distribution approaches.

While many of the categories overlap, the main challenge for marketers is to appreciate the scope of retailing and to understand the opportunities available.

Emphasis on Product Mix

Businesses in this category are best described by the kind of merchandise they offer. On a continuum, they might be arranged from extremely focused specialty stores to large operations offering a wide variety of product lines.

Specialty Stores

In colonial times, bootmakers, druggists, bakers, and others opened shops in cities. On the frontier, peddlers settled down and opened similar shops. Today, **specialty stores,** which concentrate on selling a large selection of only one line of merchandise, predominate in retailing. Most are independently owned, but a few are chains. In some cases, these stores carry specialization to an extreme, selling only mystery books, women's tennis clothes, or some other narrow product line.

Specialty Store
Store that concentrates on selling a selection of only one line of merchandise.

In River North, the Chicago neighborhood that abounds in art galleries, an unusual fashion retailer fits right in. The store, called Janis, sells "wearable art"—unique pieces made for Janis by artists and weavers from around the country and abroad. The store also sells handmade belts and jewelry.[3]

If you're interested in antiques, you might visit a specialist in that business. Refinders, of Highland Park, Illinois, specializes in artifacts of American popular culture between 1860 and 1960. At any given time, the store may display antique slot machines or Philco Predicta television sets from the 1950s.[4]

People worried about spies and terrorists might pay a visit to one of CCS Communication Control's stores. The company started out selling products to help businesspeople and diplomats discover bugs and wiretaps. Then it branched out into antiterrorist devices, including bulletproof vests hidden in Burberry raincoats and remote-control car starters to guard against bombs.[5]

Superstores Specialization enables small retailers to thrive by targeting a narrow segment of the market. Specialty stores can also succeed in the marketplace by carrying a broad selection. Large stores that carry a broad selection of one type of product at low prices are called **superstores.** These stores are sometimes called "category killers" because the selection and prices can devastate competitors.

Superstore
Large store that carries a broad selection of one type of product at low prices. Sometimes called "category killers."

Tower Records, for example, stocks as many as 75,000 record titles—25 times as many as the average mall record store. Says the company's president, Russell M. Solomon, "We might have 50 John Coltrane records and 100 different Sinatra records, not just one or two of each." Discount booksellers also are thriving. For example, Bookstop stores rely on volume to generate profits; all titles are discounted at up to 45 percent off list price. Customers use maps to find their way around the giant Bookstop stores.[6]

Department Stores

Department Store
Store that brings together a number of items under one roof.

A **department store** is an establishment that brings together a number of product lines under one roof. Many department stores originated as specialty stores, but they took on new lines as demand increased among a growing urban population after the Civil War. New York's Macy's, for example, opened in 1858 as a specialty store selling feathers, hosiery, and gloves. Year after year the store added new lines—men's clothing, towels and sheets, home furnishings—that the increase in manufactured goods made possible. Other stores, including Philadelphia's John Wanamaker's and Chicago's Marshall Field's, followed the pattern.

The distinguishing characteristic of Macy's and the other stores is their organization by departments. In a department store, responsibility for stocking a particular line (or "department") of goods is delegated to a buyer.

Some department stores have taken this concept one step further. They have arranged merchandise into boutiques of similar goods. An area might be targeted to working women, such as J. W. Robinson's "Careers Shop," or the linen department might feature one of Ralph Lauren's home furnishings boutiques.

The boutique concept is growing in popularity because it allows retailers to provide a clear focal point for consumers. (See Figure 12.1.) It is also very flexible. Colors, display decor, and graphics can be altered to feature new merchandise without disrupting the entire floor.[7]

Two other characteristics of modern department stores are important. First, they offer many services, including delivery, credit, and money-back guarantees. Their operating expenses are as high as 40 cents for every dollar's worth of goods sold. Second, department stores appeal mainly to the upper and middle classes.

Today, the major challenge is the low prices offered by superstores, discount houses, and off-price retailers. To survive, many department stores are dropping lines that yield relatively low profits. Items now rarely found in department stores include appliances and fabric. Instead, stores emphasize fashion goods and are expanding into the sale of services. For example, customers at Sears can buy insurance from Allstate, investments from Dean Witter, and real estate services from Coldwell Banker. Other stores, such as Kaufmann's in Pittsburgh, try "creative merchandising," offering the customers services that include fashion advice, investment and career counseling, and even evening college courses, all on the store premises.[8]

Supermarkets

Supermarket
Retail food store that carries dry groceries, dairy products, and fresh produce and allows customers to make their own selection.

The idea of a **supermarket,** dividing a food store into areas carrying dry goods, dairy products, and fresh produce and allowing customers to make their own selection, was introduced in the 1920s. It caught on,

Figure 12.1
The Liz Claiborne Boutique: A Focal Point for Department Store Customers

Source: Photo © 1987 Phyllis Woloshin.

however, only in the 1930s when people became more price conscious. Alert retailers recognized that if they could sell in large volume, costs—and prices—would go down. Technological advances (such as better refrigeration) and marketing advances (including consumer-sized packaging and increased advertising to presell products) also aided the development of supermarkets.[9]

Although their sales are large, most supermarkets have trouble maintaining even the industry's normal 1 percent profit margin. The market for groceries is saturated in many places. Supermarkets also face stiff competition from fast-food establishments, whose share of the American food dollar was substantial in the early 1980s. In addition, wages and energy costs account for a large part of their expenses and are rising.

An increasingly segmented population is now demanding many, often contradictory, things from supermarkets. As one analyst observed, "We want expansive displays of the provender of the land in brilliantly illuminated, air conditioned, hangar-size buildings; we want low prices and unlimited selection; generic paper towels and genuine French Roquefort; a comfortably small store around the corner, open cartons on steel shelves, one-stop shopping, all-night banking, and a place to park the car."[10]

Supermarkets are responding to the challenge of higher costs and lower profits in different ways.[11] Scrambled merchandising is one of them. Setting up delicatessens and salad bars with high-profit carry-out items is another. In addition, stores are expanding to achieve even greater savings through volume sales, and many are automating the checkout stand. Many are open longer hours, including Sundays, and offer a variety of customer services such as check cashing. To attract customers, some stores have even hosted events such as singles nights. Other developments are described in Marketing Today 12.1. The field of grocery marketing has also given rise to several new species of stores—some larger and some smaller than conventional supermarkets.

Convenience Stores

Convenience Store
Small retail outlet that provides snacks and staple groceries quickly and conveniently.

The small stores attracting today's consumers are called **convenience stores**—small retail outlets providing snacks and staple goods quickly and conveniently. Their convenience includes short lines, parking close by, long hours, and locations near busy streets and intersections. Originally concentrated in the suburbs, which lacked local food markets, and in warmer climates (where people are more apt to run to the store at night), convenience stores today are located throughout the United States. Major chains include 7-Eleven, Circle K, Cumberland Farms, and White Hen Pantry. Many stores are owned by oil companies; am/pm stores, for example, are owned by Arco.[12]

Besides groceries, convenience stores offer a variety of goods and services. These include gasoline, sandwiches, magazines, film developing, cash from automatic teller machines, and videocassette rentals. Stores are also experimenting with such diverse products as car washes and electronic ticket distribution. In addition, fast food has sold so well at convenience stores that these stores have helped slow growth at fast-food restaurants.

During the 1980s, convenience stores have been the fastest-growing segment of the retail industry. Their 1985 sales were $55 billion, compared to less than $6 billion in 1975. One 1985 research report projected that convenience store sales would double by the year 2000.

Industry observers explain the popularity of convenience stores as reflecting the rise in the number of two-income, two-career households and the greater number of single-person households. Today's consumers value time and convenience. Despite the expectations, customers of convenience stores still are predominantly blue-collar men aged 18 to 34.

The challenge for owners of convenience stores is to find a way to attract women and upscale consumers. Many are trying to do so by making their stores safer and more attractive. Circle K stores try to attract women with a line of low-calorie sandwiches. Customers in higher income brackets have been drawn to stores that include automatic teller

Marketing Today 12.1
Supermarket Update

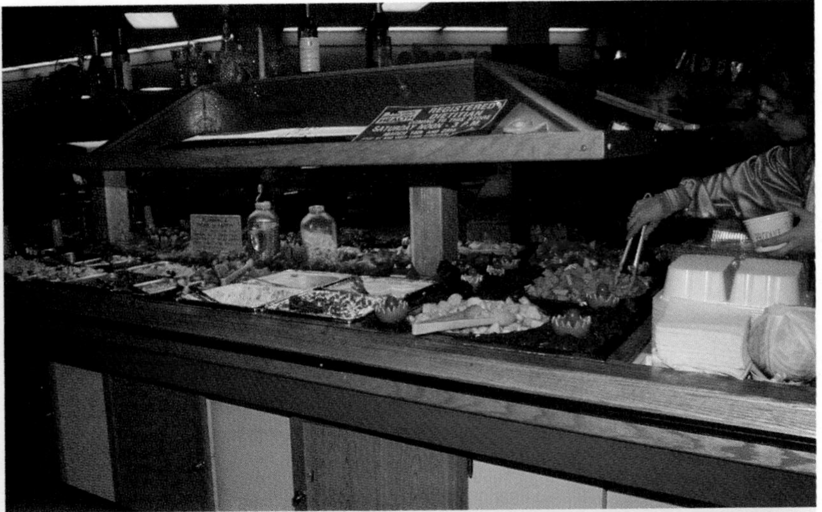
Source: Photo © 1987 Phyllis Woloshin.

The hottest growth areas in today's supermarkets are delis and in-store bakeries. Supermarket owners are attracted to them because deli and bakery food is more profitable than other products sold in supermarkets. Industry experts are recommending that supermarkets offer product samples at the deli and bakery counters and that they suggest other grocery products consumers can use with deli and bakery items.

Taking this approach one step further, many supermarkets are turning to ready-to-eat foods, such as barbecued ribs, chickens, pastas, soups, and salad bars. Some stores even provide sit-down areas for eating these products. Kroger Company has tried selling hand-dipped ice cream and has even set up a sushi bar. Perhaps the ultimate addition is at the Foodtown in Cedar Knolls, New Jersey: that store features live piano music four days a week.

Supermarket owners are also struggling with limited shelf space during a time of rapid product development. With food companies introducing 20 to 30 products a week, supermarkets must either bump slower-moving products or refuse to stock the new ones. As a result, the new products that make it onto store shelves are often those of the largest companies with the most clout. And one survey shows that over half of shoppers are unhappy that they cannot find certain items anymore.

Sources: Lynn Asinof, "Business Bulletin," *The Wall Street Journal,* February 5, 1987, p. 1; Doreen Higgins, "The Power of the Supermarket," *Advertising Age,* August 18, 1986, p. 18; Robert Johnson and Betsy Morris, "Food Companies Fight to Display More Products on Less Shelf Space," *The Wall Street Journal,* April 10, 1986, p. 35; and "Supermarket Delis Striving to Attract Shoppers with Quality, Convenience," *Marketing News,* July 4, 1986, p. 1.

machines. If convenience stores achieve their potential for growth, they will be a major force in the retailing industry.

Combination Stores and Hypermarkets

Combination Store
Combination of a supermarket and a drugstore under a single roof.

Hypermarket
Giant mass merchandiser that offers a broad selection of hard and soft goods and grocery items at discount prices on a self-serve basis.

A "combo" store, as **combination stores** are called in the retail trade, is what results when a drugstore is crossed with a supermarket. In the Chicago area, for example, shoppers at Jewel's combo stores can buy drugs, cosmetics, and hardware on one side of the store and groceries on the other side. Combo stores profit by exposing food shoppers to general merchandise.[13]

Hypermarkets are even larger mass merchandisers that offer a broad selection of hard and soft goods and grocery items at discount prices on a self-serve basis. At Fred Meyer, Inc. of Beaverton, Oregon,

Figure 12.2
Types of Stores that Emphasize Product Mix

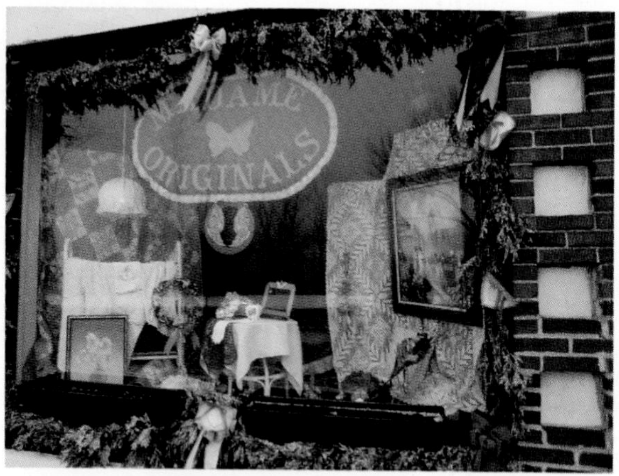

Source: Photos © 1987 Phyllis Woloshin.

shoppers can buy everything from home computers to 52 varieties of mustard. The 30 aisles at the Real Superstore of Lafayette, Louisiana, contain clothing, groceries, hardware, and jewelry; the store also features a post office, a branch bank, and a dental clinic.[14]

Hypermarkets keep costs down in a variety of ways. They typically resemble warehouses more than specialty shops. Their volume allows them to cut prices of certain products. They also spend a relatively low amount on labor. Even so, to break even, most hypermarkets must move at least $1 million worth of merchandise each week. This makes hypermarkets a risky kind of retailing.[15]

Figure 12.2 illustrates the types of stores that emphasize product mix: specialty stores, department stores, and supermarkets.

Retailing Services

Some retail establishments sell services. Service retailers include colleges, health clinics, movie theaters, hotels and motels, savings and loan institutions, and oil-change services. Hyatt Legal Services has a chain of law offices. H&R Block sells tax assistance from its storefront offices. In the United States, service retailers are growing faster than retailers of tangible products. Often, these retailers are just beginning to tap the potential of full-scale marketing.[16]

Emphasis on Price

Pricing is a critical component in any marketing strategy. Nowhere has the battle over prices been as hard fought as in the retailing industry. Off-price retailers, who sell brand names at discount prices, have launched a flurry of lawsuits against established department stores charging them with price fixing and attempting to intimidate manufacturers. While price cutting may have the retailing industry in an uproar, it has been a bonanza for consumers. Customers willing to sacrifice some of the amenities of full-price, full-selection stores have found that they can buy anything from apples to zippers at discounted prices.

Discount Stores

Discount Store
Store that sells fast-moving branded merchandise at cut-rate prices.

Discount stores, which sell fast-moving branded merchandise at cut-rate prices, became popular after World War II. The production of appliances had been halted by the war, and there was a huge demand for them when the war ended. Retailers saw an opportunity for volume sales at low prices.

To guarantee low prices, the discounters had to keep costs low. They set up stores in low-rent places, kept interiors plain, and eliminated traditional retail services such as sales assistance, credit, and delivery. The discounters did offer extended shopping hours and ample parking. The early appliance discount houses were an instant success.

Discounters soon added many other products, such as toys, cameras, luggage, and housewares. At the same time, separate discount outlets specializing in apparel sprang up, among them Zayre and Shoppers Fair. The older stores followed their lead and added clothing. Discount houses became full-line discount department stores. Other established retailers, noting the success of discount operations, started discount operations of their own.

In recent years, discounters have found that simply offering low prices does not guarantee success. Buffeted by inflation and recession, shoppers in the late 1970s and early 1980s began to focus on value rather than on price. Many were willing to pay a little more to get a quality product.[17]

Some discounters met the challenge successfully by improving their decor, expanding services (taking charge cards, offering "rain checks" for out-of-stock merchandise, and improving their return policies), and carrying more attractive lines of merchandise. Discount stores selling designer clothing are another attempt to meet the demand for quality products at low prices. Such stores include Symms, Loehmann's, and Front Row. Today, many shoppers get information at more expensive stores, then try to find the products they are interested in at discount stores. Of course, selections at the discount stores are more limited.

One of the most influential trends in the field has been the rise of the specialty discounter. The Home Economist sells gourmet foods at a discount, and the Linen Factory sells discount linens. Barnes and Noble and Crown Books sell all their books at less than list price, and establishments such as 47th St. Photo in Manhattan do a thriving business in cameras and computers.

Warehouse Stores

Warehouse Store
No-frills store that emphasizes lower prices over atmosphere and customer service.

Warehouse stores were born in the early 1970s as no-frills operations that sacrificed atmosphere and customer services in order to offer consumers the lowest possible prices. In food warehouses, items are typically displayed in original packing cases, the selection of merchandise is usually limited, and customers bag their own groceries in boxes or pay extra for shopping bags. Prices are often from 10 to 30 percent less than in traditional supermarkets.

Many warehouse stores are adding features unknown to their more primitive ancestors. A 78,000-square-foot Cub Foods warehouse store in Minnesota, for example, has 27 checkout lanes, a complete bakery, and its own sausage kitchen.

Furniture warehouses, such as Levitz and Wickes, have turned a fragmented industry into a high-volume business. At IKEA furniture stores, shoppers can select from among 14,000 different household articles stacked on flats. The store provides customers with little sales help—just a tape measure, a catalog, and a map of the store. Customers hoist their own merchandise onto carts and then assemble the furniture themselves when they get home. For many customers, this extra work is justified by low prices. A sofa bed, for example, costs about $100 less at IKEA than at a store selling comparable products.[18]

Home Improvement Centers

Home Improvement Center
Large-scale hardware store that offers one-stop shopping for around-the-house needs at prices that may be somewhat lower than those at smaller hardware stores.

Home improvement centers are really large-scale hardware stores for do-it-yourself customers. The stores stock building materials, paint, garden supplies, and tools. Their prices may be somewhat lower than traditional hardware stores, but their main attraction is one-stop shopping for around-the-house needs. Some centers sell about $2 million worth of goods each year.[19]

Catalog Showrooms

Catalog Showroom
Retail discount business based on catalog promotion and showrooms that display a limited selection of the items in the catalog. Customers receive goods from an adjacent warehouse.

Catalog showrooms combine the low prices of discount stores with catalog promotion. Retailers including Service Merchandise, Consumers Distributing, and Best Products sell a variety of brand-name hard goods, such as small appliances, jewelry, and luggage, at substantially reduced prices. Consumers receive color catalogs in the mail or travel to the showroom to page through them. The showrooms display a limited selection of the items in the catalog. Customers choose what they want, fill out an order form, and pick up their goods from an adjacent warehouse.

Catalog showrooms cut costs by buying in bulk, stocking brand-name items, leasing stores in low-rent areas, and hiring few salespeople. Customers must travel farther and receive little service, but the low prices make catalog showrooms attractive. However, with increasing competition from discount stores and sales in department stores, catalog showrooms have had to struggle to maintain sales and profits.[20]

Figure 12.3
Types of Stores that Emphasize Price

Source: Photos © 1987 Phyllis Woloshin.

Figure 12.3 shows the types of stores that emphasize price: discount stores, warehouse stores, home improvement centers, and catalog showrooms.

Emphasis on Location

At the turn of the century, little variety stores and small shops accounted for much of the retail business in America's small towns. In the cities, department stores and specialty shops clustered together to create thriving business districts. In the 1950s, suburban growth led to the rise of the shopping center, which took sales from small-town and big-city retail businesses. Nonstore retailing is now on the rise, with many consumers shopping through catalogs or electronic means.

The location of a retail business—the corner grocer or the computer terminal in the living room—has always been of critical significance. Consider now some of the issues facing retailers in traditional locations and what the future of retailing might bring.

The Importance of Retail Store Site Selection

The location decision has always been important, but today more so than ever. There are two major areas in which stores locate—in the central business district and in shopping centers.

Central Business District
Downtown shopping area of most cities, consisting of large department stores and specialty stores.

The Central Business District The **central business district** is the downtown shopping area of most cities, and it consists of large department stores and specialty stores. Downtown areas have been in decline over the past quarter century as population growth shifted to the suburbs. However, efforts to revive them are now under way, usually by reconstructing them around a central shopping mall. In St. Louis, Missouri, for example, renovated shopping areas have revived the Old Post Office and Laclede's Landing (nine blocks of 19th-century brick buildings near the riverfront). A notable addition to these efforts is the ornate Union Station, once a railroad station and today a complex of restaurants, promenades, shops, and a hotel. Shoppers can also visit a boat pond and a beer garden.[21]

Shopping Center
Group of stores planned, owned, and managed as a unit and with ample parking, usually in a suburban area.

Shopping Centers A **shopping center** is a group of stores planned, owned, and managed as a unit and with ample parking facilities, usually located in a suburban area. The owner plans not only the location and size of the stores, but also the types of stores. The three types of shopping centers, which are distinguished by size and types of store, are shown in Figure 12.4.

The neighborhood shopping center serves up to 20,000 customers and has between 5 and 15 stores—usually a supermarket and small specialty shops. A community shopping center is larger—15 to 35 stores, including both a department store and a supermarket, and it may serve 100,000 customers. The largest of all is the regional shopping center. An extreme example is the West Edmonton Mall in the province of Alberta, Canada. This shopping center contains more than 800 shops, several dozen restaurants, 34 theaters, an 18-hole miniature golf course, a 10-acre water park for swimming and sunning under tanning lamps, two dozen amusement rides, and a 360-room hotel for extended stays. All these attractions are housed under a single roof.[22]

Center-City Marketplaces Shopping centers have traditionally been a suburban phenomenon, dependent, as they were, on vast expanses of cheap land. But inner cities are now fighting back. To lure shoppers into town again, many cities have turned decaying slums or waterfront warehouse districts into fashionable shopping centers. Boston's Quincy Market and San Francisco's Ghirardelli Square were among the first. Baltimore, Philadelphia, and Pittsburgh, among others, have followed. New York City's South St. Seaport is a $351 million restoration of the old Fulton Fish Market site. Conducive to strolling and enjoyment of sidewalk cafés and other urban amenities, center-city marketplaces are enjoying great popularity.

Off-Price and Factory Outlet Shopping Centers Until recently, factory outlets and off-price retailers generally operated out of stripped-down, single-unit facilities in out-of-the-way locations. It was only a matter of time before several would decide to band together into shopping centers.

Figure 12.4
Shopping Center Types

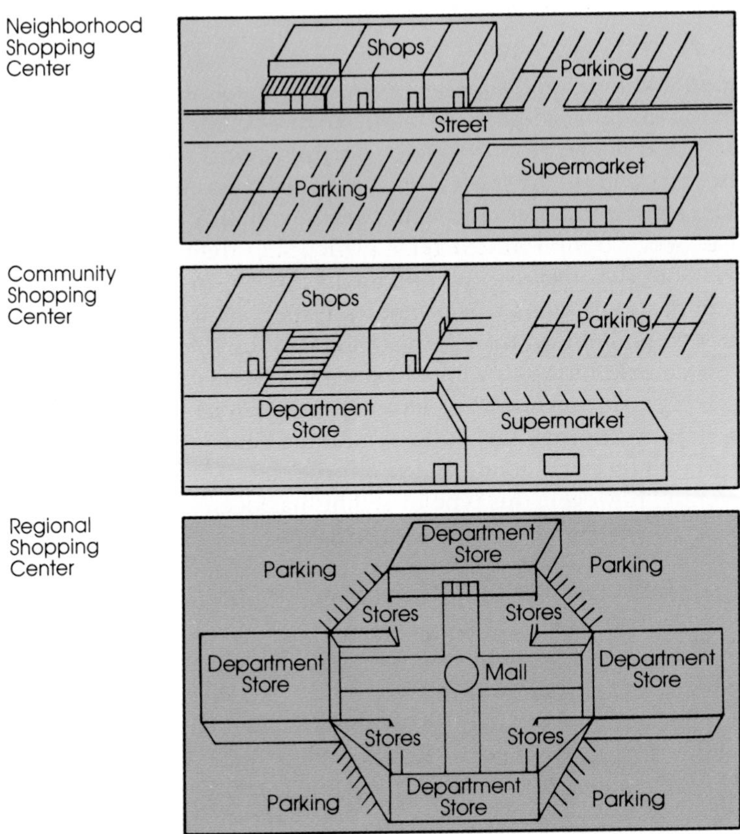

Lured by the promise of bargains in a large grouping of such stores, out-of-town shoppers from an eight-state region regularly converge on Reading, Pennsylvania. One of Orlando's most popular adult attractions, besides Disney's Epcot Center, is Factory Outlet Mall, a 350,000-square-foot extravaganza of 67 off-price and factory outlet stores and 13 kiosks. There are about 100 off-price centers in the United States.

Outlet malls tend to differ from their more traditional counterparts in a significant way: studies have shown that from 50 to 60 percent of the shoppers live outside the center's metro area. Notes one developer, "Be sure to provide parking for bus tour use, and [locate] close to major road access."[23]

Nonstore Retailing

What do a Coke machine, an encyclopedia salesperson, CompuServe videotex, and the Williams Sonoma Catalog for cooks have in common? They are all forms of nonstore retailing.

The idea for selling merchandise independent of a store site is not new. Yankee peddlers traveled the land long before the bulk rate permit was invented. While some forms of nonstore retailing are thriving, others are suffering as the demographics and life-styles of consumers change.

Door-to-Door Selling When farmers were far from a central marketplace, peddlers were the suppliers of wares that could not be made on the farm. Traveling salesmen brought knapsacks or saddlebags full of tools, buttons, medicines, or wooden utensils—and they brought the news as well. Today, the leaders in the direct-sales business include Avon Products, Dart Industries, Inc. (the parent company of Tupperware and Vanda Beauty Counselors), Shaklee (which sells detergents and cleaning products), and Grolier, Inc. (encyclopedias).

Some contemporary door-to-door salespeople are paid commissions of 50 to 100 percent on the products they sell by the companies for which they work. Others are independents who own the merchandise they sell. Most still prospect for customers by canvassing houses. A few, such as those who work for Tupperware and Shaklee, arrange in-home parties to demonstrate goods and take orders.

Recently, however, this type of selling has been experiencing some serious problems. Some companies are having trouble finding recruits. Women who demonstrated cosmetics, for example, are taking steadier jobs in other fields. Once in the work force, those same women are often reluctant to spend leisure time on selling parties, and they can afford to buy cosmetics in department stores. In addition, increased divorce rates and mobility have broken down the extended networks of relatives, friends, and neighbors that such salespeople used to rely on. As a result, party-plan selling now does best in close-knit working class and ethnic areas.[24]

Direct Marketing While department stores were developing to meet the needs of city dwellers, a new type of firm began servicing the rural countryside. The **mail-order firm** provided customers with a wide variety of goods ordered from catalogs and shipped by mail. After the Civil War, it was government policy to settle land as quickly as possible. Postal rates were kept low so that settlers could get needed supplies by mail.

Mail-Order Firm
Company that provides a wide range of goods ordered by customers from catalogs and shipped directly to them by mail.

In 1872, Montgomery Ward started a mail-order business in Chicago with a one-page leaflet that offered to accept returns of unsatisfactory goods. Ward's idea caught on because it offered shopping convenience and low prices (since no sales force or store was needed). When Sears was founded in 1886, it started putting out a store catalog. In frontier towns, the arrival of the catalogs was a regular social event.

Many of the early mail-order houses later became chain department stores, but much of their business is still conducted through the mail. About one-quarter of the business at Sears and Montgomery Ward's comes from mail-order business.[25]

Many specialty and traditional department stores send out catalogs as well. Neiman-Marcus's Christmas catalog offers his-and-her airplanes, while Hammacher Schlemmer would be happy to deliver a jet-propelled pedal boat for only $2,495. The Direct Marketing Association has predicted that by the year 2000, one-fourth of consumer expenditures will be for mail-order sales.[26] A major reason for the popularity of catalogs

Marketing Today 12.2

The Future for Catalog Entrepreneurs

An entrepreneurial spirit fueled the growth in the catalog industry. A family with an idea would gather around the kitchen table to put together a catalog, and many of those catalogs were the beginning of successful businesses. What are the odds for such a venture today?

Many experts are pessimistic. A major reason is the surge in catalog selling. In the mid-1970s, fewer than 1,500 catalogs existed. Now there are 10,000, but the number of prospective customers has not risen proportionately. When the average consumer receives 35 to 40 Christmas catalogs, it's hard for a new one to attract much attention.

The other cause for pessimism is the start-up cost. Experts agree that to start up a catalog operation now requires an investment of at least $1 million. And the operation may not be profitable for more than a year. This financial burden is certainly beyond the reach of most families.

The best prospects seem to be in catalogs selling to businesses —an area that may still grow. Another less risky approach is to start the business with a brochure advertising a single item. If that item is profitable, the entrepreneur can add other products gradually. In any case, a new business should offer unique products sold by a knowledgeable staff to a unique, proven mailing list.

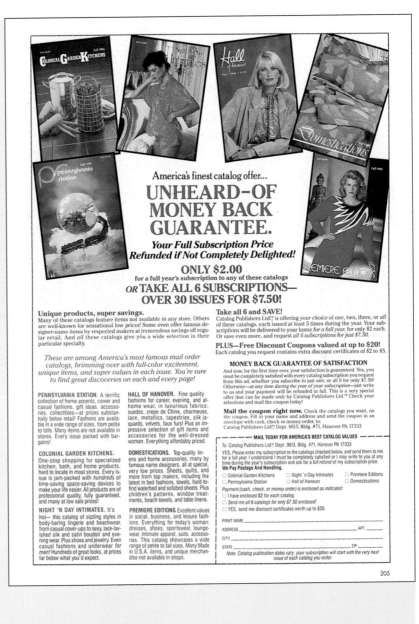

Source: Jerrold Ballinger, "What Ever Happened to the Kitchen Table Startup?" *DM News,* February 1, 1987, pp. 12–14.

is that the decline in the number of full-time homemakers means that fewer people have time to spend in stores.

Marketers have taken note of the interest in mail-order shopping, and the number of catalogs produced has soared. As a result of this competition, it has become more difficult to start a new catalog business. Marketing Today 12.2 describes some of the issues involved.

Along with direct-mail marketing, other forms of direct marketing are growing in importance. These include newspaper inserts, direct-response ads in magazines, 800-number advertising on radio and television, and telephone selling.

Telemarketing
Direct selling in which salespeople telephone potential customers.

Telephone selling, in which salespeople phone potential customers, is often referred to as **telemarketing.** According to the Direct Marketing Association, more money is spent annually in the United States on telemarketing than on direct mail. Some marketers are using computers to recite prerecorded messages or to dial phone numbers automatically. Consumers often object to the computerized phone calls, and some states limit their use. Marketers who are considering this approach must therefore first investigate consumer attitudes and legal restrictions.

Vending Machine
Device that dispenses products automatically after money is inserted.

Automatic Vending Machines **Vending machines,** which dispense goods automatically after money is inserted, are not new. The ancient Egyptians had such machines to sell sacrificial water 2,200 years ago. Vending machines became widespread in the United States only in the 1960s. Improvements, such as reliable change makers and machines to refrigerate and heat products, spurred their growth.

The four big items dispensed are candy, coffee, cigarettes, and cold drinks. Nonfood items such as stockings, newspapers, stamps, and railroad tickets are also sold through vending machines. Vending machines that sell services include coin-operated photocopiers, telephones, juke boxes, and video games.

Some vending machines take credit or debit cards instead of cash. The most common examples are automatic teller machines, which dispense cash or perform other banking services when the user inserts a banking card. Similarly, travelers can use credit cards to buy airline tickets through vending machines. Marketers are also experimenting with computer terminals that display various gift items. The terminals are located in kiosks in airports, colleges, supermarkets, office buildings, and industrial parks. Customers can select an item and order from a warehouse linked to the terminal. The success of these machines has so far been mixed; many consumers miss the interaction with a human salesperson and the immediate gratification of carrying away what they buy.[27]

The growth in the use of vending machines has been steady, but there are some problems. Mechanical breakdowns and a high pilferage rate make them an expensive way of retailing; nevertheless, they will continue to be used.

Chain Store
Group of stores centrally owned and managed that sell similar goods.

Independent Store
Store owned and managed by a single person, partnership, or corporation, usually a one-unit operation.

The Organization of Retailing

Sears, Roebuck and the little neighborhood mom-and-pop shop represent two distinct forms of organization for retail stores—the chain and the independent. Sears is a classic **chain store,** which may be defined as a group of stores centrally owned and managed that sell similar goods. By contrast, an **independent store** is usually a one-unit operation owned and managed by a single person, partnership, or corporation.[28] Not all chains are large. Chains can have only a few stores and can be in just one area or region. Similarly, not all independents are small, at least in sales volume. Strawbridge & Clothier of Philadelphia, for example, is an independent with sales of more than $300 million yearly.

There are also giant merchandising conglomerates that may own several different types of retail chains. Moreover, another form, the franchise (which represents a cross between a chain and an independent), has gained in popularity in the last 25 years.

Independents

Most retail establishments are independents. Candy stores, gasoline stations, furniture stores, and liquor stores are usually independent businesses. So are most firms that specialize in certain services—auto repair, cleaning and laundering, and hair care, for example.

Independent stores are numerous because of the advantages they offer the owner and the consumer. They are relatively easy to establish, requiring little capital. Independents offer customers three important benefits:

1. *Convenience in shopping.* Independents are often neighborhood stores.
2. *Service extras.* Most independents stay open long hours, give credit, cash checks, deliver, and offer personalized service.
3. *Timely goods.* Independents purchase frequently and in small quantities, thus they can keep abreast of rapidly changing styles and customer preferences.

Small independent retailers suffer from some limitations, however. They often must charge more than large chains because they cannot take advantage of quantity discounts from suppliers. Independent stores frequently fail. The major reasons are often related to the proprietors' lack of experience in retail management or to the particular line of goods they offer.

Chains

Chain stores developed in the 1920s, first among grocery stores and then in other retail areas. Today, chain stores account for most of the sales of department stores (Sears, R. H. Macy), discount stores (K mart, Zayre), and food stores (Safeway, Kroger), as well as for a large proportion of the sales of shoe stores (Kinney, Florsheim), and drugstores (Walgreen, People's Drug).

The main characteristics of chain stores are centralized buying and centralized management. The chain's main office buys much the same merchandise (with some regional and other variations) for all stores and receives discounts for large purchases. The main office ordinarily sets prices and creates advertising that stores run locally. Store layout may be standardized.

Sears, for example, planned in the early 1980s to overhaul its 831 stores based on a prototype store it developed in a Chicago suburb. The new design features the "boutique" within a store popularized by Bloomingdale's, diffused lighting, muted colors, and lower ceilings. Each department has its own cash register. (The "area" cashing station Sears pioneered in the late 1970s was dropped.)[29]

Centralization allows chains to overcome the drawbacks of independents. Prices are lower because costs can be spread over a large number of stores. Management hires specialists to handle advertising, window display, warehousing, and other business functions.

In the past, independents had a clear advantage in the number of services they offered, but now most stores extend credit and stay open long hours. Chains are still often at a disadvantage, however, in offering timely goods. Centralized buying requires ordering in advance and in massive quantities. Sears cannot afford to be a fashion leader in new tennis fashions or evening wear because a misjudgment of public taste may mean a huge loss.

Associations of Independents

Among independents, the trend today is to take advantage of some of the benefits of group membership without giving up freedom and flexibility. Several types of organizations have been tried.

Ownership Group
Type of department store organization in which stores keep their separate name but are owned by a corporation that centrally provides some buying and management functions.

Ownership Groups Among department stores, the **ownership group** is common. In this organization (1) stores are owned by a corporation, (2) some management functions (research, recordkeeping, finance) are performed centrally, and (3) some centralized buying for nonfashion goods may be practiced. But stores keep their separate names and do most of their buying and planning independently. Examples are Federated Department Stores (the Boston Store, Bullocks, Burdine's, Bloomingdale's, Abraham & Straus) and Allied Stores (Bon Marché, Jordan Marsh, Joske's, Donaldson's).

Franchising Arrangement
Agreement whereby an independent businessperson sells the products or services of a parent company, uses its name, and adopts its policies in exchange for an exclusive territory.

Franchises The franchising idea has been around since the beginning of the century, but it caught on, especially in food retailing, only in the 1960s. In a **franchising arrangement,** an independent businessperson agrees to sell the products or services of a parent company, use its name, and adopt its policies in exchange for an exclusive territory.

Franchise owners are neither independent operators nor mere store managers. In most cases they have the right to sell their businesses, but they operate under the rules of the parent company. They receive training from the parent company and assistance in recordkeeping and operating the business after that. The company sets prices, creates advertising programs, and may require owners to buy inventory and supplies from it.

Many store owners are glad to be relieved of these responsibilities, but some resent their lack of decision-making power, and others complain about abuses. Among the common complaints are:

1. *Franchising fees drain profits.* Either the initial purchasing price is very high or monthly royalties or rent siphon off profit. A car rental franchise (such as Hertz, Avis, or Dollar-Rent-A-Car) can cost as much as $550,000 in initial investment and start-up costs, plus royalty and advertising fees of about 7 percent of monthly rental, mileage, and collision insurance receipts.[30]
2. *National programs ignore local needs.* In Michigan, for example, ice cream has a much lower butterfat content than in New Jersey. When Dairy Queen tried to standardize its product, New Jersey owners objected, and many dropped their franchises.[31]
3. *Companies sometimes arbitrarily cancel a franchise.* During the gasoline shortage of the early 1970s, the oil companies cancelled the franchise of many service stations.[32]

Partly because of the troubled relations, many parent companies are trying to gain more control by buying back franchises and turning them into company-owned outlets. Several companies, including McDonald's and Radio Shack, are expanding overseas to avoid more competition in the saturated American market. However, franchising opportunities still exist in the United States, especially in business areas long dominated by independents—among them real estate, travel services, accounting, and home remodeling.[33]

Merchandising Conglomerates

The **merchandising conglomerate,** or "conglomerchant," as they have come to be called, is a new form of retail organization that first appeared in the 1960s and gathered steam in the 1970s. These retail empires combine several, often unrelated business units under central management. Carter Hawley Hale, for example, owns The Broadway department stores on the West Coast, the best-known department store in Dallas (Neiman-Marcus), and a large New York specialty store (Bergdorf-Goodman). Conglomerchants practice centralized buying, warehousing, and transportation, which lead to cost savings. But this form of organization is not without problems. Department stores owned by the same corporation may have to compete in the same market. Also, finding managers skilled in many different types of retailing is a problem.

Merchandising Conglomerate
Retail organization combining several, often unrelated, business units under central management.

Creating an Image

Once retail proprietors have decided on a product line, pricing strategy, location, and ownership, they must consider the type of image they want their stores to project.

Evidence suggests that consumers shop at stores that match their own self-images. A study was made of how three stores in New York were viewed by their shoppers. A profile of the three stores matched the customers' views of themselves closely. The lower-income shoppers at one store saw the store as "plain, rugged, economical." The trendy upscale shoppers described their store [Bloomingdale's] as "modern, sophisticated, extravagant." The study concluded, "The more widely separated the store image and the self-image, the less likely the shopper will find the store attractive."[34] Some shoppers will go to a prestige store to improve their own self-images, however.

Store Design

Customers often judge a retail store by external appearance. Store fixtures, lighting, carpeting, and merchandise displays all contribute to the impression that a store makes on a customer. No one design is best. What works for a supermarket might be a disaster in a specialty store and vice versa. However, studies have shown that some patterns are better than others for different categories of stores.

The first task any store designer faces is layout. Some establishments, such as supermarkets and discount houses, are laid out in a grid pattern with straight aisles. This forces customers to move in a certain direction and makes maximum use of selling areas. Modern specialty shops and department stores are more likely to use a free-form layout. Counters or racks of merchandise are placed like islands in a sea. Customers are free to roam, which encourages buying on impulse.

Atmospherics
Marketing task of creating certain effects in buyers by designing store environments.

Besides layout, other design elements that contribute to a store's image are lighting, fixtures, music, videos, and even scents. The term **atmospherics** has been used to describe the marketing task of creating certain effects in buyers by designing store environments.[35]

Marketing Mix Factors

Consumers fashion their image of a store from the elements of the marketing mix as well. Pricing definitely affects store image. Discount stores, for example, often use odd pricing (pricing below even dollar amounts) to give consumers the impression of a bargain. Quality stores, on the other hand, believe their image is portrayed best by even amounts.

Advertising also affects a store's image. Newspaper ads help distinguish stores to a certain extent. The ads of stores with a low-price emphasis feature few illustrations and a lot of type. Quality stores, in contrast, may use elegant models, little type, and a good deal of white space. (See Figure 12.5.)

The salespeople a store employs further its image as well. The sales personnel at Neiman-Marcus are urged to practice smiling. Burger King and McDonald's hire peppy young people. Clerks at certain stores that strive for an elite image are notorious for condescending attitudes. Salespeople are especially important for retailers of services, such as banks and airlines.[36] Some retailers offer special services, such as those described in At Your Service 12.1.

Figure 12.5
Comparison of How Two Stores Approach Advertising

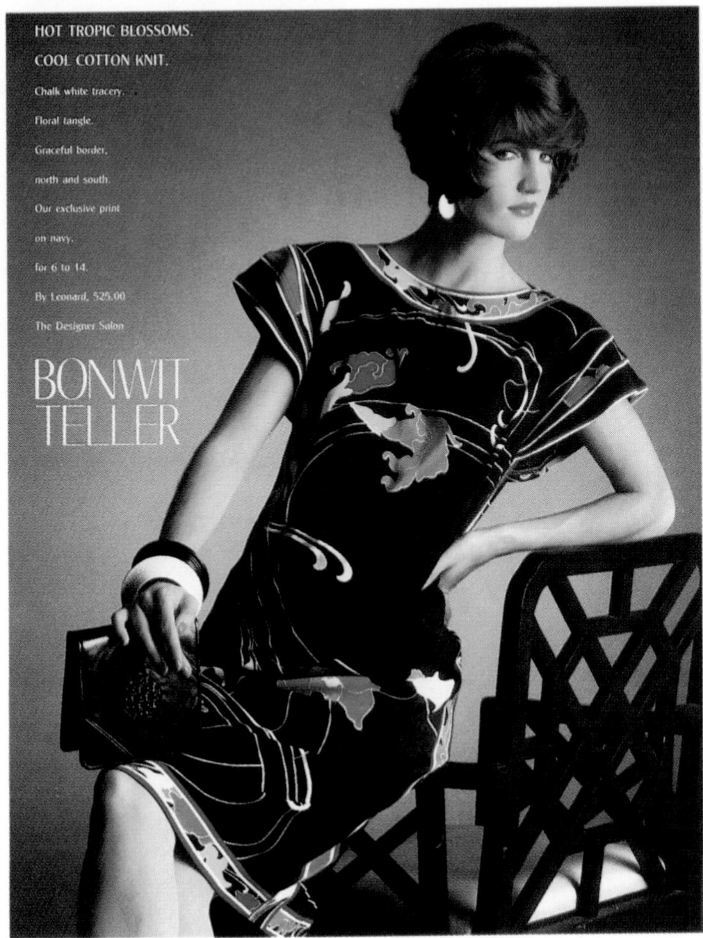

Source: Courtesy of Bonwit Teller.

Explaining Retail Changes

It has been said that the only thing that is constant in life is change. Retailing certainly bears out that observation. Marketing specialists in retailing have long tried to find patterns in retail changes and the causes of change. Two explanations have been forwarded—the wheel of retailing theory and the life-cycle hypothesis.

The Wheel of Retailing

According to Malcolm McNair, changes in retailing are cyclical. At first, a new store type challenges an existing institution by cutting prices, using simple facilities, giving few services, and offering only a limited merchandise selection. Once the store is established, however, it starts trading up its merchandise, offering more services, and improving appearances. Prices follow costs upward. The store then suffers the fate

At Your Service 12.1
Gift Registries: Special Service from Retailers

Many consumers are familiar with gift registries for couples intending to marry. The couple inform the store what china, crystal, or other gifts they would like to receive, and the store uses this information to help wedding guests select gifts.

Now some stores are expanding this service to include gift registries for babies. The babies don't register, of course; their parents do, listing everything from cribs to blankets to bottles.

A pioneer in this service is Dayton Hudson Corporation, which started its Stork Club Gift Registry in 1984. The company promotes the gift registry in newspaper ads, stuffers in bills, and special events featuring child-care experts. Besides the registry, the stores features baby products under its Stork Club private label.

Other newborn registries include Carson Pirie Scott & Company's Year One and Robinson's stores' Small Creations. These registries are an attempt to benefit from the growing number of babies born to the baby boom generation.

Source: Sarah E. Moran, "Gift Registries Can Begin from Year One," *Advertising Age,* July 21, 1986, p. 34.

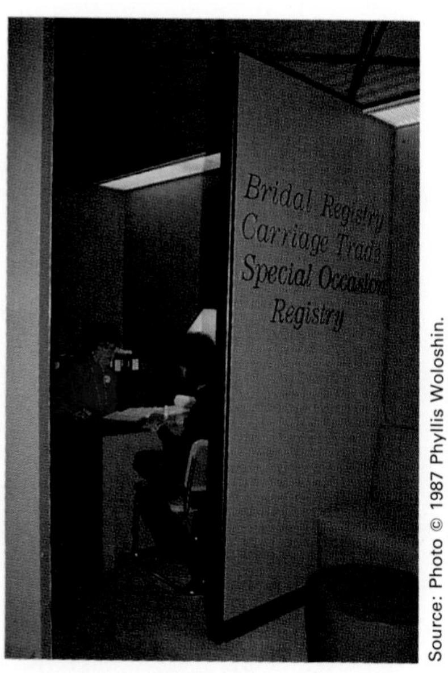

Source: Photo © 1987 Phyllis Woloshin.

of its old competitor as a new store type develops, using cost-cutting tactics. The wheel will have turned full circle.[37]

Wheel of Retailing
Theory that all retail innovators start as low-cost, low-price stores, improve services and raise prices at maturity, and decline when new types of low-cost stores challenge them.

McNair's **wheel of retailing** theory explains many changes in retailing. For example, it describes how supermarkets challenged old-fashioned grocery stores and are in turn being challenged by superstores today. But not all changes in retailing result from an effort to cut costs. Vending machines and convenience stores, for instance, are high-cost innovations that nevertheless succeeded.

The Life-Cycle Hypothesis

Retail Life Cycle
View that retail stores, like products, have life cycles that consist of phases: innovation, accelerated development, maturity, and decline.

A different hypothesis is that stores, like products, have **retail life cycles** that consist of phases: innovation, accelerated development, maturity, and decline. The movement to a new phase is brought about by competitive pressures, but they are not necessarily related to cost cutting. Maturity sets in when there are so many stores of a certain type that no room remains for new entrants.[38]

The theory has led to insights about retail change. It holds, for example, that retail life cycles are accelerating. Although it took department stores a century to reach maturity, catalog showrooms matured in less than 10 years. The speed-up of the life-cycle development means that businesspeople going into a new type of retailing have less time than ever to recover their initial investments. Retailing is becoming risky business.

The theory also suggests that just as in the case of a product, a retail store's maturity phase can be extended. This requires adjusting operations to meet the times. Macy's provides an example.

Macy's, perceived in the 1970s as stodgy compared with the fashionable Bloomingdale's, began its renaissance by pioneering a bold new approach to selling housewares. It turned its basement into a "street" of shops specializing in gourmet food and cooking equipment. "The Cellar," as the floor became known, soon was the chic place to shop for bread, pasta, fancy chocolates, and kitchen gadgetry.

Macy's also launched a pub called P. J. Clarke's and started staying open on Sundays. To establish an upscale reputation, Macy's moved aggressively into designer apparel and even echoed Bloomingdale's typography in advertising.

By the mid-1980s, Macy's, whose history extended back more than 125 years, was gaining market share, and industry analysts predicted that the trend would continue.[39]

Chapter Replay

1. **What kinds of retailers emphasize product mix?**
   Retailers that emphasize product mix include specialty stores, which may be superstores; department stores; and supermarkets. In addition, retailers have responded to changing needs with new species of supermarkets: convenience stores, combination stores, and hypermarkets.
2. **What types of retail establishments specialize in offering low prices?**
   Retailers that focus on price include discount stores, warehouse stores, home improvement centers, and catalog showrooms.
3. **Where do retailers locate their stores?**
   Retailers primarily locate stores in central business districts and in shopping centers. Shopping centers may vary in size and may include factory outlet malls.
4. **What are some ways of retailing without stores?**
   Nonstore retailing includes door-to-door selling, direct marketing (including telemarketing), and automatic vending machines.
5. **What are some ways of organizing retail establishments?**
   Retailers may be independents, chains, associations of independents (ownership groups or franchises), or merchandising conglomerates.
6. **How do retailers create an image for their store?**
   Retailers create an image through store design, including layout and atmospherics. They also use the elements of the marketing mix to create an image.
7. **How does the wheel of retailing theory attempt to explain changes in retailing?**
   According to the wheel of retailing theory, changes in retailing are cyclical. First, a new store type challenges an existing institution by cutting prices, using simple facilities, giving few services, and offering a limited selection. Gradually the store trades up in these categories, and prices follow costs upward. Eventually, a new, lower-priced type of store develops to replace this one.

8. **What is the life cycle of stores?**
The retail life cycle consists of innovation, accelerated development, maturity, and decline. The movement to each new phase is brought about by competitive pressures.

Key Terms

atmospherics
catalog showroom
central business district
chain store
combination store
convenience store
department store
discount store
franchising arrangement
home improvement center
hypermarket
independent store
mail-order firm
merchandising conglomerate
ownership group
retail life cycle
retailing
scrambled merchandising
shopping center
specialty store
supermarket
superstore
telemarketing
vending machine
warehouse store
wheel of retailing

Discussion Questions

1. What are two strategies that specialty stores can use to gain a marketing advantage?
2. How do department stores compete with the lower prices of superstores, discount houses, and off-price retailers?
3. Kevin Killroy is interested in entering the retail business. He learns that a new subdivision, Happy Acres, does not yet contain any stores. Kevin decides that a good market exists for an establishment where residents can shop for groceries. Which would you recommend that Kevin open—a supermarket, a convenience store, a combination store, or a hypermarket? Support your choice.
4. Sonya Slocum's job at an advertising agency pays just enough for Sonya to support herself and her two children in a comfortable lifestyle. Although Sonya sometimes has to stretch to pay all the bills, she almost never shops at discount or warehouse stores. Why might someone choose to pay full price elsewhere when discount stores are cheaper?
5. For each of the following products, indicate whether you would recommend selling it through direct-mail marketing or through telemarketing. Explain your choice.

   a. A line of cheeses, fruits, and chocolates packaged in fancy containers for gift giving.
   b. Subscriptions to a local newspaper.

c. A stress-management and physical fitness program at the neighborhood hospital.

d. Donations to the local orchestra in the form of $30 memberships.

6. What is the major advantage independent stores offer their owners? What are some drawbacks of independents?
7. Nancy Nonesuch is thinking of buying a car-rental franchise. What drawbacks of this retailing arrangement should she be aware of? Would she be better off starting an independent operation? Why, or why not?
8. What are some of the elements retailers consider in store design?
9. What are the stages in the retail life cycle? Based on what you read about convenience stores, at what stage of the life cycle is this type of establishment? At what stage of the life cycle are catalogs?

Case 12.1
Anderson Lumber Company

The numbers are impressive: 23 units in three states, sales of just under $90 million, more than 600 employees, an average of 12,000 stockkeeping units per store, and nearly a century of service to builders, remodelers, and, most recently, do-it-yourselfers. Nestled in the lap of the Wasatch Mountains, Ogden, Utah-based Anderson Lumber Company is fast becoming a lean, mean retailing machine.

Always strong in lumber and wood products (they account for more than 60 percent of sales), Anderson, which operates units in Utah, Wyoming, and Idaho, is pursuing a carefully crafted merchandising campaign designed to attract more D-I-Y and B-I-Y consumers—without sacrificing a large and loyal army of professional customers.

Plan of Action

At present, the company's average store is a cozy 6,500 square feet. The customer mix is dominated by professionals that account for 70 percent of sales. In the years to come, however, Anderson executives are banking on different numbers. "We're going to build major building-materials centers in the area's big markets," says James Beardall, president and chief executive officer, "and then approach the in-between spots with satellites, which will be stores with a small drive-through." In both new units and retrofits, Anderson's aim is clear: capture enough consumer business to remix the customer mix and bring it closer to 50-50.

Source: Edited from "Anderson Lumber Leaps Ahead," by Paul Kitzke, Senior Editor, *Building Supply Home Centers,* June 1986, pp. 60+. Logo courtesy of Anderson Lumber Company.

Marketing Activities

To handle the flow of new consumers, Anderson has discovered that service is the name of the game. Beefed-up desks ("Answer Centers"), better-trained salespeople ("Answer Men," "Answer Women"), and how-to classes ("Answer Clinics") are all part of a plan to keep the customers satisfied. Anderson is even trying out a line of consumer credit, the "Answercard."

To expand service, the company began an installed-sales program last year. Starting with garage-door openers, the program now includes a wide range of products and projects.

Advertising goals are changing, too. Anderson is trying to establish an image of a mass merchandiser, so its ads feature more products. Recognizing the importance of target marketing, Anderson is studying zip codes and demographics. The company has found that it may only need to send out 10,000 ad inserts in a market, not 30,000.

Management Activities

To muster skilled manpower, the company has developed a rigorous management training program. A comprehensive course in retailing, the program shapes trainees into assistant managers and, within five years, into full-fledged store managers steeped in the Anderson way of doing business.

Each store manager receives $300 a month to take a trainee. After trainees get through the first year, the managers are usually happy with them.

Soon, managing the store will mean paying closer attention to computers, says Guy Nickerson, vice president of finance. Using Dataline software and Digital hardware, Anderson has embarked on an ambitious program to link all 23 units to a mainframe computer by the end of the decade. Currently, two stores have operational minicomputers.

Though the price will be high (between $50,000 and $150,000 per store), Nickerson expects the results to go right to the bottom line. "What we've been looking for from day one was the ability to increase gross margins and control inventory," he explains. "If we can increase our gross by two points and our turns by at least one, we'll pay for the entire computer system in about a year and a half."

Focal Topics

1. To what do you attribute the success of Anderson Lumber Company?
2. What do you see as the major opportunities and problems likely to face the company in the future?
3. Discuss how some of the retailing concepts presented in this chapter can be of help to Anderson Lumber in planning for the future.

Case 12.2
McCallum Department Stores

CO

McCallum Department Stores can trace its roots back to 1907, when Charles McCallum opened a small dry goods store in a medium-sized town in Georgia. Additional lines of merchandise were added, and McCallum eventually became a full-fledged department store. Today there are 17 McCallum Department Stores in small- to medium-sized cities in Georgia and Florida. This regional chain of stores is still owned and managed by the McCallum family, with Charles' grandson Bill serving as chairman of the board and grandson Fred as president.

A Difference of Opinion

Traditional could be the best term to describe the McCallum Department Stores. Over the past years there have been a few changes in the exteriors of the stores and their physical layouts. Likewise, store buyers have attempted to keep up with the changing styles and demands for certain types of goods and services. Compared to the significant changes in department stores in major cities, however, McCallum stores are pretty much the same today as they were a decade ago. Numbers and types of lines carried, pricing strategies, and promotional activities have seen little change.

After attending a conference on emerging trends in retailing, Fred McCallum became convinced that the latest retailing evolution, off-price retailing, could have a major impact on the sales and profitability of McCallum stores. He learned that off-price sales have more than doubled since 1979 to a projected $6 billion in 1983. One retail consultant predicted that off-price stores could capture as much as 15 percent of all apparel and footwear sales by 1990.

Fred McCallum heard that off-price retailers can usually purchase merchandise at lower prices than either department stores or conventional discounters because they pay promptly and often in cash. Buying close-outs, apparel from last season, excess goods, and not asking for special allowances or returns privileges all help reduce the cost of goods for off-price retailers. Such retailers wind up selling their merchandise for 20 to 60 percent less than department stores simply by passing along their discounts. Some of the major players in off-price retailing include Marshall's (Melville Corporation), Hit or Miss and T. J. Maxx (both from Zayre Corporation), J. Brannam (F. W. Woolworth Company), Plums (Dayton Hudson), and Designer Depot (K mart).

When Fred McCallum heard rumors that some of the off-price retail chains were considering movement into McCallum's markets, he approached Bill McCallum and suggested that an offensive strategy should be developed. He proposed that McCallum stores should put in special

Sources: Factual information presented here on off-price retailing has been adapted from materials provided by Management Horizons, Inc., and Gail Benson, "Off-Price Stores Please Buyers, Rile Merchants," *U.S. News & World Report,* November 7, 1983, p. 84.

Exhibit
Traditional Apparel Stores versus Off-Price Stores

Average Piece of Merchandise (Manufacturing Cost = $40)	Traditional Apparel Stores	Off-Price Stores
Purchase Price	$ 55.00	$30.00
Initial Markup	+55.00	+25.00
Initial Selling Price	$110.00	$55.00
Markdowns and Shrinkage	−20.00	−5.00
Final Selling Price	$ 90.00	$50.00
Gross Margin	39%	40%

Source: Management Horizons, Inc.

off-price sections or perhaps open some off-price stores of their own under a different name. Bill's reaction was quick and negative. Bill challenged Fred's thinking with such statements as: "We have been quite successful with our present strategies, why change?" "We survived in the face of the larger chain stores and the onslaught of discounters." "Besides, if any of those stores open in our trading areas and if any of our vendors sell to them, we will simply stop carrying those vendors' lines."

Overview of Off-Price Retailing

Off-price retailing is really nothing new. Factory outlets have been doing business this way for a number of years. With the present proliferation of these stores, however, off-price retailing has shown signs of being a growth vehicle and a source of attractive profits for a new breed of retail specialists. Management Horizons, a leading retailing consulting firm, defines off-price retailing as a form of retailing characterized by:

1. Regular, every-day sale of medium- to high-quality products at deep discount prices.
2. Opportunistic purchase of close-out, late-season, overstocked, or slightly damaged merchandise at extremely favorable merchandise cost.
3. Conventional gross margin and high inventory turnover.

For many organizations, the economics of off-price retailing are quite persuasive. The exhibit shows some differences between traditional apparel specialty stores and off-price stores. Management Horizons notes the following points regarding this comparison:

1. Off-price stores often buy at less than the manufacturers' *full cost* of production. Some manufacturers make their money selling to traditional outlets and are sometimes willing to move merchandise at any level above *variable costs* in order to dispose of close-out, end-of-season, and irregular goods.

2. Off-price retailers take fewer markdowns, since merchandise will already be selling at bargain prices.
3. Off-price retailers can maintain a gross margin comparable to an apparel specialty store while selling virtually the same merchandise at a savings of 20 to 60 percent compared with the *original, list,* or so-called regular prices of conventional outlets. Such publicized savings do not take into account that a large percentage of the units sold by regular retailers are moved with promotional or clearance sale markdowns.

Focal Topics

1. What changes in our society and economic environment have brought about the growth and consumer acceptance of off-price retailing?
2. Do you think the growth of off-price retailers will continue? Why, or why not?
3. What do you recommend that McCallum Department Stores do if off-price retailers move into its market areas?

13 Distributing Goods

Sounding Out the Chapter

In this chapter, you will learn:

1. What activities are involved in physical distribution.
2. How companies use a total physical distribution concept.
3. The basic decisions involved in warehousing.
4. The goals of inventory management.
5. How managers decide on the amount of inventory to carry.
6. How companies keep track of inventory.
7. The modes of transportation the physical distribution manager can evaluate.
8. How companies that are too small to own or lease transportation can transport goods economically.

Source: NASDA

This Marketing Channel Ends in Space

While most cargo moves around on trucks and trains, an increasing amount is space cargo. The world's principal carrier of commercial space cargo had been the National Aeronautics and Space Administration until the *Challenger* tragedy of 1986 grounded the shuttle program. Since then, a number of organizations have moved to take over some of NASA's business.

Commercial space cargo has primarily consisted of satellites. For example, the satellites originally scheduled to be launched by NASA's space shuttles included satellites owned by GTE-Spacenet, RCA, and Western Union, as well as by communications services in Canada, Britain, and Indonesia. New York-based Terasat plans to use its Westar satellite to transmit television programming and business data for Western Union and other users. Federal Express has scheduled its Express-Star communications satellite for a 1989 launch.

Major competitors for commercial space cargo are the long-time manufacturers of the rockets used by NASA and the U.S. Air Force—Martin Marietta, McDonnell Douglas, and General Dynamics. These companies hope that their experience with NASA will give them an edge.

In addition, smaller U.S. companies are entering the competition. For example, Robert Truax, a former Navy engineer, built a rocket in the backyard of his home in Saratoga, California. He hopes to be the first private businessperson to launch commercial cargo into space.

The U.S. companies are facing stiff competition from other nations. The European space consortium Arianespace, which is led by France, had by 1987 booked all its flights through 1989. This organization is limited, however, because it can handle only about ten lift-offs a year from its launch pads in the jungles of French Guiana. A fast-growing organization is China's Great Wall Industry Corporation, which has aggressively marketed its Long March-3 booster service. Other competition comes from Japan and the Soviet Union.

Of course, most companies face more down-to-earth problems than how to launch a satellite. Nevertheless, all goods-producing firms have to find reliable and economical ways to move their products to their customers. This chapter addresses the decisions involved in getting products from manufacturers to customers.

Source: Janice Castro, "Blast-Off for Profits," *Time,* March 2, 1987, pp. 44–45.

What Is Physical Distribution?

Preceding chapters discuss how the ownership of products changes hands. The exchange may be a simple one involving just a buyer and a seller. Or, it may be a more complex transaction with several levels of wholesale intermediaries and retailers. All of the participants in the exchange make up a marketing channel.

This chapter concentrates on the physical handling and movement of goods, not ownership, although the two usually go together. Making products available where customers want them is a necessary first step to their exchange. Few realize how much effort the first step requires.

Consider buying a candy bar. The ownership exchange is simple: coins are deposited into a vending machine and, with luck, the candy drops out and the exchange is completed. But a staggering number of other activities makes that transaction possible.

Wholesale intermediaries usually stock the machine. The candy probably reaches them by a roundabout route. The wholesale customer places an order with a manufacturer. After checking inventories, the manufacturer may discover a shortage of stock and order a start-up of production. A warehouse full of raw materials transported from distant places—sugar from the West Indies, almonds from California, chocolate from Ghana—will feed the production process. Another warehouse, perhaps closer to the wholesale intermediary, may receive and store the finished product from the factory. Warehouse workers then draw up billing and shipping papers, load a truck with the amount ordered, and ship it to the wholesale customer's own warehouse. From there, wholesalers make deliveries to the hundreds of outlets they supply, including the vending machine.

Whoever named a candy product the "100 Thousand Dollar Bar" was not far off. A substantial investment in labor, storage facilities, and transportation is necessary to supply this one simple product to American consumers. The wise management of that investment is the job of those involved in physical distribution.

Physical Distribution
The process of storing and moving products along marketing channels.

Physical distribution includes all those activities required to move finished goods along marketing channels, including storing the goods along the way. The most important activities are:

1. *Warehousing*—the storage or handling of products until they are needed for production or sale.
2. *Inventory control*—the determination of the amount of stock to keep on hand for manufacturing and resale.
3. *Transportation*—the actual movement of goods to the places where they are needed for production or sale.

Service and nonprofit organizations may also have some interest in physical distribution. For example, banks are concerned with the supply of money on hand, and hospitals must know the number of beds available for patient care—both inventory problems. This topic is addressed in Chapter 18.

All members of a marketing channel are involved in physical distribution to some extent, but whoever controls the channel usually has major responsibility. This chapter focuses on the manufacturer's role in the physical distribution of goods. In the past 30 years, management ideas about that task have changed considerably.

Changing Ideas about Physical Distribution

The notion of physically storing goods and then moving them to places where they are needed is as old as recorded history. The Old Testament in the Bible tells how Joseph saved Egypt by storing grain during seven good years and selling it during the seven lean years that followed. But until recently, physical distribution has received little attention. The typical attitude of entrepreneurs was: first make the product, then worry about getting it to the customer.

Several forces came together in the 1950s to help change that attitude.[1] The marketing concept was widely adopted. The focus of firms was on consumer wants, and what consumers wanted was more convenience in purchasing. As more and more outlets were opened in the suburbs, the job of supplying them grew. That job was complicated by increases in the number of products offered to consumers. For example, the Armour-Dial company makes Dial soap in four colors and three sizes. More than 7 million bars of Dial are sold throughout the world every week. Retailers carry whichever sizes and colors sell best to their customers. Armour-Dial faces the task of making sure that consumers find the selection they want wherever they shop.[2] Keeping track of inventories and handling and shipping orders is clearly an immense challenge.

Moving more goods to more outlets raised the cost of physical distribution. When distribution charges began to significantly influence a company's bottom line, management was forced to pay attention.

The Total Physical Distribution Concept

A pioneer study in 1956 pointed the way to reduce distribution costs.[3] At that time, companies often stocked many warehouses with a full line of goods near customers. For example, Xerox kept 40 sales branches with complete inventories of supplies, parts, and chemicals for its copying machines. The study found that in many cases 80 percent of supplies were ordered very infrequently. It recommended closing several warehouses and consolidating the remaining goods in a few central locations. Salespeople worried that customer service would suffer. Days would be added in transportation time from the more distant warehouse sites. But the study suggested that goods could be shipped by air for overnight delivery, and money could still be saved.

The suggestion was revolutionary. Because of its expense, managers had never seriously considered using air freight as a routine method of transporting goods. But they had failed to weigh that cost against the cost of maintaining several warehouses. As it turned out, Xerox saved millions by closing 33 warehouses.

Figure 13.1
Management Organization under the Total Physical Distribution Concept

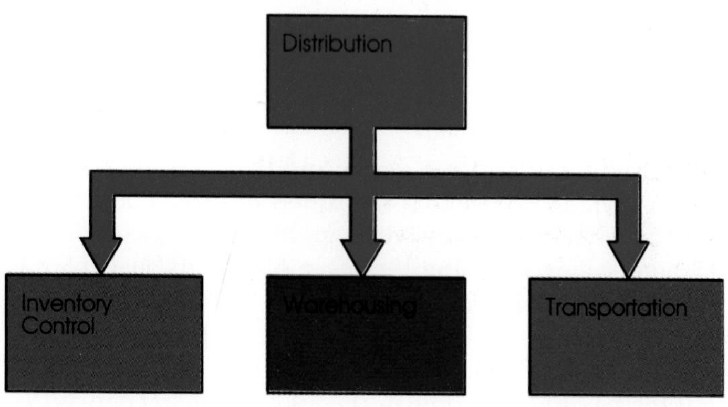

Managers had failed to recognize the potential for savings for a simple reason. Responsibility for the various areas of physical distribution was widely scattered. Warehousing was often part of the production department, and transportation was a department by itself. Costs were viewed separately. Each division was interested only in keeping its own costs down.

Total Physical Distribution Concept
Principle that all management functions related to moving products to buyers must be fully integrated.

The study gave rise to the **total physical distribution concept,** which states that all management functions related to moving products to buyers must be fully integrated. The organization chart of a firm that adopts the concept may look like Figure 13.1. Distribution is a department equal to marketing and production, and it is responsible for the three major distribution activities.

Integrating these activities is not an easy task. Each area involves an immense number of details that no one person could hope to keep track of. However, the development of the computer has made the concept a practical one.

Implementing the Concept

The total physical distribution concept has been widely adopted. According to one survey, three-quarters of companies had by 1973 given a separate department control of two or more activities in the area.[4] The head of the department, the physical distribution manager, must balance two objectives: (1) minimizing costs to the firm as a whole and (2) providing a satisfactory level of customer service.

Visible Costs
Direct and indirect costs that show up on a profit and loss statement.

Hidden Costs
Costs of doing business—for example, a cancelled order—that do not show up on a profit and loss statement.

Minimizing Costs Minimizing costs is a difficult task for two reasons. First, many costs must be considered, some of which are not obvious. Marketers refer to visible and hidden costs. **Visible costs,** which show up on a profit and loss statement, include the direct expenses of running warehouses and hiring transportation, as well as the indirect costs of insuring goods and paying property taxes. **Hidden costs,** which accountants cannot record, include losses that result from a customer failing to order or canceling an order if an item is out of stock. It is difficult to know when costs are minimized if only some of the costs are specified exactly.

Second, it is the total cost that must be kept down. Common sense suggests that the way to minimize total costs is to do things in the cheapest possible way in each area of physical distribution. But as the 1956 study showed, it sometimes pays to allow costs to increase in one area to bring down costs in others. Marketing specialists call this a **cost trade-off.**

Cost Trade-Off
Practice of allowing costs to increase in one business area to bring down costs in another.

The most frequent trade-offs are between transportation and storage costs. For example, an automaker could make sure that every car dealer has all the necessary auto parts for every possible repair. In this way, the company would avoid the expense of having to rush parts to a dealer, but the cost of carrying all those parts would be burdensome.

The cost trade-off could also involve storage and manufacturing costs. If a company stores enough of a product to handle peak demand periods, the company will avoid filling expensive rush orders, but the cost of storage will be greater.

Another trade-off is between packaging and other costs. If the company tries to save money by using the cheapest possible packaging, it might find itself incurring additional expenses to replace damaged merchandise or paying extra for special handling.

Companies therefore evaluate the total cost of distribution to find the best balance. Montgomery Ward, for example, found that the money it saved by storing its slower-moving merchandise in a single warehouse near Chicago's O'Hare Airport more than offset the additional expense of shipping items by air when necessary.[5]

For help in the task of minimizing costs, some companies are turning to computer systems. Tandy/Radio Shack uses its own microcomputers to handle the huge volume of freight originating from its plants in the United States and from sources overseas. The system speeds order-processing time and reduces the likelihood that items in Radio Shack stores will run out.[6] Other companies are turning to consultants for advice. (See At Your Service 13.1.)

Providing Customer Service In finding ways to lower costs, marketers must weigh the effects of cost savings on customer service. In some cases, customers may look elsewhere for a product that must be back ordered for several weeks or that arrives in poor condition. A summary of services that customers expect appears in Table 13.1, along with examples of the kinds of standards companies set in an effort to live up to expectations.

Sometimes customers will pay extra for superior distribution. Campbell Soup Company, for example, sells branded tomatoes that have remained on the vine longer than is typical for tomatoes sold in supermarkets. This means that the company must get them to stores faster, but many customers are willing to pay more for the riper, fresher produce. Likewise, Natural Pak sells its TomAHtoes in an airtight package that prevents decay without the refrigeration that makes other tomatoes

At Your Service 13.1
Big Savings from a Transportation Consultant

Picking the right courier can be a tricky business. For example, delivering a five-pound package from Austin to Dallas could cost anywhere from $2.30 to more than $100, depending on which carrier does the job. For help in sorting out the choices, many Sun Belt companies are turning to Sheridan Inc., a transportation management service based in Austin, Texas.

G. Richard Sheridan originally conceived the company as a travel agency for packages. However, he soon found that clients wanted more than identification of the most cost-effective courier for packages. They also wanted a company that would handle the work of getting a package shipped. Consequently, Sheridan has established accounts with 35 couriers and pools clients' packages to negotiate better rates. Sheridan shares the savings with its clients. The company will even store clients' materials in its own warehouse and ship them out on command.

Before Sheridan's service, businesses often lacked information about their choices. Observes Richard Sheridan, "Federal Express had done such a great job convincing people they needed overnight service that we found a lot of clients using them to transport packages from one side of Austin to the other." Sheridan typically saves clients between 25 and 35 percent—sometimes even 50 percent. No wonder, then, that the company is profitable and growing.

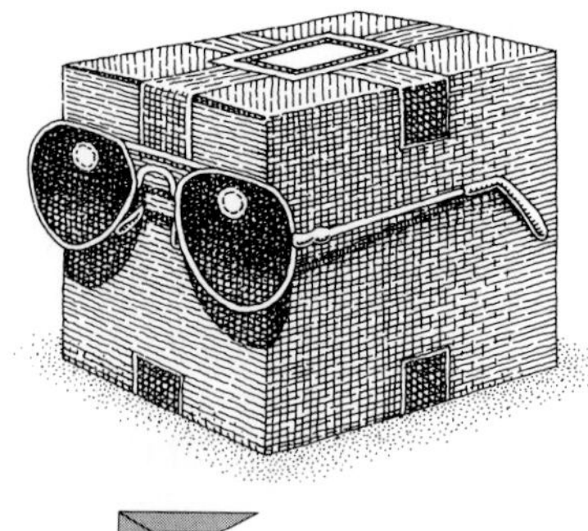

Source: Courtesy of Sheridan, Inc.

Source: Eric Christensen, "Sorting Out the Couriers," *Venture*, April 1986, pp. 112–113.

mealy and flat-tasting. While this is an added expense, the company is able to charge about 30 cents a pound extra for the tomatoes.[7]

To balance customer service and cost objectives, the company must have an in-depth knowledge of all areas of physical distribution. Since warehousing, inventory control, and transportation account for most of the costs of physical distribution (see Figure 13.2), this chapter looks at each of those areas more closely.

Table 13.1
Customer Service Standards

Service Factor	Model Standard
Speed of delivery	Delivery overnight within three days, or within the limits set by competitors
Reliability of delivery	Delivery within *X* days, 90 percent of the time
Availability of items ordered	97 percent of orders for item *X* filled from stock
Accuracy in order filling	98 percent accuracy for all orders placed
Receipt of goods in undamaged condition	97 percent of goods received undamaged

Figure 13.2
Relative Costs of Physical Distribution Components

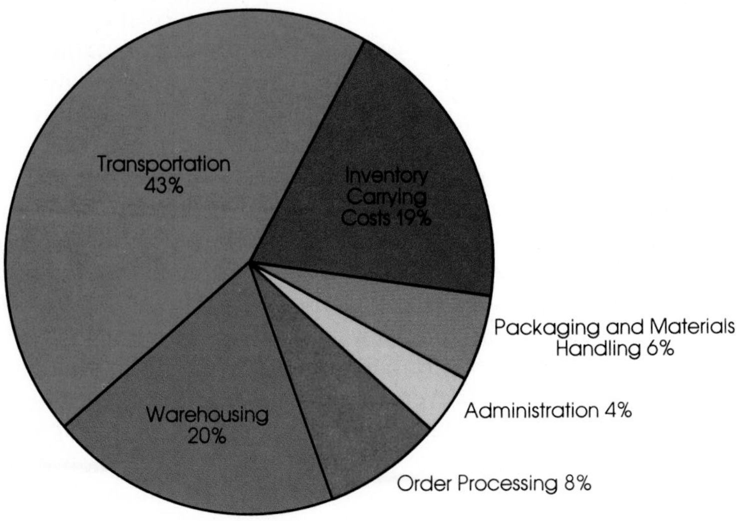

Source: Herbert W. Davis, "Physical Distribution Costs: Performance in Selected Industries—1980," *Annual Proceedings of the National Council of Physical Distribution Management,* 1980, p. 35.

Warehousing

Significant opportunities for savings, without lessening customer service, exist in the area of warehousing. That is why it is the focus of a good deal of management attention today. Three matters in particular are of interest: (1) what type of warehouse to operate, (2) whether to own or rent facilities, and (3) where to locate them.

Types of Operations

Warehouses are distinguished mainly by the functions they perform. The storage warehouse and the distribution center warehouse are the two main types.

Storage Warehouses When most people think of a warehouse, it is usually the **storage warehouse** they have in mind. In this type of facility, goods are stored for weeks, months, or years until they are needed. Companies may decide to store goods for several reasons.

Storage Warehouse
Facility in which goods are stored for weeks, months, or years until they are needed.

Some companies produce goods that are in demand only seasonally. For example, most toys are sold during the Christmas season. The Ideal Toy Company could not possibly meet all of the demand for its products by producing only in the month of December. Instead, it spreads out production through the year and stores goods in its warehouses until they are needed.

Other firms have the opposite problem. They face year-round demand but can produce only seasonally. Del Monte, for example, cans enormous quantities of peaches in the summer when supplies are plentiful and then stores them until demand catches up with supply.

The ups and downs of the business cycle provide companies with still another reason for storing goods. In periods of high inflation, manufacturers stock up on raw materials so they will not have to buy at even higher prices later. By contrast, when prices are declining, producers may hold back goods from the market until the situation improves. Farmers who store bumper crops of wheat and corn are a common example.

Some companies store goods to give them an opportunity to age. The Brown and Williamson Tobacco Company and Gallo Winemakers use large storage facilities for that purpose.

In the past, storage warehouses were often older, multistory structures that depended on labor, rather than computerized equipment, for moving goods. Recently, however, single-story **automated warehouses,** with advanced materials handling systems under the control of a central computer, have begun to replace the older facilities. Although they may cost as much as $10 to $20 million to build, they are much more efficient and can be operated with only a few employees.[8]

Automated Warehouse
Facility with advanced materials handling systems under control of a central computer.

Distribution Center Warehouses In contrast to the storage warehouse, the **distribution center warehouse** is established primarily as a temporary way-station prior to the very rapid movement of goods to customers. Thus, while storage warehouses hold goods back from markets for long periods of time, distribution centers discharge goods, usually within a week's time. (See Marketing Today 13.1.)

Distribution Center Warehouse
Facility that serves primarily as a temporary way-station before the goods are rapidly moved to customers.

The concept of the distribution center was developed after World War II. Goods in storage do not make money for a company, but instead they add to expenses. The slower that goods move, for example, the more a company must pay for insurance against spoilage or damage and for security precautions. Distribution centers decrease the cost of storage.

They also decrease other costs. Because goods move through distribution centers faster than through traditional warehouses, customers can be served through fewer facilities. Transportation costs also may be lowered, because the company ships to fewer locations. The loads are larger, and bulk loads are cheaper to transport than smaller loads.

Lower costs are not the only advantage of distribution centers; they are also more efficient than storage warehouses, primarily because they are usually more modern. All are one-story structures that eliminate the need for elevators and permit the use of modern equipment. Most are also automated, and many use computers to keep track of the flow of goods in and out of the warehouse. Tandy's main distribution center, called the Force Feed Center, is linked by computer with its six regional distribution centers. The Force Feed Center receives orders and assigns them to the appropriate regional center. In addition, the Force Feed Center automatically restocks stores with many small items.

When the Force Feed Center receives deliveries, they are immediately recorded on the center's main computer. Orders are automatically

Marketing Today 13.1

Will Success Ruin L. L. Bean? Don't Bet Your Backpack

Source: Photos courtesy of L. L. Bean, Inc.

The quaint little town of Freeport, Maine, seems an unlikely spot for the country's hottest mail-order sporting goods firm. But the family-run L. L. Bean company wouldn't have it any other way.

"There's no question," a company spokesman said, "we could make more money, in the short run at least, by changing our [unconditional, no-time-limit] guarantee, or expanding operations beyond Freeport, but we're not about to tamper with tradition."

Yet L. L. Bean, which had sales of $225 million in 1982, found that striking a balance between preserving tradition and meeting the demands posed by a highly successful business has tested its Yankee ingenuity to the limits.

The company's distribution center, a half mile away from the downtown retail store, has been operating well in excess of the facilities' original design capacity. Until a new center could be built, the company turned to industrial engineers to devise ways of coping with a system that was strained to the breaking point.

The major challenge the engineers faced was designing a system that could cope with wide fluctuations in business. About 75 percent of the company's catalog sales comes between September and the beginning of December. To cope with the crush, engineers, after analyzing operating systems, equipment, and layout, made the following suggestions:

- ☐ Since 20 percent of the orders was for 2 percent of the company's products, a "forward pick" area was developed that stores 300 of the fastest-moving items. Single orders for hot items can be filled very rapidly.
- ☐ Orders involving hand labor, such as clothing alterations or skis needing binding mounting, are split up. Orders for pants, for example, are sent directly to the alterations department to be fixed while the rest of the order is being picked. By the time the order is assembled, the pants are ready to go.
- ☐ A shipping system was designed by which a computer tracks the contents and destinations of each box and calculates the postage automatically. The packages are then sent without an actual weighing or a postage label. At the end of each day, carriers are given a printout that says, "Here's what we shipped, and here's what we owe you." Periodic audits by UPS and the U.S. Postal Service verify accuracy.

These and other modifications allow L. L. Bean to ship 53,000 packages a day at the peak of the holiday rush. The system stops well short of total automation, however. The way L. L. Bean sees it, there's not a computer yet that can do a decent job resoling a pair of hunting shoes.

Source: Richard D. Filley, "L. L. Bean's IEs Help Mail-Order Institutions Handle Success While Holding On to Tradition," *Industrial Engineering,* June 1983, pp. 47–58.

sorted on a three-level system of conveyor belts that can handle 35 cartons per minute. The system records the flow of goods by reading bar codes on the packages. The automatic sorting enables the center to load each outbound trailer in only an hour and a half.[9]

Distribution centers such as Tandy's are expensive to build, but the cost trade-off in lower operating expenses is worthwhile.

Ownership

Private Warehouse
Storage center owned or controlled by the company that uses it.

Public Warehouse
Storage center controlled by an independent, available for rent for a short time, and usually shared by a number of companies.

After physical distribution managers determine the type of warehouse that suits their needs, they must decide whether to use a private or public facility. The main feature of a **private warehouse** is that the building, equipment, and labor are company owned or controlled.[10] A **public warehouse,** on the other hand, is controlled by an independent, can be rented by anyone needing space for a short time, and is usually shared by a number of companies.

Each has advantages and disadvantages. The chief advantage of a private warehouse is that the owner has total control over operations and personnel. For example, a product such as wine may need special handling, which a public facility cannot guarantee. But private warehouses are costly to build. They are also inflexible; they are difficult to reduce or expand in periods when sales fluctuate. And, if demand shifts to another marketing area, they must either operate at a loss or be closed.

If a company does not produce enough goods to keep a warehouse constantly stocked or cannot predict sales, using public facilities may make better sense. Public warehouses issue receipts that allow companies to borrow from banks, using the stored goods as collateral.

More than 15,000 public warehouses operate in the United States today. Some offer storage and handling for general merchandise, such as furniture or industrial equipment. Others are more specialized; for example, refrigerated warehouses store perishable foods, while commodity warehouses hold unprocessed products like oil and grain. One specialized public facility is the bonded warehouse, which handles goods such as tobacco and alcohol that are taxed before release for sale.

Public warehouses may offer a variety of additional services. These include filing monthly inventory status reports, preparing transportation documents, weighing shipments, monitoring loss and damage from transportation, and assisting the company in filing claims for such losses. These services contribute to the popularity of public warehouses.[11]

Location

Factory-Positioned Warehouse
Facility used to store raw materials and fabricated parts until they are needed for manufacture or one that serves as a traditional warehouse or distribution center for finished products.

Market-Positioned Warehouse
Storage place designed to collect the products of one or more manufacturers in or near the market served before shipping goods short distances to customers.

In general, physical distribution managers have three options in deciding where to locate a warehouse. They may position a warehouse (1) near the company's factory, (2) close to the market, or (3) at an intermediate point between the two.

Factory-positioned warehouses may be used for two purposes. They may store raw materials and fabricated parts until they are needed for manufacture, or they may serve as traditional warehouses or distribution centers for finished products. The latter is especially favored by multiproduct companies that cannot economically store all of their product line near all of the markets they serve.

Market-positioned warehouses are designed to collect the products of one or more manufacturers in or near the market served before shipping the goods short distances to customers. When they are owned by a manufacturer, their purpose is simply to prevent shipping in small quantities over long distances to many customers. Retailers often make use of market-positioned warehouses.

Intermediate-positioned warehouses are usually chosen by manufacturers with several plants and widely scattered markets. The warehouses gather the products of the various plants and mix them for shipment. Tandy's regional distribution centers receive about 1,000 items from its plants in the United States and from sources overseas. The regional centers then distribute the products to more than 6,000 company-owned stores and 3,000 dealer/franchise locations.[12]

Intermediate-Positioned Warehouse
Storage place that serves manufacturers with several plants and widely scattered markets by gathering products of various plants and mixing them for shipment.

Location decisions are complex. After a general strategy for positioning a warehouse is decided on, specific sites must be chosen. Many factors should be weighed when choosing a site, including (1) availability of transportation, (2) quantity and quality of labor, (3) cost of land, (4) taxes, and (5) services provided by the local government. Computers now aid physical distribution managers in making the location decision.

Inventory Control

To manage inventory successfully, physical distribution managers must start with the company's goals for balancing costs with customer service. With those objectives in mind, the managers can then determine the proper inventory size and set up a system to keep track of it.

Goals of Inventory Management

In general, inventory managers pursue two goals: (1) to provide an adequate level of customer service by avoiding out-of-stock situations and (2) to minimize a company's investment in inventory.

Avoiding Stockouts Being out of stock of finished products can be very costly to a company. Customers easily become disenchanted and turn to competitors. One lost sale can mean the permanent loss of a large customer. On the other hand, maintaining an inventory large enough to fill nearly all orders from stock on hand can be exorbitantly expensive.

There is no hard-and-fast rule governing the percentage of orders that should be filled from stock. A well-known principle of inventory management is that usually about 20 percent of the products a company carries account for the majority of sales. Products with the largest sales should always be available so that nearly 100 percent of orders can be filled from stock. Lower levels of stock may be kept for less important products.

A technique called **ABC analysis** identifies items with the biggest sales payoffs. Items are listed by sales volume, as shown in Table 13.2. Those that account for the largest percentage of sales are classified as "A" products—those that must be stocked at all times. Lower levels of stock can be maintained for "B" and "C" products.

ABC Analysis
Inventory technique for identifying items with biggest sales payoffs by listing them by sales volume. Best sellers ("A" products) must be stocked at all times.

Table 13.2
ABC Analysis

Item		Sales Dollars		Percentage of Total Dollars	Percentage of Product Line
A	1	$20,000	$38,000	56%	20%
	2	18,000			
B	3	8,000	23,000	34	40
	4	6,000			
	5	5,000			
	6	4,000			
C	7	3,000	7,000	10	40
	8	2,500			
	9	1,000			
	10	500			
		$68,000			

Source: Edward W. Smykay, *Physical Distribution Management,* 3rd ed. (New York: Macmillan, 1973), p. 208.

Acquisition Cost
Expense incurred in preparing for manufacturing or in buying product for inventory.

Carrying Cost
Expense of holding goods over a period of time.

Cost Considerations Two costs are of particular concern in inventory management—acquisition costs and carrying costs.

Acquisition costs are expenses incurred in preparing for manufacturing or in buying the product to put in inventory. For the manufacturer, these are the costs of setting up production of the goods. For retailers and wholesalers, they are the expenses of recordkeeping and handling the paperwork for each order. They may run from a few dollars to several hundred dollars per order.

Carrying costs are the expenses involved in holding goods over a period of time. These costs vary, but they may range from 10 to 35 percent of the total costs of the goods. Thus, if a company stocks $100,000 worth of goods, it must spend from $10,000 to $35,000 to hold them in storage. Table 13.3 lists the major types of carrying costs and the percentage of the total each represents.

The table shows that the chief carrying cost is often interest, a term that deserves some explanation. If the goods stored are purchased with borrowed funds, interest must be paid to a bank. But even if goods are purchased with company funds, the company is paying "interest" for that investment. The company that keeps $100,000 in inventory does

Table 13.3
Typical Carrying Costs

Type	Percentage of Total Cost
Interest	4–15
Obsolescence and deterioration	2–8
Storage	2–5
Insurance	1–4
Taxes	1–3
Total	10–35

not have that money to invest elsewhere to gain income (in a bank, for instance, at a 10 percent return). Thus, every dollar in inventory represents an expense—in interest paid on borrowed money or interest lost by not investing elsewhere.

Because carrying costs and acquisition costs are so high, physical distribution managers have a stake in keeping down total inventory size. Avoiding stockouts while keeping inventory costs down is a delicate balancing act that requires some trade-offs.

Determining Inventory Size

To discover the correct inventory size, managers make assumptions about upcoming demand. These assumptions are really sales forecasts (discussed in Chapter 4). In general, the more accurate a company's forecast is, the less money it must tie up in excess inventory.

Physical distribution managers use sales forecasts to project the amount of inventory they need to order when it is time to replenish stock. The technical name for the amount to be reordered is the **economic order quantity (EOQ).** It is that amount of stock that costs the least to keep on hand in order to meet the average level of demand. A simple example will show how the economic order quantity is determined.

Economic Order Quantity (EOQ)
Amount of stock that costs the least to keep on hand in order to meet the average level of demand.

Suppose owners of a retail store know from sales forecasts that the store can sell 5,000 chairs in a year, but they do not know how many the store can afford to keep in stock. A tabulation, similar to that in Figure 13.3, can be constructed showing acquisition and carrying costs for orders placed only once or an increasing number of times. The figure shows that acquisition costs increase as more orders are placed. The reason is simple: paperwork must be repeated for each order. By contrast, carrying costs decrease as more orders are placed because fewer chairs must be stored in costly facilities. One cost must be traded off against the other to find the optimum order size.

In the example, the most economical number of orders per year is five. At that point, total cost (acquisition costs plus carrying costs) is the smallest. But if the store owners know from a sales forecast that the store can sell 5,000 chairs, then it may be calculated that after each order period, the store should have on hand 1,000 chairs (5,000 ÷ 5); that is, to meet the average level of demand at the least cost, the store should carry 1,000 chairs.

The economic order quantity specifies only the stock needed to meet average demand. If the sales forecast is wrong and if there is a sudden surge in demand, a stockout may result in losing customers. To guard against this, companies usually also maintain a **safety stock,** or the amount above the basic stock level, to handle emergencies.

Safety Stock
Amount above the basic stock level to handle emergencies.

Keeping Track of Inventory

Knowing how fast stock is moving is important in determining how much inventory to keep on hand. For example, the chair retailer must monitor the stock level to know if the calculations of the economic order quantity were actually equal to demand. Records of the amount of stock

Figure 13.3
EOQ Model for Chairs

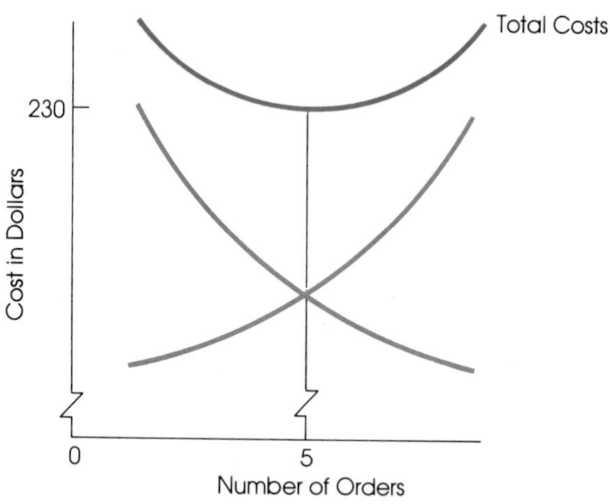

Number of Orders	Acquisition Costs	Carrying Costs	Total Costs	
1	$ 20.00	$650.00	$670.00	
2	40.00	325.00	365.00	
5	100.00	130.00	230.00	← **EOQ**
10	200.00	65.00	265.00	
20	400.00	32.50	432.00	

on hand and its rate of depletion must be kept. The two most common recordkeeping methods are physical counts and perpetual inventory.

Physical Count
Inventory practice of totaling the number of items of each line on hand at a regular interval.

A **physical count,** as the name implies, involves analyzing products on hand at a specific time. Most department stores conduct such a physical count twice a year. By comparing the results with those of a previous count, the stores know not only how much they have on hand at present, but also which items are selling well, which are in excess supply, and which must be reordered.

Perpetual Inventory
Frequently updated list of all goods in stock.

The physical inventory count tells little about the day-in, day-out flow of goods. For that, a firm needs a record of **perpetual inventory,** a list of all goods in stock, which is updated frequently. New goods are entered on the list as they arrive. Whenever goods are sold or used, they are subtracted. Manufacturers, in particular, must keep careful perpetual inventory records to know the rate of use of materials.

Until recently, most retailers could not effectively use a perpetual inventory system. Their large merchandise assortment would have made the recordkeeping operation too expensive. But computerized cash registers have changed that situation. They enable managers of large retail stores like Sears and Montgomery Ward to know, on a daily basis, which merchandise is moving and which requires reordering. Retail stores that keep a perpetual inventory may still take a physical count. Any discrepancy between the perpetual count and the physical count gives a manager some idea of how large a shoplifting problem the store has.

Transportation

The physical storage and inventorying of goods are important responsibilities, but transportation is often the single biggest headache of the physical distribution manager. For one thing, it is usually the largest expense of the three. The total annual transportation bill for General Motors, for example, amounts to more than $1 billion. Despite the expense, transportation is often a neglected area of physical distribution, and problems result. Failure to plan for transportation can result in late deliveries, excessive freight costs, and damaged merchandise.

Two areas should be of most concern to physical distribution managers: (1) the means of transportation that can best deliver a product and (2) regulations that affect the shipment of goods. After investigating both of these areas, this chapter looks at some developments that may alter the physical distribution manager's thinking about transportation in the future.

Transportation Modes

Five modes of transportation link producers and consumers: (1) railroads, (2) motor carriers, (3) water transportation, (4) air transportation, and (5) pipelines. Rail has been the most popular mode but seems to be losing ground to truck transport. Pipelines have more than doubled in importance. Motor carriers and inland water carriers have held fairly steady at roughly 20 percent of total ton-miles each. Airplanes account for less than a half percent of the total volume of freight shipped, but they too are increasing their share of the market.

Some modes are more popular than others because they meet more of the requirements shippers look for in transportation. Figure 13.4 ranks each form of transport by five important characteristics. A closer look at the transportation alternatives will reveal the reasons behind the ranking.

Railroads More than one-third of the nation's freight goes by rail. Although that is considerably less than the proportion transported by rail in the 1940s and 1950s, railroads still hold the biggest share of the market. They carry a wide variety of products (especially bulky products like coal, metal, lumber, and grain), and they serve almost every city in the United States. Railroads are the preferred means of transportation over long distances between cities.

Rail transportation, while generally cheaper over the long run, is hampered by certain limitations. First, trains generally must be used with other transportation modes to provide door-to-door service, which increases handling costs. Second, boxcars are slow, averaging only about 20 miles an hour.[13] The low average speed results from the poor condition of many roadbeds as well as from time lost at freight yards while cars are added or dropped.

With the deregulation of the rail industry in 1980, railroads have had to become more competitive. When the Interstate Commerce Commission (ICC) was setting rates for railroads, the companies sought executives skilled in dealing with the federal bureaucracy. Since deregula-

Figure 13.4
Comparing the Five Basic Forms of Transportation

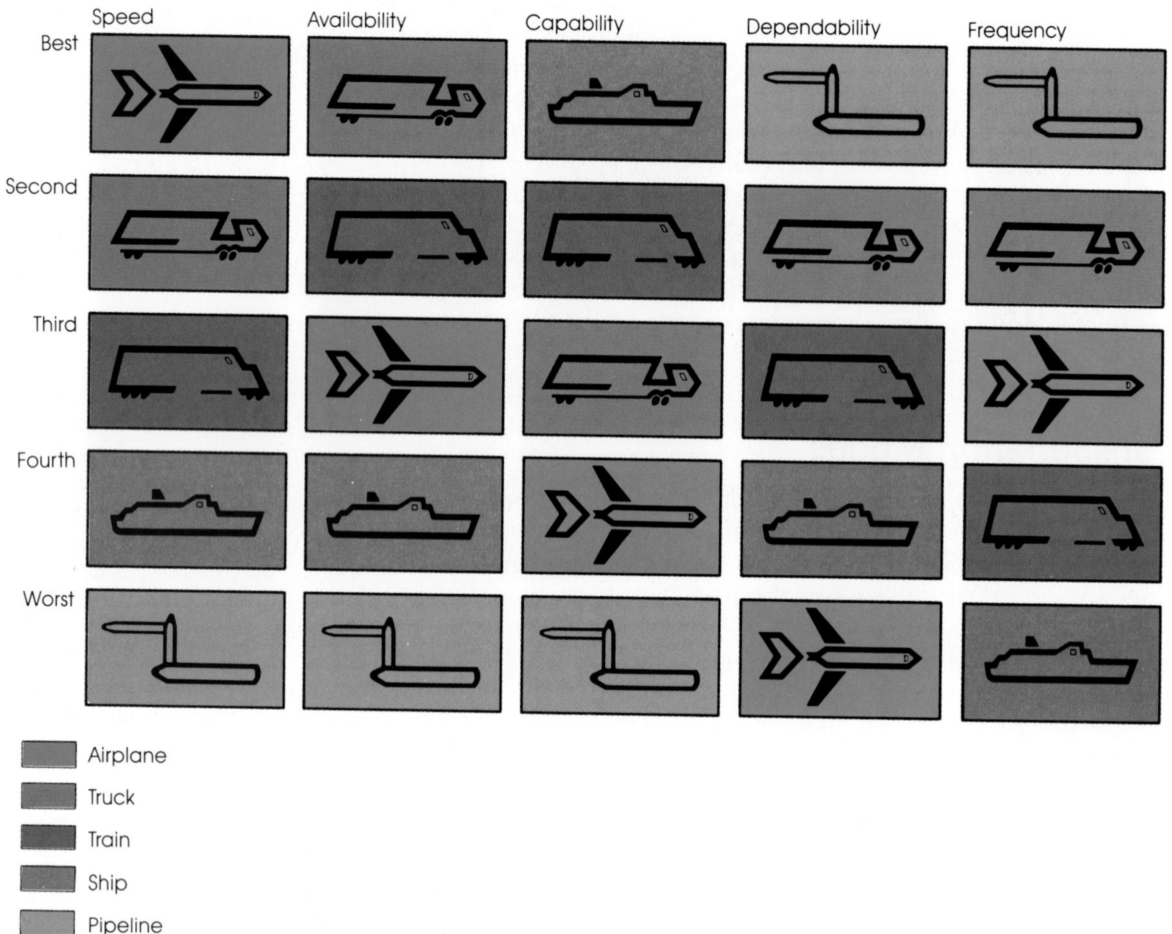

tion, the emphasis has begun to shift to marketing.[14] At Your Service 13.2 describes the experience of one railroad that has adopted a marketing orientation.

Spurred by the prospect of capturing a larger percentage of the traffic in manufactured and high-value products, the railroads have introduced several services.[15] Among the most familiar is *piggyback*—transporting truck trailers on rail cars. This technique combines the efficiency of long-haul rail transportation with the flexibility of trucking.

Another innovation is the use of *unit trains* for high-volume shipments. These trains are loaded with one commodity, such as coal, and travel nonstop between two points. When they have unloaded their cargo at the destination point, they return to the starting point to reload.

A third innovation is the *run-through train,* which avoids delays by bypassing intermediate terminals. Unlike the unit train, the run-through train may carry a variety of goods. One such train routinely covers the

At Your Service 13.2
Marketing Orientation Drives the South Shore

The Chicago South Shore and South Bend Railroad (CSS) considers its mission to be solving problems for its customers and serving as an extension of their traffic and distribution function. One way in which CSS has fulfilled that mission involved transporting molten iron between two midwestern steel companies.

A leading steel maker must shut down its two blast furnaces alternately on a four-year schedule to overhaul and reline them. Recently, so that it could fill its orders while one furnace was shut down, the company arranged to buy molten iron from a second steel company, 26 miles away.

For transportation, the steel maker turned to a major eastern railroad. In reply, the railroad recommended that, instead of molten iron, it ship slabs of metal from a plant on the East Coast, which would cost the steel company over $5 million. Besides this hefty transportation cost, the steel company would have to bear the cost of remelting the metal slabs.

CSS offered an alternative. It would transport the molten metal for a mere $800,000, but there was a hitch: the required railroad cars—called ladle cars—were each expected to weigh more than 300 tons when loaded. Because the ladle cars are designed for use inside a plant and therefore lack brakes, the train had to include nine empty gondola cars for each ladle car, to supply braking for mainline operation. These heavy trains had to pass over five bridges, which were not strong enough to hold them. To strengthen the bridges would cost CSS $500,000.

CSS's marketers turned the problem into an opportunity: if the steel company would pay for the bridge work, CSS would transport the metal. The steel company would still come out way ahead compared to paying millions for the shipment of metal slabs.

The steel company agreed, and CSS shipped 120,000 tons of molten iron over the course of 64 days, gaining a tidy profit, five strong bridges, and one delighted customer. The company's vice president proudly points out that CSS's customer orientation makes everyone a winner.

Sources: "Ladle Car Movement," entry for 1987 Modern Railroads Golden Freight Car award, Chicago South Shore and South Bend Railroad, Chicago, 1987; and interview with Jack Alexander, Vice President, Marketing, and Richard J. Hodor, General Manager of Marketing, Venango River Corporation, Chicago, March 11, 1987.

more than 2,000 miles between Chicago and Los Angeles in fewer than 48 hours.

The industry has seen an increase of mergers. Some analysts have predicted that by 1990 there may be only six to ten major rail systems serving the United States. These remaining railroads should be rich in land, energy, and cash, and may provide serious competition to other forms of freight transportation.[16]

Motor Carriers Because of this country's well-developed highway system, trucks can service any point in the United States. They also rank high in the frequency and dependability of their scheduling. Trucks are often the fastest way of shipping goods over moderate distances because they ship directly, with no intermediate unloading onto another mode of transportation. For these reasons, truck transport is the preferred mode of shipment for machinery, nonperishable food products, and compact goods such as furniture.

But trucks do have some drawbacks. They cannot economically carry bulk goods like steel because of weight load limitations. Also, truck transport is expensive. It can be five times as costly as rail for some heavy goods of little unit value like coal.

The trucking industry has also experienced major changes as a result of deregulation. In 1980, Congress passed the Motor Carrier Act, which loosened the regulatory grip of the ICC on the industry. Truckers may now set their own rates and offer a variety of services.

In the first three years following deregulation, 9,500 new trucking companies were established and massive rate-cutting ensued.[17]

Many truckers feel that future profitability will come from linking their services with other forms of transport to offer shippers an efficient and economical package.

Water Transportation By far, water transportation provides the cheapest way of carrying bulky goods over a long distance. Ocean-going vessels mainly carry oil; inland ships and barges usually transport minerals and agricultural and forestry products.

The one obvious disadvantage of water transportation is that not all buyers and sellers are on a major waterway. Ships also travel very slowly, and their scheduled runs are less frequent than other transportation modes.

A type of ship called LASH (for *L*ighter *A*board *SH*ip) is used to make ocean-going cargo more easily available to inland cities. The ship is loaded with barges that carry the cargo. These cargo-laden barges are unloaded at ocean port cities and sent inland on small rivers and canals. This development, plus increased automation of the loading process, make water transportation an even less expensive mode of transport.[18]

Air Transportation Air transportation is very important to the movement of some products. When speedy delivery over long distances is essential, as it is with perishables like flowers and fruit, airplanes cannot be matched. Goods that require special handling, such as electronic equipment and optical instruments, often go by air as well.

Cost is the major disadvantage of air. It is 20 times more expensive than rail. In addition, not all areas have airports, which limits availability. Furthermore, plane service can easily be disrupted by weather conditions.

Still, air transport appeals to an increasing number of shippers because of cost trade-offs—for example, as noted earlier, they may allow a firm to carry less inventory. Wide-bodied jets like the 747 are making possible the handling of even large, bulky products like tractors. Airlines and air express services that guarantee next day delivery have become increasingly popular, sometimes to the distress of the physical distribution manager whose job it is to control costs.

Pipelines The use of pipelines has increased tremendously since the 1950s. They transport not just oil and gas but ground coal carried in a liquid (called slurry). Dependability and low cost of operation are the main advantages of pipelines.

But pipelines are expensive to build and to maintain. The Alaska pipeline, completed in 1977, cost more than $7 billion to construct. Shipping the product to where it is needed is also a problem. Another drawback is that a pipeline has only one speed—slow. Liquids move through a pipeline at a leisurely three to four miles an hour.

Transportation Rate Structure

Transportation companies are classified by U.S. law into four categories: common carriers, contract carriers, exempt carriers, and private carriers. Some carriers are subject to strict regulation, and some are bound by no laws at all. The amount of government supervision depends on the class of carrier.

Common carriers include all those transport companies that must serve the general public. Most common carriers are airlines and railroads; they include United Air Lines, United Parcel Service, and Burlington Northern. In addition, 55 percent of pipelines, 40 percent of trucking, and 7 percent of shipping are included in the class of common carriers. The government requires that members of this class publish their rates and charge the same fees to all persons requiring transportation service. In addition, they may be restricted to operating within a certain territory.

Common Carrier
Transport company that must serve the general public.

Contract carriers are less regulated because they serve only a limited number of customers, not the general public. They may negotiate different rates with different customers, but they must publicly make known what they charge. The rates and conditions of service are specified in a contract, which usually covers no less than a six-month period. Most contract carriers are truckers. For example, the Campbell Soup Company may contract with a trucking firm to move its canned goods to regional distribution centers.

Contract Carrier
Means of transport that serves only a limited number of customers and may negotiate different rates for different customers.

Exempt carriers include all those forms of transportation that are not subject to direct federal regulation. Most ships are exempt because of a federal law that states that when a ship carries less than four kinds of commodities, it is not bound by federal law. Any carrier that transports unprocessed food products, like fish or vegetables, is also exempt. The exemption means that the government has no control over prices.

Exempt Carrier
Form of transportation not subject to direct federal regulation.

Finally, the class of **private carriers,** which includes all transportation owned by an individual company that is not primarily in the transportation business, is free from federal regulation. The private fleet of trucks owned by Macy's to make deliveries to its customers is an example. Most private carriers are truckers, although a few oil companies own their own pipelines, and some manufacturers own a 15- or 20-mile railroad running between plants.

Private Carrier
Transportation owned by an individual company that is not primarily in the transportation business.

Savings in Transportation

Small manufacturers that cannot afford to own or lease transportation have a serious problem if they do not produce in quantities large enough to warrant a full load. It is expensive to ship by common carrier in less than full truckloads or boxcar loads. Even large manufacturers may have this problem sometimes. But there is a solution.

Freight Forwarder
Company that consolidates small shipments from a number of companies for transport in full loads.

Freight forwarders collect small shipments from a number of companies, consolidate them for transport in full loads, and then see that the goods reach their final destination. They earn a portion of the savings realized by shipping in full loads. Manufacturers benefit because they pay less than they would if they shipped on their own in smaller loads. They are also relieved of most of the required paperwork.

Shippers' Associations
Organizations that serve the same function as freight forwarders, except that they work on a nonprofit basis for members of the same industry.

Shippers' associations serve the same function as freight forwarders, except that they work on a nonprofit basis for members of the same industry. Occasionally, too, some private companies near one another will consolidate loads.

Trends in Transportation

As noted previously, the total physical distribution concept has spurred marketers to think of the whole, rather than the separate parts, of an operation. The major trends in transportation concern achieving more efficiency by combining various modes.

Intermodal Transportation
Coordination of two or more transportation modes to minimize the disadvantages and maximize the strong points of each.

Intermodal transportation refers to the coordinating of two or more transportation modes to minimize the disadvantages and maximize the strong points of each. Several combinations are possible. The three most common are:

1. *Piggyback*—a truck-railroad combination.
2. *Fishyback*—a joining of truck and ship.
3. *Birdyback*—a truck and air service.

Container
Large, standard-size metal box into which goods are placed for shipping and which is sealed.

Though attempts to combine transportation modes were made in the 1920s, intermodal transportation became popular only in the 1960s, when containers were introduced. **Containers** are large, standard-size metal boxes into which goods are placed for shipping and then sealed. They eliminate the need to load and unload individual goods each time merchandise is shifted to a new mode of transport.

Containers save time and money. Consider the savings in a typical fishyback operation, when goods are transferred from ship to truck. It used to take about 200 workers a week's time to unload a large freighter. Today, 20 or 30 dock hands using a crane can unload large containers from a ship in a day's time. Damage to goods as well as loss from theft are minimized because the containers are sealed. Because fewer workers are needed to load and unload containers, unions are resisting the trend toward containerization.[19]

The easy transferability of containers has encouraged the combining of two modes. The combined use of different modes, in turn, has encouraged transportation companies to look into the possibility of owning more than one form of transport. The CSX Corporation, for example, which was formed out of a merger between the Chessie and Seaboard Coast Line railroads, started a trucking company, bought a natural-gas pipeline, acquired a barge company, and has expanded an aircraft-services concern. Such **multimodal companies,** which combine shipping modes, seek to offer shippers global door-to-door service.

Multimodal Shipping Company
Firm that combines shipping modes.

Before 1980, strict government regulation prevented companies from owning several forms of transport. Since the deregulation, however, multimodal companies are on the rise.

The implications of this change are vast. Not only should domestic transportation become more efficient and economical, but world trade should also be enchanced. The railroads should once again flourish as they carry more piggyback traffic. Decreased trucking could save American highways from deterioration, but the diminished revenues from gasoline taxes paid by trucks could pose a problem for state governments dependent on those funds. Cities like Pittsburgh, Detroit, and Cleveland, where all forms of transport converge, may experience an economic revival. Some labor unions, such as the Teamsters and the Longshoremen's Association, may see membership decline as freight is containerized, traffic is handled through fewer ports, and railroads gain business at truckers' expense.[20]

For shippers, however, these changes present great opportunities, both in achieving cost savings and in developing new markets.

Chapter Replay

1. **What activities are involved in physical distribution?**
Physical distribution includes all the activities required to move finished goods along marketing channels. This involves warehousing, inventory control, and transportation.
2. **How do companies use a total physical distribution concept?**
Companies practicing the total physical distribution concept integrate all management functions related to moving products to buyers. The person responsible for these activities is the physical distribution manager. The manager must balance the objective of minimizing costs with the objective of providing customer service.
3. **What are the basic decisions involved in warehousing?**
The physical distribution manager must decide what type of warehouse is appropriate, whether to rent or own the facility, and where the warehouse should be located.
4. **What are the goals of inventory management?**
Inventory managers pursue two goals: to provide an adequate level of customer service by avoiding out-of-stock situations and to minimize the company's investment in inventory.
5. **How do managers decide on the amount of inventory to carry?**
Physical distribution managers use sales forecasts to project how much inventory they will need. They weigh the acquisition costs and

carrying costs to determine an economic order quantity. Besides the stock needed to meet average demand, companies usually also maintain a safety stock.

6. **How do companies keep track of inventory?**
   Companies do physical counts of inventory and also keep perpetual inventory records.
7. **What modes of transportation can the physical distribution manager evaluate?**
   The manager can select from among railroads, motor carriers, water transportation, air transportation, and pipelines.
8. **How can companies that are too small to own or lease transportation transport goods economically?**
   Small manufacturers can use freight forwarders or shippers' associations to cut transportation costs.

Key Terms

ABC analysis
acquisition cost
automated warehouse
carrying cost
common carrier
container
contract carrier
cost trade-off
distribution center warehouse
economic order quantity (EOQ)
exempt carrier
factory-positioned warehouse
freight forwarder
hidden costs
intermediate-positioned warehouse
intermodal transportation
market-positioned warehouse
multimodal shipping company
perpetual inventory
physical count
physical distribution
private carrier
private warehouse
public warehouse
safety stock
shippers' associations
storage warehouse
total physical distribution concept
visible costs

Discussion Questions

1. What decisions are involved in implementing the total physical distribution concept?
2. Which of the following goods would be better kept in a storage warehouse? Which would be better kept in a distribution center warehouse? In each case, explain your answer.
   a. Fresh tomatoes on their way to grocery stores.
   b. Large quantities of tomatoes that have been canned at the end of the summer.

3. Why might a company want to use a private warehouse? What are some advantages of using a public warehouse?
4. Stan Salesperson was exasperated. He just lost an order for 200 desk chairs because the company had only 150 in stock. The customer didn't want to wait for the additional 50 chairs. "We should always keep enough inventory to fill all our orders," complained Stan. "It doesn't seem like we ever have enough for our peak period." Is Stan's complaint legitimate? If not, explain why not. If it is, describe how the company could do a better job of inventory control.
5. Sally Storekeeper runs a shoe store. Every year, she shuts down for a day to take a count of inventory. Besides this physical count, how else can Sally keep track of inventory? What kinds of information can Sally obtain from each technique?
6. Which mode of transportation best meets each of the following requirements?
   a. A steady, dependable supply of natural gas.
   b. Economical delivery of a large load of lumber over a long distance.
   c. Rapid delivery of replacement parts from a company that emphasizes customer service.
   d. Carrying furniture from a warehouse to consumers in the metropolitan area serviced by that warehouse.
7. What is the difference between a common carrier and a contract carrier? Why are common carriers regulated, while private carriers are not?
8. Larry Woodsmith runs a small company that makes dining room tables, which he sells in three states. His company doesn't make enough furniture to warrant a full truckload every time he needs to fill orders. How can Larry afford to ship his tables to his customers?

Case 13.1 Franklin International (C)

Franklin International

The Distribution Division of Franklin has two major roles in the company. One is to handle the distribution of Franklin's products from the manufacturing plant to its markets through its own trucking line and a series of regular and pool location warehouses. After deregulation of the motor carriers industry in the early 1980s, Franklin, which often has less than full truck-load quantities of its own products going to certain locations and little product or raw materials to bring back on the return hauls, established a second role for the division—to operate as a profit center involved in pooling and handling goods for other companies.

Corporation Distribution Services

The following is from the division's definition and mission statement for the corporate distribution services:

The definition of this operational function is to provide distribution expertise for all operating businesses within Franklin International. It is a cost and service departmental entity. Corporate distribution must interface with all operating businesses and staff departments. The distribution function in its true sense is driven by the marketing processes. The distribution process creates value in the economy by acting as a link between supply and demand. Franklin's products have no value unless their customers' demands are fulfilled. The Distribution Department must assist all divisions in satisfying their customers in: Lower Freight Cost; Quality Order Picking and Delivery; Consistent Delivery Performance; and Expedient Tracing Information. All these mentioned customer satisfiers will enhance the marketing efforts of all operating divisions of Franklin.

The functional definition of Corporate Distribution above is the driving force for the mission statement. The Corporate Distribution Services Mission is:

1. *Assist all business operations with distribution expertise.*
2. *Lower their cost per pound for distribution execution.*
3. *Provide consistent quality in order picking and delivery.*
4. *Provide consistent on-time delivery performance.*
5. *Help all operating businesses to open and penetrate new markets.*

Franklin Distribution (Outside Business)

The deregulation of motor carriers in June 1980 by President Carter opened new business opportunities for Franklin Distribution. The key issue for Franklin was how to formulate the business and market it to the shipping public. After much consideration, the business formulation was consummated in September 1980, and Franklin was legally recognized by the Interstate Commerce Commission as a shippers' agent.

As a shippers' agent, Franklin Distribution can consolidate the freight of other companies at the origin or the midpoint terminal location and then deliver the freight off the linehaul trailer either en route or at the delivery points. In March 1981, a subsidiary corporation, FDD, Inc., was formed. The "TOTO" decision by the ICC created new opportunities for companies to obtain for-hire operating authorities for their private-carriage operations. FDD, Inc., became Franklin's private carriage operation and at the same time a licensed motor carrier for backhaul and head-haul movements.

Focal Topics

1. Does Franklin have the proper operating philosophy as to the relationships between physical distribution and other marketing activities? Why, or why not?
2. What criteria and procedures would you recommend that Franklin use to measure the efficiency of the distribution of its products?
3. Discuss the potential advantages and disadvantages to Franklin in having its own trucking operations and the fact that other firms can ship over the system. What appeals would you use to market Franklin's trucking capabilities to outside companies?

Case 13.2
Art's Foods, Inc.

CO

James A. Art made his first potato chip in 1935. It was a difficult time to start a business, but Jim Art was a very determined young man and was willing to work long hours to make a go of it. During World War II, his firm reduced its involvement in the production of potato chips and began to provide food services to military bases in the United States. Following the war, Jim's brother Bob joined the business, and Art's Foods became a corporation. By the early 1980s, both of the original founders had retired and their sons, Jim, Jr., and Wayne, Bob's son, were running the company.

Today the company manufactures and distributes a number of snack foods such as the original potato chips, cheeze curls, popcorn, corn chips, and pretzels. The individual items in the firm's line number 24 in terms of package size and product variations.

Physical Distribution System

The market for Art's Foods covers a four-state area in the Midwest. The company has two food processing plants in different states, each producing about 50 percent of the firm's total product mix. As the snack items are produced and packaged, they are inventoried in warehouses adjacent to the plants. A fleet of company-owned tractor trailers then moves the product from the two plants to 16 company warehouses throughout the four-state marketing area. A complete product mix is inventoried at each warehouse.

Sales to the major retail stores in each of the 16 trading areas are made by Art's Foods route people who drive large panel trucks. The company employs a total of 412 route people. They visit stores on either a twice-weekly or bi-weekly basis. They check the display racks, remove any out-of-date product, bring the inventories up to proper levels, and leave a statement with the retail outlet for the amount of product sold since the last visit. The home office receives a duplicate of the statement, and the retailers are billed monthly for the total of their purchases. Smaller retail accounts in the 16 areas are served by wholesalers who periodically pick up products from an Art's Foods warehouse to stock their own warehouses.

Problem Situations

During the past few years, Art's distribution costs have outstripped price increases. Transportation costs, for example, increased 8 percent in 1987, while warehousing costs were up 7 percent. Competition in the snack food area has greatly increased in recent years, and retailers are constantly making decisions about which brands to add and which to drop. Given limited space, retailers are interested in maximizing product margins and inventory turnover.

Exhibit
Selected Customer Information

	1987	1986	1985	1984	1983
Reported Stockouts (Percentage per 1,000 items)	129.7	118.6	98.2	90.1	86.4
Overall Quality of Service[a]	2.52	2.29	2.10	1.85	1.82
Compared to Competition[a]	2.81	2.68	2.51	2.39	2.31
Number of Accounts					
Beginning of Year	43,021	44,506	43,182	42,712	41,342
Accounts Added	2,812	2,980	4,829	3,718	3,812
Accounts Dropped	4,516	4,465	3,505	3,248	2,442
End of Year	41,317	43,021	44,506	43,182	42,712

[a]For rating scale, see text.

While Art's sales have continued to increase 3 to 4 percent during each of the past five years, actual profits have remained about steady—that is, until 1987, when profits dropped 5 percent. Jim, Jr., and Wayne were obviously concerned and called a special meeting to review the trends and the facts that had been assembled.

The Exhibit shows that selected measures of customer service have deteriorated in recent years. Overall quality of service is measured by an annual retailer survey that asks respondents to rate Art's on a 5-point scale (1 = very satisfactory, 2 = satisfactory, 3 = neutral, 4 = unsatisfactory, 5 = very unsatisfactory). The comparison dimension involves asking retailers if Art's service is much better (1), better (2), about the same (3), worse (4), or much worse (5) than other snack food suppliers. Stockouts represent the number of telephone calls made by retailers to Art's warehouses indicating that one or more of the firm's products were out of stock.

When questioned about the problems, Phil Packard, manager of physical distribution, explained that operating expenses, especially warehouse costs, had significantly increased during the past five years and that he had attempted to compensate by shifting more of the inventory to the two lower-cost, larger warehouses adjacent to the manufacturing plants. This led to more stockout problems at the regional warehouses. Emergency shipments then had to be made between the various warehouses or from the two central warehouses. The net result was even greater transportation costs. He said he was working on a solution. Jim, Jr., and Wayne Art both said they certainly hoped so.

Focal Topics

The distribution problems are obviously related and did not occur overnight. For each of the following areas, what do you think Art's Foods could do, what do you recommend they do, and why?

1. Reduce total transportation costs.
2. Reduce total warehousing costs.
3. Improve overall customer service levels.

Case for Part Four

Drug Emporium

"Drug Emporium—a franchise that continues to grow because the climate is right." This statement provides the introduction to materials for people interested in obtaining a Drug Emporium franchise.

The materials go on to state, "By climate we simply mean this—when you visit any one of our Drug Emporium stores, you'll feel the enthusiasm of the store personnel. You'll sense the professional training of the management in their winning attitude. One glance down the wide, well-stocked aisles will tell you a great deal about the merchandising, know-how, and planning inherent to the franchise. Most important—only Drug Emporium offers the consumer such a tremendous assortment of quality products at *Prices So Low They Need a Shopping Cart.*"

Company Formation

In 1977, Philip Wilber founded Drug Emporium. Wilber, previously a vice president at Lane Drug Company, elected to go against conventional wisdom, which proposed that drugstores could only make money by selling products at high gross margins. He decided to operate relatively huge stores—25,000 square feet—and cut gross margins to around 20 percent, compared to the 30–35 percent margins of traditional drugstores. This allowed him to offer consumers prices that were frequently as much as 30 percent lower than competitors'.

By mid-1986, this strategy placed Drug Emporium in 24th place (up from 50th place in 1985) on *Venture* magazine's list of fast-track companies. At that time, the firm had 27 corporate stores, 16 joint venture stores, and 50 franchised stores.

Deep Discounting

Drug Emporium is part of one of the fastest-growing retailing concepts in the United States today—deep discounting. The concept began with food and is rapidly spreading to all product categories of retailing. Management Horizons, a retailing consulting firm, predicts that deep-discount drugstores will capture 4 to 5 percent of the market by 1990, with annual sales of around $3 billion.

The typical deep-discount drugstore occupies 20,000 to 30,000 square feet and can reach $12 million in annual sales at maturity, which is about eight times the volume of an average drugstore. Successful

Source: This material has been adapted from information provided by the Drug Emporium. Logo courtesy of the Drug Emporium.

drugstore discounters can usually reach breakeven sales (typically $3 to $5 million) within 12 to 18 months, with average margins of 16 to 20 percent.

Drug Emporium Operations

Drug Emporium stores purchase directly from an average of 500 vendors. Each store makes its own purchasing arrangements and attempts to buy 80 to 85 percent of merchandise on sale. The pricing strategy is to apply an 18 percent margin against its net cost on all items (reflecting all manufacturers' deals, display allowances, and volume discounts). When a manufacturer's deal is not available on a regularly represented brand and an order is necessary to maintain continuity, the product will be purchased at regular cost but will carry an 18 percent margin over net cost.

This overall pricing strategy allows Drug Emporium to offer discounts of 10 to 50 percent of the manufacturer's suggested retail price. No item is sold at a loss, so a profit is made on each sale.

Health and beauty aids account for around 45 percent of total store sales, while the pharmacy contributes 25 percent and cosmetics add 20 percent. The remaining 10 percent comes from categories such as pet supplies, household products, food and snacks, and greeting cards.

Compared to an average drugstore's 1,225 prescriptions per week, a Drug Emporium pharmacy will fill as many as 3,000. Like most other deep-discount drugstores, Drug Emporiums do not accept welfare or Medicare plans, nor do they offer senior citizen discounts.

Other operating characteristics include:

- An average inventory of $1.5 to $1.8 million.
- Inventory turns of 6 to 7 times per year.
- A population base of 100,000 people within a five-mile radius of the store.
- A policy of accepting only cash or checks for purchases; credit cards are not accepted.
- A policy of accepting manufacturers' coupons.
- An average sales per customer visit ranging from $10 to $16.

Franchising

The objective is to maintain a 50-50 balance between stores in which the company is the complete or partial owner and franchise stores.

Wilber says that the two greatest problems they have had with franchisees are violations of the chain's pricing strategy and problems with the product mix. In some ways, the firm has found it easier to work with franchisees who do not have a drugstore retailing background. According to Wilber, "There's less for them to unlearn."

Focal Topics

1. What do you see as the basic reasons for Drug Emporium's success?
2. Discuss the relative advantages and disadvantages of franchising from the perspective of Drug Emporium and that of a franchisee.
3. Do you think Drug Emporium should continue its strategy of having each store order its own merchandise directly rather than group buying and warehousing? Why, or why not?
4. What recommendations would you suggest for Drug Emporium concerning its other operating strategies?
5. What do you see as the future for Drug Emporium? Why?

For minor cuts and scrapes send for first aid.
You can't send for a doctor every time you get a little scratch or boo-boo. But you can send for help.
Just buy a specially marked box of Borateem® Bleach or 20 Mule Team® Borax. Then cut off the top and send it to us with $7.00 plus $1.50 for shipping and handling. In return, we'll send you a Johnson & Johnson First Aid Kit.
Consider it a house call from the 20 Mule Team.®
BORAX

Part Five

Promotion Strategy

Marketing Communication: The Promotional Mix

Sounding Out the Chapter

In this chapter, you will learn:

1. The activities involved in promotion of a company's product.
2. How communication occurs.
3. Some sources of misunderstanding in the communication process.
4. Advantages of communication through advertising.
5. The major advantage and disadvantage of personal selling.
6. Some functions of packaging.
7. Types of promotional strategies.
8. How marketers budget for promotion.
9. How marketers measure the effectiveness of a promotional campaign.

Source: Photo © 1987 Phyllis Woloshin.

The Power of the Package

If you never thought that packages could help sell the products inside them, consider the last time you went to the grocery store to pick up a loaf of bread. If you're like many shoppers, you left with more than bread. According to recent studies, more than two-thirds of buying decisions are made in the store—where they presumably are influenced by packaging.

While such impulse buying may sound ideal for the makers of those products, they have run into a problem. With so much effective packaging competing for your attention, marketers have to keep coming up with more attractive ideas.

One way they are doing this is by appealing to consumers' desire for convenience. For food products, this often means food that can be cooked or reheated in a microwave oven. Increasingly, makers of frozen dinners and entrees are switching from aluminum trays to microwavable plastic plates. Campbell, for example, is testing soup packaged in a plastic bowl ready to heat and serve.

Consumers are also seeing an increasing number of squeezable plastic containers. Such containers are used for a variety of products, including ketchup, barbecue sauce, jelly, mayonnaise, and salad dressings. The squeezable containers are not only convenient, they are safer to handle than glass jars. Before introducing jelly in these containers, Welch Foods conducted research and learned that many consumers were willing to pay a little extra for jams and jellies sold in plastic containers.

Milk outside refrigerated dairy cases may become another common sight. Packaging in aseptic cartons keeps milk fresh for up to three months. The challenge to marketers is to convince shoppers that this milk is the real thing, not a synthetic or watered-down product. Dairymen Inc., of Louisville, Kentucky, addressed this potential problem for its Farm Best milk with a design suggesting freshness. The carton features the Farm Best logo framing a quiet country scene. A banner labels the milk "freshly packed."

The job of convincing a shopper to buy a product typically ends with the packaging. But before that, marketers use a variety of other methods to convince people to buy a good, a service, or an idea. This chapter provides an overview of the activities involved.

Sources: Kate Bertrand, "The 6 Hottest Trends in Food Packaging," *Packaging,* January 1986, pp. 24–30, 32; Nancy L. Croft, "Wrapping Up Sales," *Nation's Business,* October 1985, pp. 41–42; Lori Kesler, "Successful Packages Turn Medium into Message," *Advertising Age,* October 13, 1986, pp. S-2–S-3; and Herbert M. Meyers, "Package Design," *Art Product News,* July/August 1986, pp. 30+.

Promotion As Communication

It is a mistake to assume that promotion is the same as advertising. While advertising is one of the most important—and perhaps the most visible—elements of a promotional strategy, it is hardly the only one. Consider these examples:

- Shortly after *Return of the Jedi* opened in movie theaters across the country, Burger King offered customers drinking glasses emblazoned with scenes from the film with every purchase of Coke. Burger King's intent was not to advertise the movie, but to sell soft drinks and hamburgers to accompany them. The glasses were a device in a strategy known as *sales promotion.*
- When Arby's Roast Beef restaurant reopened its renovated Fifth Avenue store in Pittsburgh, it celebrated by building a roast beef sandwich five feet in diameter and donating a portion of the day's roast beef sandwich sales to Children's Hospital of Pittsburgh. Pictures were in all the papers. Arby's promotional strategy was to garner free media attention through another form of promotion known as *publicity.*
- On Washington's Birthday, traditionally the biggest car selling day of the year, a stylishly dressed young couple stop to admire a new Nissan 300 ZX prominently displayed in a dealer's parking lot. As they examine the various options listed on the window sticker, a salesman ambles over. "Want to take it for a spin?" he asks. *Personal selling* is another element of the promotional mix.
- You tell your roommate that you're going to make lasagne for dinner, but when you get to the store, you realize that you're not sure exactly what goes into it. But printed on one of the boxes of lasagne noodles is a recipe that looks good and pretty simple to make. So you buy that brand of pasta even though it costs seven cents more. Since *packaging* is often called on to sell a product directly from the shelf, it is frequently included among the elements of the promotional mix.

Promotion
Marketing communication that attempts to inform and remind individuals and persuade them to accept, resell, recommend, or use a product, service, idea, or institution.

Together these methods—advertising, sales promotion, publicity, personal selling, and packaging—make up the part of the marketing mix known as **promotion.** Promotion is that marketing communications activity that attempts to inform and remind individuals and persuade them to accept, resell, recommend, or use a product, service, idea, or institution. Three points may be made about this definition.

First, promotional communication has a triple purpose: to inform, remind, and persuade. Most people do not object to the informational content of promotion because it serves to spread the word quickly about innovations. Consider how long it would have taken consumers to become aware of the availability of videocassette recorders without promotion. Similarly, most people welcome occasional reminders about products that they are already familiar with. Jell-O has been around for years, but homemakers like to see magazine ads for the product with new recipe suggestions.

The persuasive aspect of promotion, however, has been the subject of some criticism. Some would argue that such promotional messages manipulate people to want what they do not have, usually through emotional appeals. But not all persuasion is manipulative. Few would object to an ad that tried to sell a car by an appeal to its sporty looks or to a clerk's compliment on how fine one looks in a new pair of shoes. Compliments and phrases like "sporty looks" are persuasive, not informational, messages. Most marketers believe persuasion is a valid communication technique.

A second point is that not all of promotion is directed to the ultimate consumer. Some is addressed to manufacturers or institutions, some to intermediaries who specialize in resale, and some to opinion leaders who are in a position to recommend usage. Each of these markets requires a different message to be effective. A consumer may be impressed by no-drip bottles of maple syrup, but a supermarket manager is likely to be more interested in ease of shelving or amount of profit to be made on the product.

Finally, the definition implies that promotion is a useful tool for both profit and nonprofit organizations. Although promotion is often used to sell a product or service, it is being increasingly accepted in the marketing of political candidates, government institutions, and ideas. The "I Love New York" campaign has made extensive use of promotion to help stimulate tourism. The Advertising Council runs advertisements with the messages "Cocaine. The big lie" and "Just Say 'No' to Drugs" to sell the idea of staying away from drugs.

Developing Effective Promotional Communication

The one thing that all of the examples cited above have in common is that they attempt to communicate, that is, to transmit information. A marketing communication is a more specific form of information transmittal. It is one in which a seller attempts to transmit information to a buyer. At Your Service 14.1 describes some efforts of law offices to use promotional communication.

Promotion is not the only element of the marketing mix that communicates information. A product's design may convey a quality or a bargain-basement image. A price is set to reinforce the image. An exclusive or intensive distribution strategy further underlines the product quality message. Why, then, is there a need for one branch of marketing—promotion—to specialize in communication? The answer is that promotion is needed to make explicit what the other elements of the marketing mix only imply. The slogan "The quality goes in before the name goes on," featured in Zenith's advertising messages, makes consumers aware of the television's technical excellence, which they might otherwise have missed.

But communication only works if the receiver of the information (in this case, the potential buyer) *understands* what the sender (for our purposes, the seller) is trying to say. That may not seem like a particularly dramatic revelation, but consider an example.

At Your Service 14.1
Promotion Comes to the Legal World

Lawyers have been subject to legal constraints concerning how they may legally promote their firms. Typically, a lawyer would promote the firm with a soft-sell on the golf course or over a meal at the local club. But since 1977, when the Supreme Court barred states from prohibiting lawyer advertising, law firms have broadened their efforts. Economic pressures have recently quickened the pace of innovation.

Popular promotional techniques include glossy brochures and newsletters on legal developments. One firm even produced a hardcover book, *Conversations with McGuire, Woods & Battle,* which contains four chapters of "actual conversations" with partners of the Richmond, Virginia, firm. In Cleveland, Jones Day Reavis & Pogue distributes newsletters on videocassettes.

Only a few law firms advertise on television and in newspapers, but the numbers of such advertisers are growing rapidly. Observes law professor Stephen Gillers, direct selling "is the next marketing frontier."

As lawyers find their way in the marketing frontier, some errors in judgment are bound to occur. For example, a Providence, Rhode Island, firm tried to make a splash using a glossy brochure with a difference. Besides the usual photographs of the partners and the law library was a picture of two voluptuous nude women lounging in an empty bathtub.

You might wonder what this has to do with the legal profession. The caption tries to make a connection: "Like a bathtub, trial lawyers have to fill up on the facts and the law of a case. . . ."

Little wonder, then, that many law firms are turning to specialized consultants for help in planning their promotional activities.

Source: Patricia Bellew Gray, "More Lawyers Reluctantly Adopt Strange New Practice—Marketing," *The Wall Street Journal,* January 30, 1987, p. 19.

In the late 1970s, Anheuser-Busch tried to market a nonalcoholic adult soft drink called Chelsea that would provide a "socially acceptable substitute for alcohol." The product looked and was packaged like beer, although it contained less than one-half of one percent alcohol. Chelsea's advertising proclaimed it "the not-so-soft drink." Instead of understanding the slogan to mean a nonalcoholic beverage designed for adult tastes, neoprohibitionists saw the drink as "a pernicious attempt to predispose children toward beer drinking." After a storm of negative publicity and boycotts, Anheuser-Busch withdrew Chelsea from its test markets.[1]

Transmitting information is not always as simple as it may seem. For a communication to be effective, it must:

1. Gain the attention of the receiver.
2. Be understood by both the receiver and the sender.
3. Stimulate the needs of the receiver and suggest an appropriate method of satisfying those needs.[2]

How Communication Works

Many theorists have concluded that promotional communications, like all forms of communication, can take place because an orderly way of transmitting a message, similar to a telephone circuit, exists.[3] A simplified

Figure 14.1
Model of the Communication Process

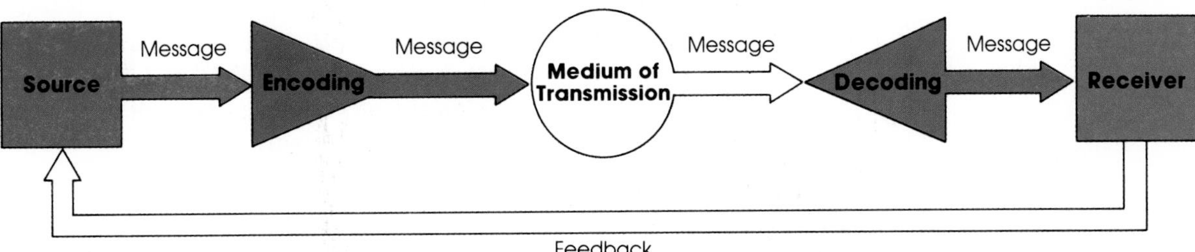

model of how communication occurs is shown in Figure 14.1. The basic elements of this communication circuit are: (1) the **source,** or originator of the message; (2) the **receiver,** the ultimate destination of the message; and (3) the **medium of transmission,** the means by which the message moves from sender to receiver. Some very important processes must occur, however, for the message to be understood. The message must be **encoded,** or put into understandable form by the source. At the opposite end, the receiver must **decode,** or retranslate the message into understandable terms. Finally, the receiver must signal the understanding by **feedback** to the source.

Source
Originator of a message.

Receiver
Ultimate destination of a message.

Medium of Transmission
Means by which a message moves from sender to receiver.

Encoding
Putting a message into understandable form by the source.

Decoding
Retranslating a message into terms the receiver understands.

Feedback
Understanding signaled by the receiver to the source.

Some Complications

The message may not be understood at all, or it may be understood in a way quite different from that intended. Recall the party game in which a group of people sit in a circle. The first person whispers a message ("Savvy businessmen wear blue suits") to the person sitting next to the first person. The game continues until the last receiver announces the message heard ("Your grandmother wears combat boots"). The garbled message usually bears little resemblance to the original. Many firms have had similar experiences. The message originally sent is unrecognizable by the time the consumer receives it. Many factors can complicate the communication model.

Source Effect Sometimes the reputation of the source affects the way a message is received. This phenomenon is known as the **source effect.** For example, one study of the effect of consumer knowledge of brands showed that if a company does not market the leading brand, it really does have to try harder to get a favorable sales response from its ads. Ad copy was prepared for three brands, two of them market leaders and the other relatively unknown. When the ad copy did not identify the brands, selected consumers judged the ads equally effective in motivating them to buy. When brand names were mentioned in the copy, however, the advertising effectiveness of the least-known brand dropped noticeably.[4]

Source Effect
Distortion of a communication resulting from the reputation of the source of a message.

The source effect impeded the unknown brand's message, but it also helped the leading brands to communicate their strengths. Using the credibility of the sender to add persuasiveness to the message is a common marketing strategy. Salespeople use their company's name, if it is well known, to gain access to buyers. And TV ads for products often lean on the credibility of people who appear in them. Candid interviews with homemakers discussing the merits of various laundry detergents are thought to be more believable than a company spokesperson touting the benefits of a brand.

Multiple Transmitters Many mistake the words of a message, whether spoken or in print, for the whole message. In fact, most messages are transmitted through more than words. Sales representatives, for example, are often very much aware of their body language. Posture, facial expression, and tone of voice can heighten a presentation or torpedo it.

Multiple transmitters also exist in print communications. The layout of an advertisement often conveys as much as the words. A discount store's ads are likely to be cluttered with notices of bargains, whereas an exclusive department store's ads may feature few words and much white space. (See page 375.) Both approaches are effective in underlining the message. The first conveys the excitement of a sale, the second the elegance associated with quality goods.

Decoding Errors Receivers do not always get the message that a source sends out. A classic example is the angry response that a Xerox television commercial aroused. The commercial showed a chimpanzee running off copies on a new machine and delivering them to the boss. The intended message was the machine's simplicity of operation. What some viewers saw—especially secretaries and reproduction clerks—was a put-down of their jobs. Xerox withdrew the advertisement.

Many decoding errors arise from selective perception and interpretation. People often see or hear only what they want. But another related problem is **noise,** interference that is either deliberately or accidentally introduced and blocks or distorts transmissions. There are three types of noise:[5]

Noise
Interference that is either deliberately or accidentally introduced and blocks or distorts transmissions.

1. Internal noise is the kind that characterizes the message itself. A message transmitted in a vocabulary unknown to the receiver creates such noise. Marketing Today 14.1 describes how one company overcame a problem with internal noise.
2. External noise is introduced accidentally from outside the communication process. Commercials telecast to viewers in barrooms have little chance of being heard.
3. Competitive noise is deliberately introduced by another source to gain a competitive advantage. A maker of bubble gum at one time attempted to break into the East Coast market by conducting a large ad campaign. Almost as soon as the gum was introduced, however, rumors spread among youngsters in the area that the gum contained spider eggs or caused cancer. The suspicion was that the product's competitors had started the rumor.[6]

Marketing Today 14.1
A Novel Marketing Technique

Creative Output faced a difficult hurdle in promoting its manufacturing-scheduling software. The software, called Optimized Production Technology (OPT), had a number of competitors, was a complicated product, and met with suspicion because it handled a common problem in an unusual way. The company would send representatives into the factory to guide users, but as soon as the reps left, the users would revert to their former way of scheduling. And the software therefore failed to live up to its promise.

So Eli Goldratt, head of Creative Output, looked for an inexpensive, attention-getting way to explain and sell his product. His solution was to write a steamy novel, a manufacturing romance titled *The Goal, Excellence in Manufacturing.* The book tells the story of Alex Rogo, a division manager for UniCo, whose plant and marriage are both about to fold. Thanks to the OPT-style advice of an old college professor, Alex manages to placate his boss and hold onto his wife.

The novel was a smashing success. Visitors to trade shows snapped it up, trade magazines serialized it, and Waldenbooks carried it. Following up on the success of the novel, Creative Output introduced a computer game using the principles of OPT. As a result of the novel and the game, potential clients are telling each other about OPT and Creative Output, and the business is rolling in. Says Goldratt, "We almost don't have to do any selling. The client is calling us before we have the chance to call him."

Source: Craig R. Waters, "One of a Kind," *Inc.*, July 1986, pp. 107–108.

Inadequate Feedback Lack of sufficient feedback to the source can stand in the way of future communications. Political candidates routinely spend thousands of dollars on polls during the course of their campaigns to determine how they are doing with various segments of the population. Inadequate feedback presents great difficulties for advertising executives. As John Wanamaker, a famous department store founder, once lamented, "Half my advertising dollars are wasted; I just don't know which half."

Elements of the Promotional Mix

In review, the major types of promotional activity are advertising, personal selling, sales promotion, publicity, and packaging. Most organizations tend to rely on either advertising or personal selling to carry most of their message and use the other tools as supplements. As forms of communication, all have important points in common. Before considering similarities, it is important to distinguish how they differ from one another. Chapters 15 and 16 discuss the various forms of promotion in more detail.

Advertising

Advertising
Any paid form of nonpersonal presentation and promotion of ideas, goods, or services by an identified sponsor.

The American Marketing Association defines **advertising** as "any paid form of nonpersonal presentation and promotion of ideas, goods, or services by an identified sponsor."[7] The key words are "nonpersonal" and "paid by an identified sponsor." Instead of communicating with customers face to face, companies that advertise ordinarily use a mass medium —television, newspapers, radio, billboards, or other well-known means of communication. When ads appear in media with editorial or program content, they are set off and clearly identified as messages paid for by a sponsor.

The cost of advertising varies by medium, but it is one of the cheapest ways to reach people. For example, at $1.1 million a minute in 1986, a television advertisement during the Super Bowl might sound expensive. But consider that those advertisements were expected to reach nearly half of the United States.[8] The cost of reaching each viewer was actually relatively small.

Efficiency is not the only advantage of advertising. Advertising captures attention because it is often quite creative. Some even claim that they enjoy ad messages more than the programs and articles that accompany them. A television commercial for the California Raisin Advisory Board features a conga line of sneaker-wearing animated raisins singing and dancing to "I Heard It through the Grapevine." On Halloween of the year the commercials hit the screen, the "in" costume was the raisin outfit. The ad was so popular that people even wrote in to say it had persuaded them to buy raisins.[9]

Another advantage of advertising is that it allows perfect reproduction of the desired message.[10] No intermediary, such as a salesperson, stands between the promoter and the potential customer to garble the message. Of course, in another way, this advantage can turn into a disadvantage. Without the personal touch, a consumer's attention can wander and the message may be lost. The advantages of advertising apparently far outweigh the disadvantages, however. Advertising expenditures in 1984 exceeded $88 billion.[11]

Personal Selling

According to the Department of Labor, about 6 percent of American workers, or about 6 million people, are engaged in sales occupations that range from the selling of encyclopedias door-to-door to the selling of computer systems to agencies of the United States government. Selling, unlike advertising, involves a one-to-one relationship with a customer. **Personal selling** is the oral presentation of a tangible or intangible product by a seller to a prospect for the purpose of completing an exchange.

Personal Selling
Oral presentation of a tangible or intangible product to a prospect for the purpose of completing an exchange.

The obvious advantage of a direct oral presentation is that it allows the salesperson to judge the reaction of customers to the sales talk. By gauging the response, the salesperson can tailor the message to the customer's needs. The price of this custom fitting is expensive, however. The average cost of a sales call on a consumer has risen to more than $100, and the average cost of a call in the industrial market to more than $150.[12] In terms of the number of people reached, this is vastly more expensive than an advertisement that costs a half-million dollars but reaches millions of potential buyers. However, since products requiring a personal sales effort are usually more expensive than those that depend on advertising, the extra cost of selling may be worthwhile.

Publicity

In November 1983, ABC-TV aired a controversial television film, "The Day After." The actual screening of the movie was almost anticlimactic. For months prior to the telecast, ABC had been building an enormous publicity campaign about the program. Taped copies were leaked into circulation and were being screened for nuclear freeze sympathizers as early as the previous July. As its air date approached, "The Day After" was being discussed on every newscast, morning talk show, and newspaper in this country—and a fair share of those abroad.[13]

Following the broadcast, ABC ran a special edition of "Viewpoint," anchored by Ted Koppel, in which notable public figures were called on to respond to issues raised in the TV movie.[14]

The network had scheduled the movie during a "sweeps week," a time when the A. C. Nielsen Company carefully monitors audience viewing habits. The network that leads in the Nielsen rating can then charge advertisers the highest prices. Despite some compelling programming on the other networks, ABC's strategy paid off. "The Day After" was watched by 100 million, making it the highest-rated made-for-TV movie.[15]

ABC's promotional efforts were a form of **publicity,** "any information relating to a manufacturer or its products that appears in any medium on a nonpaid basis."[16] This definition distinguishes publicity from advertising, which is paid for and clearly set off from news in the media. Publicity has two chief advantages over advertising. It is believable, because it appears as news rather than as a commercial message. It also costs comparatively little; the chief cost is the salaries of publicists. However, firms cannot control publicity in the same way they can control paid advertisements.

Publicity
Any information relating to a manufacturer or its products that appears in any medium on a nonpaid basis.

Publicity is only one part of a much larger task called **public relations,** which attempts to generate a favorable attitude toward a company among employees, stockholders, suppliers, the government, and customers. When a bank contributes heavily to the United Way, sponsors a showing of local art, or allows employees to donate some of their work time to community service, it has these publics in mind. Public relations, which also includes activities such as institutional advertising (see Figure 14.2) and corporate contributions to the community, is business's recognition of the necessity of maintaining a favorable public image.

Public Relations
Activities that attempt to generate a favorable attitude toward a company among employees, stockholders, suppliers, and the government, as well as among customers.

Sales Promotion

All the other promotional activities of a firm that stimulate consumer purchases or aid dealer effectiveness fall into the category of **sales promotion.** Coupons, music videos, free glasses, publishers' sweepstakes,

Sales Promotion
Promotional activities besides selling, advertising, and publicity that stimulate purchases or aid dealer effectiveness.

You're part of America's Hospitality Industry...
taking care of millions of Americans every day.

UNSUNG
HEROES!
People count on you being there when they need you. And you always are! You're a big part of what makes our world special!
OURS IS A SPECIAL WORLD!
AMERICA'S HOSPITALITY INDUSTRY
"Ours Is A Special World!" and "America's Hospitality Industry" are service marks of the National Restaurant Association and used by related hospitality associations.

and cosmetic demonstrations are just a few examples of the many forms that sales promotion may take.

The total expenditure for sales promotion in 1982, $58.1 billion, topped that for advertising. In the 1980s sales promotion activity increased markedly in importance because it was necessary to stimulate consumer buying in a sluggish economy. Sales promotion techniques are effective in doing this because they are extremely visible, often appeal to the "something for nothing" instincts in people, and usually bring about an immediate buying response. One sales promotion executive noted, "When you want awareness, you advertise. When you want immediate action, you promote."[17] Sales promotion can also be used to stimulate dealer interest. The main drawback of sales promotion techniques is that competitors tend to copy them, canceling their effectiveness.

Packaging

Packaging has become increasingly important as a promotional tool. When there is no advertising budget, a package sometimes must bear the weight of the entire promotional message.

As many marketers have discovered, the importance of packaging cannot be overestimated. Think of some of the world's great packages: the original Coke bottle, the Whitman's Sampler, or the cylindrical Quaker Oats box. Consider, too, how different the perception of a product would be if, for example, an expensive perfume came packaged in a milk carton or if a gift of Valentine candies arrived in a shabby brown box.

Marketers are so concerned with packaging that it has become a $50 billion-a-year industry in the United States. Innovations in packaging are, in fact, responsible for the success of some products. Marlboro cigarettes introduced its flip-top box in 1954, and its sales jumped from 0.3 billion cigarettes to 14.3 billion in two years' time. The advent of the aerosol can gave birth to a whole industry—hair sprays.[18] At the beginning of this chapter, you read about some more recent innovations.

The Functions of Packaging Fifty years ago, the main function of packaging was to provide a means of transport for a product between a neighborhood store and the home. Grocers scooped sugar into brown paper sacks and barkeepers filled a bucket with beer. A packaging revolution has occurred since then. Today, packages are expected to perform many functions. These include:

1. *Packages offer protection to the product and consumer.* Egg cartons, plastic wrap around record albums, and dark green wine bottles are exam-

Figure 14.2
An Institutional Advertisement for the Hospitality Industry
Source: Courtesy of the National Restaurant Association.

ples of packages that serve primarily to protect products from damage and spoilage.

In addition to protecting the product, some packages protect the consumer. One reason shampoo is sold in plastic rather than glass bottles is to avoid broken bottles in bathrooms. Manufacturers have been using increasingly sophisticated packaging to reduce the likelihood that products will be tampered with or sampled. Typical safeguards include tamper-rings on jars of nuts, heat-shrink neck bands on aspirin bottles, and shrink wrapping around ice cream cartons. One expert has suggested using hologram seals on bottles. These seals would be hard for a would-be tamperer to duplicate, and they would look unusual enough for consumers to notice whether they were there.[19]

2. *Packages increase the use of the product.* Marketers want consumers not just to try a product, but to continue to use it in greater quantities. Packaging can help. Through colorful packaging in differently shaped boxes, the makers of facial tissues have expanded use of their products from the bedroom or bathroom into other rooms of the house.
3. *Packages increase sales by adding a reuse value.* A number of packages are designed to allow package reuse for other purposes. Margarines are now sold in plastic tubs that serve as containers for leftovers when the contents are used up. Avon Products is a master at such packaging. Recent catalog offerings included bubble bath for children in an E.T. bath decanter, compass-shaped soap in a fancy tin box, and eggnog-flavored gum in a plastic gum holder.
4. *Packages promote the product.* A recent trend is toward self-service in retail stores. Discount and variety stores offer sales help only when requested, and supermarkets do not offer sales personnel. Products must sell themselves—an increasingly difficult task. This role of packaging is so important that many marketers conduct tests of packaging in an attempt to determine whether the packaging helps sales of the product. The tests consider what the package "says" about the product and how it can do it, given the selling environment—the store and the product's competition.[20]

A skillfully designed package will reinforce the information a consumer has already absorbed about the product through advertising, sales promotion, or publicity.

In some cases, packaging alone can change the way consumers feel about a product. Hanes, for example, managed by the clever packaging of L'Eggs panty hose to reverse a long-standing impression that all hosiery sold in supermarkets was of inferior quality. The egg-shaped L'Eggs package elicited perceptions of a fragile yet protected product. It also connoted fashion and sex appeal. Backed by a skillful advertising campaign, L'Eggs became the first supermarket panty hose success story.[21]

Packages might also provide a variety of other benefits:

☐ *Informing consumers about product benefits*—The package for a roll of Scotch transparent tape reads, "Stays Clear!"

- ☐ *Offering suggestions or recipes*—Boxes of Chex cereals often carry a recipe for Party Mix, a snack made with those cereals. Packaging for adjustable pliers, such as Vise Grips, might show various possible uses for this tool.
- ☐ *Announcing special value*—Two cassette tapes might be wrapped in a package labeled, "Buy Two, Get One FREE!"
- ☐ *Selling other items in the same line*—For example, some books contain a list of other books written by the same author. A box of Great Crisps! crackers shows a picture of the different flavors available.
- ☐ *Assuring protection*—Many medicine packages contain a label such as "safety sealed for your protection."
- ☐ *Highlighting special product features*—An example is toothpaste in a box labeled "Maximum Fluoride Protection."

Package Design For a package to serve many functions, it must be well designed. The task is more difficult than it may seem. Packaging is fairly standard for given types of products. All toothpaste comes in a tube, and all salt in a cylindrical box. How, then, can a package designer of a particular brand of toothpaste or salt distinguish one company's products from others on the same shelf?

Color One way is to use color effectively. Psychologists have shown that people react to certain colors in predictable ways. For impulse items, red is an effective color because it motivates people to act. As makers of expensive chocolates have discovered, gold and silver are good choices for an elegant specialty good. Men seem to buy anything that is packaged in brown, including cosmetics, perhaps because it evokes outdoor images.[22] When the Campbell Soup Company introduced Le Menu gourmet frozen dinners, it was careful to package the product in a contemporary-looking, sandstone-colored box. The company's goal was to eliminate the 1950s image associated with TV dinners.

Style Style can also serve to individualize packages. Two different styles are currently in vogue: one frequently dubbed "American Country" and the other a sleek, contemporary look.

The design of some natural cereals, picturing scenes of nineteenth-century rural America on box panels, conveys a nostalgic feeling. On the other hand, products such as Avon's *Odyssey* fragrance collection are packaged in a vertical, sculptured bottle. Avon designed it specifically for "women of the '80s [who] approach life as an adventure, journeying into new and unexplored places, propelled by an inner energy."[23]

Copy Package copy—both words and pictures—can also help distinguish a product from its competitors. In one survey, brand names were removed from packages, and people were asked to identify the product. The words "squeezably soft" on one package alerted 97 percent of those surveyed that the product was Charmin tissue. Mr. Clean's bald head and gold earring won recognition from 68 percent of those tested.[24]

Form Some variation in package form within a product category is acceptable, but not very much. When Ipana toothpaste came out with an aerosol dispenser a few years ago, it failed to catch on. Retailers resist odd shapes and sizes as much as consumers. They object to packages that take too much space, topple over, or cannot be conveniently stacked. Clearly, the requirement that packages be both attention-getting and functional puts a heavy burden on designers.

Packaging is much too critical a promotional device to be treated casually. As more and more marketers wake up to the importance of packaging, the industry has mushroomed into a multibillion-dollar business. While the development of new products accounts for a significant portion of this figure, marketers of established brands account for twice the business of new items.[25]

Promotional Objectives and Strategies

The various elements of the promotional mix have the same objectives as all other marketing activities: to bring about an exchange. But an exchange may not always be a sale. Marketers may wish to influence viewing habits ("Watch CNN"), choice of vacation sites ("Discover Alaska"), or fondness for political candidates. They may also wish to promote an idea—even if it seems contradictory to their goal of selling a product.

Less than a year after the repeal of Prohibition, Jos. E. Seagram & Sons launched an advertising campaign with copy that began, "We who make whiskey say: 'Drink Moderately.'" Since then, Seagram's has continued to promote moderation in drinking and has led the way among distillers in urging its customers not to drive if they have been drinking.[26]

The broader goal of promotion, then, may be to communicate between a producer and a public. Frequently, communication is meant to elicit an immediate and traditional exchange—a sale; at other times the goal may be more oblique—to create a favorable impression of a company, to raise consciousness for an idea, or to influence legislation that would favorably affect an industry.

Whether the desired response is concrete (redeem this coupon) or more abstract (don't be scared of computers), the promotion should be planned. This plan should map out just what is to be accomplished and how each promotional element will be used. That involves setting objectives, or goals, and then designing strategies to meet those objectives.

Objectives

Overall company and marketing goals discussed in Chapter 2 must be translated into promotional goals. This process should occur in two steps. An organization must first set very general communications objectives and then, after research, quantify them for each promotional tool used.

Figure 14.3
Effectiveness of Promotional Methods

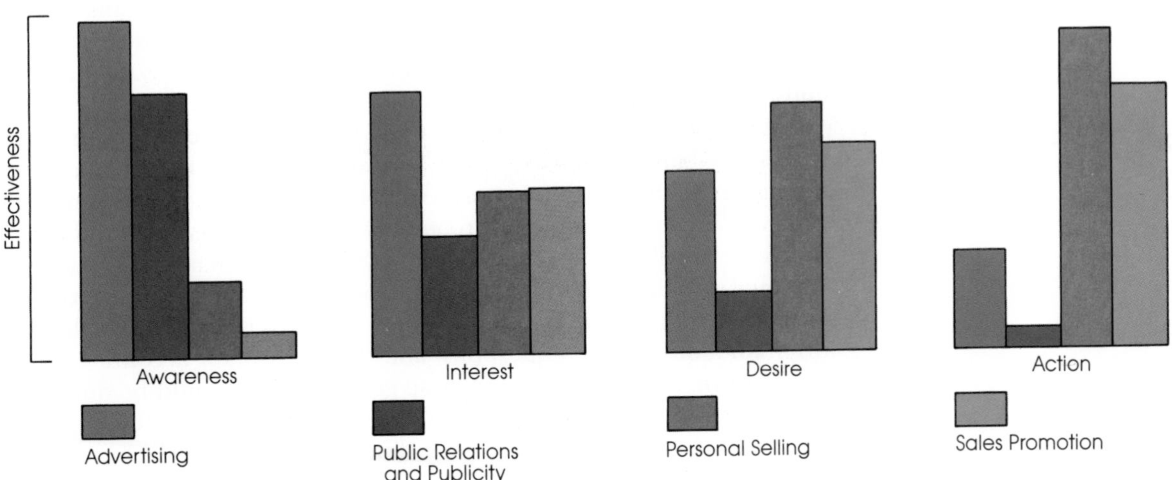

Source: Charles V. Schewe and Reuben M. Smith, *Marketing, Concepts and Applications* (New York: McGraw-Hill, 1983), p. 488.

Marketers set general communications objectives rather than specific sales goals because it is nearly impossible to measure the results of a promotional campaign by sales results. Several general communications goals may be pursued. One theory suggests that the goals of promotion coincide with the stage of product knowledge of a prospective buyer. Thus, promotion may:

1. Create *awareness,* or knowledge of the existence of a product, service, or idea.
2. Arouse *interest* in the product, service, or idea.
3. Create *desire* for the product by showing consumers how it can satisfy their needs.
4. Stimulate *action,* which may be either a purchase or the adoption of an idea.

The stages are frequently referred to by the acronym AIDA: awareness, interest, desire, and action. These sequential steps are the usual path that most consumers follow before making a purchase decision. Figure 14.3 shows the relationship between the four stages of AIDA and the effectiveness of four of the five promotional methods. Advertising, for example, is highly effective in creating awareness but less effective in stimulating action. The reverse is true for personal selling. Publicity may also serve to familiarize the public with a product, but it has little value in spurring action.[27]

To see these principles in action, consider a hypothetical bank, College National Bank, located near campus. College National has decided to build business by offering a special checking account for students who get their student loans through the bank. First, the bank wants to build *awareness,* so it sends the school newspaper press releases describing the bank's involvement with the college, its special programs for students, and financial information of interest to students.

When students begin to grow more aware of College National's programs, the bank begins its efforts to develop *interest.* It runs ads about the new checking accounts in the school paper, and it posts signs around campus. The bank then tries to build *desire* by mailing each student a brochure detailing the advantages of opening an account with College National. Finally, to stimulate *action,* College National hosts a series of lectures during which a bank representative describes what the bank can offer students, answers questions, and distributes new-account forms.

Most marketers agree that these general goals should be quantified so that results can be measured. An advertising objective for the checking account might have been "to increase brand awareness by 15 percent among students within 12 weeks"—a clear statement that could be measured by research. Similar quantitative goals could be set for the other promotional tools. All goals should be consistent with overall company and marketing objectives.

Strategies

Promotional objectives give marketers a goal; strategies tell them how to get there. Promotion managers may use either a push strategy or a pull strategy, or they may employ some combination. The major difference is in the type of promotion stressed. Figure 14.4 illustrates the differences.

Push Strategy
Urging members of a market channel to sell a product or give it adequate display.

The Push Strategy **Push strategy** got its name because it involves pushing, or urging, members of a market channel to sell a product or give it adequate display. Both personal selling and trade promotion are used by each channel member to promote the product to the channel below. Producers, for example, promote to wholesalers, wholesalers to retailers, and retailers to consumers. Producers may offer special advertising allowances or prizes to dealers to gain their support.

Pull Strategy
Creating demand for a product within a channel of distribution by appealing directly to the consumer.

The Pull Strategy An ad in *Stickers!* magazine, a publication aimed at children who collect stickers as a hobby, offered kids a chance to win free stickers if they took the entry blank featured on the page to their favorite sticker store. The ad went on to say, "With their order from us, they'll get a 10% discount and you'll be entered in a FREE sticker drawing." Promoters of this product are using a **pull strategy.** They are attempting to create demand for a product within a channel of distribution by appealing directly to the consumer. Advertising, rather than personal selling, is the primary promotional tool used for this strategy. Companies that concentrate on convenience goods, such as Procter & Gamble, specialize in this strategy, often using coupons or samples to build demand for their products. However, a pull strategy has been em-

Figure 14.4
Push and Pull Promotional Strategies

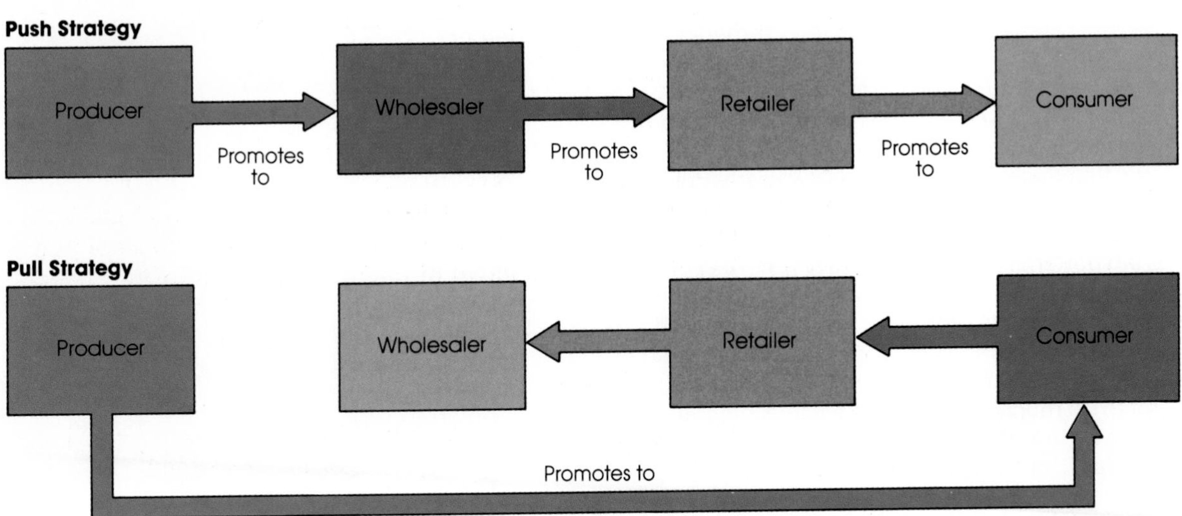

ployed successfully by industrial goods companies as well. For instance, the Farr Company, manufacturer of air filters for engines, created a demand for its product among buyers and users of trucks and locomotives, which forced equipment manufacturers to buy Farr's filters.

The Combination Strategy Most familiar consumer goods companies use a balance of selling, advertising, and other promotional techniques in a **combination strategy** to achieve their goals. For example, to promote Chaz, a line of cologne, after-shave, soap, and talc for men, Revlon ran a $150,000 "Grand Prix" Sweepstakes. Tom Selleck, star of "Magnum P.I.," was hired as spokesman, and a Ferrari sports car was offered as a grand prize.

Combination Strategy
Balance of selling, advertising, and other promotional techniques combining push and pull strategies to achieve sales goals.

Ads featuring Selleck were run in *Newsweek, Playboy,* and *Sports Illustrated* for a combined circulation of 16 million. Each ad featured an instant-winner, scratch-off game piece as a bind-in card that required participants to visit the store to determine their prize—a sales promotion technique.

A separate sweepstakes was conducted for retailers with matching prizes (excluding the Ferrari), and salespeople were motivated to exceed selling quotas with additional prizes.

Revlon received 1,502,000 sweepstakes entries, and sales increased 35 percent as a result of the promotion.[28]

Choosing the Right Strategy

The choice of a strategy is made by weighing many factors. The most important considerations are product type, the customers in the target market, and the strategy of competitors. Marketing Today 14.2 describes how Rolls-Royce takes these into account.

Marketing Today 14.2
Selective Promotion for Rolls-Royce

Rolls-Royce Motor Cars Inc. does not have a central advertising strategy. The company explains that this is because Rolls-Royce motor cars are perceived differently in each market, and buying patterns and attitudes vary. In addition, the quality image of Rolls-Royce Motor Cars is so strong that many observers suggest the company may not need to do much advertising to sustain its brand identity.

Instead, Rolls-Royce focuses on dealers. It gives local dealers incentives to spend a preset amount on advertising. Dealers also make heavy use of promotional activity—typically social occasions for potential customers, ranging from fashion shows to clay-pigeon shoots and polo matches. Once potential customers are brought together, the dealership can use direct selling to encourage sales.

A major Rolls-Royce Motor Cars dealership is the one in Beverly Hills, California. This dealership has used an ad budget of $400 per car, combined with a variety of promotional and publicity activities. The dealership sponsored a weekly classical music radio program, participated in several charities, and hosted periodic parties known as "Rolls-Royce of Beverly Hills Happenings." One of these events took place to celebrate the opening of the dealership's new service department; at this "happening," Princess Margaret was the guest of honor.

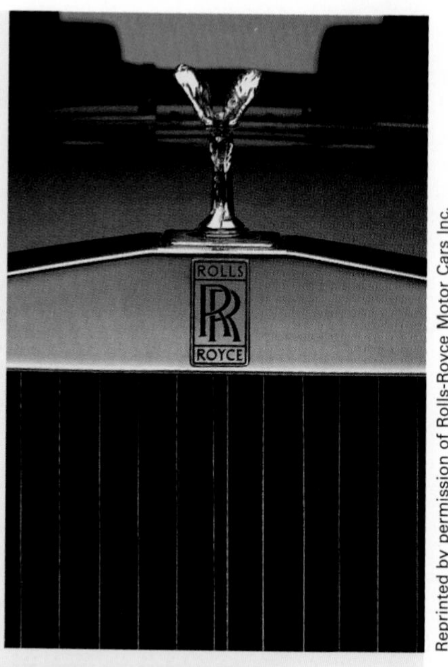

Source: Brian Oliver, "Rolls-Royce Rides on Reputation, Not Ads," *Advertising Age,* June 16, 1986, pp. S-30–S-31.

What Product Type? Some products, such as small appliances or food items, are relatively simple to promote, while others, including most industrial goods, require specialized knowledge for installation, operation, or maintenance. In general, the more complex a product, the more appropriate a push strategy. Sales personnel are the key element in IBM's business computer promotion strategy because they are needed to explain computer capabilities and to engage in the long negotiations required to close sales. No such personal effort is needed to sell an Almond Joy candy bar; a pull strategy utilizing mainly advertising is far more effective.

Some consumer products, particularly shopping goods such as clothing, autos, or large appliances, do require some selling effort because they are more costly and consumers compare values before buying. A combination strategy, therefore, is most effective. A Maytag advertisement pulls customers into stores. But Maytag sales reps are also needed to convince retailers to stock their products, and floor salespeople may be given a bonus (called "push money" or "spiffs") to put forth a special effort to sell the machines. Table 14.1. shows the relative importance of advertising to sales for different types of products. The table confirms the observation that a pull strategy (emphasizing advertising) is far more common for convenience goods than for industrial goods, and a combination strategy is more typical for shopping goods.

Table 14.1
Advertising-to-Sales Ratios, 1982

Industry	Ad Dollars as Percentage of Sales
Phonograph records	13.0
Toys and amusement, sporting goods	10.5
Perfumes, cosmetics	8.4
Drugs	8.2
Distilled beverages	7.9
Malt beverages	7.0
Soaps and detergents	6.9
Candy	6.1
Household appliances, retail	5.7
Jewelry	5.0
Books	4.6
Food products	4.2
Real estate	3.0
Heating equipment and plumbing fixtures	2.2
Industrial measuring instruments	2.0
Engines and turbines	1.8
Farm machinery	1.4
Surgical and medical instruments	1.2
Manifold business forms	0.7
Cement, hydraulic	0

Source: Schonfeld & Associates, Inc., 2550 Crawford Ave., Evanston, Ill., as seen in *Advertising Age*, August 15, 1983, p. 20.

What Customers? A firm's customers may be few and geographically concentrated or numerous and widely dispersed. Firms selling to a small, concentrated market generally rely more on personal selling—a push technique—than organizations that make a mass appeal. Thus, sellers of airplane parts can use a small sales force to cover California and Washington, the states where plane manufacturers cluster. Manufacturers of toaster ovens, on the other hand, must use sales promotion to move their products through wholesale and retail channels and advertising to create demand.

Other customer characteristics also influence the choice of a strategy. Professional purchasing agents or buyers of rare antiques, both of whom have special knowledge, are more likely to respond to a message delivered through a salesperson than through an impersonal mass medium such as a magazine.

What About Competition? Competitors affect all marketing efforts, and promotion is no exception. In most cases, it would be suicidal to neglect advertising if it is commonly used by competitors or to ignore intermediaries if a strong sales effort is required.

Rheingold Beer, a New York-based firm, discovered this the hard way when it attempted to break into the West Coast market in the 1950s. Beer sales generally depend on a combination strategy, but Rheingold chose to ignore the combination of sales effort and advertising usually used in the West. The firm bypassed the traditional wholesale distributors and tried to pull customers directly into retail outlets by ads. Moreover, their ads were placed in newspapers and magazines, not on radio and TV, which were then more commonly used for advertising beer in the West. The campaign failed, and Rheingold withdrew from the market.[29]

Exceptions exist to every rule, of course. Sometimes strategists succeed by ignoring conventional ways of doing things. Most encyclopedias, for example, rely on a push strategy, with heavy emphasis on door-to-door selling. But when Random House introduced its one-volume encyclopedia in 1977, the president of the company went on a publicity tour, and the product was heavily advertised—both pull techniques. By all accounts, this campaign was a success. Random House shipped 110,000 copies to stores during the campaign, a record for a one-volume encyclopedia.[30]

Budgeting for Promotion

Developing a workable strategy is complex, but it is by no means the only job a promotional manager must perform. Plans must be drawn up to carry out the strategy, and controls must be established. Budgeting plays a major role in both tasks. A budget guides a manager in purchasing the selling, advertising, and other services needed. It also supplies a yardstick for measuring progress, detecting flaws in strategy, and making comparisons with past performance.

How much should a firm spend on promotion? Economists say that a firm should spend only up to the point of diminishing returns. Unfortunately, managers find it quite difficult to determine when money spent is beginning to become counterproductive. More common are the other more practical methods of setting an overall budget and allocating funds discussed here.

The Percent-of-Sales Approach

Percent-of-Sales Budgeting Sales approach that fixes amount to be spent for promotion as a percentage of the previous year's sales or of anticipated sales for the coming year.

The widely used **percent-of-sales** approach fixes the amount to be spent for promotion as a percentage of last year's sales or of anticipated sales for the coming year. Both figures are arrived at by looking at company records. Thus, if a firm generally spends 7 percent of sales revenues on promotion and it expects to sell $5 billion next year, it will allocate $350 million for promotion.

Although this approach is simple, it has problems. Making advertising dependent on sales is putting the cart before the horse. If sales decline, promotion funds will also decline, although more promotion may be just what is needed to increase demand for the product. The firm is tied to spending a certain amount even though market conditions may warrant a reduction or an increase.

The Fixed-Sum-Per-Unit Method

Sometimes a promotional budget is established by putting aside a specified amount for each unit produced—the **fixed-sum-per-unit** method. This can be a useful approach when a firm produces many different brands, each of which requires a different promotional effort. For example, a number of years ago Philip Morris applied a figure of 45 cents per thousand for promoting its best-selling brand, Marlboro. Weaker brands received 70 cents per thousand for promotion, and a new brand, Benson & Hedges 100s, received $1.50 per thousand.

Fixed-Sum-per-Unit Budgeting
Allocating a specified amount for each unit produced.

The advantage of this method is that the manufacturer knows the promotional cost per unit in advance—an aid in setting the price. The disadvantage is that this method uses the past as an inflexible guide to future promotional expenditures.

The Competitive Comparison Method

Meeting competition—spending as much on promotion as the leading firms do—is the essence of the **competitive comparison** method. Although firms generally do not publicize how much they spend, trade association studies of industry averages are available.

Competitive Comparison Budgeting
Plan to spend as much on promotion as leading firms do.

This method is somewhat more sophisticated than the percent-of-sales approach because the percent figure used comes not just from one company's records, but from those of a whole industry. However, both methods rely on the past as a predictor of the future. An added disadvantage of competitive comparison budgeting is its false assumption that all companies in an industry operate under the same conditions. To cite one variation, a new firm in an industry may have to spend more on promotion than an established company. Comparisons can be misleading and thus should always be thought of as rough guides.

The Objective and Task Method

The major problem with all of the methods discussed thus far is that they are backward-looking. By contrast, the **objective and task** method recognizes that promotion leads to future sales. To be effective, therefore, promotion must be tied to future objectives, not to past sales.

Objective and Task Budgeting
Strategy that emphasizes setting goals and then fixing costs of meeting those goals for each promotional task used.

The method works in the following way. After promotional objectives are set, the tasks necessary to reach those objectives and their costs are worked out for each form of promotion to be used. Other costs, such as those for research, are then added in, and all costs are totaled to arrive at a budget. Consider a promotion for a new kind of frozen pizza. Assume that one objective is to increase brand awareness by 15 percent through advertising within six months. The tasks to accomplish this and their costs (in an extremely simplified form) might look like this:

50 network television announcements	$2,500,000
40 full-color pages in national women's magazines	1,000,000
Research costs	100,000
Administrative costs	300,000
Total	$3,900,000

This list could include publicity, sales promotion, and selling tasks if they support this effort.

From a business point of view, the approach of building up the amount to be spent on promotion makes a great deal of sense. It orients management toward the future by emphasizing goals, and it eliminates rote spending justified by past budgets. Also, objective and task budgeting provides a standard for control. If the goal of increasing brand recognition is not reached, the tasks can be reinvestigated to discover their weaknesses.

Of course, determining which tasks are most effective in reaching goals can be very difficult. In the case of advertising, for example, many choices must be made. What media should be used? What appeals should be made? When should they be scheduled? These and other questions must be answered for each task. For a multiproduct firm that uses all forms of promotion, the job is enormous. Increasingly, firms are looking to the computer to analyze data in a way that helps them in their budgeting decisions.

Evaluating and Controlling Promotion

In practice, showing which tasks fail and why is complicated and, in some cases, impossible. Measuring the effectiveness of a certain outlay by sales results may fail for several reasons, but three in particular stand out.[31] First, in good promotional programs, the tools work together. It is difficult to determine which promotional effort created the desired effect. For example, a woman buying a new Chevrolet would be hard-pressed to say which element of promotion influenced her decision most. It could have been a television commercial, a direct-mail piece sent by a local dealer, or a persuasive car salesperson. Or, none of these may have influenced her; she may simply have liked the look of her neighbor's new Chevrolet.

Another reason why measuring the effectiveness of advertising by sales results is difficult is that outside factors complicate measurement. Sometimes, no matter how much promotion is used, uncontrollable factors determine the success or failure of a campaign. Consider the weather. Officials at Toro Company, a manufacturer of snow throwers, found that among consumers the biggest barrier to buying a machine was the fear that there would not be enough snow to justify the cost. The previous year's mild winter made it likely that people would hold off buying a snow thrower until they were convinced it would be necessary. To counter the psychological resistance, Toro marketers devised a promotional gimmick that faced the issue head-on. Toro promised to refund the entire price of any of its machines purchased before December 10 if the winter's snowfall amounted to less than 20 percent of the average where the machine was bought. To protect themselves in case of a no-snow, Toro executives took out weather insurance. The scheme worked. The promotion increased sales by several thousand, and fortunately for the insurer, the Frost Belt had a very white winter.[32]

Weather is not the only uncontrollable factor. Producers can spend millions on promotion, but if retailers do not stock the item, their efforts are for naught. One author reported that in spite of all his local appearances during one month in the city of Cleveland, the sales figures for his book did not increase because local stores had not ordered his best-selling novel.

Finally, measurement is difficult because almost all promotional efforts suffer from time lag. Managers plan promotional expenditures to have an immediate impact, but what they accomplish or fail to accomplish may have resulted from a previous campaign. Advertising professionals call this phenomenon *carryover*. Part of the reason many companies switch advertising agencies frequently is a failure to recognize that a new approach takes time to penetrate and an old approach takes time to wear off. Carryover obviously complicates the task of singling out the effect of a particular commercial, coupon offer, or sales pitch.

Indirect Measurement

It would be wrong to conclude that because measuring the effect of promotion on sales is complex, no attempt should be made. Promotion managers, like other managers, must justify what they spend. Although they may not be able to say that *x* dollars in promotion produced *y* dollars in additional sales, they can measure indirect effects—the number of consumers exposed to an ad or sales talk, the number who recall what they saw or heard, and so forth. Such indirect effects can be measured before, during, or after a promotional campaign is launched.

Pretesting—measuring a promotional campaign's effectiveness before spending on a large scale—involves testing an organization's communications on a small segment of the market. For example, as part of its strategy to upgrade the image of its snacks, Austin Foods Company of Cary, North Carolina, changed its package design. Designers created a new logo, a red mill to symbolize product wholesomeness. In addition, red bands on the labels bear the message that the products—peanut butter- and cheese-filled crackers and cream-filled cookies—contain 100 percent vegetable shortening and no preservatives. The company showed the packages to potential consumers and found that people did in fact perceive the product as of higher quality than the competition.[33]

Pretesting
Measuring a promotional campaign's effectiveness before spending on a large scale.

Information secured while a promotional effort is under way, called **concurrent testing,** is also valuable. Sales reps are usually required to submit weekly, and sometimes daily, reports to managers. For measuring advertising, perhaps the most famous concurrent testing device is the Nielsen audiometer, an instrument for measuring how many viewers are tuned in to a television program and its commercials.

Concurrent Testing
Securing information while a promotional effort is under way.

Table 14.2
Indirect Measurement of Promotion

	Pretesting	Concurrent Testing	Posttesting
Personal Selling	Screening and testing of potential sales reps; field testing of sales approach	Sales reports, management field trips	Quotas, sales analysis
Advertising	Checklists, consumer juries, split runs	Consumer diaries, Nielsen audiometer, traffic counts	Readership surveys, repeat of concurrent tests
Sales Promotion	Test mailings, test markets	Coupon and entry monitoring; counts of the number of displays set up	Final counts of orders, entries, inquiries, redemptions
Publicity	—	—	Count of number of requests for reprints or inquiries
Packaging	Focus groups may discuss proposed package	Nielsen and consumer group surveys	Sales analysis, monitor customer response by mail, phone

Posttesting
Measuring the effectiveness of a full-scale campaign after it has been completed.

Posttesting, which takes place after a full-scale campaign has been completed, is commonly conducted. Sales analysis, discussed in Chapter 4, is a form of posttesting that measures the results of the sales force's effort. Many of the same measures used in concurrent testing are used in the posttesting phase for other types of promotion.

Except for publicity, the measurement of all forms of promotion is a developing art. Table 14.2 lists some of the tests used for each promotional tool. Chapters 15 and 16 discuss several tests in greater detail.

The Role of Social Responsibility in Promotion

Techniques for managing promotional tools are important for those planning a career in marketing, but they are by no means the only aspect of promotion deserving attention. Promotion has a social dimension. It is the part of the marketing mix most visible to the public. Consequently, it is the area most open to criticism. Those employed in sales, advertising, or public relations positions may at times experience a conflict between professional and personal beliefs.

Chapter 3 discusses some of the social issues marketers must keep in mind. Chapter 15 looks more closely at how the advertising community addresses its social responsibilities. Before closing this chapter, it is worth looking at one more example of a social issue facing marketers that demonstrates just how complex these problems can be.

In recent years, modern packaging practices have come under increasing attack from environmentalists and consumer groups. Both maintain that the packaging revolution has had harmful side effects. Their charges have focused public attention on the packaging industry.

Environmentalists complain that modern packaging wastes resources and pollutes the environment. Is it really necessary, they ask, to wrap slices of cheese individually? How is society to dispose of the waste materials created by overpackaged cereals?

The environmentalists have a point. The energy required to process glass, steel, and aluminum into containers is equal to a year's electric power supply for Washington, D.C., San Francisco, Boston, and Pittsburgh combined. And the cost of collecting and disposing of packaging materials is over $500 million a year. A particularly acute problem is the disposal of plastics. Many plastics resist decay, and some, like polyvinyl chloride, emit poisonous gases when burned.

Packaging experts are now paying more attention to environmentalist complaints. But consumers themselves sometimes impede their efforts. Bottlers, for example, have tried to comply with certain state and local regulations requiring that bottles be returnable. But the modest deposit fees are often not enough to motivate users to return them, and some bottlers are actually losing money.

But sometimes apparent "overpackaging" serves an important function. In the wake of the deaths caused by cyanide-laced Tylenol capsules in 1982, Johnson & Johnson quickly devised a triple safety-sealed package for protection against product tampering.

Much still remains to be done in the area of waste avoidance and economical disposal, but marketers are now more influenced by social pressures to find solutions. The problem is often one of reconciling conflicting demands for efficient, safe, yet convenient packaging.

Packaging is one obvious area in which there is room for many conflicting opinions, but it is by no means the only one. Other questions regarding marketers' social responsibilities are even more controversial. For example:

1. How much information should promotion convey? The whole truth —including a product's flaws? If not, how much can be omitted without deception?
2. Should promotion, and especially advertising, be aimed at vulnerable groups (such as children) who cannot distinguish between the persuasive and informational parts of a message?
3. In light of world shortages, should marketers promote less consumption of material goods?

These questions are raised now so that they will be kept in mind while the tools of promotion are studied in more depth. There are no easy answers. But marketers of the future should know that people on the various sides of such issues raise valid points. The challenge lies in finding a solution that takes into account the needs of individuals, businesses, and society.

☑ Chapter Replay

1. **What are the activities involved in promotion of a company's product?**
   Promotion includes advertising, sales promotion, publicity, personal selling, and packaging.

2. **How does communication occur?**
The source encodes the message, putting it into understandable form. The source sends the message through a medium of transmission. The receiver decodes the message and signals understanding by providing feedback to the source.

3. **What are some sources of misunderstanding in the communication process?**
The reputation of the source can affect the way a message is received. The multiple transmitters involved in sending a message may conflict with one another. The receiver may make decoding errors, interpreting a message in an unintended way. Inadequate feedback can cause future messages to suffer.

4. **What are some advantages of communication through advertising?**
Advertising is relatively inexpensive, measured as the cost to reach each viewer. It can be creative and can therefore be an effective way to capture attention. It also allows perfect reproduction of the desired message.

5. **What are the major advantage and disadvantage of personal selling?**
The major advantage is that it allows the salesperson to match the sales effort to the customer. The major disadvantage is the high cost of this personalized approach.

6. **What are some functions of packaging?**
Packages protect the product and the consumer. They increase the use of the product, and they increase sales if they add a reuse value. They promote the product by describing special benefits or values or by selling related items.

7. **What are the major types of promotional strategies?**
Promotional strategies include a push strategy, in which the producer promotes to intermediaries, and a pull strategy, in which the producer promotes to the consumer. Many marketers use a combination of these strategies.

8. **How do marketers budget for promotion?**
Marketers allocate funds using the percent-of-sales approach, the fixed-sum-per-unit method, the competitive comparison method, or the objective and task method.

9. **How do marketers measure the effectiveness of a promotional campaign?**
Marketers can measure effectiveness by evaluating sales results, although this method is difficult to use accurately. Often, marketers use indirect measurement through pretesting, concurrent testing, or posttesting of the promotional effort.

Key Terms

advertising
combination strategy
competitive comparison budgeting
concurrent testing
decoding
encoding
feedback

fixed-sum-per-unit budgeting
medium of transmission
noise
objective and task budgeting
percent-of-sales budgeting
personal selling
posttesting
pretesting
promotion
public relations
publicity
pull strategy
push strategy
receiver
sales promotion
source
source effect

Discussion Questions

1. How does the communication process work? What can interfere with this process?
2. The Good Life Insurance Company runs ads on television and also has a sales force of 256 salespeople, who call on prospective and current customers. If Good Life can reach a million people with a million dollars in advertising, why would it want to spend $100 a sales call for personal selling? How might the company combine these two approaches?
3. Companies have little control over the message when they use publicity as a promotional tool. Why would a company want to use publicity?
4. Bright Eyes, Inc., sells eye drops. In designing a package for the product, what issues should the company consider?
5. Tom Tremulous and Steve Subarious are preparing to open a bed and breakfast inn near a beautiful state park. Steve said, "We need to plan how to promote our inn." Tom replied, "I know, and I've got it all figured out. I'll show you my idea for some great advertisements." What steps should Tom and Steve take before planning advertisements?
6. Compare the relative merits of the different methods for developing a promotion budget.
7. Last April, Alicia Aloysius tried her first promotional campaign for her combination Italian/Mexican restaurant. She obtained publicity by sponsoring a spaghetti-eating contest, and she ran coupons for a free order of guacamole in the local newspaper. In May, her sales receipts were twice as much as her April receipts. Alicia declared her promotional campaign a success. What are some shortcomings of Alicia's evalution?
8. Consider the promotional campaign described in Question 7. How might Alicia Aloysius measure the effectiveness of this campaign indirectly?
9. Brand X Pizza Company has reformulated its pizza recipe. Now its sausage pizzas contain sausage made out of soybeans and a cheese substitute made out of tofu. The company wants to produce a promotional campaign based on the slogan, "New Improved Brand X Pizzas Are Lower in Calories." Should the company mention the

changes in its ingredients, even though its research suggests that fewer people would buy a pizza made from soybeans and tofu? Explain your answer, indicating the amount of information you think the company should be responsible for conveying.

Case 14.1 California Beef Council (E)

Based on a detailed analysis of the business and social environment, the California Beef Council (CBC) has developed a communications program that includes public and industry relations and an education program. Each of these programs is described below in terms of the relevant mission statement and broad objectives for achieving that mission.

Public Relations Program

Mission To develop and implement effective public relations programs aimed at key market segments that will increase consumer demand for beef.

Objectives

1. Position beef as part of a balanced, healthful diet among active lifestyle and health-oriented consumers. Target fitness enthusiasts through their sports publications, clubs, and athletic events.
2. Continue innovation in CBC's communications program to earn public understanding and acceptance of beef and the beef industry.
    a. Reposition beef as fashionable, convenient, and light among light and moderate users.
    b. Reinforce the traditional appeal of beef, capitalizing on current "real food" and dinner food trends.
3. Maintain the CBC's position as a reliable news source able to meet the varying needs of different consumer segments.
4. Measure program effectiveness through evaluation.

Industry Relations Program

Mission To develop an effective communications program aimed at building beef industry support for and awareness of California and the new national checkoff program.

Objectives

1. Create greater understanding and awareness of the California Beef Council and its national and statewide programs.

Source: Adapted from California Beef Council's 1987 marketing plan.

2. Extend National Beef Promotion and Research Board beef checkoff publicity programs at the state level.
3. Target communications efforts through various segments of the industry to extend the CBC program information reach.
4. Measure program effectiveness through evaluation.

Education Program

Mission To teach present and future consumers proper use and care of beef as a food product; to value it for its nutritional contributions so that consumer demand for beef as a food product is maintained/increased.

Objectives

1. Assist health care professionals to obtain and disseminate accurate nutrition information about cattle products, particularly beef.
2. Provide selected consumer audiences with accurate information about cattle products, particularly beef.
3. Maintain/improve educator information about cattle products, particularly beef, so that educators provide accurate information to the grade levels that they teach.
4. Maintain a link among the cattle industry, commodity marketing organizations, and college-level students.
5. Serve as project staff for BIC to develop and carry out programs and activities to maximize national programs.
6. Review, revise, and improve the education program through continual evaluation.

Focal Topics

1. What is your overall evaluation of the communications program planned for the CBC?
2. How would you recommend that the CBC evaluate the effectiveness of each of the three parts of its communications program?
3. What other activities would you recommend that the CBC undertake in the area of communications?

Case 14.2
Kransco

R. John Stalberger, Jr., injured his knee in 1970 before trying out for the University of Texas football team. To rehabilitate his knee after the injury, he invented what is today known as the Hacky Sack® footbag. Created as an exercise aid, the product has spawned a company, various

Source: Hacky Sack is a registered trademark of and is patented by Wham-O, Inc., a Kransco Group Company. This has been edited from the original case which appeared in *Cases for Analysis in Marketing,* by W. Wayne Talarzyk. Copyright © 1985 by CBS College Publishing. Reprinted by permission of Holt, Rinehart and Winston, Inc. Additional information and logo provided by Kransco.

footbag games, and a players' association. The ultimate goal of the association is to see footbagging become an internationally recognized sport and therefore an Olympic event.

Background Information

Stalberger developed a kicking game using a small object made of hand-stitched leather, called a Hacky Sack footbag. Because of his background in baseball, football, and other sports, he saw the game as a good off-season training and warm-up exercise. It enhanced bilateral control and versatility. Stalberger, also having a background in physical therapy, knew that such a workout for the heart and lungs was important for fitness. He wanted to develop the game as a conditioning exercise.

Stalberger poured all of his energies into developing the American Footbag Game. He was determined to make it a nationally accepted exercise game and sport. The American Footbag Game is the modern version of ancient kicking games, and it differs from all similar games in two main areas. First, using the body above the waist as a striking surface is prohibited (except in Freestyle). Second, the method of play utilizes five basic kicks that dictate the equal use of both feet.

Marketing Activities

Over the years, Hacky Sack has been promoted directly to consumers through advertisements in publications such as *National Lampoon, Sports Illustrated,* and *Boys' Life Magazine.* In a campaign in *Scholastic Coach* and *Athletic Directory,* Hacky Sack is presented to physical education teachers as an important training device for soccer, pre-sports warm-up, and other activities.

The company has also marketed its product to the sporting goods industry by participating in various trade shows and by advertising in specialized publications such as *Sporting Goods Business, The Sporting Goods Dealer, Sports Retailer,* and *Sports Merchandiser.* To support individual retailers in promoting the product, the company has developed a series of advertising slicks. Retailers can add their names and addresses to the copy and then run the advertisements in local newspapers. In addition to general themes for Hacky Sack, the company has developed segmented advertising slicks that tie the product to conditioning for other sports such as soccer, running, football, and skiing. On occasion, the company also sends Hacky Sack footbag demonstrators to retail stores for promotional programs. A Hacky Sack footbag with a book on how to play with it costs about $9.

Additional Dimensions

In connection with Frisbee, another of its products, Kransco planned to offer festivals in 50 major markets during the spring of 1987. These Hacky Sack/Frisbee Festivals, which have been run for three years, are free skill clinics and expert demonstrations. The festivals are supported by advertisements on national cable television (MTV), spot television markets (top 10 markets with the highest concentration of 12- to 24-year-old males), and youth-oriented radio stations.

Focal Topics

1. What dimensions could the company use to segment the market for Hacky Sacks?
2. Which market segments do you think would be best for Kransco to pursue? Why?
3. What marketing strategies would you recommend to reach those segments?

Advertising, Sales Promotion, and Publicity

☐ Sounding Out the Chapter

In this chapter, you will learn:

1. **The kinds of advertising marketers can use.**
2. **Reasons for advertising.**
3. **The kinds of organizations that employ the most people in the field of advertising.**
4. **The steps involved in developing an ad campaign.**
5. **Creative styles for presenting advertising messages.**
6. **The major media that advertisers use.**
7. **How advertisers and the government have responded to criticisms of advertising.**
8. **How sales promotion can increase sales.**
9. **Advantages and disadvantages of using publicity.**
10. **Activities typically included in a public relations program.**

Source: Courtesy of California Raisin Advisory Board.

Commercial Creativity

Cable TV and videocassette recorders are changing the style of television advertising. Television viewers are increasingly able to avoid commercials or to "zap" through the ones on videotaped programs. Advertising executive Jane Fuller predicts that by the year 2000 about 60 percent of television viewers will be tuning out ads. With viewers no longer a captive audience, advertisers are looking for ways to convince people to watch.

This often means commercials have a more subtle sales pitch. Hard sells and annoying jingles are being replaced with ads that try to entertain. Some are styled after music videos, while others tell mini-stories. Many use special effects. One source of the creativity is use of successful movie directors to make the advertisements. Some that have done so include Adrian Lyne *(Flashdance),* Hugh Hudson *(Chariots of Fire),* and Ridley Scott *(Alien)*.

One of the most popular of the new breed of advertisements is the California Raisin Advisory Board's dancing raisins. One woman reported that it was the only commercial she had ever gone back into the room to watch. Young people are also attracted to Max Headroom, the computer-generated creature that sells viewers on the appeal of Coke.

More down-to-earth characters are wine cooler spokesmen Fred Bartles and Ed Jaymes. They appeal to the audience with sly humor and tales of their progress in selling their product. The serial nature of the ads means that they keep changing and maintain viewers' interest.

Right Guard tells a story in a much different way. Instead of the usual scenarios of hard-working people, a Right Guard ad shows a fanciful barroom scene. A gruesome cyclops ogles an attractive woman—and is turned into a handsome man with a quick shot of Right Guard.

While not all commercials are entertaining, this style of advertising may continue to grow in popularity. As the number of commercials grows along with the opportunities for avoiding them, the job of the advertiser requires ever more creativity. This chapter discusses principles of advertising. Then it describes how marketers can reach customers through sales promotion and publicity.

Sources: "America's Favorite Campaigns," *Adweek,* March 2, 1987, p. 24; and Barbara Rosen, "And Now, a Wittier Word from Our Sponsors," *Business Week,* March 24, 1986, p. 90.

One observer of the advertising business has noted that college graduates with advertising degrees may be in for a culture shock of sorts. Trained in the sophisticated, computer-driven world of the modern college or university, these graduates often find that the real world of advertising can be less sophisticated. Nevertheless, advertising and marketing majors find they also have much to learn about putting principles to work in creative ways. The industry observer suggests that students benefit most from learning analytical tools and ways of approaching tasks.[1] This chapter attempts to begin laying that foundation.

The Nature and Growth of Advertising

Advertising as we know it today began with industrialization after the Civil War. Volume was relatively constant from 1920 to 1940. By 1950, expenditures for advertising began to climb rapidly, and between 1950 and 1960 volume more than doubled, from $5.7 billion to $11.9 billion. By 1975, companies were spending more than $28 billion annually on advertising, and 1984 expenditures reached $88 billion, more than three times the 1975 total. Principal reasons for the growth are more consumer income, greater consumer willingness to spend on services and pleasures, more competition, more products and outlets for shopping, and a rapid movement to self-service retailing.[2] The top ten national advertisers in 1985 are listed in Table 15.1.

Selective or Brand Advertising

Selective or Brand Advertising
Messages that try to increase consumer preference for a particular firm's product.

Most people associate advertising with messages that try to increase consumer preference for a particular firm's product. Advertisers refer to this as **selective or brand advertising,** because its aim is to convince consumers to "select" Wheaties, say, over Kellogg's Corn Flakes. This form of advertising is the oldest, and outwardly it has not changed much in a hundred years. In 1890, for example, the leading advertisers sold drugs, household goods, clothes, and food and drink.[3]

The theory behind most selective advertising is that a product in the mature stage of its life cycle (see Chapter 9) must be kept before the public to maintain its market share. Selective advertising also works for services. For example, the Humana chain of hospitals arranged for Mary Lou Retton to do prime-time TV testimonials as part of its national marketing campaign. Meanwhile, a competing chain, HCA, launched a national campaign of its own.[4]

Primary Demand Advertising

Primary Demand Advertising
Advertising aimed at increasing the total demand for products without distinguishing between brands.

Besides promoting a particular firm's products or services, advertising may also increase the total demand for products without distinguishing between brands.[5] **Primary demand advertising,** as it is called, is used mainly for innovative products in the first stages of their life cycle.

Table 15.1
Top Ten National Advertisers in 1985

	Total Advertising (in Millions of Dollars)
1. Procter & Gamble	$1,600.0
2. Philip Morris Companies	1,400.0
3. RJR/Nabisco	1,093.0
4. Sears, Roebuck	800.0
5. General Motors	779.0
6. Beatrice Companies	684.0
7. Ford Motor Company	614.6
8. K mart Corporation	567.0
9. McDonald's Corporation	550.0
10. Anheuser-Busch Companies	522.9

Source: *Advertising Age,* September 4, 1986, p. 1.

Mazda's first ads for its cars, for example, stressed the benefits of the rotary engine rather than the brand name. Such ads are also effective for older products that already command a large market share.

Association advertising is a special way of increasing primary demand. Members of a trade association may pool funds to promote a class of products or services. The American Florists Marketing Council hoped to spur sales of flowers by urging people to treat themselves to a bouquet. The American Association of Orthodontists encourages adults to seek orthodontic treatment by promoting the benefits of "a good-looking smile." (See Figure 15.1.)

Association Advertising Advertising sponsored by a trade association to promote a class of products or services.

Institutional Advertising

A paid message designed to build long-range goodwill for a firm rather than to sell specific goods is termed **institutional** (or **corporate) advertising.** A strong corporate image is advantageous in the marketplace. Hallmark's advertising motto, "When you care enough to send the very best," has helped to make it the dominant force in the greeting card industry for more than 20 years.

Institutional (or Corporate) Advertising Paid message designed to build long-range goodwill for a firm rather than to sell specific goods.

Controversy is another reason for using such advertising. RJR/Nabisco, for example, runs advertising suggesting ways that smokers can behave responsibly and considerately. The ads are designed to improve the company's image among nonsmokers. Similarly, Mobil runs advertisements about issues such as environmentalism and oil prices.

Other forms of institutional advertising are less controversial. Mobil Oil sponsors "Masterpiece Theater," Gulf Oil underwrites the National Geographic Specials, and American Express donated one penny of every credit card transaction and one dollar for each new card member to restore the deteriorating Statue of Liberty. Corporate advertising is also used to communicate with prospective or present employees, to signal a company's new direction or name change, or to wake up the investment

Figure 15.1
Association Advertising for Orthodontists

YOU'LL SAY IT "SMARTER" WITH A GOOD-LOOKING SMILE.

Regardless of the value of what comes out of your mouth, it's better accepted when the surroundings are attractive.

That's why so many adults who "missed" braces are turning to them now. The time you spend in treatment not only can lead to an attractive smile and a new confidence, it also can help shape your long-term oral health.

We'd like to tell you things you probably don't realize about orthodontic treatment. Not all treatment is the same. For instance, while any dental school graduate can practice orthodontics, members of the American Association of Orthodontists have at least two additional continuous years of advanced training in the specialty in a program accredited by the American Dental Association.

Send for more information, a step that's simply good business.

WE SHAPE HEALTH, NOT JUST TEETH

American Association of Orthodontists
460 N. Lindbergh Blvd.
St. Louis, MO 63141

American Association of Orthodontists
In cooperation with The Canadian Association of Orthodontists

Call toll-free 1-800-358-5858
or send this coupon for our Orthodontic Planning Kit. We'll also send information on the low cost of orthodontic/dental insurance.

Name
Street
City Phone
State Zip

Source: Courtesy of American Association of Orthodontists.

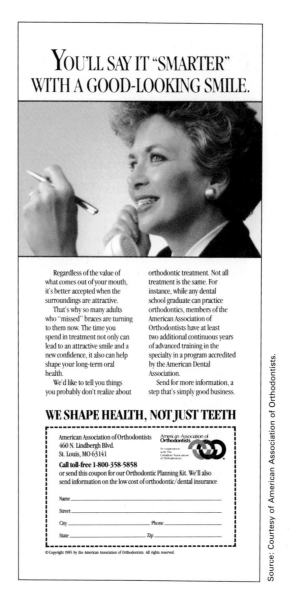

community to a company's earnings potential. They may also be used to air gripes about governmental policies.[6]

Noncommercial Advertising

Noncommercial Advertising
Paid message sponsored by nonprofit organizations.

Advertising by nonprofit organizations, **noncommercial advertising** is relatively new and rapidly growing. Philanthropic causes such as CARE are long-time advertising users. Today, however, other social and political groups are finding that it pays to advertise. The four chief users are (1) public-interest groups, (2) federal and state governments, (3) non-profit hospitals and universities, and (4) political parties. Nonprofit organizations account for about 10 percent of all money spent for advertising.

Why Advertise?

The specific reasons for advertising are as varied as the organizations that sponsor it. Most advertisers, however, seek to accomplish a few general goals.

Informing and persuading the public are among the primary reasons most companies advertise. The mixture of information and persuasion varies with the type of advertising and the stage in a product's life cycle. Primary demand and institutional advertising are usually more informative than selective advertising. Furthermore, newly introduced products usually require more informative advertising than products in the maturity phase of their life cycle.

Some experts believe that regardless of the amount of information an ad contains, ultimately it must seek to persuade its audience to buy a car or contribute to CARE. People need information, but they also need to be prodded to act. Recall from Chapter 14 that all communication, including advertising, aims not only to create awareness and arouse interest, but also to create desire and stimulate action.[7]

In addition to informing and persuading, ads also work for firms by (1) reminding consumers of a company's products or services and (2) reassuring buyers they have made the "right" purchase. Consumers must be reminded because they can remember only about 1,000 bits and pieces of ads they have seen and, as they learn new bits, they forget the old.[8] They require reassurance because buyers often experience anxiety about their decision after making a large purchase.

Ads also back up the sales force. A shopper who has seen an ad promoting a Kitchen Aid dishwasher is a better sales prospect than one who walks into an appliance dealer's showroom without having seen the ad.

Ads can also provide leads for salespeople if they contain coupons that interested prospects can fill in and return. This is particularly true for industrial advertising, although magazines such as *PC Magazine* and *House & Garden's Building and Remodeling Guide* often include bound-in cards enabling readers to send for booklets about products. Those requesting information may then be contacted by salespeople from the company that provided the booklet. In industrial advertising, such coupons may help identify people in a firm who influence purchasing decisions.

Ads can also help industrial salespeople gain entrance to a firm by building the reputation of the company for which they work. (See Figure 15.2.) Lanier Business Products, makers of dictating equipment, started as an unknown company but became widely recognized because of its ads in business magazines and its radio spots featuring the comedy team of Stiller and Meara.

Figure 15.2
Industrial Advertising As an Aid to Personal Selling

Source: Courtesy of Lanier Business Products, a Harris Company.

The Organization of Advertising

Advertising is an exciting field for a career. The common belief that only those with creative talent in writing or art are good prospects for advertising careers is not true. The advertising industry employs market researchers, broadcast production managers, account executives who act as liaisons between clients and agencies, media buyers, and fashion stylists, as well as people in traditional business fields such as accounting, personnel, and finance. The industry also employs jingle writers, arrangers, singers, actors, and even dogs.

The two organizations that employ the most people in the field are advertising departments and agencies.

The Advertising Department

Advertising departments operate within profit and nonprofit organizations. They are always responsible for setting the advertising objectives of a campaign and its budget. In many large retail stores, they also plan

Figure 15.3
The Organization of Ad Departments

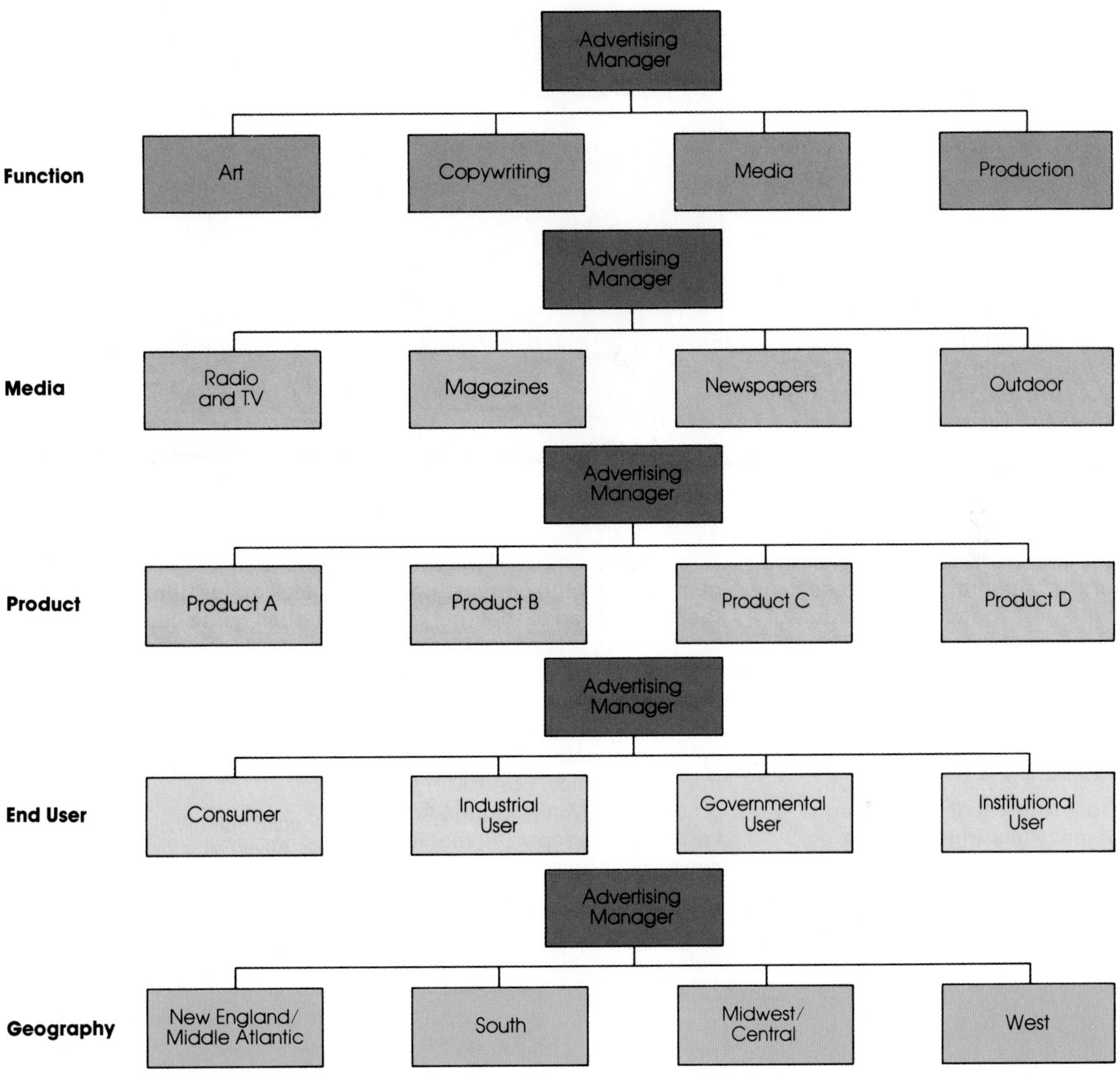

and execute the campaign. In most other organizations, however, independent advertising agencies take over these jobs, and the department reviews their work.

As Figure 15.3 shows, ad departments may be organized by function, media, product, end user, or geographical location. All are headed by an advertising manager, who usually reports to the chief marketing executive for the coordination of advertising activities with other marketing mix elements. The advertising manager's job is to oversee the plan-

At Your Service 15.1
Ad Agencies That Target Minorities

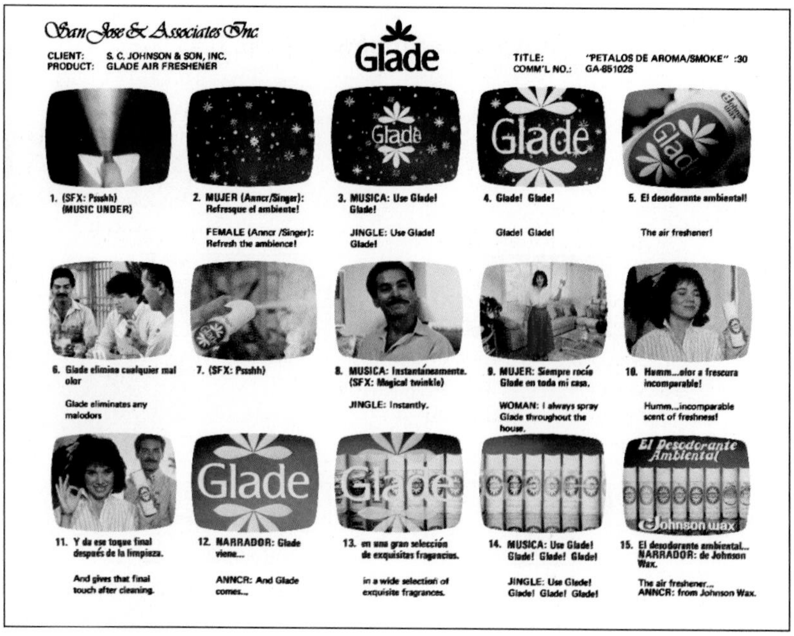

Source: Courtesy of San Jose & Associates Inc.

In an increasingly complex world, companies are frequently finding it necessary to appeal to small segments individually. In many cases, this means targeting some ads to blacks, Hispanics, and Asians.

This trend has meant more business for advertising agencies that specialize in minority markets. And some of their advertisements do so well that they are used for broader target markets. For example, Lockhart & Pettus developed an ad for Wendy's Crispy Chicken Nuggets targeted to a black audience. Using a song by Kool & the Gang, the ad urged consumers to "celebrate good times" with the product. The ad was so successful that Wendy's began using it for the product's entire campaign.

Minority ad agencies sometimes have to work harder for their business. George San Jose, president of a Chicago agency bearing his name, describes three stages of selling: (1) telling a company that the market exists; (2) convincing them that an ad to that market will result in more sales; and (3) convincing the company to use the agency.

Many companies find they need the special sensitivity of a minority agency. Frank Mingo, president of Mingo-Jones Advertising Inc., reported that in every strategy session he has attended for targeting young black males, the theme of a basketball game came up. He concludes that company managers aren't consciously stereotyping but that "their minds don't stretch beyond that."

Source: John Wall, "Minorities Slice the Advertising Pie," *Insight,* March 9, 1987, pp. 46–47.

---

ning of all campaigns, to act as a go-between in ad agency–company relations, and to control expenses.

Firms like Procter & Gamble that produce many different products have replaced the advertising manager with the product, or brand, manager. The latter has many other jobs besides advertising. The change was made because it was felt that advertising managers lack the specialized expertise needed to promote a large number of products effectively. Product managers usually oversee a few advertising specialists who give advice and work with ad agencies to create campaigns.

The Advertising Agency

About 700 advertising agencies, many of the larger ones on Madison Avenue in New York, develop and prepare most of the advertising Americans see. Agencies are useful because they bring together highly

Table 15.2
Leading Advertising Agencies in World Billings—1985

	World Billings (in Millions of Dollars)
1. Young & Rubicam	$3,575.3
2. Ogilvy Group	3,318.7
3. Ted Bates Worldwide	3,106.9
4. Saatchi & Saatchi Compton	3,033.1
5. J. Walter Thompson Company	3,009.2
6. BBDO International	2,516.0
7. McCann-Erickson Worldwide	2,302.8
8. D'Arcy Masius Benton & Bowles	2,181.3
9. Foote, Cone & Belding	1,901.0
10. Leo Burnett Company	1,868.5

Source: *Advertising Age,* March 27, 1986, p. 8.

skilled specialists. Advertisers today often prefer to work through agencies because they provide greater objectivity than an internal department and they often cost less.

The agencies themselves may specialize in handling consumer goods, industrial goods, financial services, or international business. Other agencies specialize in reaching minority target markets. (See At Your Service 15.1.) The ten largest agencies, listed in Table 15.2, handle mainly consumer goods.

Traditionally, the large established advertising agencies are paid by commission, usually 15 percent of the dollar value of the media they purchase for a company. For example, an agency may purchase $100,000 worth of space in *Mademoiselle* magazine for Revlon cosmetics. The magazine will bill the agency $85,000 ($100,000 − 15 percent commission), and the agency will bill the client the full $100,000.

Besides placing the ad, the agency may perform a number of other functions for its commission, including marketing research, product testing, and the creation and production of ad material.

As an example of how an advertising agency works, consider the efforts of Ogilvy & Mather, a large New York agency, to obtain the AT&T Advanced Information Systems account. First, the company's executive vice president and creative head assembled a team of 12 managers, account supervisors, researchers, and creative directors to develop a proposal. They, in turn, guided more than 100 writers, artists, and producers. Ogilvy & Mather had little more than two months in which to compete with nine other agencies in convincing AT&T that it had the best idea.

The company demonstrated its strengths in a credentials meeting with AT&T. While Ogilvy had little experience in the communications field, it presented eight case histories of other clients with problems similar to those of AT&T. The agency also met with a telecommunications expert to learn about the field. The agency's research department assembled a glossary of telecommunications terms for the agency's staff to refer to.

Marketing Today 15.1

Advertisements That Work

Spending a lot of money doesn't guarantee that an advertisement will get results. A New York researcher called Video Storyboard Tests confirmed this in a recent survey of television viewers. It compared how much companies spent to advertise a product with how many people remembered the ads. The result was the "cost per memory."

An example of an advertising success was the "Lee, Lee, Lee, Lee, Lee Sensation" campaign for Lee's jeans. While Lee spent less than Levi's and Wrangler, more people remembered its advertisements. But Chic, which spent the least per week to advertise, actually spent the most per 1,000 retained impressions.

Among credit cards, Visa was most efficient, with its "Everywhere you want to be" theme. For each 1,000 retained impressions, it spent only $9.10. At the other extreme was Discover, which spent $88.18 for each thousand. Discover had the hardest task, though, because it was a new product.

Source: "The Fourth Annual Measure of Efficiency," *Adweek,* March 2, 1987, pp. F.C. 22–F.C. 23+.

After the credentials meeting, AT&T provided the agency with a document asking specific questions about how the company should launch Advanced Information Systems. The media department drew up plans for placing advertisements. Team leaders met in strategy sessions and developed a campaign emphasizing product benefits. Copywriters and artists went to work. The best ideas were sorted out. The team that would present the proposal rehearsed it carefully, practicing responses to tricky questions. The final presentation was a success; the agency got the account.

Managing the Ad Campaign

We can all cite a commercial that stuck in our mind despite the fact that we saw it for only 30 seconds or glanced at it casually in a magazine. People screen out a great many of the ads they see, so breaking through their attention barrier is a real feat. (See Marketing Today 15.1.) The brief message we receive may be the product of months of work.

Among the questions that must be addressed before creating an ad that captures attention are: (1) What is the objective of this advertising campaign? (2) What is the budget? (3) How should this product be positioned? (4) What message should be used to promote it? (5) In what media should it run? and (6) How will the ad's effectiveness be measured?

Setting Advertising Objectives

Whether a company's advertising is handled in-house in an advertising department or through an independent agency, the objectives of any campaign must be in keeping with the broader promotional objectives set by the company.

There may be different goals for different types of advertising. The objective of an institutional ad may be to stimulate investor interest, while the objective of a selective or brand ad may be to encourage brand switching. In each case, goals should be quantified both in terms of degree and of time.

Establishing a Budget

Once objectives are set, a budget must be established. To determine how much of a budget should be allotted for advertising, certain factors should be taken into account. The nature of the company is probably the foremost consideration. Advertising is far less important to industrial companies than to those specializing in consumer goods. The nature of the product is also significant. Producers of soft drinks, toys, cosmetics, and tobacco products typically spend a far greater percentage of their total budgets on advertising than companies manufacturing clothing, furniture, or greeting cards. The stage in the product life cycle and the company's financial resources must also be considered. Once a budget has been agreed upon, the challenge of creating the ad can begin.

Positioning

Many advertisers today accept the theory of **positioning.**[9] The theory states that to sell a product, a company must create a unique niche or position for the product in the consumer's mind. Positioning actually involves defining a class of competitors and finding a way to distinguish the product in that class.

Positioning
Theory holding that to sell a product, a company must create a unique niche or position for it in the consumer's mind.

Are competitors really a matter of choice rather than a given? In many cases, yes. Before 1970, for example, the rule of thumb was that one drank red wines with red meats and white wines with chicken and fish. Instead of going along with this accepted rule of thumb, the agency for Blue Nun, a German white wine, had positioned it as a wine that was correct with every dish. The strategy was so successful that other companies adopted it. The company then switched its positioning to "Blue Nun Goes Everywhere," suggesting that people take the wine on picnics and to the beach. Later Schiefflin & Company, the wine's importer, again repositioned Blue Nun, this time in a by-the-glass promotion.[10]

Sometimes all the competitors in a certain class are very much alike, and one firm dominates. It may not pay to meet the competition head on. RCA discovered this when it tried to enter the computer field against IBM and failed miserably. Positioning can help to avoid direct competition. Ad agencies try to find a selling proposition that distinguishes the product. Thus, to compete with similar brands of aerobics shoes, all made of leather, Avia advertised the extra shock absorption provided by its double-wedge heel. B. F. Goodrich's campaign against Goodyear ("We're the other guys—without the blimp") was one of the most successful of all time for the company.

Creating the Message

For a successful campaign, it is not enough to find a unique position for a product. In the 1960s, for example, NoCal set itself up against Coke and Pepsi as the only sugar-free soft drink, but it soon lost out when Tab and Diet Pepsi came on the scene. The reason, according to one analyst, is that its advertising messages were bland.[11] In the hotly com-

At Your Service 15.2
Travelers Puts Its Image on Canvas

When The Travelers insurance group wanted to create an image for its organization, it turned to Bill Richards, a New York artist. The company commissioned a painting that interprets its famous red umbrella. Richards painted in front of television cameras and an enthusiastic live audience.

According to the advertising agency's creative director, Bob Joseph, showing the creator, the process of creation, and the creation itself is a visual symbol of The Travelers' ability to "turn the business of investment into an art." By showing Richards at work on various stages of the painting, the ad equates the nurturing of investments with the slow grace of the painter.

The finished painting hangs in the company's headquarters.

Source: Chuck Reece, "Travelers Turns Investment into Art," *Adweek*, July 14, 1986, p. 24.

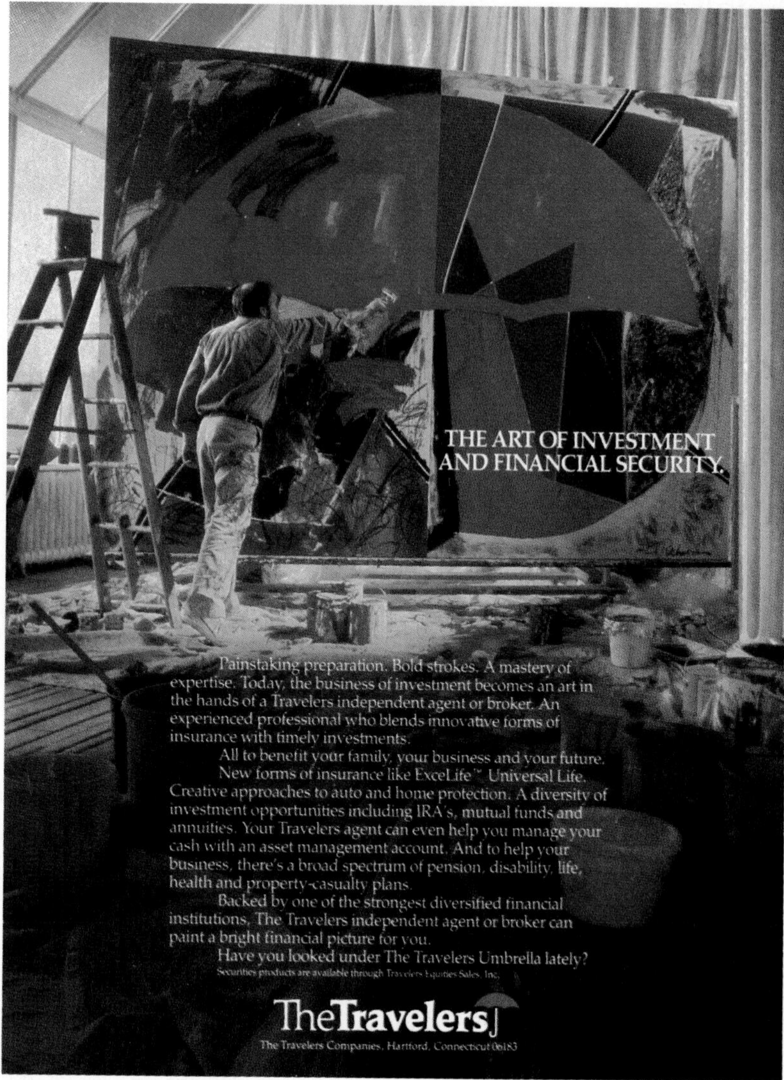

petitive advertising business, the message is just as important as the position for success.

THE ART OF INVESTMENT
AND FINANCIAL SECURITY.
Painstaking preparation. Bold strokes. A mastery of expertise. Today, the business of investment becomes an art in the hands of a Travelers independent agent or broker. An experienced professional who blends innovative forms of insurance with timely investments.
All to benefit your family, your business and your future.
New forms of insurance like ExceLife™ Universal Life. Creative approaches to auto and home protection. A diversity of investment opportunities including IRA's, mutual funds and annuities. Your Travelers agent can even help you manage your cash with an asset management account. And to help your business, there's a broad spectrum of pension, disability, life, health and property-casualty plans.
Backed by one of the strongest diversified financial institutions, The Travelers independent agent or broker can paint a bright financial picture for you.
Have you looked under The Travelers Umbrella lately?
Securities products are available through Travelers Equities Sales, Inc.
TheTravelers
The Travelers Companies, Hartford, Connecticut 06183

Over the years, several creative styles for presenting messages have evolved. Some of them have established the reputations of today's largest agencies.

The Image Sell One of the best-known approaches, the image sell, stresses the importance of creating an exclusive image for a product in ads. David Ogilvy, of the Ogilvy Group, is noted for this approach in the selling of Schweppes mixers. In his ads, he featured the elegant figure of Commander Whitehead, Schweppes' president.[12] The quality image is still with the product today, more than 30 years after it was first introduced. At Your Service 15.2 describes the creation of an image for The Travelers insurance group.

Figure 15.4
IBM's Dramatic Departure from Its No-Nonsense Image

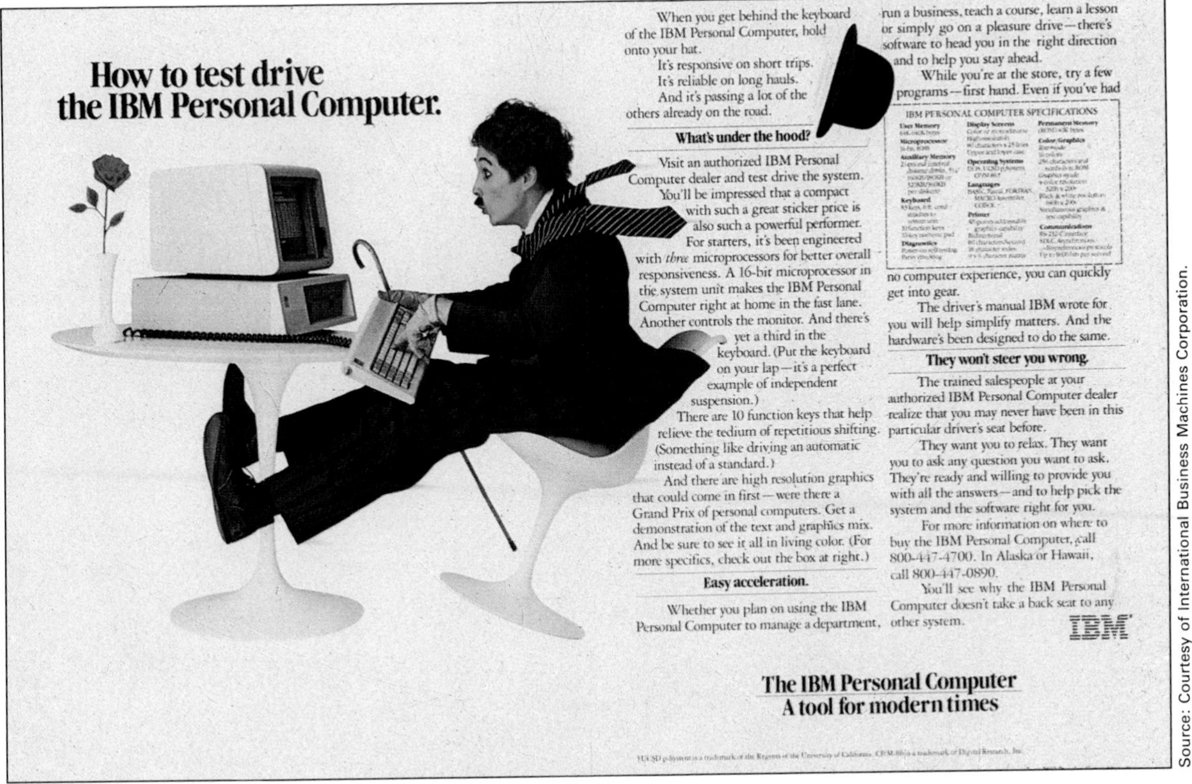

Source: Courtesy of International Business Machines Corporation.

In some cases, a successful company image in one market may be a handicap in another. IBM, for example, had built a blue-chip name in the world of office equipment, but in the mass market it was perceived as cold and efficient. To launch its first mass-market product, the Personal Computer (PC), IBM knew it had to humanize its image. The company decided to use Charlie Chaplin's Little Tramp, with his baggy trousers and ever-present red rose, to make the company—and the product—seem less threatening. (See Figure 15.4.) The strategy worked. By combining its traditional aggressive marketing with low-cost production and a new, friendly image, IBM, in two years' time, rocketed to number one in sales in the personal computer industry.[13]

Jockey International used an image of comfort and fun to introduce its line of Jockey for Her underwear. (See Figure 15.5.)

The Direct Sell The opposite of the image sell is the direct sell. This approach, advocated by Ted Bates Worldwide, relies on uncovering one unique product benefit (or "unique selling proposition") and then hammering it home through repetition. A well-known example of this format is the ad for M&Ms, "the candy that melts in your mouth, not in

LOOK WHO'S WEARING JOCKEY® NOW!
You!...Now, a free oversized T-shirt offer for all you Jockey fans.
JUST JOCKEY
For all its comforts.
To get your free, 100% soft cotton, oversized T-shirt ($9.00 retail value), send this coupon, along with the Jockey name cut from any package of Jockey men's or Jockey For Her underwear and $2.00 (to cover postage and handling) to: Jockey For Her, Free T-shirt Offer, P.O. Box 4424, Maple Plain, MN 55348.
Name
Apt.
Address
Zip
City
State
Check One Color: ☐ Mint ☐ Peach ☐ Light Blue
Allow 6-8 weeks for delivery. Valid in USA only. Offer ends
RS
Look Who's Wearing JOCKEY Now!
Look Who's Wearing JOCKEY Now!
Boxer shorts and Sierra shirt by Jockey.
Available at these and other fine stores:
SANGER-HARRIS
LAZARUS

your hands." The direct sell also lends itself to product demonstrations, such as absorbency tests for paper towels.

The Humorous or Soft Sell Ads that joke about the product were the rage of the late 1960s and early 1970s. Among the most famous were Alka-Seltzer's spots ("Try it, you'll like it"; "I can't believe I ate the whole thing"). The ad slogans became part of everyday speech, but they did little to sell the product. In fact, sales actually declined.

Later Alka-Seltzer spots were based on in-depth marketing research, which showed that heavy users of antacids are largely middle-American, upwardly mobile people. Alka-Seltzer's agency repositioned the product as an upbeat remedy for "the symptoms of stress that can come with success."[14]

Humor seems to be making a comeback in advertising, although in a new form. The newer advertising is based on a kind of humor that focuses on life's most anxious moments.

The Competitive Sell **Comparative advertising,** as the competitive sell is also known, is the creative style that uses the names of competitors. The Scali, McCabe, Sloves Agency popularized the technique after the FTC ruled in 1972 that naming competitors was in the public interest. The commission reasoned that ads identifying only "Brand X" offered too much freedom to set up imaginary competition. The battle between competitors got under way in earnest when Pepsi attacked Coke in its Pepsi Challenge taste tests and Coke counterattacked.

Comparative Advertising
Creative style that uses names of competitors.

A similar battle broke out when Burger King launched a campaign claiming that its broiled burgers are better than those of McDonald's, which are fried. McDonald's sued immediately, a response that backfired. The battle made network news, resulting in enormous free publicity for Burger King and better sales growth than for McDonald's.[15]

When competing soft drinks started advertising that they contain fruit juice, Orangina countered with comparative advertising, billing itself as "The soft drink with juice you can taste." For the company to be able to run these ads on network television, it first had to prove the difference by using focus groups. The advertisements feature crowds of angry Americans, rock singers, and a sad young woman, all complaining that they can't taste the juice in Orangina's competitors. The advertising agency's creative director explains that the ads tell Orangina drinkers, "You're smarter than other people, hipper, and you understand what's bogus in this world."[16]

Are consumers really better served by naming names? Critics say no. They maintain that citing names only contributes to information overload. Consumers remember that two names were mentioned, but they do not remember which claimed to be better. Moreover, the information

Figure 15.5
An Image Sell for Jockey
Source: Jockey International Inc., Kenosha, Wisconsin.

Table 15.3
Advertising Expenditures by Media

Medium	Percent
Newspapers	26.5%
Television	21.9
Miscellaneous*	21.7
Direct Mail	16.4
Radio	6.9
Magazines	5.4
Outdoor	1.0

*The amount identified as "miscellaneous" may include computer videotex, cinema advertising, point-of-purchase displays, and directories.

Source: *Information Please Almanac* (Boston: Houghton Mifflin, 1987), p. 66.

one competitor uses against another may be selective, providing data only in areas in which the brand excels.[17] But defenders maintain that consumers do benefit from comparisons. After Datril challenged Tylenol in ads, the price of Tylenol came down. And in a Brillo versus SOS controversy, the brand under attack changed its soap content.[18]

Selecting the Media

A campaign can still fail, despite accurate positioning and a highly creative message, if an advertisement does not reach the right audience. Media selection therefore is usually given over to experts. As used in promotion, **media** are all the different means by which advertising reaches its audience.[19]

Media
All the different means by which advertising reaches its audiences.

In some ways, media experts have an easier job today. In the 1890s, for example, there was a craze for placing ads in unusual places—on the sides of elephants at a circus, for example, or even on low-hanging clouds via a projector.[20] Today, there are only six major media—newspapers, magazines, television, radio, direct mail, and outdoor/transit signs. The division of the advertising dollar among them is shown in Table 15.3.

Besides the major media, advertisers look for new ways to draw attention to products. For example, Pepsi has tried advertising at the beginning of the videocassette version of *Top Gun*. Likewise, Target Vision uses video billboards to broadcast on college campuses via closed-circuit television. It features editorial material on the weather, entertainment, and campus activities. Advertisers buy time on these billboards.[21]

Although the number of major media is small, deciding which to use can be complex. Many factors must be considered. The nature of the product or service is one. Radio, for example, is unsuitable for conveying the features of fashion goods—they must be seen. The size of the advertising budget is another factor. A small retailer would be hard-pressed to advertise on an expensive medium like television.

Media experts also look at the strengths and weaknesses of the media themselves. There are five qualities that help distinguish them:

Table 15.4
Rating Ads by Media

When making day-to-day purchases, do you rely a great deal, some, or very little on information provided by advertising in the following media?

Media	Responses*
Newpapers	66%
In-store	58
TV	55
Magazines	53
Yellow Pages	51
Radio	42
Direct Mail	33

*Percentage of responses indicating "a great deal" or "some."

Source: *Advertising Age,* October 24, 1983, p. 18.

1. *Selectivity*—whether a medium reaches only those who are potential buyers.
2. *Flexibility*—how much time in advance an ad must be placed.
3. *Life span*—the length of time the audience is exposed to a message.
4. *Production quality*—how many human senses are engaged and how well.
5. *Reputation*—the credibility and prestige of the medium.

Some media are stronger in some of these qualities than in others, as a closer look at each will show.

Newspapers There are about 1,700 daily, 750 Sunday, and 9,000 weekly newspapers in the United States. Most are local, but a few—like *USA Today* and *The Wall Street Journal*—are national. The geographic selectivity of newspapers is one of their advantages. Local retailers need not waste advertising money on those who cannot reach their stores. Newspapers also have a reputation for credibility among the more than three-quarters of the population who read them daily. That asset is generally transferred to the advertising that appears in them. One study found that in making day-to-day purchases, consumers relied on newspapers more than any other form of advertising. (See Table 15.4.) One further advantage is that ads can be placed in newspapers almost overnight.

Newspapers get poor marks on life span and production quality, however. They are read very quickly and are saved only for about a day. Reproduction of illustrations has been poor, although modern methods of printing have lessened this problem.

Magazines The audience for magazines is vast—85 million Americans regularly read some of the 9,000 consumer, farm, and business magazines. Despite the large overall audience, most magazines are highly targeted because they appeal to special interests (fashion, sports, specific hobbies). Even mass-circulation magazines like *Time* have regional editions so that advertisers can select the areas where they want their messages to appear. In addition, magazines are strong where newspapers are weak. They have a comparatively long life span (as well as a high pass-along rate), and they offer high-quality illustrations for products like fashion and food.

The quality that magazines lack most is flexibility. Monthly magazine ads, for example, must be placed 60 to 90 days in advance. Magazines also appeal to only the sense of sight, which limits their effectiveness for some products.

Television The reasons for advertising on TV are clear: more American homes are equipped with a television set than with a bathtub, and the average set is on about seven hours a day. Although television is a mass medium, it can be selective. Ads may be placed nationally on one of the three networks, in specific geographic areas (or "spots"), or locally on one station. In addition, the programming guarantees some demographic selectivity (for example, "Gimme a Break" appeals primarily to teenagers, "One Day at a Time" to women). Television also scores high on production quality. It is excellent for product demonstrations because it reproduces both pictures and the human voice. The skillful advertiser can benefit from the flexibility of being able to combine words, graphics, actors, and music. For example, research has suggested that the use of background music can affect how certain viewers respond to television commercials.[22]

For television, however, national advertisements usually must be booked months in advance, although local stations are more flexible. The life of a TV commercial is at most 60 seconds, and usually only 30. And, finally, television commercials are expensive. The cost of a TV commercial grew 230 percent between 1970 and 1982—far more than costs in any other medium. Typically, prime-time 30-second network spots now cost more than $100,000. Add to that the cost of producing the commercial itself, which has exceeded $1 million, and it is clear that television is a medium ordinarily affordable only by larger advertisers. (National advertisers spent $10.56 billion on TV in 1982, accounting for 27 percent of all advertising expenditures.[23])

One response to skyrocketing television advertising costs has been the birth of the "split 30." Under this arrangement, one advertiser can run commercials for two different products as long as the ad's total length is no more than 30 seconds. Alberto-Culver, for example, could buy one time slot and advertise Alberto VO5 shampoo and Sugar Twin sweetener. Advocates claim split 30s are the only way to cope with rising costs. Critics say they only create unmanageable commercial clutter, lead to less creativity in advertising, and sell products less effectively.[24] Advertisers fear the increase in "zapping," whereby viewers with remote control devices simply change stations when commercials appear. Nevertheless, some advertisers have tried even shorter, 15-second ads.

Despite its disadvantages, television advertising is expected to grow in the future. Some advertisers have begun to sponsor low-budget programs on cable TV, whose content often fits neatly with a sponsor's products. While the audiences for these shows are much smaller than for network programming, they have the advantage of being highly targeted. An audience of car enthusiasts is virtually guaranteed, for example, for "STP's Pitstop" show, which runs during stock-car races on a sports cable channel.[25]

Radio Radio is experiencing one of the most innovative and competitive periods in its history. Satellite transmission means that local stations can tap into a broad range of national programming. AM stations, while they are struggling to regain lost market share,[26] can broadcast in stereo. Computers are being used to transmit fast-breaking news stories. Government deregulation of requirements governing licensing has resulted in the creation of from 600 to 800 new stations, bringing the total close to 9,000.

Radio is attractive to advertisers for many reasons. In drawing power, radio dominates television through most of the day. Radio's audience is broad. There are more than 456 million radios in the United States (about 5.7 per household).[27] Radio is also far more selective than TV. Most programs originate locally, and special formats (all-news, talk, rock music, country music) help segment the audience. Scheduling is generally more flexible for a radio commercial as well, and total cost is also usually less.

Radio commercials, like television's, are brief. But their chances of being heard may be greater because there are over 93 million radios in cars alone, and many of those are tuned in during "drive time," the period spent commuting to and from work. In addition, nearly 12 percent of the population now owns some form of walkabout radio, so potential consumers may hear an advertiser's message while out jogging, walking the dog, or working on a tan at the beach.[28]

With television ad prices becoming astronomical, many analysts believe that radio will emerge as an even stronger medium in the future.

Direct Mail In 1981, nearly $9 billion was spent on various forms of direct mail, including sales letters, catalogs, postcards, and house organs (periodicals published by organizations), among others.

Direct mail combines many of the qualities that advertisers look for in a medium. With the aid of computers, potential customers can be targeted in an infinite variety of ways, and messages can be personalized.

Direct mail is also flexible. With the help of a cooperative printer and first-class postage (rarely used, however, because of the expense), a rush campaign could take only days from conception to a consumer's mailbox. Direct mail is also the medium in which it is easiest to track results. Given a generous budget, direct mail can incorporate magazine quality art—or even a sample of the product.

Among its drawbacks are its association with "junk mail" and its relatively high cost. In addition, its growing popularity among marketers has led to such an increase in volume that it is easy for one company's message to be lost among those of so many competitors jamming a consumer's mailbox. One trade association has estimated that the average American home receives 80 catalogs a year—but those with a history of buying by mail may receive two to three times that number.[29]

Nonetheless, direct mail is big business. Increasingly, U.S. companies are looking to the international market as a vast, relatively untapped area for expansion.

Outdoor/Transit Media Outdoor advertising, which may include billboards, blimps, joggers' T-shirts, taxicabs, and more, accounts for about 2.8 percent of all advertising expenditures.[30] Although this medium fell from favor somewhat following the passage of the Highway Beautification Act of 1965, it subsequently experienced a rebirth of interest.[31] During 1980, advertisers spent an estimated $700 million to put their messages on billboards.[32]

Besides being relatively inexpensive, outdoor media are selective of local audiences, and they have a long life span—often 30 days or more. However, traffic jams aside, passersby are generally exposed to billboards for only about five to ten seconds, which limits the message they can carry.

The San Diego Zoo has overcome this limitation by using a series of three billboards with a simple message. (See Figure 15.6.) The first board shows a snake that flicks its tongue as it slithers toward a birthday cake. A quarter mile away, another board shows the same snake, mouth open and closer to the cake. Another quarter mile away, the snake has swallowed the cake, and now-curious motorists see a message that explains the pictures: "Celebrate the San Diego Zoo's 70th Birthday."

Other companies are regular users of billboards and transit posters despite their limitations. The tobacco and liquor industries are by far the biggest investors in outdoor media.

Some firms are trying novel ideas for outdoor advertising that go far beyond run-of-the-road billboards. One company makes inflatable advertising pieces in the shape of corporate products and characters—sometimes as high as 30 feet tall. Its clients include Miller Brewing Company, McDonald's, and Coca-Cola.[33] Another enterprising advertiser affixes message-carrying, 8-foot-long blimp-shaped balloons to mopeds, and has riders cruise the highways simulating moving billboards.[34]

Testing Advertising Effectiveness

The cost of producing—writing, casting, filming, and editing—a single uncomplicated TV commercial can run to $100,000. Added to that is the cost of purchasing time. Magazines can be expensive as well. A single page in *Newsweek* magazine, for example, can cost more than $50,000.

With that kind of money at stake, advertisers want some assurance that their messages will bring results. Advertisers try to measure such things as whether the intended audience was exposed to, is aware of, or can recall their messages. A few common ways of testing effectiveness are noted in Table 15.5.

Figure 15.6
A Series of Billboards That Tell a Story

Celebrate the San Diego Zoo's 70th birthday.

Source: Client: San Diego Zoo; Agency: Phillips-Ramsey. Used with permission.

Advertising: Criticisms and Constraints

Creating a major advertising campaign is a complex process, involving a good measure of art, an equal dose of science, a hefty amount of money, and a small army of people. At its best, advertising can be an amusing, informative, creative, and cost-effective way of communicating information about a product. But because it is such a powerful means of delivering a message, it has also been the focus of a great deal of criticism.

Advertising has been accused of being deceptive, manipulative, wasteful, and irritating. Critics say that advertising often degrades women,

Table 15.5
Techniques for Measuring Advertising Effectiveness

Pretesting

Evaluation of advertising before the campaign.

Opinion and Attitude Tests

Consumer juries —carefully selected panels of people are asked to rate the effectiveness of various ads.

Theater-type tests —test TV commercials are screened by an audience that indicates likes and dislikes by pressing a button.

Attitude scales —respondents are asked to rate their feelings toward a particular advertisement on an attitude rating scale.

Mechanical Laboratory Methods

Tachistoscopes —a mechanical device that measure how long it takes respondents to get the point of an illustration, a headline, etc.

Eye camera —a camera that photographs the movement of people's eyes while they read an ad to gain information on the placement of a headline, the length of the copy, etc.

Psychogalvanometer —similar to a lie detector, this instrument measures a subject's emotional reaction to an ad.

Pupillometer —this device measures a subject's pupil size while viewing an ad; wider pupils indicate interest or emotional involvement.

Projective Techniques

Depth interviewing —a trained interviewer probes a respondent about underlying feelings about an ad, for example, "What does this ad tell you about yourself?"

Word association and sentence completion tests —a researcher selects certain words or phrases from an ad to test consumer reaction to their meaning.

Concurrent Testing

Evaluation of TV and radio advertising at the time it is aired.

Nielsen audiometer —electronic device used to record audience tuning of TV sets.

Consumer diaries —booklets in which members of a representative sample record what they are actually viewing or listening to.

Posttesting

Evaluation of advertising after it has appeared in various media.

Readership (recognition) tests —at a certain point after the receipt of a magazine, an interviewer asks a reader to go through the publication and indicate which ads were read.

Recall tests —similar to a readership test, but respondents are asked to tell what they remember about an ad without having the magazine before them.

Attitude change measures —a survey of the change in consumer attitudes about a product following an advertising campaign by using a similar precampaign study as a benchmark.

insults men, and takes advantage of children who are too young to distinguish between programming and commercials.

The advertising community is understandably concerned about these charges. To counter what it feels is unfair criticism, it has mounted an advertising campaign of its own to attempt to change consumer percep-

Table 15.6
Some FTC Programs Regulating Advertising

Substantiation. The FTC may require an advertiser to submit all test studies, research, and other data to support a questioned advertising claim. Products that are potentially harmful (such as drugs) or are widely used (such as autos, gasoline, and appliances) receive special surveillance.

Disclosure of Information. The FTC considers as deceptive advertising the failure to provide important information, which could then lead to a purchase decision based on false assumptions. The FTC is especially interested in expensive products, such as automobiles and appliances, and products using excessive amounts of energy.

Endorsements. A product endorsement by an expert must be based on that person's actual use of the product and can be used only as long as that person continues to use the product.

Corrective Advertising. If consumer research determines that lasting false beliefs have been created about a product through advertising, the FTC may require that corrective advertising be run to dispel those beliefs. One of the best-known examples of this ruling occurred when the FTC required Warner-Lambert to specify in its ads that Listerine did not cure colds or sore throats.

Children's Advertising. The FTC has been particularly concerned about advertising to children, especially those under the age of eight. This area promises to be a continued source of controversy, especially with regard to the licensing of toy characters for television series and specials.

---

tions about advertising. The campaign featured an advertisement with the heading "This ad is full of lies." The advertisement went on to provide arguments against the "lies" that advertising makes people buy things they don't want, makes things cost more, helps bad products sell, and is a waste of money.

Individual advertisers have also responded to complaints. For example, a single father wrote to Sears to complain about brochures for cleaning products that were explicitly directed to "mother." The director of public affairs at Sears wrote to the unhappy father, promising that the company would henceforth try to substitute the word *parent* for *mother* or *father*.[35]

But many of the criticisms leveled against advertising are more serious than simply an unpopular public image. In the past, some advertising has been deceptive, and some downright false. As noted in Chapter 3, the advertising industry has formed a self-governing body, the National Advertising Review Board (NARB), to help guard against such abuses. In addition, various governmental agencies have the power to regulate advertising. The most powerful of these groups is the Federal Trade Commission (FTC). The FTC's most important programs for regulating advertising are cited in Table 15.6.

While there is no denying that many of the criticisms of advertising have been justified, the general public still seems to think that the benefits of advertising outweigh its possible hazards. A recent study showed that 93 percent of respondents agreed or strongly agreed that advertising is an important part of the American economy; 59 percent said they enjoyed the advertising they read, saw, or heard; and a surprising 53 percent said they would like their children to be employed in the advertising business.[36]

The Role of Sales Promotion

Sales promotion covers promotional efforts that cannot be classed as personal selling, advertising, or publicity. Factory tours, cents-off coupons, trade show exhibits, and message-bearing beer mugs are all examples of the forms sales promotion can take.

As they do with advertising, marketers should begin a sales promotional campaign by establishing objectives and a budget. For the consumer market, objectives might include encouraging brand switching, attracting new users, or getting established customers to buy greater quantities. For intermediaries, objectives might include encouraging retailers to carry a new product line or a higher level of inventory, building brand loyalty, or offsetting a competitor's promotion. For the sales force, objectives might include building support for a new product or model, encouraging more sales calls, or stimulating off-season sales.[37]

Sales promotion often is designed to assist the efforts of the sales force. In some cases, the aid is direct, as when it paves the way for a sales rep's call. For example, American Telecom Inc., a low-profile supplier of telecommunications equipment, developed a sweet way to introduce potential distributors to its new line. Instead of sending them the usual telegram, brochure, or pamphlet, the company sent each dealer a box containing a three-and-a-half-pound solid chocolate telephone, a sample contract, some introductory literature, and the business card of the ATI regional sales manager. The cost of the mailing was high—$50 per piece—but the response more than justified the expenditure. Every single dealer expressed interest in handling the new line, and ATI found itself in the enviable position of being able to pick the dealers it wanted to form its distributor network.[38]

Like ATI's gift, many sales promotion tools are aimed at intermediaries. The theory is that a wholesaler or retailer deals with thousands of products and must be offered an extra incentive to "push" those of a particular firm. But sales promotions can also be directed toward consumers and the sales force. When consumers are the target, the producer tries to pressure intermediaries indirectly by creating consumer demand (a "pull strategy"). When the target is the sales force, the purpose is to fire up enthusiasm or keep members informed.

Table 15.7 lists the tools of sales promotion by target audience, and Figure 15.7 shows the relative importance of some of them.

Promoting to the Sales Force

Perhaps the most common form of sales promotion to the sales force is the annual sales meeting. Here new product lines are introduced and selling techniques refreshed. Since salespeople who sell directly to consumers encounter more rejections than others, their meetings are often more like pep rallies.

Besides sales meetings, contests and incentive campaigns are common promotional motivators. Each year, for example, Ciba-Geigy Corporation, a pharmaceutical company, gives Distinguished Performance Awards to its top sales reps. Winners get pewter bowls, publicity in the

Table 15.7
Types of Sales Promotion

For Sales Reps	For Intermediaries	For Consumers
Sales meetings	Sales meetings	In-store demonstrations
Sales manuals	Contests	Premiums
Product demonstration models	Push money	Samples
Contests and incentive campaigns	Dealer gifts	Coupons
Sales letters and bulletins	Point-of-purchase materials	Trading stamps
	Trade shows and exhibits	Refunds
	Advertising allowances	Contests and games
	Business catalogs	Direct mailings

Journal of the American Medical Association (which is read by their physician customers), and a three-day vacation. Increases in sales of about 20 percent are common during such campaigns.[39]

Promoting to the Intermediary

Some promotional tools aimed at sales reps—including sales meetings, contests, and gifts—can also be used effectively with intermediaries. Others—such as trade shows, point-of-purchase materials, and advertising allowances—are targeted specifically for wholesale intermediaries and retailers.

Trade Shows Every year nearly 6,000 manufacturers exhibit their goods at **trade shows** to audiences of nearly 80 million people. The main purpose of these expositions is to allow salespeople to display their new products to dealers, to make new contacts, and to develop mailing lists for future use. In some industries, such as apparel, they also provide a marketplace where sales are made.

Trade Show
Exposition that allows salespeople to display their new products to dealers, to make new contacts, and to develop mailing lists for future use.

Point-of-Purchase Materials Posters and signs, display racks, banners, and price cards are some of the promotional tools classified as **point-of-purchase (POP) materials.** In addition, POP materials today are more sophisticated, incorporating materials such as interactive video and displays that emit product aromas.[40]

Point-of-Purchase (POP) Materials
Promotional tools such as posters, display racks, and price cards.

Marketers spend billions of dollars each year on POP displays. Perhaps the largest array of such displays is found in supermarkets. With thousands of products competing for consumer attention, an impressive POP device can give a product a competitive edge. Surveys have shown that the addition of POP materials to an advertising program can increase awareness of the entire program by up to 50 percent.[41]

Today, a growing trend is for retailers to take control of POP displays. Many retailers have been disappointed over the quality of some POP materials, so they use materials they generate themselves. These

Figure 15.7
The Importance of Selected Promotional Tools

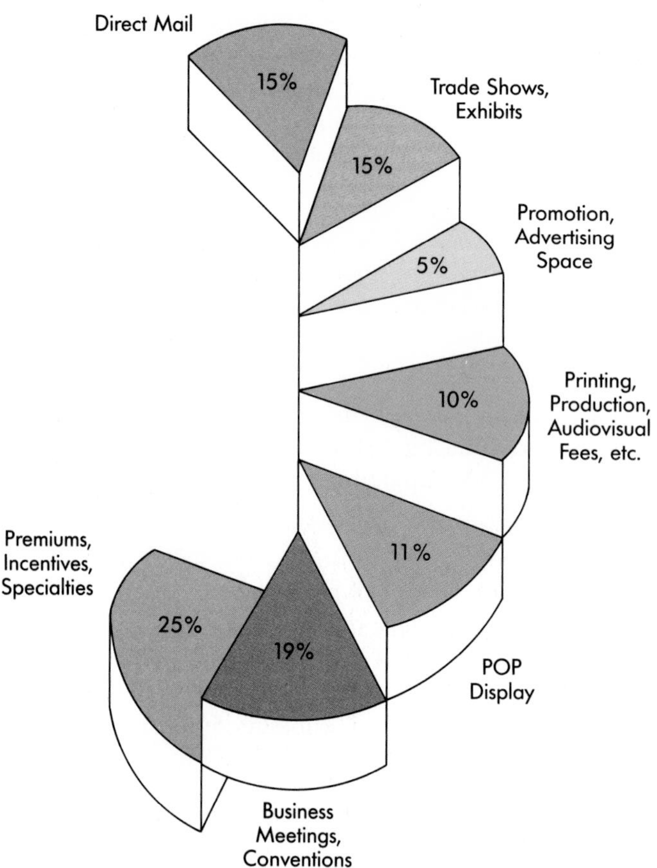

Source: Adapted from Roger A. Strang, "Sales Promotion—Fast Growth, Faulty Management," *Harvard Business Review* (July–August 1976): 118.

materials guide customers through the store and have a unified design. In response, some manufacturers are working closely with retailers to design POP materials. The aim is to prepare materials that work most effectively for both the manufacturer and the retailer.[42]

Advertising Allowance
Reimbursement by a manufacturer for part of the cost of local advertising run by retailers and wholesalers.

Advertising Allowances Frequently retailers, and sometimes wholesalers, are reimbursed in part by a manufacturer for running the company's ad in a newspaper or on local broadcast media. Such **advertising allowances** are commonly given to department stores by appliance manufacturers and cosmetics companies. "Cooperative advertising," as it is also known, can be very attractive to dealers. Often the added business that the ads bring in will cost retailers much less because of the money refunded by the manufacturer for running the ad.

Promoting to Consumers

Sales promotions to consumers are often dated to encourage an immediate impact on sales or on a company's competitive position. Unfortunately for the initiator, most sales incentives are easily duplicated, and therefore may have only a short-term effect before competitors' defensive maneuvers erode any sales increases.

Coupons In 1985, producers of packaged goods issued 180 billion **coupons,** with a face value of about $50 billion—about double the value of coupons issued only three years earlier. The consumers who redeemed these coupons cut their shopping bills by about $2 billion.[43] Beginning in 1986, however, the pace of growth seems to have slowed. Some evidence indicates that companies may now be shifting to less use of coupons and greater use of other kinds of promotional activity, such as advertising.[44]

Coupon
Sales promotion tool aimed at consumers that offers a certain amount off the price of an item.

Most coupons are distributed through the mail, in newspapers and magazines, within a package, or on the back of cash register tapes. Large food-processing companies such as General Mills and Pillsbury are among the largest providers of coupons to the public.

One reason coupons have been popular among manufacturers is the increasing costliness of advertising rates. Coupons enable manufacturers to maintain a price while stimulating sales with a price break. Coupons also can be effective in inducing consumers to try a new product. They are relatively flexible and easy to use, consumers find them appealing, and they are suitable for a number of marketing objectives.

One drawback of coupons is that they may be redeemed fraudulently by people who didn't actually buy the product. While manufacturers have tried to fight the problem in various ways, including the use of decoy coupons, the problem persists.[45] In addition, persistent use of coupons can "train" consumers to wait for a price break before buying.[46]

Samples and Premiums Manufacturers offer **samples,** or giveaways in a trial size, for products whose benefits cannot be fully conveyed through advertising. Computer software companies, for example, sometimes have demonstration diskettes bound into issues of computer magazines such as *PC World.* This enables subscribers to sample new programs.

Sample
Giveaway in a trial size for products whose benefits cannot be fully conveyed through advertising.

Samples may also be mailed, given away in stores, or handed out on streets. They are expensive, but they gain attention.

Premiums are items offered free or at a low cost as a reward for buying a product. They may keep customers loyal and, if properly selected, reinforce the product's image. Bob Valenti Chevy Oldsmobile in Mystic, Connecticut, used premiums that generated a lot of attention. The dealership had trouble selling five Toronados, so it advertised that consumers who bought a Toronado would get a free Yugo. Within a month, all five Toronados were off the lot. Some people who looked at the cars came from 200 miles away.[47]

Premium
Item offered free or at a low cost as a reward for buying a product.

Blending Sales Promotion Tools

The strongest sales promotion programs tie together the tools aimed at various groups. Revlon cosmetics offers an excellent example. In a typical large department store such as Macy's, Revlon's program might employ the following promotional tools:

1. Bonuses for retail sales personnel.
2. Training for in-store demonstrators.
3. Cooperative advertising funds.
4. Installation of cosmetic counters and fixtures.
5. Consumer gifts with purchases.
6. Special clinics for teenagers.

Revlon's program includes something for everyone—sales personnel, store owners, and consumers. Any one of the elements listed may help to increase sales. Working together, however, they produce a whole that is greater than the sum of its parts.

Marketers can also blend sales promotion tools with other types of product promotion. For example, Charles of the Ritz combines free samples with advertising. In ads for eye shadow, readers can pull back tabs to find samples of the makeup to try on immediately. Some observers are optimistic that this technique will give a big boost to makeup sales.[48]

The Role of Publicity

When Grete Waitz crossed the finish line as the women's champion of the 1983 New York Marathon, millions of people were watching. It was no coincidence that prominently displayed on Ms. Waitz's uniform were the words "Team Xerox." Subsequent photos of Ms. Waitz in the press and on television news broadcasts carried the Xerox message to millions of additional viewers. While the company paid the runners to wear the uniform, it didn't have to pay for the media coverage.

After studying their potential customer base, Xerox marketers had determined that sponsorship of sports events was an efficient way to reach the market they had targeted. Marathon running seemed a natural tie-in with their new line of photocopiers. The company decided to sponsor 15 major marathon events around the world. It also assembled "Team Xerox," consisting of world-class runners Grete Waitz, Bill Rogers, and Rob de Castella, who agreed to wear Team Xerox uniforms whenever allowed.[49]

The company carefully reinforced the marathon tie-in by running advertising for the photocopier featuring a marathon runner in the business press. Xerox demonstrated a skillful use of publicity, both for its new product line and for the company's corporate image.

Publicity, as defined in Chapter 14, refers to any information relating to a manufacturer or its products that appears in any medium on a nonpaid basis. This definition hints at the major differences between

Table 15.8
Major Differences between Advertising and Publicity

Advertising	Publicity
Paid for	No charge for media coverage
Selling slant	News slant
Sometimes lacks credibility	High credibility
Ads scheduled close together	Items infrequently used more than once
Placer has complete control	Media share control

publicity and advertising, which are summarized in Table 15.8. For one thing, because the medium providing the coverage doesn't charge for the time or space, publicity is less controllable than advertising. A 300-word publicity release submitted to a newspaper may be cut to 50 words or run on a slow news day instead of on the day the publicist preferred. Also, unlike advertisements, which can be repeated until the public recalls them, a publicity item usually appears only once.

Despite these disadvantages, publicity can be a valuable promotional tool used in conjunction with advertising or by itself. It appears as news and therefore is as believable as news. An advertisement by Exxon saying that it is doing its best to find new energy sources may be met with skepticism. A news item prepared by an Exxon publicist that tells the story of a new oil find and its importance may be a more effective way of helping the company's image. Because publicity is highly believable, organizations and professionals who would normally not advertise have found it an effective means of promotion.

In addition to news releases, which are usually 300-word pieces sometimes accompanied by a photograph, there are four other publicity tools:

1. *Feature articles*—500- to 3,000-word articles that often appear in the business and family-living sections of newspapers.
2. *Press conferences and personal appearances*—Businesses use these for major announcements, such as executive changes.
3. *Records and films*—Radio and television stations often need "fillers."
4. *Editorials*—Firms sometimes supply editors with material for their editorial pages.

These forms of publicity may be used alone or in combination for maximum effectiveness.

Besides publicity, which is often part of a broader communication strategy, an organization's public relations program may include:

☐ *Opinion research*—amassing information regarding public attitudes that may be used in drafting speeches, making decisions regarding operating policies, preparing news releases, or taking a stand on legislation.

At Your Service 15.3
Toll-Free Customer Service

Part of the public relations effort at some companies is conducted through toll-free numbers. The numbers are printed on packages, and consumers can call the company to complain or get information.

The first company to use this approach was Procter & Gamble. It first tried the approach in 1974, and by 1982, all of its consumer products carried a toll-free number on their labels. P&G now employs about 50 agents at its answering center. Approximately one-third of the calls it receives are complaints. Top management receives monthly reports on the types of calls received for each product, so that they can spot needed changes.

Typically, consumers call to ask about ingredients, calories, and nutrition. Food companies also get requests for recipes.

General Foods spokesperson Naomi Martin admits that it is difficult to measure the impact of public relations. But she reports that the initial results of General Foods' use of toll-free numbers "showed it improved the way of making the corporation more accessible to the consumer."

Source: Linda Keslar, "Getting the Customer to Talk Back," *Adweek,* November 10, 1986.

- *Lobbying*—promoting legislative or administrative action for an organization or against an adverse interest. It can also include obtaining government cooperation of sponsorship for a cause (such as National Fire Prevention Week).
- *Public affairs*—promoting an organization's total concept of corporate citizenship. This function is usually confined to large corporations and conglomerates.
- *Fund raising and membership drives*—primarily the province of private health, education, and welfare agencies that depend on contributions for their survival.[50]

At Your Service 15.3 describes how some companies are using toll-free numbers as part of their programs.

Like other forms of promotion, a publicity program should begin with objectives consistent with an overall marketing program. These may be to generate sales inquiries, to promote a new product image, to gain visibility for new applications for a mature line, or to promote new distributors.[51]

Measuring the effectiveness of a public relations campaign can be difficult. Although numbers of news stories, photographs, and personal appearances can be counted, it is often difficult to determine if all that coverage really had an impact. In some cases, publicity programs can use the same tactics as other forms of promotion to measure results:

1. *Controlled market comparisons*—sales results can be compared in test markets where public relations was included as part of the marketing mix versus those where it was not.
2. *Direct response*—public relations can sometimes generate cost-effective, direct customer response. Mensa, an organization for people with high IQs, succeeded in placing an "IQ Quiz" in *Reader's Digest* that drew 75,000 inquiries.
3. *Communication with the sales force*—by providing the sales force with reprints of publicity for merchandising to customers, and then surveying salespeople for customer response, a public relations department can get an idea of the effectiveness of a campaign.[52]

Chapter Replay

1. **What kinds of advertising can marketers use?**
The various types of advertising include selective or brand advertising, primary demand advertising, institutional advertising, and noncommercial advertising.
2. **What are some reasons for advertising?**
Advertisers inform the public and try to persuade them to buy certain products. Ads remind consumers of an organization's products and reassure buyers that they have made the right purchase. Ads also back up the sales force and provide leads for salespeople.
3. **What kinds of organizations employ the most people in the field of advertising?**
The organizations that employ the most people are advertising departments, which operate within for-profit and nonprofit organizations, and advertising agencies, which prepare most ads and which may specialize in certain kinds of advertising.
4. **What steps are involved in developing an ad campaign?**
In developing an advertising campaign, marketers must set objectives, determine a budget, define a positioning strategy, decide on a message, choose media, and develop ways to measure the effectiveness of the campaign.
5. **What are some creative styles for presenting advertising messages?**
Advertisers can use an image sell, a direct sell, a humorous or soft sell, or a competitive sell.
6. **What major media do advertisers use?**
The six major media are newspapers, magazines, television, radio, direct mail, and outdoor/transit signs.

7. **How have advertisers and the government responded to criticisms of advertising?**
Individual advertisers try to modify messages that consumers find objectionable. As a whole, the advertising community prepares messages describing the benefits of advertising. The government has formed the Federal Trade Commission and passed laws regulating advertising.
8. **How can sales promotion increase sales?**
Through contests, sales meetings, and incentives, sales promotion can motivate the sales force and intermediaries. Through coupons, point-of-purchase materials, samples, and premiums, it can also stimulate consumers to act.
9. **What are some advantages and disadvantages of using publicity?**
The user of publicity pays nothing for the media coverage. In addition, publicity offers a news slant and high credibility. But publicity items are rarely used more than once, and the organization generating the publicity gives up some control to the media.
10. **What activities are typically included in a public relations program?**
An organization's public relations program may include publicity, opinion research, lobbying, public affairs, and fund raising and membership drives.

Key Terms

advertising allowance
association advertising
comparative advertising
coupon
institutional (or corporate) advertising
media
noncommercial advertising
point-of-purchase (POP) materials
positioning
premium
primary demand advertising
sample
selective or brand advertising
trade show

Discussion Questions

1. Why might an organization use primary demand advertising rather than brand advertising?
2. Brand Z Corporation uses a highly trained sales force to sell pharmaceuticals to doctors and hospitals. Why would the company want to advertise when it already spends a lot of money on salespeople?
3. What activities do advertising agencies typically perform for their clients?
4. In general terms, describe how a chain of fast-food restaurants might use an image sell. How might it use a direct sell? A competitive sell?
5. Rita Jones is responsible for advertising for her company, which sells tents and sleeping bags. She determines that the company can afford

either to advertise in magazines that appeal to campers or to buy mailing lists from those magazines and sent out brochures to the readers. Based on the information in this chapter about magazines and direct mail, which of these approaches would you recommend? Why?

6. Why are some manufacturers reluctant to use coupons extensively? Besides coupons, what sales promotion methods do manufacturers use to reach consumers?
7. The Big Museum of Natural History has been dissatisfied with its publicity program. For the last few years, the museum has sent out press releases every month or so but rarely receives media coverage. The Big Museum therefore hired a new publicity director, Paul Plum. What publicity techniques might Paul use besides press releases?
8. What are some ways of measuring the effectiveness of a public relations campaign?

Case 15.1
Exxon Office Systems

Given the uncertainties of the world market for oil and gas, Exxon, for a number of years, had been looking for new sources of long-term earnings growth. It is estimated that the company invested $1 billion in synthetic fuels research and development before curtailing investments in the area. An additional $1 billion was invested in acquiring Reliance Electric Company, an investment that has been filled with problems and has shown disappointing returns. Major sums also went into mining and nuclear fuels, where a number of business lines have shown profitable returns.

One significant investment outside the area of oil was in office automation systems. Several hundred million dollars have been invested in building an office systems business. The company's three major office product lines—the Qwip telephone facsimile transmission unit, Qyx electronic typewriter line, and Vydec word processor line—were merged in 1981 to form Exxon Office Systems (EOS).

Initial Communications Effort

In 1981, after its organization, EOS spent almost $5 million in an advertising campaign designed to bring instant recognition and credibility to the new company. Some industry observers felt that the campaign fell short of the mark. In fact, there were many rumors that Exxon was going to cut its losses and get out of the office automation business. Exxon management repeatedly denied the rumors.

Source: Adapted from Robert Raissman, "Exxon Out to Boost Its Sagging Office Unit," *Advertising Age,* June 28, 1982, p. 50; and Edward D. Sheffe, "Campaign: Getting Away from Gas Pumps," *Madison Avenue,* September 1983, pp. 60–66.

During the first half of 1982, the company spent $500,000 on a one-month print campaign designed to reinforce the fact that Exxon was still aggressively pursuing the word processing market and planned to develop new technology. The advertisements developed by Marsteller, Inc., featured statements of commitment by various EOS officers in the headlines. In the initial advertisement, the president of EOS was quoted as saying, "Remember . . . when you buy our word processing systems . . . you buy our commitment to your future." The company's other advertising activities for various new and existing products utilized television and direct mail, as well as the print media.

Another Campaign

In many people's minds, Exxon was still not firmly established as an office automation company. At the same time, EOS had received some unfavorable responses from the trade press. One publication implied that some of its earlier products had become outmoded and expensive. The situation posed two immediate problems for the company: (1) establish popular awareness among its target audience and (2) overcome the unfavorable comments about its products and future in the marketplace.

The first issue was addressed by a series of new product introductions, carefully designed and timed to create and maintain excitement in the marketplace. A basic objective was to get the proper message about EOS to the industry consultants. The company actively participated in trade shows and pursued major consultants in the industry. At the same time, efforts were under way to develop an aggressive advertising campaign to try to fix the "tigers-and-gasoline" image problem.

While many of the office automation firms were directing their communications to departmental or individual user levels, EOS people felt that the decision-making authority was moving up the organization, especially as systems representing significant capital investments were considered. The objective was perceived as getting Exxon's message across to middle- and senior-level managers in larger companies—people who might not be highly technically oriented. Once it was decided to focus on network television as the primary vehicle, animation was considered as the logical choice for the campaign. Such an approach had the key elements of universal appeal, flexibility, and even credibility if done right.

Marsteller created three 60-second and five 30-second television spots. They focused on EOS's corporate identity, the Exxon 500 series information processor, the Qwip facsimile, the new Exxon 965 Ink Jet Printer, and the communications capabilities and integration of the products. Three of the spots specifically stressed the theme, "At Exxon Office Systems, we bring the high-tech office down to earth." An animated executive, created by Arnie Levin, a well-known *New Yorker* cartoonist, was shown strolling through an office with information processors growing out of the top of each desk. The stylized machines were very much in evidence, but the emphasis was more on smiling, productive people. Narrated by John Huston, the assurance throughout the commercials was that Exxon Office Systems is here to stay and can help ease the trauma as people and companies make the transition to "The Future . . . without the shock."

The commercials ran in major markets from October through November and April to mid-June 1983. To reinforce the broadcast media, an ongoing print campaign ran in national and local newspapers and in general business, trade, and office publications.

Focal Topics

1. Why do you believe the earlier campaigns for Exxon Office Systems did not create the desired position in the marketplace?
2. How would you measure the effectiveness of EOS's later advertising campaign?
3. From Exxon's perspective, the initial results of the campaign were favorable. The key question is whether the campaign will have staying power. What are your advertising recommendations to Exxon, if and when the campaign seems to have run its course? Be specific about objectives, creative themes, and media selection.

Case 15.2 California Beef Council (F)

The California Beef Council's 1987 advertising plan has four basic objectives:

1. To communicate the light, low-in-calories, good-for-you beef message by positioning beef as the "ideal food for the way we eat and live today."
2. To target the message at active life-style groups in order to change their attitudes about beef and reverse the trend of decreasing serving frequency among light users and to maintain the beef usage level of heavy and medium users.
3. To provide methods for program evaluation to measure attitudinal change.
4. To explore, evaluate, and place additional advertising to meet regional marketing opportunities.

First Three Objectives

The first three objectives are the stated objectives of the national advertising campaign supported by the CBC since 1982. This year, the CBC must invest $1,154,000 in direct support of the two national boards (Beef Promotion and Research Board and the Beef Industry Council) and their programs to ensure program continuity and effective advertising expenditures for targeted markets. Support of the national advertising program offers a specific advantage for California. The CBC will

Source: Adapted from the California Beef Council's 1987 marketing plan.

receive $3 for every $1 spent to support the California national investment.

Target Audience The target audience is active, contemporary women and men. Key indicators of this life-style are age, income, and VALS group*: (1) Age 25–54, emphasis 25–44, (2) income $30,000+, and (3) VALS groups of "Achievers" and "Societally Conscious." Other indicators include (1) education—some college or more, (2) employment—women who tend to work either full- or part-time, and (3) presence of children.

Rationale Concentrating efforts toward a more selective audience (women versus all adults) enables greater impact against that group, particularly necessary in light of limited available funds. Achievers and Societally Conscious VALS groups represent the groups that tend to have less favorable attitudes towards beef but (a) are likely to respond positively to the creative message and (b) tend to be trendsetters. Households with children are more likely to purchase and consume beef (thereby accounting for more volume) than singles or adults living together.

Fourth Objective

California's Hispanic population continues to grow at a faster rate than any other segment in California. CBC research has shown they are strong consumers of beef. In 1987, the marketing thrust for Hispanics will be continued through a combination of public relations, publicity, and advantageous media placements on radio, TV, and print.

Advertising flights will run in cooperation with the national media schedule to increase impact in California and the regional thrust of the national plan. Media selection will target the active life-style and convenience-oriented consumer. Materials should communicate the "real food" national campaign message.

Based on the success of the CBC's cooperative ad program in 1986, a similar program will be undertaken in 1987, with offers open to retailers, wholesalers, packers, purveyors, and other industry groups and offers matching funds up to $2,000 for any one cooperative advertising venture.

Focal Topics

1. Discuss your overall evaluation of the advertising plan presented here.
2. What creative themes would you use in CBC's (a) television commercials, (b) radio commercials, and (c) magazine advertisements? Support your recommendations.
3. What other media could be used as part of the CBC's advertising program? Which, if any, would you recommend?
4. How would you measure the effectiveness of the CBC's advertising plan?

*See California Beef Council (C) in Chapter 6 for additional information on VALS.

Personal Selling and Sales Management

Sounding Out the Chapter

In this chapter, you will learn:

1. The circumstances under which personal selling is most important in the marketing mix.
2. Basic types of sales jobs.
3. The decisions an organization must make with regard to its sales force.
4. How the sales manager can organize the sales force.
5. How companies screen applicants for sales positions.
6. The tasks of the sales manager.
7. The stages of the selling process.
8. How salespeople are compensated.
9. How sales managers evaluate the performance of salespeople.

Source: *Sales and Marketing Management,* January 1987, p. 44.

Selling the Corporate Caterer

If you're having lunch at your desk in New York City, you might want to send out to Fisher & Levy, a corporate caterer that specializes in delivery. Instead of corned beef on rye, you'll be able to enjoy, say, a chicken provençale sandwich attractively presented along with specially printed napkins and packaged mints.

The owners of Fisher & Levy are Doug Levy, a chef, and Chip Fisher, the marketing department. Fisher started a sales career upon graduating from Harvard with a degree in English. At that time, he took a position selling computers for IBM. He wanted to work for IBM because he thought selling for that company was an excellent marketing position. Working there taught him a lot about selling a premium product for a premium price.

Selling is Fisher's forte. He keeps a map of the buildings in midtown New York, and about every six weeks he heads out to drum up new business. Starting with a briefcase full of menus, he goes door to door in the city's office buildings. He starts at the top of each building, because he finds the wealthiest clients there.

Fisher has polished sales tactics. He dresses to look like a young professional and walks into buildings with the air of someone heading to an appointment. That way, he minimizes the chance that a building manager or security guard will discover he's soliciting and ask him to leave. For the same reason, he avoids being seen on different floors by the same person.

For most salespeople, the receptionist is a hurdle, but for Fisher this person is a prospect. He explains, "I guess 90 percent of the people in offices go to the receptionist for information about where to get food." After a polite, friendly introduction, he drops off a few menus and then heads for the next office.

Evidently, Fisher's selling technique is working. In the two years between 1984 and 1986, Fisher & Levy's sales doubled.

Personal selling is often crucial to a company's success. This chapter takes a more detailed look at how companies can make the most of this important marketing function.

Source: Bill Kelley, "Gourmet to Go," *Sales and Marketing Management,* January 1987, pp. 43–44.

Table 16.1
Factors Affecting the Importance of Personal Selling in the Promotional Mix

	Personal Selling is likely to be more important when	Advertising is likely to be more important when
Consumer is:	geographically concentrated, relatively small in numbers	geographically dispersed, relatively large in numbers
Product is:	expensive, technically complex, custom-made, special handling required, trade-ins frequently involved	inexpensive, simple to understand, standardized, no special handling, no trade-ins
Price is:	relatively high	relatively low
Channels are:	relatively short	relatively long

Source: Louis E. Boone and David L. Kurtz, *Contemporary Marketing,* 5th edition (Hinsdale, Ill.: The Dryden Press, 1986), p. 436. Copyright 1986 by The Dryden Press, a division of CBS College Publishing. Reprinted by permission.

Personal Selling's Place in the Promotional Mix

A firm may have an outstanding product that it offers at a competitive price, an efficient distribution system, award-winning advertising, eye-catching sales promotional displays, and headline-making publicity. But, as the late Red Motley, an outstanding sales trainer, once said, "Nothing happens until somebody sells something."

In the increasingly self-service world of retailing, the role of personal selling is not always immediately apparent. Nonetheless, it is still an essential part of any firm's marketing plan. While Nabisco's sales force, for example, may not be lurking in the cookie aisle of the local supermarket urging shoppers to sample their new line, they are probably a very real presence to the store's owner or manager. In fact, Nabisco fields a small army of 3,000 salespeople who regularly visit supermarkets to inspect and position the baked goods.[1] And back at the company's headquarters, many other personal sales must take place before one cookie can come off a conveyor belt. Someone had to sell Nabisco flour, chocolate chips, plant machinery, transportation services, warehousing facilities, advertising assistance, tax advice, office forms, typewriters, and soap for the washrooms.

All this activity makes a sales career one that can be both financially rewarding and practically recession-proof. American firms spend heavily on their millions of salespeople. Many new college and university graduates become salespeople every year. Marketing Today 16.1 describes attitudes of students toward selling careers.

As discussed in Chapter 7, personal selling is generally the most important element in the promotional mix of industrial marketers. The other circumstances in which personal selling is of primary importance are summarized in Table 16.1.

Types of Sales Jobs

Despite dramatic changes in the way products are now sold, selling still suffers from the negative stereotypes of its occasionally disreputable past. Certainly the snake-oil salesmen who roamed the frontier and

Marketing Today 16.1
Student Interest in Selling

While women have played an important role in marketing, they have been underrepresented in the field of personal selling. Recently, two researchers tried to determine whether this reflected a lack of interest. They surveyed 296 students at three Ohio universities, asking them to rate 10 marketing careers on a five-point scale from 1 (least preferred) to 5 (most preferred).

The male and female respondents gave significantly different answers. Women were more interested than men in public relations, advertising, and retail management. Men were more interested than women in wholesale sales, manufacturer sales, industrial buying, distribution management, and product management.

When asked about the attributes of sales careers, women were more likely to agree with statements that a sales career entails responsibility, requires high-pressure sales tactics, and has too little monetary reward. Men were more likely to agree that sales careers require much travel and high skills and that salespeople are money-hungry. In explaining these differences, the researchers noted that more women than men indicated that their contact with salespeople has mostly been limited to sales clerks. The authors suggest that recruiters might emphasize female role models for sales positions.

While women expressed less interest in a sales career, neither group was particularly enthusiastic. Thus, sales managers must make extra efforts to attract qualified college graduates to sales positions.

Source: Photo © 1987 Phyllis Woloshin.

Source: Robert W. Cook and Timothy Hartman, "Female College Student Interest in a Sales Career: A Comparison," *Journal of Personal Selling and Sales Management* 6 (May 1986): 29–34.

Arthur Miller's tragic play "Death of a Salesman" have done little to make selling seem like an appealing profession. But today's salesperson is likely to be part of a sophisticated team of professionals, highly skilled in the demands of a particular field, a creative problem solver rather than product pusher, and an important source of information for clients.

Many of the misconceptions about selling arise because of failure to recognize the variety of jobs included under the heading "sales." A widely accepted classification of selling jobs by Robert McMurry shows how diverse selling is. His classification, which distinguishes sales jobs by the degree of creativity they involve, include the following categories of sales personnel:[2]

Merchandise Deliverer Salesperson who sees that buyers receive their purchases.

1. **Merchandise deliverers.** People in this category have no responsibility for creative selling, but they provide essential support to the sales effort by seeing that buyers receive their purchases. Truck wholesalers, such as those who sell and deliver bakery products directly to supermarkets, fall into this category.

Order Taker
Salesperson whose main function is to write or ring up orders.

2. **Order takers.** Salespeople who may suggest an article for purchase but whose main function is to write or ring up orders are called order takers. "Inside" order takers may work within a store or take telephone orders at direct-mail firms or sales offices. "Outside" order takers work in the field. For instance, the junior "sales reps" for Del Monte check grocery displays and shelves and reorder when supplies of the canned products are low. They also gather information on competitive products and feed it back to headquarters.

Missionary
Salesperson whose role is to build goodwill or to educate potential customers rather than to make a direct sale.

3. **Missionaries.** These are salespeople whose job is to build goodwill or to educate potential customers rather than to make a direct sale. Drug companies like Upjohn send missionary salespeople (often called "detailers") to doctors to describe the uses of new drugs and leave free samples. Other manufacturers sometimes use missionaries to supplement the efforts of independent wholesale distributors who handle their products.

Technical Salespeople
Technicians in sales positions who act as consultants and sometimes help to design products or systems to meet a client's needs.

4. **Technical salespeople.** Technicians in sales positions who act as consultants and sometimes help to design products or systems to meet a client's needs are technical salespeople. They are high on the creativity scale. Reynolds Aluminum once used members of its sales staff with engineering backgrounds to convince Ford to switch from steel to aluminum bumpers. The deal was closed after three years when the sales staff came up with a model strong enough to withstand banging by Ford negotiators, but light enough to be lifted with one hand.[3]

Creative Salespeople
Individuals charged with determining customers' needs, helping them solve problems, and getting orders.

5. **Creative salespeople.** Those charged with determining customer needs, helping them solve problems, and getting orders are properly called "creative" salespeople. They may work within a company or in the field, and they may sell tangible products or intangible services. New products require a large measure of creative selling, since potential customers must be made to see how an innovation can solve their problems. Many trainees start as order takers or missionaries, but their goal is to reach senior positions that involve creative selling.

Of course, not all jobs fit neatly into one of the categories listed here. Clothing salespeople at a retail store, for example, may write orders, but they are also responsible for creating customer goodwill; in addition, they may have enough technical knowledge of clothing design to advise a customer on a well-made coat. It is useful to classify them as order takers because they spend the largest part of their time processing orders. But all selling jobs, if well done, may involve a degree of creativity.

As might be expected, the more knowledge, creativity, and responsibility a sales job requires, the greater its compensation will be. In 1986, for example, salespeople earned on average between $21,922 and $56,865, depending on their experience and level of responsibility. In general, those who sold services earned most, followed by industrial goods and consumer goods salespeople. College graduates taking sales positions were offered on average more than $20,000.[4] At the other extreme, top commission-only salespeople earned an average of more than

$185,000 in 1985, four times the figure paid to the top salary-only salespeople.[5] A sales career can clearly offer much satisfaction in the area of personal achievement—and an opportunity for substantial financial rewards.

Making Sales Force Decisions

Once a company decides to field a sales force—for any of the reasons cited—many decisions must be made, among them: (1) the goals of the sales force; (2) the size force the company requires; and (3) how the sales force should be structured.

Establishing Sales Force Objectives

The first step in determining the role of the sales force is to set objectives. This process is less evident than it may seem. While selling products is any sales force's foremost objective, it is often not the only one. Other objectives may include presales activity, such as identifying new customers and educating them about a company's products and services, and postsales activity, such as offering technical assistance and further problem-solving advice. At the time of the sale, a salesperson may help to arrange financing and assist with the mechanics of delivery. Some of these goals—such as providing technical assistance—are hard to quantify. But whenever possible, sales organizations try to specify objectives as precisely as possible. One company may set a goal, for example, of increasing overall sales by 6 percent within a year or propose that each salesperson open two new accounts monthly.

Finally, one of the most valuable functions of a sales force is to provide feedback from customers on the effectiveness of an advertising or promotion campaign, the success—or problems—of a new product, and the activities of competitors. In their travels, salespeople may pick up ideas for new products or suggestions for improvements on old ones. A marketing organization that uses its sales force effectively can find it an invaluable source of information.

Determining Sales Force Structure

Once objectives have been set, a sales manager must determine how to organize the sales force for maximum efficiency. Structures include organizing by:

1. *Territory.* Most textbook publishers, for example, have eastern, southern, midwestern, and western divisions.
2. *Product.* Because Dow Chemical manufactures a diverse line of technically complex products, the company's sales reps specialize in selling chemicals, plastics, metal products, medical products, consumer products, or packaging.

3. *Market.* Eastman Kodak, maker of photographic equipment, organizes its sales force around a business system market and a consumer market.
4. *A combination.* If a company sells many products to different types of customers over a wide geographical area, it may choose to organize the sales force by a combination of methods. For example, in one company, a sales representative may be responsible for selling a certain product throughout the country. Another company may further organize its sales force so that each representative sells a certain product line to a specified market in a well-defined territory.

Within the framework of this overall work force design, sales managers must answer the question, "How much territory can an individual salesperson cover effectively?" The answer depends on many factors, including the nature of the product, the number and location of buyers, and the type of selling required. For example, an IBM computer sales rep may cover only a few city blocks in Chicago because the product is complex, potential customers—large business firms—are densely clustered, and the job requires creative selling. The situation of a sales rep for Union Carbide's agricultural pesticides is just the opposite. The territory may cover three or four western states because farms are widely scattered and the product may not require as much creative selling.

Some sales managers also must consider how the salesperson's time should be spent. Technical and creative salespeople usually allocate their own time, but the routes and schedules of order takers and missionary salespeople may be determined at headquarters. Regular routes and schedules mean that repeat buyers get service they can rely on and that the sales force's time is being used efficiently.

Decisions regarding sales force structure have taken on great importance as the cost of an average sales call has skyrocketed. Sharp increases in the cost of meals, lodging, and gasoline have pushed the average cost to almost $200.[6]

Managing efficient use of time and territory is critical to a salesperson's success. Executives surveyed in over 400 industries indicated that, for the future, sales managers will emphasize the importance of time and territory management to their sales personnel. The way salespeople invest available sales time may well be one of the most critical factors influencing territory sales-cost ratios.[7]

Determining Sales Force Size

One method of determining the size of the sales force is to use the company's sales forecast for a given period to determine sales potential for individual regions or districts. The company then decides how much one salesperson must sell to have a profitable territory. The size of the sales force is then determined by dividing the company's sales potential by the sales that the individual salesperson must generate.

Another method begins by determining the number of accounts and categorizing them on the basis of their sales and potential importance.

The accounts with higher sales warrant frequent calls; smaller accounts might be visited less often. To calculate the total number of sales calls, add the number of calls to large accounts to those for smaller accounts. For example:

Large customers:

$$1 \text{ call per month} \times 1{,}000 \text{ accounts} = 12{,}000 \text{ calls}$$

Small customers:

$$\begin{aligned} 1 \text{ call per quarter} \times 2{,}000 \text{ accounts} &= \underline{8{,}000} \text{ calls} \\ \text{Total number of calls per year} &= 20{,}000 \text{ calls} \end{aligned}$$

Then the number of calls each salesperson can make in one year is determined. For example:

$$4 \text{ calls per day (or 20 calls/week)} \times 50 \text{ weeks} = 1{,}000 \text{ calls}$$

The total number of calls per year is then divided by the number of calls one salesperson can make in the course of a year to arrive at the number of salespeople required:

$$20{,}000 \text{ calls} \div 1{,}000 \text{ calls per salesperson} = 20 \text{ salespeople}$$

Established companies may have simpler methods. For every $500,000 in sales, a company may add one salesperson. Procter & Gamble uses population figures to determine sales force size. The company calculates that there will usually be 120 to 130 grocery stores for every 60,000 people, and that number of retail accounts represents sufficient sales potential to support one salesperson.[8]

Staffing the Sales Force

A company now has the broad outlines of the sales force sketched in. What remains is as much an art as a science: recruiting and selecting the best possible sales force.

Are Creative Salespeople Born or Made?

Much has been written about whether good salespeople are born or made. Most of the research has centered on drawing up lists of traits common to all good salespeople. The result: no two researchers seem to agree on the qualities that ensure superior selling ability. Some researchers stress a high level of energy and self-confidence as common to all good salespeople; others think superior selling ability springs from a feeling of being unwanted and unloved and the need to overcome that feeling.[9] (See Figure 16.1.)

Such obvious disagreement seems to discredit the notion that an individual must be born with certain characteristics to succeed in selling.

Figure 16.1
Do You Have What It Takes to Be a Super Salesperson?

What motivates the super salesperson? One study of several thousand top producers isolated seven motives common to most:

Need for Status—The best salespeople seek recognition as proof of their ability and performance. They enjoy power and authority and are strongly aware of image and reputation.

Need for Control—Successful sellers like people, enjoy being with them, and delight in influencing them. They seldom care deeply whether others like them, a trait that enables them to use emotion without falling prey to it.

Need for Respect—They want to be seen as experts on what is right, best, or appropriate. They regard themselves as well-intentioned people, willing to help and advise others.

Need for Routine—Contrary to the popular belief that top salespeople are impulsive and somewhat undisciplined, most like routine and hate having it interrupted.

Need for Accomplishment—Material comforts—a nice house, expensive clothing, a fancy car—are only the beginning. Money starts as a prime motivator, but the top salespeople earn so much that as one said, "Money loses its ability to inspire you." The superstars constantly create new challenges and go after the "impossible sales" to maintain their enthusiasm.

Need for Stimulation—Top producers are normally calm, relaxed people who thrive on challenge. They have more physical energy than most people and welcome outside stimulation as a way to channel their energy in satisfying ways.

Need for Honesty—The best salespeople have such a strong need to believe in the product that they will switch jobs if the company's reputation slips or if they have serious doubts about a new product line. They are not rigidly moralistic; experience has taught them to accept imperfections, in people and products, of the real world.

Source: Donald J. Moine, "The Fire Within." Reprinted with permission from *Psychology Today,* March 1984, p. 44. Copyright 1984 American Psychological Association.

Because there is such a diversity of selling jobs, the qualities that make for a good salesperson in one field may not work in another. The intellectual and psychological requirements desirable for selling computers may not be so desirable for selling encyclopedias. One job may require an MBA and problem-solving ability, while the other may be filled by someone with little formal education but a great deal of perseverance. Companies attempt to screen out those who are obviously unsuitable for the kinds of selling they require. They then supply those selected with extensive training.

The Screening Process

Sales trainees are recruited from a number of sources. They may come from nonselling jobs within a company or be "pirated" from competing companies. More frequently today they are recruited from college campuses because of the degree of technical ability most professional sales jobs require.

Many highly industrialized companies, however, do not insist that applicants have technical backgrounds. Half of Bethlehem Steel's recruits, for example, major in business oı economics, a quarter to a third in engineering, and the rest in liberal arts. At IBM, the personnel director noted, "We search for individuals who are intelligent, quick learners, problem solvers. We don't look for specific academic backgrounds. We've hired some music majors, because they have very logical minds"[10]

Companies use a wide variety of tools to sort out the qualifications of applicants. Sales managers rely heavily on application forms and job interviews. The biographical data that these tools reveal help match the backgrounds of job applicants and customers. In the field of life insurance, for example, a study in the 1960s demonstrated a relationship between similarity in the buyer's and seller's ages and success in making a sale.[11]

Companies may also use various tests to determine if candidates have the traits that spell success. One approach many experts recommend is to give a company's top salespeople tests that measure the traits usually found in people who do well in selling. The results are then used to build a profile of the characteristics most important in that particular sales field. Candidates for sales jobs can then be measured against that profile.[12]

Few companies rely solely on test scores for hiring. Almost all intelligence, personality, and vocational interest tests have been found to be poor predictors of good performance in sales work. This fact seems to bear out the notion that training rather than innate sales ability has more to do with selling success.

Companies take the job of hiring salespeople seriously. The process is not only time-consuming, but expensive. One electronics firm estimated that the cost of hiring a salesperson was well in excess of $25,000. Out-of-pocket expenses for the first six months included:

Advertising costs	$ 1,500
Base salary (first 6 months)	12,000
Samples and equipment	2,000
Initial training	750
Miscellaneous expenses	1,500
	$17,750

Add to that the cost of management time spent in the hiring process and sales and profits lost while a territory is inadequately covered, and the costs become enormous.[13]

A company must make its selections carefully for at least one other reason: damage done to customer relations and company reputation by a poor salesperson can take years to overcome.

Managing the Sales Force

With the sales force in place, work can begin on translating the goals and objectives set by management into results. The responsibility for that job usually falls to a sales manager. With so much riding on sales force performance, its management is a crucial task. **Sales management** involves recruiting, selecting, and training salespeople, supervising and motivating them on the job, and evaluating their performance. Why is

Sales Management
Marketing function that embraces recruiting, selecting, and training salespeople, supervising and motivating them, and evaluating their performance.

sales management so important? Because without proper training, efficient assignment of work, and adequate incentives, the sales force drifts aimlessly. Block Drug, makers of Polident denture cleanser and Tegrin shampoo, found that out the hard way.

Twenty years ago, Block, lacking competition, regarded its sales reps mainly as order takers. But when Procter & Gamble entered the market with Head & Shoulders, and Warner-Lambert with Efferdent, Block had to alter its strategy. Instead of depending mainly on advertising, the company tried a new push strategy that required an increased sales effort to retailers. Cast in their new roles as creative salespeople, Block's reps floundered. There were three problems. First, they had never been trained in the skills necessary for creative selling. Second, their schedules called for them to maintain a six-calls-a-day average, even though they were assigned more duties. Third, although the company wanted them to increase sales by penetrating a new market—mass merchandising outlets such as discount stores—it offered no pay incentives. The results were disastrous. Sales declined, and shelf space and market share decreased.

When Block discovered its mistake, it attacked the problem systematically. The company divided its 10,000 accounts into two groups—large orders and small. Sales reps were assigned to cover only the top 3,750 customers; the rest would be contacted by mail. This action freed the sales force to seek out new accounts. But before doing that, sales reps were called in for retraining. Their base pay was increased, and they were given bonuses for meeting management objectives. The new program succeeded. Block reported a 20 percent increase in sales and a 10 percent increase in profits after its reorganization.[14]

The Block example shows how management's involvement and support of sales staff efforts can make the difference in an entire firm's success in the marketplace.

Training

In general, all applicants who are hired go through a formal or informal training program. The length of the program may vary from a few weeks to many months, depending on the complexity of the product or service being sold. Dow Chemical's training program for its industrial sales reps last from 25 to 30 weeks. At IBM, a training program can take as long as two years. Regardless of the type of company, training is expensive, costing tens of thousands of dollars. The sheer size of a company's investment in training is a good indication of how high a regard managers have for the selling job.

Role Playing
Training method for salespeople in which one person acts the part of the salesperson and the other takes the part of the customer.

Training can take place on or off the job. Good training programs like Dow's combine the two. One unusual on-the-job program, that of Roche Laboratories, a drug company, requires missionary sales reps to spend two weeks in a hospital learning the regimen of interns and physicians. Training off the job ordinarily occurs in a classroom setting, although learning by doing is stressed. The Xerox Corporation uses **role playing,** in which one person acts the part of the salesperson and the

Marketing Today **16.2**

Training for Telephone Sales

Telemarketing is increasingly popular in light of the high cost of sales calls. But many companies are finding that people who sell on the phone could be doing a lot better. To improve performance, they are turning to sales trainers.

One company that offers training in telemarketing is Dylnamics. This company emphasizes relationship building. The 9-hour Dylnamics workshop trains telemarketers in the principles of behavioral science. They learn specific skills for making positive initial contacts with potential customers and for following up to build receptiveness, interest, and involvement. After the sessions, the salespeople can receive additional counseling—by phone, of course.

Another company, Learning International, teaches courses called Professional Telephone Selling Skills and Telephone Prospecting. These courses combine written exercises, interactive video and audio, role playing, games, discussions, and self-instructional follow-up. The courses teach techniques for overcoming a potential customer's resistance to spending time on the phone with a salesperson and ways to control the conversation.

Source: Courtesy of Burgoyne *Consumer Views.*

Sources: "Communication Key to Training TSRs," *Marketing News,* August 1, 1986, p. 12; and "Selling You by Phone," *INC,* April 1986, p. 99.

other the customer. The scene is videotaped, so that trainees can evaluate their performance. Some companies also use tapes and cassettes for home self-instruction. Marketing Today 16.2 describes some training programs for telephone sales reps.

During the training program, companies try to impart both knowledge and sales skills. Three sorts of factual information are stressed:

1. *Knowledge of the company*—its history, objectives, sales policies, officers, and organizational setup.
2. *Knowledge of the product*—its physical features and manufacture and the benefits customers can expect.
3. *Knowledge of the competition*—product strengths and weaknesses, price, and the promotional support it receives.

In addition to this information, sales reps are also expected to learn a general approach to selling. Two approaches are often taught—the AIDA theory of selling and the want-satisfaction theory.

The AIDA Theory In Chapter 14 we discussed the communication theory, which suggests that promotional goals be keyed to the stage of product knowledge of a prospective buyer. This theory can also be used to guide a prospect through the various stages (Awareness, Interest, Desire, and Action) leading to a purchase decision. Some companies prepare a standard presentation for trainees—including prescribed phrases and appropriate pauses and gestures for each stage—which is why the theory is often referred to as the "canned approach."

This approach to selling allows a great deal of company control over the sales message, which means less chance to be misunderstood. But in concentrating on the salesperson's message, it neglects the customer. Not all customers, for instance, pass through all of these stages. Some may already be aware of the product and have an interest. A sales representative who insists on points aimed at bringing the buyer through all four stages may be wasting his time and the customer's. Firms that cannot afford long training periods or that have customers with similar needs and no special problems may find this approach satisfactory, however. Door-to-door salespeople are often trained using this approach.

Want-Satisfaction Approach
Sales theory that stresses that the salesperson must first determine what a buyer really wants or needs before launching a sales talk.

The Want-Satisfaction Theory Unlike the AIDA theory, the **want-satisfaction approach** stresses that the salesperson must first determine what a buyer really wants or needs before launching a sales talk. This requires skillful questioning and, above all, an ability to listen. Office equipment salespersons, for example, may be accustomed to stressing the speed of the typewriters they are selling. However, they may find after some probing that certain office managers are more concerned with typist accuracy. If they had pursued their preconceived notion of what buyers wanted, they might have lost an important sale.

For most creative and technical selling jobs, training in the want-satisfaction theory is probably best. At this level, salespeople can expect to encounter a wide range of customers with different problems. A formula approach simply may not work. Also, the high-caliber person attracted to such selling positions may be turned off by a pre-established pattern of selling. The want-satisfaction method takes longer to master, but it usually results in more profitable sales.

Job Performance

Selling is a skill like running. Both require training, but no amount of it can substitute for the proving ground—the race for the runner and the sales situation for the salesperson.

A company can enhance the performance of its salespeople by providing them with the proper tools; increasingly, this means computers. Hewlett-Packard, for example, gave its salespeople an edge by equipping each of them with a portable personal computer and software selected to address their top concerns. The software includes a time management program and *Lotus 1-2-3* to help salespeople keep track of accounts. The company is also planning to make greater use of programs that give sales reps access to information that helps them prepare bids, contact the office, and obtain leads on hot prospects.

HP expects that the computers will accomplish three goals:

1. Increase the amount of time salespeople spend with customers instead of doing paperwork and visiting the office.

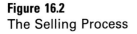

Figure 16.2
The Selling Process

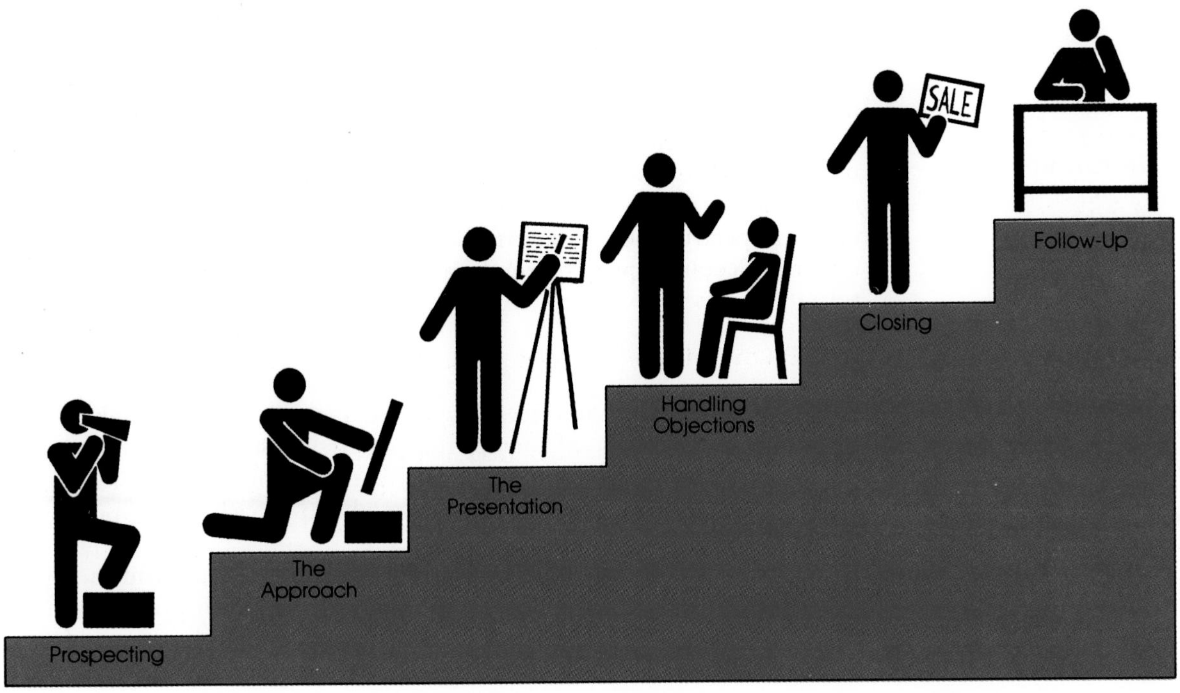

2. Increase the company's visibility—customers will remember Hewlett-Packard as the company whose sales reps use computers.
3. Improve motivation among salespeople by giving them tools that make them feel more professional.

Initial results suggest that HP is meeting all of these goals.[15]

No two sales are exactly alike in the problems encountered, but the process of selling itself does not vary. It consists of six stages. (See Figure 16.2.) The actual meeting of buyer and seller takes place in the four middle stages—the approach, presentation, handling of objections, and the close. However, the preparation for that meeting in the prospecting stage and the follow-up afterward can be crucial.

Prospecting and Qualifying Rarely do the builders of better mousetraps find lines waiting outside their doors. They must actively seek out buyers, which is termed **prospecting.** Even order takers in retail stores sometimes prospect. For example, the salespeople in exclusive department stores such as Saks Fifth Avenue keep records of customers who might be interested in seeing designer clothing as it comes in. Finding new accounts is absolutely essential to field sales reps.

Prospecting
Actively seeking out buyers.

There are many new ways of finding new prospects. Sales reps from Fuller Brush may use the cold-canvass method of going from door to door. Insurance sales agents and other field personnel often use a less hit-and-miss approach: asking present customers or acquaintances for referrals. Trade association mailing lists and business magazine ads by manufacturers aid salespeople who sell to industry. Some salespeople offer rewards to anyone whose lead develops into a sale.

Qualifying
Determining whether prospects have the authority to buy and the money to pay for the purchases.

Not all prospects turn into buyers, however. Consumers may not have the money, or industrial contacts the authority, to purchase. To avoid wasting time in visiting them, salespeople **qualify** prospects. That means they determine whether prospects have the authority to buy and the money to pay for purchases. Qualifying prospects may involve making preliminary phone calls, checking credit, or simply chatting with secretaries. Keeping records on 3 × 5 cards or in other ways is useful if repeat business is expected. If a prospect looks promising, an appointment is made.

Approach (Warm-Up)
Beginning of sales presentation intended to secure attention and to establish rapport and credibility with the client.

The Approach The sales presentation begins with the **approach,** or **warm-up.** The purpose of the approach is first to secure attention and then to establish rapport and credibility with the client. At Your Service 16.1 describes the experiences of people who approach selling personal services.

One unique attention getter used by a very successful insurance salesman involves handing the prospect a $50 bill and informing him that he may keep it if he cannot save at least that much by switching insurance firms. The salesman reports that he has never lost the money. The device is effective because it appeals to curiosity. The offer of a free sample by a door-to-door Avon salesperson has the same effect. A less flashy but still serviceable attention-getting device is dropping the name of a mutual friend or a firm that is known and respected by the client.

Besides getting attention, the approach should also establish rapport between seller and buyer by involving the prospect in the sale. Sometimes this can be accomplished by a pertinent question to the prospect. For example, a sales representative for a jewelry manufacturer might inquire of a retailer, "That display in your front showcase is eye catching, but has it increased sales?"

An approach that is both attention getting and involving is ideal. Consider the following anecdote:

A timid-appearing young insurance agent entered the office of a dynamic sales manager, shyly approached the desk, and then softly uttered, "You don't want to buy any life insurance, do you?" "No!" snarled the manager. "That's what I was afraid of," sighed the embarrassed agent, starting to leave. "Just a minute," demanded the aggressive manager. "I've been dealing with salespeople all my life, and you, without a doubt, are the worst I've ever seen. Don't you realize that you have to inspire confidence, and that to do it you must have confidence in yourself? To help you gain that confidence to make a sale, I'll sign for a $40,000 policy." As he signed, the manager advised, "You have to learn some effective techniques for approaching customers and then use them." "Oh, but I have," replied the young agent enthusiastically. "I have an approach for almost every kind of businessperson. The one I just used on you was my standard approach for sales managers."[16]

At Your Service 16.1
The Perils of Selling Yourself

The classic case of selling oneself is through a resume or in a job interview. Selling unusual services requires a more unusual approach—and can introduce some unusual perils.

Ann Haggerty started a service called Rent a Wife, which performs a variety of the tasks that traditional wives have performed: shopping, ironing, planning parties, running errands, watering the plants. Explains Haggerty, "We do anything to save people time, to make their lives a little nicer, the way things were 40, 50 years ago when home was really home . . . because people had time to do things that enhanced their lives." Unfortunately, some people have inferred from the company's name that it performs some intimate services that are not offered. Heavy breathers will be disappointed to find that Rent a Wife installed an answering machine.

Rent-a-Nerd offers quite a different service. Mike MacDonald modeled his service after a Halloween character he invented named Hornby K. Fletcher. Hornby wears outrageous clothes and taped hornrim glasses, and he fills his pockets with at least 100 pennies, five combs, calculator, transparent ruler, two slide rules, dental floss, styptic pencil, tape, rubber bands, extra shoestring, and a couple of 2-inch screws removed from his ankle following recovery from a bicycle accident. Who would hire a nerd? Many people seem to need one for parties, bar mitzvahs, office events, and other occasions.

Sources: Clarence Petersen, "Rent a Wife—Up to a Point," *Chicago Tribune,* February 8, 1987, sec. 3, p. 1; and "Rent-a-Nerd Transforms Former Programmer into the Life of Your Party," *Advertising Age,* February 16, 1987, pp. 46–47.

Source: Reprinted with permission from *Advertising Age,* February 16, 1987. Crain Communications, Inc. Mary Herlehy, photographer.

The agent's approach certainly gained attention. But more important, it involved the prospect by offering him a rather imaginative benefit: the ability to show off his own sales ability by helping the young man out.

The Presentation On average, a salesperson has between ten minutes and half an hour to convince a prospect to buy.[17] To make maximum use of that time, he or she must plan a **presentation.** The AIDA approach to selling obviously requires planning, but so does the want-satisfaction method. Even if the sales talk is not memorized, the seller can prepare a list of benefits that may interest the customer.

Presentation
Stage of selling process during which a salesperson translates the features of a product into benefits the customer can understand.

One way of doing this is to jot down the product's features and to translate each of these into a benefit that the client may derive from the feature.[18] For example, an automobile salesperson may translate the product feature "fuel injection system" into the customer benefit "savings on gasoline bills." After doing so for a number of product features, the salesperson can establish an order of importance, draw up a checklist or outline, and commit it to memory. In the sales presentation, the salesperson may choose not to follow the outline, but will remember the points.

In addition to planning what to say, a salesperson should also think of a way to demonstrate the product. *Sales and Marketing Management* once did a survey showing that after three days, people remember only 10 percent of what is said to them; however, they recall 65 percent of what is both told and shown them. Besides aiding memory, demonstrations also help maintain interest during the presentation by inviting the prospect's participation. The salesperson can use demonstration materials as a jumping-off point for questioning the prospect's understanding of a product's benefits. Booklets, flip-charts, slides, movies, and product samples are often used to help make a sales presentation.

More and more today, old-fashioned sample cases are giving way to VCRs or compact portable computers that can be used to display products. The new electronic sales tools often serve two purposes. On the one hand, video presentations can quickly and precisely show off a complicated product's assets—often more dramatically than a salesperson can. On the other hand, some companies have begun using video equipment to give a presentation the "something extra" that distinguishes its product from those of the competition. Said one marketing executive of a soft-drink company, "The ability to interact in a sales meeting is an attention-getting device. It's much better than flopping an old printout on the bottler's desk."

But most companies agree that video presentations are no replacement for personal contact. "I'd be fooling myself if I thought the customer was going to stand up and give the salesman an order because of the tape I made," said one senior product specialist. "It's just one part of the [sales] puzzle."[19]

Handling Objections Someone once defined selling as the art of getting used to the unexpected. Objections are the unexpected in selling. The more experienced the salesperson, the more easily objections can be handled. Five categories of objections are identifiable:

1. *Delay or time objections:* "I have to talk it over with my wife."
2. *Product objections:* "I don't care for that brand."
3. *Vendor objections:* "We always deal with the Squibb Company."
4. *Product service objections:* "You don't have enough service centers for this imported bicycle."
5. *Price objections:* "I can't afford to pay that much for a suit."

For the most part, objections are a healthy sign: they show a prospect is listening. Moreover, they can be overcome. If an objection comes early in the presentation, a salesperson can sidestep it by saying, "I'm coming to that." Sometimes an objection can be turned into a sales point. A prospect who objects to the price of a product may be convinced that its durability is worth the extra cost. In general, it is wise to avoid arguing. Experienced salespeople use the "Yes, but" technique:

Table 16.2
Closing Techniques

Technique	Description	Example
Direct approach	Ask for the order	When would you like that delivered?
Preference close	Give the prospect a choice	Will that be cash or charge?
Multiple acceptance approach	Obtain a series of agreements	So you like the color? And the fit seems all right? Would you like me to box it for you?
Special offer close	Provide an inducement	If you order today, I can have it for you by the end of the week.
Last chance offer	Use when supply is limited	By next week we expect to be out of this special purchase.
List of features close	Summarize the benefits	The machine can produce twice the output of your present equipment and in the long run will save you money.
Fair-minded approach	Compare advantages and disadvantages	You may have to sacrifice now to pay for this house, but you'll pay no more rent and someday the house will be yours.
Assumption close	Assume the buyer will purchase	To save us time, I've written up this order.

"I can understand why you feel that way; however. . . ." That technique offers assurance without arousing hostility. Coming to a sales presentation armed with a few answers to the most common objections is also a good idea.

Closing The point at which a prospect agrees either to buy or not to buy is called the **closing.** Despite the name, a closing does not have to occur at the end of a sales presentation. Salespeople have been known to talk themselves out of a sale by speaking too long. When prospects are ready to buy, they will give a signal. It may be a physical action such as reading the order form. Or it may be a simple statement or question: "When can you make delivery?" The signal is not always clear, so a salesperson may have to make several trial closes during the course of the transaction. Some well-tested closing techniques are listed in Table 16.2.

Closing
Point of the selling process at which a prospect agrees to buy or decides not to buy.

Not all closes are equally successful with every customer. And some customers may turn down the offer to purchase flatly. According to one source, the typical encyclopedia salesperson suffers 179 turndowns for every sale.[20] A ratio of five refusals to one sale is much more common.

Follow-Up A survey to determine why people did not return to the dealer who had sold them their last car revealed that over two-thirds left because they felt the salesperson did not care.[21] The moral: repeat business requires continuing contact with customers. The **follow-up,** as such contact is called, can serve a number of purposes. Customers often experience doubt after a major purchase; they may need reassurance. Also, if special terms were agreed to, such as a rush delivery, the salesperson is responsible for checking them. And, for a servicing problem, the sales rep is often the customer's only contact in the company. So the follow-

Follow-Up
Stage of the selling process during which a salesperson checks to see that orders have been filled and the customer is satisfied.

up call, a few days or a few weeks after the sale, can solve problems and create goodwill. To remind themselves, salespeople sometimes keep a **tickler file,** composed of cards containing data on the sale and times to call back.

Tickler File
Reminder file, often composed of cards, containing data on a sale and times to call back.

Follow-up calls can also be useful in determining why a sale was lost. One marketing director at Sperry Rand, after losing a major sale of computers, returned to the buyer. He discovered that the sale had fallen through because he had failed to make clear how the buyer's present equipment could be converted to work with the new computers. As a result of the follow-up, Sperry Rand developed a series of conversion tools for their sales reps aimed at solving the problem.[22]

Compensation

Good salespeople are among any company's greatest assets. Consequently, developing a compensation plan that attracts and motivates effective sales personnel, and then keeps them from seeking greener pastures elsewhere, is one of a sales manager's most important responsibilities. Sales personnel are usually compensated in one of three ways: straight salary, commission, or some combination.

Straight Salary
Pay plan under which salespeople are guaranteed a regular income.

About 17 percent of all companies use a **straight salary** plan that guarantees salespeople a regular income.[23] It is widely used in industries in which a salesperson has to perform functions other than creative selling. For example, a salesperson for Chanel perfumes may be charged with the task of arranging attractive displays in major department stores. An order taker in the field, such as a beer wholesaler who must cover a great number of stores and whose main function is restocking rather than finding new accounts, may also receive a straight salary. Straight salaries are relatively easy for management to administer, but they may not motivate salespeople to do their best.

Commission
Pay plan under which salespeople are paid a percentage of the sales they close.

Sellers who are expected to create new business may work solely on **commission,** receiving a percentage of sales. Only about 6 percent of the businesses in the United States rely exclusively on commissions for compensation. The selling staff of clothing manufacturers commonly receives commissions for displaying and selling sample lines. Commissions spur sales and help control costs. A firm with a 5 percent commission plan is assured that its selling costs will approximate 5 percent of sales. But straight commissions are not widely favored by sales reps themselves because most want more financial stability.

When salespeople must divide their time equally between selling and nonselling activities, a salary plus commission or bonus is best. A commission represents payment on a percentage of sales, whereas a bonus is paid as a flat fee. Most industries use a combination plan of some sort, typically 80 percent salary and 20 percent commissions.[24] When Green Giant converted to sales plus bonus, it offered its food brokers bonus points for exceeding quotas of cases sold. At the end of the year, points were converted into sizable lump-sum payments. The plan was an effective motivator.[25]

Selling is one of the few careers in which the amount of effort expended is most clearly reflected in a person's paycheck. In some industries the top salespeople routinely earn six-figure incomes—often more than the company's president.

Besides compensating employees with money, companies can reward them in other ways. They can offer benefits such as insurance, paid vacations, a company car, and a pension. In addition, compensation can include such intangibles as self-respect, opportunity for advancement, and recognition inside and outside the organization.[26]

Motivation

Selling can be exhilarating or deflating. The high of closing a large sale may be followed by weeks of depressing, flat refusals. The effort of catering to other people's needs can be exhausting. Conventional wisdom has often held that "the key to motivating salespeople is money," but recent studies have shown that the task is not that simple.[27]

While no one would deny that a compensation plan that rewards sales performance is a powerful motivating factor, other psychological issues are also important. Because good salespeople typically have strong needs for accomplishment, it is critical that they be able to see the correlation between their efforts and sales results. This relationship has been termed **sales task clarity.** Designing a system in which sales tasks are clear often presents a real challenge to even the most able sales manager.

Sales Task Clarity
The visible relationship between a salesperson's efforts and sales results.

A drug company salesperson, for example, spends a great deal of time calling on doctors to educate them about the advantages of a new medicine. But without a later audit of prescriptions written by those doctors for that product and competing ones, it is hard to determine if a sale was ever made. This can be extremely frustrating to a salesperson who has no way of knowing if sales efforts are bearing fruit.

Recognizing this problem, sales managers should strive to find ways in which to set goals that are as concrete as possible. Even in ambiguous situations, such as those faced by drug retailers, it is possible to set specific objectives and enhance feedback. Salespeople might be asked to add five new qualified prospects to an account list each month, for example, or computerized systems might be designed to track sales more effectively.

Sales task clarity has been found to be 50 percent more important in determining motivation than innate personality traits such as need for achievement. And it is nearly three times as important as the type of pay plan a company offers.[28]

Once salespeople meet the objectives set out for them, they should be recognized and rewarded. Sales contests, "salesperson of the month" and "most interesting sale of the week" awards are ways some companies recognize and motivate salespeople.

Evaluation

Salespeople lead an independent life. Still, they need guidance, and their performance must be evaluated to determine who deserves rewards and who requires help. Both sales reps and managers have a role in measuring performance.

Table 16.3
Measurements of Sales Effectiveness

Type	Description	Example
Sales-volume quota	Sets amount to be sold in dollars or units	Sales rep will sell $100,000 or 5,000 cases
Gross-profit quota	Measures profitability of goods sold	Sales rep will return $50,000 in profit
Activity quota	Sets number of calls to be made, orders to be gotten, displays set up, and so on	Sales rep will make 4 calls a day, bring in 2 new orders a week, set up 6 special displays, and so on
Expense quota	Limits the amount sales rep can spend	Sales rep can spend up to $10,000 in travel, lodging, food, and so on this year

Sales Quota
Quantitative measure of the effectiveness of salespeople.

The Sales Manager's Role **Sales quotas** are quantitative measures of the effectiveness of salespeople. They may be expressed as goals to be reached, levels of minimum performance, or ceilings not to be exceeded. Sales managers establish quotas on the basis of past records and sales forecasts. Table 16.3 describes common types of sales quotas, with examples.

In the past, sales-volume quotas expressed in dollar amounts were the standard yardstick. Managers discovered, however, that large sales do not always mean large profits. Some products may cost a great deal to sell in relation to what they return. Sales personnel who sell many products that return different rates of profit are now given gross-profit quotas instead. Gross-profit quotas encourage them to sell high-profit products rather than low-profit items that may be easier to sell.

The two other quotas in Table 16.3—activity and expense quotas—also aid in the evaluation of the sales force. But they should not be used alone to measure effectiveness. Sales reps can make their records look better by increasing calls per day, for example, but the added calls may produce no further sales and may actually hurt sales by not giving accounts adequate attention.

The Salesperson's Role Quotas can be gross exaggerations or reasonable measures of what a salesperson can be expected to produce. Effective sales managers keep in touch with field sales reps so that they know what is reasonable. Reports are one way of doing so. Most field sales personnel are required to file, on a weekly or monthly basis, call reports of their visits to prospects and expense reports detailing costs of meals, hotels, transportation, and so forth. Some salespeople also file reports on product complaints, lost orders, and market conditions.

The number one complaint of sales forces has been that there is too much paperwork. New technology seems destined to make that complaint obsolete. As more companies invest in computer systems that are capable of "talking" to one another, "paperless ordering" is becoming more common.[29]

In other companies, salespeople can update computer records daily by making a simple phone call from the field. The computer can then analyze the cost of each call, the cost of each customer, the cost of serving each territory, and the relationship between the cost of a particular sales call and the profit it generates. This can help a sales manager decide which customers to concentrate on, how frequently to call on them, and how much money to spend servicing an account.[30]

Chapter Replay

1. **Under what circumstances is personal selling most important in the marketing mix?**
Personal selling is likely to be most important when consumers are geographically concentrated and relatively few; when the product is expensive, technically complex, custom-made, requires special handling, and involves trade-ins; when the price is relatively high; and when the marketing channels are relatively short.
2. **What are the basic types of sales jobs?**
Classified by degree of creativity, sales jobs include merchandise deliverers, order takers, missionaries, technical salespeople, and creative salespeople.
3. **What decisions must an organization make with regard to its sales force?**
The organization must establish goals for the sales force, decide what size force the company requires, and determine how the sales force should be established.
4. **How can the sales manager organize the sales force?**
The manager can organize the sales force by territory, by product, by market, or by some combination of these. In so doing, the manager must consider how much territory each salesperson can cover effectively.
5. **How do companies screen applicants for sales positions?**
To screen applicants, companies use application forms, job interviews, and various tests.
6. **What are the tasks of the sales manager?**
The sales manager recruits, selects, and trains salespeople; supervises and motivates them on the job; designs compensation plans that will attract and keep effective personnel; and evaluates the sales force's performance.
7. **What are the stages of the selling process?**
The stages of the selling process are prospecting and qualifying, the approach, the presentation, handling objections, closing, and follow-up.
8. **How are salespeople compensated?**
Sales personnel are usually compensated with straight salary, straight commission, or—most commonly—some combination of the two. In addition, companies offer salespeople benefits and intangible rewards.

9. **How do sales managers evaluate the performance of salespeople?** Managers measure the salesperson's performance against quotas, including sales-volume quotas, gross-profit quotas, activity quotas, and expense quotas.

Key Terms

approach (warm-up)
closing
commission
creative salespeople
follow-up
merchandise deliverer
missionary
order taker
presentation
prospecting
qualifying
role playing
sales management
sales quota
sales task clarity
straight salary
technical salespeople
tickler file
want-satisfaction approach

Discussion Questions

1. For each of the following products, identify whether personal selling or advertising is likely to play a more important role in the promotional mix.
   a. Specialized accounting and tax preparation software that is geared to a doctor's or lawyer's private practice and, among other things, prepares tax returns for Michigan state taxes.
   b. Relatively unsophisticated spreadsheet software that competes on the basis of price and adaptability to many situations (which also means that the user has to work harder to apply it to a situation).
   c. Soft drinks.
2. What are the types of sales positions? Which type would a company likely hire to sell an innovative financial service it has just developed?
3. Third National Bank is planning to hire telephone sales reps to sell individual retirement accounts. Besides a goal for the volume of new accounts, what other objectives might the bank establish for the sales reps?
4. What are some methods by which a company can decide how many salespeople to hire?
5. How do companies use test scores in screening applicants for sales positions?
6. Liza Dooalot is the new sales manager for Long Life Insurance Company. Her boss, Jack Cracker, gave her information about two sales training programs and suggested that she select one of these for

training the company's salespeople. One of the training programs uses the AIDA theory; the other uses the want-satisfaction theory. Which would you recommend that Liza use?

7. John Dough got a summer job selling encyclopedias. He practiced his presentation over and over until he could deliver it flawlessly. He researched neighborhoods and picked one in which he thought sales would be best. The he rang his first doorbells. When someone answered the door, John would say, "Hi! Please let me show you these encyclopedias." After a number of days of trying, John found that no one would give him a chance to deliver his presentation. What in John's technique might account for his lack of success? How might he improve his technique?
8. What are some signs that a prospect is interested in buying? What is likely to happen if a salesperson keeps trying to push a product after that point?
9. The sales reps for Acme Business Forms are paid a straight salary. Lately, sales have declined somewhat, and Acme's sales manager suspects that the problem is the motivation of the sales force. In what ways might the sales manager use compensation and other factors to better motivate the sales reps?
10. Why shouldn't managers use activity quotas and expense quotas alone to evaluate performance?

Case 16.1 Educational Marketing Associates, Inc.

Educational Marketing Associates, Inc. (EMA) is an organization that sells advertising for desk pads that are distributed free of charge to college students. Eric Kingson, founder and president of EMA, realizes that the salespeople have a difficult product to sell. Kingson, faced with a high turnover rate of salespeople, is looking for ways to improve selection, training, motivation, and compensation to decrease turnover.

Desk Pad Description

The desk pads distributed by EMA are 18 inches by 22 inches. Each pad includes a perforated topsheet of coupons to be torn off and kept for use throughout the term and 10 identical 18- by 22-inch sheets that actually make up the desk pad. The 10 sheets are fastened to the desk pad base on three sides to prevent corners from curling up.

Approximately one-third of the space on the 10 desk pad sheets is blank and can be used by the students for reminders or doodling. The remaining two-thirds is used for advertising. An average of 30 advertisers appear on each desk pad. A calendar and sports schedules for the term are also printed on the desk pad.

The Selling Environment

EMA salespeople have a difficult selling job. They are not selling a tangible product such as a computer. The company itself does not have an image comparable to a firm such as IBM. Many of the companies EMA sales representatives call on are small businesses. Often it is difficult to convince the proprietor of a small business that the advantages of participating outweigh the initial cost. Furthermore, many of the businesses in a campus environment come and go, which makes it difficult for a salesperson to establish a stable customer base.

The hours that an EMA salesperson works may be long and unpredictable. For example, many pizza places do not open until the dinner hour. Thus, the salesperson not only has to call on the potential client after normal business hours, but the client may be too busy preparing pizzas to discuss advertising. In fact, the salespeople are constantly faced with discouragement. As many as 10 calls may be made before a sale is obtained.

Eric Kingson thinks that the high turnover of salespeople is in part due to the selling situation. He has tried to combat the turnover problem by recruiting individuals who could handle frequent rejection and training the recruits to sell this particular product. Furthermore, he has tried to effectively motivate and compensate the salespeople to encourage them to stay with the job. However, Kingson has never been satisfied with the results of efforts in any of these areas. The following section describes what he has done or has thought about doing in terms of recruitment, training, compensation, and motivation.

Managing the Sales Force

Kingson has recruited salespeople directly out of college, with limited sales experience, with work experience but not sales experience, and with extensive sales experience. He has interviewed potential sales representatives from college campus placement offices and employment agencies. He has placed ads in the newspaper for salespeople and has a bonus program for current employees who bring in recruits who are later hired.

Kingson has experimented with a variety of training programs such as (1) field training—where the trainee observes the supervisor, the supervisor observes the trainee, and a combination of both; (2) a three-day classroom training program, with the trainee then going into the field with or without supervision; and (3) a week-long, intensive training session with video presentations, role playing, and other techniques.

Kingson has tried several methods of compensation, including straight commission, no draw; draw against commission; straight salary; and salary plus bonus. Kingson has never given salespeople expense accounts, but he has tried car allowances, car and food allowances, and company cars.

Kingson believes that one of the useful methods of motivating salespeople is through recognition. EMA, therefore, publishes a weekly newsletter to publicize the performance of the top salesperson of the week. Each week, the best performing salesperson wins a gift certificate to a local restaurant. Monthly contests are also held. The salesperson of the month, the super salesperson of the month, and the sales trainee of the month are all recognized and awarded prizes.

Focal Topics

1. What are the advantages and disadvantages of the compensation alternatives Eric Kingson has tried? Which compensation plan do you recommend (you may develop a new plan)?
2. Suggest several ways to improve the morale and motivation of the sales force at EMA.
3. Give your recommendations on how recruiting and training procedures at EMA might be improved.

Case 16.2
Hyde-Phillip Chemical Company

Michael Claxton, a recent marketing graduate of a well-known college, has been assigned the task of evaluating Hyde-Phillip Chemical Company's methods of selling the firm's products. Hyde-Phillip currently utilizes a mix of company salespersons, merchant wholesalers, and agent wholesalers to present its products to current and potential users. While this combination of selling forces is somewhat unusual, it reflects the orientation of management over time to the relative values of alternative forms of sales representation. Claxton's challenge is to review the data that has been gathered on the three types of sales efforts, determine if additional information is needed, and make recommendations as to what changes, if any, should be made in the firm's approach to sales representation.

Information on the Company

Hyde-Phillip was formed in the early 1960s through the merger of Hyde Industrial Chemicals and Phillip Laboratories. Both firms had a broad range of experience in the development and production of certain types of chemicals and related supplies for a variety of industrial users. While the two firms had a few overlapping product lines, each brought to the merger some exclusive product offerings. The resulting combination of the two firms yielded a new organization capable of marketing a complete line of chemicals for industrial use.

Prior to the merger, Hyde Industrial Chemicals had utilized a group of industrial distributors (merchant wholesalers) to market its products. Phillip Laboratories, on the other hand, had several manufacturers' agents (agent wholesalers) who sold its product offering. The new firm, after the merger, retained some of the industrial distributors and some of the manufacturing agents and then began to develop its own sales force.

Source: This case has been edited from an earlier one that appeared in *Cases for Analysis in Marketing*, by W. Wayne Talarzyk.

Exhibit
Available Data on Sales Territories

Territory Number	Level of Sales	Type of Representation	Use of Sales Support	Geographic Location
1	2	1	2	3
2	3	1	3	3
3	2	2	1	1
4	1	1	1	1
5	2	3	1	1
6	2	1	2	1
7	3	3	2	3
8	1	2	1	2
9	2	1	2	2
10	2	1	2	3
11	1	2	1	1
12	1	1	1	2
13	2	2	2	2
14	2	3	2	1
15	1	1	2	3
16	2	3	2	2
17	2	1	3	1
18	1	2	1	2
19	2	3	2	2
20	3	1	3	2
21	1	3	1	3
22	2	2	1	3
23	3	3	1	1
24	3	1	3	2
25	3	2	3	1
26	1	2	1	2
27	2	1	2	2
28	1	2	1	3
29	2	3	3	3
30	2	3	2	3

Codes: Level of sales: 1 = more than \$2 million; 2 = \$1–2 million; 3 = less than \$1 million.
Type of representation: 1 = company sales force; 2 = industrial distributor; 3 = manufacturers' agent.
Use of sales support: 1 = extensive user; 2 = moderate user; 3 = light user.
Geographic location: 1 = Northern; 2 = Southern; 3 = Eastern.

Today, Hyde-Phillip serves 30 sales territories in states east of the Mississippi through its own sales force of 50 individuals (6 women and 44 men), 9 industrial distributors, and 9 manufacturers' agents. The 50 salespeople are about evenly allocated across 12 of the sales territories. Each of the industrial distributors and manufacturers' agents has exclusive selling rights in one of the 18 remaining sales territories. Individual distributors and agents have from 5 to 30 people working for them and many represent other noncompeting manufacturers. The 30 sales territories were originally established to represent areas of approximately equal sales potential for Hyde-Phillip's products.

Data on Sales Territories

As a first step in beginning his analysis, Claxton asked his assistant to compile the available information on each of the 30 sales territories. This information is presented in coded form in the Exhibit.

In terms of level of sales, 9 territories have annual sales in excess of $2 million, 15 have sales between $1 and $2 million, and 6 have sales less than $1 million. As already indicated, in 12 of the territories the firm is represented by its own sales force, and industrial distributors and manufacturers' agents each represent the company in 9 territories.

Based on estimates provided by the sales support department, 12 of the territories make extensive use of the available sales support programs, 12 are moderate users, and 6 are light users. Each of the firm's sales territories is also divided into one of three geographic divisions—Northern, Southern, or Eastern. As indicated in the Exhibit, each of these geographic locations includes 10 sales territories.

Claxton's initial reaction was that the firm should consider replacing part of its own sales force and the manufacturers' agents with more industrial distributors. He was concerned, however, with what other variables should be taken into account to more fully analyze and evaluate Hyde-Phillip's current approach to sales representation.

Focal Topics

1. From the perspective of Hyde-Phillip, discuss the relative advantages and disadvantages of each of the following forms of sales representation: company sales force, industrial distributors, and manufacturers' agents.
2. Based upon the data in the case, which form of sales representation seems "best" for Hyde-Phillip at this time?
3. Based on your analysis of the case, what would be your specific recommendations to the company at this time?

Case for Part Five

Chrysler Corporation

"He's an American legend, the tough-talking, straight-shooting businessman who brought Chrysler back from the brink and in the process became a media celebrity, a newsmaker, and a man many have urged to run for President." This description appears on the front flap of the cover of *Iacocca, An Autobiography.* This man, when removed as president of Ford Motor Company, was told by his wife, Mary, "Don't get mad, get even."

As part of the revival of Chrysler, and, in some ways how he got even, Lee Iacocca signed many of Chrysler's print advertisements and appeared in many of the company's television advertisements.

Spokesman Iacocca

In his autobiography, Iacocca states that he was asked to personally appear in television advertisements shortly after he came to Chrysler. At that time, several companies were using their presidents as company spokesmen. But acting on instinct and professional advice from friends, Iacocca declined. He did not feel that the time was appropriate.

About a year later, after he had signed some of Chrysler's print advertisements, the firm's advertising agency, Kenyon & Eckhardt, asked him to reconsider appearing in the television advertisements. Their logic: "Everyone thinks Chrysler's going bankrupt. Somebody has to tell them you're not. The most believable guy to do that would be you. First, you're well known. And second, the viewers know very well that after you make the commercial, you have to go back to the business of making the cars you touted. By appearing in these ads, you're putting your money where your mouth is."

At first, Iacocca only delivered tag lines to the commercials, such as "I'm not asking you to buy one of our cars on faith, I'm asking you to compare" and "If you buy a car without considering Chrysler, that'll be too bad—for both of us."

Later his statements became bolder: "You can go with Chrysler, or you can go with someone else—and take your chances." In one line, which was his own creation and which has been parodied in many ways, he said, "If you can find a better car—buy it." As conditions continued to improve at Chrysler, Iacocca began to do fewer television commercials and finally stopped completely.

Sources: Lee Iacocca with William Novak, *Iacocca, An Autobiography* (Bantam Books, 1984); "100 Leading National Advertisers," *Advertising Age,* September 4, 1986, pp. 63+; Michelie Krebs, "Chrysler Credit to test two plans," *Automotive News,* March 24, 1986, p. 32; and Raymond Serafin and Patrick Strnad, "Iacocca back in pitchman seat for '87," *Advertising Age,* September 22, 1986, pp. 50+. Logo courtesy of the Chrysler Corporation.

Promotional Activities

Over the years, Chrysler has used a variety of promotional activities to reach consumers. Some examples include the following:

- ☐ At one point when sales were low, Chrysler's advertising agency came up with: "We want to get you to consider a Chrysler product. Come in and test-drive one of our cars. If you do, and if you then end up buying a car from one of our competitors, we'll give you fifty bucks just for considering us."
- ☐ Another marketing first: "Buy one of our cars, take it home, and within thirty days, if you don't like it *for any reason,* bring it back and we'll refund your money." The only catch was a depreciation charge of $100, since the car could not be resold as new. The total number of returns worked out to less than two-tenths of 1 percent.
- ☐ The company has placed major emphasis on its 5-year, 50,000-mile warranty program, with emphasis on "setting new standards of performance."
- ☐ In July 1986, the company set new sales incentives of 5.5 percent financing or up to $1,500 rebates on most models.
- ☐ Chrysler Credit Corporation, the automotive financing arm of Chrysler, tested two financial programs: balloon note financing and variable-rate financing. With balloon note financing, the buyer makes monthly payments that are lower than with traditional financing for a specified number of months. A lump sum (or balloon payment) is due at the end of the period. The consumer has the choice of paying the lump sum and keeping the car or turning it over to the financial institution. With variable rate financing, the interest rate on the loan is adjusted periodically, based on market conditions, with the number of monthly payments increased or reduced.

Recent Advertising

In the fall of 1985, Chrysler continued the theme, "All the Japanese you need to know" to advertise its 1986 vehicles imported by Mitsubishi Motors. The objective was to set its captive imports apart from its domestically built cars by positioning them as Japanese. Colt four-door sedans and a new, four-wheel-drive Colt Vista received extra television and print advertising that was aimed predominantly at women.

According to *Advertising Age,* "Chrysler's September-breaking ads for 1986 models were patriotic and comparative. The positioning reflected thinking that Chrysler faces a long-term competitive disadvantage against imports. Chrysler used more daytime and prime-time TV, radio, and cable TV in 1986."

In terms of its overall corporate objective, Chrysler's aim was to "be the best." Plymouth's theme was "Born in America," and Dodge focused again on being "An American Revolution." Advertisements for Chrysler stated, "Chrysler technology makes 'Made in America' mean something again."

Iacocca Returns

To show that the company is not "resting on our laurels," chairman Lee Iacocca returned as spokesman for Chrysler's 1987 advertising program. In one advertisement for a 1988 luxury model, Iacocca said, "It ain't cheap but neither is caviar." The Maserati-built Chrysler luxury coupe was expected to be priced at around $30,000.

Specific corporate advertising that featured Iacocca focused on the new Chrysler LeBaron coupe and convertibles, new compacts Plymouth Sundance and Dodge Shadow, new mid-size pickup Dodge Dakota, and the restyled Dodge Daytona.

"Best-built, best-backed American cars and trucks" remained as the basic advertising theme in all corporate and divisional print advertisements. Corporate advertisements used these lines: "Working together to be the best" and "Fastest-growing car and truck company in America."

Focal Topics

1. How important do you think Iacocca's presence in Chrysler's advertising was in turning the company around?
2. What are the main reasons why a consumer chooses one automobile over another?
3. How important do you think advertising is for Chrysler at the corporate level, at the divisional level, and at the dealer level?
4. What advertising–promotion recommendations would you make to Chrysler?
5. Do you think it is a good move for Chrysler to again use Iacocca for its advertising? Why, or why not?

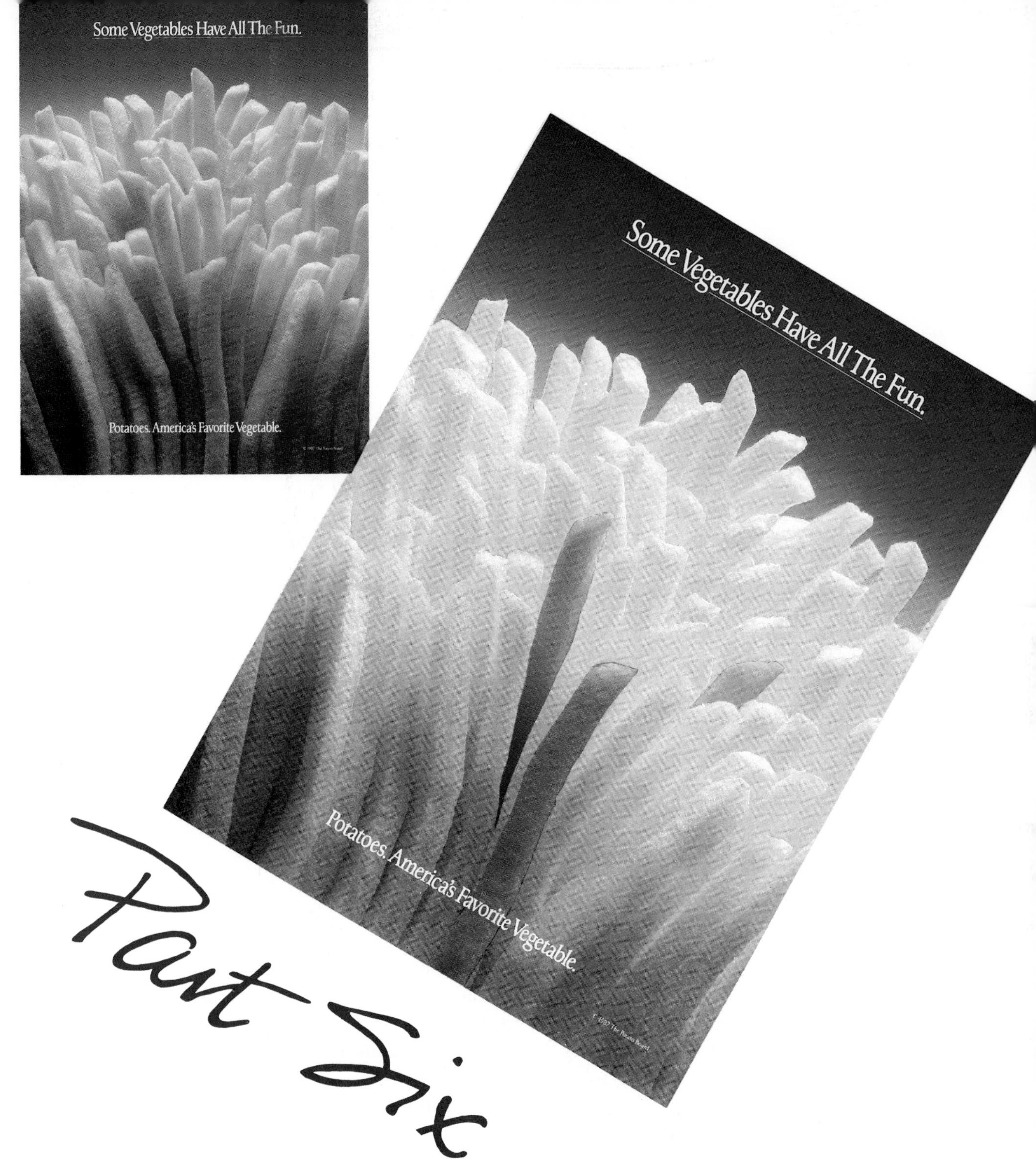

Special Marketing

17

International Marketing

☐ Sounding Out the Chapter

In this chapter, you will learn:

1. **The differences between foreign trade, foreign marketing, and multinational marketing.**
2. **Ways in which businesses can penetrate foreign markets.**
3. **Economic characteristics marketers consider in evaluating international markets.**
4. **Some cultural differences marketers must be aware of.**
5. **How governments affect a marketer's involvement in a country.**
6. **Limitations on researching foreign markets.**
7. **Issues marketers must consider in developing products for international markets.**
8. **The pricing decisions international marketers must make.**
9. **The major types of intermediaries American companies use to place their products in foreign markets.**
10. **Reasons marketers may have to modify promotions for foreign markets.**

Source: Courtesy of Vanport Manufacturing Inc.

U.S. Lumber Crosses the Pacific

Producers in the Northwest once enjoyed a seemingly perpetual boom for their lumber, fruit, and grains. In the 1980s, that began to change. Other regions and other countries began to make inroads into markets where the Northwest had once been the dominant supplier. The companies that have survived the change have often done so by finding new markets for their products.

One such company is Vanport Manufacturing Inc., a small lumber company in Portland, Oregon. Vanport's owner, Adolf Hertrich, decided that the lumber industry's potential lay across the ocean, in Japan. Japanese firms rarely bought finished lumber from Oregon because it didn't meet their rigorous standards. Hertrich decided that his company would change that pattern.

Hertrich traveled extensively in Japan, meeting with prospective customers and inspecting the facilities of Japanese lumber companies. Because Vanport was such a small company, the Japanese companies didn't take Hertrich seriously, and he was able to take photographs and make careful notes. He then redesigned Vanport's entire mill, adapting it to Japanese needs.

Vanport's willingness to adapt to the culture of its overseas customers was a powerful strategy. Today, while many of Vanport's Oregon competitors are idle, its workers labor two shifts. Of the company's 1986 sales, 90 percent were to Japan.

Another Oregon lumber company, Gregory Forest Products Inc., has found a different approach to attract the Japanese market. Instead of adapting operations to the traditional Japanese style, company owner Bill Gregory determined that a market segment in Japan is interested in Gregory's standard products. Specifically, the Japanese market for traditional American houses is growing. Gregory is hoping to capitalize on this trend.

Other conditions make the Japanese market attractive for northwestern lumber companies. Transportation is one; containerized shipping makes it cheaper to send lumber by boat to Japan than by truck or rail to Texas. In addition, the dollar's value relative to the Japanese yen has been falling since 1985, making American lumber cheaper for Japanese customers.

Companies in many industries have found their future in foreign markets. This chapter describes some of the issues marketers confront in selling across national boundaries.

Source: Joel Kotkin, "The New Northwest Passage," *Inc.*, February 1987, pp. 92–94, 96.

Marketing Abroad

Anyone familiar with pocket calculators knows the name Hewlett-Packard. The firm specializes in producing the Cadillacs of electronic devices. The company was founded 40 years ago by two young men with only $538 and a garage for working space. Today, it designs over 3,000 products in 22 plants. An important reason for the firm's success is its expansion into overseas markets.

Hewlett-Packard's international marketing activity began in the late 1940s when the firm exported a few products outside the United States. Overseas exports grew until they reached 10 percent of sales volume ten years later. Sensing a vast, untapped market in Europe, the company then increased its foreign commitment by setting up a marketing headquarters in Geneva, Switzerland, with its own sales force. To supply the increased demand, the firm also established factories in Germany and England. By 1980, foreign sales—many of them from German-developed products—were larger than domestic sales.[1]

International Marketing Performance of marketing activities across national boundaries.

Hewlett-Packard's experience is typical of those firms that engage in **international marketing,** or the performance of marketing activities across national boundaries.[2] Not all firms market abroad. In fact, only about 10 percent of American businesses are involved in the international marketplace. But for those that are involved—more than 25,000 organizations—it is a profitable field.

More than $2 trillion in goods moved across national borders in 1984. United States exports in that year accounted for $364 billion.[3] Services are an important and rapidly growing area of international trade; unfortunately, however, statistics about the international exchange of services are scanty. Some of the best-known U.S. companies make between 40 and 60 percent of their profits abroad. Indeed, in the 1970s, foreign sales grew faster than domestic sales for many American businesses.

Reasons for International Marketing

Firms seek markets overseas for two reasons: because they are pushed out of their home markets or because they are pulled by promising market prospects abroad.[4]

Many factors push companies out of domestic markets. Heavy competition at home is one of them. Fast-food outlets are found at nearly every American intersection, so the companies look to Europe, where they are still a novelty. Some of that competition comes from abroad. For example, as imported automobiles gained popularity in the United States, the response of U.S. automakers included increased development of overseas markets.

Another push can come from unfavorable government policies. High corporate taxation and minimum-wage laws have contributed to the decisions of American television manufacturers to establish plants abroad. Finally, excess production capacity at home may push firms into selling abroad. American farmers engage in international marketing because of surplus production.

The major force pulling manufacturers abroad is the market potential of other countries. About 95 percent of the world's population and three-quarters of its purchasing power exist outside the United States.[5] These numbers draw U.S. firms to other countries. Concurrently, the relative affluence and large number of U.S. buyers leads many foreign marketers to target U.S. markets. (See Figure 17.1.) For example, Canadian singers generally seek popularity among listeners in the United States as well as Canada. An increasingly popular way to market in the United States is direct ownership. Howard Johnson restaurants are British-owned, and many farms in the United States have owners overseas.[6]

Also, if a company finds it more profitable to produce in greater quantity, it might determine that an overseas market is particularly receptive to its product. Many smaller firms lack the funds to undertake international marketing and the personnel to handle its complexities. But for firms with sufficient resources, the opportunities seem unlimited.

Modes of International Marketing

International marketing is a complex field because it can encompass a number of activities.[7] The term used to be a synonym for **foreign trade,** which involves home production and the export of products across national boundaries. When Hewlett-Packard first started selling abroad, its international marketing was limited to foreign trade.

Foreign Trade
Home production and the export of products across national boundaries.

But many companies, including Hewlett-Packard, have discovered that both sales and profits can be improved by operating within the foreign country where goods are to be sold. This mode of international marketing is known as **foreign marketing.** Firms that engage in foreign marketing generally have a serious international commitment, and their organizational structure usually expands to reflect this.

Foreign Marketing
Operating within the foreign country where goods are to be sold.

A company that decides to market in one foreign country usually expands to several countries eventually. At this point, international marketing activities must be coordinated for maximum efficiency. Integrating marketing activities carried out in a number of countries is referred to as **multinational marketing.** The difference between firms that engage in foreign trade and foreign marketing, on the one hand, and those involved in multinational marketing, on the other, is worth emphasizing.

Multinational Marketing
Integrating marketing activities carried out in a number of countries.

Multinational corporations not only trade with but operate out of several countries and obtain much of their profit from such operations. Furthermore, they make decisions based on alternatives available anywhere in the world. For example, they convert their cash on hand into currencies that are strongest. And they produce component parts wherever costs are lowest. Thus Ford assembles its cars in the United States, but it produces engines in Germany, electrical systems in Canada, and transmissions in England.

True multinational corporations no longer emphasize the distinction between home and foreign markets, but most have a national identity. About half of all sales by multinationals are made by U.S.-based firms. Eight of the ten largest multinationals are American, most of them car manufacturers or oil companies. But there are some giant foreign-based

If you could see us now Mom—
Our beach is 3 steps away from a quaint marketplace.
The people are so nice, and the prices are so good, we need a trunk to send everything home!
Oh the trials and tribulations of honeymooning in Mexico.

Love,
(The brand new)
Mrs. Newell

FEEL THE WARMTH OF MÉXICO.

For more information call your travel agent or write to:
Mexico Tourism, P.O. Box 8013-GMAG, Smithtown, N.Y. 11787

Turismo de México

multinationals that are familiar in America, including Shell (British-Dutch), Bayer (German), and Nestlé (Swiss).

Multinational companies are receiving increasing attention. It is important to keep in mind, however, that their mode of operation represents only one type of involvement in international marketing.

Routes of Expansion Abroad

In addition to distinguishing the types of involvement in international marketing, most experts also differentiate the ways that businesses can penetrate foreign markets. The routes of expansion abroad include exportation, licensing, joint ventures, and direct investment. Foreign trade is usually associated with exportation alone. But both foreign trade and foreign marketing can take place by any one or all of those means.

Marketers choose a route based on a variety of considerations, including the amount of time and resources they want to commit and the level of risk they are willing to bear. The different routes also give organizations different degrees of control over the marketing activity abroad. As Figure 17.2 shows, exportation provides a company with the least amount of control, whereas direct investment allows maximum control.

Exportation American companies exported a total of $370 billion in goods and services in 1985, posting more than a 65 percent increase in just three years. Although exports have increased, they represent less than 10 percent of the U.S. gross national product.[8] Many other nations export far more of their gross national products (GNP). West Germany, for example, exports nearly one-quarter of its GNP, and Belgium almost half.

Exporting is usually the first step in international marketing, because it requires the smallest financial commitment. For example, firms with surplus production find exporting a convenient way of ridding themselves of the excess while picking up a contribution to their costs. Or a company that detects a demand for its products overseas may find it worthwhile to hire additional workers or add another shift. In the United States, the leading exports are machinery, transportation equipment, agricultural products, chemicals, and consumer goods. They are sold mainly in Canada, Europe, and Japan.[9]

Firms that engage in exporting may do so in two ways. Those with the least amount of exporting experience usually start by using intermediaries who work for or are in contact with buyers in foreign markets. When companies become more experienced and their sales volume increases, they may choose to sell directly to buyers, as Hewlett-Packard did.

Figure 17.1
Targeting a Relatively Affluent Market—U.S. Consumers
Source: Reprinted with permission of the Secretaria de Turismo.

Figure 17.2
Routes of Entry and Degree of Control

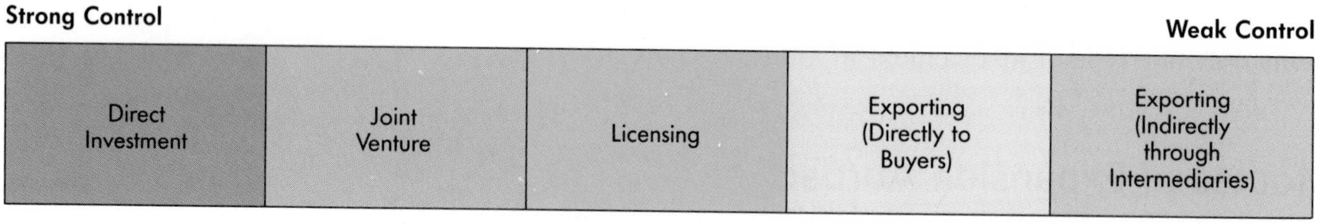

Strong Control				Weak Control
Direct Investment	Joint Venture	Licensing	Exporting (Directly to Buyers)	Exporting (Indirectly through Intermediaries)

Licensing
Arrangement under which a company (the licensor) grants a foreign firm (the licensee) the rights to patents, trademarks, and the use of technical processes in exchange for a royalty or fee for use.

Licensing A company with a limited amount of money to invest but a need for greater control over marketing may try **licensing.** In this arrangement, a company (the licensor) grants a foreign firm (the licensee) the rights to patents, trademarks, and the use of technical processes in exchange for a royalty or fee for use. Usually the licensor will also agree to provide management assistance.

Some companies use licensing extensively. Philip Morris has licensing agreements for its tobacco products in six Western European and four Eastern European countries. An automotive equipment manufacturer had almost 500 different licensing agreements in foreign countries, which brought in millions of dollars in royalties and were the source of valuable technical developments.[10] Franchising is a form of licensing that is becoming increasingly popular.

The main advantages of licensing are that a firm risks no capital in granting a license and that it gains direct access to foreign markets. The latter is especially important, since governments often limit the number of goods from abroad, blocking access to markets by exportation.

One drawback is that control over quality may be limited. Government-owned companies in Egypt produce Pepsi-Cola under license, and dealers complain it lacks the flavor of beverages produced by private companies.[11] Another disadvantage is that after a time the licensee may adapt the licensed product and become an independent competitor. Japanese companies have done so in the past with transistor radios and are now challenging Americans in producing power tools, microwave ovens, and outboard motors. Other entry routes are sometimes safer.

Joint Venture
Partnership with a foreign firm under which both partners invest money and share ownership and control in proportion to their investment.

Joint Ventures Companies wishing even more control over marketing may choose a **joint venture,** or partnership with a foreign firm. Both partners invest money and share ownership and control in proportion to their investment. Kentucky Fried Chicken's arrangement with the Mitsubishi Corporation of Japan is an example. Each company contributed 50 percent of the capital for start-up. In addition, KFC supplies marketing expertise and Mitsubishi provides the chickens, cooking equipment, and real estate for store sites.[12]

Until recently, most joint ventures involving U.S. firms were set up for activities in other countries. However, a growing number of these ventures are now operating in the United States, especially with Japanese companies. An example of such a setup is the arrangement between the world's two largest automakers, General Motors and Toyota, to manufacture subcompacts in a retooled GM plant in Fremont, California. GM hopes to learn more about manufacturing small cars, and Toyota hopes to maintain its market position in the face of rising protectionist sentiment.[13]

Besides pooling complementary areas of expertise, companies that conduct joint ventures can derive several other benefits. A joint venture allows a company to share risks with another or to take advantage of another company's existing lines of distribution. Also, because a joint venture can enter a market faster than a new company alone, this arrangement can give a company a head start or at least allow it to keep up in a fast-changing environment. Pooling resources is also important in industries with soaring costs, such as the aircraft industry.

Despite these advantages, not all joint ventures work out well. Dow Chemical Company and Germany's BASF set up a joint venture in the United States; BASF provided the technology to make chemical raw material and fibers, and Dow provided the marketing expertise. But even though the enterprise was making a profit, the partners dissolved it, because BASF wanted to expand, while Dow was reluctant to invest further in a venture that made a product—fibers—outside of Dow's main business—chemicals.[14]

This example illustrates one of the major drawbacks of a joint venture: conflicting objectives. Other major disadvantages are the lack of total control and the risk of investment loss. And one partner may use its experience in the venture to improve its ability to compete with the other partner.

Nevertheless, firms sometimes are forced into agreeing to partial ownership by government decree. For example, India, Japan, and Mexico deny foreigners majority ownership of any venture in their countries.[15] Firms may accept such a restriction if they feel a local firm can provide them with needed knowledge of an unfamiliar marketplace.

Direct Investment In the 1960s and early 1970s, **direct investment,** or total control of production and sales of goods in a foreign country, became the most popular route for American firms expanding abroad. While American companies continue to invest overseas, a major trend in recent years has been direct investment of foreign companies in the United States. From the mid-1970s to the mid-1980s, foreign direct investment in the United States has quadrupled.[16]

Direct Investment
Total control of production and sales of goods in a foreign country.

American firms have invested heavily overseas for three reasons:

1. To sidestep trade barriers, such as tariffs erected against American imports in foreign countries.
2. To take advantage of cheaper labor abroad.
3. To overcome the inflated prices of American exports caused by the high value of the dollar relative to other nation's currencies.

To some extent, those conditions have less effect today. Tariff barriers have been negotiated downward. Labor is still cheaper in many countries, but not so in Europe, where most of the investment had traditionally taken place. While somewhat lessened in recent years, the strength of the dollar continues to hurt the U.S. trade balance by making imports cheap and American exports expensive in other currencies.

Direct investment allows a company superior control over operations. On the other hand, it also exposes a company to expropriation, or seizure, of facilities if hostility develops between the host country and the foreign company. Firms must weigh both benefits and risks before deciding on this route for expanding abroad.

The Environment of Marketing Abroad

In deciding whether to market abroad, a company needs to consider the opportunities and limitations of the international marketplace. This includes the conditions within countries, as well as the broader issues of marketing internationally.

The principles of analyzing the international marketplace are basically the same as those involved in learning about the domestic external environment. The marketer examines economic, cultural, and political/legal characteristics of the marketplace to identify opportunities and select target markets. Nevertheless, the process may be more complex. For example, American companies marketing abroad typically have to contend with trade restrictions and agreements, a language barrier, competition among national interests, and attitudes toward U.S. companies in general. Thus, the following discussion of economic, cultural, and political/legal characteristics applies some familiar principles to some new situations. The perspective is that of an American marketer.

Economic Differences

The world population is approaching the 5-billion mark, of which only about 5 percent live within the United States. Moreover, the population of most of the rest of the world is growing at a faster rate than the U.S. population. Typically, the more developed and affluent the country, the lower the birth rate. The fastest growth is occurring in oil-producing countries of the Middle East.[17]

Per-Capita Income
A country's gross national product divided by its population.

But people are considered part of a market only if they have purchasing power. One way to measure this is to use **per-capita income,** which is a country's gross national product divided by its population. Per-capita income figures vary widely among nations. The United States is among the wealthiest, with a 1985 per-capita income of $13,451. Oil-rich Kuwait was doing even better in 1983, with a per-capita income of $18,000. At the other extreme are Cambodia and Chad, with 1984 per-capita incomes of only $100 and $88, respectively. (The dates vary because not every country provides this information every year.) According to the World Bank, about half of the world's population lives in countries with an average per-capita income of $270.[18]

This breakdown is important to marketers. If markets are people with money, over 50 percent of the world is unattractive for marketing. Some trading in raw materials and agricultural products between less-developed countries and the rest of the world does go on. But direct investment for manufacturing and selling abroad is confined to about a dozen industrialized countries and a handful of other countries that are developing industrially.

Developing countries may, in fact, become increasingly important to marketers in the future. Competition in industrialized countries is becoming so intense that certain developing countries, among them Egypt, Spain, Chile, and China, are beginning to look like attractive and less-crowded markets. That is why Canada Dry, 7-Up, and Coca-Cola are challenging Pepsi-Cola's dominance in Egypt. The market is, as one executive put it, "like a sponge," and it may offset some of the losses soft-drink companies expect to suffer at home because of the shrinking youth market.[19]

Per-capita income should be evaluated with care, as it often hides extremes. In addition, marketers should consider other measures of economic differences. One common classification divides countries according to their industrial structure:[20]

☐ *Subsistence economies,* in which most people engage in simple agriculture and consume most of their output.

☐ *Raw-material-exporting economies,* which are rich in natural resources and receive most of their revenue from exporting them.

☐ *Industrializing economies,* in which manufacturing accounts for about 10 to 20 percent of the economy and a small middle class is forming.

☐ *Industrial economies,* which are major exporters of manufactured goods and investment funds and have large middle classes.

In considering a classification such as this, marketers assess the kinds of products demanded in the different economies, the prospects for growth, and the likelihood that an economy is shifting from one type to another. As an example, industrializing economies provide a market for selling raw materials to manufacturers and selling luxury goods to those who have become wealthy from the manufacturing. Notably, some industrializing nations—South Korea, for example—also are becoming an important source of competition for manufacturers in industrial economies.

Besides data on income and industrial structure, marketers must also study a country's **economic infrastructure.** That refers to facilities such as paved roads, communication and transportation services, banks, and distribution organizations that make marketing possible.

Economic Infrastructure
Facilities such as paved roads, communication and transportation services, banks, and distribution organizations that make marketing possible.

Outside the United States, even in largely industrial countries, the infrastructure is not always well developed. For example, U.S. marketers commonly facilitate sales by allowing customers to charge purchases on credit cards. But in many countries, few consumers have credit cards. This has hampered the expansion of home shopping via cable television.[21]

Cultural Differences

Marketers sometimes assume that the beliefs, values, and customs most familiar to them apply everywhere. When they enter a foreign market, they find themselves in culture shock.

When the Campbell Soup Company first entered the Dutch market, it neglected to notice a difference in customs. Dutch housewives were familiar with canned soups, but not condensed soups, which require adding a can of water. Many failed to read the cooking instructions on the can and complained of the soups' bitter taste. Campbell lost millions in sales before it discovered the problem and ran informational ads.[22]

Failure to take account of cultural differences is responsible for many, if not most, marketing failures abroad. Language, aesthetic perceptions, social organization, and values differ widely from country to country.

Language Most marketers are aware of language differences when they enter a foreign market. But they are sometimes less conscious of the difficulties of translating expressions from one language to another.

Examples of translation errors are numerous. When Frank Perdue's advertising agency tried to translate his slogan, "It takes a tough man to make a tender chicken," into Spanish, it came out, "It takes a sexually excited man to make a chicken affectionate." And breweries have had their share of problems with Spanish translations. One claimed to sell "the beer that would make you more drunk," and a light beer boasted that it is "Filling. Less delicious."[23] Translating into Asian languages can be particularly challenging, and the mistakes startling. Coca-Cola, for example, once found that it was promoting itself with Chinese characters that translated to "bite the waxy tadpole."[24]

Language can be a very difficult problem when marketers must sell in multilingual countries. The situation is bad enough in a bilingual country like Canada, where labels and packages must be in both English and French. But imagine the problems of marketing in India, where 203 languages and dialects are spoken.

Aesthetic Perceptions Ideas concerning beauty and good taste are almost as internationally varied as languages. These aesthetic differences also influence marketing.

Consider the meanings people give to various colors. White, often a symbol of joy in this country, is usually associated with mourning in the Far East, and is therefore unsuitable for packaging. Major marketing errors have resulted from ignoring the importance of color. For example, a yellow cologne failed to sell in Africa because consumers associated it with animal urine. Only when the product was tinted green did it succeed.[25]

People's ideas about beauty in design also may vary. One marketing expert has observed that many consumer products have universal appeal in the United States, Japan, and the European Community—the countries that account for most of the demand for these goods. Higher education levels and exposure to television have led citizens of these countries to develop similar tastes. Nevertheless, modifications are needed at times. For example, piano interiors are basically the same, but preferences for the exterior vary. In North America, consumers like wood grains, but in Japan, where pianos are used for children's education, consumers prefer black enamel. In contrast, watches and motorcycles sold around the world can have universal designs.[26]

Social Organization All societies have families in some form, but roles within the family may differ markedly from culture to culture.

Women seldom enjoy equality with men outside industrialized countries, and that can affect marketing. For example, in some less-developed countries, men do the shopping because women are confined to the home. Advertising must therefore appeal to men. Even in industrialized and developing countries, women's activities outside the home are limited. Thus, in Spain or Turkey, marketers might not be able to draw together a group of working-class women for panel discussions on products.[27]

The role of children in the family also varies from country to country. In the United States, because children have a voice in some purchasing decisions, advertising can be directed at them. But in England, children have a more limited role and advertising aimed at them is considered inappropriate.

In the United States, the social revolution that affects women in particular is beginning to spread worldwide. Therefore, some of the generalizations about social organization that are valid today may break down in the near future. Marketers must be alert to such changes.

Values The term *value* can refer to a religious or moral belief or merely a practical attitude that sums up a person's experience. Values are perhaps the most variable cultural item discussed thus far, and they too can affect marketing success.

Wendy's would probably have little or no success in India because of the Hindu prohibition against eating beef. Similarly, a drug firm selling contraceptives would encounter difficulties in Latin America, with its large Roman Catholic population. Religious or ethical values sometimes restrict certain kinds of advertising.

The unwitting violation of another culture's beliefs is one sort of dilemma marketers face. A quite different problem arises when marketers are confronted with values their culture finds unethical. For example, in many foreign countries, bribery of officials to cut through red tape is an accepted way of life. But in 1975, when over 400 large American companies admitted making payoffs abroad, the American public was shocked.

Since then, Congress has passed legislation requiring the disclosure of payments made to foreign officials and setting penalties for such payments. Some feel that these restrictions unfairly burden American firms and put them at a competitive disadvantage. The issue is a complex one. But marketers are now alerted that they must take care not to violate their own ethical standards while respecting those of other cultures.[28]

Political and Legal Differences

The U.S. regulations concerning bribery indicate the importance of political climate and law in shaping international marketing decisions. Foreign regulations governing business are sometimes even more restrictive than American laws. The reason is that there are important political differences among countries. The political differences result in a variety of laws, and firms must become aware of them before marketing abroad.

Government Policy Government policies can affect a marketer's involvement in a country. Governments control marketing activities in four major ways:

Tariff
Tax on imports.

Import Quota
Restriction on the number of goods entering a country.

1. By imposing **tariffs,**[29] or taxes on imports.
2. By setting **import quotas,** or restrictions on the number of goods entering a country.
3. By restricting the amount of currency that can be taken out of a country by a foreign multinational.
4. By setting maximum prices on goods sold within their borders.

Tariffs and quotas are intended to make goods and services produced within the country more competitive with imports. Presumably, they make the country's businesses more profitable and increase its level of employment; unfortunately, they also can increase prices paid by consumers.

Dumping
Practice of selling goods overseas at a lower price than a company charges in its own home market.

Traditionally, the American philosophy has been to support free trade, that is, minimal restrictions on importers and exporters. In recent years, however, competition from foreign companies has been on the rise, and some observers have complained that American workers are losing jobs as a result. Some foreign firms have even been accused of **dumping** in the United States, or selling products in the United States for less than in the company's domestic market. As a result, the protectionist measures of tariffs and quotas have become more popular in the United States. For example, in response to claims that the Japanese were dumping semiconductors, the U.S. government in 1987 imposed duties of 100 percent on several Japanese products, ranging from television sets to X-ray film. A huge trade imbalance with Japan probably influenced the decision to take such drastic measures.[30]

Governments may also restrict exports as a matter of foreign policy. For example, the United States restricts sales of computer products to the Soviet Union so that it can maintain an edge in technology. Trade with some countries may be forbidden altogether. Recent U.S. restrictions include prohibitions of trade with Vietnam, Cambodia, Cuba, and North Korea.

Governments can also move to encourage business. For example, following a two-year period of sluggish U.S. direct investment in the Netherlands, the office of the Dutch Industrial Commissioner in New York mounted an advertising campaign stressing the country's location and transportation network.[31] Other countries offer investment incentives and site location services.

In addition to laws about international trade, antitrust laws apply to U.S. firms marketing abroad. A company can be held in violation of antitrust laws if it commits an action abroad that affects business activity in the United States.

Political Life Abroad Marketers must learn two important facts of life about marketing overseas. First, government participation in economic affairs is far greater in most countries than in the United States. Second, many countries are politically unstable, which makes marketing there a risky venture.

In communist countries, where the government owns the means of production, the government is the only customer. This affects marketing planning. For example, in the People's Republic of China, technical experts and state planners decide what products will be imported. Chinese trade experts recommend that all advertising contain technical information rather than persuasive appeals.[32]

Sometimes, no matter what a government does to encourage marketing interest, violence erupts and marketers caught in the turmoil lose their investments. One company that provides political risk insurance for American investors in developing countries, for example, had to pay out more than $14 million in claims to businesses hurt in the 1979 Iranian revolution. The IT&T Corporation claimed losses of $92.5 million when the Chilean government took over its properties.[33]

Marketers must try to evaluate the risk of outbreaks before entering new markets. To do so, they may use both subjective means, such as talks with political and business leaders and assessments by educated experts, and objective means, including extrapolation from past events.[34] A company interested in investing in Indonesia, for example, might undertake a study of past trends of political instability in that country and then prepare a forecast of future risk. If the risk of political upheaval seemed too high, the company might then reconsider its plans for expansion.

International Law and Agreements While there is no international law-making body, police force, or court system (with the limited exception of the World Court in The Hague), international "laws" do exist in the form of treaties, conventions, and agreements among nations. The European Community, for example, has been standardizing the laws of its member nations.[35] The United Nations has been working on development of an international commercial code.[36]

An agreement that is particularly important for U.S. marketers is the General Agreement on Tariffs and Trade (GATT), an international trade agreement designed to reduce the level of tariffs.[37] More than 120 nations are members or associates of the GATT. The GATT is based on two main principles:

1. *Nondiscrimination*—GATT members grant others the same tariff rate.
2. *Consultation*—GATT provides a forum for discussing trade disagreements. Since 1947, GATT has sponsored several major tariff negotiations, resulting in reduced tariff rates for tens of thousands of items.

Large multinational companies have legal staffs that keep up with this vast and expanding body of laws. Marketers must stay on top of legal developments. Their success in the marketplace often depends on their doing so.

Strategic Planning for International Markets

Environmental analysis makes marketers aware of the difficulties they may encounter in several possible markets worldwide. With that kind of background knowledge, marketers can plan the strategy they wish to pursue. (See Marketing Today 17.1 for a description of the global strategies of two soft-drink companies.) As noted in Chapter 2, planning marketing strategy is a two-step process involving (1) selection of the target market and (2) design of the marketing mix.

Targeting relates to selection of the market or markets a company can serve best. To do that, marketers must engage in research to determine the demographic, sociological, and psychographic characteristics of potential customers. On the basis of such research, product, price, placement, and promotion policies can be tailored to meet the needs of customers.

Researching Foreign Markets

The goals and methods of research are the same for both the American market and foreign markets. But research of international markets can be more difficult.

Market research, as noted in Chapter 4, usually begins by gathering secondary data. Published information about market size and customer behavior is not always as available for other countries as for the United States. Possible sources of information are listed in Table 17.1. Government bodies such as the U.S. Department of Commerce and international organizations are good starting points, although more data are likely to be available for industrialized countries than for developing or less-developed countries.

All secondary data must be evaluated carefully. National pride sometimes stands in the way of statistical accuracy, and information about income level or demand for a product may be exaggerated. Another difficulty is that data collected from various sources are not always comparable. For example, collecting statistics on alcohol consumption in Europe may be complicated by the fact that beer is considered an alcoholic beverage in the north, whereas in the south it may be categorized with soft drinks.[38]

When secondary data are unavailable or questionable, primary data must be collected. But difficulties also arise in this area. One researcher noted the following typical problems:

- ☐ Telephone research is nearly impossible, even in industrialized countries such as England and West Germany, where only about one-third of all households have phones.

Marketing Today 17.1
Coke and Pepsi Seek Global Appeal

Source: Uzzle/ARCHIVE.

Around the world, consumers enjoy soft drinks. Cola makers have responded to this broad appeal by adopting a global strategy, selling the same product, packaging, and upbeat message in many nations. For the two leading brands—Coca-Cola and Pepsi—the competition has been stiff, resulting in aggressive promotion.

Worldwide volume for Coca-Cola is double that for Pepsi. Consequently, Pepsi has responded by competing selectively. For example, the company promoted heavily in Canada and edged out Coke there. When Coke introduced Cherry Coke in Canada, Pepsi countered with Cherry Pepsi. Pepsi's advertising campaign uses the theme "We Got the Taste," a message designed to communicate flavor superiority. Pepsi also acquired Seven-Up International (which does not include U.S. operations), to give the company greater muscle and enable it to compete with Coca-Cola's Sprite.

Coke's global brand strategy is based on "availability, affordability, and acceptability." Coke sees its biggest opportunity as growth in per-capita consumption of its product. U.S. consumers drink about eight times as much as the overseas market. To take advantage of the growth opportunity, Coca-Cola positions its brands not merely as the most satisfying soft drink, but as the most satisfying beverage. This means that in Japan, for example, Coke's biggest competition isn't Pepsi, it's tea.

Source: Jeffry Scott, "The Cola Wars Go Global," *Adweek,* September 22, 1986, p. B.R. 18.

- Mail surveys are not easily conducted in countries with high illiteracy rates such as Italy and Spain.
- Long questionnaires are not acceptable in Hong Kong, which is a rush society; but even short questionnaires may turn out to be long in Brazil because citizens are conscientious answerers.[39]

Educational and cultural differences make primary research difficult but not impossible. In increasingly competitive international markets, such research is becoming an absolute necessity.

Table 17.1
Sources of Information for Marketing Abroad

I. For Major Producing and Exporting Countries
- A. Official government statistics
  - —Production
  - —Foreign trade (imports and exports)
  - —Statistical abstract
- B. Foreign industry associations
  - —Production, consumption, in use, saturation
  - —Industry directory (list of member firms, product scope, etc.)
  - —Industry magazines
- C. Foreign periodicals
  - —Magazines directed to wholesale and retail trade

II. International Marketing Indicators
- A. United Nations
- B. International Monetary Fund
- C. U.S. Department of Commerce
- D. Regional organizations
  - —Organization for Economic Cooperation & Development (OECD)

III. General Background Information
- A. Complementary or service industry publications
  - —Frozen foods, coffee, steel, shipbuilding
- B. International press and newsletters
  - —*Business International*
- C. Research organizations
  - —Ford Foundation
- D. International banking publications

IV. U.S. Sources of Industry Information
- A. U.S. industry associations' international publications
  - —E.I.A. *International News*

V. U.S. Department of Commerce
- A. U.S. import and export statistics
- B. Overseas business reports
- C. BDSA short market surveys and trade reports
- D. Foreign service dispatch loan service
- E. *International Commerce*

VI. Competition
- A. Annual reports of major competitors, U.S. and foreign

Source: R. J. Dickensheets, "Basic and Economical Approaches to International Marketing Research," *1963 Proceedings of the American Marketing Association* (Chicago: American Marketing Association, 1963), p. 364.

Selecting Target Markets

Information gleaned from market research helps the organization select target markets. The organization may choose to develop a marketing mix aimed at certain nations or groups within nations, or it may decide to prepare a single marketing mix to appeal to a broad segment of the world marketplace. The first approach is called *multinational marketing;* the second, *global marketing.*

With global marketing, the organization tries to identify needs held in common around the world and to design a single marketing mix to meet those needs. Some observers have noted that American companies more typically plan a product for the U.S. market, and then try to sell it internationally, making modifications if deemed necessary. This is not global marketing, because it starts with a single country's needs and preferences, rather than identifying commonalities among nations.[40]

True global marketing can require more creativity, because marketers must go beyond the differences in what people say they want; instead they try to identify underlying needs. Buyers may be willing to change their expectations if the marketer offers a product at a lower price than they pay for existing products. Standardized products that have sold successfully around the world include automobiles, agricultural commodities, banking and insurance services, McDonald's hamburgers, and Hollywood movies.[41]

After examining a number of researchers' reports, one marketing expert has concluded that a global strategy is most appropriate for firms with less ambitious sales goals, a greater emphasis on cost control, fewer production plants, and fully owned subsidiaries overseas. By contrast, the organizations most likely to benefit from a multinational strategy are those with ambitious goals for sales and market share, operations in many foreign markets, extensive financial and managerial resources, a global production network, and significant joint-venture operations.[42]

When the organization has selected its international target markets, it is ready to plan the elements of the marketing mix.

Product Planning

Marketers must determine whether to sell the same product abroad as at home, modify it for the new market, or develop an entirely different product. At Your Service 17.1 describes a company that helps marketers make decisions of this nature.

The tactic of selling the same product around the world is practical if culture has no influence on the way the product is used or prepared. Many consumer products, such as soft drinks and cosmetics, are the same no matter where they are sold. For example, Oil of Olay is formulated the same for American and European markets, and, in the past, commercials have shown beautiful women around the world praising the product in their native language.

In the case of food products and many other consumer or industrial products, however, modifications must be made for a variety of reasons. For example, Exxon reformulates its gasoline to meet climatic conditions; Nestlé sells dozens of varieties of coffee to meet local taste preferences; and Burroughs, an office equipment manufacturer, adapts the voltage of its machines to the electrical power systems of various countries.[43]

Sometimes a product must be redesigned entirely to meet the needs of a population. For example, Ford has developed a type of model-T truck appropriate for low-income Asian countries, and Coca-Cola markets a protein- and vitamin-fortified drink to sell to markets in need of a diet supplement.[44]

The physical makeup of a product is, of course, only one aspect of the total product. Service, another consideration, is especially important

At Your Service 17.1
Company Helps Marketers Plan Marketing Strategy

Many companies try to learn from what sells overseas; adapting an existing product can be much simpler than developing one from scratch. But cultural differences can make it difficult to predict which products will succeed. Food preferences, in particular, vary greatly. For example, Nabisco's Life Savers subsidiary has found that the most popular flavors of hard candy in Britain are currant and violet, and in South Africa, musk—not exactly the top flavors in the United States.

For help in predicting how foreign products will fare domestically, many companies turn to research services. One of these is Product Initiatives, a Toronto company that conducts annual surveys of consumer interest in foreign products.

Product Initiatives will put a client's products on the shelf to see how they sell. It also tests use of the products once they have been purchased and provides user profiles of heavy users. Product Initiatives asks questions intended to determine the product's image and the reasons underlying consumers' reactions to a product.

For example, General Foods had an opportunity to license its Freeze Flo technology in Canada. Freeze Flo allows frozen foods to remain soft and pliable; jams and pie fillings packaged with this technology taste fresher and more like home-made. General Foods turned to Product Initiatives, which studied the product potential and helped the company refine prototypes, communications, and package design. When it appeared that the product would be a success, the company even gave General Foods' ad agency a briefing on the type of advertising message that would be most effective.

Source: Photo © 1987 Phyllis Woloshin.

Sources: "Alert! A Reliable, Diagnostic Assessment for New Brand Propositions," brochure from Product Initiatives, Toronto, Ontario; Ronald Alsop, "U.S. Concerns Seek Inspiration for Products from Overseas," *The Wall Street Journal,* January 3, 1985, p. 13; and "General Foods Exploits Exciting New Technology," Product Initiatives Case History, Product Initiatives, Toronto, Ontario.

in selling a foreign product. Singer sewing machines have an excellent reputation in Europe because of the company's liberal service policy.

In addition to the service component, branding is a significant part of the total product. Brand-name choice is a difficult problem. Some firms such as Coca-Cola believe it is important to establish a worldwide image for a product by using the same name. Other firms feel that an American name in foreign markets may arouse hostility. Kodak dropped its brand name in Latin American markets because of high nationalist sentiment there.[45]

Of course, the tactic of downplaying an American brand name can backfire. One American firm in Mexico picked a Spanish name for its product, assuming Mexicans would prefer a product identified with their country. In fact, the market for the product was highly class conscious and preferred the status that goes with buying American-made goods.[46]

Pricing Strategies

Marketing managers face two different pricing problems, depending on what mode of international marketing activity they select. One problem concerns how to price exports, and the other has to do with how to price component parts or goods transferred between a company and its overseas subsidiary.

Export Pricing Chapter 10 notes that prices can be set on a cost-plus basis or on the basis of demand. Ideally, costs and the amount of consumer demand should both be considered.

Marketers must determine whether to charge the same price at home and abroad, or whether to charge a higher or lower price. Seldom are the costs of selling at home the same as the costs of selling overseas. Higher prices abroad might be justified because (1) there may be additional taxes in the form of tariffs, (2) special packaging and documentation may be required, (3) the costs of distribution may be greater, or (4) inflation may be higher abroad.

On the other hand, exporting does not always mean higher costs. Sometimes domestic sales may be sufficient to cover research and overhead costs, so that any sales made abroad may be looked on as "gravy"—a contribution to profit. A lower price, therefore, may be justified. In some cases it may even be required, if competition abroad charges less than the home market price or the foreign government controls prices.

Some studies have revealed that certain goods sold abroad are very much lower in price than their counterparts sold in the United States. Companies selling goods overseas at a lower price than what they charge in their own home markets may be accused of dumping. The practice is prohibited in many countries if it significantly harms home competitors. General Electric Company, Zenith Radio Corporation, and four U.S. labor organizations, for example, petitioned the Commerce Department to investigate several South Korean and Taiwanese companies thought to be dumping color television sets in the United States. An antidumping battle in the 1960s led Sony and Matsushita Electric Industrial Corporation to recast their marketing strategy by building large production facilities in the United States.[47]

Transfer Pricing When a company establishes marketing operations abroad, it must decide how much to charge subsidiaries for goods or parts shipped to or from them. This pricing within the corporate family is known as **transfer pricing,** and it is controversial.

Transfer Pricing
Pricing within a corporate family, perhaps used to avoid taxes.

Some experts claim that multinational corporations use transfer pricing to better their profits. For example, transfer pricing can be used to evade high taxes. Thus, if American corporate income taxes are higher than Switzerland's tax rate, an American company may underprice what it sells to its Swiss subsidiary or overprice what it buys from it in order to minimize profits and its resulting tax bill in the United States. Many governments have passed laws against pricing aimed specifically at avoiding taxes.

Studies in the last ten years indicate that American multinationals no longer widely use transfer pricing to solve their tax problems. Instead,

Arm's-Length Policy
Policy that requires a firm's subsidiary to charge or be charged the same price available to any buyer outside the firm.

they follow an **arm's-length policy** in transfer pricing. That policy requires the subsidiary to charge or be charged the same price available to any buyer outside the firm. When there are no outside buyers to provide a standard price, problems may arise. Also, the means to police whether companies are actually charging the same price are sometimes absent. For these reasons, many countries are now calling for stiffer international controls to prevent abuses.[48]

Placement Decisions

Firms can choose a number of arrangements to place their products in foreign markets. Several factors are involved in the decision, including degree of control desired. Firms that need special control to provide servicing may set up their own sales force abroad as Singer does. Other organizations may simply prefer to sell franchisees the right to use their name. For example, H&R Block has almost 2,000 outlets abroad.[49]

Some organizations prefer to work through intermediaries. An organization that has an existing channel through an intermediary typically uses the same intermediary when introducing a new product. Marketers also prefer intermediaries when selling products that are susceptible to heavy competition and when operating in non-Western markets (that is, the ones with which they are least familiar).[50]

The major types of intermediaries that link American manufacturers and foreign markets are:

1. Resident buyers within the United States who work for foreign firms.
2. Overseas representatives of foreign firms.
3. Independent intermediaries who either buy goods for sale abroad (foreign merchant wholesalers) or arrange to bring buyers and sellers together (foreign agents).

Some companies that sell many different types of products use several of these routes.

The relative size and number of wholesalers varies greatly from country to country. In general, the industrialized nations have large wholesaling organizations serving many retailers, while wholesaling in developing countries is likely to be fragmented. A notable exception to this rule is Japan, where wholesalers sell to other wholesalers. Because wholesaling in most countries is more fragmented and operates on a smaller scale than in the United States, wholesalers in other countries often provide less service than they do in the United States.[51]

Retailing, too, may vary. Many countries have smaller retail outlets than in the United States. Retailers also may provide fewer services and may expect wholesalers to extend credit over lengthy periods.

The problem of inefficient channels of distribution is often worsened overseas by poor physical distribution facilities. Transportation is especially troublesome in less-developed countries. In Zaire, for example, a typical shipment of goods must be loaded and unloaded four times to reach the African interior because of a disjointed transportation system.[52]

At Your Service 17.2
Ad Agencies Help Marketers Sell in China

Selling in China involves so many cultural differences that many companies find they need more than the usual services from advertising agencies. Advertising agencies in China help clients find their way through the bureaucratic maze and advise them about the bewildering differences in culture, language, and media. Agencies also guide companies in translating their name and trademark into a Chinese dialect understood by the target market.

In sum, agencies serve as advisers, helping their clients create a positive image and avoid blunders. Cultural blunders in advertising include misusing the color white and the number four (both associated with death), as well as preparing ads that refer to politics or sex or overtly promote Western life-styles.

When Sperry and Burroughs merged to form Unisys, they turned to DYR/Beijing for help with promotion in China. Rather than merely translating the American ad into Chinese, the agency started by making sure the Chinese staff really understood the themes of the ad: brain power, world power, staying power, and "the power of two [companies combined]." The agency spent a lot of time in discussions of the meaning of the concepts and then rewrote them to make them understandable to a Chinese audience. In selecting a name for the company, Unisys settled on a rough translation of United Information Systems. Finally, the ad was rewritten so that it rhymed, an elegant practice by Chinese standards.

Sources: Karen Singer, "The China Card: A Giant Reawakens to Advertising," *Adweek,* February 23, 1987, p. 17; and Karen Singer, "Commerce in China Requires an Eye toward Custom," *Adweek,* March 2, 1987.

Warehousing is a problem everywhere, even in industrialized countries. Storage facilities may be small, old-fashioned, and ill-equipped. Inadequate transportation or warehousing adds to costs and may even stand in the way of successfully marketing products abroad.

Besides getting products to customers, placement involves extending credit to facilitate a purchase. Because governments generally want to promote exports, they may help companies that want to extend credit on exports. For U.S. companies, this help comes from the Export-Import Bank.

Extending credit internationally can be quite risky. Not only individuals and corporations, but even many nations have had trouble keeping up with debt payments. Exporters that want to extend credit may buy special insurance policies to protect themselves against the risk that the foreign debtor will be unable to pay because of certain commercial and political risks. In the United States, this insurance is available from the Foreign Credit Insurance Association.[53]

Promotional Considerations

The purpose of promotion is communication. But because communication takes place within a culture, promotional programs in different countries may require widely varying approaches. To reach the target audiences, messages must be varied, one perhaps stressing an emotional theme and the other making a more rational appeal. Media and timing of messages also vary with the target audiences. Many companies turn for help to agencies that specialize in promoting to foreign markets. (See At Your Service 17.2.)

Figure 17.3
Standardized Advertising for Corvette

Source: Courtesy of General Motors Corporation and McCann-Erickson, Inc.

Not all companies try for a unique message in different markets. For example, jeans manufacturer Levi Strauss keeps ads uniform from country to country, believing that Levi customers speak a common language—the language of youth.[54] Similarly, ads for General Motors' Corvette are carefully designed to be able to cross international markets with only a change in language. While the wording in the ad shown in Figure 17.3 is in either Arabic, Dutch, English, French, German, or

Spanish, the background is purposely vague. It could be a desert or a misty morning on the Highlands. Furthermore, no human models are used.[55]

Standardized campaigns are not always possible, however. Ad messages may have to be changed for a number of reasons. Language, mentioned earlier, is one. The "Un-Cola" slogan of 7-Up could not be translated into other languages and still retain its special meaning.[56] Differing values and attitudes also sometimes stand in the way of a common message. Club Mediteranée finds that it must vary its message to appeal to different segments of the European market. The Swiss don't like to vacation with their children, so Club Med puts less emphasis on family ambience in its Swiss ads. The resort chain promotes sunny beaches to the Germans, but not to Italians, who have sunny beaches at home and are more attracted by the activities Club Med offers.[57]

The media used to convey the messages may also have to be locally tailored. Media availability and impact vary widely. For example:

- ☐ TV is present in most industrialized countries, but commercial time is often severely limited. The Scandinavian countries have banned commercials altogether, although this is beginning to change somewhat.[58]
- ☐ Newspapers are fragmented along political lines in much of Europe, requiring marketers to place ads in a dozen papers to achieve the coverage of one or two newspapers in the United States.
- ☐ Unusual media, such as movies featuring commercials, are often required to reach illiterate audiences in developing countries.[59] In Thailand, a highly successful campaign to promote vasectomies used slogans painted on the hides of water buffalo.[60]

When media are restricted or unavailable, sales promotion techniques become important. Free samples, coupons, and contests have been used to arouse product interest abroad. But sometimes governments have acted to restrict the use of these techniques as well. In Greece, Colgate was once sued for giving away razor blades with its shaving cream.[61]

Different national attitudes toward advertising and sales promotion carry over to the field of personal selling. In Europe, smiling Avon callers are not well received because European women regard at-home sales calls as an intrusion. On the other hand, European industrial buyers do not like to be seen with salespeople in public. At trade shows, costly floor space must be set aside for private compartments where customers can deal out of view of competitors.[62] Marketers may find adaptations such as this a nuisance, but in many cases they are absolutely necessary to carry on a successful marketing program.

Packaging is also a significant part of the total promotional mix. Packaging must conform not only to the aesthetic preferences of customers, but also to their income limitations and shopping habits. Large economy-size packages may be practical in an affluent United States where many customers shop once a week, but smaller packages are needed in poorer countries where people may shop daily.

The success of Miller High Life in Canada has been attributed at least partially to packaging. According to the marketing manager of a competing brand, "The consumer was looking for something new and different. If Miller had come out in the traditional stubby brown bottle [instead of its U.S.-style long neck shape], it wouldn't have gotten to first base."[63]

Standardizing or Adapting the Marketing Mix

The preceding review of marketing mix elements may make a global marketing strategy sound impossible. But that is not the case. Differences have been stressed because marketers have tended to ignore them in the past. Where circumstances are similar, however, marketing managers would be foolish to introduce unnecessary adaptations.

Standardization
Practice of transferring all parts of a successful marketing mix from one country to another.

Modified Standardization Approach
Practice of changing one or more elements of the marketing mix.

Standardization—the practice of transferring all parts of a successful marketing mix from one country to another—may be desirable to keep costs down, to make products easily identifiable among travelers, and to simplify planning and control.

When cultural, economic, and legal differences make complete standardization undesirable or impossible, a **modified standardization approach,** changing one or more elements of the marketing mix, may be more appropriate. For example, the same product may be sold worldwide, but different advertising approaches may be used.

While a standardized approach to marketing is often the most cost efficient, it should not be used indiscriminately. What works fine in St. Paul may be disastrous in São Paulo, as even retailing giant Sears, Roebuck learned to its chagrin. Sears withdrew its entire operation from Brazil after a series of marketing mistakes. As retail marketing became fiercely competitive in Brazil, Sears ceased to innovate. The apparel it offered was widely regarded as lacking style. Its store sites, chosen in the 1950s and 1960s, were no longer choice locations, and its advertising was inappropriate to the local customs. In Brazil, even kitchen stoves and blenders are featured in lively and amusing television commercials. Sears failed to use television, and its print ads were unexciting. According to one São Paulo shopper, the ads "were filled with weird gray drawings of little things like vegetable drainers and pea podders on sale that week." One analyst observed that Sears, more than most multinationals, is run from its U.S. headquarters, with little local input. "[Marketing] solutions are sent by telex from Chicago. It's 'send down promotion package No. 84.' "

To add further insult to injury, Sears' stores featured shelving at American heights—although Brazilians are several inches shorter than the average American. And Sears failed to offer financing, although Brazilians, accustomed to triple-digit inflation, prefer to finance everything from irons to television sets in 24 monthly payments.

After watching its sales slide steadily for several years, Sears decided to sell out to a Dutch conglomerate.[64]

International marketing is a complex task. In devising marketing strategies, managers must consider both similarities and differences between their own country and the country they wish to penetrate. Shortcuts based on unresearched assumptions are the surest road to market failure. But, as McDonald's, Coca-Cola, Levi Strauss, and many other companies have shown, when handled properly, international marketing can be an area of boundless opportunity.

Chapter Replay

1. **What are the differences between foreign trade, foreign marketing, and multinational marketing?**
   Foreign trade involves producing goods or services at home and exporting them. Foreign marketing involves operating within the foreign country where goods are to be sold. Multinational marketing refers to integrated marketing activities carried out in a number of countries.
2. **In what ways can business penetrate foreign markets?**
   The routes of expansion abroad include direct or indirect exportation, licensing, joint ventures, and direct investment.
3. **What economic characteristics do marketers consider in evaluating international markets?**
   Marketers compare different countries' per-capita income, industrial structure, and economic infrastructure.
4. **What are some cultural differences marketers must be aware of?**
   Marketers must take account of differences in language, aesthetic perceptions, social organization, and values.
5. **How do governments affect a marketer's involvement in a country?**
   Governments control marketing activities by imposing tariffs, by setting import quotas, by restricting the flow of currency, and by setting price ceilings. Governments may restrict imports to protect domestic businesses or restrict exports to protect national security. In addition, marketers are subject to international trade agreements such as the General Agreement on Tariffs and Trade.
6. **What are some limitations on researching foreign markets?**
   Published secondary information is not always available or accurate. Information from different sources is not always comparable. Educational and cultural differences make primary research difficult.
7. **What issues must marketers consider in developing products for international markets?**
   Marketers must consider whether to sell a single version of a product or to modify it for various submarkets. The company must give special attention to service and choose brand names that are understandable and positive in foreign markets.
8. **What pricing decisions must international marketers make?**
   International marketers must decide whether to charge a different price for exports than for products sold domestically. They also must decide how much to charge foreign subsidiaries for goods or parts shipped to or from them.

9. **What are the major types of intermediaries American companies use to place their products in foreign markets?**
The major types of intermediaries are resident buyers within the United States who work for foreign firms, overseas representatives of foreign firms, and independent intermediaries who either buy goods for sale abroad or arrange to bring buyers and sellers together.
10. **What are some reasons marketers may have to modify promotions for foreign markets?**
Messages may have to differ to overcome language barriers, to adapt to differing values and attitudes, to reflect the availability and impact of various media, to respond to differing national attitudes toward advertising and selling, and to accommodate income limitations and shopping habits.

Key Terms

arm's-length policy
direct investment
dumping
economic infrastructure
foreign marketing
foreign trade
import quota
international marketing
joint venture
licensing
modified standardization approach
multinational marketing
per-capita income
standardization
tariff
transfer pricing

Discussion Questions

1. When American farmers have a bumper crop, they look for foreign buyers. Are they engaging in foreign trade, foreign marketing, or multinational marketing? Besides surplus production, what other forces lead companies to enter foreign markets?
2. Feel Good Inc. runs a chain of health care centers offering emergency care and outpatient surgery. Because competition in the health care business is so stiff in the United States, the company is thinking of expanding to some foreign markets. What routes to expansion are available to Feel Good Inc.? Which do you recommend the company use? Why?
3. The per-capita income of Country Z, an industrializing nation, is only $1,630 (compared to $13,451 for the United States). Does this mean that a manufacturer of luxury goods shouldn't bother trying to sell in Country Z? Why, or why not?
4. What are some sources of cultural differences that marketers should be aware of?
5. What are some reasons why governments regulate imports and exports? What are some actions governments take to encourage international trade?

6. When Wondrous Cleaning Products wants to add to its line of home-cleaning products in the United States, it researches the market by conducting a telephone poll and holding a focus group interview of homemakers. Why might these research techniques fail when Wondrous expands operations into Turkey?
7. What are some advantages of selling a single product globally? When is this approach appropriate?
8. NiftyTek Computers sells computers through its own distribution network in the United States and Canada but relies on independent intermediaries for its sales in Indonesia. What might account for the different placement strategies?
9. Bob Baxter, owner of Big Bus Tours, is planning to set up bus tours in the capitals of the world's 15 largest nations. Bob and Big Bus's marketing director, Lynette Long, meet with a marketing consultant, Pat Prognosticator. Pat uses elaborate diagrams to illustrate her view that Big Bus Tours should hire 15 advertising agencies—one in each city—to devise 15 different advertising campaigns. "You have to meet the unique needs of each marketplace," explains Pat.

   After Pat leaves, Lynette exclaims, "That's crazy! All we need to do is hire our usual agency in New York to prepare some ads. Then we'll get some translators to translate the words. Pat's ideas would cost us a fortune."

   Who is right—Pat or Lynette? Why?

Case 17.1 Hard Rock Cafe

Co

On November 22, 1986, the Dallas edition of the Hard Rock Cafe opened with much fanfare. Dan Aykroyd, a partner in the company, reunited the original Blues Brothers Band for the black-tie party that marked the opening. Commenting on the Dallas location, Aykroyd said, "If the New York Hard Rock is the Grand Central, this baby is the Supreme Court of rock 'n' roll."

Background

The original Hard Rock Cafe was created in 1971 in London by Issac Tigrett of Jackson, Tennessee, who, along with his partners, felt that Europe should sample the best of American cooking—"the best down-home, righteous meals at reasonable prices." That location, in the fashionable area of Mayfair and just around the corner from Buckingham Palace, showed a first-year net profit of $7,000. Today it grosses some $2 million a year and is the third British restaurant company ever to be listed on the London Stock Exchange.

Source: Edited from Richard David Story, "Hard Rock Story," *USA Today*, November 20, 1986, pp. 01+, and *Hard Rock Cafe Hall of Fame Guide* from original London location.

Hard Rock Cafes have been added in such cities as New York, Stockholm, Dallas, Houston, Boston, and Chicago. A sister company has restaurants in Los Angeles and San Francisco. More locations are planned. All cafes are based on the philosophy of genuine value for money, along with a simple spiritual message—"Love All—Serve All"—with each meal.

Restaurant Atmospherics

The Hard Rock Cafe represents what *People* magazine called "The Smithsonian of rock 'n' roll." According to Sotheby, the cafes feature "Truly the largest collection in the world of musical memorabilia." Among the most famous items are Elvis Presley's velvet suit, John Lennon's first stage suit, Elton John's psychedelic piano, Keith Richards' five-string guitar, B. B. King's "Lucille" guitar, and over 200 authentic Gold Albums awarded to the Beatles, the Beach Boys, and other famous recording groups. The collection circulates among the various restaurant locations.

"From the very beginning, rock was the uniting force," Tigrett says. The total collection of rock memorabilia on walls, ceilings, and floors of Hard Rock Cafes is estimated at close to $3 million.

Music is a constant companion at each Hard Rock Cafe. For example, the Dallas location features a $700,000 sound system with 32 amplifiers. The resulting 3,000 amps makes the restaurant a rock 'n' roll haven.

The Offering

Along with the rock 'n' roll atmosphere, Hard Rock Cafes offer what are billed as the most reasonably priced hamburgers, french fries, milkshakes, pig (barbequed pork) sandwiches, and T-bone steaks. The Dallas restaurant also serves *fajitas* and buffalo stew.

Individual restaurants sell a variety of personalized clothing items. Students on most college campuses around the world wear T-shirts, sweatshirts, jackets, caps, and other items that carry the Hard Rock Cafe emblem along with the city of origin.

Focal Topics

1. How would international markets differ from domestic markets for Hard Rock Cafes?
2. How would you explain the success of the Hard Rock Cafe in London?
3. What do you see as the greatest potential problems facing Hard Rock Cafes as they move into more international markets? How can the company best cope with these problems?

Case 17.2
Franklin International (D)

As indicated in part A of this case, Franklin was started in 1935 as a manufacturer of animal glues for the furniture industry. The Industrial Division (originally the Franklin Glue Company) was the first manufacturer of synthetic aliphatic resin glues to be used in the furniture manufacturing process.

Background

The superior technical ability of its salespeople has always been a key differentiating factor in comparing Franklin to the competition. In addition, a substantial application and research laboratory has provided backup and analysis for the customer's use of Franklin's products. Eleven warehouses throughout the country inventory products and provide pickup service when desired. The Industrial Division has also been able to provide customers with a special product when needed, such as adding a colored dye to the adhesive in order to match the wood or finish being used.

Because of these additional services, the Industrial Division has always positioned itself as the quality, premium-priced adhesive producer in the marketplace. Management determined some time ago that it did not want to participate in markets that were based only on price and that if satisfactory margins were not available from a product, then they would not carry that product.

Some of the major market segments that the Industrial Division serves are:

- Household Furniture—assembly of components and complex furniture pieces.
- Wood Dimension—laminating edge and face pieces to main material surfaces.
- Fingerjointed Stack—gluing smaller pieces of wood together to form wider, thicker, or longer pieces.
- Replacement Truck Flooring—assembly of wood pieces to replace worn floors in trucks.
- Modular Housing Fabrication—using adhesive products in the production of mobile and manufactured housing.
- Polyfoam Laminating—gluing various insulating materials to various surfaces.

International Dimensions

Franklin International has never had a major export operation. As recently as 1980, the firm sold only thirteen 55-gallon drums of its products overseas. Those were delivered to Central America. By 1983, how ever, the international demands for the company's products had increased significantly but still represented a very small component of total industrial sales.

Imports have become an increasing factor in furniture marketing in the United States. In some cases, completed pieces of furniture are shipped to this country. In other instances, components are assembled in foreign countries and then shipped to the United States for final assembly and finishing. Some of the assembly facilities are owned by U.S. firms; others are owned by foreign companies that do component assembly outside the United States. Franklin found that many of the foreign firms were interested in using Franklin adhesives to assemble the components or complete furniture pieces.

In analyzing its export sales, Franklin found that about 75 percent were going to European countries. Yugoslavia, site of the 1984 Winter Olympic Games, turned out to be the major purchaser. In that country, individual wood furniture consortiums were purchasing the glues primarily to assemble furniture components. Franklin reached the European market through a Yugoslavian agent who has dual citizenship and lives in New York City. Franklin would like to expand the distribution of its products into Poland, Romania, and Czechoslovakia. The company is also thinking about developing a warehouse facility in Trieste. By shipping to such a location, the products could then be forwarded to other locations at lower tariff rates.

The other 25 percent of Franklin's export sales were going to Asian countries, such as Singapore and Korea, and to Taiwan. To reach those markets, the company worked through agents in California who serve local representatives in the various countries. Furniture manufacturers in those countries are typically involved in producing case goods (bedroom and dining room furniture) and knocked-down furniture that is assembled by the ultimate consumer.

Franklin is exploring the option of selling directly to the representatives in Southeast Asian countries. In addition, the company may have an interesting opportunity to engage in a barter relationship with a chemical plant that is being developed in Taiwan. That plant will produce, among other chemicals, vinyl acetate monomer and polyvinyl alcohol, both basic components in the manufacture of the polymer that is used in the manufacture of adhesive products. Franklin possibly could trade its finished products for the raw materials.

Focal Topics

1. What do you see as the possible advantages and disadvantages of Franklin's expanding the export of its adhesive products?
2. What alternative ways are available for Franklin to increase its international sales? Which do you recommend that it use?
3. What is your overall evaluation of the potential to barter with the chemical facility in Taiwan?

18 Nonprofit Marketing

☐ Sounding Out the Chapter

In this chapter, you will learn:

1. The basic types of nonprofit marketing.
2. How nonprofit organizations market ideas.
3. Major categories of nonprofit organizations.
4. Ways in which nonprofit organizations differ from businesses.
5. The major similarities of nonprofit and for-profit organizations.
6. Why environmental analysis is especially important for nonprofit organizations.
7. Characteristics of the marketing mix for nonprofit organizations.
8. The major ways to measure marketing success in the nonprofit sector.

LEAPIN' LIZARDS!
It's Dinosaur Days at the Sloan Museum.

JANUARY 8 - FEBRUARY 28, 1987
See the gigantic, moveable model dinosaurs on special exhibit at the Sloan Museum.
SPONSORED BY NBD GENESEE BANK • SLOAN MUSEUM, 1221 E. KEARSLEY ST., 762-1169

Source: Courtesy of GNB Genesee Bank.

The Fine Art of Marketing Culture

"Museums can't be marketed like a bar of soap." Not so long ago, that was a typical response of museum directors who scorned the idea of promoting their institutions with crass sales techniques. But in the face of massive cutbacks in government funding and a slower economy in some regions, museums and other cultural institutions are embracing marketing zealously. The results are often a pleasant surprise.

Consider a few examples:

- ☐ New York's prestigious Metropolitan Museum of Art has opened museum shops at the New York Public Library and at Macy's department store. The institution also routinely advertises its exhibits on subway posters, in newspaper print ads, and on the radio.
- ☐ In Chicago, the Victory Gardens Theater raises funds by auctioning the rights to participate in a play, with direction from Victory Gardens staff. Parts for actors sell for $900–$2,200; other supporters buy rights to play in the orchestra—or to watch at $35 a ticket. Besides raising $29,000 in 1987, the theater built a strong bond with a large group of supporters.
- ☐ The Denver Symphony Orchestra has tried attracting younger people by holding "blue jeans" concerts at which everyone is invited to attend wearing blue jeans. Many young listeners prefer the more casual atmosphere.
- ☐ To promote an exhibit of antique armor, the Seattle Art Museum suited up a horseman in full regalia and trotted him through downtown Seattle.

Forces other than funding cutbacks have combined to persuade museums that they must market more aggressively or lose their audiences. As the director of marketing for the Henry Ford Museum and Greenfield Village in Dearborn, Michigan, noted, "We're in competition with every other leisure activity. Our market is the same people who go to theme parks, who buy videotape equipment, who attend movies and sporting events, who spend their weekends at home gardening."

While marketing is a new development among cultural institutions, only a few doubt that its future in those institutions is bright. The same is true for many other kinds of nonprofit organizations. This chapter examines how the general principles of marketing apply to the specific needs of the nonprofit sector.

Sources: Alan Rosenthal, "Museums Jump into the Marketing Game," *Advertising Age,* September 27, 1982, p. M-2; "Weekend Edition," National Public Radio, March 28, 1987; and "All Things Considered," National Public Radio, March 31, 1987.

THIS IS A HOSPITAL?

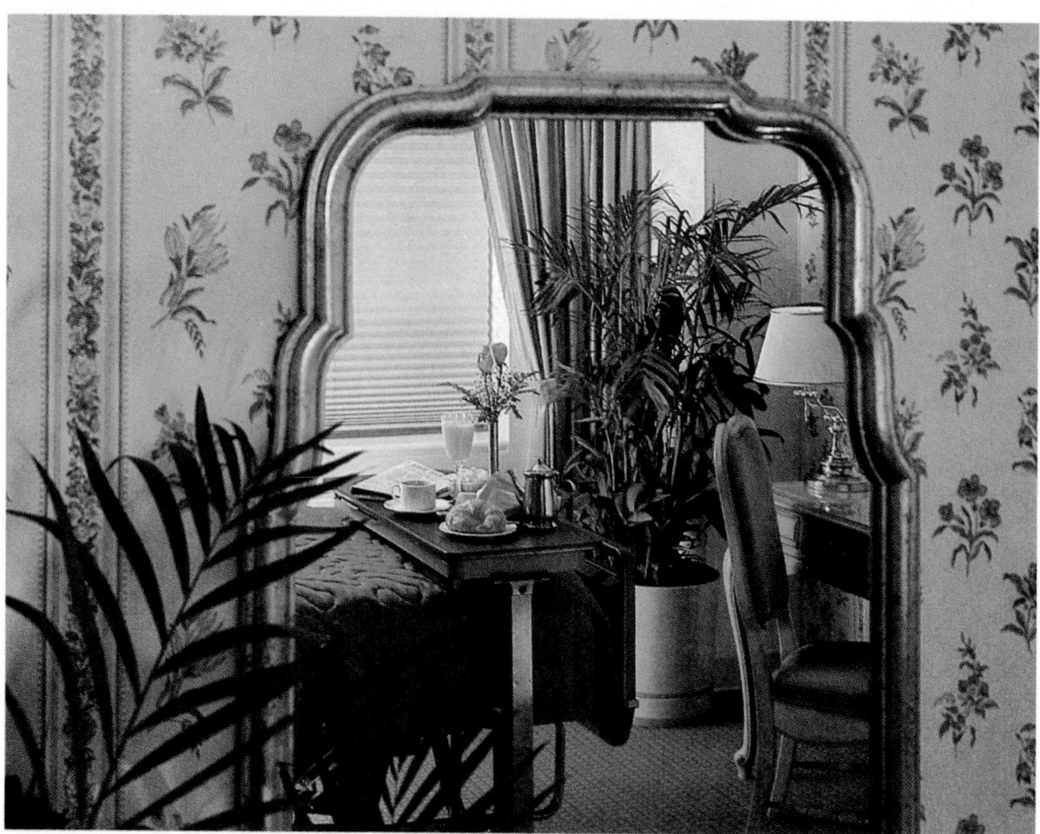

Believe it or not, this is a hospital room. A Signature Suite at Christ Hospital & Medical Center. With an ambience so luxurious, private and restful that you may find yourself getting well faster than you imagined.

Custom-designed furniture throughout. Golden bath fixtures. Sterling silver service to reflect your menu selections prepared by a gourmet chef. Coordinated linens and your own fluffy terry cloth robe. The daily paper of your choice. Cable TV with SportsVision® programming. Genuine imported Godiva chocolates at day's end. Plus a special food tray for a visitor. Even your own stylish pen and stationery. Cost? Only nominally more than a regular hospital room.

For more information on Signature Suites, mail this coupon today. Or call 857-5940 and ask for the charge nurse.

Signature Suites
Christ Hospital & Medical Center
4440 West 95th Street
Oak Lawn, Illinois 60453 (Please print)

Name ______________________

Address ______________________

City ____________ State ________ Zip ______

SIGNATURE SUITES
AT CHRIST HOSPITAL

It's Like a Hotel in a Hospital

Christ Hospital & Medical Center, Oak Lawn • Good Samaritan Hospital, Downers Grove • Good Shepherd Hospital, Barrington • Bethany Hospital, Chicago

The Scope of Nonprofit Marketing

Most of this book concentrates on organizations that operate for profit. But an important part of the American economy—some say as much as 20 percent—operates for some other reason besides making a profit. Included in the nonprofit sector are religious organizations, human services organizations, museums, private libraries, secondary schools, hospitals, colleges and universities, symphony orchestras, labor unions, government bodies, political parties, and other organizations. These organizations employ a variety of service workers and professionals.

What do the Minneapolis Police Department, the Red Cross, Miami Valley Hospital, and the Los Angeles Philharmonic have in common? All of those nonprofit organizations face serious problems that can be solved, at least in part, by the application of marketing principles. The existence of problems in the nonprofit sector is not hard to document:

- Police departments nationwide face growing public fear of crime at a time when their employees must ask for higher wages from taxpayers. They have a serious public relations problem.
- Charities and cultural institutions are hard-pressed for funds because people now give less, as a percentage of their annual income, than in previous years, and there are now more charities and cultural institutions competing for donations than ever before.
- Studies have shown that today's patient has input over 60 percent of the time in selecting where to be hospitalized.[1] To compete in an increasingly competitive health care market, many hospitals have had to devise ways of making their institutions appealing to consumers. (See Figure 18.1.)

These people and resource problems are the kinds of problems marketing people can help solve.

The idea of applying marketing to nonprofit organizations is comparatively recent. The marketing concept took hold in the business world in the late 1950s and early 1960s. As business managers began to be called upon to volunteer their time in the nonprofit sector, they started to see the usefulness of the marketing discipline outside business.

Theorists such as Robert Bartels and Richard Bagozzi gave a sound conceptual basis to business volunteers' intuition by defining marketing as "exchange." As explained in Chapter 1, exchange is a broader concept than buying and selling. When a product and money change hands, that is one type of exchange. But another kind of exchange occurs when political promises are traded for votes or when volunteer labor is offered for a feeling of doing good.[2]

Whenever an exchange occurs—whether or not it involves money—marketing principles can be applied. This chapter explores the usefulness of marketing in not-for-profit situations.

Figure 18.1
Promotion of a Hospital's Services
Source: Courtesy of Christ Hospital and Medical Center.

Types of Nonprofit Marketing

In the nonprofit sector, marketers apply their skills mainly to organizations. But persons and ideas can also be "sold" by using marketing techniques.

Person Marketing

Person Marketing
Efforts directed toward cultivating the attention, interest, and preference of a target market toward a person.

Person marketing involves "an effort to cultivate the attention, interest, and preference of a target market toward a person."[3] An interesting example of this is the New York man who advertised his availability for dating on billboards. Nearly 5,000 women responded, and he contracted to write a book about his experiences.

A more typical example of person marketing occurs in the political arena. In the 1984 Democratic primary, for example, candidates scrambled to carve out images that would differentiate them from others in the initially crowded race. John Glenn hired a successful advertising producer to build a media campaign around Glenn's image as a man with the "right stuff." Gary Hart found that his "yuppie" image was a hindrance among blue-collar workers, and therefore appeared in ads that positioned him as a friend to minorities and union workers. The Mondale organization researched the issues important in each state and then ran targeted ads contrasting Mondale's positions with those of the opposition.

Political advertising has often received criticism. Some legislators have even tried to limit the kinds of advertising a candidate may run. But whether advertising is manipulative of voters is subject to debate. The candidate who spends the most on ads is not always the winning candidate.

Besides advertising, political marketing uses promotional materials such as campaign buttons and bumper stickers, informational brochures, and efforts to obtain publicity by staging media events. In addition, campaigners conduct marketing research to determine voters' interests and to measure the success of promotional efforts.

Idea Marketing

Idea Marketing
Offering a cause in exchange for public acceptance.

Social Marketing
Use of marketing techniques to increase the acceptability of a social idea, cause, or practice in a target group.

The essence of **idea marketing** is the offering of a cause in exchange for public acceptance. It might be argued that all marketing is idea marketing, whether it be to promote the idea that getting sunburned is bad and that Coppertone Shade can help, or that encouraging a child's creativity is good and Crayola products will do the trick. One particular type of idea marketing is **social marketing.** Social marketing is the use of marketing techniques to increase the acceptability of a social idea, cause, or practice in a target group(s).[4]

Many causes have been marketed to the American public, including adoption of the Equal Rights Amendment, positions for and against the ownership of handguns, and the case for and against legalized abortions. Reader's Digest sponsored a contest among advertising agencies to develop posters discouraging drunk driving. The Reader's Digest Foundation, the company's philanthropic arm, underwrote the cost of sending a set of posters to every U.S. high school.[5] One of those posters is shown in Figure 18.2.

Marketing an idea is not synonymous with promotion, though that is an important tool. Other marketing mix variables such as price (the "cost" of acceptance by the audience) and even placement (convenient locations for blood pressure screening, for example) must also be carefully considered. The use of the various elements of the marketing mix to market ideas is discussed at greater length later in this chapter.

Organization Marketing

The biggest share of nonprofit marketing can be classified as **organization marketing,** which attempts to influence others to accept the goals of, receive the services of, or contribute in some way to an organization. There are countless types of nonprofit organizations, but they can be classified into three categories.[6]

Organizational Marketing
Activities that attempt to influence others to accept the goals of, receive the services of, or contribute in some way to an organization.

One category is composed of **service organizations.** These are institutions, such as hospitals, colleges, and museums, that provide a service for clients, sometimes in exchange for a fee. However, because the price charged for the service does not cover costs, these organizations usually must depend on others—contributors—to make up the difference. Service organizations thus have at least two large markets to reach—clients (patients, students, museum-goers, and so on) and donors.

Service Organization
Institution, such as a hospital, college, or museum, that provides a service for clients, sometimes in exchange for a fee.

A second category of nonprofit organizations consists of **mutual benefit associations.** Political parties, unions, clubs, and churches fall into this category. (See Figure 18.3 on page 558.) These associations are organized for the benefit of members, not outsiders. Marketing activities are carried on primarily to increase membership, although they are also sometimes performed to win the support of outsiders. For example, the International Ladies' Garment Workers' Union's (ILGWU) campaign—"look for the union label"—was designed to urge Americans to buy American-made clothing and to persuade Congress to pass legislation limiting imports.[7]

Mutual Benefit Association
Association organized for the benefit of members, not outsiders.

The final category of nonprofit organizations includes **government organizations,** which serve the interests of the public at large. All government agencies, including post offices, military services, and police and fire departments, need professional marketing to win goodwill and improve their operations. For example, the military uses marketing to encourage enlistment. According to army recruiters, advertising with the slogan "Be All That You Can Be" has had broad appeal. Other elements of the marketing mix are important, too. An attractive element of the product that the army offers to recruits has been its Army College Fund.[8]

Government Organization
Nonprofit agency that serves the interests of the public at large.

Organization marketing is the focus of much of the rest of the chapter, but it is important to keep in mind that what is said also applies to the other two kinds of nonprofit marketing—person marketing and idea marketing.

THERE ARE NO HEROES IN THIS LOCKER ROOM.

Please Don't Drink and Drive.

Marketing for Profit and Nonprofit Organizations: A Comparison

General Motors and General Foods produce vastly different products, but both companies use the principles described in this text to market their products. The gap between what General Motors offers the public and what a college provides may seem even wider. Yet the same principles apply. There are some differences, however.

Differences

The most obvious difference between General Motors and a college is the dissimilarity in marketing objectives. An organization like General Motors exists to make a profit for its stockholders, and it does so by stimulating as much demand for its auto models as possible. By contrast, a college's main purpose is to provide a service—education—and its existence would be threatened if it took in as many students as wanted that service. That is why there are admission standards. In general, nonprofit organizations work with limited resources and cannot afford to stimulate as much demand as possible. Only in very rare cases are profit-making organizations similarly constrained over the long run.

A second difference is noticeable in the markets served. General Motors meets its profit-making objectives by marketing to a single public—the buying public. But a college and many nonprofit organizations must consider several markets. The student body is an important market for all schools, but so are alumni and legislators who may provide funds, and parents and teachers who may influence students' choices of college. Those who directly use the "product" exchanged by nonprofit organizations are called **client publics,** and those who have an indirect interest are referred to as **general publics.**[9] Not all nonprofit organizations have two or more distinct markets or publics to serve. But many do, and that complicates the marketing task.

Client Public
Those who directly use the product exchanged by nonprofit organizations.

General Public
Those who have an indirect interest in a nonprofit organization's goods or services.

Nonprofit organizations, moreover, have a more difficult time than profit-making organizations in setting control standards. General Motors has sales data and market share figures to guide it in knowing whether it is meeting objectives, for example. Sometimes nonprofit organizations have difficulty finding similar measures.

The difficulty is not unconquerable. A college may have as its objective "to provide a quality education for students"—a standard not subject to exact measurements. But it can substitute indirect measures (such as achievements of students or accreditation of the school). Control may be more difficult in nonprofit organizations, but it is not impossible.[10]

Figure 18.2
Promotion of a Cause
Source: Courtesy of Reader's Digest.

Similarities

Nonprofit and profit-making organizations are more similar than dissimilar. The major similarities may be stated as follows:

1. Both need to plan objectives and analyze their environments to operate efficiently. Chapter 2 points out that objectives tell an organization where it is going, and environmental analysis lists the obstacles to getting there. Businesses need such planning to avoid being sidetracked and to anticipate trouble. Operating with more limited funds, nonprofit organizations need such planning even more.
2. Both need to know their clients to serve them well. By engaging in target-market analysis, businesses decide whether to serve the mass market or to cater to one or more segments. Nonbusiness organizations can benefit from the same kind of analysis. Complaints about "government bureaucracy" or "unresponsive churches" arise from the failure to analyze publics and their needs.
3. Both work with the same marketing elements—the four "Ps"—in serving customer needs. In the case of a nonprofit organization, the product may be more intangible, the price of exchange nonmonetary, the distribution channels more direct, and the promotional effort more dependent on publicity and volunteer salespeople. Still, all four elements are present.
4. Both need to check whether objectives are being reached and marketing programs implemented. As noted previously, measuring results may be more difficult for nonprofit organizations, but they must try to check on public satisfaction.[11]

This abstract statement of similarities is more convincing when applied to actual situations. The remainder of the chapter will explore some of these similarities.

Marketing Objectives and Environmental Analysis

Generally speaking, the objectives of business organizations named in Chapter 2 are not the same as those of nonbusiness organizations because profit is not central to the latter's purpose. Nevertheless, nonprofit organizations must have clear objectives, and, like businesses, they must evaluate how realistic their objectives are in light of environmental conditions.

Nonprofit Organizational Objectives

As noted in Chapter 2, two kinds of objectives interest marketers: (1) general organizational objectives, which direct the organization as a whole; and (2) marketing objectives, which state what marketers can do

Figure 18.3
Promotion of an Organization
Source: Reprinted with permission of The Catholic Health Association of the United States © 1987.

Table 18.1
Objectives of Typical Nonprofit Organizations

Organization	General Organizational Objectives	Marketing Objectives
Hospital	To deliver quality medical care to the community.	To become recognized in the treatment of multiple sclerosis among 65 percent of U.S. physicians. To attract *x* dollars for research next year.
Post office	To serve the public with efficient mail service.	To cut operating costs 6 percent this year by informing customers about zip codes. To obtain favorable ratings from 85 percent of U.S. businesses.
Union	To raise the living standard of members.	To increase consumption of union goods by 20 percent over 2 years. To recruit *x* new members in 6 months.

to support the overall objectives. Table 18.1 lists a few hypothetical examples of both types for a hospital, a post office, and a union.

Note that the organizational objectives listed in the table are stated not in terms of a product or service offering but of a public to be served. Organizations that are product oriented may become locked in to limited objectives and disappear as conditions change. Firms that are public oriented may adapt to a changing world.

The Advertising Council provides an interesting example of how a nonprofit organization adapted its purpose to meet changing times. The Council was founded during World War II to mobilize the American public behind the war effort by conducting advertising campaigns. When the war ended, its objective to mobilize American public opinion remained, but its "product" was no longer the war effort. Instead, it promoted various public causes, such as the prevention of forest fires and the encouragement of safe driving.

After flexible organizational objectives are determined, marketing objectives to meet overall goals can be set. Whenever possible, marketing objectives should be quantified. As Table 18.1 shows, fund-raising or recruiting goals may be conveniently assigned a dollar or number value. Other goals, such as convincing or informing the public, are harder to attach numbers to, but some effort should be made.

For example, one of the post office's main marketing objectives currently is to improve efficiency by persuading the public to use a nine-digit zip code. That objective can be specified further: to achieve 75 percent public cooperation on first-class mail within five years of the changeover. The new objective is specific and realistic in light of past experience involving the introduction of zip codes. It will also be useful for control purposes later.

The Environment of Nonprofit Organizations

Recall that three distinct environmental levels must be analyzed to determine whether objectives are realizable. The internal, operating, and general environments affect the operation of profit-making and nonprofit organizations alike. In a sense, nonprofit organizations must be even more environmentally sensitive than businesses because their existence often depends on the goodwill of donors and taxpayers as well as the public they serve.

The Internal Environment The internal environment, consisting of the tangible and intangible resources an organization needs to operate, can make or break the marketing efforts of a nonprofit organization.

Like businesses, many nonprofit organizations have tangible resources such as buildings and financial reserves. For example, the Chicago Historical Society's assets include its building, the inventory at its museum store, millions in investments, and its museum collection.[12] Likewise, a religious organization's assets may include its house of worship, its educational facilities, and the money currently available to it.

Such tangible assets are important because they determine the kinds of programs the organization can pursue. But most nonprofit organizations are restricted in the amount of money available to them in a given year. Organizations such as the American Heart Association fund all of their programs in one year from money raised in the preceding year. They cannot borrow or issue new stock, as businesses can. That is why fund-raising is so important. Marketing Today 18.1 describes how one organization has marketed with limited resources.

Intangible resources can be as important as tangible ones. The experience of the American March of Dimes supports this statement. In the early 1960s, the organization had to decide whether to continue or to cease operation. The charity had been founded to combat polio, which had been conquered by the Salk and Sabine vaccines. Although its reason for being had ended, market analysis showed that the organization had two significant intangible assets: (1) widespread name recognition by the public and (2) a dedicated core of volunteers. With those assets and some sound marketing planning, the March of Dimes was able to survive while pursuing a new objective—the conquest of birth defects.[13]

The Operating Environment The factor of most concern in the operating environment of nonprofit organizations is competition. It has intensified for many reasons. For example, the lowered birth rate of the 1970s has resulted in a fierce battle by colleges to recruit a reduced number of student candidates. Hospitals, too, are trying a variety of approaches to attract patients, offering special services and investing in advertising.

Another reason for increased competition in the nonprofit sector is changing values. Churches are especially affected. For example, recently "parish shopping" by Catholics has become a growing trend. Although the practice is common among Protestants, the Roman Catholic tradition

Marketing Today 18.1
Fun Image Makes Zoo a Success

At the Lincoln Park Zoo in Chicago, admission is free, so the zoo has to find other sources for funds to maintain and expand its facilities. When Barbara Whitney became the zoo's executive director in 1975, the zoo was struggling; Whitney's goal was to make it the finest urban zoo while keeping admissions free.

She started with a quarter-million dollars and a marketing strategy: use communication power to gain people power to obtain a broad and diverse base of support. She sent out a mailing designed to give the zoo a light-hearted and fun image. One slogan was "You Belong in the Zoo."

Whitney also sought out trendsetting people to participate on volunteer boards. These people gave her ideas and also acted as catalysts to bring in other volunteers and funds.

A third part of Whitney's marketing program is special events to attract people to the zoo and recruit members. The events include the Zoo Ball, the Super Zoo Picnic, and Christmas caroling to the animals. (This last event attracts publicity as well as people.) In addition, the zoo sponsors a program by which people can "adopt" an animal by making a contribution to the zoo.

The marketing program has brought the zoo out of the doldrums. In Barbara Whitney's first ten years on the job, membership has increased from 2,000 to 14,000, and annual revenues from $250,000 to $4.5 million.

Sources: JoAnn D. Hinz, "Is Your Business a Zoo?" *The Exponent* (University of Chicago Women's Business Group), August 1985, pp. 2, 5; and Sue Weeks, "Marketing: Creating a Product Image," *The Exponent,* June 1985, p. 1.

ADOPT
ADOPT
ADOPT
It's true!
Animals Depend On People, Too...
People who care
People who love animals
People who want to help improve the zoo

Source: Courtesy of Lincoln Park Zoological Society.

has always been to belong to the parish one lives in. Now, however, families are choosing to travel to a parish that they find more spiritually nourishing. This practice has led to big gains in some congregations—and big losses in others. Since a church's operating expenses are generally funded by donations from parishioners, a decline in membership can have dire effects. Many churches, responding to this competition, have begun improving the "product" they offer by developing livelier services, which sometimes incorporate guitar music, slide shows, interpretive dance, laity participation, and altar girls. As one professor at the Catholic Theological Union in Chicago noted, "It's the good old American system: you come up with something good or fold."[14]

In the past, nonprofit organizations tended to ignore the importance of competition, believing it to exist only among businesses. But the federal government's budget cutbacks have brought home to organizations the fact that the supply of funding is limited. Any exchange relationship involves potential gains or losses to participants. Organizations that can promise and deliver more benefits, whether tangible or intangible, are likely to win a greater following.

The General Environment The four most important factors in the general environment are economic developments, technological advances, legal and governmental actions, and social expectations and values. Nonprofit organizations, like businesses, must evaluate all of these.

Economic forces can affect demand. Inflation, for example, has had a negative effect on college enrollment by driving up the cost of tuition. It has also hurt charitable fund-raising since the segment that accounts for 50 percent of all giving (those with incomes below $20,000) is hardest hit. Cultural organizations (museums, symphonies, and so on) may not be as hard hit because they are supported mainly by those in the highest income bracket, who can manage to stay ahead of inflation. In states such as Texas that depend heavily on the oil industry, the decline in oil prices in the latter half of the 1980s dried up funds for a wide variety of nonprofit organizations.

Technological developments must also be considered in the nonprofit sector. A technological advance in sorting equipment is one of the reasons why the post office is marketing a nine-digit zip code. Hospitals are interested in technological developments that advance the fight against disease because well-equipped hospitals attract patrons (both patients and donors).

Legal developments may seem unimportant because most antitrust and consumer laws that restrict business marketing practices are not applicable in the nonprofit sphere. Government actions can affect nonprofit organizations, however. City colleges in New York City, for example, were forced to impose tuition on students when the city found it was no longer able to support the colleges solely with taxes. In effect, the city limited the market for those colleges to those who could pay the new tuition fees. Laws affecting the tax status of charitable organizations are another example of the influence of the legal environment on the nonprofit sector.

Equally important to the survival and prosperity of most nonprofit organizations is the social climate in communities where they operate. Occasionally, nonprofit marketing programs are controversial. Family planning centers sometimes meet with opposition from local church groups. Federal agencies charged with building nuclear power plants may face opposition in some communities. Environmental analysis allows marketers to anticipate such problems and cope with them through marketing programs.

Target Marketing

Chapter 7 introduced target marketing, which consists of determining (1) whether to treat all members of the market as the same or to distinguish various segments and (2) if segments are distinguished, whether to market to one or a number of them. The decisions are the same in the profit and nonprofit spheres.

For most nonprofit organizations, it pays to distinguish market segments. In fact, for those nonprofit institutions that cater to both a client public and a general public, it is absolutely necessary. Public television stations serve an educated viewing public but raise most of their operating funds from businesses, the federal government, and private foundations. They must have separate marketing objectives and strategies for the viewing public and the giving public.

But even for organizations supported by the same members they serve, it pays to consider segmentation if members have different needs. A nonprofit organization can choose to concentrate its marketing effort on one segment or on many segments, as can a business. For example, Dallas has targeted suburban commuters in promoting its mass transit system. The city made arrangements with a local laundry to offer these riders a special service. In the morning, commuters can drop off their dirty laundry at a heavily used bus stop; when they return in the evening, the riders get their clothes back, clean and neatly folded, for just $.85 per pound. Other possible services include film processing and shoe repair.[15] At Your Service 18.1 describes how some nonprofit organizations in Washington used a targeted strategy.

The same basis used to segment markets in the profit sector may be used in the nonprofit sphere. In the case of hospitals, benefit segmentation is the usual method of distinguishing clients. For charities, usage-rate segmentation is of some value. For example, a market research study for the American Cancer Society found that ACS donors in California contributed to more nonprofit organizations in the past five years than nondonors (an average of 7.0 versus 3.2).[16]

Marketing Mix Variables

Nonprofit marketers work with the four "Ps" just as business marketers do. For example, marketers for a political candidate can see their task as offering a product (the candidate), at a price (the electorate's vote), by various promotional means (television ads, publicity releases, the candidate's personal appearances), and through various outlets (town meetings, small clubs, whistle stops, television debates). The meaning of the four "Ps" varies somewhat, but many of the same considerations apply.

Product Considerations

A product is a complex entity, even in a business setting. In nonbusiness organizations, a product can be still more difficult to define. Often what is offered for exchange is completely intangible. A symphony offers a musical performance. A charity may offer its donors a good feeling. Of course, not all the products of a nonprofit organization are so intangible. A library provides books, and a family-planning organization offers contraceptives.

When the product is highly intangible, as in the case of an idea, marketers may try to embody it in a more concrete form. The idea of safe driving, marketed by the National Safety Council, is "sold" in such

At Your Service 18.1
Target Marketing of a Forest

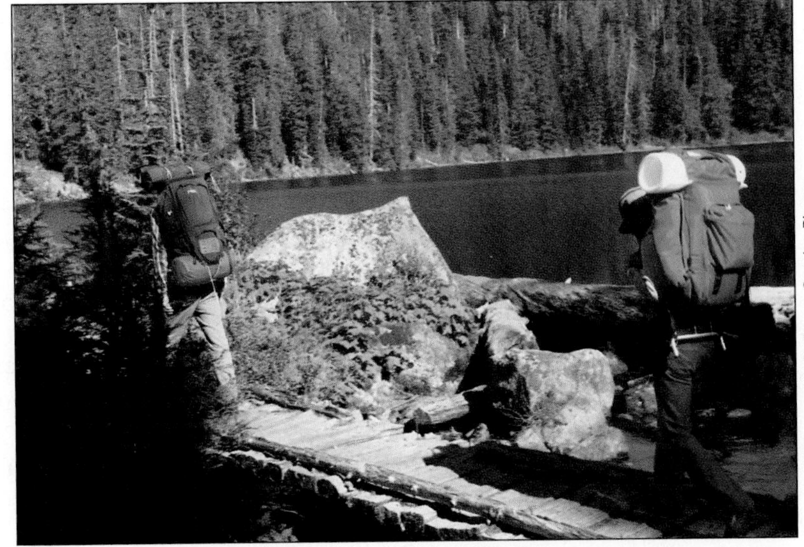
Source: Courtesy of U.S. Forest Service Photos.

Hikers are the target market for a special service in Washington State. Seattle residents can use a computer at one of three locations to find out about trails in the Mount Baker/Snoqualmie National Forest. The information, provided through the Trails Information System, is free.

The user can tell the computer the kind of trail desired—say, moderately difficult, uncrowded, free of snow, two hours away, and close to fishing. The computer then prints out a list. The user can ask for a profile of one of the hikes on the list. The computer gives the trail length, directions to the trailhead, elevation gain, type of setting, and whether dogs are allowed. It even reports on snow conditions, number of people in the area, and biting bugs.

The project is sponsored by the U.S. Forest Service, the Seattle Public Library, and Recreational Equipment Inc. The Forest Service is considering expanding the system nationwide.

Source: Andy Dappen, "Future Hikes," *Outside,* February 1987, p. 11.

---

tangible forms, or "packages," as defensive driving courses and lower-premium insurance policies for good drivers.[17] In promoting its mission—health of body, mind, and spirit—the YMCA offers a wide variety of programs: child care, aquatics, youth employment, health and fitness, camping, youth sports, international exchange, and other volunteer and family activities. (See Figure 18.4.)

Many of the concepts introduced previously about business products apply to nonbusiness products as well. For example, Procter & Gamble provides a broad mix of products for the market (from Pampers to Pringle's to Dove), but so does New York's Metropolitan Museum of Art. The museum offers a permanent collection, special shows such as the Yves Saint Laurent retrospective at the museum's Costume Institute, slides of its collection for school groups, and reproductions in its museum shops.[18] In this respect, the agencies of the federal government offer perhaps the widest mix of goods and services in the nonprofit sector.

Another product concept application in both the business and nonbusiness spheres is the product life cycle—the notion that all goods and services move through stages that call for a different marketing strategy. A good example in the nonprofit sector is the Scholastic Aptitude Test, designed by Princeton's Educational Testing Service (ETS), a nonprofit group. The test, taken by many college applicants, measures verbal and

No one comes out the same.

The YMCA has a way of changing people's lives.

And it doesn't seem to matter if you're young, old, or somewhere in between.

For example, with our fitness programs you might have a change in your body. Or because of our youth, family and volunteer programs, you might feel a change inside, about yourself and your relationship with others.

In any case, the Y affects different people in many ways. With all kinds of different programs and activities. Yet one thing doesn't seem to change. And that is, when you go into the YMCA, you don't come out the same. You come out a little *better.*

The YMCA. It's for all of you.™

mathematical skills. Demand for the test, introduced in 1947, grew throughout the 1960s, but slackened as college enrollment declined. The test has reached the maturity stage, the point at which it must be remarketed to gain new life. As part of a remarketing program, ETS is now selling the test, with modifications, to nonacademic institutions such as business firms that want to measure prospective employees' academic skills.[19]

The products of nonprofit organizations may also require demarketing when they go into a decline. A university, for example, may want to phase out a resource-draining graduate school and concentrate on undergraduate education. It may accomplish this by offering graduate courses on only one campus.

Pricing Considerations

The concept of price varies depending on what is being marketed in the nonprofit sector. When ideas are marketed, the price is often nonmonetary. The price of commitment to the idea of equal rights for women may be simply a letter to a legislator. Some ideas that are marketed extract a psychological price as well. A "quit smoking" campaign calls on the public to pay for better health by giving up the perceived pleasure of that habit.

In the marketing of organizations, the notion of price can also have varied meanings. Mutual benefit associations, such as unions and clubs, often charge dues or membership fees that must cover the cost of services to members. The price for the services of a government organization is the tax citizens pay.

Service organizations, which have both donor and client markets, charge both a monetary and nonmonetary price. Frequently the monetary charge to clients does not cover costs. Symphonies and museums charge admission fees but do not run solely on those funds. Benefactors make up the difference. The nonmonetary charge by service organizations is often psychological or intangible. The American Cancer Society asks its donors for a personal commitment of time as well as money. Its marketing slogan at one time was, "Fight cancer with a checkup and a check."

Setting prices when both monetary and nonmonetary considerations are involved is difficult.[20] The goal in determining the nonmonetary price is to encourage involvement; therefore, the psychological costs must be minimized. In setting the monetary price, the goal is usually to cover costs.

Occasionally, however, nonprofit pricing is demand oriented rather than cost oriented. Some organizations charge a high price and try to stimulate demand. (See Marketing Today 18.2.) Or the price is set to encourage or discourage demand. For example, Sunrise Hospital in Las

Figure 18.4
Promotion of an Intangible Product—Fitness
Source: Courtesy of the YMCA of the USA.

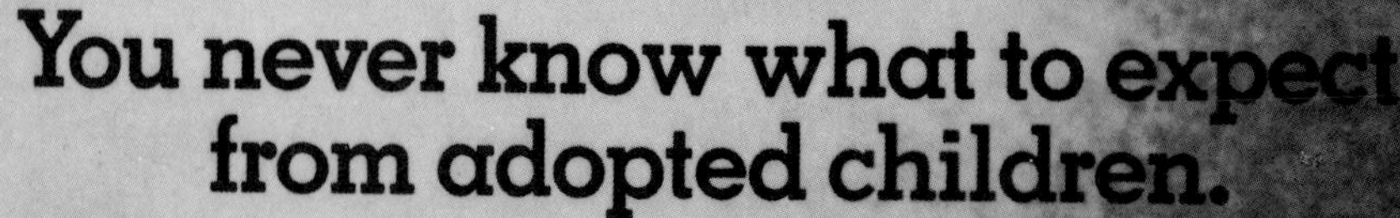

You never know what to expect
from adopted children.

This one became President.

In 1916, Gerald R. Ford Jr. was
adopted by his stepfather.

In 1974, he became President of the United States.

ADOPTED KIDS HAVE GREAT EXPECTATIONS.

National Committee for Adoption, P.O. Box 33366, Washington, D.C. 20033

Marketing Today 18.2

Business School Builds Demand for Its Pricey Education

Students at Duke University's Fuqua School of Business pay a high price. But even though tuition reached $11,400 a year in the fall of 1987 (compared with $11,900 at Harvard), full-time enrollment doubled between 1980 and 1987. Evidently, the school must have found the right target market and delivered the right product.

A key part of Fuqua's marketing strategy has been development of a superior product. The school lures high-quality faculty with North Carolina's warm climate, support for research, the exciting atmosphere of a growing institution, and, of course, money. The school also developed an emphasis on computer literacy and cultivated ties to the business community.

Another marketing strategy involved inviting executives to speak in classes. Professors make sure their classes are prepared to ask intelligent questions and then pamper their guests out of class at social gatherings. As the word has spread that Fuqua is worth visiting, the school has built awareness among business leaders. This is especially helpful when it comes time to find jobs for graduates.

An education at Fuqua may be expensive, but thanks to these efforts, many students evidently find it worth the price.

Source: Ed Bean, "By Practicing What It Preaches, Fuqua Wins a Place among Top Business Schools," *The Wall Street Journal,* May 13, 1986, p. 33.

Vegas, notorious for its "have surgery and win a cruise" campaign, began a maternity ward price war when it cut its charge for delivering babies by 46 percent. The move was made not only to fill beds, but to help cover the costs of often idle equipment and full-time staff. The price cut had two results: a competing hospital slashed prices 40 percent, and the number of deliveries at Sunrise increased 15 percent from the two months preceding the offer.[21]

Placement Considerations

Since most of the products marketed by nonprofit organizations are ideas or services, their distribution (or placement in the consumer's hands) tends to be direct, without the use of intermediaries.

For ideas, the channels of distribution are the same as the media used to communicate them. Channel width is an important consideration: How many different media should be used to make people aware of the idea? A "save the whales" campaign may be handled best by an exclusive distribution strategy, using only direct mailings to members of conservationist organizations. By contrast, to promote a consolidated position on adoption and give a positive image to being adopted, the National Committee for Adoption wanted to reach a broad national audience. So it placed its message on television and in general circulation magazines such as *People, Time,* and *Us.* (See Figure 18.5.)[22]

The placement of services is similar to the distribution of goods in many respects. Services must be delivered through retail-like outlets. Thus, the University of Michigan distributes its educational services

Figure 18.5
A Message Targeting a Broad Audience

Source: © National Committee for Adoption, Incorporated. All rights reserved. Ad created by Tim Love Advertising.

through its main Ann Arbor campus, but also through its Flint and Dearborn "branches." In general, sites must be selected carefully in order to reach the maximum number of customers. Charities usually set up chapters in major metropolitan areas in order to take advantage of the large number of volunteers and major donors usually found there.

The Institute of Medicine uses more diverse distribution channels for its product (information). The institute aggressively promotes its research results and makes them available in book and videotape form. The institute's president makes personal trips to Capitol Hill to bring information directly to Congress. In addition, chairpersons of institute study committees testify at congressional hearings. People receive information from the institute in many ways; the greater visibility gives the institute the prestige that attracts high-caliber members and interests potential donors in backing the institute's work.[23]

Promotional Considerations

All of the means of promotion used by business—personal selling, advertising, publicity, and sales promotion—can be used by nonprofit marketers as well. Some variation in emphasis is noticeable, however.

In the nonprofit sector, the most important promotional element is often personal selling. Some organizations, particularly larger ones, hire experts to raise funds, recruit members, or sell ideas or services. Another approach is to recruit people with high status or income to participate on a board of advisers or board of directors. These board members can then tap friends or colleagues in high places and ask for their support. Many people are willing to help but are waiting to be asked directly. Sometimes a direct request can bring a substantial contribution.

Nonprofit organizations are making increased use of telemarketing. In an unusual twist to telephone selling, the San Antonio Zoo took advantage of a common April Fool's joke: leaving a co-worker a message to call, say, a Ms. Ella Funt or a Mr. G. Raffe at the number of the zoo. When such calls came in, the zoo's telephone operator would ask, "Who gave you that note?" and suggest playing a trick on that person. The trick was for the zoo to call the prankster and ask him or her to match the donation of the original caller. In 1987, the zoo raised $11,000 in pledges that way.[24]

Volunteers are an important part of the sales force in the nonprofit sector. They help not just in soliciting funds but in attracting clients. For example, Alcoholics Anonymous uses its rehabilitated members to explain their experiences to alcoholics. Personal contact work requires training, supervision, and motivation. Training may be more informal and supervision less close than in business. And psychological motivators are more important than monetary rewards, although some charities offer prizes to their most successful fund-raisers.

Besides personal selling, nonprofit marketers have found advertising to be a highly effective way of communicating with the public. Many cities and states are discovering just how powerful advertising is. Tired of its frostbitten image, Syracuse, New York, for example, launched a multimillion-dollar advertising campaign to help sell the city as a comfortable place to live and work. The campaign generated 1,750 responses in its first six months, 250 of them from companies outside the United States.[25] New York State's "I Love New York" campaign, which has been running since 1977, is considered among the most successful advertising campaigns for any product. Between 1976 and 1982, the revenue attributed to tourism in New York more than doubled, from $5.5 billion annually to $11.5 billion. The promotion has launched a host of imitators, ranging from takeoffs on the slogan ("I Love Great Danes") to takeoffs on the idea ("Cleveland's a Plum," "Miami's for Me," and "Delaware . . . Small Wonder" are just a few).[26]

Some of the advertising available to nonprofit organizations is free. Advertising agencies volunteer their services through the Advertising Council, and the media run the resulting campaigns at no charge. For example, the ads promoting the Peace Corps ("the toughest job you'll ever love") are credited with recruiting 100,000 volunteers, including former President Jimmy Carter's mother, who signed up after seeing a commercial on local television.[27] Advertising of this sort resembles publicity in that it is nonpaid. Other forms of publicity—including press conferences and news releases—are very important to nonprofit marketers with limited funds.[28]

Sales promotion tools are also valuable instruments to gain public attention. Exhibits, leaflets, and dramatic events are the principal tools of sales promotion for nonprofit organizations. In recent years, for example, the American Cancer Society has held golf tournaments to raise funds and has sponsored "Great American Smokeout" days, when smokers are asked to abstain for 24 hours.[29]

The most effective promotional strategy coordinates all of the tools mentioned here. The military's campaign to fill the ranks of an all-volunteer service is an excellent example of a coordinated program. The personal selling efforts of 12,000 recruiters in high schools was one leg of that program. Another was the $129 million for paid advertising in magazines and newspapers and on posters and billboards. Finally, sales promotion activities, such as lending military bands to high-school functions and providing tours of military bases, were included in the total program. The program has been so successful that some divisions have waiting lists of qualified applicants. When the Department of Defense asked young adults if they could recall its advertising, 40 to 50 percent sang out the theme tunes of each branch with no prompting.[30]

A more troubling question than the degree of success of the government's promotional program is whether the government should be involved in promotion at all. Some critics charge that promotion, and especially advertising, by the government lends itself to abuse of power and wasteful spending. In 1976, for example, the U.S. Postal Service filmed a television commercial urging Americans to write letters. The ad was scrapped after airing in a few test markets. Viewers had complained that sponsoring advertising was not an appropriate use of tax dollars.[31] Since the government is an important part of the nonprofit sector, its marketers must give serious consideration to this issue and many others as they prepare government promotional campaigns.

Marketing Control

Even a well-planned marketing program can fail if marketers ignore controls. The process of control involves four steps: (1) setting well-defined objectives, (2) measuring actual results against planned results, (3) finding reasons for deviation from the plan, and (4) taking corrective action.

Objectives established in the planning phase set goals to be reached. For nonprofit marketers, the most difficult job in the control phase is to find measurements that indicate progress toward objectives. The kinds of measures needed in the nonprofit sector are not so different from those needed by business.[32] The most important measures are:

1. *Total marketing response.* In business, this refers to additional sales resulting from a marketing program. In the nonbusiness sector, it could mean increased patronage for a symphony or museum or additional funds raised by a charity in response to the marketing strategy.
2. *Market share.* This is actually a measure of how well an organization is doing relative to its direct competitors. Not all nonprofit organizations have direct competitors. A city police department has no direct competitors, though it certainly competes for limited funds with other city agencies. Hospitals, on the other hand, do compete and must measure their performance against competitors. Slippage in the number of patients in one hospital while other hospitals are experiencing an increase might indicate a marketing failure.
3. *Cost per dollar of marketing response.* In the process of meeting objectives, marketing programs should not financially strain an organization. Costs must be weighed carefully against results. For example, a test market of a March of Dimes campaign showed that a new marketing approach stressing direct mail to heavy contributors and additional radio and television advertising added to expenses by 14 percent but increased contributions by 33 percent.[33]
4. *Marketing attitudes.* Measuring customer satisfaction is important. Businesses sometimes make return sales calls, or they survey panels of product users. Nonbusiness marketers can use similar checking techniques. The post office, for example, checks on customer satisfaction by making available customer service cards, which postal users can fill out with complaints or remarks about service.

One or more of these measures can be used to gauge progress toward objectives. If total market response or market share falls short of plans, if costs run too high in relation to public response, or if customer attitudes are negative, reasons must be found for the failure and corrective actions must be taken.

Corrective action by the post office, for example, consists of forwarding every complaint received on its customer service cards to the local postmaster for action. The postmaster must explain how the problem was resolved to a consumer affairs bureau in Washington. The Washington bureau spot checks complaints to see if follow-up action was actually taken.[34] Since an important marketing objective of the post office is to raise its public image, the control program is a key to meeting that objective. Other nonprofit organizations might benefit from imitating the example.

Chapter Replay

1. **What are the basic types of nonprofit marketing?**
   Nonprofit marketing includes person marketing, idea marketing, and organization marketing.
2. **How do nonprofit organizations market ideas?**
   They use social marketing—they apply marketing techniques to increase the acceptability of a social idea, cause, or practice in one or more selected target groups.
3. **What are the major categories of nonprofit organizations?**
   Nonprofit organizations include service organizations, mutual benefit associations, and government organizations.
4. **In what ways do nonprofit organizations differ from businesses?**
   Nonprofit organizations usually have limited resources, often serve general publics as well as client publics, and may have more difficulty establishing control standards.
5. **What are the major similarities of nonprofit and for-profit organizations?**
   Both need to plan their objectives and analyze their environments in order to operate efficiently; both need to know their markets; both work with the same elements of the marketing mix; and both need to keep track of whether they are meeting objectives.
6. **Why is environmental analysis especially important for nonprofit organizations?**
   It is important because the existence of nonprofit organizations often depends on the goodwill of donors and taxpayers as well as the public they serve.
7. **What are the characteristics of the marketing mix for nonprofit organizations?**
   The elements of the marketing mix are the same as for business marketing. In the nonprofit sector, the product may be a person, an idea, or an organization. The price may be monetary, nonmonetary, or a combination of the two. Distribution channels are usually direct. Promotion often relies heavily on personal selling, which may depend on volunteers. Advertising may be nonpaid.
8. **What are the major ways to measure marketing success in the nonprofit sector?**
   The most important measures of marketing success are total marketing response, market share, cost per dollar of marketing response, and marketing attitudes.

Key Terms

client public
general public
government organization
idea marketing
mutual benefit association
organizational marketing
person marketing
service organization
social marketing

Discussion Questions

1. What kinds of products do nonprofit organizations market?
2. What are the major differences between nonprofit and business organizations? What are the similarities?
3. Revise the following proposed marketing objectives to quantify them.
   a. For a college: Attract good students.
   b. For a community organization: Start a day care center.
   c. For a mass transit system: Increase ridership.
4. In deciding whether to add a new wing, what are some characteristics of the environment that an art museum should consider?
5. To sell season tickets, a local opera company is considering placing an advertisement in the entertainment section of a local newspaper, running ads on the radio station that plays classical music, or sending a brochure to the names on the mailing list of people who bought symphony orchestra tickets last year. The budget allows for only one of these approaches. Which do you recommend? Why?
6. A group of lawyers started a legal aid clinic to provide services in a neighborhood where most people have low to middle incomes. The goal of the clinic is to make legal services available to people who otherwise could not afford them. In setting prices, should the lawyers use a demand-oriented or a cost-oriented strategy? Why?
7. Personal selling is a major part of promotion for many nonprofit organizations. Who are the salespeople in a nonprofit organization?
8. How can a nonprofit organization measure the success of its marketing efforts?
9. Is it ethical for an organization such as a charity or a church to spend money on a radio or newspaper ad when it could be spending the money on helping the needy? Why, or why not?

Case 18.1
March of Dimes Birth Defects Foundation

The National Foundation for Infantile Paralysis was founded in 1938 by President Franklin D. Roosevelt. It was set up as a permanent, nonstock, nonprofit organization, incorporated under the Membership Corporation Law of New York. When the victory over polio was assured in the 1950s, the National Foundation was faced with a decision of how best to utilize the knowledge, experience, and volunteer leadership developed over a 20-year period. Extensive analysis indicated that the foundation's specialized programs in research, patient services, and professional and public health education could address another major health concern—the vast and, at the time, largely unexplored field of birth defects.

The March of Dimes, a name initially coined for the annual fundraising campaign of The National Foundation, over the years became so closely identified with the organization that it was adopted in 1979 as the formal corporate name—the March of Dimes Birth Defects Foundation.

The mission of the March of Dimes is to unify, lead, and direct the fight to prevent birth defects and their consequences. In its efforts to protect the unborn and the newborn, the approaches it employs to attain its goals remain the same as in the effort against polio:

1. Research seeks causes of birth defects; faster, and more accurate, diagnostic methods; and more effective treatment and prevention techniques.
2. Health services strive to improve delivery of health care and programs of prevention related to genetic disorders, low-birthweight babies, and high-risk pregnancies.
3. Professional education disseminates knowledge gained through research and trains health professionals to improve and expand maternal/newborn health care.
4. Community services implements chapter programs to inform and educate the American public about birth defects prevention, and to develop volunteer leadership and advocacy initiatives.

Professional Education

The March of Dimes attains its goals through a historic partnership of medical professionals and volunteers. It fights birth defects with a broad spectrum of programs supported by voluntary contributions. The national organization and its local chapters are leaders in educating health professionals and lay people about developments in the prevention and treatment of birth defects.

Varied, innovative professional education programs make research and health services results available to a wide range of health care professionals. Up-to-date information about birth defects, genetics, and perinatal health are reported in such publications as the *March of Dimes Reprint Series* and the *Original Article Series.* Other printed and audiovisual materials on outreach education, adolescent pregnancy, nutrition, nursing research, newborn behavior, and intensive care are also disseminated.

The March of Dimes supports the International Clearinghouse for Birth Defects Monitoring Systems, a resource for reporting and exchanging information on birth defects incidence among a score of countries. The foundation sponsors medical conferences, symposia, and seminars to transmit and encourage discussion and exchanges of information and ideas concerning the study and treatment of birth defects.

Public Education through Community Services

Community services programs inform and educate the public about risks posed by birth defects and low birthweight to the unborn and newborn. Since early, regular prenatal care is recognized as the most important factor in the health of a mother and baby, every effort is made to communicate this to all sectors of society. Community services programs use print materials, audiovisuals, and exhibits to support group and individual behavior patterns conducive to healthy childbearing. Grants are awarded to schools, hospitals, and community agencies to assist in preventive health education programs.

The March of Dimes takes a leading role in developing the national Healthy Mothers/Healthy Babies public health education campaign of a coalition of federal, professional, and voluntary health agencies.

The foundation offers prenatal health education programs in the workplace—such as Good Health Is Good Business—to reach potential parents, particularly the increasing number of working women. In addition, the March of Dimes maintains a continuing effort to communicate its preventive message through the media, including news releases, feature articles, public service announcement campaigns, and video news reports, on risks during pregnancy and how to minimize them. The goal of all community service and publicity efforts is to achieve maximum awareness and understanding of birth defects and the need for their prevention and treatment.

Fund-Raising

Many of the ways in which the March of Dimes raises money annually are linked to its informational and educational prevention programs. Fund-raising activities are a primary way of informing the public about the need to prevent birth defects. Through an initial involvement with fund-raising, volunteers are recruited for service and community programs. As a result, the March of Dimes over the years has chosen not to participate in the United Way or other locally oriented campaigns. In its early years, the foundation adopted this policy to assure its independent ability to launch emergency appeals for funds during polio epidemics.

March of Dimes fund-raising events are conducted nationally and locally and depend on volunteer involvement for planning and execution. National events include the telethon, which carries the message of prevention coast-to-coast while raising millions of dollars annually. Similar events include the annual Mothers March and WalkAmerica. Chapters sponsor a broad range of other fund-raising events to fund national programs and others at the community level.

Focal Topics

1. What basic marketing concepts are being used by, or could be helpful to, the March of Dimes?
2. What advantages and disadvantages result from the Foundation's conducting its own separate campaign for support instead of joining a local organization such as the United Way? How can these advantages be maximized and disadvantages be minimized?
3. Indicate what strategy the organization should use to communicate its objectives, projects, results, and needs to its public.

Case 18.2
Simpson Road Church

In early 1984, Simpson Road Church observed its 50th anniversary. A variety of worship services, guest speakers, church dinners, and special ceremonies and events were held to celebrate the occasion. The membership was proud of its church and the many accomplishments realized during its first 50 years.

As the pastor and leaders of the church began to think about the future of Simpson Road Church, however, they realized that the church needed a plan, a set of goals and objectives, or some sort of strategy as it entered its second half-century of religious service. Toward that end, a Vision Committee was formed to help develop an understanding of where Simpson Road Church was at that time and where it should be headed in the future.

Church Characteristics

As a prelude to developing a set of plans and objectives for Simpson Road Church, the Vision Committee compiled a list of salient characteristics of the church.

- It is in the downtown area of a major midwestern metropolitan community with a population of around 900,000.
- The present church structure is about 40 years old, has been fairly well maintained, but is in need of some major renovations to minimize future maintenance problems.
- As shown in the Exhibit, the church's 1983 membership, according to its rolls, was 526. Average attendance at morning worship was 169 for the year, while average attendance at Sunday school was 109.
- Also, as shown in the Exhibit, financial contributions decreased in 1983 after showing increases in the previous three years.
- Present seating capacity of the church, including a currently closed balcony, is for 825 people.
- During the week, the church makes its facilities available to local organizations for meetings. Some of the organizations using the facilities include Boy Scout groups, Lamaze classes, and some inner-city counseling groups.
- The church has an annual budget of just over $105,500, with approximately 80 percent coming from contributions to the church and the remaining coming from interest on the church's endowment fund and memorial gifts.

Source: Much of the information here is based on an actual church. The name and certain facts have been modified.

Exhibit
Membership, Attendance, and Offering Statistics, 1977–1983

Year	Total Members	Members Gained	Members Lost	Worship Average	Sunday School Average	Total Offerings
1983	526	25	9	169	109	$84,672
1982	511	32	16	175	113	86,366
1981	495	5	8	156	104	72,641
1980	498	9	20	165	101	69,894
1979	509	8	16	168	108	69,525
1978	517	17	15	185	121	74,726
1977	515	10	22	210	133	76,220

- ☐ A variety of programs is provided for all age groups—men's monthly prayer breakfasts, weekly meetings for various women's groups, and an active youth program including Sunday evening sessions along with monthly special activities. Individual Sunday school classes also hold special studies and social get-togethers several times a month.
- ☐ The church supports an active ministry in the downtown area where individuals and families in need can receive food, clothing, and temporary shelter.

Proposed Membership Research

In developing plans for the future, the Vision Committee considered it essential to have information on the attitudes, feelings, and understandings of its members toward the church and its activities. A special subcommittee, chaired by George McCormick, was formed to design, implement, and interpret a comprehensive research study of Simpson Road's membership.

George, in preparing for the first subcommittee meeting, looked to the book of Hebrews: "Consider how we may spur one another toward love and good deeds . . . do not give up meeting together . . . but to encourage one another" (Hebrews 10:24,25). This led him to the conclusion that the purpose of the research would be to obtain information that would help the church continue its goal of building up the church body. He felt that a good approach to gathering the needed membership input would be to design a detailed questionnaire to be completed by each person in the church 12 years and older. Specific information to be compiled included the members' feelings, attitudes, and understanding of the church for its members and the community.

Focal Topics

1. Do you believe that it is appropriate to use marketing concepts in religious organizations? Why, or why not?
2. What marketing concepts might be appropriate for Simpson Road Church to use in planning for the future?
3. How would you design the membership survey form? Be specific about types of questions and ways of asking them.

Case for Part Six

Live Aid Concert

In retrospect, it was the largest, single-day fund-raising event in history. On July 13, 1985, fans sweated and cheered—90,000 in Philadelphia and 72,000 in London—and an estimated 1.5 billion people tuned in via television through the magic of satellite television. Live Aid, the brainchild of Irish rock musician Bob Geldof, raised over $60 million for famine relief in Ethiopia and other African countries.

Background

In 1984, Bob Geldof, lead singer of the Boomtown Rats, recruited other British recording artists to tape the hit song, "Do They Know It's Christmas/Feed the World." Proceeds, which exceeded $11 million, were used for African famine relief by the organization British Band Aid. Not to be outdone, a galaxy of American pop music stars got together and recorded an overwhelmingly well-received, "We Are The World." Proceeds from that recording went to USA for Africa.

Geldof then had the vision of bringing together the world's greatest rock musicians for a huge, live benefit concert. An organization called Worldwide Sports and Entertainment, formed to put together mega-events, got the massive concert idea rolling.

The Event

The international, 16-hour rock 'n' roll extravaganza was held on July 13, 1985. Artists performed live on stages in Philadelphia and London. By connecting together 13 satellites to reach over 128 countries simultaneously, and shipping four hours of videotaped highlights to 22 additional countries, Live Aid was delivered to audiences of more than 1.5 billion people, more than a third of the world's population.

Some 56 acts performed during the concert. Among the artists were Mick Jagger; Paul McCartney; Tina Turner; Duran Duran; Joan Baez; Bob Dylan; and Peter, Paul, and Mary.

The Results

Estimated costs to put on the Live Aid concert came to a little over $4 million. Total revenue from all sources was expected to reach over $60 million, leaving some $56 million for famine relief in Africa.

Sources: Michael Goldberg, "Live Aid take may hit $60 million," *Rolling Stone,* August 29, 1985, pp. 17+; and Allan Dodds Frank, "It's only rock 'n' roll but they like it," *Forbes,* September 23, 1985; p. 140.

MTV broadcast the entire 16 hours in the United States and donated all of its $750,000 advertising revenue to the relief fund. ABC paid about $1.5 million for the rights to run its three-hour special, and a syndicate of 105 independent television stations paid about $2.5 million in rights fees and revenue for advertising. According to ABC, as many as 40 million people saw at least part of its broadcast. An additional $6 million came in from television rights fees from other countries.

The biggest portion of Live Aid revenue, roughly $36 million, came from the telethons that were held in some 22 countries. Amounts from selected countries included $10 million (United States), $18.9 million (the United Kingdom), $1.4 million (Canada), $2.0 million (New Zealand), $4.9 million (Ireland), and $3.5 million (Australia). In the United States, the average amount contributed per call during the telethon was $30.

Ticket sales and merchandising activities accounted for an additional $9.5 million in Live Aid revenue. Four corporate sponsors—AT&T, Pepsi, Kodak, and Chevrolet—contributed a total of $5 million for exposure during the concert, including having their names displayed on banners across the stage for all of the world to see.

John Costello, Pepsi's senior vice-president of marketing, estimates that his soft-drink company received 350 million favorable impressions in the United States alone for about one-third the cost of reaching that audience in prime time. That exposure was from the 26 minutes of advertising that Pepsi bought on MTV and various syndicated broadcasts.

The Future

Expenditure of Funds Various organizations involved with Live Aid established relationships with most of the reputable agencies already at work in the famine-stricken countries and asked them to submit funding requests for needed projects. Some of the money raised was used to purchase food and supplies to be distributed through the established relief agencies. Funds were also used to obtain and distribute medical supplies and equipment. Trucks and other vehicles were purchased to transport the food and supplies to the areas of need.

Much of the money raised was devoted to longer-term projects in an effort to prevent the African tragedy from happening again. Investments were made in agricultural development projects, including water-drilling rigs to help with irrigation.

Additional Events The success of Live Aid led to a number of other large-scale fund-raising events. Farm Aid was designed to assist financially stricken farmers in the United States. A worldwide torch relay race, First Earth Run, was held in September 1986 to raise funds for UNICEF. Live Aid sequels called Sport Aid and Farm Aid II were also held in 1986.

On May 25, 1986, the Los Angeles-based USA for Africa sponsored "Hands Across America." This event, involving over 6 million people and a number of corporate sponsors, sought to link hands from New York to Los Angeles with the objective of raising money to aid the hungry and homeless in the United States.

While these and other similar events seemed to be well received by individuals and corporate sponsors, some questions are beginning to be raised. Might the sheer number of such events, coupled with a fatigue factor, undermine interest in the massive fund-raisers?

Focal Topics

1. What do you think are the reasons that made Live Aid so successful?
2. Beyond the aid recipients, who else benefits from such fund-raising events? In what ways do they benefit?
3. How would you promote an event like Live Aid to get more people around the world to watch it?
4. What suggestions do you have for additional ways to generate revenue from an event like Live Aid?
5. What do you see as the future for massive international fund-raising events?

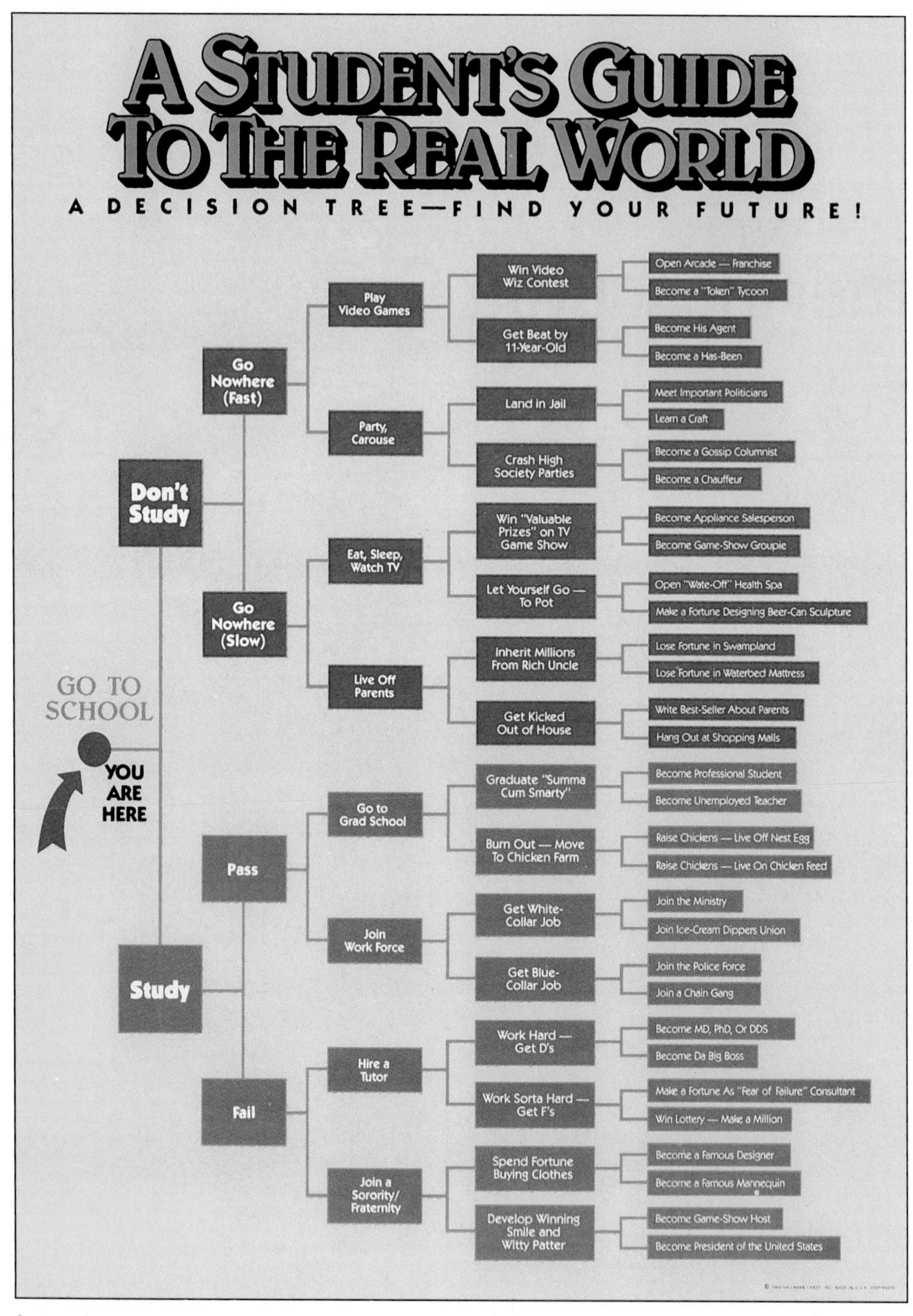

Source: Copyright Hallmark Cards Inc.

Appendix A
Career Resource Guide

The purpose of this appendix is to help students target their ambitions in selecting an entry-level position in the field of marketing. We will describe some of the most prevalent entry-level jobs in the areas of sales, advertising, sales promotion, public relations, marketing research, retailing, wholesaling, telemarketing, and entrepreneurship. We will also explain how internships help students become more qualified in the job market.

Sales

According to a recent survey at Lansing Community College in Lansing, Michigan, nearly 80 percent of students graduating with an associates degree in marketing had planned to join the work force in a sales position. Selling jobs are plentiful, and some are especially attractive to graduating students.

Wholesale Sales

Wholesale selling involves the sale of goods and services to intermediaries who in turn resell the goods to others for a profit. Examples include selling to retailers, wholesalers, and industrial and commercial firms. A *wholesaler representative* would be responsible for selling to retailers while

This appendix was written by Professor Deleski Smith of Lansing Community College.

working for a wholesaler, jobber, and/or distributor. Wholesale selling often involves selling a vast number of products—in some cases up to 50,000 items. This is accomplished by selling from a catalog or series of catalogs because there are too many items to memorize. A wholesaler rep usually represents more than one supplier or manufacturer and, in some cases, may represent competitors in the marketplace. For many years wholesale reps were considered order takers, but with increasing competition in the field, they have become order seekers through their sales efforts. Among their objectives are communicating enthusiasm to the prospective buyers and helping them feel the need to carry a new or improved product.

A *merchandising salesperson* sells to retailers. The main area of responsibility for these salespeople is developing a territory that will produce the maximum volume of business for a particular product. Their job description might include the following tasks: checking inventory to find out exactly what the customer needs; discussing and taking regular orders, including recommending the amount of product the customer needs to take care of business on a regular basis; showing customers the monthly and quarterly specials offered by the companies they represent; and presenting special sales to get the companies' goods on display or in the dealers' advertising.

Industrial Sales

In the area of industrial sales, a *manufacturers' representative* works directly for and is employed by the manufacturer. These salespeople call on wholesalers, dealers, and distributors. They are also contact and promotional people, sales supervisors, complaint handlers, adjusters, and public relations people. Entry-level positions in this area of selling are scarce and are filled by assertive, innovative, and emotionally well-adjusted people who must be able to manage time and accept rejection. They not only must be knowledgeable about the company and its products and services, they should also know all areas of marketing, including product and product development, pricing and discount policies, physical distribution, promotion, and sales promotion. The manufacturers' representative relays customers' needs to the firm's research and development department so new products may be planned and developed for the marketplace. This job usually involves a great deal of traveling.

Retail Sales

Generally speaking, the *retail salesperson* positions are not sought out by college graduates. The main reason for this is because most of these positions are minimum wage jobs and offer limited chance for advancement. If advancement is to come, it usually takes a very long time. A good professional retail salesperson can be a great asset to a retail company and usually is paid on a commission basis. This type of sales position would normally involve a "big ticket" item such as furniture, appliances, fences, and floor coverings.

Direct Sales

Our discussion of direct sales positions is limited to the most common types. Let's begin with the *account executive trainee* in an advertising agency. Trainees frequently receive formal training, some on the job and some in a classroom. They work in various departments of the agency, including media, creative, production, traffic, customer service, and customer relations. Their tasks may be menial, but they are exposed to all aspects of the agency and have contact with successful account executives. Trainees also work with assistant account executives. By so doing, they make client contact, help put ideas together, "chase" material and people, and contribute to decision making.

A *specialty advertising salesperson* works for a company that sells specialty advertising items such as calendars, T-shirts, caps, pens, pencils, and rulers. The selling includes making cold calls and servicing repeat business. The salesperson's objective is to encourage customers to "get their name out before their buying public." One specialty advertising salesperson said, "If you can get the item to hold still for thirty seconds, we'll get your name on it and you can give it to your customer."

The key to successful specialty advertising selling is to first develop the customer's need for a specialty item and then develop a plan for the distribution of that item. Developing a distribution plan is especially important: many repeat sales have been lost because the item never got into the hands of the person who made the buying decision. Because there are about 15,000 different specialty advertising items, the salesperson must be able to suggest those items that would be most appropriate to deliver the customer's message. Roger Shuneson began his career in specialty advertising as a salesman for Brown & Bigelow, one of the largest firms in the business. After five years of selling, he was promoted to district manager and then regional manager. According to Shuneson, go-getters do well in the business. He says, "There's always a need for talented salespeople who want to make a lot of money."

Real estate selling is another direct sales area that rewards those with initiative. Many *real estate salespeople* have made a fortune. Some have even gone on to start their own firms. Selling real estate involves more than just listing and selling houses, vacant lots, and businesses. An important part of the job is developing a list of prospects. This may be done in many ways, from receiving calls made to the real estate company for a particular house listed to making cold calls in a neighborhood that has the potential for profitable sales. In the trade, the latter is known as "farming" a neighborhood, whereby salespeople make themselves known to the residents of an area by making calls, introducing themselves, and letting the residents know of the services they provide.

Real estate selling is a career in which the recent college graduate can excel from the first year and generate an excellent income. Compensation is usually on a straight commission basis. Because most real estate salespeople are independent contractors, they do not receive many of the benefits of company employees. This means that they are responsible for their own benefits, such as insurance. They also take full responsibility for paying their own withholding and Social Security taxes.

Moving Up
JO FOXWORTH
Founder
Jo Foxworth Advertising, Inc.

Source: Photograph by Meifert & Heal.

A Mississippi native, Jo Foxworth received a journalism degree from the University of Missouri and began her career selling advertising for a newspaper in McComb, Mississippi, for $10 a week. Following that, she worked in retailing and advertising in Louisville and at Nan Duskin in Philadelphia before moving to New York in 1955.

In New York, she began her advertising career in earnest with a job at J. M. Mathes and soon after moved to McCann-Erikson, where she worked as a copywriter on the Coca-Cola, Westinghouse, Nestlé, and Liggett & Myers accounts. After stints at a few other agencies, she decided to start her own shop with D'Agostino supermarkets as her first client. Soon after, J. C. Penney, Celanese Corporation, and United Fruit Company were added to the roster.

Jo Foxworth is probably best known for a speech she gave in which she set forth the "Nine Commandments for Women in Business." Among them: *"Thou shalt try harder; thou need not be only number two." "Thou shalt know when to zip thy lip and listen quietly." "Thou shalt watch thy language; there may be gentlemen present."*

Source: Bart Cummings, "The Benevolent Dictators," *Advertising Age*, February 20, 1984, pp. M-4–5, M-51.

Some salespeople specialize in certain areas such as residential, commercial, or industrial real estate. All selling, however, requires a people orientation and a desire to serve clients. Satisfying clients is especially important in selling real estate because new business is often generated from referrals. Lynne Van Deventor, a realtor associate at a Century 21 office in Lansing, Michigan, attributes her success to a good referral business and customer follow-up. Van Deventor is one of many women who have prospered in this field of selling. In a recent year she sold over $12 million of residential, commercial, industrial, and vacant land real estate and has been the leading salesperson in her office for the past 11 years.

Advertising

An *assistant art director* has a general knowledge of marketing and an art background. Creativeness is essential, even though the assistant often begins in the paste-up room putting together advertisements. Communication skills are also important because the assistant interacts with the art director, copywriters, and production people. The assistant art director graphically projects what the copywriter has written. Assistants may be assigned to a small account, working under the supervision of the art director. Some of their time may be spent with a photographer or illustrator and in brainstorming sessions for innovative ideas.

Moving Up

LENORE COONEY
Account Supervisor
Dudly-Anderson-Yutzy
Public Relations

"What can you say about a 100-year-old bridge in need of refurbishment?" Lenore Cooney asked herself the day she got the Brooklyn Bridge account. Plenty, as it turned out. The 100th birthday party for the bridge on May 24, 1983, became such an extravaganza that one reporter called it "this year's version of the royal wedding."

Behind all this hoopla was Lenore Cooney, who had spent 18 months researching stories, finding angles, providing photographs, filling airtime, and otherwise servicing the insatiable media monster.

By the time the last fireworks display had vanished into the New York night sky, the stack of newspaper clippings about the event had reached six feet, articles had appeared in every magazine from *Life* to *Popular Mechanics,* total U.S. television coverage had run to 18 hours, and TV crews from Brazil, Japan, and five European countries covered the event.

While selling the Brooklyn Bridge seems like a singular marketing challenge, according to Cooney it wasn't much different from selling bananas or pain relievers or floppy disks. Public relations success in any of these areas, says Cooney, requires that a marketer find a theme, develop the news angles, and "then follow-up, follow-up."

Source: Curtis Hartman, "Selling the Brooklyn Bridge," *Inc.,* November 1983, p. 58.

A *sales promotion assistant* can work for an advertising agency or a wholesaler. Sales promotion is one of the most important links in the marketing process: it gets the product or service into the distribution process and the sell-through process.

Sales involves interfacing with different vendors for promotion ideas. The other part of the job is sales merchandising, which entails sending bulletins to the field on current promotions. A third part of the position involves helping brand groups when they need assistance in the selection of promotional pieces by developing various promotional materials and screening outside ideas that come in.

Public Relations

Working with the public relations staff, an *assistant public relations reporter or writer* assists in gathering important information, interpreting the information, and then writing press releases from this data. An assistant usually compiles and checks press lists, helps set up and confirm arrangements for public relations events, researches background facts and figures for a supervisor, and develops a network of contacts, which is a valuable source of information. This area of marketing requires excellent verbal and writing skills as well as the ability to communicate with clients, other staff members, and the media. Developing good relationships with media personnel is especially important because they publish or air the message about a company's product, service, or image. An assistant could be promoted to a public relations officer or director of public relations.

Moving Up

DAVID P. FORSYTH
Vice-President—Research
McGraw-Hill Publications Company

From the time he was young, David Forsyth always knew he wanted to be a newspaper reporter. In high school he worked for a weekly newspaper that covered coal mining in central Utah. At Brigham Young University he majored in newspaper journalism and went on for a master's degree in magazine journalism at Northwestern University.

After completing his degrees, he took a teaching job at the University of Iowa. While there, he took some research courses and got hooked. He then went to Chilton to get some experience in business publishing and after eight years left to form his own media and marketing research organization. His company was asked by McGraw-Hill to conduct a special research project. McGraw-Hill was impressed enough by his work to ask him to become their first vice-president—research.

Forsyth believes that to be a successful marketing researcher, "You must not only have the marketing research training, you must have an understanding for the whole concept of marketing—and enthusiasm."

Source: *Advertising Age,* January 2, 1984, p. M-11.

Source: McGraw-Hill, Inc.

Marketing Research

Collecting information is the primary task of a *marketing research assistant.* Most of the information is collected through telephone calls. An assistant might also work with an assistant marketing analyst in compiling information for a project. For this, familiarity with computers and computer reports is necessary. Advancement in marketing research requires at least a bachelor's degree but preferably a master's degree.

Retailing

Most graduates begin their careers in retailing as an *executive trainee.* Trainees are often assigned to a buyer and a group manager so they are exposed to both the merchandising and the managerial aspects of retailing. Initial tasks might include assisting the assistant buyer to ensure that correct merchandise has been received and is moved to the proper selling area at the right time, and working on temporary price changes.

In moving up the retail ladder, a trainee could become an assistant buyer, a buyer, a divisional merchandise manager, and finally a general manager. Those who advance quickly are bright and innovative and have a lot of ambition and desire to keep on learning.

Executive trainees can also move into sales management positions. A *sales manager* is responsible for a small number of classifications under the divisional group manager's authority. The sales manager organizes and staffs the department and handles financial planning, quota setting,

Moving Up
DAWN MELLO
President
Bergdorf Goodman

Reflecting on her career in retailing, Dawn Mello notes that she has been a saleswoman since she was 10 years old. At that tender age, she started on the path to the upper ranks of retailing by selling pine cones and pine boughs at Christmas time. Then, at age 15, she went to work in a store wrapping packages because she wasn't old enough to sell.

After doing stints at May Department Stores and B. Altman & Company, Mello came to Bergdorf Goodman as vice-president and director of fashion merchandising. She was promoted to president in October of 1983.

For Dawn Mello, the field of retailing has always held a special fascination. "Being on the sales floor and listening to the customers is a most exciting world, which always held a special magic for me—still does, I suppose."

Although Mello isn't on the selling floor as much as she once was, she hasn't lost touch with her customers. As president of the store, she now gets much of the mail from customers who believe in taking their complaints "right to the top!"

Source: Bergdorf Goodman.

Source: *Working Woman,* February 1984, p. 64.

---

and territory management. The sales manager must constantly train and evaluate the sales force, motivating them to excel through appropriate incentives and compensation.

Wholesaling

One entry-level position in the physical distribution area of marketing is an *order processing rate clerk,* whose main task is processing orders. This involves identifying the appropriate storage and transportation rates, examining new equipment purchase details, and performing routine financial and inventory control. Clerks frequently use computers to perform these functions. They also assist the terminal manager with planning and analysis, customer service, traffic and transportation, warehouse operation, and inventory control. This experience helps prepare them for a promotion to terminal manager and then regional manager.

Another entry-level position is a *traffic scheduler,* who is responsible for comparing transportation costs and then processing the necessary paperwork to accomplish this task. The job includes scheduling, customer service, selecting a carrier (on a limited basis), and tracing shipments. The traffic scheduling person would assist the traffic manager in his main responsibility, cost savings. They must find the most dependable, accessible, least expensive carrier that can deliver the goods on time and in the quantity needed.

Another wholesaling job available to graduating students is that of the *production or warehouse line*. People work with the inventory coordinator by moving the product upward through the channels as rapidly as possible. This position includes writing and expediting orders, handling

Moving Up
TERRY CONWAY
Owner
John T. Handy Company

In Crisfield, Maryland, Terry Conway has become something of a local legend. Conway is the man who gave up a hefty, six-figure salary and a vice presidency at Perdue Farms, Inc. to switch from the chicken business to the packaging and selling of soft-shell crabs. In 1981, Conway purchased a family-owned seafood packing business for $500,000. Three years later, the business had grown to a multimillion-dollar food concern.

Conway's strategy has been to develop a top quality product and to zero in on a select market of gourmet five-star restaurants across the United States. To reach this market, he launched an aggressive advertising campaign in food and restaurant magazines.

Not content to corner the gourmet crab market only in the United States, Conway recently struck a deal with several restaurants in Tokyo. If Conway has anything to do with it, Maryland soft-shell crabs may soon become as famous and treasured as French foie gras or Beluga caviar.

Source: Courtesy of John T. Handy Co., Inc.

Source: "From Chicken to Crabs," *Venture,* June 1984, p. 18.

---

manufacturing relations, and maintaining records on inventory counts. Establishing good communications with the channel members is a top priority. Promotions may lead to inventory coordinator and then inventory control manager.

An *assistant brand manager* works with sales promotion managers in developing theories, strategies, techniques, and credibility for the brand. For the consumer goods wholesaler and manufacturer, the assistant brand manager assists the sales promotion manager in trying to develop appropriate promotions that will improve the business of the brand groups. They perform creative tasks similar to those of an advertising agency. They often recognize an opportunity, approach the brand group with an idea, and then work with the necessary support groups to develop, implement, and measure the success or failure of the promotional event. An assistant brand manager may be promoted to a promotional assistant and then a planning coordinator.

Telemarketing

The fastest-growing business in the United States, according to some studies, is telemarketing. By 1990, there will be 8 million jobs for *telemarketers,* who sell everything from newspapers to computers. The owner of a telemarketing business says telemarketers must have a good voice and maintain excellent voice techniques. A good command of the English language and proper grammar usage are essential. Telemarketers study product characteristics and learn sales scripts. They must be sincere and capable of conveying the excitement of the product they are selling without the benefit of face-to-face contact with prospective buyers.

Entrepreneurship

A classroom survey revealed that over 50 percent of students studying business would like to become entrepreneurs.[1]

With this amount of interest, it is important to address the possibilities of owning a business after graduation. During a recent interview with Ms. Priscilla Peterson, Manager of Management Recruiters and owner of Office Mates in Lansing, Michigan, she stated, "I came here to become a *management recruiter executive*. I liked the business so well I became the manager and then started my own business called Office Mates." In Office Mates, office support people are placed around the immediate area, "usually not over 50 miles from Lansing," says Ms. Peterson. "This is known as a 'head hunting' business," Ms. Peterson goes on to say "and it would be a very good experience for a college graduate to become a business owner." In this business they try and match possible employees with companies that need talented individuals. The management recruiter would be responsible for the development of client companies and the servicing of those companies by finding people to fill their needs. Their duties and responsibilities include the following: 1) develop new client companies through telephone calls; 2) write orders; 3) recruit, when necessary, to fill openings for clients; 4) interview applicants; 5) present job openings to qualified candidates; 6) reference check applicants; 7) arrange interview dates and times; 8) prepare applicants for job interviews; 9) follow up interviews with applicants and employers; 10) close and finalize placements; 11) make necessary "key accounts" visits; 12) plan the next day's activities during the planning hour; and 13) keep records on daily statistics of placements.

Ms. Peterson states, "For one to be acceptable in this business, one should possess several traits. Among these are enthusiasm, positive attitude, internal motivation, good self-image, some kind of previous success, a curious mind, common sense, good listening skills, and integrity." She went on to say, "90% of this job is telemarketing." This is an attractive business that a college graduate may well be qualified to run.

Internships

An excellent way to become familiar with many entry-level marketing jobs is to become an intern. An internship is a cooperative arrangement between businesses and colleges or universities whereby students work part-time and receive college credit for their on-the-job training. Interning gives students the opportunity to determine whether or not they are suited to a certain type of job.

About 50 percent of all intern students are hired by the companies they worked for during their college years. An internship can be a vital part of a college education. It gives students a chance to practice what they have learned in the classroom, it exposes them to the workplace and teaches them how to function in a controlled setting, and it provides them with an opportunity to develop interpersonal skills and attitudes involving relationships with others. Internships also help students to develop proficiency in judgment and decision making, to understand the functions of marketing and management, and to realize the importance of dependability, appearance, and promptness.

Internships are available in many areas of marketing—selling, marketing research, retail sales, telemarketing, and office management.

Appendix B Marketing Arithmetic

Many decisions that marketers make are based on an analysis of their company's financial statements. To arrive at these business decisions, marketers must be able to perform some basic marketing arithmetic.

Marketing arithmetic deals with simple arithmetic ideas, such as percentages and ratios. This appendix presents three major areas of marketing arithmetic: the operating statement, analytical ratios, and pricing.

The Operating Statement

The *operating statement* can also be called the profit-and-loss statement, or the income statement. This statement presents a summary of a company's sales and expenses *over a specific period of time*—a month, a quarter, or a year—and one of the major tools for analyzing a company's financial performance is the operating statement.

Another important financial statement is the *balance sheet,* which shows the assets, liabilities, and net worth of a company *at one point in time.* Both of these financial statements are used by marketers to arrive at decisions.

For the marketer, however, the operating statement is the more important of the two financial statements. Besides showing whether a company had a net profit or net loss, it provides much of the information needed to figure the analytical ratios used in marketing decision making.

Table B.1 shows the operating statement for Jones & Smith Clothiers, Inc., a small retail company. This is the type of operating statement that a company would provide to its marketers. It has six main parts:

Table B.1

Jones & Smith Clothiers, Inc.
Operating Statement
for December

Revenues			
Gross sales		$54,000	
Less: Sales returns and allowances	$ 3,000		
Net sales			$51,000
Cost of goods sold			
Beginning inventory, January 1 (at cost)		$10,000	
Gross purchases during year	$25,000		
Less: Purchase discounts	1,000		
Net purchases	$24,000		
Plus: Freight in	800		
Net purchases (total delivered cost)		24,800	
Cost of goods available for sale		$34,800	
Less: Ending inventory, December 31 (at cost)		8,000	
Cost of goods sold			$26,800
Gross margin			$24,200
Operating expenses			
Selling expenses			
Sales salaries and commissions	$ 6,000		
Advertising	2,000		
Delivery charges	2,000		
Total selling expenses		$10,000	
General expenses			
Office salaries	$ 4,000		
Rent and utilities	3,000		
Miscellaneous general expenses	1,000		
Total general expenses		$ 8,000	
Total operating expenses			$18,000
Net income before taxes			$ 6,200

gross sales, net sales, cost of goods sold, gross margin, operating expenses, and net profit before taxes.

Gross sales are the total sales revenue received by a company during a specific period of time. In the case of Jones & Smith, gross sales were $54,000 for the month of December.

Net sales are the revenue retained by a company after subtracting the amount paid to customers for sales *returns* and *allowances*. If a customer returns merchandise and receives a refund or credit, this is considered a sales return. If a customer returns a damaged item and is given a price reduction on the item, this is considered an allowance. The net sales for Jones & Smith in December were $51,000.

Cost of goods sold is the total amount that a company paid for the merchandise it sold. Jones & Smith's cost of goods sold was $26,800. This figure was determined by first adding the *beginning inventory,* or goods on hand at the beginning of the year, to the net purchases (including transportation cost) and then subtracting the ending inventory amount.

If Jones & Smith were a manufacturing company instead of a retail company, the purchases section of the operating statement would be replaced by a cost of goods manufactured section. This section includes the cost of raw materials, labor, and factory overhead (light, heat, power). It is important to remember that for retailers the cost of goods sold is the cost of merchandise purchased for resale.

The next line on the operating statement is *gross margin,* or gross profit. This figure is obtained by subtracting the cost of goods sold from net sales. Jones & Smith's gross margin was $24,200. Gross margin is the total amount that a company has to cover operating expenses and to provide a net profit.

Operating expenses are all the expenses, other than the cost of goods, that a company has during the time covered by the operating statement. Included in this part of the operating statement are selling expenses and general expenses. Some companies also list administrative expenses separately within this section. Selling expenses are sometimes listed as marketing expenses.

Jones & Smith Clothiers' selling expenses included salaries and commissions for sales personnel, advertising, and delivery charges. General expenses covered office salaries, rent and utilities, and miscellaneous expenses such as office supplies and insurance. By adding the total selling expenses of $10,000 to the total general expenses of $8,000, Jones & Smith Clothiers find that total operating expenses were $18,000.

Total operating expenses are then subtracted from gross margin to determine *net income before taxes,* or net profit before taxes. This part of the operating statement is often referred to as the "bottom line." If a company has a loss rather than a profit for the operating period, the bottom line reads:

Net Income (Loss) before Taxes

Jones & Smith's net income before taxes was $6,200. This amount is used to cover federal and state taxes as well as profits for owners or shareholders. Net income *before* taxes is important because a company's operating performance is evaluated on this basis.

The Jones & Smith operating statement is an example of a *multistep* statement. This is the form of statement that marketing personnel within a company would use to analyze the company's performance. Another type of operating statement, the *single-step* statement, arrives at net profit before taxes in one step: expenses are subtracted from net sales; no other information is provided. Companies use the single-step form in their reports to stockholders or in other public documents.

Analytical Ratios

In addition to showing a company's net sales and net profit, the operating statement provides data for figuring important *analytical ratios,* or performance ratios. These ratios enable marketers to evaluate their com-

Table B.2
Analytical Ratios Commonly Used in Marketing

Ratio	Formula
Gross Margin Ratio (Percentage)	$\frac{\text{Gross Margin}}{\text{Net Sales}} = \text{Gross Margin \%}$
Operating Expense Ratio (Percentage)	$\frac{\text{Total Operating Expenses}}{\text{Net Sales}} = \text{Expense \%}$
Net Profit Ratio (Percentage)	$\frac{\text{Net Income before Taxes}}{\text{Net Sales}} = \text{Net Profit \%}$
Stock Turnover Rate (STR) (Based on Cost)	$\frac{\text{Cost of Goods Sold}}{\text{Average Inventory at Cost}} = \text{STR}$
	$\text{Average Inventory} = \frac{\text{Beginning Inventory} + \text{End Inventory}}{2}$
Return on Investment (ROI)	$\frac{\text{Net Profit}}{\text{Net Sales}} \times \frac{\text{Net Sales}}{\text{Investment}} = \text{ROI}$
Markup Percentage (Based on Selling Price)	$\frac{\text{Dollar Markup}}{\text{Selling Price}} = \text{Markup \%}$
Markdown Ratio (Percentage)	$\frac{\text{Markdown} + \text{\$ Allowance}}{\text{Net Sales for Item}} = \text{Markdown \%}$

pany's performance by comparing it with their performance in previous operating periods or with the performances of similar companies in their industry. Dun & Bradstreet, Robert Morris Associates, U.S. Department of Commerce, and various trade associations are sources for these kinds of comparative data.

Operating Ratios

Operating ratios are analytical ratios obtained by dividing each item on the operating statement by the amount of net sales. These ratios are expressed as a percentage of net sales, with net sales as a base of 100 percent. Although an operating ratio can be calculated for each line on the operating statement, the most important and most commonly used operating ratios for marketers are gross margin ratio, operating expense ratio, and net profit ratio. The formulas for calculating these ratios and other marketing ratios are given in Table B.2.

The *gross margin ratio* shows the percentage of net sales dollars available to cover operating expenses and to provide a profit after paying for the cost of goods sold. Using the information from Table B.1, the gross margin ratio for Jones & Smith is calculated as follows:

$$\text{Gross Margin Ratio} = \frac{\text{Gross Margin}}{\text{Net Sales}}$$

or

$$\frac{\$24{,}200}{\$51{,}000} = .475 \text{ or } 47.5\%$$

The higher the gross margin ratio, the more dollars a company has left for expenses and profit.

The *operating expense ratio* indicates the percentage of each net sales dollar needed to cover total operating expenses. If this ratio is high, it means that the company is spending a great deal on salaries, commissions, and advertising. The marketer can then calculate the ratio for each item within the operating expenses section to determine which expenses were too high.

Jones & Smith's operating ratio is figured as follows:

$$\text{Operating Expense Ratio} = \frac{\text{Total Operating Expenses}}{\text{Net Sales}}$$

or

$$\frac{\$18{,}000}{\$51{,}000} = .353 \text{ or } 35.3\%$$

The *net profit ratio* reveals the percentage of each net sales dollar that is left *after* all expenses have been paid, but *before* payment of federal and state income taxes. Some companies, however, figure net profit ratio *after* taxes have been deducted. When comparing the net profit ratios of several similar companies, marketers must know whether the ratios were calculated before or after taxes.

Net profit ratios vary widely from one industry to another. Thus marketers should know the industry average before evaluating their company's net profit ratio. For example, a 1 percent net profit ratio is average in the supermarket industry but low in the retail clothing industry.

Jones & Smith's net profit ratio is figured as follows:

$$\text{Net Profit Ratio} = \frac{\text{Net Income before Taxes}}{\text{Net Sales}}$$

or

$$\frac{\$\ 6{,}200}{\$51{,}000} = .122 \text{ or } 12.2\%$$

Question 1 If a company had net sales of $110,000, gross sales of $112,000, gross margin of $55,800, and expenses of $43,000, what would the gross margin ratio, expense ratio, and net profit ratio be?

Stock Turnover Rate

Another kind of analytical ratio that helps measure a company's performance is the *stock turnover rate*. This is the number of times that a company's average inventory is sold, or turns over, during a specified period of time—usually a year. Average inventory can be figured by adding beginning and ending inventories, then dividing by 2.

$$\text{Average Inventory} = \frac{\text{Beginning Inventory} + \text{Ending Inventory}}{2}$$

Stock turnover rate can be computed in three different ways, depending on the kind of figures available. The formulas for computing stock turnover rate are:

$$\text{Stock Turnover Rate} = \frac{\text{Cost of Goods Sold}}{\text{Average Inventory at Cost}}$$

$$\text{Stock Turnover Rate} = \frac{\text{Net Sales}}{\text{Average Inventory at Selling Price}}$$

$$\text{Stock Turnover Rate} = \frac{\text{Sales in Units}}{\text{Average Inventory in Units}}$$

The most commonly used formula is based on cost of goods sold because all the data are easily available on the operating statement. By using the first formula and information from Jones & Smith's operating statement, the stock turnover rate is calculated as follows:

$$\text{Average Inventory at Cost} = \frac{\$10{,}000 + \$8{,}000}{2} = \$9{,}000$$

$$\text{Stock Turnover Rate} = \frac{\$26{,}800}{\$\ 9{,}000} = 2.98$$

This means that Jones and Smith's inventory turned over 2.98 times during the year.

Average stock turnover rates, like net profit ratios, also vary from one industry to another and from one department to another in the same company. For example, the turnover rate of a grocery store should be much higher than the turnover rate of a furniture store. Within the grocery store, the meat department should have a much higher turnover rate than the canned goods department.

Usually, a high stock turnover rate shows that a company's management is efficient and is turning a profit. However, if the stock turnover rate is too high, it might mean that a company is maintaining too low an average inventory. A reduced stock turnover rate from one year to the next shows that a company is carrying some unpopular items in its inventory. Thus the stock turnover rate is an important figure for evaluating a company's performance.

Question 2 Compute the stock turnover rate for a company whose cost of goods sold was $54,200, with beginning inventory of $26,000 and ending inventory of $24,000.

Return on Investment

Return on investment (ROI) is an analytical ratio that compares a company's profits with the amount of investment the company needs to make or sell a product. *Investment* is a company's total assets, such as land, factory or store, equipment, and inventory minus the firm's liabilities. The ROI shows how well a company has used its assets to generate sales and make a profit. Thus it is an important ratio for marketers.

To figure a company's ROI, a marketer needs both the balance sheet and the operating statement. The amount of investment is obtained from the company's balance sheet. The operating statement provides the net sales and net profit before taxes figures. The formula for calculating ROI follows:

$$\text{ROI} = \frac{\text{Net Profit}}{\text{Net Sales}} \times \frac{\text{Net Sales}}{\text{Investment}}$$

If Jones & Smith's balance sheet for December 31, 1983, showed \$30,000 for total investment, the ROI would be figured in this way:

$$\text{ROI} = \frac{\$6{,}200}{\$51{,}000} \times \frac{\$51{,}000}{\$30{,}000}$$

$$= .1215 \times 1.7 = .2066 \text{ or } 20.66\%$$

Question 3 By using this formula a company can determine how to increase its ROI either by increasing its net profit or decreasing its investment. If Jones & Smith increased sales to \$75,000, how would the ROI be affected? This would happen no matter how much sales were increased. Now figure Jones & Smith's ROI, with sales of \$75,000 and investment reduced to \$25,000. Then figure Jones & Smith's ROI using the original figures, but increasing the net profit to \$10,000.

Pricing

Another major area of marketing arithmetic involves pricing. Marketers should know how to calculate selling prices using the formulas for markups and markdowns. Both markups and markdowns are expressed as percentages.

Markups

A *markup* is the dollar amount added to the cost of goods to determine the selling price. Markup is closely related to gross margin because both are expected to cover operating expenses and net profit. Markups can be figured as either a percentage of cost or as a percentage of selling price:

$$\begin{array}{c}\text{Markup Percentage}\\ \text{Based on Cost}\end{array} = \frac{\text{Dollar Markup (Amount Added to Cost)}}{\text{Cost}}$$

$$\begin{array}{c}\text{Markup Percentage}\\ \text{Based on Selling Price}\end{array} = \frac{\text{Dollar Markup (Amount Added to Cost)}}{\text{Selling Price}}$$

If Jones & Smith bought ties at a cost of \$6 a piece and set a selling price of \$10 for them, the markup would be \$4. The markup percentage could be figured in these two ways:

$$\text{Markup Percentage Based on Cost} = \frac{\$4.00}{\$6.00} = 66.67\%$$

$$\text{Markup Percentage Based on Selling Price} = \frac{\$4.00}{\$10.00} = 40\%$$

Although the *dollar* markup used in both formulas is the same, the *percentages* of markup differed because one formula was based on cost and the other formula was based on selling price.

For marketers to make valid comparisons between markups on identical items from one store to another, they must know what the markup percentage was based on. For this reason, *markup percentages are usually stated as percentage of selling price*—unless indicated otherwise.

Suppose Jones & Smith bought suits at $90 a piece and knew that their usual markup based on selling price is 40 percent. The selling price could be determined by using the following formula:

$$\text{Selling Price} = \frac{\text{Cost in Dollars}}{100\% - \text{Markup Percentage Based on Selling Price}}$$

or

$$\text{Selling Price} = \frac{\$90.00}{100\% - 40\%} = \frac{\$90.00}{60\%} = \$150.00$$

Sometimes marketers wish to convert the markup percentage from one base—cost or selling price—to the other. This can be done by using one of the following formulas:

$$\text{Markup Percentage Based on Cost} = \frac{\text{Markup Percentage Based on Selling Price}}{100\% - \text{Markup Percentage Based on Selling Price}}$$

$$\text{Markup Percentage Based on Selling Price} = \frac{\text{Markup Percentage Based on Cost}}{100\% + \text{Markup Percentage Based on Cost}}$$

If Jones & Smith had calculated only one markup percentage for the ties, they could convert that markup percentage in one of the following ways:

$$\text{Markup Percentage Based on Cost} = \frac{40\%}{100\% - 40\%}$$

$$= \frac{40\%}{60\%} = 66.67\%$$

$$\text{Markup Percentage Based on Selling Price} = \frac{66.67\%}{100\% + 66.67\%}$$

$$= \frac{66.67\%}{166.67\%} = 40\%$$

Most marketers, however, have tables to convert one markup percentage to another.

Markup percentages are sometimes affected by the stock turnover rate of particular items. For example, high turnover rates for fresh food items in a supermarket mean a lower markup percentage, but lower turnover rates for cosmetics in the same supermarket mean a higher markup percentage.

Markdowns

When customers will not buy an item at its original selling price, the marketer must *mark down,* or reduce the selling price. Markdowns may be made for soiled or damaged goods, for end-of-season clearances, or for a special sales promotion. Often, however, markdowns are made because the store's buyer bought items that required too high a markup. For this reason, the markdown ratio is an important measure of a company's operating efficiency.

Markdowns and sales allowances are similar because in both instances an item's price is reduced. To compute a markdown ratio, the dollar amount of markdown is added to the dollar amount of allowances, and then divided by net sales for that item only. The markdown formula is as follows:

$$\text{Markdown Percentage} = \frac{\text{Dollar Markdown} + \text{Dollar Allowances}}{\text{Net Dollar Sales per Item}}$$

If Jones & Smith priced ten suits at $150 each, sold four suits at the original selling price, marked down the remaining six suits to $110 and sold four of them, and gave an allowance of $15 on one of the originally priced suits, the markdown ratio would be computed as follows:

$$\text{Markdown Percentage} = \frac{(\$40.00 \text{ Markdown} \times 6 \text{ Suits}) + \$15.00 \text{ Allowances}}{(\$150.00 \times 4 \text{ Suits}) + (\$110.00 \times 4 \text{ Suits})}$$

$$= \frac{\$240.00 \text{ Markdown} + \$15.00 \text{ Allowances}}{\$300.00 + \$440.00}$$

$$= \frac{\$255.00}{\$740.00} = 34.46\%$$

Thus the markdown ratio included all ten suits—the four that sold at the original selling price, the four that sold at the markdown price, and the two that remained unsold. The total markdown ratio was 34.46%.

Summary

Effective marketers should be able to analyze their company's operating statements and balance sheets in order to make sound marketing decisions. By computing analytical ratios based on data from the operating statement, marketers are able to measure their company's performance in relation to industry averages.

The stock turnover rate tells marketers whether or not management is efficiently turning a profit. By calculating the return on investment (ROI) ratio, marketers can measure how well their company has used its assets to generate sales and to make a profit. Determining markup and markdown percentages is also a task for the marketer.

Answers to Appendix Questions

Question 1

$$\text{Gross Margin Ratio} = \frac{\$55{,}800}{\$110{,}000} = 50.7\%$$

$$\text{Expense Ratio} = \frac{\$43{,}000}{\$110{,}000} = 39.1\%$$

$$\text{Net Profit Ratio} = \frac{\$12{,}800}{\$110{,}000} = 11.6\%$$

Question 2

$$\text{Average Inventory at Cost} = \frac{\$26{,}000 + \$24{,}000}{2} = \frac{\$50{,}000}{2} = \$25{,}000$$

$$\text{Stock Turnover Rate} = \frac{\$54{,}200}{\$25{,}000} = 2.168$$

Question 3

ROI with sales increased to $75,000:

$$\text{ROI} = \frac{\$\ 6{,}200}{\$75{,}000} \times \frac{\$75{,}000}{\$30{,}000} = .0826 \times 2.5 = .2065 \text{ or } 20.65\%$$

ROI with investment reduced to $25,000:

$$\text{ROI} = \frac{\$\ 6{,}200}{\$75{,}000} \times \frac{\$75{,}000}{\$25{,}000} = .0826 \times 3 = .2478 \text{ or } 24.78\%$$

ROI with net profit increased to $10,000, sales of $51,000, and investment of $30,000:

$$\text{ROI} = \frac{\$10{,}000}{\$51{,}000} \times \frac{\$51{,}000}{\$30{,}000} = .1960 \times 1.7 = .3332 \text{ or } 33.32\%$$

Appendix C Marketing for Small Businesses

Studies of marketing often cite the strategies of large corporations as examples. Product positioning at firms such as General Motors, Anheuser Busch, and IBM illustrates marketing strategy. Professional marketing research departments are often described as an essential part of the corporate staff while research and development of new products is viewed as an on-going process.

Although the activities of large corporations serve as excellent examples, students should realize that proper marketing is essential for small businesses as well as large ones. This section is provided to illustrate the contribution of small business to the United States marketing environment and to provide an example of the marketing activities of one small firm.[1]

Small businesses provide many benefits to the marketing environment that typically go unnoticed by the general public. Over 500,000 new businesses are started each year, each attempting to provide consumers with a new product, better service, or a more convenient location. Occasionally, completely new industries have germinated through the efforts of entrepreneurs like Steven Jobs, who invented the personal computer. New products such as Softsoap and herbal, decaffeinated tea were developed by individuals who acted upon their ideas.

Small businesses often provide goods and services to markets the large corporations consider too small. For example, one entrepreneur developed and marketed K-9 Cola, a nutritious soft drink for dogs. Al-

This appendix was written by Professor Peggy Lambing of the University of Missouri — St. Louis.

though the product may have a sales potential sufficient to provide the entrepreneur with an excellent income, large pet food manufacturers such as Ralston Purina may consider the market too small to be of interest.

Small businesses also provide goods and services to large corporations. For example, General Motors purchases goods and services from over 30,000 small businesses. Similarly, large aircraft manufacturers such as McDonnell Douglas, Boeing, and Lockheed subcontract with thousands of small machine shops to provide them with necessary products and services.

Small businesses, then, contribute much to the marketing environment, but they face many problems that large corporations do not. Small businesses often have very limited financial and human resources. They must compete effectively without adequate funds to complete research projects or run a sufficient amount of advertising. The entrepreneur is often the marketing manager, as well as the manager of personnel, finance, and production. The entrepreneur is often not prepared for this overwhelming burden; while good decisions bring rewards, bad decisions can be catastrophic.

The following case provides an example of one entrepreneur's new business and her marketing strategies. As with most successful small businesses, she fills a niche in the market that large business have neglected. Her customers appreciate her quality products and service, and therefore return to her shop to make their purchases.

The K & K Aquarium and Pet Center: A Case Study

Company History

As Kathy Fessler walked around her shop, she gently stroked a snake that coiled around her arm. The snake contentedly rested its head near Kathy's wrist, seemingly unaware of the activity around it. Kathy explained that although someone had expressed interest in purchasing the snake, she had become so attached to it she may no longer have wanted to sell it.

For Kathy Fessler, whose home is also home to horses, dogs, rabbits, cats, and a variety of other animals, owning a pet shop is a natural extension of daily activities. Her pet shop developed from her hobby of breeding tropical fish, which she began approximately six years ago. As a member of the Missouri Aquarium Society, she won several awards for the quality and color of her fish. Eventually, she had 27 tanks in her basement and spent all day each Saturday cleaning them. As the fish multiplied, she began to sell the offspring to local pet shops, using the income to offset the cost of her expanding hobby. In 1984, Kathy and her twin sister Karen started K & K Aquarium Maintenance, selling and maintaining aquariums in offices and private homes.

Although the business grew and prospered, K & K found its sales limited because the maintenance service was operated out of their homes and offered no opportunity to display aquariums. For the business to grow, a retail outlet seemed essential. In January 1986, Kathy and Karen opened K & K Aquariums and Pet Center, a retail outlet in Fenton, Missouri. Although the business is legally a partnership, Karen is not actively involved in the management of the store.

The company mission of K & K Aquariums and Pets, as described by Kathy, is to help people enjoy their pets. This is accomplished by providing people with the healthiest pets possible and teaching the customers about proper care for the animals. Kathy's philosophy is that a sale is not as important as insuring correct pet care. In keeping with this philosophy, employees are instructed not to rush customers, not to sell unnecessary products, and to provide customers with complete instructions.

Products and Services

The company now consists of both a retail outlet and the maintenance service. The retail outlet sells a variety of pets including cats, birds, tropical fish, hamsters, guinea pigs, snakes, and iguanas. Pet supplies are also available, as are books on the proper care of specific animals. The outlet sells many name-brand products including Tetra fish products, Science Diet dog and cat food, and Victory Veterinary Formula flea products. Kathy purchases both name-brand and less well-known products for her inventory, as long as the products meet her high standards of quality. A 48-hour guarantee is offered on all animals, and customer satisfaction is guaranteed on all purchases. However, few customers return products or animals. The time spent with customers prior to the purchase often helps to insure that they make the correct purchase.

A layaway plan is also available to allow customers to finance major purchases. This plan is often used by customers purchasing animals for gifts since it can be timed to have the purchase paid off immediately before the gift is needed. This insures that the customer's choice of a specific animal will not be sold to anyone else and that the animal will receive proper care until the customer wishes to pick it up.

The aquarium maintenance service provided by K & K includes cleaning and general tank maintenance, emergency visits for sick fish, and moving and setting up tanks for people who relocate within the metropolitan area. General tank maintenance consists of two visits per month to each customer during which the water is changed, purified, and checked for the proper pH level. The fish are checked for diseases and any necessary medication is administered. All equipment such as filters, air stones, and so forth are checked and replaced if they are not functioning properly.

Customer Groups

The store serves a wide variety of customers of all ages, but they do fall into several general categories. Customers for the retail outlet include families, hobbyists, and gift purchasers. The constant stream of parents and small children into the store is one indication that families are a major customer group for K & K.

Hobbyists also are a major group of customers. K & K offers a 15 percent discount to members of animal and fish clubs, such as the Missouri Aquarium Society, in an attempt to promote better animal health care and awareness of the pet industry. Many hobbyists purchase animals and supplies at K & K because of the high quality of the products and expert advice.

Gift purchasers also represent a customer group. Birthdays, anniversaries, Christmas, and Mother's day are a few of the special occasions for which purchases are made. Many gift certificates are also purchased by customers who are unsure of making correct choices.

Families, hobbyists, and gift purchasers are also customer groups of the aquarium maintenance service. Many families and hobbyists enjoy owning tropical fish but do not wish (or lack the time) to maintain the aquariums. K & K will visit the customers' homes to provide the necessary service. An aquarium maintenance contract can also be purchased as a gift, if desired.

The maintenance service has one additional customer group. Organizations and businesses often purchase aquariums and maintenance contracts for offices, retail outlets, and so forth. The aquariums are displayed to provide a diversion for customers who must wait for service. An accounting firm that had an aquarium maintained by K & K found that customers are more relaxed and don't mind waiting if they can watch the fish in the aquarium. Similarly, a retail outlet found that the aquarium makes children calmer and more patient while their parents are shopping. The maintenance service is also available to these firms so that the care of the fish does not become burdensome.

Competition

K & K's competition for the maintenance service comes primarily from two companies, Tanks A Lot and Aquarium Maintenance of St. Louis. Although several other firms provide similar services, Kathy believes they are not strong competition. K & K's competitive advantage consists of two factors. For the first, K & K will clean any size tank, at a price based on the number of gallons. Many competing firms do not want to clean smaller tanks because it is more cost effective to clean larger ones.

K & K's second competitive advantage is its use of a diatom, a piece of equipment for cleaning the tanks. Although a tank can be cleaned in other ways, the diatom results in a noticeable improvement immediately. Kathy believes that the use of a diatom convinces the customer that the tank is well cared for and therefore helps maintain customer satisfaction.

The competition for retail sales consists primarily of the Fenton Pet Shop, located approximately 2.5 miles from Kathy's outlet, and the Walmart store, located 2 miles away. Although Walmart sells fish and birds at lower prices than K & K, Kathy does not try to compete on price. K & K's competitive advantage over Walmart comes from quality products, total pet care, and as much help and instruction as needed. Many customers come to Kathy's shop to purchase an animal after they have visited Walmart and decided they want more instructions, better quality pets, and continued support after the purchase. K & K's competitive advantage over the Fenton Pet Shop is location. Traffic in the Fenton shopping district where Fenton Pet Shop is located is congested, and residents often seek more accessible stores.

Environmental Factors

Numerous environmental factors affect the operation of a pet shop. These factors include both legal considerations and technological changes.

Many federal, state, and local legal restrictions have been established to insure the proper care of animals. For example, K & K does not sell dogs because local zoning laws require special enclosures and ventilation. Because these additional fixtures would have resulted in much higher startup costs, Kathy decided not to sell dogs.

For similar reasons, K & K does not sell turtles. Turtles cannot be sold unless they meet specific size requirements. Also, turtles may carry salmonella bacteria that could be transmitted to a person, and a pet owner shop could be held liable if this should occur. Kathy is concerned that a child might not wash carefully after handling a pet turtle and might contract the salmonella bacteria. Because the bacteria could result in the illness or death of a child, Kathy has decided not to carry turtles.

The state of Missouri also has laws regulating the sale of any wildlife of the state. To sell animals such as crayfish, snakes, birds, and fish that live naturally within the state, a retail outlet must have a bill of sale from a licensed dealer. This prevents a pet shop owner from selling an animal taken from its natural habitat.

Technological changes have also helped to improve the care of pets. In the tropical fish industry, better filters, tank cleaning tubes, and water testing kits have improved the care and breeding of fish. Because of research on cats, dogs, and a variety of other animals, better flea-control products and more nutritious foods have been developed. Research, technology, and law interact to improve the pet industry and insure the highest standards of quality. The pet shop owner must be aware of all of the factors and constantly monitor the changes that occur.

Suppliers

K & K uses many suppliers in an effort to obtain quality animals at reasonable prices. Suppliers for tropical fish include Beltz Aquarium, a large wholesaler in St. Louis County, and Fritz's, located in St. Charles, Missouri. Kathy prefers to pick up inventory from these wholesalers because, although both of these wholesalers will deliver, they offer a 10 percent discount if delivery is not requested.

K & K has also started ordering from Eastside Hatchery in Caseyville, Illinois. Kathy believes Eastside offers better prices and delivery while also providing larger, higher-quality fish. The owner of Eastside Hatchery will replace any of his fish lost because of diseases or other factors, while Beltz and Fritz's give only a 48-hour guarantee. Kathy believes Eastside gives better service because it is a smaller business and Kathy's account is important to the company.

K & K uses local private breeders to supply many of the other animals such as hamsters, guinea pigs, and parakeets. Use of local suppliers eliminates the need to ship animals long distances. This is important because the stress of shipment results in a high loss rate. Many of the local breeders can also provide very high quality animals. For example, one breeder who raises parakeets for shows sells K & K the birds that do not meet show quality. Although many birds do not meet show quality standards, they are still excellent birds. Customers of K & K have become aware of these birds and are willing to wait to get one. Proof of customer loyalty became evident when the supplier went out of town for a short time, and K & K sold all of its parakeets. By the time the supplier came back in town, K & K had a waiting list of customers.

K & K also has established a working relationship with Bentley Animal Hospital, located near K & K. When medical supplies or advice is needed, Kathy calls the veterinarians at Bentley. Similarly, if a customer comes to the shop to purchase supplies for a sick animal, Kathy will call Bentley (or refer the customer to them) for a serious problem.

Company Strengths

Location

K & K is located in Fenton, Missouri, a rapidly growing suburb in St. Louis County. The municipality is a community of approximately 2,800 people and 500 businesses, however the unincorporated area around the municipality includes many other residents and businesses. Fenton includes densely populated residential areas, as well a a few farms and industrial parks. The area has many middle income families with young children, one of the major target markets of K & K.

K & K Aquarium and Pet Center was one of the first businesses to open in Brookwood Center, a new neighborhood shopping center in a heavily residential area. The shopping center is located at the corner of Highway 141 and Bowles Avenue, one of the busiest intersections in Fenton. Highway 141, the main road leading to Interstate 44, has a daily traffic count of 19,410. Bowles Avenue, which also serves as a thoroughfare to the Interstate, has a daily traffic count of 13,240. Bowles Avenue was recently widened to handle the increasing traffic volume, and there are plans to widen Highway 141. Many new shopping centers are planned for the surrounding area to help meet the needs of the increasing population.

Before deciding on Brookwood Center, Kathy and Karen looked at many other sites, many with lower rental costs. However, they chose Brookwood Center because of the high traffic counts and good accessibility. They leased a 1,800-square foot space at the third storefront from the end of the shopping center. They chose this space because it is near Highway 141 and has excellent visibility. Although they would have preferred the storefront at the very end (because it has even better visibility), it had already been leased by a video tape rental store. Kathy is pleased with her location and believes that the continued growth of the area will be a definite advantage for her store.

Knowledge and Reputation

Kathy's knowledge of pet care and the store's reputation for quality products and complete service are the primary intangible resources for the firm. Kathy's willingness to take as much time as necessary with each customer has helped to establish the reputation of caring, not just selling.

Kathy's contacts with others in the industry also have helped to establish a network for exchanging information. Her membership in the Missouri Aquarium Society, friendly relationships with competitors, and a referral system with Bentley Animal Hospital all serve to increase her knowledge of the industry and her awareness of the changes that are occurring.

The store's reputation for high-quality products and knowledgeable service is also a major intangible strength of the company. Many customers visit the store because they were referred by another satisfied customer. This reputation is one of the factors that helps differentiate K & K from its competitors.

Long-Term Goals

One of Kathy's goals for her store is to increase the products and services offered. She hopes eventually to carry more salt water fish, and to add puppies to her product line. She would also like to offer a dog grooming service to help generate revenue during the summer months when aquarium sales generally decline. She has considered expanding into the storefront next to hers (if the current tenant moves) in order to accomplish these goals.

Eventually, Kathy hopes to own more than one shop. This would give her more buying power with suppliers and help increase her profit margin. She also believes that this would help her to get the best advertising for her money, because with several outlets radio advertising would be cost-effective.

Short-Term Goals

Kathy's more immediate goals are to expand the number of customers for the aquarium maintenance service, to increase productivity in the store so that sales per employee increase, and to try to obtain the greatest effectiveness for the advertising dollars that she spends. These goals will help increase revenue and profit and lead to future expansion.

As with many small business owners, Kathy is knowledgeable about the industry, but has no formal business background. Therefore, one of her short-term goals is to learn more about all aspects of business management. Kathy believes that more knowledge of business management will also help to increase the productivity and profits of the store.

K&K AQUARIUMS

914 BROOKWOOD CENTER FENTON, MO.
(At Bowles & 141)
343-0620

48 HR. GUARANTEE ON ALL BIRDS, FISH REPTILES & CRITTERS

K&K AQUARIUM COUPON

FREE 1 LB. BULK FOOD

NO PURCHASE NECESSARY!
(Offer Good With This Coupon Only)

- HAMPSTER
- GERBIL
- RABBIT
- GUINEA PIG
- CANARY
- COCKATIEL
- PARAKEET
- PARROT
- DOVE
- FINCH

GOOD THRU APRIL 19, 1986

K&K COUPON
TANK MAINTENANCE
2 FREE MONTHS
WITH PURCHASE OF 55 GAL. AQUARIUM OR LARGER AND 6 MO. CONTRACT. Offer Good With This Coupon Only.
EXPIRES APR. 24,'86

K&K COUPON
15% Off
All Fish
FOOD
WITH THIS COUPON
EXP. APR. 24,'86

We Now Have
LARGE
GOLDFISH
FOR
YOUR
POND!

3 STEP FLEA & TICK CONTROL SYSTEM

$5.00 CASH REFUND

(When you buy one Victory 5™ or Victory® Flea & Tick collar and any two Victory Veterinary Formula™ or Victory® Products.)

VICTORY 5™
FLEA & TICK COLLARS
Kills Fleas & Ticks
Up To 5 Months!
(Contains Sendran)

VICTORY VETERINARY FORMULA™
FLEA & TICK KILLER SHAMPOO FOR DOGS.
Contains 1/3 more Pyrethrins than most regular flea and tick shampoos!

VICTORY VETERINARY FORMULA™
FLEA & TICK KILLER DIP FOR DOGS
Kills Fleas Up To 28 Days!
Kills Ticks Up To 21 Days!

K&K AQUARIUMS

914 BROOKWOOD CENTER FENTON, MO.
(At Bowles & 141)
343-0620

48 HR. GUARANTEE ON ALL BIRDS, FISH REPTILES & CRITTERS

25% OFF
ALL FROZEN FISH FOOD IN STOCK
WHILE SUPPLIES LAST

FERRETS
REG. $69.99
SALE
$55.99

WE NOW HAVE SALTWATER FISH

WE NOW CARRY
HILL'S SCIENCE DIET.
DOG & CAT FOOD

DOVES
REG. $9.99
SALE $7.99

AQUARIUMS

ILLUSTRATION ONLY

30 Gal. Black
Reg. $54.67
Now $46.47

30 Gal. Woodgrain
Reg. $57.45
Now $48.83

OFFER EXPIRES 6-2-86

AQUARIUM MAINTENANCE PROGRAM

DO YOU WANT AN AQUARIUM IN YOUR OFFICE BUT DON'T HAVE THE TIME TO CLEAN IT? LET US CLEAN IT FOR YOU! ASK ABOUT OUR AQUARIUM MAINTENANCE PROGRAM. WE SET UP & MAINTAIN AQUARIUMS IN OFFICES. ALL YOU DO IS FEED THE FISH AND ENJOY YOUR AQUARIUM.

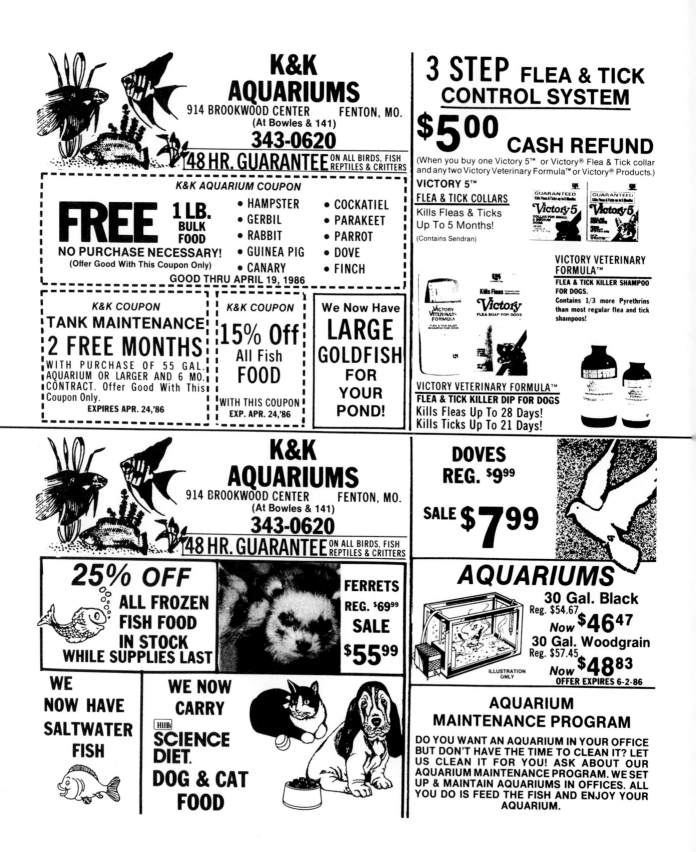

Promotion

K & K has no specific advertising budget, although Kathy believes one should be developed. Most advertising runs in local publications that are distributed free of charge to consumers. These publications include two TV program guides, *The TV Weekly* and *TV Fanfare,* both distributed free at the local supermarkets. *TV Fanfare* is a small weekly publication with a distribution of 500 per month. Advertising rates are affordable, with a front cover ad costing only $20. *The TV Weekly* has a distribution of 22,000 per week. Advertising rates range from one-eighth of a page at $42 per week to a full page for $150 per week. Another publication that K & K uses periodically is *The Green Apple,* which is mailed to homes in the Fenton area. *The Green Apple* is primarily an advertising circular. It provides coupons and promotional information from local businesses to 112,000 homes. Advertising rates vary with the placement and frequency of the ad, however an average cost for a 3 by 5 inch ad is $70.

Of all of these advertising methods, Kathy prefers *The TV Weekly,* not only because of its good response rate, but also because the staff at *The TV Weekly* provides assistance in ad design. Often if Kathy has an idea for a specific type of promotion, she can just explain the idea and the employees at *The TV Weekly* then design an effective ad. Kathy is very pleased with the publication's use of eye-catching phrases and pictures, which help to improve the ad's effectiveness. For Kathy, who must handle so many other responsibilities, this assistance with advertising is invaluable.

Ads run all year long, even though the business is very seasonal. Kathy uses advertising to capitalize on the peak season and offset slow periods. The busiest months come in winter when people spend more time inside and have time to devote to their hobbies. In the summer months, when sales usually decline, Kathy uses promotional efforts to generate customer traffic. This helps to maintain a more consistent monthly volume.

K & K often runs institutional advertising to publicize the company, the product lines available, and the quality image of the store. These ads feature the company name along with the brand name products and the discounts offered to members of animal and fish clubs. These ads are designed to appeal to customers, often hobbyists, looking for a high-quality store.

K & K also runs sale ads and product ads to appeal to the families in the area. These ads may feature a specific animal, such as a "Snake Sale," or a "Ferret Sale," or they may announce discounts or "buy one, get one free" specials.

All ads give the company name, location, and phone number. Many ads list the store hours, product guarantee policy, and the availability of the lay-a-way payment plan. (Figure C.1 provides an example of two K & K ads.)

Figure C.1
Ads Promoting the K & K Aquarium and Pet Center

One of the best forms of advertising for K & K is generated by the store's reputation for quality and service. Referrals from previous customers are a major source of promotion. This not only helps to generate business from local residents but also brings customers from other areas. It is not uncommon for out-of-state customers to come to the shop when they are visiting relatives in Fenton merely because it was highly recommended by a family member.

As with many business owners, though, Kathy is baffled by consumer behavior. An ad run at two different times often generates an excellent response one time and almost no response the next. In addition, customer response is often delayed, making measurement more difficult. Kathy once ran a snake special that generated no immediate customers. Three weeks after the ad ran, however, many customers came in to buy snakes. For a small business owner with no access to formal market research, this type of consumer behavior can be frustrating.

Current advertising is designed primarily for families, hobbyists, and gift purchasers. Advertising and promotion will be developed in the future to create more awareness among the organizational customer group. This promotion will include direct mail literature about aquariums and the maintenance service as well as direct sales calls by K & K staff members. Kathy believes that this major promotional effort to companies should only be undertaken after personnel are completely trained and knowledgeable and have developed sales skills. Only then can a highly professional, quality image be conveyed to other businesses.

Conclusion

Like all small business owners, Kathy faces many challenges in trying to operate her store. It is not easy for Kathy to find employees who know enough about pet care and meet her standards of quality. In addition, the need for Kathy to be a jack-of-all-trades and manage many different factors is sometimes overwhelming. However, Kathy sees many opportunities for growth and is optimistic about the future of the pet industry in general and her business in particular.

Questions

1. What are the major factors contributing to K & K's success?
2. For a small business like K & K that lacks a marketing research department, what is the best way to develop effective advertising?
3. K & K currently has no specific advertising budget. Why should one be developed?
4. In addition to developing a budget, what additional planning should be done concerning promotional efforts?

Notes

Chapter 1

[1]Peter Drucker, *The Practice of Management* (New York: Harper & Row, 1954), p. 38.

[2]LeRoy C. Blake, " 'Marketing': What's in a Name?" *Industrial Marketing,* March 1983, p. 110.

[3]"AMA Board Approves New Marketing Definition," *Marketing News,* March 1, 1985, p. 1.

[4]William J. Winston, "Topic: Internal Marketing—Key to a Successful Professional Service Marketing Program," *Journal of Professional Services Marketing* 1 (Fall 1985/Winter 1985–1986): 16.

[5]Economic Indicators, January 1987 (Washington, D.C.: U.S. Government Printing Office, 1987).

[6]Philip Kotler, "A Generic Concept of Marketing," *Journal of Marketing* (April 1972): 48.

[7]Explanation adapted from Richard P. Bagozzi, "Marketing as Exchange," *Journal of Marketing* (October 1974): 77–81.

[8]Louis E. Boone and David L. Kurtz, *Contemporary Business,* 5th ed. (Hinsdale, Ill.: The Dryden Press, 1987), p. 332.

[9]The classic study of how marketing benefited the toy industry is Robert Steiner, "Economic Theory and the Idea of Marketing Productivity" (Working Paper, Marketing Science Institute, Cambridge, Mass., December 1974).

[10]This list of marketing functions is similar to one proposed by Edmund McGarry, "Some Functions of Marketing Reconsidered," in *Theory of Marketing,* edited by Reavis Cox and Wroe Anderson (Homewood, Ill.: Irwin, 1950), pp. 269–273.

[11]The history of changing business philosophies is traced in Richard R. Weeks and William J. Marks, "The Marketing Concept in Historical Perspective," *Business and Society,* Spring 1969, pp. 24–32.

[12]The evolution of The Pillsbury Company's business philosophy is traced by Robert J. Keith, "The Marketing Revolution," *Journal of Marketing* (January 1960): 35–38.

[13]Louis E. Boone and David L. Kurtz, *Contemporary Marketing,* 5th ed. (Hinsdale, Ill.: The Dryden Press, 1986), p. 12.

[14]Eric N. Berkowitz, Roger A. Kerin, and William Rudelius, *Marketing* (St. Louis, Mo.: Times Mirror/Mosby College Publishing, 1986), p. 17.

[15]Marvin Bower, "The Role of Marketing in Management," in *Handbook of Modern Marketing,* edited by Victor Buell (New York: McGraw-Hill, 1970), pp. 1–7.

[16]LeRoy C. Blake, " 'Marketing': What's in a Name?"

[17]Jerome McCarthy, *Basic Marketing: A Managerial Approach,* 5th ed. (Homewood, Ill.: Irwin, 1975), p. 75.

[18]This and other studies on brand loyalty are cited in Thomas Exter, "Looking for Brand Loyalty," *American Demographics* (April 1986): 32–33, 52–56.

[19]Frederick E. Webster, Jr., "Top Management's Concerns about Marketing: Issues for the 1980s," *Journal of Marketing* (Summer 1981): 15.

[20]Eric N. Berkowitz et al., *Marketing,* p. 83.

[21]Peter F. Drucker, *Management: Tasks, Responsibilities, Practices* (New York: Harper & Row, 1973), p. 64.

[22]"The Soda Wars: Citrus Takes on Caffeine," *Newsweek,* September 15, 1986.

[23]Franklin S. Houston, "The Marketing Concept: What It Is and What It Is Not," *Journal of Marketing* 50 (April 1986): 82.

[24]Ibid., pp. 81–87.

[25]Roger C. Bennett and Robert G. Cooper, "The Misuse of Marketing: An American Tragedy," *Business Horizons,* November–December 1981, p. 52.

[26]LeRoy C. Blake, " 'Marketing': What's in a Name?"

[27]"Japan vs. America: Same Goal, Different Tactics," *Sales and Marketing Management,* October 1986.

[28]See Philip Kotler, *Marketing Management: Analysis, Planning, and Control,* 5th ed. (Englewood Cliffs, N.J.: Prentice-Hall, 1984), p. 29; and Andrew Takas, "Societal Marketing: A Businessman's Perspective," *Journal of Marketing* (October 1974): 2–7.

[29]Jerry W. Anderson, Jr., "Social Responsibility and the Corporation," *Business Horizons,* July–August 1986.

Chapter 2

[1]William M. Bell, "Marketing—More than Selling," in 1974 *Combined Proceedings of the American Marketing Association,* edited by Ronald C. Curhan (New York: AMA, 1975), p. 527.

[2]See O. C. Ferrell and William M. Pride, *Fundamentals of Marketing* (Boston: Houghton Mifflin, 1982), pp. 401–403.

[3]Yoplait examples are based on information from Andrew C. Brown, "The Many Uses of Hot Air," *Fortune,* January 12, 1981, p. 106; Beatrice Trum Hunter, "Yogurt," *Consumers' Research Magazine,* January 1980, pp. 30–32; and *Progressive Grocer,* June 1983, pp. 39–40.

[4]These differences are discussed in greater detail in Kenneth R. Davis, *Marketing Management,* 5th ed. (New York: Wiley, 1985).

[5]The problem of defining company mission too narrowly is discussed by Theodore Levitt, "Marketing Myopia," in *Modern Marketing Strategy,* edited by Edward C. Bursk and John F. Chapman (Cambridge, Mass.: Harvard University Press, 1964), pp. 24–48.

[6]See Peter Vanderwicken, "What's Really Wrong at Chrysler?" *Fortune,* May 1975, pp. 176–178ff.

[7]William J. Hampton, "The Next Act at Chrysler," *Business Week,* November 3, 1986, pp. 66–69, 72.

[8]This section borrows heavily from Scott, Warshaw, and Taylor, *Introduction to Marketing Management,* 5th ed. (Homewood, Ill.: Irwin, 1985), pp. 19–38.

[9]Robert Ball, "Volkswagen's Struggle to Restore Its Name," *Fortune,* June 27, 1983, pp. 100–104.

[10]Ann M. Morrison, "The General Mills Brand of Managers," *Fortune,* January 12, 1981, pp. 99–100.

[11]"Airlines in Turmoil," *Business Week,* October 10, 1983, pp. 98–102.

[12]Gay Jervey, "Parker Bros. Puts Its Chips on New Boards," *Advertising Age,* August 22, 1983, pp. 4, 52–53.

[13]See David Snyder, "Fitness Pitch Adds Zip to Quaker Rice Cakes," *Crain's Chicago Business,* July 14, 1986, p. 8.

Chapter 3

[1]For a more in-depth analysis of the market types, see E. Jerome McCarthy and William D. Perreault, Jr., *Essentials of Marketing* (Homewood, Ill.: Irwin, 1985), pp. 100–104.

[2]Louis E. Boone and David L. Kurtz, *Contemporary Business,* 5th ed. (Hinsdale, Ill.: The Dryden Press, 1987), p. 15.

[3]Philip Kotler and Gary Armstrong, *Marketing: An Introduction* (Englewood Cliffs, N.J.: Prentice-Hall, Inc., 1987), p. 295.

[4]Julie Franz and Brian Lowry, "Produce Marketers Take Fresh Approach," *Advertising Age,* October 13, 1986, pp. 4, 92.

[5]NAD/NARB, *A Review and Perspective on Advertising Industry Self-Regulation, 1971–1977* (New York: The National Advertising Review Council, 1978), p. 13.

[6]"The 99th Congress: What Was Left Undone," *Insight,* November 17, 1986, p. 24.

[7]For a more in-depth discussion, see George A. Steiner and John F. Steiner, *Business, Government, and Society* (New York: Random House, 1985), pp. 438–470.

[8]Stephen Koepp, "Pul-eeze! Will Somebody Help Me?" *Time,* February 2, 1987, pp. 48–55.

[9]George A. Steiner and John F. Steiner, *Business, Government, and Society,* pp. 438–470.

[10]"Eyelashes at 20 Paces," *Time,* September 15, 1986, p. 57.

[11]Luthans and Hodgetts, *Social Issues in Business,* pp. 261–263; see also "Taking the Profit out of Pollution," *Business Week,* December 19, 1977, p. 27.

[12]Stephen Goode, "EPA Standards," *Insight,* December 8, 1986, p. 55.

[13]Don McLeod, "Waste Not, Pay Anyway: Most Firms Foot Cleanup Bill," *Insight,* November 17, 1986, pp. 18–19.

[14]See George A. Steiner and John F. Steiner, *Business, Government, and Society,* pp. 212–214.

[15]GE and Whirlpool models for social responsibility are discussed in Lawrence P. Feldman, *Consumer Protection: Problems and Prospects* (New York: West, 1976), pp. 250–251.

[16]Bernice Kanner, "Stale Mallomars and Other Outrages," *New York,* September 5, 1983, pp. 16–20.

[17]C. Jackson Grayson, cited by Judson Gooding, "It's No Easy Trick to Be the Well-Informed Executive," *Fortune,* January 1973, p. 87.

[18]"The Squeeze on the Product Mix," *Business Week,* January 5, 1974, p. 50.

[19]Philip Elmer-DeWitt, "The Wall Comes Tumbling Down," *Time,* February 2, 1987, p. 68; and Bill Howard and William G. Wong, "Compaq Leads the Way to Speed and Compatibility," *PC Magazine,* November 25, 1986, pp. 134–139.

[20]John D. Baxter, "#1 Lead Indicator Is Consumer Spending," *Iron Age,* November 19, 1982, pp. 27–29.

[21]Fabian Linden, "Up the Ladder," *Across the Board,* October 1979, pp. 70–74.

[22]Cheryl Russell and Thomas G. Exter, "America at Mid-Decade," *American Demographics* (January 1986): 22–29.

[23]These and most of the other figures in this section are from Cheryl Russell and Thomas G. Exter, "America at Mid-Decade."

[24]"It's 9 a.m.: Do You Know Where Your Mother Is?" *Sales and Marketing Management,* October 1986, p. 32.

[25]"High Tech Temps in Growing Demand," *High Technology,* February 1987, p. 9.

[26]John W. Wilson, "The Chip Market Goes Haywire," *Business Week,* September 1, 1986, pp. 24–25.

[27]Alicia Hills Moore, "Where the U.S. Stands," *Fortune,* October 13, 1986, pp. 28–37.

[28]Ibid., p. 28.

Chapter 4

[1]For these and other examples, see "National Firms Find That Selling to Local Tastes Is Costly, Complex," *The Wall Street Journal,* February 9, 1987, p. 17.

[2]GM's story is documented in Daniel J. Boorstin, *The Americans: The Democratic Experience* (New York: Vintage Books, 1973), pp. 551–555.

[3]Russell I. Haley, "Benefit Segments: Backwards and Forwards," *Journal of Advertising Research* 24 (February/March 1984): 19–25.

[4]Ibid.

[5]George Miaoulis and Michael D. Kalfus, "Benefit Segmentation Analysis Suggests Marketing Strategies for MBA Programs," *Marketing News,* August 5, 1983, p. 14.

[6]Russell I. Haley, "Benefit Segments."

[7]Philip Kotler, *Principles of Marketing,* 3rd ed. (Englewood Cliffs, N.J.: Prentice-Hall, 1986), p. 173.

[8]An application of this method is described in Russell I. Haley, "Benefit Segments," pp. 22–24.

[9]"How Colgate Brand Managers Applied Psychos to Market and Media for Irish Spring," *Media Decisions,* December 1976, pp. 70–71ff.

[10]Jack A. Lesser and Marie Adele Hughes, "The Generalizability of Psychographic Market Segments across Geographic Locations," *Journal of Marketing* 50 (January 1986): 18–27.

[11]Adapted from "Survey of Industrial Purchasing Power," *Sales and Marketing Management,* April 24, 1978, p. 32.

[12]Robert Haas discusses use of such sources in detail in "SIC System and Related Data for More Effective Market Research," *Industrial Marketing Management,* 1977, pp. 429–435.

[13]"Variations on a Theme," *Inc.,* May 1984, p. 148.

[14]Ellen Paris, "Massacre on the Miracle Mile," *Forbes,* April 26, 1982, pp. 40–41.

[15]John Koten, " 'Real' Cigarets Prove True Disappointment Despite Their Merit," *The Wall Street Journal,* February 26, 1980, p. 18.

[16]Al Urbanski, "Wells Fargo's Sales Force Tames the Wild West," *Sales and Marketing Management,* January 1987, pp. 38–41.

[17]"Lipton Goes on the Offensive," *Business Week,* September 5, 1983, pp. 102–104.

[18]See Eric N. Berkowitz, Roger A. Kerin, and William Rudelius, *Marketing* (St. Louis, Mo.: Mosby College Publishing, 1986), pp. 208–215; and John C. Chambers et al., "How to Choose the Right Forecasting Technique," *Harvard Business Review* (July–August 1971): 45ff.

[19]See Eric N. Berkowitz et al., *Marketing,* pp. 208–215; and John C. Chambers et al., *An Executive's Guide to Forecasting* (New York: Wiley, 1974), p. 16.

[20]For subjective methods of demand estimation, see Donald S. Tull and Del I. Hawkins, *Marketing Research,* 3rd ed. (New York: Macmillan, 1984).

[21]For a more in-depth discussion of time-series projection, see Steven P. Schnaars, "Situational Factors Affecting Forecast Accuracy," *Journal of Marketing Research* 21 (August 1984): 290–297.

Chapter 5

[1]Kim Foltz, "What's in a Name?" *Newsweek,* October 21, 1985, pp. 64, 66.

[2]Ibid., p. 64.

[3]This and many of the following examples are based on Donald F. Cox and Robert E. Good, "How to Build a Marketing Information System," *Harvard Business Review* (May–June 1967): p. 146.

[4]Darrell E. Owen, "SMR Forum: Information Systems Organizations—Keeping Pace with the Pressures," *Sloan Management Review* 27 (Spring 1986): pp. 59–68.

[5]Robert Levy, "Scanning for Dollars," *INC.,* September 1986, pp. 63–64.

[6]Philip Kotler, *Principles of Marketing,* 3rd ed. (Englewood Cliffs, N.J.: Prentice-Hall, 1986), p. 86.

[7]"Skil Finally Breaks the Profit Barrier," *Business Week,* November 25, 1972, pp. 50–54.

[8]Cox and Good, "How to Build a Marketing Information System," p. 146.

[9]Kotler, *Principles of Marketing,* pp. 98–99.

[10]Robert L. Yeager, "Engineering the Customer-Oriented Marketing Strategy," *Business Marketing,* November 1985, pp. 66, 68.

[11]"Key Role of Research in Agree's Success Is Told," *Marketing News,* January 12, 1979, pp. 14–15.

[12]Stephen A. Greyser, "Research-Management Partnership Proves Best," *Advertising Age,* November 14, 1985, p. 34.

[13]Herbert L. Aist and Bayne Sparks, "Market Research," *H & H,* May 1972, p. 102.

[14]Alexa Smith, "Researchers Must Control Focus Group—and Those behind the Mirror as Well," *Marketing News,* September 12, 1986, pp. 33–34, 36.

[15]Amanda Bennett, "Once a Tool of Retail Marketers, Focus Groups Gain Wider Usage," *The Wall Street Journal,* June 3, 1986, p. 31.

[16]Eugene H. Fram, "How Focus Groups Unlock Market Intelligence: Tapping In-House 'Researchers,' " *Business Marketing,* December 1985, pp. 80, 82.

[17]Kotler, *Principles of Marketing,* pp. 97–98.

[18]William G. Zikmund, *Exploring Marketing Research,* 2nd ed. (Hinsdale, Ill.: The Dryden Press, 1986), pp. 145–154.

[19]This case is presented in full in Robert S. Wheeler, "Marketing Tales with a Moral," *Product Marketing,* April 1977, p. 41.

[20]Julian L. Simon, *Basic Research Methods in Social Science: The Art of Empirical Investigation* (New York: Random House, 1969), p. 4.

[21]"Researching at the Checkout," *New York Times,* May 15, 1983, sec. 3, p. F15.

[22]Frederick C. Klein, "Researcher Probes Consumers Using Anthropological Skills," *The Wall Street Journal,* July 7, 1983, p. 21.

[23]Roy G. Stout, "Developing Data to Estimate Price-Quantity Relationships," *Journal of Marketing* (April 1969): 34–36.

[24]Mason Haire, "Projective Techniques in Marketing Research," *Journal of Marketing* 14 (April 1950): 649–656.

[25]Philip Kotler and Gary Armstrong, *Marketing: An Introduction* (Englewood Cliffs, N.J.: Prentice-Hall, 1987), p. 100.

[26]E. Jerome McCarthy and William D. Perreault, *Essentials of Marketing,* 3rd ed. (Homewood, Ill.: Irwin, 1985), p. 122.

[27]For more detail on survey methods, see Rena Bartos, "Qualitative Research: What It Is and Where It Came From," *Journal of Advertising Research* 26 (June/July 1986): RC-3–RC-6; Charles S. Mayer, "Data Collection Methods: Personal Interview"; Paul L. Erdos, "Data Collecting Methods: Mail Surveys," and Stanley L. Payne, "Data Collecting Methods: Telephone Surveys," in *Handbook of Marketing Research,* pp. 2-82–2-123; and Charles Overholser, "Quality, Quantity, and Thinking Real Hard," *Journal of Advertising Research* 26 (June/July 1986): RC-7–RC-12.

[28]Lee Adler, "Confessions of an Interview Reader," *Journal of Marketing Research* (May 1966): 194–195.

[29]For more information on the theory of sampling, see Paul B. Sheatsley, "Survey Design," in *Handbook of Modern Marketing,* especially pp. 17–76; Thomas T. Semon, "Basic Concepts," in the same work, pp. 217–229; and Zikmund, *Exploring Marketing Research,* pp. 436–437.

[30]These statistical techniques are discussed at length in *Handbook of Marketing Research,* pp. 2-307–2-498.

[31]The case is reported in Chester R. Wasson, "Use and Appraisal of Existing Information," in *Handbook of Marketing Research,* p. 2–12.

Chapter 6

[1]The definition of the scope of consumer behavior comes from Leon G. Schiffman and Leslie Lazar Kanuk, *Consumer Behavior,* 2nd ed. (Englewood Cliffs, N.J.: Prentice-Hall, 1983).

[2]For a good overview of the contribution of these disciplines to marketing, see James F. Engel, Roger D. Blackwell, and Paul W. Miniard, *Consumer Behavior,* 5th ed. (Hinsdale, Ill.: The Dryden Press, 1986), pp. 15–17.

[3]The uses and users of consumer behavior studies are explored in David W. Cravens et al., *Marketing Decision Making,* rev. ed. (Homewood, Ill.: Irwin, 1980), pp. 370–371.

[4]Philip Kotler, *Marketing Management,* 5th ed. (Englewood Cliffs, N.J.: 1984).

[5]The example is from David Dutton, "Does American Marketing Strategy Work Abroad?" *Proceedings of the 1966 World Congress of the American Marketing Association,* edited by John S. Wright and Jack Goldstrucker (Chicago: AMA, 1966), pp. 687–693.

[6]"Great American Stampede to Vacation Overseas," *U.S. News and World Report,* July 18, 1983, pp. 49–50.

[7]"Americans' New Quest: Seeking Safety of the Cocoon," *Marketing News,* November 7, 1986, p. 27.

[8]Henry Tischler et al., *Introduction to Sociology* (New York: Holt, Rinehart & Winston, 1983), p. 93.

[9]Jeffrey Kovack, "Minority Sell: Ads Target Blacks, Hispanics, but . . .," *Industry Week,* November 11, 1985.

[10]Ed Fitch, "Marketing to Hispanics: Buying Power Bursts Poverty-Stricken Image," *Advertising Age,* February 9, 1987, pp. S-1–S-2+.

[11]Richard Edel, "Outdoor Boards Are Growing in Stature," *Advertising Age,* August 11, 1986, pp. S-2, S-4.

[12]Richard Edel, "Losing Something in the Translation," *Advertising Age,* August 11, 1986, pp. S-2, S-4.

[13]Ed Fitch, "Asians Share Certain Hispanic Values," *Advertising Age,* February 9, 1987, pp. S-2, S-6.

[14]George E. Barna, "Typology Offers Perspectives on Growing Christian Market," *Marketing News,* September 16, 1983, p. 12.

[15]Joan Kron, *Home Psych: The Social Psychology of Home Decoration* (New York: Clarkson Potter, 1983).

[16]Good overviews of class differences in consumption behavior are found in James F. Engel et al., *Consumer Behavior,* Chapter 14; and Schiffman and Kanuk, *Consumer Behavior.*

[17]See Francis S. Bourne, "Group Influence in Marketing and Public Relations," in *Some Applications of Behavioral Research,* edited by Renais Likert and S. P. Hayes (Paris: UNESCO, 1957), pp. 208–224; and James F. Engel et al., *Consumer Behavior,* pp. 318–319.

[18]Francis S. Bourne, "Group Influence in Marketing and Public Relations."

[19]M. Wayne DeLozier, *The Marketing Communication Process* (New York: McGraw-Hill, 1976), pp. 158–159.

[20]Paul F. Lazarsfeld et al., *The People's Choice* (New York: Duell, Sloan & Pearce, 1948).

[21]James F. Engel et al., *Consumer Behavior,* pp. 543–546, devote more attention to these differences.

[22]For further discussion of the differences in purchase behavior in each phase and alternatives to the traditional stages, see James F. Engel et al., *Consumer Behavior,* pp. 277–292.

[23]Thayer C. Taylor, "Markets That Marketers Pursue Are a Changin'," *Sales and Marketing Management,* July 28, 1980, p. A-19.

[24]Cheryl Russell and Thomas G. Exter, "America at Mid-Decade," *American Demographics* (January 1986): 22–29.

[25]Richard Kern, "USA 2000," *Sales and Marketing Management,* October 27, 1986, pp. 8–10+.

[26]See Harry L. David and Benny P. Rigaux, "Perception of Marital Roles in Decision Processes," *Journal of Consumer Research* (June 1974): 51–62.

[27]See Scott Ward and Daniel Wackman, "Purchase Influence Attempts and Parental Yielding," *Journal of Marketing Research* (August 1972): 316–319.

[28]*Publishers Weekly,* September 23, 1983, p. 16; Jeffrey A. Trachtenberg, "Big Spenders: Teenage Division," *Forbes,* November 3, 1986, pp. 201, 204.

[29]Richard Kern, "USA 2000," p. 12.

[30]Paul B. Brown, "Last Year It Was Yuppies—This Year It's Their Parents," *Business Week,* March 10, 1986, pp. 68+.

[31]Richard Kern, "USA 2000," p. 12.

[32]See Abraham Maslow, *Toward a Psychology of Being* (New York: Van Nostrand, 1968), pp. 189–215.

[33]Kenneth E. Runyon, *Consumer Behavior,* 2nd ed. (Columbus, Ohio: Charles E. Merrill, 1980), p. 209.

[34]C. Glenn Walters, *Consumer Behavior: Theory and Practice,* 3rd ed. (Homewood, Ill.: Irwin, 1978), p. 237.

[35]Reported in James F. Engel et al., *Consumer Behavior,* p. 235.

[36]See James F. Engel et al., *Consumer Behavior,* pp. 115–116.

[37]Kathleen A. Hughes, "Coffee Makers Hope New Ads Will Reverse Declining Sales," *The Wall Street Journal,* September 1, 1983, p. 21.

[38]Elaine Donelson, *Personality: A Scientific Approach* (Pacific Palisades, Calif.: Goodyear, 1973), p. 3.

[39]See Russell L. Ackoff and James R. Emshoff, "Advertising Research at Anheuser-Busch, Inc. (1968–74)," *Sloan Management Review* (Spring 1975): 1–15.

[40]Jack A. Adams, *Learning and Memory: An Introduction* (Homewood, Ill.: Irwin, 1976), p. 6.

[41]E. Jerome McCarthy and William D. Perreault, Jr., *Basic Marketing,* 8th ed. (Homewood, Ill.: Irwin, 1984), p. 204.

[42]See Wayne DeLozier, *The Marketing Communications Process* (New York: McGraw-Hill, 1976), pp. 56–61.

[43]The description of VALS is based on Del Hawkins, Roger J. Best, and Kenneth A. Coney, *Consumer Behavior,* 3rd ed. (Plano, Tex.: Business Publications, Inc., 1986), pp. 429–445.

[44]The following discussion relies on that presented in Leon G. Shiffman and Leslie Lazar Kanuk, *Consumer Behavior,* 3rd ed. (Englewood Cliffs, N.J.: Prentice-Hall, 1983).

Chapter 7

[1]*Statistical Abstract of the United States, 1986* (Washington, D.C.: U.S. Government Printing Office, 1986).

[2]Richard E. Plank, "Industrial Marketing Education: Present Conditions and Future Prospects," working paper, Montclair State College, Upper Montclair, N.J., July 1982.

[3]*Statistical Abstract of the United States, 1986,* p. 744.

[4]"1986 Survey of Industrial and Commercial Buying Power," *Sales and Marketing Management,* April 28, 1986, p. 24.

[5]Ibid., p. 20.

[6]This chapter draws heavily from Michael D. Hutt and Thomas W. Speh, *Industrial Marketing Management,* 2nd ed. (Hinsdale, Ill.: The Dryden Press, 1984). This section is from Chapter 2.

[7]William K. Stevens, "Town Worries about Its Future with the Coming of Volkswagen," *New York Times,* July 20, 1976, p. 9.

[8]Hutt and Speh, *Industrial Marketing Management.*

[9]Donald R. Lehmann and John O'Shaughnessy, "Difference in Attribute Importance for Different Industrial Products," *Journal of Marketing* (April 1976): 36–42; Lowell E. Crow and Jay D. Lindquist, "Impact of Organizational and Buyer Characteristics on the Buying Center," *Industrial Marketing Management,* February 1985, pp. 49–58. See also Lehmann and O'Shaughnessy, "Decision Criteria Used in Buying Different Categories of Products," *Journal of Purchasing and Materials Management* (Spring 1982): 9–14.

[10]Thomas V. Bonoma and Gerald Zaltman, eds., "Introduction," in *Organizational Buying Behavior* (Chicago: American Marketing Association, 1978), p. 8.

[11]See Paul F. Anderson and Terry M. Chambers, "A Reward/Measurement Model of Organizational Buying Behavior," *Journal of Marketing* 49 (Spring 1985): 7–23; and Michael Kutschker, "The Multi-Organizational Interaction Approach to Industrial Marketing," *Journal of Business Research* 13 (October 1985): 383–403.

[12]Thomas V. Bonoma, "Major Sales: Who Really Does the Buying?" *Harvard Business Review* (May–June 1982): 111.

[13]H. Lazo, "Emotional Aspects of Industrial Buying," in *Proceedings of the American Marketing Association,* edited by R. S. Hancock (Chicago: American Marketing Association, 1960), p. 265.

[14]"Computer Shock Hits the Office," *Business Week,* August 8, 1983, p. 46.

[15]Ibid., p. 53.

[16]Bonoma and Zaltman, *Organizational Buying Behavior,* pp. 3–4.

[17]This section is drawn from Philip Kotler and Gary Armstrong, *Marketing: An Introduction* (Englewood Cliffs, N.J.: Prentice-Hall, Inc., 1987), pp. 185–186.

[18]F. E. Webster and Yoram Wind, "A General Model for Understanding Organization Buyer Behavior," *Journal of Marketing* (April 1972): 17.

[19]For more discussion of this point, see Jean-Marie Choffray and Gary Lilien, "Assessing Response to Industrial Marketing Strategy," *Journal of Marketing* (April 1978): 29–30.

Chapter 8

[1]Philip Kotler, *Principles of Marketing,* 3rd ed. (Englewood Cliffs, N.J.: Prentice-Hall, 1986), p. 6.

[2]"New Products: Still Rising . . . Finding a Winner . . . Hassles," *The Wall Street Journal,* November 3, 1983, p. 27.

[3]Kevin Brown, Sandra Davis, and Julie Doherty, "Intros Bring New Wine, Old Bottles," *Advertising Age,* January 5, 1987, p. 52.

[4]Kevin T. Higgins, "Home Delivery Is Helping Pizza to Battle Burgers," *Marketing News,* August 1, 1986, pp. 1, 6.

[5]Lisa Miller Mesdag, "The Appliance Boom Begins," *Fortune,* July 25, 1983, pp. 52–57.

[6]For refinements of the consumer product classification system, see Louis P. Bucklin, "Retail Strategy and the Classification of Consumer Goods," *Journal of Marketing* (January 1963): 50–55; and Leo V. Aspinwall, "The Marketing Characteristics of Goods," in *Four Marketing Theories* (Boulder: University of Colorado, 1961).

[7]"Crayola Draws a New Image," *Marketing and Media Decisions,* November 1981, pp. 70–71, 108–109.

[8]Pat Sloan, "Benetton Readies Its First Fragrance," *Advertising Age,* October 6, 1986, p. 34.

[9]Pamela G. Hollie, "Monopoly Loses Its Trademark," *New York Times,* February 23, 1983, p. D1; and Joani Nelson Horchler, "Is the Trademark 'Monopoly' Doomed?" *Industry Week,* March 21, 1983, pp. 70–71.

[10]See Laurie Freeman, "Battle for Shelf Space," *Advertising Age,* February 28, 1985, p. 16; and Bill Saporito, "Has-Been Brands Go Back to Work," *Fortune,* April 28, 1986, pp. 123–124.

[11]Laurie Freeman, "Battle for Shelf Space."

[12]"Generics Now Hurting Private Label," *Supermarket Business,* September 1982, p. 8.

[13]Mary McCabe English, "Calm after the Storm," *Advertising Age,* March 15, 1982, p. 18.

[14]Martha R. McEnally and John M. Hawes, "The Market for Generic Brand Grocery Products: A Review and Extension," *Journal of Marketing* 48 (Winter 1984): 75–83.

[15]Bill Kelley,"Zenith Labs on a New Product High," *Sales and Marketing Management,* October 1986, pp. 42–45.

[16]Ibid., p. 44.

[17]Kotler, *Principles of Marketing,* p. 267.

[18]See M. Ven Venkatesan, "Characteristics of Services Necessitate a Different Approach than Product Marketing," *Marketing News,* May 27, 1983, p. 14.

[19]Clare Ansberry, "Merit Awards Spark Revival at Small College," *The Wall Street Journal,* February 4, 1987, p. 25.

[20]William J. Winston, "Topic: Internal Marketing—Key to a Successful Professional Service Marketing Program," *Journal of Professional Services Marketing* 1 (Fall 1985/Winter 1985–86): 15–18.

[21]George Russell, "Where the Customer Is Still King," *Time,* February 2, 1987, pp. 56–57.

[22]Ibid., p. 56.

[23]Many of the concepts summarized here are expanded in G. Lynn Shostack's excellent article, "Breaking Free from Product Marketing," *Journal of Marketing* (April 1977): 73–80.

[24]"Big Sam's: The Hair Club," recruiting brochure from S.M.R. Enterprises, Inc., Memphis, Tennessee.

[25]Dan R. E. Thomas, "Strategy Is Different in Service Businesses," *Harvard Business Review* (July–August 1978): 158–165.

[26]"Accountants to Zoologists," *Time,* February 2, 1987, p. 52.

Chapter 9

[1]Hiotaka Takeuchi and Ikujiro Nonaka, "The New New Product Development Game," *Harvard Business Review* (January–February 1986): 137–146.

[2]Ibid., p. 137.

[3]Peter Finch, "Intrapreneurism: New Hope for New Business," *Business Marketing,* July 1985, pp. 32–34+.

[4]Anastasia Toufexis, "Going Crazy over Calcium," *Time,* February 23, 1987, pp. 88–89.

[5]See Nariman K. Dhalla and Sonia Yuspeh, "Forget the Product Life Cycle!" *Harvard Business Review* (January 1976): 102–112, for the view that generalizations about the average length of life cycles are useless and may mislead managers into killing off brands prematurely. For an opposite view, see John E. Smallwood, "The Product Life Cycle: A Key to Strategic Marketing Planning," *MSU Business Topics* (Winter 1973): 29–35; Ben M. Enis et al., "Extending the Product Life Cycle," *Business Horizons,* June 1977,

pp. 46–56; and "Keeping Products Alive and Well in the Market," *Product Marketing,* November 1977, pp. 46–53.

[6]E. Jerome McCarthy and William D. Perreault, Jr., *Essentials of Marketing,* 3rd ed. (Homewood, Ill.: Richard D. Irwin, 1985), p. 242; and Sak Onkvisit and John J. Shaw, "Competition and Product Management: Can the Product Life Cycle Help?" *Business Horizons,* July/August 1986, pp. 51–62.

[7]Joshua Hyatt, "Cat Fight," *Inc.,* November 1986, pp. 82+.

[8]Hirotaka Takeuchi and Ikujiro Nonaka, "The New New Product Development Game."

[9]Neil Ulman, "Sweating It Out: Time, Risk, Ingenuity All Go into Launching New Personal Product," *The Wall Street Journal,* November 17, 1978, pp. 1, 41.

[10]John A. Prestbo, "At Procter & Gamble Success Is Largely Due to Heeding Customers," *The Wall Street Journal,* April 29, 1980, p. 1.

[11]Joshua Hyatt, "Cat Fight."

[12]"The Lower Birthrate Crimps the Baby Food Market," *Business Week,* July 13, 1974, p. 47.

[13]Shelby H. McIntyre and Meir Statman, "Managing the Risk of New Product Development," *Business Horizons,* May–June 1982, pp. 51–55.

[14]Philip Kotler, *Marketing Management: Analysis, Planning, and Control* (Englewood Cliffs, N.J.: Prentice Hall, 1984), p. 205.

[15]Caryn James, "Publishers' Confessions—Rejections I Regret," *New York Times Book Review,* May 6, 1984, pp. 1, 34–37.

[16]Lawrence Incrassia, "There's No Way to Tell if a New Food Product Will Please the Public," *The Wall Street Journal,* February 26, 1980, pp. 1, 23.

[17]"Test Marketing: The Most Dangerous Game in Marketing," *Marketing Insights,* October 9, 1967, p. 16.

[18]Carol Galginaitis, "What's Beneath a Test Market?" *Advertising Age,* February 9, 1981, p. S-2.

[19]Richard Edel, "New Graphics Energize Magazines' Appeal," *Advertising Age,* October 17, 1983, p. M46.

[20]O. C. Ferrell and William M. Pride, *Fundamentals of Marketing* (Boston: Houghton Mifflin, 1982), p. 194.

[21]Judann Dagnoli, "Walking Shoes May Open Gait to Big Profits," *Advertising Age,* July 7, 1986, pp. 12, 47.

[22]Charles D. Schewe and Reuben M. Smith, *Marketing Concepts and Applications* (New York: McGraw-Hill, 1983), p. 315.

[23]"Home Computer Firms," *The Wall Street Journal,* September 12, 1983, p. 1.

[24]Theodore Levitt, *Marketing for Business Growth,* 2nd ed. (New York: McGraw-Hill, 1974), pp. 162–165.

[25]Ann M. Morrison, "The General Mills Brand of Managers," *Fortune,* January 12, 1981, pp. 99–107.

[26]"Dannon Expands on the Diet Market," *Marketing and Media Decisions,* November 1981, pp. 74–75, 130–131.

[27]Lynn Asinof, "Business Bulletin," *The Wall Street Journal,* February 5, 1987, p. 1.

[28]See Carl R. Anderson and Carl P. Zeithaml, "Stage of the Product Life Cycle, Business Strategy, and Business Performance," *Academy of Management Journal* 27 (March 1984): 5–24; Roger A. Kevin et al., "Cannibalism and New Product Development," *Business Horizons,* October 1978, pp. 25–31; and Sak Onkvisit and John J. Shaw, "Competition and Product Management."

[29]This example is from Chester R. Wasson, *Product Management: Product Life Cycles and Competitive Marketing Strategy* (St. Charles, Ill.: Challenge Books, 1971), pp. 183–184.

[30]See Philip Kotler, "Harvesting Strategies for Weak Products," *Business Horizons,* August 1978, pp. 15–22.

[31]Ferrell and Pride, *Fundamentals of Marketing,* p. 198.

Chapter 10

[1]*Marketing News,* November 11, 1983, p. 1.

[2]Philip Kotler, *Principles of Marketing,* 3rd ed. (Englewood Cliffs, N.J.: Prentice-Hall, 1986), p. 366.

[3]Jeffrey H. Birnbaum, "Pricing of Products Is Still an Art, Often Having Little Link to Costs," *The Wall Street Journal,* November 25, 1981, p. 29.

[4]"The More Expensive a Product, the Better the Quality, Right?" *The Wall Street Journal,* December 22, 1977, p. 1.

[5]Eitan Gerstner, "Do Higher Prices Signal Higher Quality?" *Journal of Marketing Research* 22 (May 1985): 209–215.

[6]"The Price TI is Paying for Misreading a Market," *Business Week,* September 19, 1983, pp. 61–64; "Round Two for Computer Makers," *Business Week,* September 19, 1983, pp. 93–95; and "Why TI Will Return to Home Computers," *Business Week,* November 14, 1983, pp. 48–49.

[7]David W. Cravens, Gerald E. Hills, and Robert B. Woodruff, *Marketing Decision Making: Concepts and Strategy,* rev. ed. (Homewood, Ill.: Irwin, 1980), Chapter 14.

[8]Daniel J. Boorstin, *The Americans: The Democratic Experience* (New York: Vintage Books, 1973), p. 108.

[9]David W. Cravens et al., *Marketing Decision Making,* p. 326.

[10]See S. Prakesh Sethi, "One Way to Punish a Corporation: Jail the Boss," *New York Times,* February 12, 1978, p. 3; see also Donald I. Baker, "Price Fixers Beware!" *Across the Board,* February 1977, pp. 37–43; and Jean A. Briggs, "For Whom Does the Bell Toll?" *Forbes,* June 25, 1979, p. 33.

[11]"A Stretched Definition of Price Fixing," *Business Week,* December 27, 1976, pp. 28–30. See also David F. Lean, Jonathan D. Ogur, and Robert P. Rogers, "Does Collusion Pay . . . Does Antitrust Work?" *Southern Economic Journal* 51 (January 1985): 828–841.

[12]"The First Big Test of a New Antitrust Law," *Business Week,* September 12, 1977, pp. 48–49.

[13]"Sears, FTC Settle Case on 'Bait and Switch,' " *Advertising Age,* March 8, 1976, p. 3.

[14]Gerald Badler, director of the Strategy Planning Institute, as quoted in "Flexible Pricing," *Business Week,* December 12, 1977, p. 80.

[15]Birnbaum, "Pricing of Products Still an Art," p. 29.

[16]George P. Sproles, "New Evidence on Price and Product Quality," *Journal of Consumer Affairs* (Summer 1977): 69–73.

[17]This point is made by Martin R. Schlessel in "Pricing in a Service Industry," *MSU Business Topics* (Spring 1977): 37–48. The author studied the pricing of exterminator services and concluded that most firms price with the market. However, some industry members got away with above-market

pricing because buyers lacked objective criteria for judging the quality of service before the purchase.

[18]Laura Landro, "Technology, Competition Cut Prices of Electronics Gear as Quality Rises," *The Wall Street Journal*, December 1, 1981, p. 37.

[19]The classic article discussing new product pricing is Joel Dean, "Pricing Policies for New Products," reprinted in *Harvard Business Review* (November–December 1976): 141–153. See also the chapter on pricing in Richard H. Buskirk and Percy J. Vaughn, Jr., *Managing New Enterprises* (New York: West, 1976).

[20]See Kent Monroe, *Pricing: Making Profitable Decisions* (New York: McGraw-Hill, 1979), Chapter 13.

[21]See "Airline Takes the Marginal Route," *Business Week*, April 20, 1963, pp. 111–112+; and Brenton Walling, Jr., "Why Price-Cutting Backfires in the Airline Industry," *Business Week*, October 10, 1977, pp. 116, 118.

[22]David J. Rachman and Michael H. Mescon, *Business Today* (New York: Random House, 1982), p. 289; and George W. James, "Airline Deregulation: Has It Worked?" *Business Economics* (July 1985): 11–14.

[23]David J. Rachman and Michael H. Mescon, *Business Today*, p. 289.

[24]Ibid.

[25]Ibid.

[26]For the arguments that cost-plus pricing is also competitively smart and socially fair, see Philip Kotler, *Marketing Management*, 5th ed. (Englewood Cliffs, N.J.: Prentice-Hall, 1984), p. 517.

[27]Jeffrey Birnbaum, "Location, Volume, Marketing Make Prices Vary Widely in NYC," *The Wall Street Journal*, December 3, 1981, p. 31.

[28]See Louis W. Stern and Adel I. El-Ansary, *Marketing Channels* (Englewood Cliffs, N.J.: Prentice-Hall, 1977), pp. 339–340.

[29]H. J. Maidenberg, "Misadventures of Cocoa Trade," *New York Times*, February 25, 1979, pp. F1, 41; Hershey Foods Corporation.

[30]See "Consumers Find Firms Are Paring Quantities to Avoid Price Rises," *The Wall Street Journal*, February 15, 1977, pp. 1, 21.

[31]Dik Warren Twedt, "Does the '9 Fixation' in Retail Pricing Really Promote Sales?" *Journal of Marketing* (October 1975): 54–55.

[32]Jeffrey H. Birnbaum, "Pricing of Products Is Still an Art."

Chapter 11

[1]The argument to include services in marketing channels is presented at length in James H. Donnelly, Jr., "Marketing Intermediaries in Channels of Distribution for Services," *Journal of Marketing* (January 1976): 55–70.

[2]Michelle Bekey, "Empire Building with Ice Cream," *Working Woman*, August 1986, pp. 37–39.

[3]For other examples, see Donnelly, "Marketing Intermediaries." See also Louis W. Stern and Adel I. El-Ansary, *Marketing Channels*, 2nd ed. (Englewood Cliffs, N.J.: Prentice-Hall, 1982).

[4]Susan Fraker, "Making a Mint in Nuts and Bolts," *Fortune*, August 22, 1983, pp. 131–134.

[5]William Harris, "Fashion Is Fickle," *Forbes*, June 22, 1981, pp. 102–103.

[6]David W. Cravens, Gerald E. Hills, and Robert B. Woodruff, *Marketing Decision Making: Concepts and Strategy*, rev. ed. (Homewood, Ill.: Irwin, 1980), pp. 287–288.

[7]See Robert E. Weigand, "Fit Products and Channels to Your Markets," *Harvard Business Review* (January–February 1977): 95–105, for a complete discussion. Some of the examples used here are from that article.

[8]The case is from Phil Fitzell, "Distribution: How Welch Cracked the Soft Drink Market," *Product Marketing*, June 1977, pp. 19–23.

[9]James D. Hlavacek and Tommy J. McCuistion, "Industrial Distributors—When, Who, and How?" *Harvard Business Review* (March–April 1983): 96–101.

[10]The food brokers mentioned in the Welch example are, contrary to their name, actually a type of manufacturers' agent. See Joseph S. Siebert, *Concepts of Marketing Management* (New York: Harper & Row, 1973), pp. 381–382.

[11]"High Court Places Curbs on Transshipping, Strengthens Role of Independent Distributor," *Merchandising*, August 1977, pp. 6–7; and Ralph Blumenthal, "Legal Storm over Discounting," *New York Times*, February 3, 1979, pp. D1, D4.

[12]Arthur Bragg, "When Your Sales Team Yells, 'Foul!' " *Sales and Marketing Management*, July 1, 1985, pp. 66–67.

[13]The classic article on this problem is Warren J. Wittreich, "Misunderstanding the Retailer," *Harvard Business Review*, May–June 1962, pp. 147–152+.

[14]Barry Stavro, "Bottleneck," *Forbes*, January 16, 1984, pp. 88–89.

[15]Bruce Mallen, "Conflict and Cooperation in Marketing Channels," *Progress in Marketing*, edited by L. George Smith (New York: American Marketing Association, 1964).

[16]Robert W. Little, "The Marketing Channel: Who Should Lead This Extra Corporate Organization?" *Journal of Marketing* (January 1970): 31–38.

[17]These techniques are discussed more thoroughly in Bruce Mallen, "Conflict and Cooperation in Marketing Channels." See also "Distributor Incentive Programs—You Both Should Win," *Sales and Marketing Management*, September 8, 1975, pp. 45–48.

[18]Robert E. Weigand and Hilda C. Wasson, "Arbitration in the Marketing Channel," *Business Horizons*, October 1974, pp. 39–47.

[19]The advantages of vertical marketing systems are discussed at length in Bert C. McCammon, Jr., "Perspectives for Distribution Programming," in *Vertical Marketing Systems*, edited by Louis P. Bucklin (Glenview, Ill.: Scott, Foresman, 1970), p. 44.

[20]The experience of O. M. Scott Company is discussed in Louis W. Stern and Adel I. El-Ansary, *Marketing Channels*.

[21]Phillip Bagozzi, *Principles of Marketing Management* (Chicago: Science Research Associates, 1986), pp. 575–576.

Chapter 12

[1]Philip Kotler, *Principles of Marketing*, 3rd ed. (Englewood Cliffs, N.J.: Prentice-Hall, 1986), p. 444.

[2]David J. Rachman and Michael H. Mescon, *Business Today* (New York: Random House, 1982), pp. 323–324.

[3]Cecelia Reed, "Janis Specializes in Works of Art that Wear Well," *Advertising Age,* July 7, 1986, p. 30.

[4]Cecelia Reed, "Gift for Serendipity Leads Treasure Hunter Where the Past Hides," *Advertising Age,* November 3, 1986, p. 54.

[5]"Here's a Shop that Counters Spies," *Changing Times,* April 1986, p. 9.

[6]Steven P. Galante, "Bookshop 'Superstore' Reflects the Latest Word in Retailing," *The Wall Street Journal,* February 23, 1987, p. 21; Steve Weiner, "With Big Selection and Low Prices, 'Category Killer' Stores Are a Hit," *The Wall Street Journal,* June 17, 1986, p. 31.

[7]"Satisfaction of Consumer Needs," in Raymond A. Marquardt, James C. Makens, and Robert G. Roe, *Retail Management,* 3rd ed. (Hinsdale, Ill.: The Dryden Press, 1983), p. 237.

[8]Barbara Toman, "Department Stores Start Adding Seminars and Services to Attract Working Women," *The Wall Street Journal,* July 5, 1982, p. 17.

[9]Louis W. Stern and Adel I. El-Ansary, *Marketing Channels,* 2nd ed. (Englewood Cliffs, N.J.: Prentice-Hall, 1982).

[10]Kenneth Wylie, "A Perspective on Today's Grocer," *Advertising Age,* October 10, 1983, pp. M9–M10.

[11]See Danny N. Bellenger, Thomas J. Stanley, and John W. Allen, "Food Retailing in the 1980s: Problems and Prospects," *Journal of Retailing* (Fall 1977): 59–70; and Larry Edwards, "Soft Sales Challenge Food Marketers," *Advertising Age,* October 30, 1978, pp. 27, 103.

[12]This section draws from information in Lisa Gubernick, "Stores for Our Times," *Forbes,* November 3, 1986, pp. 40–42; and Jeremy Schlosberg, "The Demographics of Convenience," *American Demographics* (October 1986): 36–40.

[13]Anna Sobczynski, "Cashing in on the Best of Both Worlds," *Advertising Age,* October 10, 1983, p. M-22.

[14]Annetta Miller, "Filling a Tooth at the Grocer: Off to the Hypermarket," *Newsweek,* November 10, 1986, p. 59.

[15]Ibid.

[16]Philip Kotler and Gary Armstrong, *Marketing: An Introduction* (Englewood Cliffs, N.J.: Prentice-Hall, 1987), p. 366.

[17]"Playing the Department Store Game," *Chain Store Age,* August 1983, pp. 65–68.

[18]Kimberly Carpenter, "Help Yourself: IKEA Bets on Rock-Bottom Prices and Bare-Bones Service," *Working Woman,* August 1986, p. 56.

[19]"Home Improvement Center: It's a Big Business . . .," *Merchandising,* August 1977, pp. 15–21.

[20]"Why Analysts Like Catalog Showrooms," *Business Week,* October 10, 1977, p. 105; Philip Kotler and Gary Armstrong, *Marketing: An Introduction,* p. 369; and David J. Rachman and Michael H. Mescon, *Business Today,* p. 329.

[21]Kurt Andersen, "New Gilded Age Grandeur," *Time,* September 2, 1985, pp. 46–47.

[22]William Dunn, "Edmonton's Eighth Wonder of the World," *American Demographics* (February 1986): 20.

[23]"Shopping Center Futures," *Stores,* May 1983, pp. 28–30.

[24]Dean Rotbart and Laurie P. Cohen, "The Party at Mary Kay Isn't Quite So Lively, as Recruiting Falls Off," *The Wall Street Journal,* October 28, 1983, pp. 1, 18.

[25]Suzy Hagstrom, "Consumers' Turn of Page Fuels Catalog Sales Picture," *Sentinel Star,* February 23, 1982, pp. 1E, 8E.

[26]Lori Kesler, "Marketing's Stepchild Comes into Its Own," *Advertising Age,* November 28. 1983, p. M-9.

[27]Rifka Rosenwein, "Whir, Click, Thanks: Merchandisers Turn to Electronic Salesmen in 24-Hour Kiosks," *The Wall Street Journal,* June 23, 1986, p. 23.

[28]Some independents have branch operations, but having several stores does not qualify an organization as a chain.

[29]Robert Reed, "Wood Prepares for Selling the 'New Sears,' " *Advertising Age,* May 9, 1983, pp. 1, 88.

[30]"Opportunities in Car Rentals," *Venture,* January 1984, p. 39.

[31]Agis Salpukas, "50 Dairy Queen Operators Secede over Recipe Dispute," *New York Times,* July 25, 1977.

[32]For the legal issues involving franchises, see *Franchising in the Economy: 1975–77* (Washington, D.C.: U.S. Government Printing Office, 1977), pp. 15–18.

[33]See Thomas J. Murray, "Franchising Comes of Age," *Dun's Review,* August 1977, pp. 58–60; "Things Are Looking Up for Franchises," *U.S. News and World Report,* May 10, 1976, p. 65; and Shelby D. Hunt, "The Trend toward Company-Operated Units in Franchise Chains," *Journal of Retailing* (Summer 1973): 3–12.

[34]Irving Burstiner, "A Three-Way Mirror," *Journal of Retailing* (Spring 1974): 24–36+.

[35]See Philip Kotler, "Atmospherics as a Marketing Tool," *Journal of Retailing* (Winter 1973–1974): 48–64. For examples of the use of fashion videos, see Pat Sloan, "Fashion Videos Dress for Work," *Advertising Age,* July 28, 1986, p. 36.

[36]The issue is discussed by William R. George in "The Retailing of Services—A Challenging Future," *Journal of Retailing* (Fall 1977): 85–97. See also Richard M. Bessom and Donald W. Jackson, Jr., "Service Retailing: A Strategic Marketing Approach," *Journal of Retailing* (Summer 1975): 75–84.

[37]For a more detailed discussion, see Stanley C. Hollander, "The Wheel of Retailing," *Journal of Marketing* (July 1960): 37–42.

[38]This hypothesis has been developed by several writers. See Bert C. McCammon, Jr., "Future Shock and the Practice of Management," in *Attitude Bridges the Atlantic,* edited by Philip Levine (Chicago: American Marketing Association, 1975), pp. 84–86; and William R. Davidson, Albert D. Bates, and Stephen J. Bass, "The Retail Life Cycle," *Harvard Business Review* (November–December 1976): 89–96.

[39]Pat Sloan, "Bloomingdale's Future in Expanding Its Mystique," *Advertising Age,* pp. 3, 58.

Chapter 13

[1]For a full discussion of these, see Peter M. Lynagh, "Physical Distribution Seventies Style," *Business Perspectives,* Summer 1973, pp. 28–31.

[2]Charles D. Schewe and Reuben M. Smith, *Marketing: Concepts and Applications* (New York: McGraw-Hill, 1983), pp. 453–454.

[3]Howard T. Lewis, James W. Cullition, and Jack D. Steele, *The Role of Air Freight in Physical Distribution* (Boston: Divi-

sion of Research, Harvard University Graduate School of Business Administration, 1956).

[4]Peter M. Lynagh, "Physical Distribution Seventies Style," p. 30.

[5]Roy D. Shapiro, "Get Leverage from Logistics," *Harvard Business Review* (May–June 1984): 119–125.

[6]Jack W. Farrell, "Computers Cut Distribution Network Down to Size," *Traffic Management,* February 1986, pp. 64–67.

[7]Christopher S. Eklund, "Will a Tomato by Any Other Name Taste Better?" *Business Week,* September 30, 1985, p. 105.

[8]Philip Kotler, *Principles of Marketing,* 3rd ed. (Englewood Cliffs, N.J.: Prentice-Hall, 1986), p. 435.

[9]Jack W. Farrell, "Computers Cut Distribution Network Down to Size."

[10]Eric N. Berkowitz, Roger A. Kerin, and William Rudelius, *Marketing* (St. Louis, Mo.: Mosby, 1986), pp. 390–391.

[11]Jack W. Farrell, "Computers Cut Distribution Network Down to Size," p. 64.

[12]Association of American Railroads, *Railroad Facts* (Washington, D.C.: Association of American Railroads, 1974), p. 45.

[13]Bill Paul, "Freight Transportation Is Being Transformed in an Era of Deregulation," *The Wall Street Journal,* October 20, 1983, pp. 1, 18.

[14]These developments are described in Louis E. Boone and David L. Kurtz, *Contemporary Marketing,* 5th ed. (Hinsdale, Ill.: The Dryden Press, 1986), pp. 358–359.

[15]Bill Paul, "Freight Transportation Is Being Transformed," p. 18.

[16]Bill Paul, "Trucks' Rates on Small Loads Stir Big Fight," *The Wall Street Journal,* July 28, 1983, p. 19.

[17]See Patrick Gallagher, "Politics and New Services Shape Ocean Transportation," *Handling and Shipping,* March 1977, pp. 48–53.

[18]See David F. White, "Issue behind Dock Strike: Ocean Shipping Revolution," *New York Times,* October 8, 1977; and Joseph A. Austin, "Domestic Containerization: Wave of the Future," *American Import and Export Bulletin,* July 1976, pp. 367–371.

[19]Bill Paul, "Freight Transportation Is Being Transformed."

Chapter 14

[1]"Felled by a Head of Foam," *Fortune,* January 15, 1979, p. 96.

[2]Wilbur Schramm, *The Nature of Communication between Humans,* rev. ed. (Urbana: University of Illinois Press, 1971), pp. 3–53.

[3]See, for example, Wilbur Schramm, ed., *The Process & Effects of Mass Communications* (Urbana: University of Illinois Press, 1955), pp. 3–26; and John Ball and Francis C. Byrnes, eds., *Principles and Practices in Visual Communications* (Washington, D.C.: National Education Association, 1960).

[4]Marjii F. Simon, "Influence of Brand Names on Attitude," *Journal of Advertising Research* (June 1970): 28–30.

[5]These types of noise are discussed in James A. Constantin et al., *Marketing Strategy and Management* (Dallas: Business Publications, Inc., 1976), p. 361. See also Terrence Shimp and M. Wayne DeLozier, *Promotion Management and Marketing Communication* (Hinsdale, Ill.: The Dryden Press, 1986), pp. 27–28.

[6]"Ballooning Fortunes of Bubble Yum," *New York Times,* March 25, 1977.

[7]Ralph S. Alexander, ed., *Marketing Definitions* (Chicago: American Marketing Association, 1964), p. 9.

[8]"Super Bowl XX: Who Bought the Million-Dollar Minutes," *Business Week,* February 3, 1986, p. 94.

[9]Charlyne Varkonyi, "Raisins Gain Day in Sun," *Chicago Tribune,* January 22, 1987, sec. 7, p. 10.

[10]This feature is discussed by James U. McNeal in "Promotion: An Overview." See his collection *Readings in Promotion Management* (New York: Appleton-Century-Crofts, 1966), p. 5.

[11]*Advertising Age,* May 6, 1985.

[12]Richard Kern, "From a Reporter to a Source: A New Survey of Selling Costs," *Sales and Marketing Management,* February 16, 1987, pp. 12–14.

[13]"The Nightmare Comes Home," *Time,* October 24, 1983, pp. 84–86.

[14]Craig Reiss, "ABC the Big Victor," *Advertising Age,* November 28, 1983, pp. 1, 104.

[15]Diane Mermigas, " 'Day' Blasts ABC to Top," *Advertising Age,* November 28, 1983, p. 2.

[16]David J. Rachman and Michael H. Mescon, *Business Today,* 3rd ed. (New York: Random House, 1982), p. 308.

[17]Leo LeFort, "We've Come a Long Way, Baby," *Advertising Age,* August 22, 1983, p. M-12.

[18]For other packaging advances, see Walter Stern, "The Top Ten Packaging Advances Since 1927," *Modern Packaging,* July 1977, pp. 44+. See also the articles cited in the opening vignette for this chapter.

[19]Cynthia Crossen, "Tamperproof Packaging: Inventors Say It Can't Be Done—but They Keep Trying," *The Wall Street Journal,* February 26, 1986, p. 27; and Melissa Larson, "Food Packagers Add Tamper-Evident Features," *Packaging,* January 1986, pp. 62–64, 66.

[20]John Lister, "To Research or Not to Research," *Advertising Age,* September 22, 1986, p. 80; and William H. Motes and Arch G. Woodside, "Field Test of Package Advertising Effects on Brand Choice Behavior," *Journal of Advertising Research* 24 (February/March 1984): 39–45.

[21]"Packaging Remains an Underdeveloped Element in Pushing Consumers' Buttons," *Marketing News,* October 14, 1983, p. 3.

[22]Color as a motivational tool in packaging is discussed in Walter P. Margulies, *Packaging Power* (New York: The World Publishing Company, 1970), pp. 110–118.

[23]Denise Lenci, "Packaging Is Key As Avon Fragrance Scores," *Drug and Cosmetic Industry,* November 1982, p. 50.

[24]Walter Margulies, "How Many Brands Can You Spot with Names Off Packages?" *Advertising Age,* August 21, 1972, pp. 37–40. For other examples of good package design, see Roy Parcels, "Ten Steps to Profitable Packages," *Advertising Age,* September 5, 1977, pp. 31+; Lori Kesler, "Successful Packages Turn Medium into Message," *Advertising Age,* October 13, 1986, pp. S-2–S-3; and Herbert M. Meyers,

"Package Design," *Art Product News,* July/August 1986, pp. 30–31, 34.

[25]Bernice Kanner, "Wrapping It Up," *New York,* June 6, 1983, p. 12.

[26]"Liquor's Other Campaigns," *Advertising Age,* August 15, 1983, p. M-40.

[27]Charles D. Schewe and Reuben M. Smith, *Marketing: Concepts and Applications,* 2nd ed. (New York: McGraw-Hill, 1983), p. 488. For research into the relationship of the factors leading to action, see David W. Stewart, "The Moderating Role of Recall, Comprehension, and Brand Differentiation on the Persuasiveness of Television Advertising," *Journal of Advertising Research* (April/May 1986): 43–47.

[28]William S. Robinson, "Best Promotions of the Year," *Advertising Age,* May 9, 1983, p. M-54.

[29]This case is discussed in detail in Thomas Berg, *Case Histories of Marketing Misfires* (New York: Doubleday, 1970), pp. 132–156.

[30]Reported in *Sales and Marketing,* January 1978, p. 38.

[31]These three reasons are discussed in Rolie Tillman and C. A. Kirkpatrick, *Promotion: Persuasive Communication in Marketing* (Homewood, Ill.: Irwin, 1972). See also William H. Motes and Arch G. Woodside, "Field Test of Package Advertising Effects on Brand Choice Behavior"; Simon Broadbent and Stephen Colman, "Advertising Effectiveness: Across Brands," *Journal of the Market Research Society* 28 (January 1986): 15–24.

[32]Bill Richards, "Executives at Toro Are Dreaming of a White Winter—Very White," *The Wall Street Journal,* December 20, 1983, p. 27.

[33]Nancy L. Croft, "Wrapping Up Sales," *Nation's Business,* October 1985, pp. 41–42.

Chapter 15

[1]Bob Lauterborn, "What Should Ad Majors Learn?" *Advertising Age,* January 19, 1987, pp. 18, 20.

[2]See *Advertising Age,* January 8, 1979, p. S-8.

[3]A complete list of the early leading advertisers can be found in Maurice I. Mandell, *Advertising,* 2nd ed. (Englewood Cliffs, N.J.: Prentice-Hall, 1974), p. 37.

[4]"Hospitals Discover Some Marketing Savvy," *Sales and Marketing Management,* September 1986, p. 164.

[5]David J. Rachman and Michael H. Mescon, *Business Today,* 3rd ed. (New York: Random House, 1982), p. 297.

[6]Cecilia Reed, "Reading the Board Room Message Right," *Advertising Age,* January 23, 1984, p. M-9.

[7]For more on the persuasive function of advertising, see C. H. Sandage, "Basic Functions of Advertising," in *Issues in Advertising,* edited by Robert E. Karp (New York: MSS Information Corp., 1972), pp. 14–30.

[8]Harry D. Wolfe and Dik Twedt, *Essentials in the Promotional Mix* (New York: Appleton-Century-Crofts, 1970), p. 54.

[9]See Lawrence Wolf, "How to Make Your New Product Advertising Work Harder," *Advertising Age,* October 21, 1974, pp. 57–60; Ted Morgan, "New! Improved! Advertising!" *New York Times Magazine,* January 25, 1976, pp. 12–15+; and Thomas J. Reynolds and Jonathan Gutman, "Advertising Is Image Management," *Journal of Advertising Research* 24 (February/March 1984): 27–36.

[10]"Shiefflin Tests Dual-Positioned Red Wine," *Marketing News,* November 11, 1983, p. 4.

[11]Leo Greenland, "No This Is Not the Era of Positioning," *Advertising Age,* July 10, 1972, pp. 43–44, 46.

[12]For an account of Ogilvy's other image sells, see *Confessions of an Advertising Man* (New York: Atheneum, 1964).

[13]"Softening a Starchy Image," *Time,* July 11, 1983, p. 54.

[14]Bernice Kanner, "The Fizz Bizz," *New York,* January 16, 1984, pp. 10–16.

[15]For more information on this battle, see Bill Abrams, "Some New Ads May Rekindle Burger Battle," *The Wall Street Journal,* March 4, 1983, pp. 1, 31; "The Fast Food War: Big Mac under Attack," *Business Week,* January 30, 1984, pp. 44–46; and Anna Sobczynski, "Serving Up a Variety of Choices," *Advertising Age,* November 21, 1983, pp. M-9–M-10.

[16]Debbie Seaman, "Orangina Spots May Start 'Juice Wars,'" *Adweek,* August 4, 1986.

[17]See Gordon H. G. McDougall, "Comparative Advertising: Consumer Issues and Attitudes," in *Contemporary Marketing Thought: 1977 Educators' Proceedings,* edited by Barnett Greenberg and Danny Bellenger (Chicago: American Marketing Association, 1977), pp. 286–291; Edmond M. Rosenthal, "Comparative Ad—Weapon or Fad?" *Marketing Times,* September–October 1976, pp. 10–15; and Edwin McDowell, "Oh, for the Good Old Days of Brand X," *New York Times,* April 22, 1979, pp. F1, F9.

[18]These claims were made by an FTC spokesman on the "MacNeil/Lehrer Report," August 10, 1977.

[19]David J. Rachman and Michael H. Mescon, *Business Today,* p. 298.

[20]For more unusual "media," see Ed Brennan, *Advertising Media* (New York: McGraw-Hill, 1951), pp. 210–211.

[21]"Do Top Guns Swig Diet Pop?" *Time,* March 9, 1987, p. 65; Dottie Enrico and Mary Huhn, "Target Vision Aims for Travelers, Students," *Adweek,* September 15, 1986, p. 62.

[22]C. Whan Park and S. Mark Young, "Consumer Response to Television Commercials: The Impact of Involvement and Background Music on Brand Attitude Formation," *Journal of Marketing Research* 23 (February 1986): 11–24.

[23]Bill Abrams, "Advertisers Growing Restless over the Rising Cost of TV Time," *The Wall Street Journal,* July 19, 1983, p. 37; "Super Bowl XX: Who Bought the Million-Dollar Minutes?" *Business Week,* February 3, 1986, p. 94.

[24]Bill Abrams, "Planned Rise in TV Ads Stirs Debate," *The Wall Street Journal,* December 1, 1983, p. 31; Craig Reiss, "Opponents of Split 30s Fear Basic Change in TV," *Advertising Age,* October 31, 1983, pp. 3, 96.

[25]Nancy E. Marx, "Sponsors Start Making Shows to Plug Goods on Cable TV," August 25, 1983, p. 17.

[26]Andrew Jaffe and Jua Nyla Hutcheson-Brewster, "Radio Biz Eyes Anti-Drug Push," *Adweek,* September 15, 1986, p. 17.

[27]David J. Rachman and Michael H. Mescon, *Business Today,* p. 301.

[28]J. Fred MacDonald, "New Tools, New Tunes," *Advertising Age,* July 11, 1983, pp. M-9–M-10.

[29]Bill Abrams, "Entrepreneur's Slick Catalog for Affluent Is Pacing the Growing Direct-Mail Business," *The Wall Street Journal,* March 1, 1984, p. 25.

[30]Kevin Higgins, "Often Overlooked Outdoor Advertising Offers More Impact and Exposures than Most Media," *Marketing News,* July 22, 1983, pp. 1, 10.

[31]Philip H. Dougherty, "Advertising: Forecast of Future for Six Major Fields," *New York Times,* October 25, 1976; see also Stan Luxenberg, "For Billboards, the Signs Are Bullish," *New York Times,* June 25, 1978, p. F-3.

[32]*New York Times,* August 26, 1980.

[33]Bill Johnson, "Advertiser Thrives by Making Inflatables of Firms' Products," *The Wall Street Journal,* September 26, 1983, p. 25.

[34]Laurie P. Cohen, "Thought Goodyear Had the Corner on This Market? Keep Looking Up," *The Wall Street Journal,* September 26, 1983, p. 25.

[35]Jack Feuer, "Activists, Industry Rethinking Men's Place in Ads," *Adweek,* September 29, 1986, pp. 56, 60.

[36]Nancy Millman, "Consumers Rate Advertising High," *Advertising Age,* October 24, 1983, pp. 1, 18.

[37]Philip Kotler, *Principles of Marketing,* 3rd ed. (Englewood Cliffs, N.J.: Prentice-Hall, 1986), pp. 528–529.

[38]"Sweet Sell Garners 100% Response for Phone Equipment Manufacturer," *Marketing News,* April 1, 1983, p. 3.

[39]Sally Scanlon, "Let's Hear It for Recognition," *Sales and Marketing Management,* April 12, 1976, p. 44; see also James O'Hanlon, "Even a Millionaire Couldn't Buy Something Like That," *Forbes,* November 1, 1977, pp. 88–90.

[40]J. Max Robins, "Making Point of Purchase More Pointed," *Adweek,* November 10, 1986, pp. P.G. 8, P.G. 10.

[41]"Cosmetics Display Walls Spearhead Boom in Point-of-Purchase Media Use," *Marketing News,* February 18, 1983, p. 18.

[42]J. Max Robins "Making Point of Purchase More Pointed," p. P.G. 10.

[43]Felix Kessler, "The Costly Coupon Craze," *Fortune,* June 9, 1986, pp. 83–84.

[44]Joanne Lipman, "Firms Bid to Cut Sales Coupons, Other Incentives," *The Wall Street Journal,* February 3, 1987, p. 37.

[45]Jennifer Alter and Nancy Giges, "Industry Losing $350 Million on Coupon Misredemption," and Nancy Giges, "New Coupon Trap Set," both in *Advertising Age,* May 30, 1983, pp. 1, 57.

[46]Joanne Lipman, "Firms Bid to Cut Sales Coupons, Other Incentives."

[47]Timothy K. Smith, "Buy One Car, Get One Free: Marketers Experiment with Freebies on Grand Scale," *The Wall Street Journal,* March 16, 1987, p. 23.

[48]Bernice Kanner, "Teaser Strips," *New York,* March 17, 1986, pp. 24, 27.

[49]"Marathon Sponsorship Is Promotion Centerpiece for Xerox Photocopier Line," *Marketing News,* February 17, 1984, pp. 1, 10.

[50]This section is based on Scott H. Cutlip and Allen H. Center, *Effective Public Relations,* 5th ed. (Englewood Cliffs, N.J.: Prentice-Hall, 1982), pp. 8–11.

[51]David P. McClure, "Publicity Should Be Integrated in Marketing Plan," *Marketing News,* December 10, 1982, p. 6.

[52]Roy R. Bumsted, "How to Measure Effectiveness of PR Campaign," *Marketing News,* March 18, 1983, p. 13.

Chapter 16

[1]Gay Sands Miller, "Nabisco Sees Its Sales Force Providing Promotional Services for Other Firms," *The Wall Street Journal,* April 21, 1980, p. 20.

[2]Robert N. McMurry, "The Mystique of Super-Salesmanship," *Harvard Business Review* (March–April 1961): 114.

[3]"How a Salesman Urges Auto Companies to Use More Aluminum Parts," *The Wall Street Journal,* June 13, 1977, p. 1.

[4]"1987 Survey of Selling Costs: Compensation," *Sales and Marketing Management,* February 16, 1987, pp. 51–59.

[5]"Top Commission-Only Reps' Average Take: 185 Gs," *Sales and Marketing Management,* October 1986, pp. 26–27.

[6]Richard Kern, "From a Reporter to a Source: A New Survey of Selling Costs," *Sales and Marketing Management,* February 16, 1987, pp. 12–14.

[7]Charles Futrell, *Sales Management: Behavior, Practice, and Cases* (Hinsdale, Ill.: The Dryden Press, 1981), p. 147.

[8]Ibid., pp. 185–189.

[9]See, for example, Robert N. McMurry, "The Mystique of Super-Salesmanship," for the notion that self-confidence is essential to successful selling. The opposite view is forwarded by Gerard W. Ditz, "Status Problems of the Salesman," *MSU Business Topics* (Winter 1967), especially p. 77. A more recent assessment of needed traits is found in Lawrence M. Lamont and W. J. Lundstrom, "Identifying Successful Industrial Salesmen by Personality and Personal Characteristics," *Journal of Marketing Research* (November 1977): 517–529.

[10]William B. Mead, "The Life of a Salesman," *Money,* October 1980, pp. 117–124.

[11]Franklin B. Evans, "Selling as a Dyadic Relationship—A New Approach," *American Behavioral Scientist,* May 1963, pp. 76–79.

[12]John Wolfe, "How to Hire the Best Possible Sales Force," *INC.,* November 1980, p. 120.

[13]Ibid.

[14]"Block Drug Takes the Cure," *Sales and Marketing Management,* June 14, 1976, pp. 33–35.

[15]Thayer C. Taylor, "Hewlett-Packard Gives Sales Reps a Competitive Edge," *Sales and Marketing Management,* February 1987, pp. 36–38+.

[16]Stan Kossen, *Creative Selling Today* (San Francisco: Canfield Press, 1977), p. 140.

[17]"What Makes a Good Presentation? It Depends on Where You Sit," *Sales and Marketing Management,* January 22, 1973, p. 45.

[18]More detail on this suggestion can be found in W. J. E. Crissy et al., *Selling and the Personal Force in Marketing* (New York: Wiley, 1977), pp. 247–250.

[19]"Rebirth of a Salesman: Willy Loman Goes Electronic," *Business Week,* February 27, 1984, pp. 103–104.

[20]Marvin A. Jolson, "Direct Selling: Consumer vs. Salesman," *Business Horizons,* October 1972, pp. 87–95.

[21]Cited in David L. Kurtz et al., *Professional Selling* (Dallas: Business Publications, Inc., 1976), p. 238.

[22]"The New Supersalesman—Wired for Success," *Business Week,* January 6, 1973, p. 48.

[23]William J. Stanton and Richard H. Buskirk, *Management of the Sales Force,* 7th ed. (Homewood, Ill.: Irwin, 1987), p. 326.

[24]John A. Byrne, "Motivating Willy Loman," *Forbes,* January 30, 1984, p. 91.

[25]Some firms use a "draw against commission" combination. They pay their salespeople a fixed amount regularly, but the amount is deducted from commissions they make. Salespersons whose draws regularly exceed their commissions are, of course, not long for the sales force.

[26]William J. Stanton and Richard H. Buskirk, *Management of the Sales Force,* pp. 301, 325.

[27]John Wolfe, "How to Hire the Best Possible Sales Force," p. 121.

[28]Benson P. Shapiro and Stephen X. Doyle, "Make the Sales Task Clear," *Harvard Business Review* (November–December 1983): 75–76.

[29]"Rebirth of a Salesman: Willy Loman Goes Electronic."

[30]Yovovich, *Advertising Age,* June 14, 1983, p. M-22.

Chapter 17

[1]Hewlett-Packard's story is told at length in George Leroy, *Multinational Product Strategy: A Typology for Analysis of Worldwide Product Innovation and Diffusion* (New York: Praeger, 1976), pp. 74–77. See also Vern Terpstra, *International Marketing,* 4th ed. (Hinsdale, Ill.: The Dryden Press, 1987), p. 307.

[2]Vern Terpstra, *International Marketing,* p. 4.

[3]Ibid., pp. 24–25.

[4]Philip Kotler, *Marketing Management,* 5th ed. (Englewood Cliffs, N.J.: Prentice-Hall, 1984).

[5]Vern Terpstra, *International Marketing,* p. 9.

[6]John S. McClenahen, "Who Owns U.S. Industry?" *Industry Week,* January 7, 1985, pp. 30–34.

[7]We are grateful to Professor J. J. Boddewyn of Baruch College for the distinctions made in this section.

[8]*Economic Indicators, January 1987* (Washington, D.C.: U.S. Government Printing Office, 1987).

[9]See Silver and Schwartz, "The U.S. Industrial Marketer's Position in International Trade," pp. 343–345.

[10]Vern Terpstra, *International Marketing,* pp. 360–363.

[11]"Egypt an Oasis for Soft Drinks," *New York Times,* August 1, 1978, p. D1.

[12]"Will Big Mac Meet Its Match in the Land of the Rising Sun?" *Forbes,* May 15, 1978, p. 118.

[13]"Are Foreign Partners Good for U.S. Companies?" *Business Week,* May 28, 1984, pp. 58–60.

[14]Ibid., p. 59.

[15]Vern Terpstra, *International Marketing,* p. 365.

[16]John S. McClenahen, "Who Owns U.S. Industry?"

[17]Vern Terpstra, *International Marketing,* p. 55.

[18]Vern Terpstra, *International Marketing,* p. 59; and *The World Almanac 1987* (New York: Pharos Books, 1987), pp. 545–634.

[19]See "Egypt an Oasis for Soft Drinks," p. D4; and Fox Butterfield, "The China Trade: Companies Mob Peking," *New York Times,* February 4, 1979, sec. 12, p. 58.

[20]Philip Kotler and Gary Armstrong, *Marketing: An Introduction* (Englewood Cliffs, N.J.: Prentice-Hall, 1987), pp. 478–479.

[21]Judann Dagnoli, "Home Shopping Beams to Japan," *Advertising Age,* January 19, 1987, p. 8.

[22]José de la Torre, "Product Life Cycle as a Determinant of Global Marketing Strategies," *Atlanta Economic Review,* September–October 1975, p. 14.

[23]Joshua Hyatt, "Bad Translations Turn Ads from Mild to Spicy," *INC.,* November 1986, p. 18.

[24]Karen Singer, "Commerce in China Requires an Eye toward Custom," *Adweek,* March 2, 1987.

[25]Eliyahu Tal, "Advertising in Developing Countries," *Journal of Advertising* (Spring 1974): 21.

[26]Perry Pascarella, "In Search of Universal Designs," *Industry Week,* July 22, 1985, pp. 47, 49, 52.

[27]A. Graeme Cranch, "Modern Marketing Techniques Applied to Developing Countries," *1972 Proceedings of the Spring and Fall Conference of the American Marketing Association,* edited by Boris W. Becker and Helmut Becker (Chicago: American Marketing Association, 1972), pp. 183–186; and Lee Adler, "Special Wrinkles in International Marketing Research—Part I," *Sales and Marketing Management,* July 12, 1976, p. 63.

[28]See Hans Scholhammer, "Ethics in an International Business Context," *MSU Business Topics* (Spring 1977): 54–63; and "Coping with the New Rules of Conduct," *Business Week,* October 10, 1977, pp. 76–77.

[29]There are two general classes of tariffs: protective tariffs, which seek to raise the price of an imported product to match or exceed a similar domestic product; and revenue tariffs, designed to raise funds for the government. See David L. Kurtz and Louis E. Boone, *Contemporary Marketing,* 5th ed. (Hinsdale, Ill.: The Dryden Press, 1986), pp. 526–527.

[30]Stephen Koepp, "Fighting the Trade Tilt," *Time,* April 6, 1987, pp. 50–51.

[31]"Netherlands Woos U.S. Companies," *The Wall Street Journal,* March 7, 1984, p. 30.

[32]See Gerry Semmel, "Developing Trade with the People's Republic of China," *Industrial Marketing,* July 1976, pp. 70–72.

[33]Clyde H. Farnsworth, "Easing a Company's Risks Overseas," *New York Times,* April 25, 1982, sec. 3, 6:3.

[34]R. J. Rummel and David A. Heenan, "How Multinationals Analyze Political Risk," *Harvard Business Review* (January–February 1978): 67–76. See also Frank Vogl, "Protection against Political Upheaval," *New York Times,* January 28, 1979, sec. 3, pp. 1, 12.

[35]Vern Terpstra, *International Marketing,* p. 134.

[36]Ibid., p. 130.

[37]For a more in-depth discussion of GATT, see Vern Terpstra, *International Marketing,* pp. 34–35.

[38]Lee Adler, "Special Wrinkles in International Marketing Research," p. 63.

[39]For other types of marketing research problems, see Charles S. Mayer, "The Lessons of Multinational Marketing Research," *Business Horizons,* December 1978, pp. 7–13.

[40]Theodore Levitt, "The Globalization of Markets," *Harvard Business Review* (May–June 1983): 92–102; and Perry Pascarella, "In Search of Universal Designs," p. 49.

[41]Theodore Levitt, "The Globalization of Markets."

[42]Peter G. P. Walters, "International Marketing Policy: A Discussion of the Standardization Construct and Its Relevance for Corporate Policy," *Journal of International Business Studies* (Summer 1986): 55–69.

[43]Vern Terpstra, *International Marketing,* p. 244; Ulrich Weichman, "Integrating Multinational Marketing Activity," *Columbia Journal of World Business* (Winter 1974): 12–13; and Norris Willatt, "How Nestlé Adapts Product to Its Markets," *Business Abroad,* June 1970, pp. 31–33.

[44]Richard D. Robinson, *International Business Management* (New York: Holt, Rinehart & Winston, 1973), p. 27; and Edwin McDowell, "Coke's Hi-C Aims to Raise Food Value of Soft Drinks," *New York Times,* April 24, 1978, pp. D1–D2.

[45]Vern Terpstra, *International Marketing,* pp. 254–255.

[46]S. B. Prasad and Y. Krishna Shetty, *An Introduction to Multinational Management* (Englewood Cliffs, N.J.: Prentice-Hall, 1976), p. 155.

[47]Eduardo Lachica, "Some South Korean and Taiwan Firms Face Possible Dumping Duties on T.V. Sets," *The Wall Street Journal,* February 27, 1984, p. 8.

[48]See Vern Terpstra, *International Marketing,* pp. 539–545; and Stephan H. Robock et al., *International Business and Multinational Enterprises* (Homewood, Ill.: Irwin, 1977), pp. 465–468.

[49]Vern Terpstra, *International Marketing,* p. 234.

[50]Erin Anderson and Anne T. Coughlan, "International Market Entry and Expansion via Independent or Integrated Channels of Distribution," *Journal of Marketing* 51 (January 1987): 71–82.

[51]Vern Terpstra, *International Marketing,* pp. 388–390.

[52]Ibid., p. 408.

[53]Ibid., pp. 534–535.

[54]Ibid., p. 445.

[55]Ralph Gray and Jessee Snyder, "GM Mapping Future on Truly Global Scale," *Advertising Age,* March 12, 1984, pp. 3, 64.

[56]David I. McIntyre, "Multinational Positioning Strategy," *Columbia Journal of World Business* (Fall 1975): 109.

[57]Claire Wilson, "Going European: Club Med Tries for Broader Appeal with New Pan-Regional Campaign," *Advertising Age,* January 19, 1987, p. 50.

[58]Jack Burton, "Swedish Shops Using PSA Spots to Improve Ad Quality," *Advertising Age,* January 19, 1987, p. 50.

[59]See Christine D. Urban, "A Cross-National Comparison of Consumer Media Patterns," *Columbia Journal of World Business* (Winter 1977): 53–64; and Cranch, "Modern Marketing Techniques Applied to Developing Countries," p. 414.

[60]Mary McKinney, "McCann-Erickson Gets Thai Birth Control Account," *Advertising Age,* February 6, 1984, p. 35.

[61]S. B. Prasad and Y. Krishna Shetty, *An Introduction to Multinational Management,* p. 159.

[62]Douglas and Dubois, "Looking at the Cultural Environment for International Marketing Opportunities," p. 107; and Blair R. Gettig, "Some Basic Lessons for the U.S. Adman Whose Company Is Going Multinational," *International Marketing,* November 1976, p. 70.

[63]Carolyn Hulse and Mike Diebert, "Miller's Canadian Launch Is a Hit," *Advertising Age,* October 17, 1983, p. 47.

[64]Laurel Wentz, "Marketing Errors Doomed Sears in Brazil," *Advertising Age,* May 16, 1983, p. 32.

Chapter 18

[1]"Hospitals Go Courting," *American Demographics* (September 1986): 14–15.

[2]See Chapter 1. See also Philip Kotler, "A Generic Concept of Marketing," *Journal of Marketing* (April 1972): 46–54; Robert Bartels, "The Identity Crises in Marketing," *Journal of Marketing* (October 1974): 73–76; and Richard P. Bagozzi, "Marketing As an Exchange," *Journal of Marketing* (October 1975): 32–39.

[3]Philip Kotler, *Marketing for Nonprofit Organizations* (Englewood Cliffs, N.J.: Prentice-Hall, 1975), p. 365.

[4]Philip Kotler, *Principles of Marketing,* 3rd ed. (Englewood Cliffs, N.J.: Prentice-Hall, 1986), p. 693.

[5]". . . And We'd All Been Drinking," *Reader's Digest,* June 1986.

[6]The categories are those of Peter M. Blau and W. Richard Scott, *Formal Organizations* (San Francisco: Chandler, 1962), pp. 45–58.

[7]See *General Executive Board Report 1977,* 36th Convention, International Ladies' Garment Workers' Union, Hollywood, Florida, May 27, 1977, pp. 78–86.

[8]Jim Brosseau, "Recruiters: Keep Best of Army Campaign," *Adweek,* January 26, 1987.

[9]Philip Kotler, *Marketing for Nonprofit Organizations,* p. 19.

[10]These differences are discussed more fully in George Wasem, "Marketing for Profits and Nonprofits," *Banker's Monthly Magazine,* March 15, 1975, pp. 23–24; and Franklin S. Houston and Richard E. Homans, "Public Agency Marketing: Pitfalls and Problems," *MSU Business Topics* (Summer 1977): 36–40.

[11]For a more detailed discussion, see George Wasem, "Marketing for Profits and Nonprofits," pp. 25–27; and Ray O'Leary and Ian Iredale, "The Marketing Concept: Quo Vadis?" *European Journal of Marketing* (1976): 146–157.

[12]Chicago Historical Society, *Annual Report 1985–1986.*

[13]William A. Mindak and H. Malcolm Bybee, "Marketing's Application to Fund Raising," *Journal of Marketing* (July 1971): 14.

[14]Lawrence Ingrassia, "Some Catholics Try Shopping about a Bit to Find Best Parish," *The Wall Street Journal,* July 6, 1982, pp. 1, 4.

[15]"My Beautiful Laundry Ride," *Time,* March 2, 1987, p. 55.

[16]Daniel F. Hansler, "American Cancer Society's Market Planning Process," *Fund Raising Management,* August 1983, pp. 32–40.

[17]See Philip Kotler and Gerald Zaltman, "Social Marketing: An Approach to Planned Social Change," *Journal of Marketing* (July 1971): 7.

[18]Other examples of the widening product mix of museums can be found in Roger Ricklefs, "Museums Merchandise

More Shows and Wares to Broaden Patronage," *The Wall Street Journal,* August 14, 1975, p. 1.

[19]See "The Pleasures of Nonprofitability," *Forbes,* November 15, 1976, pp. 90–94.

[20]A good summary of the complexities of pricing for nonprofit organizations is found in Benson P. Shapiro, "Marketing for Nonprofit Organizations," *Harvard Business Review* (October 1973): 130.

[21]Barry Witt, "Having a Baby? You Might Be Able to Save Some Money in Las Vegas," *The Wall Street Journal,* July 12, 1983, p. 37.

[22]Dottie Enrico, "DFS Breaks Ads for Adoption Group," *Adweek,* December 22, 1986.

[23]Alan L. Otten, "When Institute of Medicine Speaks, People Listen, Because Newest President Won't Let It Be Ignored," *The Wall Street Journal,* March 31, 1987, p. 64.

[24]Andrea Rothman, "Ms. Buffy Lowe and Friends Made a Tidy Profit on April Fool's Day," *The Wall Street Journal,* April 3, 1987, p. 29.

[25]*The Wall Street Journal,* December 28, 1982, p. 17.

[26]Linda Charlton, "New York Just *Loves* Its Tourists," *Boston Globe,* June 26, 1983, p. 54.

[27]Bernice Kanner, "This Ad Is Your Ad," *New York,* April 4, 1983, p. 16.

[28]See Philip Kotler, *Marketing for Nonprofit Organizations,* pp. 211–213.

[29]American Cancer Society, *1983 Annual Report.*

[30]See A. J. Martin et al., "Marketing Research Applications in Recruiting: Meeting Manpower Requirements in the All-Volunteer Armed Forces," *1978 Proceedings of the American Marketing Association* (Chicago: American Marketing Association, 1978), p. 363; Philip Kotler, *Marketing for Nonprofit Organizations,* pp. 397–399; and Bernice Kanner, "This Ad Is Your Ad."

[31]Bernice Kanner, "This Ad Is Your Ad."

[32]The measures discussed are suggested by Philip Kotler in *Marketing for Nonprofit Organizations,* pp. 250–251.

[33]William A. Mindak and H. Malcolm Bybee, "Marketing's Application to Fund Raising," p. 17.

[34]"Why People Are Sore at Postal Service," *U.S. News and World Report,* March 15, 1976, p. 19.

Appendix A

[1]Based on surveys in marketing, sales, and sales management classes at Lansing Community College and in an advertising class at Michigan State University.

Appendix C

[1]*Small business* has been defined in many ways by various organizations. The Small Business Administration, a government agency, classifies businesses as small according to number of employees and sales volume. The specific guidelines vary though, depending on the industry. For example, a construction company is small if sales do not exceed $12 million. In contrast, a retail variety store must have sales of less than $2.5 million in order to be considered small. Some manufacturing plants are considered small only if they have less than 500 employees, while others can have as many as 1,000. "Small business," then, includes the mom-and-pop store, but also many other firms.

Glossary

ABC Analysis
Inventory technique for identifying items with biggest sales payoffs by listing them by sales volume. Best sellers ("A" products) must be stocked at all times.

Accessory Equipment
Less expensive industrial product necessary to the final product's manufacture though not part of it—for example, hand tools and office equipment.

Acquisition Cost
Expense incurred in preparing for manufacturing or in buying product for inventory.

Administered System
Vertical marketing system in which one member secures agreement from other members of a channel on certain plans concerning price, display, and advertising.

Advertising
Any paid form of nonpersonal presentation and promotion of ideas, goods, or services by an identified sponsor.

Advertising Allowance
Reimbursement by a manufacturer for part of the cost of local advertising run by retailers and wholesalers.

Agent
Wholesale intermediary who merely arranges for the buying and selling of goods but never actually acquires ownership or possession of the goods.

Approach (Warm-Up)
Beginning of sales presentation intended to secure attention and to establish rapport and credibility with the client.

Arm's-Length Policy
Policy that requires a firm's subsidiary to charge or be charged the same price available to any buyer outside the firm.

Aspirational Group
Reference group with which a person may want to be identified.

Association Advertising
Advertising sponsored by a trade association to promote a class of products or services.

Atmospherics
Marketing task of creating certain effects in buyers by designing store environments.

Attitude
State that includes a person's beliefs about and feelings toward some object, combined with a tendency to behave in a certain way with respect to that object.

Attitude Scale
Technique for measuring consumer attitudes that poses statements about which respondents are asked to indicate the intensity of their agreement or disagreement.

Auction Company
Agent wholesaler that works on a one-time basis for a commission; may send catalogs to prospective buyers and take bids at time of auction.

Automated Warehouse
Facility with advanced materials handling systems under control of a central computer.

Average Markup
Single percentage used to determine the selling price of each item in a given product line.

Bait Pricing
Illegal practice of advertising a "special" at a cut-rate price with no intention to sell at the price advertised.

Basing-Point Pricing
Policy of calculating freight charges not from their factories but from a city or cities designated by members of an industry.

Benefit Segmentation
Division of a market into classes on the basis of benefits that members of each class seek.

Breakeven Analysis
Way for price setters to determine what will happen to profits at various price levels.

Broker
Agent wholesaler who brings buyers and sellers together, acting on behalf of one or the other and used on a one-time basis.

Business Analysis
Process of estimating future sales and profit potential of a new product.

Buyer
Person, often called purchasing agent, with the formal responsibility of placing orders.

Buyer Behavior
Study that provides marketing managers with an understanding of what is behind the decision to spend money, time, and effort on consumption-related items.

Buyer's Market
Market in which there is an abundance of goods and services.

Buying Center
Group involved in purchasing for an industrial market.

Cannibalization
Process by which a company's new product takes sales away from existing products in the same company's line.

Carrying Cost
Expense of holding goods over a period of time.

Cash-and-Carry Wholesaler
Limited-function merchant wholesaler who does not give credit.

Cash Discount
Reduction from list price made for early payment.

Catalog Showroom
Retail discount business based on catalog promotion and showrooms that display a limited selection of the items in the catalog. Customers receive goods from an adjacent warehouse.

Census
Complete canvass of every member of a population under study.

Central Business District
Downtown shopping area of most cities, consisting of large department stores and specialty stores.

Chain Store
Group of stores centrally owned and managed that sell similar goods.

Channel Captain
Member of a marketing channel with power or ability to set and enforce policy.

Channel Length
Number of links (intermediary types) in a particular marketing chain.

Channel Member Type
Kind of wholesaling intermediaries and retailers in a marketing channel.

Channel Number
Quantity of different marketing channels to use in order to reach buyers.

Channel Width
Number of outlets or individual firms to employ at each level in a channel.

Client Public
Those who directly use the product exchanged by nonprofit organizations.

Closing
Point of the selling process at which a prospect agrees to buy or decides not to buy.

Cluster Sampling
Probability sampling in which the population under study is divided into subgroups and then parts of the group are chosen at random to be sampled.

Combination Store
Combination of a supermarket and a drugstore under a single roof.

Combination Strategy
Balance of selling, advertising, and other promotional techniques combining push and pull strategies to achieve sales goals.

Commission
Pay plan under which salespeople are paid a percentage of the sales they close.

Commission Merchant
Agent wholesaler who markets the output of small farmers for a commission; may store goods but does not take title.

Common Carrier
Transport company that must serve the general public.

Comparative Advertising
Creative style that uses names of competitors.

Competitive Comparison Budgeting
Plan to spend as much on promotion as leading firms do.

Concentrated Marketing
Practice of dividing the market into market segments and selecting only one segment to serve with a marketing mix.

Concurrent Testing
Securing information while a promotional effort is under way.

Consumer Market
Individuals who buy either for their own or for their family's personal consumption.

Consumer Products
Goods sold to individuals or households for their personal use.

Consumer Responsibility
Buyers' obligation to know their rights and to make informed judgments.

Consumerism
Movement to increase the influence, power, and rights of consumers in their dealings with institutions of all types.

Container
Large, standard size metal box into which goods are placed for shipping and which is sealed.

Contract Carrier
Means of transport that serves only a limited number of customers and may negotiate different rates for different customers.

Contractual System
Vertical marketing system based on a formal agreement among channel members to cooperate on such matters as buying, advertising, accounting practices, and other functions. Forms are franchises, retail-sponsored cooperatives, and wholesale-sponsored voluntaries.

Contribution (Incremental) Pricing
Special type of cost-plus pricing that allows companies to produce unprofitable items to cover variable costs.

Convenience Goods
Products that individuals buy quickly and often.

Convenience Sample
Nonprobability sample in which subjects are chosen on the basis of convenience to the researcher.

Convenience Store
Small retail outlet that provides snacks and staple groceries quickly and conveniently.

Corporate System
Vertical marketing system in which one channel member fully or partially owns the business operations of two or more channel levels.

Correlation Analysis
Statistical method of forecasting used to find factors that change in advance of changes in product demand.

Cost-Benefit Analysis
System for weighing economic costs against economic benefits.

Cost-Plus Pricing
Policy of setting prices by totaling costs and adding a margin of profit.

Cost Trade-Off
Practice of allowing costs to increase in one business area to bring down costs in another.

Coupon
Sales promotion tool aimed at consumers that offers a certain amount off the price of an item.

Creative Salespeople
Individuals charged with determining customers' needs, helping them solve problems, and getting orders.

Culture
A people's shared customs, beliefs, values, and artifacts that are transmitted from generation to generation.

Cumulative Discount
Policy that permits a customer to total up consecutive orders to qualify for the discount.

Customary Pricing
Pricing some types of products—usually small-value items—at a certain level to avert consumer resistance at higher levels.

Customer Sampling
Survey conducted to sample customers' intentions to buy.

Data Bank
Marketing information system's storehouse of information gathered from internal and external environments and used to retrieve data selectively; also called a data base.

Decider
Manager with authority to make the final choice.

Decline Phase
Stage of product life cycle during which products start losing a significant number of customers without replacing them.

Decoding
Retranslating a message into terms the receiver understands.

Demarketing
Promotion aimed at persuading the public that there are valid economic reasons for withdrawing a product.

Demographic Segmentation
Division of a market into classes on the basis of geographic proximity or some shared socioeconomic trait.

Department Store
Store that brings together a number of items under one roof.

Depression
Phase of the business cycle characterized by a radical drop in business activity and consequent high unemployment and business failure.

Derived Demand
Demand by industrial users that depends on consumer demand for the finished product.

Differential Advantage
Special edge over competition an organization may have or develop by working with the elements of the marketing mix.

Differentiated Marketing
Practice of marketing to many market segments, each with a different marketing mix.

Direct Investment
Total control of production and sales of goods in a foreign country.

Discount
Deduction made from the list price and offered to wholesalers and retailers.

Discount Store
Store that sells fast-moving branded merchandise at cut-rate prices.

Discretionary Income
Any money remaining from disposable income that a family or individual is free to spend for luxuries or save.

Disposable Income
Any money that remains after taxes are paid and that is spent for necessities.

Dissociative Group
Reference group from which a person may want to dissociate himself or herself.

Distribution
Activity directed toward placing goods and services where they are needed and when they are wanted.

Distribution Center Warehouse
Facility that serves primarily as a temporary way-station before the goods are rapidly moved to customers.

Drop Shipper
Limited-function merchant wholesaler who neither maintains a warehouse nor carries inventories but who takes title to goods and is responsible for billing and collecting payment.

Dumping
Practice of selling goods overseas at a lower price than a company charges in its own home market.

Economic Forecast
Prediction of how the economy will fare as a whole in light of changes in the national and international business climate.

Economic Infrastructure
Facilities such as paved roads, communication and transportation services, banks, and distribution organizations that make marketing possible.

Economic Order Quantity (EOQ)
Amount of stock that costs the least to keep on hand in order to meet the average level of demand.

Elastic Demand
Relationship that holds between price and revenue if total revenue increases with a price drop or decreases with a price rise.

Elasticity of Demand
Rate at which demand changes in response to price changes.

Emergency Items
Products bought when an unexpected need arises.

Encoding
Putting a message into understandable form by the source.

Environmental Analysis
Examination of the environment and identification of the circumstances and conditions that can cause the greatest problems or offer the greatest opportunities.

Exchange
Process by which two or more parties freely give something of value to one another to satisfy needs and wants.

Exclusive Distribution
Selling a product through only one wholesaler or retailer in a given area.

Executive-Panel Survey
Means for sales forecasting using opinions of company officials.

Exempt Carrier
Form of transportation not subject to direct federal regulation.

Experimentation
Research method that establishes cause and effect relationships.

F.O.B. Pricing
Practice of having the buyer choose and pay for transportation from the time goods are loaded on a carrier ("free on board"). The buyer takes title at that time.

Factory-Positioned Warehouse
Facility used to store raw materials and fabricated parts until they are needed for manufacture or one that serves as a traditional warehouse or distribution center for finished products.

Fad
Product with a short life cycle, usually no more than two years.

Family Brand
Brand that covers many products under one brand name.

Family Life Cycle
Traditional stages through which families pass, from the unmarried state through child rearing, empty nest, and loss of a spouse.

Feedback
Understanding signaled by the receiver to the source.

Fixed Costs
Costs that do not vary with a firm's output; also called overhead.

Fixed-Sum-per-Unit Budgeting
Allocating a specified amount for each unit produced.

Flanker Product
Item related to an already established product and bearing the same brand name.

Fluctuating Demand
Demand in the industrial sector that may vary widely in response to changing economic conditions or changes in consumer tastes.

Focus Group Interview
Method of determining customer attitudes by interviewing a relatively homogeneous group assembled to discuss a topic.

Follow-Up
Stage of the selling process during which a salesperson checks to see that orders have been filled and the customer is satisfied.

Forecasting
Predicting demand in the marketplace over a given period of time.

Foreign Marketing
Operating within the foreign country where goods are to be sold.

Foreign Trade
Home production and the export of products across national boundaries.

Form Utility
Value added to a product by converting raw materials into a finished good.

Four "Ps"
Elements of the marketing mix, which are product, price, promotion, and placement.

Franchising Arrangement
Agreement whereby an independent businessperson sells the products or services of a parent company, uses its name, and adopts its policies in exchange for an exclusive territory.

Freight Forwarder
Company that consolidates small shipments from a number of companies for transport in full loads.

Full-Service Merchant Wholesaler
Wholesale intermediary who performs a wide variety of distribution tasks such as assembly, storage and delivery, and financing, and may provide market information.

Gatekeeper
Organizational member who controls the flow of information into the buying center.

General (Macro) Environment
Economic, technological, legal, and social forces that are largely outside the control of marketers and that affect the success or failure of marketing plans.

General Public
Those who have an indirect interest in a nonprofit organization's goods or services.

Generic Product
Product that is unbranded and marketed with minimal advertising.

Goals
Organizational objectives that have been made specific with regard to size and time.

Goods
Tangible objects exchanged in marketing.

Government Organization
Nonprofit agency that serves the interests of the public at large.

Growth Phase
Stage of product life cycle during which product availability and marketing efforts expand and sales and profits surge upward.

Halo Effect
Transfer of goodwill from one product in a company's line to another.

Heterogeneous Shopping Goods
Products that a consumer will buy only after making a comparison of the style or quality of brands—for example, a dress or suit.

Hidden Costs
Costs of doing business—for example, a cancelled order—that do not show up on a profit and loss statement.

Home Improvement Center
Large-scale hardware store that offers one-stop shopping for around-the-house needs at prices that may be somewhat lower than those at smaller hardware stores.

Homogeneous Shopping Goods
Products that a consumer buys only after making price comparisons among sellers—consumers see them as essentially the same.

Hypermarket
Giant mass merchandiser that offers a broad selection of hard and soft goods and grocery items at discount prices on a self-serve basis.

Hypothesis
Educated guess about the relationship between things or what will happen in the future.

Idea Marketing
Offering a cause in exchange for public acceptance.

Import Quota
Restriction on the number of goods entering a country.

Impulse Items
Products bought on the spur of the moment.

Incubation Phase
Stage of product life cycle during which a product is conceived, developed, and tested.

Independent Store
Store owned and managed by a single person, partnership, or corporation, usually a one-unit operation.

Individual Brand
Distinct name given to each product a company produces.

Industrial Distributor
Wholesaler who sells to the industrial market.

Industrial Market
Businesses, governments, and organizations that buy goods and services for resale or for use in producing other goods and services.

Industry Forecast
Prediction of likely sales for a class of products.

Inelastic Demand
As it relates to consumer behavior: Demand that remains relatively constant despite price changes. *As it relates to price setting:* Relationship that holds between price and revenue if total revenue increases with price rises or declines with price cuts.

Influencer
One who can affect the decision process by assisting in evaluating alternative products.

Innovator
Person who is first to find out about and use a new product.

Input
Facts not in a consumer's control that may affect decisions to buy.

Installation
Large, expensive, industrial product necessary for the production of final products but not a part of those goods —for example, industrial plants and major equipment.

Institutional (or Corporate) Advertising
Paid message designed to build long-range goodwill for a firm rather than to sell specific goods.

Intensive Distribution
Selling a product through almost all available wholesale or retail outlets.

Intermediate-Positioned Warehouse
Storage place that serves manufacturers with several plants and widely scattered markets by gathering products of various plants and mixing them for shipment.

Intermodal Transportation
Coordination of two or more transportation modes to minimize the disadvantages and maximize the strong points of each.

Internal (Micro) Environment
Factors in an organization (such as financial resources and employees) capable of being influenced but not totally controlled by marketing managers.

International Marketing
Peformance of marketing activities across national boundaries.

Intrapreneurship
Entrepreneurial activity within an organization.

Introductory Phase
Stage of product life cycle during which a company brings a new product to the marketplace.

Joint Demand
Market condition when demand for one product will be affected by the availability of another product with which it is used.

Joint Venture
Partnership with a foreign firm under which both partners invest money and share ownership and control in proportion to their investment.

Judgment Sample
Nonprobability sample composed of subjects who are specially qualified in the area of interest of a study.

Law of Demand
Economic rule that states more goods generally are sold at a lower price than at a higher one.

Learning
Any change in an individual's response or behavior resulting from practice, experience, or mental association.

Legal Environment
Laws that compel businesses to operate under competitive conditions and to observe specified consumer rights.

Licensing
Process by which designer or character names or identities are leased to businesses for use on their products in exchange for royalties.

Life-Style
Person's pattern of living expressed in activities, interests, and opinions.

Limited-Function Merchant Wholesaler
Merchant wholesaler who provides only a few services for customers.

List Price
Selling price quoted to buyers.

Loss Leader
Item priced below cost to attract customers.

Mail Order Firm
Company that provides a wide range of goods ordered by customers from catalogs and shipped directly to them by mail.

Mail-Order Wholesaler
Limited-function merchant wholesaler who does not en-

gage in personal selling; sales catalogs are sent to retail firms or other wholesalers.

Manufactured Materials (Manufactured Parts)
Industrial goods that have in some way been shaped or finished and are incorporated into another product.

Manufacturers' Agent
Agent wholesaler who handles marketing in areas a manufacturer chooses not to cover with the manufacturer's own sales force.

Market
For business, those who are willing to buy a firm's output and have the purchasing power to do so. For nonprofit firms, those who have an interest in a product and are willing to exchange something in return (whether monetary or nonmonetary).

Market Potential
Total of all sales that might be generated in a market segment.

Market Segment
Group of individuals, groups, or organizations in a market that share similar characteristics that cause them to have similar wants or needs.

Market Share
Percentage of total industry sales that a particular firm can claim.

Marketing
Activities performed by individuals, businesses, and not-for-profit organizations that satisfy needs and wants through the process of exchange.

Marketing Concept
Business philosophy emphasizing that (1) companies should produce only what customers want; (2) management must integrate all company activities to develop programs to satisfy those wants; and (3) long-range profit goals should guide management.

Marketing (Distribution) Channel
The people and organizations involved in making a product available to a user.

Marketing Information System (MIS)
Orderly procedure for regular collection of raw data internally and externally and conversion of those data into information for use in making marketing decisions.

Marketing Manager
Chief marketing executive who coordinates the work of the members of a marketing department.

Marketing Mix
Plan that specifies what will be offered to customers (the product) and how (its price, promotion, and placement).

Marketing Objectives
Stated goals of the marketing department that specify quantitatively how marketing will contribute to meeting overall organizational objectives.

Marketing Research
Method for collecting, on a one-time basis, data pertinent to a particular marketing problem or opportunity.

Marketing Strategy
Concrete plan for achieving marketing objectives by using a specified marketing mix to reach a specified target market.

Market-Positioned Warehouse
Storage place designed to collect the products of one or more manufacturers in or near the market served before shipping goods short distances to customers.

Markup
Difference between the cost of an item and its selling price.

Markup Percentage
Markup expressed as a percentage.

Mass Marketing
Practice of directing the marketing mix at all potential buyers rather than a particular subgroup.

Maturity Phase
Stage of product life cycle during which the number of buyers continues to grow, but more slowly, until sales level off.

Media
All the different means by which advertising reaches its audiences.

Medium of Transmission
Means by which a message moves from sender to receiver.

Membership Group
Reference group to which a person may belong—for ex-

ample, family, friends, neighbors.

Merchandise Deliverer
Salesperson who sees that buyers receive their purchases.

Merchandising Conglomerate
Retail organization combining several, often unrelated, business units under central management.

Merchant Wholesaler
Independent who buys goods from manufacturers, takes physical possession of them, and sells them to other intermediaries.

Missionary
Salesperson whose role is to build goodwill or to educate potential customers rather than to make a direct sale.

Modified Rebuy
Repurchase in which the buyer wants to modify product specifications, prices, terms, or suppliers.

Modified Standardization Approach
Practice of changing one or more elements of the marketing mix.

Monopolistic Competition
Situation in which there are many sellers in a market who rarely engage in price competition but compete by trying to establish brand preferences among consumers.

Monopoly
Situation in which one company is the exclusive provider of a product or service.

Motivation
Inner state that activates or moves people toward goals.

Multimodal Shipping Company
Firm that combines shipping modes.

Multinational Marketing
Integrating marketing activities carried out in a number of countries.

Multiple Brand Strategy
Corporate practice of promoting individual brands that compete with one another.

Mutual Benefit Association
Association organized for the benefit of members, not outsiders.

National Brand
Branded item distributed by national manufacturers.

Need Hierarchy
Theory of Abraham Maslow that there is an order in which human needs arise. When one need is at least partially satisfied, the need at the next highest level arises.

New Product
Good or service new to the company producing it.

New Product Committee
Group of top-level executives and representatives of several departments that meets regularly to consider new products.

New Product Department
Permanent committee that works on new product ideas on a day-to-day basis.

New Product Venture Team
Group that usually assumes total responsibility for a new product from conception through decline.

New Task
Purchase of a good or service for the first time.

Noise
Interference that is either deliberately or accidentally introduced and blocks or distorts transmissions.

Noncommercial Advertising
Paid message sponsored by nonprofit organizations.

Noncumulative Discount
One-time reduction for larger-than-usual order.

Nonprobability Sample
Sample that involves personal judgment in the selection of sampled items.

Objective and Task Budgeting
Strategy that emphasizes setting goals and then fixing costs of meeting those goals for each promotional task used.

Observation
Research method that involves either the personal or mechanical viewing of subjects or physical phenomena.

Odd Pricing
Retail practice of adjusting prices to end with an odd number or just under a round number (for example, $7.99).

Oligopoly
Situation in which a few firms dominate the market, set similar prices, and make entry by other firms difficult.

One-Price Policy
Policy of offering goods purchased at the same time and in the same quantity at a single price to all.

Operating Environment
Individuals and organizations outside a firm (such as dealers and competitors) that help shape marketing plans and can, in turn, be shaped by them to some extent.

Opinion Leader
Member of a group who is capable of influencing others in it.

Order Taker
Salesperson whose main function is to write or ring up orders.

Organizational Marketing
Activities that attempt to influence others to accept the goals of, receive the services of, or contribute in some way to an organization.

Organizational Objectives
Overall goals a firm pursues, such as increasing sales or maintaining a quality image.

Output
Actual purchase and postpurchase evaluation by a consumer.

Ownership Group
Type of department store organization in which stores keep their separate name but are owned by a corporation that centrally provides some buying and management functions.

Ownership Utility
Value added to a product by giving consumers a way to obtain ownership of it.

Penetration Pricing
Policy of setting initial price for a new product very low in order to achieve the largest possible market share quickly.

Per-Capita Income
A country's gross national product divided by its population.

Percent-of-Sales Budgeting
Sales approach that fixes amount to be spent for promotion as a percentage of the previous year's sales or of anticipated sales for the coming year.

Perception
Process by which an individual becomes aware of the environment and interprets it so that it fits into his or her frame of reference.

Perpetual Inventory
Frequently updated list of all goods in stock.

Person Marketing
Efforts directed toward cultivating the attention, interest, and preference of a target market toward a person.

Personal Selling
Oral presentation of a tangible or intangible product to a prospect for the purpose of completing an exchange.

Personality
Sum of characteristics that make a person what he or she is and distinguish each individual from every other individual.

Physical Count
Inventory practice of totaling the number of items of each line on hand at a regular interval.

Physical Distribution
The process of storing and moving products along marketing channels.

Place Utility
Value added to a product by making it available where buyers want it.

Placement
Means of delivering a product; also called distribution.

Point-of-Purchase (POP) Materials
Promotional tools such as posters, display racks, and price cards.

Positioning
Theory holding that to sell a product, a company must create a unique niche or position for it in the consumer's mind.

Posttesting
Measuring the effectiveness of a full-scale campaign after it has been completed.

Premium
Item offered free or at a low cost as a reward for buying a product.

Presentation
Stage of selling process during which a salesperson translates the features of a product into benefits the customer can understand.

Pretesting
Measuring a promotional campaign's effectiveness before spending on a large scale.

Price Collusion
Joint fixing of prices by competitors.

Price Discrimination
Price cuts that are not offered equally to every buyer.

Price Leader
Dominant member of an industry that announces pricing

policies other companies often follow.

Price Lining
Practice of grouping merchandise into classes by means of price.

Pricing
Placing a value on a product.

Pricing Objectives
Long-range goals that managers wish to pursue in their pricing decisions.

Pricing Policies
Pricing plans for dealing with situations in the future that generally recur.

Primary Data
Original information gathered for a specific research project.

Primary Demand Advertising
Advertising aimed at increasing the total demand for products without distinguishing between brands.

Private Carrier
Transportation owned by an individual company that is not primarily in the transportation business.

Private (Distributor) Brand
Product sold under the name of a retailer or wholesale intermediary.

Private Warehouse
Storage center owned or controlled by the company that uses it.

Probability Sample
Sample in which each member of a given population is selected on some objective basis not controlled by the researcher.

Procompetitive Legislation
Laws that sustain and protect competition.

Product
Anything that can be offered to a market for attention, acquisition, use, or consumption that might satisfy a want or need.

Product Life Cycle
Five phases through which a product passes: (1) incubation, (2) introduction, (3) growth, (4) maturity, and (5) decline.

Product Position
Image that a product has in consumers' minds, especially in relation to competing products.

Product Positioning
Decisions marketers make to create or maintain a certain product concept in consumers' minds.

Production Orientation
Business philosophy emphasizing that (1) anything that can be produced can be sold; (2) the most important managerial task is to keep the cost of production down; and (3) a company should produce only certain basic products.

Profit
What remains for a business after expenses are deducted from revenues or income.

Promotion
Marketing communication that attempts to inform and remind individuals and persuade them to accept, resell, recommend, or use a product, service, idea, or institution.

Prospecting
Actively seeking out buyers.

Prosperity
Period in business cycle of generally high income, employment, and business growth.

Psychographic Segmentation
Division of the market into classes on the basis of the life-styles of members.

Public Relations
Activities that attempt to generate a favorable attitude toward a company among employees, stockholders, suppliers, and the government, as well as among customers.

Public Warehouse
Storage center controlled by an independent, available for rent for a short time, and usually shared by a number of companies.

Publicity
Any information relating to a manufacturer or its products that appears in any medium on a nonpaid basis.

Pull Strategy
Creating demand for a product within a channel of distribution by appealing directly to the consumer.

Pure Competition
Situation in which there are many sellers, no seller dominates a market, and the products sold are interchangeable.

Push Strategy
Urging members of a market channel to sell a product or give it adequate display.

Qualifying
Determining whether prospects have the authority to buy and the money to pay for the purchases.

Quantity Discount
Reduction in list price to intermediaries for buying in large volume.

Quota Sample
Nonprobability sample composed of subjects chosen on the basis of characteristics thought pertinent to a study.

Rack Jobber
Full-service merchant wholesaler who supplies grocery and other retail stores with nonfood items on display racks and who owns the goods and racks.

Random Sample
Probability sample in which each member of a population under study has an equal chance of being selected.

Raw Material
Natural resource such as crude oil or a cultivated product such as wheat used in the production of finished products.

Recall
Power of certain federal agencies to require manufacturers to notify customers that a product may be hazardous and may be exchanged or repaired.

Receiver
Ultimate destination of a message.

Recession
Phase of the business cycle characterized by decreasing income, employment, and growth rate.

Reciprocity
In industrial marketing, the relationship between buyer and seller that influences purchasing decisions rather than economic or performance factors.

Recovery
Upswing in the business cycle characterized by a gradual rise in business and consumer economic well-being.

Reference Group
Group that serves as a model for an individual's behavior and frame of reference for decision making.

Research Design
Method for carrying out a marketing study.

Retail Life Cycle
View that retail stores, like products, have life cycles that consist of phases: innovation, accelerated development, maturity, and decline.

Retailer
Intermediary who sells directly to consumers.

Retailing
All activities involved in selling goods or services directly to final consumers for their personal, nonbusiness use.

Role
In sociology, a kind of specialization of task. Family roles include those concerning decisions that may be wife-dominated, husband-dominated, or autonomous (either spouse may decide).

Role Playing
Training method for salespeople in which one person acts the part of the salesperson and the other takes the part of the customer.

Safety Stock
Amount above the basic stock level to handle emergencies.

Sales Analysis
Breakdown of a company's sales data by product or customer demand, territorial volume, and salesperson performance.

Sales Branch
A manufacturing firm's service center and stock storehouse.

Sales-Force Survey
Means for sales forecasting using estimates of company salespeople.

Sales Forecast
Prediction of actual sales a company can expect to make in a certain market or segment.

Sales Management
Marketing function that embraces recruiting, selecting, and training salespeople, supervising and motivating them, and evaluating their performance.

Sales Office
Headquarters for a sales force away from a company's plant.

Sales Orientation
Business philosophy emphasizing that (1) finding buyers for products is management's chief concern; and (2) convincing buyers to purchase a firm's output is management's chief task.

Sales Promotion
Promotional activities besides selling, advertising, and pub-

licity that stimulate purchases or aid dealer effectiveness.

Sales Quota
Quantitative measure of the effectiveness of salespeople.

Sales Task Clarity
The visible relationship between a salesperson's efforts and sales results.

Sample
In promotion, giveaway in a trial size for products whose benefits cannot be fully conveyed through advertising. In research, limited canvass of a representative part of a population under study.

Scrambled Merchandising
Practice, by previously specialized retailers, of selling many unrelated lines of goods.

Screening
First attempt to separate ideas worth pursuing from those that are not.

Seasonal Discount
Special price for buying out of season.

Secondary Data
Information that exists before a particular study is conducted and that was collected for another purpose.

Selective or Brand Advertising
Messages that try to increase consumer preference for a particular firm's product.

Selective Distribution
Use of more than one but less than all firms that might carry a product.

Selective Exposure
Process of filtering out information that is not of interest.

Selective Perception
Process of filtering out or modifying information that conflicts with one's ideas or beliefs.

Selective Retention
Memory of only what supports one's ideas or beliefs.

Seller's Market
Market in which there is a shortage of goods and services.

Selling Agent
Agent wholesaler who handles marketing for the entire output of small manufacturers.

Service
Intangible benefit exchanged in marketing.

Service Organization
Institution, such as a hospital, college, or museum, that provides a service for clients, sometimes in exchange for a fee.

Shippers' Associations
Organizations that serve the same function as freight forwarders, except that they work on a nonprofit basis for members of the same industry.

Shopping Center
Group of stores planned, owned, and managed as a unit and with ample parking, usually in a suburban area.

Shopping Goods
Products that a consumer buys only after making comparisons among competing stores.

Skimming
Pricing policy under which new products are often priced high, and their price is gradually lowered as they mature.

Social Class
Group distinguished by characteristics such as occupation, education, possessions, and values.

Social Environment
Climate of public opinion that affects marketers' practices.

Social Marketing
Use of marketing techniques to increase the acceptability of a social idea, cause, or practice in a target group.

Social Responsibility
Moral obligation of businesses to consider the effects of their decisions on society and to accomplish social benefits.

Societal Marketing
Concept that balances concern for profits with concern for satisfying individual wants and societal needs.

Source
Originator of a message.

Source Effect
Distortion of a communication resulting from the reputation of the source of a message.

Specialty Goods
Products that a consumer is willing to make a special effort to obtain.

Specialty Store
Store that concentrates on

selling a selection of only one line of merchandise.

Standard Industrial Classification (SIC) Code
Numbering system followed by the U.S. government for categorizing businesses by economic activity.

Standardization
Practice of transferring all parts of a successful marketing mix from one country to another.

Staple Items
Products bought through habit—for example, milk.

Storage Warehouse
Facility in which goods are stored for weeks, months, or years until they are needed.

Straight Rebuy
Repurchase without any modifications to the product, terms, or suppliers.

Straight Salary
Pay plan under which salespeople are guaranteed a regular income.

Strategic Marketing Planning
Process of establishing an organization's goals, assessing opportunities, and developing marketing objectives; results in marketing strategies.

Stratified Sampling
Probability sampling in which subgroups are identified and than randomly sampled.

Subculture
Subgroup within a larger culture that has distinctive lifestyles, values, norms, and beliefs.

Supermarket
Retail food store that carries dry groceries, dairy products, and fresh produce and allows customers to make their own selection.

Superstore
Large store that carries a broad selection of one type of product at low prices. Sometimes called "category killers."

Supplies
Industrial products needed for the maintenance or repair of equipment or for the operation of a business.

Survey Research
Study using direct or indirect interviews.

Target Market
Market segment an organization designs its marketing mix to reach because that segment is considered likely to demand the product being marketed.

Target Marketing
Practice of dividing the market into segments and devising a marketing mix to appeal to one or more targeted market segments.

Target Rate of Return
Goal stated as a certain percentage of return on sales or investment.

Tariff
Tax on imports.

Technical Salespeople
Technicians in sales positions who act as consultants and sometimes help to design products or systems to meet a client's needs.

Technology
Application of principles of science to the solution of practical problems.

Telemarketing
Direct selling in which salespeople telephone potential customers.

Test Marketing
Trial marketing in a limited area chosen as representative of an entire market.

Theory of Conditioned Learning
View holding that learning takes place by association.

Theory of Instrumental Learning
View that people learn to act in a certain way when some responses are rewarded (or reinforced) and others are punished.

Tickler File
Reminder file, often composed of cards, containing data on a sale and times to call back.

Time-Series Projection
Statistical method for forecasting sales based on past patterns projected into the future.

Time Utility
Value added to a product by making it available when buyers need it.

Total Physical Distribution Concept
Principle that all management functions related to moving products to buyers must be fully integrated.

Trade Discount
Reduction to "the trade" (wholesalers and retailers) from list price.

Trade Show
Exposition that allows salespeople to display their new products to dealers, to make new contacts, and to develop mailing lists for future use.

Transfer Pricing
Pricing within a corporate family, perhaps used to avoid taxes.

Transfer Principle
Principle that all functions of the marketing channel are vital and when not performed by one channel member must be taken over by another.

Truck Wholesaler
Limited-function merchant wholesaler who performs all the functions of full-service organizations except financing; operates by selling and making deliveries directly from a truck.

Turnover
Number of times average inventory is sold during a given period.

Uniform-Delivery Pricing
Practice of quoting a single price to all sellers regardless of location, reached by averaging the transportation charges of all buyers and adding that figure to the selling price.

Usage-Rate Segmentation
Division of a market into classes on the basis of the rate at which members buy and use products.

User
Member of a buying center who works with the products purchased.

Utility
Want-satisfying power of goods or services.

Variable Costs
Costs that increase or decrease with the amount of output.

Variable-Price Policy
Policy that allows special prices for different customers.

Vending Machine
Device that dispenses products automatically after money is inserted.

Vertical Marketing System (VMS)
System in which one channel member owns, controls, or coordinates the operations of other channel members.

Visible Costs
Direct and indirect costs that show up on a profit and loss statement.

Want-Satisfaction Approach
Sales theory that stresses that the salesperson must first determine what a buyer really wants or needs before launching a sales talk.

Warehouse Store
No-frills store that emphasizes lower prices over atmosphere and customer service.

Wheel of Retailing
Theory that all retail innovators start as low-cost, low-price stores, improve services and raise prices at maturity, and decline when new types of low-cost stores challenge them.

Wholesale Intermediary
Link that sells to retailers, other wholesaling intermediaries, or industrial users.

Wholesale Merchant
Full-service merchant wholesaler who supplies mainly retailers or institutions.

Wholly Owned Wholesaler
Distribution arm of manufacturer that sets it up. Can be manufacturers' sales branches or sales offices.

Zone-Delivery Pricing
Policy under which sellers divide the country or market into two or more zones, charging the same rate within a zone but different rates among zones.

Name and Company Index*

**Companies that are discussed in end-of-chapter or end-of-part cases appear in boldface type along with the page number(s) on which they appear.*

Subject Index*

Words appearing in boldface type are glossary terms defined in text. The boldface page numbers indicate the pages on which the key terms are defined.